THE NEW YORK TIMES **INTERNATIONAL COOK BOOK**

BOOKS BY CRAIG CLAIBORNE: *The New York Times International Cook Book*

Cooking with Herbs and Spices

Craig Claiborne's Kitchen Primer

The New York Times Menu Cook Book

The New York Times Cook Book

The New York Times

HARPER & ROW, PUBLISHERS, NEW YORK

GRAND RAPIDS, PHILADELPHIA, ST. LOUIS, SAN FRANCISCO

LONDON, SINGAPORE, SYDNEY, TOKYO, TORONTO

1817

by Craig Claiborne

International Cook Book

Drawings by James J. Spanfeller

ISBN: 0-06-010788-x

LIBRARY OF CONGRESS CATALOG CARD NUMBER: 70-156514

Designed by Sidney Feinberg

90 91 92 93 94 19 18 17 16 15 14 13

For Velma Cannon

Contents

Recipes by Category

Consult the index for page numbers.

Inlagd Sill
Marinated Herring
Matjes Herring in Horseradish
  Sauce
Matjes Herring in Sherry
Pickled Herring in Milt Sauce
Rollmops

Mackerel

Mackerel au Vin Blanc
Seviche
Soused Mackerel

Pike

Chinese Braised Fish with Green
  Onions
Quenelles de Brochet

Porgies

African Fish Stew
Fish au Citron

Red Snapper

Red Snapper Antiboise
Red Snapper Creole

Salmon

Coulibiac
Pickled Salmon

Sole

Fillets of Sole in Shrimp Sauce
Fish, Portuguese Style
Sole Judic
Sole Monte Carlo
Sole with Mushrooms

Swordfish

Swordfish Shish Kebab
Swordfish Steak, Spanish Style

Trout

Stuffed Trout with Fish Mousse
Trout Amandine
Trout Grenobloise
Trout Meunière
Truites au Bleu

Tuna

Tuna Soup Martinique
Vitello Tonnato

Whitefish

Serbian Fish

Whiting

Fish Fillets Piemontese
Spaghetti with Fish Balls

Clams

Clam Bisque
Clam Chowder from Long
  Island
Clam Pie à la Springs
Clams au Beurre Blanc
Clam Soup, French Style
Clam Soup, Italian Style
Fish Soup
Linguine with Red Clam Sauce
New England Clam Chowder
Spaghetti with Anchovy and
  Clam Sauce
Stuffed Clams
Stuffed Clams Florentine

Crabmeat

Crabmeat Wrapped in Phyllo

Lobster

Cheese Soufflé with Lobster
Lobster Américaine
Lobster Bisque
Lobster Cantonese
Lobster Cardinal
Lobster Fra Diavolo
Lobster with Linguine
Lobster Marseillaise
Lobsters Cooked in Sea Water
Lobster Thermidor

Mussels

Billi Bi
Cozze alla Marinara
Francillon Salad
Media Dolma

Moules Marinière
Mussels Vinaigrette
Pilaf of Mussels
Risotto with Mussels
Spaghetti with Mussels
Stuffed Mussels

Scallops

Breaded Scallops
Broiled Scallops with Lemon
Coquilles Saint-Jacques
Crème Saint-Jacques
Scallops au Citron

Shrimp

Baked Fresh Shrimp with Feta
  Cheese
Baked Shrimp in Cream Sauce
Boiled Shrimp with Anchovy
  Butter
Cauliflower with Shrimp and
  Dill Sauce
Chawanmushi
Chinese Shrimp Toast
Fillets of Sole in Shrimp Sauce
Glorified Bulljoul
Greek-Style Shrimp
Har-Gow
Korean Saewu Jun
Nasi Goreng
Palusami
Paprika Shrimp with Sour
  Cream
Peas and Shrimp
Puffed Shrimp
Puree of Pumpkin and Shrimp
Roman Shrimp
Sambal Goreng Udang
Sautéed Shrimp with Broccoli
Scampi
Scampi Spaghetti
Shrimp and Artichokes aux
  Câpres
Shrimp Baratin
Shrimp with Black Bean Sauce
Shrimp aux Câpres
Shrimp Dahomienne
Shrimp Granados
Shrimp with Hoi Sin Sauce

Shrimp with Hot Fish Sauce
Shrimp Marinara
Shrimp Marseillaise
Shrimp and Pork Egg Rolls
Shrimp with Saffron
Shrimp Scorpio
Shrimp Tarragon

Stir-Fried Shrimp in Shells
Stuffed Shrimp
Szechwan Shrimp

Snails

Aïoli
Escargots à la Bourguignonne

Snails Provençale on Toast
Snails, Sicilian Style

Squid

Calamari Ripieni
Squid in Tomato Sauce
Squid Vinaigrette

MEATS

Beef

Armenian Steak Tartare
Baked Kibbee
Beef Esterhazy
Beef Fillet with Madeira Sauce
Beef à la Lindstrom
Beef au Madère
Beef Périgourdine
Beef Picadillo
Beef Ragoût
Beef Salade Vinaigrette
Beef Stew with Quinces
Beef Stroganoff
Beef Teriyaki
Bistec a la Caserola
Boeuf en Daube Provençale
Boeuf à la Mode en Gelée
Boiled Beef
Bracciole in Tomato Sauce
Brasciole all'Oreste Cianci
Carbonnades of Beef à la Fla-
    mande
Carne Mechada
Ceylon Curry
Chinese Pepper Steak
Cocido Bogotano
Couscous
Cutleti
Daube de Boeuf en Gelée
El Harirah
Fondue Bourguignonne
Grilled Steak Sandwiches with
    Tartar Sauce
Hungarian Beef Goulash
Israeli Sweet and Sour Meat
    Balls
Italian Beef Roll
Italian Beef Stew with Rose-
    mary
Kebab and Kofte

Koftas in Sour Cream
Korean Beef Shreds
Korean Bul-Kogi
Korean Meat Salad
Mahashes
Meat Balls Paprikash
Meat Balls Smitane
Moussaka
Mussala
Norwegian Meat Balls in Cream
Oriental Flank Steak
Paprika Meat Balls
Pastels
Pastitsio
Petite Marmite
Picadinho a Brasileira
Pot Roast Provençale
Potted Steak, Burgundy Style
Ribs of Beef au Vin Rouge
Rolladen
Roulades de Boeuf
Saffron Beef
Sauerbraten
Sauerbraten, Czechoslovakian
    Style
Sauté of Beef, Hungarian Style
Shabu-Shabu
Shchi
Short Ribs of Beef with Caraway
Short Ribs à la Française
Sicilian Meat Balls
Sicilian Round Steak
Sliced Beef with Soy Sauce
Spaghetti with Meat Balls and
    Bracciolini
Spaghetti with Stuffed Peppers
Steaks à la Crème
Steak aux Échalotes
Steak and Kidney Pie
Steak au Poivre

Steak au Poivre à la Crème
Stuffed Green Peppers, Tuscany
    Style
Tournedos Ismal Bayeldi
Tournedos Rossini
Triple Goulash
Turkish Meat Balls on Skewers
Vindaloo Beef Curry

Ham

Boiled Ham
Braccioline
Ham Braised in Cider
Ham and Endive Mornay
Pipérade with Ham
Swedish Christmas Ham
Veal Shanks with Prosciutto
    and Peas
Zampino or Ham with Beans
    Bretonne

Lamb

Armenian Stuffed Meat Balls
Braised Lamb with Eggplant
Cassoulet
Charcoal-Grilled Lamb Proven-
    çale
Couscous
Cracked Wheat with Lamb and
    Chick-Peas
Curried Lamb à la Française
English Lamb Chops
Haricot de Mouton
Kebab and Kofte with Cherry
    Tomatoes
Lamb Chops Rouennaise
Lamb with Dill
Lamb Marrakech
Lamb and Sauerkraut Stew

Lamb Shanks Côte d'Azur
Lamb Shanks au Vin Rouge
Lamb Shreds with Cellophane Noodles
Lamb on Skewers
Lamb Stew Forestière
Lamb Stew, Spanish Style
Macaroni with Greek Lamb Sauce
Meat Balls, Middle Eastern Style
Moussaka
Mussala
Noisettes d'Agneau à l'Estragon
Parsleyed Rack of Lamb
Podarakia Arniou
Raw Kibbee
Roast Baby Lamb
Roast Lamb à la Française
Sate Kambing
Spit-Roasted Leg of Lamb
Stuffed Artichokes Armenian Style
Les Truffes au Mouton
Turkish Meat Balls on Skewers

Pork

Bakonyi Pork
Barbecued Spareribs
Bavarian Pork and Veal Roast
Bracciole in Tomato Sauce
Braised Pork, Hungarian Style
Cassoulet
Chawanmushi
Chicken and Pork Español
Chinese Roast Pork
Chinese Spareribs with Black Beans
Chou Farci
Cretons Français
Ginger and Pork Fried Rice
Grilled Pork Chops
Hwang Kua Jo Tang
Italian Stuffed Pork Chops
Melton Mowbray Pie
Mexican Spareribs
Mushrooms Stuffed with Pork and Veal
Oven-Roasted Pork Loin
Pearl Balls

Pork Boulettes
Pork Chops with Mustard
Pork Chops Teriyaki
Pork Chops Vera Cruz
Pork Goulash
Pork with Sauerkraut
Puerco en Adobo
Ragoût de Pattes
Ragoût of Pork au Vin Rouge
Roast Loin of Pork au Vin Blanc
Roast Pig with Danish Fruit Stuffing
Santiago Pork Roast
Sate Babi
Sauerkraut with Pork Balls
Shrimp and Pork Egg Rolls
Spaghetti Carbonara
Steamed Pork Balls
Stuffed Cabbage
Stuffed Pork Chops in Sour Cream
Stuffed Veal or Pork Chops aux Pistaches
Szechwan Pork
Tomato Sauce with Meat Balls and Sausages
Tourtière
Transylvanian Pork and Sauerkraut
Trinidad Roast Pork
Triple Goulash
Zampino or Ham with Beans Bretonne

Veal

Anchovy-Stuffed Breast of Veal
Baked Veal Stew
Bavarian Pork and Veal Roast
Blanquette de Veau
Bracciolini
Braised Veal Ravioli Stuffing
Braised Veal Shanks
Breaded Veal Scallops
Danish Stuffed Cabbage
Deep South Veal Grillades
Hungarian Veal
Kalvekarbonader
Mushrooms Stuffed with Pork and Veal

Norwegian Veal Chops
Oiseaux sans Tête
Paupiettes de Veau
Roast of Veal à la Française
Roast Veal Ménagère
Spaghettini with Little Veal Cubes
Stuffed Veal or Pork Chops aux Pistaches
Stuffed Veal Steak with Onions
Tomato Sauce with Tarragon Veal Balls
Triple Goulash
Uccelleti Scappati
Veal Birds Salsicciana
Veal Blanquette with Dill
Veal Bon Appetit
Veal Bordelaise
Veal Chops with Anchovies
Veal Chops Beau Séjour
Veal Cordon Bleu
Veal Cutlets from Ouchy
Veal Cutlets Provençale
Veal Goulash
Veal Marengo
Veal Oreganata
Veal Piccata
Veal Roast with Frankfurters
Veal Sauté with Mushrooms
Veal Scallops Chasseur
Veal Scallops with Cheese
Veal Scallops with Mushrooms
Veal Scaloppine with Lemon
Veal Scaloppine with Marsala
Veal Scaloppine with Parmesan
Veal Shanks, Greek Style
Veal Shanks with Prosciutto and Peas
Veal Stuffing for Ravioli
Veal, Swiss Style
Veau aux Amandes
Vitello Tonnato
Wienerschnitzel

Miscellaneous and Variety Meats

Bigos
Black Pudding
Calves' Feet Poulette
Cassoulet

Cau Yang Roh
Cervelas
Charcutier Salad
Cocida Español
Curried Kidneys, English Style
Fondue Bourguignonne
Hor Gwo
Italian Sausages Marchigiana
Kidneys on Skewers
Kori Kuk
Leverpostej
Liver Pâté
Mayeritsa Avgolemono
Mongolian Grill
Oxtail Ragoût
Pâté à l'Auberge
Pâté Barbara
Peperoni Pizza
Pigs' Feet Sainte-Menehould
Poor People's Stew
Pork Sausage with Fennel

Pot au Feu
Ragoût Toulousaine
Rice with Chicken and Sausage
Rosemary-Stuffed Zucchini
Sausage with Savoy Cabbage
Sausage with White Beans
Souse
Spaghetti with Chicken Livers
Spaghetti with Meat Balls and Bracciolini
Spaghettini with Sausages
Steak and Kidney Pie
Stuffed Lettuce Balls
Swedish Liver Pâté
Swedish Meat Balls
Sweetbreads Florentine
Sweetbreads Maréchale
Sweetbreads Périgourdine
Sweet Meat Balls for Couscous
Tarragon Spaghetti with Meat Balls and Sausages

Three-Day Sauerkraut with Champagne
Tomato Sauce with Meat Balls and Sausages
Tripe Soup
Veal Birds Salsicciana
Veal Roast with Frankfurters
Ziti with Marinara Sauce, Sausage, and Cheese

Game

Cabrito Asada
Jamaican Curried Goat
Lapin Gibelotte
Perdrix au Choux
Quail Mole
Rabbit with Wine
Roast Venison
Terrine of Pheasant
Terrine Sauvage

POULTRY

Chicken

Barbecued Chicken
Breasts of Chicken Gismonda
Caldo Xochitl
Ceylon Curry
Chalupas
Chicken with Almonds
Chicken with Beet Khuta
Chicken Bengal
Chicken Breasts Albuféra
Chicken Breasts à l'Empereur
Chicken Breasts Hungarian
Chicken Breasts alla Parmigiana
Chicken Breasts in Port
Chicken Breasts Siena Style
Chicken Canzanese
Chicken in Champagne Sauce au Pavillon
Chicken with Champagne Sauce
Chicken Chasseur
Chicken Colombiana
Chicken in Cream with Tomatoes
Chicken Croquettes
Chicken Cutlets Pojarski
Chicken El Parador

Chicken Español
Chicken Fricassee
Chicken, Hungarian Style
Chicken Jambalaya
Chicken with Lemon
Chicken Mole Pablano
Chicken Mousse
Chicken and Mushroom Crêpes Florentine
Chicken with Noodles Parisien
Chicken and Noodles in Wine Sauce
Chicken Paprikash
Chicken Parmigiana
Chicken Paysanne
Chicken with Peppers
Chicken and Pork Español
Chicken Rea
Chicken Romarin
Chicken with Saffron Cream Sauce
Chicken Sauté au Parmesan
Chickens Demi-Deuil
Chicken with Squash and Corn
Chicken Tandoori
Chicken with Tarragon and Sour Cream

Chicken Vallée d'Auge
Chicken in Velouté
Chicken with Velouté Sauce
Chicken Vieille France
Chicken with Walnut Sauce
Chilaquiles
Chinese Smoked Chicken
Cold Roast Chicken
Cold Tarragon Chicken
Escabeche of Chicken
Fricassee of Chicken with Tarragon
Fricasseed Chicken
Galician Soup
Kotopita
Lemon Chicken
Mahashes
Mulligatawny Soup
Mussala
Nasi Goreng
Noodles and Chicken Campanini
Oyako Domburi
Paella
Petite Marmite
Picante de Gallina

Pollo alla Cacciatore
Pollo Estofado
Pot au Feu
Poulet au Riesling
Poulet au Riz
Ragoût de Poulet
Ragoût Toulousaine
Rice with Chicken and Sausage
Salat Olivet
Serbian Chicken Casserole
Smothered Chicken Smitane
Sopa de Mazorca con Pollo
Soto Ajam
Southern Fried Chicken
Stuffed Chicken (for Pot au Feu)

Suimono
Szechwan Chicken
Truffled Steamed Chicken
Turmeric Chicken
Viennese Chicken
Waterzooie
White Cut Chicken
Wiener Backhendl

Duck

Cantonese Roast Duck
Duck Fermière
Duck Montmorency
Duck Nivernaise
Duck and Rutabaga Stew
Five-Spice Duck

Foh Opp
Galantine of Duck
Peking Duck
Soya Duck
Spanish Duck, Mountain Style

Rock Cornish Hens

Rock Cornish Hens Ménàgere

Squab

Stuffed Squab
Stuffed Squab with Madeira Sauce

Turkey

Turkey with Noodles Florentine

EGGS, CHEESE, RICE AND OTHER CEREALS, AND PASTA

Eggs

Aïoli
Caviar Eggs in Aspic
Chawanmushi
Cheese Soufflé with Lobster
Egg Pancakes (for Nasi Goreng)
Eggplant Soufflé
Eggs in Aspic
Eggs in Green Sauce
Eggs with Sauce Gribiche
Eggs in Tomato Shells
Har-Gow
Mushroom and Fines Herbes Omelet
Pipérade with Ham
Poached Eggs
Soufflé Laurette
Spatzle

Cheese

Baked Fresh Shrimp with Feta Cheese
Cheese Crisps
Cheese Soufflé with Lobster
Chilies Rellenos con Queso
Cream Cheese Pastry
Fondue Bruxelloise
Gruyère Crêpes with White Truffles
Gruyère Potatoes

Hungarian Cheese
Lasagne for a Crowd
Liptauer Cheese
Manicotti
Mozzarella in Carrozza
Pasta with Ricotta
Pastellios
Potato and Cheese Mayonnaise alla Romana
Rigatoni con Quattro Formaggi
Spanakopetes
Surullitos
Tiropetes
Tostadas with Cheese
Túrós Delkei
Veal Scallops with Cheese
Ziti with Marinara Sauce, Sausage, and Cheese

Rice and Other Cereals

Armenian Rice Pilaf
Arroz con Gandules
Baked Kibbee
Baked Rice
Coucou
Couscous
Cracked Wheat with Lamb and Chick-peas
Eggplant with Cumin Rice
Eggplant and Rice Provençale
Farofa

Ginger and Pork Fried Rice
Jamaican Rice and Beans
Nasi Goreng
Oyako Domburi
Paella
Poulet au Riz
Raw Kibbee
Rice Albuféra
Rice Andalouse
Rice Bujambura
Rice with Chicken and Sausage
Rice for Pilaf of Mussels
Rice Salad
Risotto
Risotto Milanese
Risotto with Mussels
Tabbouleh
Valencian Rice
White Risotto with Mushrooms
Yellow Rice
Young Jewel Fried Rice

Pasta

Cappelleti in Brodo
Chicken and Noodles with Wine Sauce
Chicken with Noodles Parisien
Cocida Español
Cozze alla Marinara
Fettuccine Alfredo
Fettuccine alla Romana

Green Noodles with Garlic
Homemade Noodles with a Machine
Lamb Shreds with Cellophane Noodles
Lasagne for a Crowd
Linguine with Red Clam Sauce
Lobster with Linguine
Macaroni with Greek Lamb Sauce
Macaroni Leonardo
Noodles and Chicken Campanini
Noodles Florentine
Pasta e Fagioli
Pasta with Ricotta

Pasta with Seafood
Pastitsio
Pesto Genovese
Ravioli
Rigatoni con Quattro Formaggi
Rotelle with Mushrooms
Scampi Spaghetti
Spaghetti with Anchovy and Clam Sauce
Spaghetti Carbonara
Spaghetti with Chicken Livers
Spaghetti with Fish Balls
Spaghetti with Fresh Peas
Spaghetti with Meat Balls and Bracciolini
Spaghetti with Mussels

Spaghettini Estivi
Spaghettini with Little Veal Cubes
Spaghettini with Sausages
Spaghetti all 'Ortolana
Spaghetti with Peas
Spaghetti with Pesto and Vegetables
Spaghetti with Stuffed Peppers
Spaghetti with Tarragon Meat Balls and Sausages
Tortelloni di Biete
Turkey with Noodles Florentine
Ziti with Marinara Sauce, Sausage, and Cheese

VEGETABLES

Cappon Magro
Cocida Español
Elaborate Tempura
Fuji Foo Young (for Elaborate Tempura)
Gado-Gado
Koo Chul Pan
Málaga Gazpacho
Ratatouille
Spaghetti with Pesto and Vegetables

Artichokes

Aïoli
Artichokes in Oil
Artichokes à l 'Orange
Artichokes for Roast Lamb
Artichokes Roman Style
Shrimp and Artichokes aux Câpres
Stuffed Artichokes, Armenian Style

Asparagus

Asparagus Vinaigrette Salad

Avocados

Guacamole

Bananas and Plantains

Bananas a Brasileira
Boiled Green Bananas

Broiled Bananas (for Nasi Goreng)
Fried Plantains
Fried Plantains, Jamaican Style

Beans

Aïoli
Bean Soup
Black Bean Soup
Cassoulet
Chilled White Bean Casserole
Chinese Spareribs with Black Beans
Cuban Black Beans
Dhal (Lentil) Curry
Dried Fava Bean Salad
Flageolets Bretonne
Green Beans with Shallots
Haricot de Mouton
Indian Sambhar
Jamaican Rice and Beans
Lentil Salad
Lentil Soup
Lentils with Tomatoes
Pasta e Fagioli
Sausage with White Beans
Zampino or Ham with Beans Bretonne

Beets

Beet and Onion Salad
Borscht

Chicken and Beet Khuta
Pickled Beets

Broccoli

Sautéed Shrimp with Broccoli
Sicilian Broccoli

Cabbage

Bigos
Borscht
Cabbage in Caraway Cream
Cabbage Mornay
Cabbage Strudel
Choucroute Garnie
Chou Farcie
Danish Stuffed Cabbage
German Cabbage Salad
Kim Chee
Lamb and Sauerkraut Stew
Palusami
Perdrix au Choux
Pork with Sauerkraut
Sauerkraut with Pork Balls
Sauerkraut with Sherry Wine
Sauerkraut Soup
Sausage with Savoy Cabbage
Savoy Soup
Shchi
Stuffed Cabbage
Sweet and Sour Cabbage
Three-Day Sauerkraut with Champagne

Transylvanian Layered Cabbage
Transylvanian Pork and Sauerkraut

Carrots

Aïoli
Carrot Puree
Cream of Carrot Soup
Moroccan Carrot Appetizer

Cauliflower

Aïoli
Cauliflower with Shrimp and Dill Sauce
Indian Gobhi Musallam

Celery

Bagno Caldo with Celery
Celery Root Rémoulade

Chestnuts

Puree of Chestnuts

Coconuts

Coconut Cream
Coconut Milk Made in a Blender
Coconut Side Dish

Corn

Mexican Corn Soup
Pollo con Calabacitas
Sopa de Mazorca con Pollo

Cucumbers

Cucumber and Sour Cream Salad
Cucumbers with Yogurt, Greek Style
Danish Cucumber Salad
Hwang Kua Jo Tang
Pickled Cucumbers
Raita
Swedish Cucumber Salad
Yogurt with Cucumbers for Curry

Eggplant

Baba Ghanouj
Braised Lamb with Eggplant
Cold Eggplant with Pine Nuts
Eggplant Arlésienne
Eggplant with Cumin Rice
Eggplant Curry
Eggplant Parmigiana
Eggplant with Rice Provençale
Eggplant Soufflé
Greek Eggplant
Indian Eggplant Rayatha
Moussaka
Sautéed Eggplant Slices
Smoked Eggplant Chutney
Spaghetti all'Ortolana
Stuffed Eggplant all'Italiana

Endive

Braised Endive
Ham and Endive Mornay

Escarole

Escarole Soup

Leeks

Leek and Potato Soup

Lettuce

Braised Lettuce
Stuffed Lettuce Balls

Mushrooms

Baked Mushrooms in Cream
Chicken and Mushroom Crêpes Florentine
Deep-Fried Mushrooms
Duxelles
Funghi Trifolati
Mushroom and Fines Herbes Omelet
Mushroom Piroshki
Mushroom Pizza
Mushroom Puree
Mushroom Soup
Mushrooms Parmigiana
Mushrooms Smitane
Mushrooms in Sour Cream
Mushrooms Stuffed with Anchovies
Mushrooms Stuffed with Pork and Veal
Pickled Mushrooms
Rotelle with Mushrooms
Sole with Mushrooms
Stuffed Mushrooms
Veal Sauté with Mushrooms
Veal Scallops with Mushrooms
White Risotto with Mushrooms
Wild Mushroom Soup

Okra

Coucou

Onions

Beet and Onion Salad
Deep-Fried Onion or Garlic
French Onion Tart
Glazed Onions
Onion Relish
Onion Soup Chablisienne
Onion Soup Gratinée
Onion Soup, Lyonnaise Style
Stuffed Veal Steak with Onions

Parsley

Fried Parsley

Peas

Arroz con Gandules
Cracked Wheat with Lamb and Chick-Peas
Green Peas à la Française
Hummus
Indian Chana
Peas and Shrimp
Petits Pois à la Française
Pureed Peas
Soupe aux Pois Canadienne
Spaghetti with Fresh Peas
Spaghetti with Peas
Veal Shanks with Prosciutto and Peas

Peppers

Bagno Caldo with Peppers
Chicken with Peppers
Chilies Rellenos con Queso
Chinese Pepper Steak
Mahashes
Roasted Italian Peppers
Sopa de Chilies Poblanos
Spaghetti with Stuffed Peppers
Stuffed Green Peppers, Tuscany Style

Bread Sauce for Poultry
Brown Sauce
Caper Sauce
Cardinal Sauce
Chicken Velouté
Chive Hollandaise Sauce
Cream Sauce
Curry Sauce
Danish Mustard
Dumpling and Hor Gwo Sauce
  for One
Fiji Cream Sauce
French Sardine Butter
Fresh Tomato Sauce
Ginger-Pepper Sauce
Gotamare
Herb Sauce
Homemade Hot Mustard
Hot Pepper Sauce
Italian Tomato Sauce
Lobster Butter
Madeira Sauce
Marinara Sauce
Martinique Sauce Chien
Mexican Tomato Sauce

Mushroom Sauce
Mustard-Egg Sauce
Mustard à la Russe
New Orleans Remoulade
  Sauce
Paprika Sauce
Paprika Sauce for Chicken Cut-
  lets Pojarski
Peking Duck Sauce
Pesto
Poivrade Sauce
Ponzu
Poulette Sauce
Rainbow Fish Sauce
Red Chili Sauce
Salsa
Salsa Fria
Salsa de Tomate Verde
Sauce Aurore
Sauce Belle Aurore
Sauce Charcutière
Sauce Chasseur
Sauce Diable
Sauce Diane

Sauce for Gado-Gado
Sauce Nantaise
Sauce Orly
Sauce Piquante
Sauce Portugaise
Sauce Robert
Sesame-Flavored Sauce
Sicilian Tomato Sauce with
  Meat Balls
Sour Cream and Horseradish
  Sauce
Szechwan Sauce for Dumplings
Tartar Sauce
Tempura Sauce
Tomato and Caper Sauce
Tomato and Green Chili Sauce
Tomato Sauce
Tomato Sauce with Meat Balls
  and Sausages
Tomato Sauce with Tarragon
  Veal Balls
Walnut Sauce
Yogurt
Yogurt Sauce

RELISHES AND PRESERVES

Atjar
Hot Herb and Tomato Relish
Kim Chee
Onion Relish
Pickled Beets

Pickled Cucumbers
Pickled Mushrooms
Pickled Lemons
Quince Compote
Quince Jelly

Quince Preserves
Raita
Smoked Eggplant Chutney
Yogurt with Cucumbers for
  Curry

BREADS, PANCAKES, BATTERS, DUMPLINGS, AND STUFFINGS

Blini
Chalupas
Chicken and Mushroom Crêpes
  Florentine
Chinese Fried Dumplings
Christmas Stollen
Corn Bread Stuffing
Coulibiac
Croutons
Crouton Triangles
Dumplings
Fritter Batter Orly

Garlic Croutons
Gruyère Crêpes with White
  Truffles
Har-Gow
Hot Cross Buns
Italian Olive Stuffing
Krupuk
Lumpia Goreng
Manicotti
Mozzarella in Carrozza
Mushroom Pizza
Pancakes (for Koo Chul Pan)

Peperoni Pizza
Pissaladière
Pizza
Seafood Crêpes
Shrimp and Pork Egg Rolls
Steamed Pancakes
Tempura Batter
Tostadas with Cheese
Tsoureki
Túrós Delkli

Fruit Desserts

Baked Papaya
Bananas, Brazilian Style
Bananas au Rhum
Cherries Jubilee
Dessert Crêpes with Pears
Indian Neruppu Vazhai
Oranges with Glazed Peel in Grand Marnier Syrup
Les Oranges aux Liqueurs
Pears in Port Wine
Pineapple Flambée
Poached Pears with Chestnuts
Red Fruit Pudding with Frozen Berries
Strawberries in Liqueur

Cakes and Torten

Amaretti Torte
Apple Nut Torte
Cheesecake
Cheesecake with Genoise
Coach House Chocolate Cake
Danish Loaf Cakes
Date Torte
Gâteau Bretonne
Genoise
Jamaican Rub-Up Cake
Kirsch Torte
Laggtarta
Marzipan Cake
Nut Torte
Queen Mother's Cake
Quince Torte
Ravani
Sacher Torte
Spanische Windtorte
Sponge Cake
Sponge Jelly Roll
Sponge Roll
Trinidad Torte
Vienna Speckle Cake
Viennese Apple Torte
Yogurt Dessert
Zuppa Inglese

Cookies and Candies

Austrian Hazelnut Tarts with Chocolate Icing
Candied Orange Peel
Cream Cornets
Danish Cones with Whipped Cream
Filled Marzipan Cookies
Florentines
Koulourakia
Pfeffernüsse
Viennese Crescents
White Spritz Cookies

Pies and Pastries

Brandy Alexander Pie
Cheese-Filled Danish Pastries
Chestnut-Chocolate Tarts
Date Wonton
Dessert Crêpes
Dessert Crêpes with Pears
Gali
Juiced Apple Pie
Lemon Chess Pie
Lime Pie
Martinique Pineapple Tart
Pecan Pie
St. Joseph's Cream Puffs
Sicilian Cannoli
Tarte au Sirop d 'Érable
Tarte au Suif
Tarte Tatin
Zeppole di San Giuseppe

Creams, Custards, Puddings, and Soufflés

Almond Crème Brûlée
Almond Curd
Bavarian Cream
Bavarois à l'Orange
Bread-and-Butter Custard
Cazuela
Chocolate Bavarian Cream
Chocolate Soufflé
Chocolate Zabaglione Dessert

Chongos
Coeurs à la Crème with Sauce
Coffee Charlotte
Cold Chocolate Soufflé
Crème Brulée
English Custard with Chestnuts
English Trifle
Farina Pudding Mold
French Bread-and-Butter Pudding
Lemon Soufflé
Lemon Sponge Custard
Marquise de Chocolat
Mont Blanc with Chestnut Puree
Oeufs à la Neige
Papuan Rice Pudding
Paschka
Pineapple Flan
Pots de Crème
Red Fruit Pudding with Frozen Berries
Rice Pudding à la Française
Riz à l'Impératrice
Rum Custard
Rum Custard Pudding
Schokoladendunstkoch
Soufflé Sarah Bernhardt
Soufflés à l'Orange
Spanish Caramel Custard
Spiced Apple Charlotte
Templeque

Mousses, Frozen Desserts, and Meringues

Banana Ice Cream
Biscuit Tortoni
Bombe al Zabaglione
Chestnut Mousse
French Vanilla Ice Cream
Frozen Lemon Cream
Lady Sholl's Pavlova
Lemon Mousse
Oeufs à la Neige
Sherbet with Liqueur
Soufflé Glacé with Candied Fruit

Strawberry Ice Cream
Vanilla Soufflé Glacé

Fillings and Frostings

Buttercream Filling
Buttercream Frosting
Buttercream Mousseline
Chestnut-Chocolate Filling

Chocolate Frosting
Chocolate Icing
Custard Filling
Mocha Frosting
Orange-Flavored Icing
Pear Conserve
Rich Vanilla Cream Filling
Ricotta Filling

Dessert Sauces

Chocolate Sauce
Crème Anglaise
Crème Fraîche
Crêpe Sauce
Date Honey
Sauce Amandine

BEVERAGES

French Rum Punch
Glögg
Margharita

Pineapple Rum Punch
Rum Punch
Sangrita

Tequila, Mexican Style
Tequila Sour
Trinidad Punch

Preface

It was my particular good fortune where this book is concerned to have lived in the one city in the world that offered—and offers—in the private homes of its inhabitants and in its restaurants the greatest variety of the world's dishes. It is true that several hundred of the recipes here were gathered in the course of several thousand miles of travel around the world. Those recipes were painstakingly translated, measured, and put into workable form either in my own kitchen or in the test kitchen of the *New York Times*.

But New York is the home of thousands of nationalities—socialites and diplomats and clerks and "people who are just passing through." I have known many of those who cared most earnestly about food and cooking, those who wanted to communicate their culture via their kitchen to the rest of the world. In their own kitchens here they adapted their cooking as authentically as possible to the American scene, and I shared many of the good things of their tables. It has been their extraordinary diversity and dedication to their own culture that remarkably simplified my task. And it is they who made a book of this scope—and accuracy—feasible. I am indebted to hundreds for their generosity and willingness to share their foods with me. The list is long and has included:

Florence and Sam Aaron, Mrs. Sihwati Nawangwulan Abdulgani, Mrs. Claus Adam, Victor and Kathleen Allan, Bunny and Jeri Allen, Mrs. Marian Argo, Roger Baldwin, Christos and Josephine Bastis, Mrs. Loran Bayley, Mr. and Mrs. Louis Benoist, Anna Beranek, Odette Berry, Marion Gorman Braun, Philip Brown, Mrs. Luca Buccellati, René Buch, Rev. Robert Farrar Capon

Bruno Caravaggi, Eleazar de Carvalho, Mrs. Luc Castonguay, Mrs. Nash Castro, Giorgio Cavallon, Samuel and Narcissa Chamberlain, Mrs. Haig Chekenian, Mrs. Sang Kook Choo, Grace Chu, Helen Corey, Mrs. Lilian Cornfeld, Anneliese von der Cron, Joseph Czarnecki, Mrs. Djoka Damar, Julie Dannenbaum, Elizabeth David, Joseph and Anyuka Davis, Mrs. George T. Delacorte, Mrs. Ellsworth Donnell

Mrs. Dudley Dougherty, David H. Dugan, Jr., Mildred Dunnock, Juliette Elkon, Mrs. Raphael Elmaleh, Mrs. Nuri Eren, Mrs. Michael Fama, Roger Fessaguet, Mr. and Mrs. Shelby Foote, Mr. and Mrs. Paul de Francis, Dagmar Freuchen, Mrs. Paul Fussell, Rosa de la Garza, Antoine Gilly, Ed Giobbi, Gerald Godfrey, Marcel Gosselin, Mrs. Gary Graffman, Mable Grimes

Albert Grobe, Inga Hansen, Mrs. Victor Hazan, Nika Hazelton, Maida Heatter, Geoffrey Holder, Mr. and Mrs. Peter Hyun, Vincent Iannoli, Helen Jacobson, Carlos Jacott, Madhur Jaffrey, Mr. and Mrs. Abdeslam Jaidi, Mrs. Alan Kamman, Diana Kennedy, Mrs. Huyn Chul Kim, Mildred Knopf, Jerry Komarek, Mrs. George de Kornfeld, Emily Kwoh

Alma Lach, Camela Labastide, Suzy Larochette, Mr. and Mrs. David Lawrence, Jim Lee, Virginia Lee, John Leong, Kay and Warner LeRoy, Leon Lianides, Florence Lin, Mrs. Lydia Ling, Mrs. Jacques Lipchitz, Mrs. Herbert Loebel, Dione Lucas, Lee Lum, Nancy Chih Ma, Gloria Mandelstam, Margaret de Marcy, Copeland H. Marks

Mrs. Sudarmo Maronagoro, Paule Marshall, Glen McCaskey, Bill and Joie McGrail, Marquesa Mercedes Ocio de Merry del Val, Mrs. Robert Meyers, Gloria Bley Miller, Mr. and Mrs. Burton Moore, Tim Moore, Ruth Norman, Richard Olney, Elizabeth Lambert Ortiz, Lita Paniagua, Peter Paone, James Paul, James Pearsall

Mrs. John S. Pearson, Jacques Pepin, Gianni Peri, Bernard Pfriem, June Platt, Mrs. Gregori Portnov, Mrs. Gusuf Ramli, Mrs. George W. Renchard, Elizabeth Rich, Ignacia (Maggie) Rini, Ann Roe Robbins, Gino Robusti, Jane Rohan, Carmine Rosa, Rosalina Santa Cruz, J. Tunkie Saunders, Frank Schoonmaker, Jack Denton Scott, Mrs. Helen Sebillon, May de Sena, Ann Seranne

Courtney Shabazian, Nell and Ted Shepherd, Richard Shiner,

Jacques and Rachel Siboni, Mrs. Peter Sichel, Seloti Sikivou, Mr. and Mrs. Myron Simons, Mrs. Chand Balbir Singh, André Soltner, Suzanne Taylor, Mrs. Bernard Tilakaratna, Michael and Irene Tong, Mrs. Richard Toupin, Jennie Tourel, Shizuo Tsuji

Dr. Elisabeth Turnauer, Carlo Urbani, Luis and Carmen Valldejuli, Mrs. M. Varadarajan, Jean Vergnes, Mrs. Aijiro Wakita, Mrs. Stanton Waterman, Bernard White, Lucia Wilcox, Charles Williams, Eva Zane, Pablo Zappi-Manzoni, Elena Zelayeta, Bruno Zirato, Mrs. Maxine-Leopold Zollner, Mrs. Adrian Zorgniotti.

And finally, thanks to my great, good friend Pierre Franey, former chef of Le Pavillon during its days of glory and now vice president of Howard Johnson. Together he and I have spent untold hours in my kitchen in East Hampton creating the vast majority of the French dishes that appear here. My debt to him both as a friend and colleague is beyond measure. If there are others whose names do not appear here, I beg forgiveness.

CRAIG CLAIBORNE

THE NEW YORK TIMES INTERNATIONAL COOK BOOK

Armenia

Armenian Steak Tartare

4 servings

1 pound top round steak, trimmed of all
   fat and ground 3 times
1 cup very fine burghul (cracked wheat)
½ cup cold water, approximately
1 teaspoon salt
½ teaspoon black pepper
½ teaspoon paprika
½ cup finely chopped green pepper
1 cup finely chopped green onions
1 cup finely chopped parsley

1. Place the meat in a mixing bowl and
add the burghul, water, salt, pepper, and
paprika. Knead until very smooth, about
five minutes.

2. Add half of the green pepper, green
onions, and parsley and knead well again,
adding a few drops of water until you have
a very smooth mixture.

3. Shape the mixture into a round, flat
shape about one inch high. Put on a serving
plate and sprinkle with the remaining green
peppers, green onions, and parsley. Cut into
wedges and serve with French bread or
Armenian peta bread.

Lamb and Sauerkraut Stew

4 servings

1 pound lamb riblets, cut into serving
   pieces
3 tablespoons vegetable oil
1 cup small pearl barley
1½ cups sauerkraut, drained
½ cup Fresh Tomato Sauce (page 279), or
   canned tomato sauce
1½ teaspoons salt

1. Wash the meat and pat dry. Heat the oil
in a skillet and brown the meat lightly. Transfer the meat to a heavy casserole. Add the
barley and water to cover and simmer for
forty-five minutes.

2. Add the sauerkraut, tomato sauce, and
salt. Cover and continue simmering for
thirty minutes longer.

1

Armenian Stuffed Meat Balls

About 2 dozen

STUFFING:

1 pound lamb, not too lean, ground
4 medium onions, sliced
¼ cup finely chopped green pepper
2 tablespoons chopped parsley
¼ teaspoon chopped mint
1 teaspoon salt
1 teaspoon freshly ground pepper

MEAT BALLS:

1 pound very lean lamb, ground twice
1 cup very fine burghul (cracked wheat)
   Salt and freshly ground pepper to taste
1 small onion, finely chopped
1 tablespoon finely chopped parsley
   Water
4 cups boiling Beef Stock (page 115)

1. To make the stuffing, sauté the lamb over medium heat, stirring occasionally. Add the onions and cook over low heat for thirty minutes, stirring occasionally. Add the green pepper, parsley, and mint and cook ten minutes. Add salt and pepper and simmer for five minutes.

2. When cool, chill for at least two hours. (The filling can be made a day ahead.) After it is thoroughly chilled, shape into the size of small marbles (about one teaspoonful for each).

3. To make the meat balls, combine the meat, burghul, salt, pepper, onion, and parsley and knead the mixture as you would dough, adding a few drops of water as you go along. Knead the mixture for twenty minutes, until the mixture is like a medium-soft dough.

4. Dip the hands in a bowl of cold water and make balls the size of walnuts. Make a dent in the middle of each ball with your thumb and press all around the inside wall to make a round opening for the filling. The wall should be fairly thin.

5. Place one marble-shaped filling in each shell and bring the edges together to close. Smooth the surface with wet fingers and flatten slightly by gently pressing between the palms.

6. Drop the meat balls into the boiling stock and cook for ten minutes, or until the meat balls come to the surface. Remove with a slotted spoon without puncturing. Serve at once with Armenian Rice Pilaf (below) or serve in the broth.

Armenian Rice Pilaf

4 to 6 servings

1 tablespoon vegetable oil
¼ cup very fine egg noodles
1 cup uncooked long-grain rice
   Salt and freshly ground pepper to taste
¼ cup butter
2 cups boiling Chicken Stock (page 115)

1. Preheat the oven to 325 degrees.

2. Heat the oil in an ovenproof casserole and cook the noodles until slightly brown.

3. Add the rice, salt, pepper, butter, and chicken stock. Stir over a low flame until the butter is melted. Cover tightly and bake twenty-five to thirty minutes, or until all the liquid has been absorbed.

4. Remove the casserole from the oven and remove the cover. Cover the casserole with a kitchen towel, replace the cover, and let stand for five minutes.

Stuffed Artichokes Armenian Style

4 servings

The artichoke, one of the most elegant of vegetables, depends—like snails and spaghetti—on embellishments to heighten its appeal. These may be sauces like hollandaise or mayonnaise or vinaigrette; or stuffings that range from seafood (even pureed oysters) to beef and pork and lamb. Artichokes are not the simplest of vegetables to cook because of that fuzzy "choke" in the center, but they're worth the effort.

4 artichokes
1 onion (¼ pound), peeled
  Salt to taste
¼ cup burghul (cracked wheat)
¾ pound lean lamb, ground
  Freshly ground pepper to taste
⅓ cup finely chopped parsley
½ teaspoon paprika
7 tablespoons cold water
¼ cup pignoli (pine nuts)
⅓ cup each chopped celery, onion, and carrots
2 sprigs parsley
1 bay leaf
1 cup Chicken Stock (page 115)
4 teaspoons butter

1. Prepare the artichokes for stuffing and baking according to the method below.
2. Preheat the oven to 350 degrees.
3. Peel the onion and grate it on a coarse grater into a mixing bowl. Sprinkle with salt and let stand about ten minutes.
4. Place the burghul in a mixing bowl and add cold water to cover.
5. Place the lamb in a mixing bowl. Empty the grated onion mixture into a small length of cheesecloth, squeeze the onion juice into the lamb, and then discard the grated onion.
6. Drain the burghul and squeeze it in a clean towel or cheesecloth. Add it to the lamb, then add salt and pepper and knead well. Add the parsley, paprika, water, and pignoli and knead again with the hands. Spoon equal parts of the mixture into each of the artichoke centers, then push the leaves together to regain the artichoke shape.
7. Scatter the celery, onion, carrots, parsley sprigs, and bay leaf over the bottom of a buttered deep, metal baking dish. Arrange the artichokes over all and pour in the chicken stock. Place a teaspoon of butter over the filling of each artichoke. Cover loosely with foil and bring to a boil on top of the stove. Place the casserole in the oven and bake one hour or longer, or until the artichoke bottoms are tender. Remove the foil for the last fifteen minutes of baking. Serve hot, with Tomato Sauce I (page 278) on the side.

PREPARING ARTICHOKES FOR STUFFING AND BAKING:

Pull off a few of the bottom leaves of the artichokes and cut off the tips of some of the larger leaves. Cut off the tips of the artichokes, about an inch from the top.

Bring enough water in a deep kettle to boil to cover the artichokes. Add the juice of one lemon. To keep the green color of the artichokes, blend two tablespoons of flour with about half a cup of cold water. Pour this through a strainer into the kettle. Add salt to taste.

Cut off the stems of the artichokes and immediately rub the cut portion with a lemon half to prevent discoloration. Drop the artichokes immediately into the kettle and cover with a piece of cheesecloth. Bring to a boil. Simmer fifteen minutes, then drain.

Open the centers of the artichokes with the fingers. Using the fingers, pull away the center leaves to expose the fibrous "choke" at the bottom. Use a spoon or a melon-ball cutter to scrape away the "choke," taking care to disturb the meaty bottom as little as possible.

The artichokes may now be filled, pushing the leaves together to regroup them.

Australia

5. Beat the egg whites with the salt until stiff but not dry. Adding one-third of the egg whites at a time, fold carefully into the chocolate mixture. Pour into the prepared pan and bake twenty minutes. Reduce the oven temperature to 350 degrees and bake forty-five minutes longer. Remove from the oven, place on a wet towel, and cool.

6. When cool, remove the cake from the pan. If the top is uneven, level it with a thin, sharp knife. Place the cake on waxed paper and pour the icing over. Using a spatula, completely cover the top and sides. Let stand until the icing sets, then transfer to a cake platter.

Queen Mother's Cake

12 servings

Fine bread crumbs
6 ounces fine-quality sweet chocolate
¾ cup sweet butter
¾ cup granulated sugar
6 eggs, separated
6 ounces finely grated almonds
Pinch of salt
Icing (see below)

1. Preheat the oven to 375 degrees.
2. Butter a nine-inch spring-form pan. Line the bottom with waxed paper and butter the paper. Dust the sides and bottom with fine bread crumbs. Set aside.
3. Melt the chocolate in the top of a double boiler. Remove from the heat and cool.
4. Cream the butter and sugar very well. Add the egg yolks, one at a time, and beat until smooth. Stir in the cooled chocolate and almonds.

ICING:
½ cup heavy cream
1 rounded teaspoon decaffeinated instant coffee
8 ounces fine-quality sweet chocolate, broken into pieces

Heat the cream in a heavy saucepan until it just barely begins to boil. Add the instant coffee and stir to dissolve, then add the chocolate. After a minute or two, remove the saucepan from the heat and stir constantly until the chocolate is completely melted. Let cool a few minutes, until just barely tepid. Stir well.

Lady Sholl's Pavlova

8 or more servings

4 egg whites
½ teaspoon salt
1 cup granulated sugar
2 teaspoons cornstarch
2 teaspoons vinegar
3 to 4 cups sliced bananas, crushed pine-apple, strawberries, or canned passion fruit
Whipped cream

1. Preheat the oven to 300 degrees.

2. Butter an eight-inch cake pan, cover the bottom with a round of waxed paper, and butter the paper. Dust the paper lightly with cornstarch.

3. Beat the egg whites in a large mixing bowl, and when foamy, add the salt. Continue beating until stiff. Gradually add the sugar, beating well after each addition. When the meringue is glossy, combine the cornstarch and vinegar and fold into the meringue.

4. Spoon the meringue into the prepared cake tin and smooth around to the edges, leaving a slight indentation or "well" from the edges to the center.

5. Place the tin in the oven and immediately turn down the temperature to 250 degrees. Bake one and one-quarter hours. Remove the meringue from the oven and let stand at room temperature until cool, then remove from the tin and place on a serving dish. Drain the fruit and spoon it into the meringue. Cover with whipped cream and serve immediately.

Austria

Beef Esterhazy

8 servings

3 pounds fillet or other good quality beef, sliced thin
  Salt and freshly ground pepper to taste
1 tablespoon plus 1 teaspoon all-purpose flour
6 tablespoons butter
2 tablespoons finely chopped onion
1 tablespoon finely chopped fresh parsley
1 cup sour cream
½ cup Beef Stock (page 115), approximately
1 teaspoon chopped capers
1 teaspoon chopped anchovy fillet

1. Sprinkle the beef slices with salt and pepper and arrange the pieces on a flat surface. Dust lightly on one side with the tablespoon of flour.

2. In a large skillet heat two tablespoons of the butter. Sauté the beef quickly on both sides.

3. Heat the remaining butter in a casserole and add the onion. Cook until lightly glazed. Add the parsley.

4. Sprinkle the mixture with the remaining one teaspoon flour and stir. Add the sour cream and enough stock to make a smooth sauce, then add the meat and cook until tender. If fillet is used, it is ready to serve when heated through. Lesser cuts of beef will require longer cooking. When ready to serve, stir in the capers and anchovy.

Mushroom Soup

4 to 6 servings

4 cups Beef Stock (page 115)
1 cup thinly sliced mushrooms
4 to 6 teaspoons dry sherry

1. Combine the stock and mushrooms in a saucepan and bring to a boil. Simmer one minute.

2. Ladle the soup into hot cups and add one teaspoon of sherry to each cup.

6

Breaded Veal Scallops

6 servings

6 veal slices, each ¼ inch thick, pounded thin
All-purpose flour
Salt and freshly ground black pepper
1 egg
1 tablespoon water
1 cup fresh bread crumbs
⅓ cup plus 1 tablespoon butter
1 medium onion, minced
1 cup sliced mushrooms
⅓ cup Chicken Stock (page 115) or sherry
1 tablespoon chopped parsley
Pinch of dried tarragon

1. Coat each piece of meat with flour seasoned with salt and pepper. Dip in the egg beaten with the water, then in the crumbs. Press the meat lightly with the flat side of a knife to make the crumbs stick.

2. Heat the one-third cup butter in a skillet and cook the meat slowly for four to five minutes on each side, or until golden brown. Transfer the scallops to a warm serving platter.

3. Add the remaining tablespoon butter to the skillet. Add the onion and mushrooms and cook until lightly browned. Add the chicken stock, bring to a boil, and simmer two minutes. Add the parsley and tarragon. Pour the vegetables and sauce over the meat.

Viennese Chicken

4 servings

2 tablespoons butter
1 onion, finely chopped
1 chicken (2 to 3 pounds), cut into serving pieces
1 green pepper, chopped
2 carrots, chopped
6 mushrooms, sliced
1 tomato, skinned and diced
1 cup Chicken Stock (page 115)
1 teaspoon paprika
½ teaspoon salt
⅛ teaspoon freshly ground black pepper
1 tablespoon all-purpose flour
¼ cup sour cream

1. Melt the butter in a heavy skillet. Add the onion and sauté until tender but not browned. Add the chicken pieces and brown on all sides.

2. Add the green pepper, carrots, mushrooms, tomato, stock, paprika, salt, and pepper. Bring to a boil. Cover and simmer twenty-five to thirty-five minutes, until the chicken is tender.

3. Blend the flour with the cream and stir into the skillet. Reheat while stirring, but do not allow to boil.

Vienna Speckle Cake

8 to 10 servings

¾ cup cake flour
¾ cup grated unsweetened chocolate
6 egg yolks
1 cup granulated sugar
¾ teaspoon vanilla extract
¼ teaspoon almond extract
¼ teaspoon salt
7 egg whites
  Whipped cream
  Fruit, if desired, for filling

1. Preheat the oven to 350 degrees.
2. Sift the flour, add the grated chocolate, and set aside.
3. Beat the egg yolks until thick and lemon colored, then add the sugar and beat until thick and fluffy. Add the vanilla and almond extracts. Add half of the flour mixture and beat until thoroughly mixed.
4. Add the salt to the egg whites and beat until stiff. Fold the remaining flour mixture into the egg whites. Fold the egg white mixture into the egg yolk mixture.
5. Pour the batter into an ungreased nine-inch tube pan and bake for forty-five minutes. Invert to cool.
6. Cut the cake into halves to form layers. Fill with whipped cream and fruit or any desired filling. Cover the entire cake with whipped cream.

Wiener Backhendl

6 to 12 servings

12 chicken thighs
   Salt
½ cup all-purpose flour
2 eggs
1 teaspoon water
1½ cups fresh bread crumbs
   Solid vegetable shortening

1. Bone the thighs or have them boned by the butcher.
2. Sprinkle the boned thighs on all sides with salt and let stand one hour.
3. Coat the thighs with flour.
4. Break the eggs into a glass pie plate or baking dish, beat lightly, and stir in the water. Dip the flour-coated thighs in egg, then in the bread crumbs.
5. Heat the shortening to a depth of one-quarter inch in a large, heavy skillet. Cook the thighs over medium heat until golden brown on one side, then turn and cook until golden brown on the other. Drain on paper towels. If the chicken is not to be served immediately, it may be kept warm in a very low oven (150 degrees).

Coach House Chocolate Cake

12 to 16 servings

4 cups sifted all-purpose flour
1½ cups butter
½ pound semisweet or sweet chocolate
⅓ cup warm water
½ teaspoon salt
2 cups heavy cream
1 pound finest-quality sweet chocolate
  Confectioners' sugar
  Chocolate curls

1. To make the cake layers, place the flour in a bowl. Using a pastry blender, two knives or the fingertips, work the butter into the flour, as though making pastry, until the mixture resembles coarse oatmeal. Do not allow the butter to become oil.

2. Melt the semisweet chocolate very slowly over hot water, then beat in the water and salt until the mixture is smooth. Fold the chocolate mixture into the flour and butter.

3. Divide the dough into three parts, wrap each part in waxed paper, and chill twenty minutes, or until firm, in the refrigerator.

4. Roll each third of the dough, in turn, between sheets of waxed paper, into a rectangle about eight by twelve inches. Peel off the top paper and fold the rectangle into threes, peeling the bottom paper off as you go. Wrap in fresh waxed paper and chill about twenty minutes. Repeat the rollings between waxed paper, folding and chilling twice more, a total of three times.

5. Wrap each third of dough in waxed paper and chill until very firm, about two hours.

6. Preheat the oven to 325 degrees.

7. Roll out each third of dough, between sheets of waxed paper, into a circle and remove the top sheet of waxed paper. Cut a nine- to ten-inch circle with a sharp knife, leaving a round of waxed paper beneath the layer. Place the circle, waxed-paper side down, on an ungreased baking sheet. Bake thirty minutes, or until done. Cool on the sheet. Repeat with the other two thirds of the dough. (Alternately, the thirds of dough can be rolled into four-by-eighteen-inch rectangles and baked as above to make a long rectangular cake for cutting into slices rather than a round cake to cut into wedges.)

8. When the layers are completely cold, place the cream in a chilled bowl buried in ice.

9. Melt the chocolate very slowly over hot water and when it is melted but still only lukewarm, fold it into the cream, which has been whipped until stiff.

10. Spread the chocolate cream filling between the round or rectangular layers; it will be quite thick. Sprinkle the top with confectioners' sugar and garnish with chocolate curls. Chill well.

11. The cake should be removed from the refrigerator at least an hour before it is to be served. Use a sharp, serrated knife for cutting.

Note: This cake freezes well.

Kirsch Torte

10 to 12 servings

That clear white spirit called kirsch, a fine brandy distilled from cherries, imparts a seductive flavor to many European desserts. The torte described below is among the most agreeable of kirsch-flavored desserts. Note, please, that imported kirsch—from Switzerland, Germany, or France's Alsace—is infinitely superior to our domestic product, which is not even an acceptable imitation.

1½ cups (approximately) Jelly Filling (page 11)
  2 Meringue Layers (see below)
  1 9-inch Sponge Cake (see below)
    Kirsch Solution (page 11)
    Buttercream Frosting (page 11)
⅓ cup chopped toasted almonds
    Red jelly (optional)

1. Spread one-half of the filling on one of the meringue layers. Put the sponge cake on top. Pour the kirsch solution over the sponge cake. Spread the remaining jelly filling over the sponge cake and top with the second meringue layer.

2. Frost the torte with the buttercream frosting over the top and around the sides. Using the fingers, cover the sides of the torte with the chopped almonds. If desired, make a design on top of the torte with the red jelly well beaten.

Note: This torte tastes best if made at least twenty-four hours before serving.

SPONGE CAKE:

1 9-inch sponge cake

4 eggs
¾ cup granulated sugar
½ teaspoon baking powder
¾ cup sifted cake flour
¼ teaspoon salt

1. Preheat the oven to 325 degrees.

2. Place the eggs and sugar in a bowl and warm very gently over warm water, stirring occasionally to prevent drying.

3. When the mixture is lukewarm, beat with an electric mixer until very thick and pale lemon-colored.

4. Sift together the baking powder, flour, and salt and fold into the egg mixture.

5. Turn into a nine-inch spring-form pan that has been lightly greased and floured on the bottom only. Bake fifty to sixty minutes, or until the cake rebounds to the touch when pressed gently in the center.

6. Turn upside down in the pan to cool.

MERINGUE LAYERS:

2 meringue layers

3 egg whites
⅛ teaspoon cream of tartar
⅞ cup superfine granulated sugar
1 tablespoon vanilla sugar (see note)
1 cup finely ground almonds

1. Preheat the oven to 250 to 275 degrees.

2. Beat the egg whites and cream of tartar until the mixture forms peaks. Gradually, a tablespoon at a time, beat in the sugar, mixed with the vanilla sugar, so that no graininess remains.

3. Fold in the nuts. Turn the mixture into two nine-inch greased Teflon-lined pans, preferably lined on the bottom with parchment paper.

4. Bake one hour. Turn off the oven and leave the layers in the oven with the door closed for another hour. Cool on a rack.

Note: Vanilla sugar is available in the spice section of most specialty stores. Do not attempt to make these layers on a damp or humid day.

JELLY FILLING:

About 1½ cups

3 tablespoons cornstarch
½ cup granulated sugar
1 cup milk
4 tablespoons currant jelly
¾ cup butter
2 drops red food coloring (optional)

1. Blend together the cornstarch, sugar, and one-quarter cup of the milk.

2. Heat the remaining milk to boiling. Remove from the heat and add to the above mixture.

3. Bring the mixture to a boil once, stirring. Remove from the heat and add the jelly. Cool to barely lukewarm.

4. Blend the butter until creamy. Add the jelly mixture to the butter a tablespoon at a time, blending continuously. If a deeper color is desired, add the food coloring. Refrigerate until the proper spreading consistency is reached.

KIRSCH SOLUTION:

About ½ cup

6 tablespoons water
3 tablespoons granulated sugar
6 tablespoons kirsch

Bring the water and sugar to a boil. Stir until the sugar is dissolved. Cool, then stir in the kirsch.

BUTTERCREAM FROSTING:

About 2 cups

⅔ cup granulated sugar
⅓ cup water
⅛ teaspoon cream of tartar
5 egg yolks
1 cup soft butter
1 teaspoon vanilla extract

1. Combine the sugar, water, and cream of tartar in a small saucepan. Bring to a boil, stirring until the sugar dissolves.

2. Continue to heat, without stirring, until the mixture registers 238 to 240 degrees on a candy thermometer or forms a soft ball in cold water.

3. Beat the egg yolks until very thick and light.

4. Pour the hot syrup in a fine stream into the egg yolks, beating all the time. Continue to beat until the mixture starts to thicken. Cool to room temperature, then beat in the butter and the vanilla. Chill until firm enough to spread.

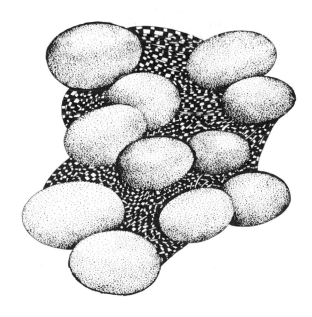

Date Torte I

6 servings

2 eggs, separated
1 cup corn syrup or honey
1 cup chopped, pitted dates
1 teaspoon vanilla extract
¼ cup chopped pecans or hazelnuts
1 cup sifted bread crumbs
¼ cup sifted all-purpose flour
½ teaspoon salt
½ teaspoon baking powder
¾ cup heavy cream
2 tablespoons superfine granulated sugar

1. Preheat the oven to 375 degrees.
2. Place the egg yolks in a mixing bowl and add the corn syrup. Beat with an electric mixer or a rotary beater until well blended. Stir in the chopped dates, vanilla extract, and nuts.
3. Sift the bread crumbs once more with the flour, salt, and baking powder, then fold the mixture into the batter. Beat the egg whites until stiff and fold them in.
4. Butter a nine-inch layer cake pan (one and one-half inches deep) and add the batter. Bake twenty-five minutes.
5. Cut the torte into wedges while still warm. Whip the cream, season with sugar, and serve with the warm cake.

Date Torte II

18 to 24 servings

2 cups sifted dry bread crumbs
½ cup sifted all-purpose flour
Dash of salt
1 teaspoon baking powder
4 eggs, separated
2 cups honey
2 cups chopped, pitted dates
1 cup chopped walnuts
2 teaspoons vanilla extract
Whipped cream

1. Preheat the oven to 375 degrees. Grease a cake pan (13 x 9 x 2 inches).
2. Sift together the bread crumbs, flour, salt, and baking powder. Set aside.
3. Beat the egg yolks lightly. Add the honey and mix thoroughly. Add the dates, walnuts, vanilla, and sifted dry ingredients. Mix well.
4. Beat the egg whites until stiff peaks are formed. Fold gently into the batter.
5. Pour into the prepared pan. Bake for twenty-five to thirty minutes, until the cake rebounds to the touch when pressed gently in the center. Remove the cake from the oven, cut into squares, and serve hot with whipped cream.

Sacher Torte

10 servings

8 egg yolks
10 egg whites
⅛ teaspoon salt
¾ cup granulated sugar
½ cup sweet butter
6½ ounces (6½ squares) semisweet chocolate
1 teaspoon vanilla extract
1 cup sifted all-purpose flour
Frosting (see below)
½ cup apricot preserves

1. Preheat the oven to 350 degrees.
2. Grease three nine- or ten-inch layer pans; line the bottoms with waxed paper and grease the paper.
3. Place the egg yolks in a medium-sized bowl and the egg whites in the largest bowl of the electric mixer.
4. Add the salt to the egg whites and beat until peaks just form. Add the sugar, a tablespoon at a time, continuing to beat constantly. Continue to beat three to four minutes after all the sugar is added. The mixture should be very thick and glossy.
5. Meanwhile, melt the butter and chocolate together in a heavy pan or over hot water in a double boiler. Cool slightly, then add, along with the vanilla extract, to the egg yolks, using a wire whisk to combine. This will be a thick mixture.
6. Add one quarter of the meringue to the butter, chocolate, and egg yolk mixture and incorporate with the whisk. Pour this mixture over the remaining whites and sprinkle the flour over the top. Fold all together with the whisk or the hands so there are no lumps of white showing, being careful not to under- or overmix. Overmixing will produce a hard cake, while undermixing will result in large holes.
7. Pour into the prepared pans and bake twenty-five to thirty minutes, depending on the size of pans, or until done.
8. Turn onto a rack to cool and peel off the waxed paper. The layers will shrink as they cool.
9. While the cake is baking, or several hours ahead, make the frosting.
10. When the cake is cool, spread the preserves between the layers, and setting the cake on a piece of waxed paper to catch the drips, pour the cooled frosting over. Transfer to a serving platter and refrigerate two to three hours to set the frosting. Before serving, allow the cake to reach room temperature.

FROSTING:
3 ounces (3 squares) unsweetened baking chocolate
1 cup heavy cream
1 tablespoon corn syrup
1 cup granulated sugar
1 egg, lightly beaten
1 teaspoon vanilla extract

1. Combine the chocolate, cream, corn syrup, and sugar in a small, heavy pan. Heat, stirring, until the chocolate is melted and the sugar dissolved.
2. Raise the heat to medium and cook until the mixture reaches 224 to 226 degrees on a candy thermometer or forms a soft ball when dropped into water, stirring only enough to prevent sticking.
3. Using a small wire whisk, beat the hot mixture into the beaten egg. Cool to room temperature, then stir in the vanilla extract.

Spanische Windtorte

12 servings

Ask a pastry chef to name the most fragile, tenderest, and most delicate of desserts and chances are he will mention vacherin, *the gossamer-light, sculptured, baked meringue that is generally served with a mound or filling of whipped cream.* Vacherin *is the French word for the sweet; the Austrians and Germans have a special name for it. They call it* Spanische Windtorte, *or Spanish wind torte, which is romantic indeed. Here is the recipe for this airy dessert.*

12 egg whites, at room temperature
⅛ teaspoon salt
¾ teaspoon cream of tartar
 3 cups superfine granulated sugar
    Parchment paper or unglazed brown paper
 4 cups heavy cream, whipped
 3 tablespoons confectioners' sugar
 1 quart strawberries

1. Preheat the oven to 150 to 200 degrees.
2. Place eight of the egg whites in a large electric mixer bowl. Add half the salt. Beat until frothy, then add one-half teaspoon of the cream of tartar. (The whites can also be beaten in a copper bowl with a balloon whisk.)
3. Continue to beat and gradually add, a tablespoon at a time, one and three-quarters cups of the superfine sugar. Beat until the mixture is smooth and glossy and there is no hint of graininess when the mixture is felt between the fingers.
4. Fold in one-quarter cup more of the superfine sugar and transfer the mixture to a large piping bag fitted with a no. 8 plain tube.
5. Place sheets of parchment paper on slightly damp baking sheets and mark off five eight-inch circles.
6. Starting in the center of the first circle, make a snail-like pattern, going around and around until the edge of the circle is covered. This will be the bottom layer of the cake.
7. On the next three circles, make a ring of piped meringue, two layers high, around the outside edge. These will form the sides of the cake.
8. On the last circle, using a no. 6 star tube this time, pipe the meringue into a fairly thick, single-layer ring around the edge. Fill in the center with crisscrossed lattice work substantial enough to enable this layer to be lifted off and used for the top of the cake.
9. Bake, or rather dry, all five circles of meringue for two to three hours, or until they are crisp but have not taken on any color. When they are dry, they will be easily removable from the parchment paper if care is taken.
10. Beat the remaining four egg whites, with the remaining salt, until frothy. Add the remaining quarter teaspoon cream of tartar and beat until peaks form.
11. Gradually, a tablespoon at a time, beat in three-quarters cup of the remaining superfine sugar. Beat until the mixture is smooth and glossy and does not feel grainy. Fold in the remaining one-quarter cup superfine sugar.
12. Place the solid circle on a serving plate. Dot around the edges with meringue and put the first ring in place. Dot the top of this ring and position the second ring. Repeat with the third ring.
13. With a spatula, use meringue to frost all around the outside of the cake shell to make a smooth surface. Transfer the remaining meringue to a piping bag fitted with a no. 6 star tube and decorate the cake around the bottom and on the sides. Bake, or dry, at 200 degrees, or below, several hours or overnight.
14. To serve, combine the whipped cream

with the confectioners' sugar and strawberries, sliced except for a few left whole for garnish. Pile into the cake shell. Top with the lattice meringue top and garnish with the whole strawberries.

Note: For best results this dessert should not be attempted on a damp or humid day.

If baked meringue breaks, it can be mended by "gluing" it together with unbaked meringue.

Viennese Apple Torte

8 or more servings

PASTRY:
½ cup butter
1 cup sifted all-purpose flour
2 tablespoons granulated sugar
1 egg yolk
Grated rind of 1 lemon

FILLING:
2½ pounds tart apples, peeled, cored, quartered, and sliced
¼ cup granulated sugar
¼ cup lemon juice
2 tablespoons water
¼ cup raisins

TOPPING:
1 pound tart apples, peeled, cored, quartered, and cut lengthwise into ⅛-inch slices
1 egg white, lightly beaten
Juice of ½ lemon

GLAZE:
½ cup apricot preserves, put through a sieve
2 tablespoons granulated sugar

1. Prepare the pastry first. Place the butter, flour, sugar, egg yolk, and grated lemon rind in a mixing bowl and work until smooth. Wrap in waxed paper and refrigerate half an hour.

2. Roll out the pastry on a lightly floured board.

3. Butter and lightly flour an eight-inch spring-form pan or a nine-inch pie plate. Arrange the pastry in the prepared pan. Chill.

4. Prepare the filling. Place the apples in a heavy enameled saucepan and add the sugar, lemon juice, water, and raisins. Cover tightly and bring to a boil. Simmer 10 minutes. Set aside to cool.

5. Preheat the oven to 300 degrees.

6. Pour the filling into the pastry shell and prepare the topping. Cover the filling with the apple slices, arranging them in a circular pattern with the slices slightly overlapping. Brush the topping with the egg white and sprinkle with the lemon juice.

7. Bake the torte until the crust is brown, about one hour.

8. Prepare the glaze by combining the apricot preserves with the sugar in the top of a double boiler and stirring until smooth.

9. Spread the glaze over the top of the torte. Serve at room temperature.

Austrian Hazelnut Tarts with Chocolate Icing

About 3½ dozen

6 tablespoons unsalted butter
1½ cups sifted all-purpose flour
1 egg yolk
1½ cups ground hazelnuts
½ cup granulated sugar
    Apricot jam
    Chocolate Icing (see below)
    Almonds, blanched and halved

1. Preheat the oven to 250 degrees.
2. With a fork, blend the butter into the flour until well mixed. Fold the egg yolk and ground nuts into the sugar and mix with the flour and butter mixture. Roll out on a dusted board and cut with a cookie cutter one inch in diameter. Bake until lightly browned, about twelve to fifteen minutes. Let cool.
3. Place two cookies atop each other and put some apricot jam in between. (Dilute the jam with a little water to make it spread more easily.) Frost with chocolate icing and place half a blanched almond in the center of each.

CHOCOLATE ICING:

About 1 cup

4 semisweet chocolate cubes (German chocolate)
1 cup granulated sugar
6 tablespoons water
1 teaspoon unsalted butter

Melt the chocolate in the top of a double boiler. Cook the sugar and water together, stirring constantly, until the mixture becomes a thick syrup. Mix the syrup into the melted chocolate and stir until smooth. Remove from the stove and add the butter to make the icing shiny.

Schokoladendunstkoch

(Chocolate Pudding)

6 or more servings

6 tablespoons softened butter
¾ cup granulated sugar
6 egg yolks
5 squares (5 ounces) semisweet chocolate
1 cup milk
8 small slices firm bread, crusts removed, cut into small cubes (about 2 cups cubes)
⅓ cup ground almonds
    Grated rind of ½ lemon
6 egg whites, stiffly beaten but not dry
2 tablespoons cracker crumbs
    Whipped cream
    Chocolate Sauce (page 17)

1. Cream the butter and sugar and beat in the egg yolks, one at a time.
2. Melt the chocolate over low heat and beat into the creamed mixture.
3. Add the milk to the bread cubes. Soak five minutes, then squeeze dry, discarding the milk. Crumble the bread cubes and add to the chocolate mixture, along with the almonds and lemon rind. Mix well, then fold the egg whites into the pudding.
4. Prepare a two-quart mold for steaming by buttering the inside and sprinkling with cracker crumbs. Pour the pudding mixture into it and seal with a tight-fitting cover or aluminum foil and string.
5. Place two to four inches of water in a kettle and bring to a boil. Place the sealed mold on a rack in the kettle, cover, and steam one hour. To serve, unmold while hot and make a border of whipped cream and a little of the chocolate sauce. Serve the remaining chocolate sauce separately.

Chocolate Sauce

About 2½ cups

2 cups plus 2 tablespoons water
1 cup granulated sugar
1 teaspoon vanilla extract
4 squares (4 ounces) semisweet chocolate
1 teaspoon cornstarch
2 tablespoons butter

1. Combine two cups of the water and the sugar in a saucepan and bring to a boil. Stir until the sugar is dissolved. Add the vanilla and chocolate and stir until dissolved.

2. Blend the cornstarch with the remaining water. Add to the chocolate mixture and return to a boil. Stir in the butter and serve.

Viennese Crescents

3 dozen

¼ vanilla bean
1½ to 2 cups sifted confectioners' sugar
2½ cups sifted all-purpose flour
1 cup plus 1 tablespoon butter, at room temperature
2 cups granulated sugar
1 cup almonds, finely chopped

1. Prepare vanilla sugar by pulverizing the bean and mixing it into the sifted confectioners' sugar. Let stand overnight, closely covered.

2. Preheat the oven to 350 degrees.

3. With the fingers, mix the flour and butter. Add the granulated sugar and chopped almonds and mix well. Shape the dough, a teaspoon at a time, into small crescents.

4. Bake on an ungreased cookie sheet for fifteen to twenty minutes. Allow to cool briefly. While still warm, sift the vanilla sugar over the cookies.

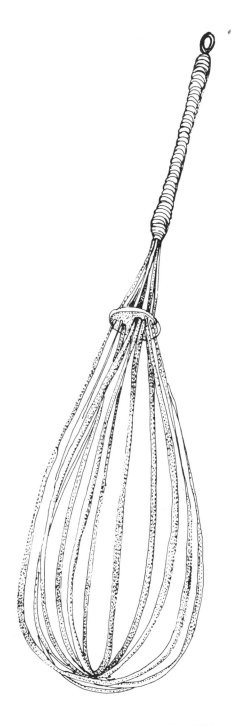

Barbados

Barbadian Funji or Coo-Koo with Codfish Sauce

4 to 6 servings

CODFISH SAUCE:
- 1 pound dried salted codfish
- 2 tablespoons olive oil
- 1 cup thinly sliced onions
- 1 clove garlic, finely minced
- 1 no. 2 can tomatoes with juice
  Freshly ground pepper to taste
- 1 teaspoon dried thyme
- ½ cup clam broth or water
- 1 small fresh or dried hot pepper (optional)

FUNJI:
- 1½ pounds fresh whole baby okra or 2 10-ounce packages frozen okra
- 2 quarts water
- 1 tablespoon salt
- 1 cup fine yellow cornmeal

1. Soak the cod in cold water to cover for twenty-four hours. Cut into three or four large pieces and place in a skillet. Add cold water to cover and bring to a boil. Simmer about ten minutes, then drain and let cool. Remove any skin and bones and break the cooked fish into slightly larger than bite-sized portions.

2. Heat the oil in a saucepan and cook the onion and garlic until the onion is wilted. Add the tomatoes, pepper, thyme, broth, and hot pepper. Add the cod and simmer slowly thirty minutes.

3. If fresh okra is used, rinse in cold water. Cut each pod of okra, fresh or frozen, in half and place in a kettle. Add the two quarts of water and the salt and bring to a boil. Simmer until the okra is tender.

4. Drain the okra, reserving both okra and cooking liquid. Add one quart of the cooking liquid to a saucepan and bring to a fast boil. Gradually add the cornmeal, stirring rapidly and continuously with a wire whisk. When the mixture is thickened and smooth, add the okra. Continue cooking, stirring frequently, fifteen to twenty minutes, adding more of the reserved cooking liquid as necessary. When done, this will be a thickened mush. It must not be soupy.

5. Spoon the hot mush into hot buttered soup bowls and cover with codfish sauce.

Souse

10 to 12 servings

6 pigs' feet, split
6 pigs' ears
3 pigs' snouts
3 pork tongues
  Salt
5 whole peppercorns
1 bay leaf
1 clove garlic, split
  Tabasco to taste
½ lime
4 cucumbers, peeled and sliced (part of this may be used later as a garnish)
  Juice of 6 limes
2 medium onions, finely minced
1 green pepper, cored, seeded, and finely chopped
1½ teaspoons chopped fresh basil or ¾ teaspoon dried basil
½ cup finely chopped parsley
3 fresh hot red peppers, seeded and finely chopped
  Freshly ground pepper to taste
3 cups water

1. Thoroughly clean and scrub the pigs' feet, ears, snouts, and tongues. Place them in a kettle and add cold water to cover. Bring to a boil, then remove from the heat and drain well. Return the pigs' feet to the kettle and add hot water to cover. Set aside the ears, snouts, and tongues.

2. Add one tablespoon salt, the peppercorns, bay leaf, garlic, Tabasco, and lime to the kettle and bring to a boil. Simmer about forty-five minutes. Add the reserved meats and, if necessary, enough water to cover all. Simmer, partly covered, until all the meats are fork tender, about forty-five minutes longer.

3. Drain the meats and cut them into bite-sized pieces. Place them in a bowl.

4. Combine all the remaining ingredients, plus salt to taste. This mixture is called a "peth." Pour the peth over the meats and let stand or "soak," as they say in Barbados, three to four hours or longer. Serve at room temperature.

Black Pudding

12 or more servings

7 or 8 lengths of whole chitterlings
  Lime juice
  Salt
10 pounds sweet potatoes (not the brick-red
  Southern yams)
2 pounds fresh beets, peeled
4 teaspoons dried thyme
1 cup finely chopped fresh parsley
8 green onions, finely chopped, green part
  and all
  Freshly ground pepper to taste
4 fresh hot red peppers, seeded and chopped
⅓ cup butter
⅓ cup pork lard
½ cup salad oil
1 tablespoon granulated sugar
6 cloves, crushed

1. The chitterlings must be thoroughly cleaned inside and out with lime juice and salt. Discard the fat from the chitterlings without breaking them. Place them in a large bowl and pour boiling water over them. Let stand.

2. Grate the sweet potatoes and beets into a large bowl. Add salt to taste and the remaining ingredients, with the exception of the chitterlings. Blend well.

3. Tie one end of each chitterling and stuff, sausage fashion. As each is filled, tie the untied end.

4. Cover the bottom of a large kettle with a flat steamer or metal plate. This is to keep the sausages, or black puddings, from sticking. Add enough water to cover all the puddings. Bring the water to a boil and carefully lower the puddings into it. Bring to a boil and simmer about one hour, or until a toothpick will come out clean when used to pierce the puddings. Serve hot or cold. Leftover puddings may be fried.

Rum Punch

12 or more servings

  Juice of 6 to 8 limes
1 cup granulated sugar
2 cups water (see note)
1 fifth bottle dark rum
4 or 5 dashes Angostura bitters
  Grated nutmeg

Combine the lime juice, sugar, water, rum, and bitters. Pour the mixture into a large pitcher and chill thoroughly. Serve in small tumblers, adding a dash of nutmeg to each drink.

Note: The water is sometimes replaced with equal amounts of blended orange and pineapple juice. If desired, each serving may be garnished with slices of lime or orange or pineapple slivers.

Belgium

Carbonnades of Beef à la Flamande

6 to 8 servings

3 pounds round steak or chuck, cut into 1-inch cubes
Salt and freshly ground black pepper
¼ pound salt pork, finely diced
5 tablespoons butter
6 cups thinly sliced onions
½ pound mushrooms, thinly sliced
3 tablespoons all-purpose flour
2 cups light beer
1 cup Beef Stock (page 115)
1 tablespoon wine vinegar
1 teaspoon brown sugar
1 clove garlic, finely minced
1 leek, trimmed and washed well
3 sprigs parsley
2 sprigs fresh thyme or ½ teaspoon dried thyme
1 bay leaf

1. Preheat the oven to 325 degrees.
2. Sprinkle the meat with salt and pepper.
3. Place the salt pork in a small saucepan and cover with water. Simmer one minute and drain well. Heat one tablespoon of the butter in a large skillet and add the salt pork cubes. Cook over moderate heat until brown. With a slotted spoon, remove the pork and drain on paper towels. Brown a few cubes of beef at a time in the remaining fat, and, as the meat browns, transfer it to a heavy casserole with a lid.
4. Heat the remaining butter in the skillet and cook the onions, stirring frequently, just until they are golden brown. Add the mushrooms and cook three to four minutes. Add the flour to the skillet and cook, stirring, over very low heat until the flour starts to brown. Gradually add the beer and stock, stirring and scraping vigorously with a wire whisk. When the mixture is thickened and smooth, add the vinegar, sugar, and garlic and return to a boil. Add the sauce and salt pork cubes to the meat.
5. Tie the leek, parsley, thyme, and bay leaf into a small bundle and add to the casserole. Sprinkle with salt and pepper. Cover and bake one and one-half to two hours or until the meat is fork tender. Before serving, remove the leek bundle. Serve with buttered noodles or steamed potatoes.

Waterzooie

4 to 8 servings

2 chickens (2½ pounds each), cut into serving pieces
Salt and freshly ground pepper to taste
½ cup butter
6 ribs celery
2 carrots, trimmed and scraped
8 sprigs fresh parsley
4 leeks, trimmed, split, and rinsed well under cold running water
12 peppercorns
1 blade dried mace or nutmeg to taste
5 cups boiling Chicken Stock (page 115)
Juice of 1 lemon
4 egg yolks
½ cup heavy cream
4 thin slices fresh lemon, seeds removed

1. Sprinkle the chicken pieces with salt and pepper to taste.

2. Heat the butter in a heatproof casserole and add the chicken. Cover and simmer, turning the chicken pieces occasionally, about ten minutes. The chicken should more or less stew in the butter without browning.

3. Add the ribs of celery, carrots, parsley, leeks, peppercorns, and mace. Add the boiling stock and cover once more. Simmer over low heat about thirty minutes, or until the chicken is tender.

4. Remove the chicken to a hot dish and cover to keep warm. Strain the broth into another casserole and add the lemon juice. Heat.

5. Beat the egg yolks lightly and add the cream. Gradually add this to the hot broth, stirring vigorously. Add the chicken. Let cook, without boiling, until the sauce thickens slightly. Do not overcook or the sauce may curdle. Serve in hot soup bowls garnished with lemon slices. Serve rice separately.

Fondue Bruxelloise

8 to 12 servings

¼ cup butter
All-purpose flour
2 cups milk
¼ pound Gruyère or Swiss cheese, grated
1 cup grated Parmesan cheese
⅛ teaspoon cayenne pepper
¼ teaspoon nutmeg
5 egg yolks
Salt and freshly ground pepper to taste
3 eggs, lightly beaten
2 teaspoons cold water
1 tablespoon peanut oil
3 cups fresh bread crumbs, approximately
Oil for deep frying
Fried Parsley (page 249)

1. Melt the butter in a large saucepan and stir in six tablespoons flour, using a wire whisk. Add the milk, stirring rapidly until the mixture is thickened and smooth. Simmer five minutes.

2. Remove the sauce from the heat and add the Gruyère, Parmesan, cayenne pepper, nutmeg, egg yolks, and salt and pepper to taste. Return the sauce to the heat and stir rapidly with the whisk. Cook, stirring, until it thickens further, but do not allow it to boil.

3. Generously butter a thirteen-by-nine-inch or a nine-inch-square pan and pour the sauce into it. Spread it smooth with a rubber spatula. Cover with buttered waxed paper and refrigerate overnight or longer.

4. Cut the firm mixture into squares, rectangles, rounds, or diamond shapes.

5. Beat the eggs until frothy, then beat in the water, oil, and salt and pepper to taste. Coat the cutouts on all sides with flour, then dip them into the egg mixture. Finally coat with crumbs, tapping lightly with the flat side of a knife so crumbs will adhere.

6. Heat the oil in a deep-fat fryer to 360 degrees and cook the cutouts until golden. Drain on paper towels. Serve hot, garnished with fried parsley.

BELGIUM 23

Brazil

Picadinho a Brasileira

6 to 8 servings

½ cup olive oil
 1 large onion, finely chopped
 4 cloves garlic, coarsely chopped
 2 pounds lean beef, preferably fillet, ground
 6 eggs
 2 ribs celery, including leaves, finely chopped
 1 green pepper, cored, seeded, and finely chopped
 1 cup finely chopped parsley
 2 cans (1-pound 1-ounce each) tomatoes, preferably Italian style
    Salt and freshly ground pepper to taste
1½ cups dry red wine
    Hot red pepper flakes to taste

1. Heat the oil in a large, deep saucepan and add the onion and garlic. Cook until golden brown, stirring frequently.

2. Meanwhile, place the meat in a large bowl. Add the eggs, celery, green pepper, parsley, and tomatoes. Work the mixture thoroughly with the hands. Add the mixture to the saucepan and cook, stirring, until well blended and the meat loses its red color.

3. Cook the mixture fifteen minutes and add salt, pepper, and one cup of the wine. Cover and cook fifteen minutes longer. Add the remaining wine and red pepper flakes, then partly cover and cook, stirring occasionally, one hour or longer. Note that in the beginning the picadinho will seem quite liquid. When done, however, most of the liquid will be absorbed. Raise the heat, if necessary, to hasten evaporation. Serve with rice, Farofa (page 25), and Bananas a Brasileira (page 25).

Note: If desired, various seasonings, flavors, and other foods may be added to a picadinho, including pitted green olives, capers, chopped pimento, green peas, and raisins.

Beef Picadillo

4 servings

½ cup raisins
¼ cup hot Beef Stock (page 115)
2 tablespoons olive oil
1 clove garlic, finely minced
⅓ cup finely chopped green onion
¾ pound round of beef, ground
¼ pound lean pork, ground
1 teaspoon salt
¼ teaspoon freshly ground black pepper
1½ cups canned tomatoes
1 tablespoon vinegar
1 small hot pepper, finely chopped
¼ teaspoon ground cumin (optional)
   Pinch of ground cloves
½ cup slivered blanched almonds

1. Soak the raisins in the hot beef stock for ten minutes.
2. Heat the oil in a saucepan and sauté the garlic, green onion, beef, and pork for about five minutes.
3. Add the salt, black pepper, tomatoes, vinegar, hot pepper, cumin, cloves, and soaked raisins. Bring to a boil and simmer for thirty minutes. Stir in the almonds. Serve hot, with rice.

Farofa

6 to 8 servings

¼ pound butter
2 eggs
1 cup farinha de manioca (Brazilian farina)
   Salt to taste

1. Melt the butter in a skillet.
2. Beat the eggs with a fork and add them to the skillet. Cook as for scrambled eggs, but while they are still runny and soft, stir in the farina. Stir constantly so the farina will be coated with the egg and butter mixture. Add salt and serve hot, with Picadinho a Brasileira (page 24).

Bananas a Brasileira

8 servings

4 firm, barely ripe bananas
2 eggs, lightly beaten
1½ cups fresh bread crumbs
   Vegetable oil or butter for shallow frying

1. Peel the bananas and cut each into four sections.
2. Roll the banana pieces first in egg, then in bread crumbs. Heat the oil or butter or a mixture of both in a skillet and cook the banana sections until golden brown on all sides. Serve as a side dish with Picadinho a Brasileira (page 24).

Bananas Brazilian Style

6 servings

6 medium bananas
½ cup fresh orange juice
1 tablespoon fresh lemon juice
¼ cup brown sugar
⅛ teaspoon salt
2 tablespoons butter
1 cup grated fresh coconut

1. Preheat the oven to 400 degrees.
2. Peel the bananas and cut them lengthwise into halves. Place in a buttered casserole.
3. Combine orange and lemon juices, sugar, and salt and pour over the bananas. Dot with butter.
4. Bake for ten to fifteen minutes, then remove from the oven. Before serving, sprinkle the bananas with the grated coconut. Serve as a dessert.

Canada

Soupe Aux Pois Canadienne

(Canadian Yellow Pea Soup)

6 to 8 servings

1 pound dried whole yellow peas
2½ quarts water, approximately
½ pound salt pork, rind removed, rinsed under cold water, and dried
2 medium onions, coarsely chopped
1 carrot, scraped and diced
1 teaspoon salt
½ teaspoon dried sage
  Salt and pepper to taste
  Freshly chopped parsley

1. Rinse the dried peas in cold water; pick over and discard any that are discolored. Drain.

2. Transfer the peas to a large, heavy soup kettle, pour in the two and one-half quarts water and bring to a boil. Boil the peas for two minutes, remove from the heat, and let soak for one hour.

3. Cut the salt pork into quarter-inch dice and render it in a frying pan, stirring frequently, for about ten minutes, until golden. Remove the dice with a slotted spoon and set aside. Discard the fat.

4. Return the soaked peas to the heat and bring to a boil, skimming if necessary. Add the pork dice, chopped onions, carrots, salt, and sage.

5. Partially cover the pot and simmer for at least two and one-half hours. During the last hour of cooking, uncover the pot and stir the soup occasionally; as it cooks it tends to stick to the bottom of the pan. Add an additional cup or two of water if the soup becomes too thick.

6. Before serving, add salt and freshly ground pepper to taste and sprinkle with freshly chopped parsley.

Ragoût de Pattes

(Pork Hocks in Brown Sauce)

4 servings

4 medium pork hocks, each split in half
2 cloves garlic, peeled and quartered
   Salt and freshly ground pepper
¼ teaspoon ground cloves
¼ teaspoon ground nutmeg
¼ teaspoon ground allspice
3 to 4 tablespoons vegetable oil
2 medium onions, coarsely chopped
¼ cup all-purpose flour mixed with ½ cup
   water
   Chopped parsley

1. Dry the hocks, make a small slit in the meaty part and stuff with a sliver of garlic. Combine one tablespoon salt, one-half teaspoon pepper, the cloves, nutmeg, and allspice and roll the meat in the mixture until each piece is well coated.

2. Heat the vegetable oil in a large frying pan. Brown the hocks as much as possible on all sides, turning frequently. Transfer the hocks to a heavy kettle, remove any browned pieces of garlic from the pan, and cook the onions in the remaining fat until they are soft and lightly browned. Add to the kettle.

3. Pour off the fat from the frying pan, add one cup water to the pan, and bring to a boil. Pour over the meat in kettle. Cover the hocks with enough additional boiling water to cover them completely.

4. Partially cover the pot and simmer the hocks for about one and one-half hours, or until the skin and meat begin to fall away from the bones.

5. Stir in the moistened flour and continue stirring until sauce has thickened. Continue simmering for another ten minutes.

6. Before serving, add salt and pepper to taste and sprinkle with chopped parsley. Serve while the hocks are still hot.

Note: A bowl of plain boiled potatoes or crusty French bread would be an ideal accompaniment. The sauce is generous in amount and particularly flavorsome.

Cretons Français

(Potted Pork with Cracklings)

3 cups

¾ pound fat salt pork, cut into 2-inch pieces
1 pound lean pork, cubed
2 medium onions, quartered
½ teaspoon ground cinnamon
¼ teaspoon ground cloves
¼ teaspoon ground allspice
¼ teaspoon freshly ground pepper
2 tablespoons dry bread crumbs
   Salt

1. Sauté the pieces of salt pork in a pan until golden and somewhat crisp. Remove the cracklings and reserve the remaining fat.

2. Put the pork, onions, and cracklings through a meat chopper. Combine the chopped mixture with the cinnamon, cloves, allspice, and pepper, mixing very thoroughly.

3. Place the mixture in a frying pan and cook over low heat, stirring occasionally, for one and one-quarter to one and one-half hours.

4. Remove from the heat, stir in the bread crumbs, and season with salt to taste.

5. Pour into a one-quart mold, or into individual molds, previously rinsed in cold water.

6. Cool to room temperature. If sufficient fat has not risen to cover the top of the meat, pour on a thin film of the reserved fat.

7. Chill thoroughly, preferably at least eight hours, then unmold and spread on crackers, Melba toast, or between slices of French or rye bread. Serve as an appetizer.

Tourtière

(French-Canadian Pork Pie)

6 servings

- 1 onion, finely chopped
- 1 clove garlic, finely chopped
- 2 tablespoons butter
- 1½ pounds pork, ground
- ½ teaspoon ground cloves
- ½ teaspoon ground cinnamon
- ½ teaspoon ground savory
- 1 bay leaf
- ¾ cup boiling pork stock or water
  Salt and freshly ground black pepper
  Pastry Shell (page 289; see note) for a
  2-crust pie
- 1 egg

1. Cook the onion and garlic in butter until wilted. Add the pork and continue cooking, breaking up the meat and stirring frequently. Add the cloves, cinnamon, savory, bay leaf, pork stock, and salt and pepper to taste. Continue cooking, stirring, about thirty minutes. Place the filling in the refrigerator and chill thoroughly.

2. Preheat the oven to 425 degrees.

3. Line a pie plate with half the pastry and spoon in the filling. Cover with the remaining pastry, pressing to seal the edges. Prick the top to allow steam to escape. Brush with a beaten egg mixed with a little water. Bake ten minutes, then lower the heat to 350 degrees and bake forty minutes longer. The pie, many Canadians declare, is best if frozen, then reheated before serving.

Perdrix au Choux

(Partridges with Cabbage)

4 servings

- 2 partridges, weighing about 1 pound each when cleaned
- ¾ pound lean salt pork, cut in slices about ¼ inch thick
- ¾ pound garlic sausage
- 1 medium head cabbage, preferably Savoy
- 2 carrots, scraped, quartered, and cut into ½-inch strips
- 2 ribs celery, tops removed, ribs cut in quarters
- 4 small white onions, peeled
- 2 whole cloves
  Salt and pepper
- ½ cup water
- 2 tablespoons butter

1. Preheat the oven to medium (350 degrees).

2. Split the birds in half, rinse, and dry thoroughly.

3. In a heavy frying pan, slowly fry the salt pork until the slices are golden. Remove the pork from the pan, then brown the split birds in the remaining fat. Set the partridges aside with the pork slices.

4. Cover the sausage with boiling water and simmer for five minutes. Drain and pat dry. Remove any hard casing and cut the sausage into eight diagonal slices.

5. Core the cabbage, leaving the head intact. Boil for five minutes in a large amount of water. Remove the cabbage and peel off the individual leaves, dropping each leaf into a bowl of cold water. (If peeling becomes difficult as you proceed, return the cabbage to the boiling water and cook a few minutes longer, or until all the leaves come away easily.) Drain and dry the cabbage leaves.

6. In the bottom of a roasting pan with cover or a heavy shallow casserole, place a layer of cabbage, using about one-third of

the leaves. Arrange the pork slices over the bed, then the partridges, skin side up, and surround each half with carrots and celery. Stick two of the onions with cloves, then add all four onions to the other vegetables. Sprinkle with salt and pepper. Cover with another layer of cabbage, again using about a third of the leaves.

7. Arrange the slices of sausage over the second layer of cabbage, then cover the sausage with the remaining cabbage. Dot the top layer with butter, then add salt and pepper to taste. Pour in the water, cover the pot, and bake in the preheated oven for one to one and one-half hours, or until the partridges are tender.

8. Serve at once, arranging half a partridge, slices of pork and sausage, cabbage, and vegetables on each plate, and spooning some of the hot liquid over each serving.

Tarte au Sirop d'Érable

(Maple Walnut Tart)

6 to 8 servings

This French-Canadian maple walnut tart, or pie if you prefer, has a certain kinship with American pecan pie, although its top crust may come as a surprise to some. If the sweetness of the tart is overpowering, accompany each serving with a wedge of lemon.

Pastry for a 2-crust 8-inch pie (see note)
1 cup pure maple syrup
½ cup water
3 tablespoons cornstarch
3 tablespoons water
2 tablespoons butter
1 cup (3¾ ounces) shelled walnuts, coarsely chopped

1. Preheat the oven to 400 degrees.

2. Prepare the pastry and refrigerate it to chill slightly while the filling is being made.

3. Bring the maple syrup and water to a boil; continue to boil for two minutes. Mix the cornstarch and water together in a small bowl and add to the boiling syrup, stirring constantly for about two minutes, or until the mixture thickens. Remove from the heat, stir in the butter, and cool quickly by placing the pan in the refrigerator.

4. Line an eight-inch pie pan with the pastry, pour in the cooled syrup and sprinkle the walnuts on top. Cover with the top crust, crimping the edges to seal, and cut a few slashes in the center of the pastry to allow steam to escape.

5. Bake for thirty minutes in the center of the oven. Serve warm or at room temperature.

Note: To make the pastry for the crust, use any recipe for a two-crust pie pastry or double the recipe for Pastry Shell (page 289).

Tarte au Suif

(Suet Apple Tart)

6 to 8 servings

Pastry for a single-crust pie (see recipe for Pastry Shell, page 289)

3 medium tart apples, cored, peeled, and chopped into small pieces (enough to make 2½ cups)

½ cup finely minced beef suet (raw beef fat)

½ cup dark brown sugar

¼ teaspoon salt

Freshly grated nutmeg

1. Preheat the oven to 400 degrees.

2. Line an eight-inch pie pan with the pastry.

3. Place the apples, suet, brown sugar, and salt in a bowl and toss about only enough to combine. Transfer the apple-suet mixture to the pie pan. Sprinkle the top with as much freshly grated nutmeg as desired.

4. Bake in the 400-degree oven for ten minutes, then reduce the heat to 350 degrees and continue baking for another thirty minutes. Serve while still warm.

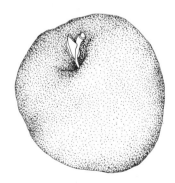

Ceylon

Ceylon Curry

(Beef or Chicken Curry)

6 servings

2 pounds lean stewing beef or chicken
2½ teaspoons salt
½ teaspoon freshly ground pepper
1 tablespoon vinegar
1 1-inch piece cinnamon
3 tablespoons Curry Powder (page 33)
2 cloves garlic, crushed
1 teaspoon chopped fresh ginger or ¼ teaspoon powdered ginger
3 bay leaves
2 cardamom seeds
  Cayenne pepper to taste (optional)
3 tablespoons butter
2 onions, chopped
1 green pepper, seeded and sliced
1 cup Coconut Milk Made in a Blender (page 34) or cow's milk
1 tablespoon lemon juice

1. Cut the beef or chicken into small chunks. Place the meat in a bowl and add the salt, pepper, vinegar, cinnamon, curry powder, garlic, ginger, two bay leaves (crushed), one cardamom seed, and cayenne. Mix well. Let stand about two hours.

2. Heat the butter in a saucepan and add the onion, the remaining bay leaf and cardamom seed and the green pepper. Cook briefly, stirring, over medium heat, then add the seasoned meat. Cook, stirring, until the liquid is partly absorbed. Cover and cook about thirty to forty-five minutes over low heat. When the meat is tender, add the milk and simmer ten to fifteen minutes. Add the lemon juice just before taking the saucepan off the heat, but keep stirring until it is removed.

Yellow Rice

8 to 12 servings

4 cups uncooked rice
3 tablespoons butter
1 cup thinly sliced onions
2 cardamom seeds
1 1-inch piece cinnamon, broken
12 peppercorns
8½ cups hot water
    Salt to taste
¼ teaspoon turmeric powder
¼ teaspoon lemon juice
    Vegetable oil
¼ cup raisins
¼ cup sliced almonds
1 hard-cooked egg, sliced
    Chopped parsley

1. Wash and drain the rice one hour in advance.

2. Heat the butter in a saucepan and add one-half cup of the onions, the cardamom seeds, cinnamon, and peppercorns. Cook, stirring, until the onions are golden. Then add the drained rice and cook five minutes, stirring. Add the hot water, salt, and turmeric. Cover and cook thirteen to fifteen minutes, then stir with a two-pronged fork. When the water is absorbed, add the lemon juice; stir and cover. Continue cooking over low heat until the rice is tender but firm, about twenty minutes.

3. Heat one-half inch of oil in a skillet and cook the raisins briefly. Remove with a slotted spoon and drain on paper towels. Add the almonds to the skillet and cook until brown, then remove and drain on paper towels. Add the remaining sliced onions to the skillet and cook until brown, stirring. Drain on paper towels.

4. Spoon the rice onto a hot platter and garnish with raisins, almonds, onions, hard-cooked egg slices, and chopped parsley.

Eggplant Curry

6 servings

1¾ pounds eggplant
    Salt to taste
½ teaspoon turmeric powder
    Vegetable oil for deep frying, plus 1 tablespoon
1 tablespoon chopped onion
1 bay leaf
2 cloves garlic, chopped
1 teaspoon chopped fresh ginger or ¼ teaspoon powdered ginger
1 1-inch piece cinnamon
1 medium tomato, sliced
1 tablespoon Curry Powder (page 33)
1½ tablespoons dry mustard
1 teaspoon paprika
1 cup Coconut Milk Made in a Blender (page 34) or cow's milk
½ teaspoon lemon juice

1. Cut the eggplant lengthwise into strips and then into one-and-one-half-inch pieces. Soak in cold water for about one-half hour, then drain the pieces and press the pieces lightly between paper towels to remove excess water. Season the eggplant with salt and turmeric and fry in deep oil at 375 degrees until light brown but not crisp. Drain on paper towels.

2. Heat the one tablespoon oil in a saucepan and add the onion, bay leaf, garlic, ginger, and cinnamon and cook, stirring, until the onions are golden. Add the tomato slices, curry powder, mustard, and paprika and cook, stirring, to a paste, about five minutes.

3. Add the milk to the onion-tomato mixture and then add the fried eggplant. Cook for five minutes. Add the lemon juice and remove from the heat.

Kirsch torte (Austria

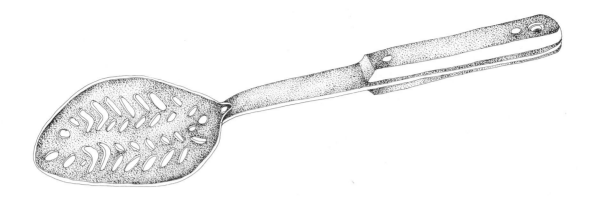

Dhal (Lentil) Curry

About 8 servings

1 cup red split lentils
3 cups water
1 cup chopped onion
1 2-inch piece cinnamon, broken
3 cloves garlic, peeled and sliced
   Freshly ground black pepper to taste
¼ teaspoon turmeric powder
   Salt to taste
1 teaspoon lemon juice
1 tablespoon vegetable oil
½ teaspoon black mustard seeds
½ to ¾ cup Coconut Milk Made in a Blender (page 34) or cow's milk

1. Wash the lentils in cold water, then drain. Let stand one hour.

2. Put the lentils in a saucepan and add the three cups water, one-half cup of the chopped onion, cinnamon, two cloves of the garlic, pepper, turmeric, and salt. Cook until the lentils are soft and most of the water is absorbed, about fifteen minutes. Stir in the lemon juice.

3. Heat the oil in a saucepan. Add the remaining chopped onion and garlic and cook until brown. Then add the mustard seeds and cook briefly, stirring. Pour in the cooked lentils, add the milk, and cook five minutes, stirring.

Curry Powder

About 1¼ pounds

Whenever a recipe for a curry appears, if curry powder is not listed among the ingredients there are always letters and telephone calls protesting the supposed omission. It may be laboring the point, but we will say again that the best curries have never known the commercial mixture called curry powder. There is no such thing as a curry bush or curry tree; curry powder is a blend of spices, as you will see in the recipe below.

1 pound coriander
¼ pound small cumin seed
1 tablespoon sweet cumin seed
1 tablespoon black mustard seeds
1 1-inch piece cinnamon
2 cardamom seeds
½ teaspoon freshly ground black pepper

1. Preheat the oven to 250 degrees.

2. Put all the ingredients in a baking pan and bake about 15 minutes. Grind while hot in an electric blender or mortar with pestle.

Note: This curry powder will keep for six months in an airtight jar.

Coconut Milk Made in a Blender

About 4 cups

2 coconuts
4 cups hot water

1. Crack the coconuts. Pour out and discard the white water in the center. Use a knife to extract the coconut meat from the shell. Pare away the dark outer coating of the meat, then cut the white, fleshy coconut meat into cubes.

2. Pour two cups of hot water into the container of an electric blender. Add the coconut meat and blend on high speed until thoroughly blended.

3. Line a mixing bowl with cheesecloth and pour the blended mixture into it. Squeeze and twist the cheesecloth to extract most of the liquid. Pour the liquid into a quart jar. Return the squeezed coconut to the blender and add the remaining two cups of hot water. Blend as before, then pour back into the cheesecloth-lined mixing bowl and squeeze again. Pour the liquid into the quart jar and discard the pressed coconut. The liquid in the jar is coconut milk. Shake before using.

China

Curry Puffs

(Baked Curried Deem Sum)

About 2 dozen

- 2 cups sifted all-purpose flour
- ⅔ cup butter
- ⅓ cup ice water, approximately
- 1 teaspoon peanut oil
- 1 pound pork, ground
- 1 tablespoon dry sherry
- 1 teaspoon Curry Powder (page 33), or to taste
- 1½ tablespoons soy sauce
- 1½ teaspoons salt
- 1½ teaspoons granulated sugar
- 1 cup finely chopped onion
- 1 cup mashed potatoes
- 1 egg, well beaten

1. Combine the flour and butter in a mixing bowl and work with the fingertips until the mixture forms bits the size of small peas. Stir with a fork and, while stirring, moisten with ice water. Use just enough water to hold the dough together. Shape the mixture into a ball, wrap in waxed paper, and chill at least one hour.

2. Preheat the oven to 400 degrees.

3. Heat the oil in a wok (Chinese cooking utensil) or large skillet. Cook the pork, stirring to break up lumps. When the meat loses its color, add the sherry, curry powder, soy sauce, salt, and sugar. Mix well, then spoon into a mixing bowl. Add the onions to the wok or skillet. Cook, stirring, until wilted. Add to the pork mixture, then add the mashed potatoes and blend thoroughly. Let cool.

4. Place the dough on a lightly floured board. Using a rolling pin, roll with light, quick strokes until one-eighth inch thick. Cut into two-inch circles with a biscuit cutter. Place a bit of filling in the center of each pastry circle and fold one side of the circle over the filling to meet the other edge. Press the edges of the circles together with the fingers to make crescents, then crimp the edges decoratively. Arrange on a cookie sheet and brush with beaten egg. Prick the top of each with a fork. Bake fifteen minutes, or until golden brown. Serve hot, as an appetizer.

Date Wonton

(Sweet Deem Sum)

About 2 dozen

1 cup sifted all-purpose flour
1 egg, lightly beaten
1 to 2 tablespoons water
1 6-ounce package pitted dates
½ cup finely chopped walnuts
2 teaspoons grated orange rind
  Fat for deep frying
  Confectioners' sugar

1. Mix the flour and egg in a mixing bowl. Stir in the water, a little at a time, to form a stiff dough. Divide the dough into two equal parts and roll out one part at a time, covering the part not being rolled. To roll the dough, place it on a well-floured board and roll until wafer thin. Cut into two-inch squares.

2. Chop the dates into five pieces each and blend with the walnuts and orange rind. Place a small portion of filling on one edge of a dough square and roll jellyroll fashion. Pinch the dough together along the seam but leave the ends open. Continue until all the filling is used.

3. Heat the fat to 300 degrees and deep-fry the wonton until golden brown. Drain on paper towels.

4. When the wonton are cool, sprinkle with confectioners' sugar. Serve as an appetizer or, if desired, as a dessert or with tea.

Chinese Shrimp Toast

6 servings

6 slices sandwich bread
½ pound cooked shrimp, finely chopped
¼ pound fat pork, finely chopped
2 tablespoons minced onion
1 teaspoon salt
1 teaspoon granulated sugar
½ teaspoon monosodium glutamate
1 tablespoon cornstarch
2 eggs, lightly beaten
  Fine dry bread crumbs
2 cups cooking oil

1. Trim the crusts from the bread and spread the slices out to dry for a few minutes.

2. Mix all the remaining ingredients except the bread crumbs and the oil. Spread the mixture over the bread and cover with the bread crumbs, pressing the crumbs into the surface. Cut each slice into four squares or triangles.

3. Heat the cooking oil to 375 degrees. Sauté the bread, shrimp side down, until golden brown. Turn and cook the other side. Drain on absorbent paper and cool slightly to crisp. Serve as an appetizer.

Hwang Kua Jo Tang

(Cucumber Sliced-Pork Soup)

6 servings

2 medium pork chops
2 medium cucumbers
4 cups Chicken Stock (page 115)
1 teaspoon salt
1 tablespoon light soy sauce
¼ teaspoon monosodium glutamate

1. Remove the bones and fat from the pork chops and cut them into one-quarter-inch slices. Peel the cucumbers and cut them lengthwise into halves. Remove the seeds, then cut the halves into one-quarter-inch slices.

2. Heat the stock with the salt, soy sauce, and monosodium glutamate. Add the pork and bring to a boil. Boil for five minutes, then add the cucumber slices and again bring to a boil. Boil for about four minutes, until the cucumber slices are translucent. Serve hot.

Mandarin Soup

6 to 8 servings

4 dried Chinese mushrooms
¼ pound lean pork
½ cup bamboo shoots (2 ounces)
2 pieces of fresh bean curd
4 cups Chicken Stock (page 115)
1 teaspoon salt
1 tablespoon soy sauce
2 tablespoons cornstarch mixed with ¼ cup water
1 egg
1 green onion, chopped
1 tablespoon sesame oil

1. Soak the mushrooms in warm water for twenty minutes. Drain, reserving the liquid.

2. Cut the pork, bamboo shoots, mushrooms, and bean curd into thin strips. Set aside.

3. Combine the stock and the reserved mushroom liquid in a saucepan. Bring the mixture to a boil. Add the salt, soy sauce, pork, bamboo shoots, and mushrooms. Cover and simmer for five minutes.

4. Add the bean curd and again bring the mixture to a boil. Add a small amount of the hot liquid to the cornstarch paste, stirring. Add this mixture to the pan and cook for one to two minutes longer.

5. Beat the egg lightly and slowly add it to the hot soup. Stir once gently. Remove the soup from the heat and pour into a large soup tureen. Sprinkle with the chopped green onion and sesame oil. Serve hot.

HOT AND SOUR SOUP:

To make hot and sour soup, add two table-spoons vinegar and one-quarter teaspoon freshly ground black pepper to the mixture above.

Wonton Soup

5 to 6 servings

2 cups sifted all-purpose flour
2 eggs
1 teaspoon vegetable oil
1 tablespoon water, approximately
1 pound pork, ground
1 teaspoon grated fresh ginger
2 tablespoons chopped green onion, green part and all
1 teaspoon sesame oil
Salt to taste
¼ teaspoon monosodium glutamate
1 teaspoon finely chopped Chinese parsley (fresh coriander leaves or cilantro)
¼ teaspoon granulated sugar
1 teaspoon dry sherry
Boiling hot Chicken Stock (page 115) or pork broth. Roast pork strips, shredded cooked chicken, fresh spinach leaves, slices of soaked dried mushrooms (optional)

1. Place the flour in a mixing bowl and make a well in the center. Crack the eggs into the well and add the oil. Start mixing and kneading the dough with the fingers, adding just enough water so that the dough is workable. Knead it thoroughly and shape it into a ball. Wrap it closely in plastic wrap and let it stand thirty minutes.

2. Combine all the remaining ingredients in a mixing bowl.

3. Roll out the dough as thinly as possible and cut it into twenty-five to thirty triangles or circles. Spoon a teaspoon or so of filling into the center of each triangle or circle and rub a little cold water around the perimeter of each triangle or circle. Fold the dough over the filling to enclose it, pressing down the edges with the fingers to seal. Drop the wonton into boiling, salted water and simmer until done, ten to fifteen minutes. Serve in boiling hot chicken stock or pork broth with, if desired, a garnish of roast pork strips, shredded cooked chicken, fresh spinach leaves, and/or slices of soaked dried mushrooms.

Braised Soy Fish

4 servings

1 sea bass (2 to 3 pounds), cleaned and scaled but left whole, with head intact
1 teaspoon salt
All-purpose flour
3 slices fresh ginger
1 to 2 green onions
1 cup water
4 tablespoons soy sauce
2 tablespoons sherry
½ teaspoon granulated sugar
4 to 6 tablespoons vegetable oil

1. Rinse the fish in cold water and score both sides with diagonal cuts.

2. Sprinkle the fish with half the salt and let stand ten minutes. Coat lightly with flour.

3. Mince the ginger and green onions and set aside. Combine the water, soy sauce, sherry, sugar, and remaining salt.

4. Heat the oil in a heavy pan until almost smoking. Add the fish and fry over high heat, one minute on each side. Reduce the heat to medium and fry one and one-half minutes on each side. Baste with the hot oil. Remove all but one tablespoon of the oil.

5. Pour the ginger and green onion mixture over the fish and bring to a boil. Cook, covered, over medium heat until done, fifteen to twenty minutes, turning the fish halfway through cooking.

Bok Sui Ngui

(Poached Sea Bass, Chinese Style)

2 servings

1 fresh sea bass or, if not available, porgy (about 1½ pounds), cleaned and scaled but with head and tail left on
1 tablespoon dark soy sauce
1 tablespoon light soy sauce
1 teaspoon monosodium glutamate
1 teaspoon granulated sugar
¼ cup peanut oil or vegetable oil
1 teaspoon sesame oil (optional)
2 cloves garlic, peeled and left whole
4 thin slices fresh ginger, shredded
4 green onions, trimmed and cut into 1½-inch lengths
2 pieces cha ga (Chinese canned sweet pickles) or 2 sweet gherkins, sliced

1. It is important to have all vegetables chopped and all ingredients ready before making this dish.

2. Use a fish cooker or another utensil just large enough to hold the fish. Add enough water to cover the fish when it is put in and bring to a boil. Place the fish on the rack of the fish cooker or in a sling made of cheesecloth. Gently lower the fish into the boiling water and immediately shut off the heat. The water should not boil again. Cover the pot and let the fish stand in the water fifteen to twenty minutes. The fish is done when the eyes are white and pop out of their sockets.

3. While the fish is poaching, combine the soy sauces, monosodium glutamate, and sugar in a small mixing bowl.

4. Heat the oils in a saucepan and add the garlic. Cook over low heat until the garlic starts to turn brown, then discard the garlic. Keep the oil warm.

5. Remove the fish from the water and drain. Place on a serving platter and pour the soy sauce mixture over it.

6. Reheat the oil and add the ginger. When light brown, pour the oil and ginger over the fish. The oil may splatter, so hold the saucepan at arm's length. Sprinkle the fish with green onions and pickles and serve immediately.

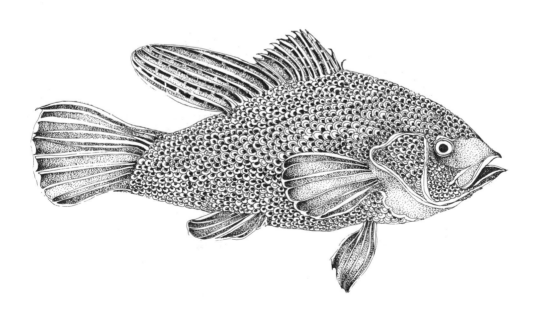

Steamed Sea Bass

2 to 4 servings

1 sea bass (about 1½ pounds)
1 teaspoon shredded fresh ginger
2 green onions, trimmed and chopped
1 teaspoon fermented black beans
1 tablespoon dry sherry
1 teaspoon sesame oil
¼ cup plus 1 tablespoon soy sauce
½ teaspoon monosodium glutamate
1 teaspoon granulated sugar
¼ cup peanut oil
2 cloves garlic, peeled
2 green onions, trimmed and cut into one-and-one-half-inch lengths, green part and all, for garnish
1 whole preserved cucumber, finely shredded, for garnish

1. The fish must be thoroughly cleaned, with gills removed but head and tail left on. Place it in an oval or round heatproof dish just large enough to hold it and put the dish in a steamer. If you do not have a steamer, you can improvise one (see note).

2. Combine half the ginger, the chopped green onions, black beans, sherry, half the sesame oil, and one tablespoon soy sauce and pour over the fish. Cover tightly and steam fifteen to twenty minutes.

3. Meanwhile, combine the remaining soy sauce, monosodium glutamate, and sugar and stir until the sugar dissolves. When the fish is done, ladle this mixture over.

4. Heat the peanut oil and the remaining sesame oil in a small skillet. Add the garlic and brown lightly. Discard the garlic, then quickly add the remaining shredded ginger. Pour the hot oil and ginger over the fish. Sprinkle the fish with the green onions and cucumber and serve immediately.

Note: To improvise a steamer, select a deep kettle or other cooking utensil large enough to hold the food to be steamed or the dish it is in. Place a rack in the kettle and add about eight cups of boiling water.

Place the food or dish on the rack, making certain that the rack is high enough to prevent the water from getting into the food or dish when the water boils again.

Steamed Fish

4 to 6 servings

2 tablespoons finely shredded fresh ginger
2 green onions
1 sea bass (1½ to 2 pounds), cleaned and scaled but with head and tail left on
1 tablespoon dry sherry
3 tablespoons vegetable oil
3 tablespoons soy sauce
1 teaspoon granulated sugar
 Fresh Chinese parsley (fresh coriander leaves or cilantro) (optional)

1. Prepare the ginger and set it aside.

2. Trim the green onions and cut into two-inch lengths. Cut each length into shreds. Set aside.

3. Rinse the fish in cold water and pat dry with paper towels. Place the fish on a heatproof platter or shallow dish and sprinkle with sherry. Place the platter in a steamer or substitute for one (see note above), making certain that the water in the steamer does not come into the platter. Cover closely and steam the fish exactly fifteen minutes.

4. Heat a wok (Chinese cooking utensil) or small skillet for thirty seconds. Add the oil and swirl to coat the bottom of the pan. Add the shredded ginger and cook over moderate heat for one minute, then add the shredded green onions, soy sauce, and sugar. Pour the mixture over the steamed fish. Garnish with Chinese parsley.

Rainbow Fish

4 servings

2 or 3 dried Chinese mushrooms
½ pound flounder fillets
¼ cup (1 ounce) Smithfield ham
½ cup tightly packed spinach leaves
1 small bamboo shoot
1 egg white
½ teaspoon salt
1 tablespoon dry sherry
2 teaspoons cornstarch
2 teaspoons vegetable oil
   Rainbow Fish Sauce (see below)

1. Soak the mushrooms for twenty minutes in warm water. Drain.

2. Cut the fish, ham, mushrooms, spinach, and bamboo shoot into thin strips. Mix with the egg white, salt, sherry, cornstarch, and oil.

3. Form the mixture into balls the size of walnuts and arrange evenly on an oiled plate. Steam for five minutes by covering the plate with a cover or foil and placing over a pan of rapidly boiling water. (An alternate method is to place a coffee can with both ends removed in a pan of rapidly boiling water and rest the covered plate on the can. Cover the pan.) Serve the steamed fish topped with the following sauce.

RAINBOW FISH SAUCE:

½ cup

½ cup Fish Stock (page 116), or canned
   clam broth
1 teaspoon cornstarch
1 tablespoon water
¼ teaspoon salt

Bring the stock to a boil in a saucepan. Mix the cornstarch and water to a paste and stir into the boiling stock. Add the salt (if canned broth is used, omit the salt). Simmer and stir until the sauce is smooth and thickened.

Fried Fish Wrapped in Paper

4 to 6 servings

2   teaspoons sesame oil
½   pound boneless fish fillets such as striped
    bass, flounder, or sea bass
1   teaspoon salt
1   tablespoon sake or dry sherry
    Freshly ground pepper to taste
12 thin slices fresh ginger
12 small snow peas
12 small strips of green onion
12 slices fresh mushrooms
    Vegetable oil for deep frying

1. Cut twelve six-inch squares out of waxed paper and brush each on one side with a little sesame oil.

2. Cut the fish into twelve pieces of approximately equal size. Sprinkle the fish with salt, sake, and pepper.

3. Place one piece of fish on an oiled square of waxed paper and top each piece with a slice of ginger, a snow pea, a strip of green onion, and a mushroom slice. Fold the pieces of paper envelope fashion, tucking in the ends securely so that no steam can escape.

4. Heat the oil to 180 degrees and deep-fry the envelopes about three minutes, or until lightly brown. Serve the envelopes unopened.

Chinese Braised Fish with Green Onions

4 servings

1 pike (3 to 4 pounds), cleaned and scaled but with head and tail left on
½ cup peanut oil
½ teaspoon salt
1 cup plus 2 tablespoons water
3 tablespoons gin
2 tablespoons soy sauce
6 green onions, trimmed and cut into 1-inch lengths
4 bamboo shoots, cut into thin rounds and then shredded
10 wafer-thin slices peeled fresh ginger
1 teaspoon cornstarch
6 sprigs fresh coriander (Chinese parsley)

1. Rinse the fish well in cold water and pat it dry with paper towels. If a long, oval fish cooker with a rack is available, use it. If not, use a small oval roasting pan with a rack large enough to hold the fish. In the beginning, however, remove the rack from the cooker.

2. Pour the oil into the cooker and sprinkle with the salt. When it is hot, add the fish and cook five minutes on each side, turning once. Carefully remove the fish from the cooker with a pancake turner, taking care that it does not break. Transfer the fish to the rack and return it to the cooker.

3. Pour one cup of water, the gin, and the soy sauce over the fish. Cover the fish cooker closely and steam the fish over medium-low heat for about twenty minutes. Do not overcook. Remove the cover and scatter the onions over the fish. Add the bamboo shoots and ginger, then cover and steam five minutes longer.

4. Remove the rack from the cooker. Transfer the fish to a warm serving platter and cover with foil to keep warm.

5. Blend the cornstarch with the two tablespoons of water. Bring the drippings in the fish cooker to a boil and stir in the cornstarch. When the sauce boils, stir it rapidly, then remove from the heat and pour over the fish. Garnish with coriander sprigs.

Lobster Cantonese

4 to 6 servings

2 tablespoons salad oil
¾ pound lean pork, ground
1 tablespoon finely chopped carrot
1 tablespoon finely chopped celery
¼ cup chopped green onion, including green part
½ clove garlic, finely minced
½ teaspoon grated fresh ginger (optional)
Salt and freshly ground pepper to taste
2 lobsters (1½ pounds each), boiled and shelled
1 cup Chicken Stock (page 115)
1 egg
2 tablespoons cornstarch
1 tablespoon soy sauce
¼ cup water

1. Heat the oil in a skillet and add the pork, carrot, celery, green onion, garlic, ginger, and salt and pepper to taste. Stir quickly with a metal kitchen spoon to break up the meat.

2. Meanwhile, cut the meat from the lobsters into bite-sized pieces. Add the lobster meat and chicken stock to the pork mixture, cover, and let simmer ten minutes.

3. Beat the egg lightly but do not overblend. Add to the lobster and pork mixture and simmer two minutes, stirring constantly. Blend the cornstarch, soy sauce, and water; stir into the sauce. Cook until thickened. Serve with rice.

Shrimp with Black Bean Sauce

4 servings

1 pound raw shrimp
3 tablespoons peanut oil
2 green onions, cut in 2-inch pieces
2 teaspoons dry fermented black beans
1 clove garlic, crushed
¼ cup plus 2 tablespoons water
2 tablespoons dry sherry
2 tablespoons soy sauce
1 tablespoon cornstarch
1 egg, slightly beaten

1. Shell, devein, wash, and drain the shrimp. Split each in two lengthwise.

2. In a skillet or wok (Chinese cooking utensil), heat the oil and quickly stir-fry (cook and stir) the green onions, black beans, and garlic. Discard the garlic.

3. Add the shrimp and cook, stirring continuously, for about two minutes, or until the shrimp turn pink. Add the one-quarter cup water, the sherry, and the soy sauce.

4. Dissolve the cornstarch in the remaining two tablespoons water and add to the shrimp mixture, stirring. When thickened, stir in the beaten egg and turn off the heat immediately. Serve hot.

Shrimp with Hoi Sin Sauce

4 servings

2 teaspoons cornstarch
½ cup water
⅓ cup hoi sin deung (sweet bean sauce)
2 tablespoons oyster sauce or light soy sauce
2 pounds medium shrimp, shelled or unshelled
¼ cup vegetable oil
⅛ teaspoon salt
2 slices fresh ginger, shredded
1 clove garlic, minced
6 green onions, cut into 1½-inch lengths
¼ cup whisky or gin

1. Mix together the cornstarch mixed in the water, the sweet bean sauce, and oyster sauce and put aside.

2. Wash the shrimp and dry with paper towels.

3. Heat a wok (Chinese cooking utensil) or pan hot and dry. Add the oil, then the salt. Turn the heat down to medium, then add the ginger and garlic. As soon as the garlic and ginger have turned light brown, add all the shrimp at once and stir gently until they turn pink, about four minutes.

4. Add the green onions and stir well. Add the cornstarch-sauce mixture. Mix with the shrimp and cover to cook two minutes longer. Stir in the whisky just before serving.

Shrimp with Hot Fish Sauce

4 to 6 servings

24 medium raw shrimp (about 1 pound)
 1 pound pork, ground
 3 tablespoons dark soy sauce
1½ tablespoons cornstarch
 1 egg, beaten
 1 tablespoon finely chopped garlic
 1 tablespoon finely chopped fresh ginger
 ¾ cup finely chopped green onion, green part and all
 ¼ cup chopped fresh hot green and/or red peppers
 2 tablespoons dry sherry or Chinese wine
 1 tablespoon sesame oil
 1 teaspoon granulated sugar
 2 teaspoons Chinese hot sauce
 2 tablespoons hot chili paste with garlic
 ⅓ cup salad oil
   Salt to taste
   Chinese parsley (fresh coriander leaves) for garnish (optional)

1. Rinse the shrimp and drain. Using a pair of kitchen shears, cut through the shell of each shrimp down the back, but do not peel. Hold the shrimp, one at a time, under cold running water and pull and rinse away the dark vein down the back. When all the shrimp are cleaned (but with the shell left on), drain and pat dry. Set aside.

2. Combine the pork, soy sauce, cornstarch, and egg in a mixing bowl and blend well with the fingers. Set aside.

3. Blend the garlic, ginger, green onions, and hot peppers and set aside.

4. Combine the wine, sesame oil, sugar, hot sauce, and chili paste and set aside.

5. Heat the oil in a wok or large skillet and cook the shrimp, stirring, until they turn red all over. Remove them with a slotted spoon and set aside.

6. Add the pork mixture and cook, breaking up the lumps with the side of the spoon,

until the meat loses color. Stir in the garlic and ginger mixture, then the liquid mixture. Add salt to taste. Return the shrimp to the sauce and, when piping hot, pour the mixture into a hot serving dish. Garnish with Chinese parsley and serve with rice.

Puffed Shrimp

4 servings

12 large raw shrimp (about 1½ pounds)
   Juice from 1 clove garlic, put through a press
   Salt
   Monosodium glutamate
 1 cup sifted all-purpose flour
 2 tablespoons cornstarch
 1 tablespoon plus ½ teaspoon baking powder
 5 to 6 tablespoons peanut oil or vegetable oil for batter
 ¾ cup water, approximately
   Vegetable oil for deep frying
   Parsley or watercress

1. Shell the shrimp but leave the last tail segment on. With a sharp knife, cut through the underside of each shrimp almost but not quite to the back. Do not sever the halves completely. Rinse the shrimp to remove the dark vein down the back and drain on paper towels. Pat dry. Arrange the shrimp, split side up, on a plate and rub with the garlic juice. Sprinkle with a little salt and monosodium glutamate.

2. Put the flour, cornstarch, baking powder, and one-half teaspoon salt in a mixing bowl. Mix thoroughly. Add the peanut oil, a little at a time, stirring with a wooden spoon or fork. Continue stirring and adding oil until the mixture forms a ball and leaves the sides of the bowl.

3. Add water, a little at a time, stirring until the dough has the consistency of pancake batter. The thicker the batter, the thicker the crust will be on the cooked shrimp.

4. Heat the oil in a wok (Chinese cooking utensil) or other deep-frying utensil to a temperature of 180 degrees. Place the shrimp and batter near the cooking utensil.

5. Take each shrimp by the tail, dip it into the batter, then drop, one at a time, into the hot oil. Turn once with tongs. When golden brown all over, drain on paper towels. Serve on a bed of lettuce leaves with a garnish of parsley or watercress.

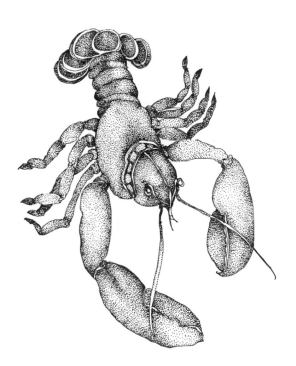

Sautéed Shrimp with Broccoli

4 servings

1 pound raw shrimp
½ teaspoon ginger juice (see note)
3 teaspoons cornstarch
1 small bunch broccoli
5 tablespoons peanut oil
1 teaspoon salt
1 teaspoon granulated sugar
2 teaspoons sake or dry sherry
1 tablespoon water

1. Shell and devein the shrimp.

2. Combine the ginger juice with two teaspoons of the cornstarch and add to the shrimp, stirring until the shrimp are coated. Let stand five minutes.

3. Separate the broccoli into small flowerets and drop into boiling water. Simmer briefly, until crisp and tender. Drain and set aside.

4. Heat the oil in a skillet or wok (Chinese cooking utensil) and add the shrimp. Cook over high heat, stirring and shaking the skillet, until the shrimp turn pink. Add the broccoli, salt, sugar, and sake and continue to cook, stirring, until all the ingredients are coated with oil. Combine the remaining cornstarch with the water and add it, stirring. When thickened, serve hot.

Note: Slice fresh ginger and put it in a garlic press. Squeeze hard to extract the juice.

Szechwan Shrimp

2 to 6 servings

"The cuisine of Szechwan is a brilliant freak that breaks all the rules and gets away with it," according to Hsiang Ju Lin and Tsuifeng Lin in their book Chinese Gastronomy *(Hastings House). The cuisine of this province in Southwest China is "freakish," because hot peppers and a certain oiliness are characteristic. "One is shocked by the first taste," the authors note, "then one begins to see . . . a different logic." New Yorkers have become increasingly attracted to this "different logic" during the past decade. The really excellent Szechwan shrimp dish that follows was served in the home of Michael Tong, of the Shun Lee Dynasty restaurant.*

  1 pound small raw shrimp
  1 egg white
1½ tablespoons cornstarch
 ¼ cup finely diced bamboo shoots
 ½ cup finely chopped green onion, green part and all
 ¼ cup chopped hot green pepper
  1 teaspoon hot red pepper flakes
  1 tablespoon chopped garlic
  1 tablespoon grated fresh ginger
 ½ cup Chicken Stock (page 115)
  5 tablespoons tomato catsup
 ¼ teaspoon monosodium glutamate (optional)
 ½ teaspoon soy sauce
  2 tablespoons dry sherry
 ½ teaspoon sesame oil
  2 cups plus 2 tablespoons peanut oil
    Salt to taste

1. Shell the shrimp and devein them. Rinse in cold water and pat dry with paper towels.

2. Beat the egg white lightly, then beat in the cornstarch. Add the shrimp and stir to coat. Let stand five hours.

3. Combine the bamboo shoots, green onions, green pepper, red pepper flakes, garlic, and ginger and set aside.

4. Blend the chicken stock, catsup, monosodium glutamate, soy sauce, sherry, and sesame oil. Set aside.

5. Have two cooking utensils ready, a small deep-fryer (a small deep casserole will do) and a wok (Chinese cooking utensil) or skillet. Heat the two cups of oil to medium hot in the deep-fryer. The fat must not be too hot.

6. Place the shrimp in a sieve or small wire basket and lower into the oil. Cook, without browning, about one minute in all. Lift the sieve from the oil.

7. Heat the two tablespoons of oil in a wok over high heat and add the shrimp and the bamboo shoot mixture. Cook quickly, stirring constantly. Add the catsup mixture and cook quickly until the shrimp are coated and piping hot. Add salt to taste and serve with rice.

Stir-Fried Shrimp in Shells

4 servings

  1 pound raw shrimp
  3 tablespoons vegetable oil
 ½ teaspoon salt
  1 clove garlic, crushed
  2 slices fresh ginger, finely chopped
  1 green onion, cut into ½-inch pieces
  2 tablespoons catsup
  2 tablespoons sherry
  5 tablespoons water
  1 tablespoon cornstarch
  1 teaspoon granulated sugar
 ⅛ teaspoon freshly ground black pepper

1. Wash the shrimp and remove the legs. Slit along the back, using scissors or a sharp knife, but do not remove the shell. Remove the vein with the aid of a toothpick.

2. Heat two tablespoons of the oil in a wok (Chinese cooking utensil) or large skillet.

3. Add the salt and garlic and stir-fry (cook and stir), over high heat, until the garlic browns. Add the shrimp and fry until pink, two to three minutes. Remove from the pan.

4. Add the remaining oil to the pan; add the ginger and green onion and stir-fry a few times. Mix the catsup, sherry, and two tablespoons of the water and stir into the pan.

5. Return the shrimp to the pan and stir to reheat.

6. Mix the cornstarch, sugar, pepper, and remaining water and stir into the shrimp mixture. Cook, stirring, until the mixture thickens.

Hor Gwo

(Chinese Chrysanthemum Pot or Chinese Hot Pot)

Serves any number, within reason

1. Use a regular Chinese hot pot with a water jacket if available. Use charcoal as a source of heat or Sterno as a substitute. An electric skillet may be used for this dish, or a basin of some sort set on a heating unit that will assure continuous boiling as foods are cooked. A fondue dish could conceivably be used, but for no more than one or two people. Provide each guest with chopsticks or fondue fork and a bowl of dipping sauce (Dumpling and Hor Gwo Sauce for One, page 63), or give the guests the various ingredients and let them mix their own.

2. Add a quart or more of boiling water to the water jacket, electric skillet, or whatever, depending on the size of the utensil and the number of guests to be served. Keep boiling throughout the meal.

3. Arrange thinly sliced lamb or beef and/or breast of chicken and/or sea bass, shrimp, or other seafood on chilled plates, keeping chilled until ready to serve. Count on about half a pound of meat and/or fish per person. Meats and/or fish are generally cooked and eaten first, then the vegetables, and so on.

4. Supplement this, if desired, with a combination of bean curd cut into thick strips, coarse-cut Chinese cabbage, coarse-cut spinach, watercress, thin-sliced mushrooms, cellophane noodles soaked in boiling water until wilted, onion rings, and so on.

5. Let each guest serve himself by picking up various ingredients with chopsticks or spearing them with forks. Guests dip one morsel at a time into the boiling liquid and cook quickly (or to the desired degree of doneness). As each bite is cooked it is dipped quickly into the sauce, then eaten immediately, while hot.

6. When all the foods have been cooked and eaten, the broth remaining may be poured into the remaining sauce bowls and drunk.

Note: For each pound of cleaned, deveined shrimp, sprinkle before serving with one teaspoon of cornstarch and two tablespoons of dry sherry. Let stand one hour before serving.

Chinese Pepper Steak

4 servings

1 pound round steak, 1 inch thick
¼ cup butter
1 clove garlic, minced
½ teaspoon salt
¼ teaspoon freshly ground black pepper
4 tablespoons soy sauce
½ teaspoon granulated sugar
1 cup bean sprouts, fresh or canned
2 tomatoes, quartered, or 1 cup canned tomatoes
2 green peppers, seeded and cut into 1-inch pieces
½ tablespoon cornstarch
2 tablespoons cold water
4 green onions, chopped

1. Slice the steak as thinly as possible in short crosswise pieces.

2. Heat the butter in a skillet and add the garlic, salt, and pepper. Add the beef and cook until brown on both sides.

3. Add the soy sauce and sugar, cover, and cook over high heat for five minutes. If canned bean sprouts are used, rinse under cold running water and drain. Add the bean sprouts, tomatoes, and green peppers. Cover and cook for five minutes, then stir in the cornstarch dissolved in the cold water and cook, stirring, until the sauce is thickened. Sprinkle with chopped green onions. Serve with rice.

Oriental Flank Steak

8 or more servings

1 flank steak (3 to 4 pounds), well trimmed
½ cup soy sauce
3 tablespoons vegetable oil
3 tablespoons honey
1 teaspoon grated fresh ginger or ¾ teaspoon ground ginger
1 clove garlic, crushed

1. Place the steak in a large stainless steel, enamel, or glass dish. Combine the remaining ingredients and pour over the meat. Let the meat stand in the mixture for several hours, turning occasionally.

2. Broil the steak or grill it over hot charcoal to the desired degree of doneness. For rare steak, broil or grill about five minutes to the side. Cut the steak into thin slices on the diagonal, using a sharp knife.

Spiced Beef with Soy Sauce

About 8 servings

3 to 4 pounds boneless chuck of beef
1 cup water
1 tablespoon dry sherry
⅓ cup soy sauce
2 slices fresh ginger
½ tablespoon star anise cloves
2 tablespoons granulated sugar

1. Place all the ingredients in a heavy pot. Bring to a boil and cover.

2. Simmer over very low heat for three hours, or until the meat is very tender. Turn the meat occasionally as it cooks. If necessary to prevent dryness, add a little more water as the meat cooks. Serve hot or cold.

Cau Yang Roh

(Mongolian Grilled Meat)

4 to 8 servings

2 pounds frozen boneless meat, preferably
mutton, although lamb or beef may be
used
6 cups water
3 tablespoons star anise
1½ tablespoons whole peppercorns
¾ cup soy sauce
1 cup shao-shing (Chinese wine) or medium dry sherry
3 cups finely shredded green onion
2 cups fresh coriander (cilantro or Chinese parsley) or ½ teaspoon ground
coriander seeds
Sesame seed rolls or, preferably, Armenian or Syrian sesame bread

1. The meat must be frozen so it may be
easily sliced. Cut the frozen meat into the
thinnest possible slices. If the meat is too
solidly frozen, let it defrost slightly. Divide
the sliced meat into eight equal portions
(about one-quarter pound each). Arrange
the slices of each portion in one layer,
slightly overlapping, on one of eight large
dinner plates. (The use of eight dinner plates
is purely for purposes of organization; the
dish is for four persons.)

2. Prepare a fire in a charcoal grill, preferably using pine cones as burning material.

3. Meanwhile, combine the water, star
anise, and peppercorns in a saucepan and
bring to a boil. Simmer about ten minutes
and remove from the heat. Pour into a
pitcher and let cool slightly.

4. Pour one to one and one-half cups of
the still hot or warm liquid into each of four
individual serving bowls. To each bowl add
three tablespoons soy sauce, one-quarter cup
wine, three-quarters cup green onion and
one-half cup fresh coriander (or one-eighth
teaspoon ground). Adjust the seasonings to
taste.

5. Add the contents of one plate to each
of the bowls and let stand ten or fifteen minutes.

6. Using chopsticks or a fork, lift the meat
and vegetables, a portion at a time, onto the
hot grill, spreading the slices around as neatly
as possible. Turn once or twice, but cook
quickly and do not overcook. Immediately
serve the meat, sandwich style, on sesame
bread or toasted sesame rolls. As the meat is
removed from each of the bowls, add another
portion and continue cooking.

Lamb Shreds with Cellophane Noodles

4 servings

½ pound leg of lamb, boned
1 egg white
1 teaspoon salt
1 teaspoon cornstarch
1 cup plus 2 tablespoons peanut oil
1 tablespoon soy sauce
¼ teaspoon hot pepper oil or Tabasco
1 ounce dry cellophane noodles

1. Slice the lamb into thin, matchlike
shreds and mix with the egg white, one-half
teaspoon of the salt, and the cornstarch. Let
stand five minutes.

2. Heat the two tablespoons peanut oil in
a skillet or wok (Chinese cooking utensil)
and quickly stir-fry (cook and stir) the lamb
for about two minutes. Add the soy sauce
and pepper oil. Mix well and place on a warm
platter.

3. Heat the remaining peanut oil to 375
degrees and deep-fry the cellophane noodles
for a second or two. Do not burn. Drain on
paper towels. Sprinkle with the remaining
salt and place at both ends of the lamb
shreds.

Chinese Spareribs with Black Beans

4 to 6 servings

1 rack lean spareribs (about 2½ pounds)
2 cloves garlic
1 tablespoon fermented black beans
2 tablespoons vegetable oil
3 tablespoons soy sauce
2 teaspoons granulated sugar
2 tablespoons dry sherry
1 cup plus 1 tablespoon water
1 teaspoon cornstarch

1. With a heavy cleaver or heavy knife, chop the spareribs crosswise into one-and-one-half-inch lengths. Separate the ribs by cutting between them. If the ribs are fatty, cut off the excess fat.

2. Crush the garlic and set aside. Chop the beans and set aside.

3. Heat a two-quart saucepan for thirty seconds. Add the oil and swirl it over the bottom. Add the spareribs and cook, stirring, for three to four minutes, or until lightly browned. Add the soy sauce, sugar, sherry, garlic, and fermented beans. Stir to coat the ribs. Add the one cup water and bring to a boil. Cover and simmer about one hour, stirring once in a while. When cooked, there should be about half a cup of sauce in the pan. Let the spareribs stand for half an hour, then remove them. Leave the sauce in the pan.

4. Skim off any excess fat from the sauce and discard the garlic. Combine the cornstarch and the remaining one tablespoon water and stir into the sauce. Cook, stirring, until the sauce clears. Add the spareribs and stir to coat well. Serve hot.

Chinese Roast Pork

6 to 8 servings

1 pound boneless lean pork, preferably pork tenderloin
2 tablespoons grated fresh ginger
2 cloves garlic, finely minced
1½ tablespoons hoi sin deung (sweet bean sauce)
1 teaspoon anise seed, crushed
¼ cup dry sherry
3 tablespoons soy sauce
Salt to taste
¼ cup honey
1 tablespoon red food coloring

1. Cut the pork into strips (1½ x 1½ x 4).

2. Combine the remaining ingredients, then add the pork. Let stand, turning occasionally so the pieces are well coated, about two hours.

3. Preheat the oven to 350 degrees.

4. Using wire from unpainted coat hangers, make several large S-hooks. Cut the wire to three-inch lengths and bend each piece in the shape of an S. Insert one end of each hook into each piece of pork.

5. Use only one rack in the oven, placing it as high in the oven as it will fit. Suspend the pork, on the hooks, from the center of the rack. Put about three cups of water in a baking dish and place it beneath the pork to catch the drippings.

6. Roast the pork for thirty-five minutes, then increase the oven heat to 450 degrees and continue roasting the pork thirty minutes longer. Serve sliced, hot or cold. Leftover roast pork keeps well, and is good shredded in soups, egg rolls, etc.

Szechwan Pork

2 to 6 servings

  1 pound lean pork
  1 egg white
1½ tablespoons cornstarch
  4 dried Chinese mushrooms
  1 cup thinly sliced or chopped fresh mushrooms
  1 cup chopped Chinese cabbage
  ½ cup chopped green pepper
  ½ cup thinly sliced bamboo shoots
  1 tablespoon chopped fresh ginger
1½ tablespoons chopped fresh garlic, or to taste
  1 or more finely shredded hot green peppers
  ¼ cup chopped green onion
  5 tablespoons hoi sin deung (sweet bean sauce)
  1 teaspoon sesame oil
  2 tablespoons dry sherry
  ½ teaspoon granulated sugar
  2 cups plus 2 tablespoons peanut oil

1. Partially freeze the pork to facilitate slicing. Cut the pork against the grain into very thin slices and cut each slice into shreds.

2. Beat the egg white lightly and beat in the cornstarch. Add the pork shreds and stir to coat. Let stand five hours.

3. Meanwhile, pour boiling water over the dried mushrooms and let stand twenty minutes. Drain and chop. Combine these in a bowl with the sliced mushrooms, cabbage, green pepper, and bamboo shoots. Set aside.

4. In another bowl combine the chopped fresh ginger, garlic, hot peppers, green onion, hoi sin deung, sesame oil, sherry, and sugar. Set aside.

5. Have two cooking utensils ready, a small deep-fryer (a small deep casserole will do) and a wok (Chinese cooking utensil) or skillet. Heat the two cups of oil to medium hot in the deep-fryer. The fat must not be too hot.

6. Place the pork in a sieve or other small wire basket and add the mushroom mixture. Lower this into the oil and cook without browning. Cook about thirty seconds in all and lift the sieve from the oil.

7. Heat the two tablespoons of oil in a wok over high heat and add the pork mixture. Cook quickly, stirring constantly. Add the ginger and garlic mixture and stir. When all is blended and piping hot, serve immediately with rice.

Pearl Balls

(Rice-Coated Meat Balls)

About 2 dozen

  4 dried Chinese mushrooms
    Lukewarm water to cover
  ½ cup glutinous rice
  1 pound ground pork
  6 water chestnuts, finely chopped
  1 green onion, finely chopped, green part and all
  1 tablespoon soy sauce
  1 teaspoon salt
  ½ teaspoon granulated sugar
  1 teaspoon cornstarch

1. Soak the mushrooms in lukewarm water thirty minutes, or until soft. Drain and chop.

2. Wash the rice and soak it in water to cover fifteen minutes.

3. Combine the pork with the mushrooms and all ingredients except the rice. Scoop up about one tablespoon of filling and shape into a round ball. Drain the rice and roll the ball in it. Press gently until well coated. Continue shaping balls and rolling in rice until all the filling is used.

4. Arrange a damp cloth on a steamer rack (see note page 40), arrange the meat balls on the cloth and steam, covered, thirty minutes. Serve hot.

Steamed Pork Balls

6 servings, about 36 balls

1 cup uncooked rice
1 pound lean pork, ground
1 to 2 green onions, finely chopped
2 slices fresh ginger, finely chopped
1 egg, lightly beaten
2 tablespoons imported soy sauce
1 tablespoon sherry
1 tablespoon water
2 teaspoons cornstarch
1 teaspoon granulated sugar

1. Cover the rice with cold water and soak for three hours. Drain.

2. Mix the pork well with all the ingredients except the rice, but do not overhandle. Form into balls the size of walnuts.

3. Spread the rice on a flat plate and roll the pork balls, one at a time, in the rice to coat them.

4. Arrange the balls on the trays of an oriental bamboo steamer or on an ovenproof plate, allowing one-half-inch spaces between the balls. Steam in the bamboo steamer over a wok (Chinese cooking utensil) of boiling water or place the plate on a rack in a skillet of boiling water. Cover the plate with foil that has been pierced at several points with a food pick. Cover the steamer or skillet and steam for about an hour, or until the pork is well cooked and the rice is tender. Serve with hot mustard and soy sauce.

Chicken with Peppers

4 servings

½ chicken (about 1 pound)
2 tablespoons sake or dry sherry
3 tablespoons soy sauce
5 teaspoons cornstarch
  Vegetable oil for deep frying
3 small green peppers
3 tablespoons peanut oil
1 or 2 hot dried red peppers or Tabasco to taste
1 whole clove garlic, peeled
3 slices fresh ginger
1 teaspoon granulated sugar
¼ teaspoon monosodium glutamate
½ cup water

1. Cut and chop the chicken, bones and all, into bite-sized pieces.

2. Sprinkle the chicken with one tablespoon sake, one tablespoon soy sauce, and three teaspoons cornstarch. Stir so all the pieces are coated.

3. Heat the oil to 350 degrees and cook the chicken until crisp and brown. Do not overcook.

4. Remove cores and seeds from the green peppers and cut the peppers into quarters. Heat the peanut oil and cook the red pepper, garlic, and ginger over high heat for one minute, stirring. Add the green peppers and cook, stirring, until coated with oil. Add the chicken, the remaining sake, the sugar, the remaining soy sauce, and the monosodium glutamate. Cook, stirring, until the liquid boils. Combine the remaining cornstarch with the water and add, stirring. When thickened, serve hot.

Lemon Chicken

4 servings

One of the most interesting of Chinese dishes is a creation of highly skilled chef Lee Lum. Called simply Lemon Chicken, it consists of boneless chicken breast, coated with water chestnut powder, crisply fried, and served over crisp vegetables in a sweet and pungent lemon sauce whose extraordinary flavor comes from the ounce of lemon extract that is added at the last moment. The recipe is given here for home cooks who would like to duplicate Lee Lum's triumph.

4 whole chicken breasts, boned and skinned
2 tablespoons light soy sauce
¼ teaspoon sesame oil
1 teaspoon salt
1 tablespoon gin or vodka
3 egg whites, beaten until frothy
1 cup water chestnut flour or powder
   Peanut or salad oil
¾ cup granulated sugar
½ cup white vinegar
1 cup Chicken Stock (page 115)
1 tablespoon cornstarch
2 tablespoons water
1 teaspoon monosodium glutamate
   Juice of 1 lemon
   Thin yellow rind of 1 lemon, finely chopped
¼ head iceberg lettuce, finely shredded
3 small carrots, cut in thinnest possible strips (julienne)
½ large green pepper, cut in thinnest possible strips (julienne)
3 green onions, cut in thinnest possible strips (julienne)
½ cup shredded canned pineapple
1 1-ounce bottle lemon extract

1. Place the chicken in a shallow earthenware dish or bowl. Combine the soy sauce, sesame oil, salt, and gin or vodka and pour over the chicken. Toss to coat and let sit thirty minutes.

2. Drain the chicken and discard the marinade. Add the chicken pieces to the beaten egg whites and toss to coat. Place the water chestnut flour on a plate and use to coat the chicken pieces.

3. Add peanut oil to a skillet to a depth of one-half inch and heat to 350 degrees. Add the chicken pieces, a few at a time if necessary, and brown on both sides. Drain.

4. Meanwhile, place the sugar, vinegar, stock, cornstarch mixed with water, monosodium glutamate, and lemon juice and rind in a small pan. Bring to a boil and cook stirring, until the mixture thickens.

5. Cut the drained chicken into one-inch crosswise slices and place it on top of the shredded lettuce on a serving platter. If necessary, keep warm in a 200-degree oven.

6. Add the vegetables and pineapple to the sauce. Remove from the heat and stir in the lemon extract. Pour over the chicken.

Szechwan Chicken

2 to 6 servings

1 pound skinned, boned breast of chicken (there should be about 1 pound of meat after skinning and boning)
1 egg white
1½ tablespoons cornstarch
⅓ cup finely shredded hot green pepper
¼ cup chopped green onions
1 tablespoon coarsely chopped garlic
1 tablespoon finely chopped fresh ginger
1 tablespoon dry sherry
¼ teaspoon monosodium glutamate (optional)
1 teaspoon white vinegar
1 teaspoon granulated sugar
1 tablespoon soy sauce
2 cups plus 2 tablespoons peanut oil
Sprigs of fresh coriander leaves (cilantro or Chinese parsley) (optional)

1. Partially freeze the chicken meat to facilitate slicing. Cut the chicken, with the grain, into lengthwise strips, the thinnest possible (julienne).

2. Beat the egg white lightly, then beat in the cornstarch. Add the shredded chicken and stir to coat well. Let the coated chicken stand five hours.

3. In one bowl combine the hot green pepper, green onions, garlic, and chopped ginger.

4. In another bowl combine the sherry, monosodium glutamate, white vinegar, sugar, and soy sauce. Stir to blend thoroughly.

5. Have two cooking utensils ready, a small deep-fryer (a small deep casserole will do) and a wok (Chinese cooking utensil) or skillet. Heat the two cups of oil to medium hot in the deep-fryer. The fat must not be too hot.

6. When ready to cook, fluff up the chicken shreds with the fingers, then add to a sieve or small wire basket. Lower into the oil and cook just until the shreds turn white,

about one minute or less. Do not brown. Lift the sieve from the oil.

7. Heat the two tablespoons of oil in a wok over high heat and add the chicken plus the green onion mixture. Stir to blend, then add the sherry and vinegar mixture. Cook briefly, stirring rapidly and constantly, until the mixture is bubbling and thoroughly hot. If desired, garnish with coriander leaves.

Chinese Smoked Chicken

4 to 6 servings

1 roasting chicken (about 4 pounds)
2 tablespoons salt
5 tablespoons brown sugar
2 teaspoons sesame oil

1. Wash the chicken, dry with paper towels inside and out, and rub inside and out with the salt. Let stand overnight.

2. Place the chicken in a steaming utensil. To improvise, place the chicken in a colander and suspend the colander in a kettle large enough to hold it. Add water to within one inch of the bottom of the colander. Cover tightly with a cover or aluminum foil. Steam the chicken for forty-five minutes over rapidly boiling water. Add more boiling water as the original water boils away.

3. Heat the brown sugar in a large saucepan lined with aluminum foil. Place a wire grill, such as a cake rack or roasting pan rack, on sugar-covered foil and set the chicken on it. Cover the pan with a lid wrapped in aluminum foil; this will keep the lid clean and prevent smoke from escaping. Smoke the chicken for ten minutes over medium heat.

4. Turn off the heat and let the pan stand, covered, for three or four minutes. Remove the chicken and rub with sesame oil. Cut into small pieces and serve hot or cold.

White Cut Chicken

4 to 6 servings

6 to 8 cups Chicken Stock (page 115)
4 thin slices fresh ginger
1 green onion, trimmed and cut into 2-inch
  lengths
1 chicken (3½ to 4 pounds)

1. Heat the stock in a kettle and add the ginger root and green onion. There should be enough stock to completely cover the chicken when it is added.

2. Place a metal teaspoon inside the chicken to help retain the heat, then add the chicken to the stock. If the stock does not completely cover the chicken, add boiling water to make up the difference.

3. When the stock starts to boil, reduce the heat to a simmer. Cover and simmer twenty minutes. Turn off the heat and leave the chicken in the stock for two hours, then remove from the stock and cut into two-and-one-half-inch cubes. Serve with Sesame-Flavored Sauce or Ginger-Pepper Sauce (see below).

SESAME-FLAVORED SAUCE:

About 5 tablespoons

1 tablespoon sesame oil
¼ cup soy sauce

Combine the oil and soy sauce and blend. Serve as a dip with White Cut Chicken (see above) or pour the sauce over the chicken.

GINGER-PEPPER SAUCE:

About ½ cup

1 tablespoon finely shredded fresh ginger
4 green onions, white part only, trimmed
  and shredded
½ teaspoon granulated sugar
¼ cup vegetable oil
1 teaspoon salt
½ teaspoon hot pepper flakes or chopped
  hot green or red pepper

1. Place the ginger, green onions, and sugar in a small heatproof dish.

2. Heat the oil and salt until hot but not smoking. Add the hot pepper and pour the mixture over the ginger mixture. Let cool. Serve as a dip for White Cut Chicken (see above) or pour the mixture over the chicken as a sauce.

Roast Peking Duck

4 servings

One of the famed delights of Chinese cooking is Peking duck. It must, almost invariably, be ordered twenty-four hours in advance. Professional chefs sometimes use a pump to blow air between the skin and flesh of the duck. Then, when the duck is roasted, the fat simply flows out, leaving the crisp skin that is cut into pieces and eaten with the duck meat, green onions and sauce—all wrapped in Chinese pancakes. The method for cooking Peking duck given here does not call for a pump. Instead, the skin is separated from the flesh with the fingers and a sharp knife—a technique that brings Peking duck into the sphere of the home kitchen and the home cook.

1 duck (5 to 6 pounds)
1 tablespoon salad oil
1 green onion, cut into 2-inch lengths and shredded (julienne)
   Rind of ½ orange, cut into thinnest possible strips (julienne)
1 clove garlic, finely minced
3 tablespoons hoi sin deung (sweet bean sauce)
1 teaspoon granulated sugar
3 tablespoons honey
¼ cup water
   Salt to taste
   Fresh coriander sprigs (Chinese parsley) for garnish (optional)
   Steamed Pancakes (page 57)
   Peking Duck Sauce (page 57)
   Green Onion Flowers (page 57)

1. The most important thing about making this recipe is to separate the skin from the flesh of the duck, keeping both skin and flesh intact. You must work cautiously to avoid piercing the skin, although if it is pierced it may be sewn together again.

2. Cut off the wings of the duck. The holes thus left will be sewed up later.

3. Start at the neck of the duck and, using the fingers and a sharp paring knife, start separating the skin from the flesh. Continue working toward the tail section of the duck, pulling with the fingers, cutting where essential with the knife. The principal danger area is at the cartilage-like point of the breastbone. Use a little ingenuity and your sharp knife to leave a bit of this cartilage intact so as not to rip the skin. Work the fingers around the drumsticks, but leave the tips of each drumstick intact. Do not skin the duck completely. When you have nearly reached the tail section, pull the skin back over the flesh of the duck to reshape it entirely.

4. Heat the oil in a small saucepan and add the shredded green onion, orange rind, and garlic. Cook briefly, stirring, and remove from the heat. Add the hoi sin deung and sugar and stir. Push this mixture into the cavity of the duck.

5. Use a needle and thread to sew up the neck opening of the duck, the holes where the wings were, and any places where the skin was torn.

6. Bring a large kettle of water to a boil and add the duck. Using a two-pronged fork to keep the duck immersed, keep the duck in the boiling water for five minutes, then remove it. Drain thoroughly and wipe the outside dry with paper towels.

7. Combine the honey and the one-quarter cup water. Bring just to a boil. Brush the duck all over with the mixture. Sprinkle the duck with salt.

8. Put a hook through the tail bone of the duck and hang it, neck side down, on the hook. Let it stand eight to ten hours in a cool, airy place, or place it before an electric fan for three to four hours to dry or partially dry the skin.

9. When ready to cook, preheat the oven to 375 degrees.

10. Place the duck breast side up on a rack in a shallow roasting pan. It will not be necessary to baste the duck. Place the pan on

the lower shelf of the oven and roast thirty minutes.

11. Reduce the oven heat to 250 degrees. Pour off the fat from the roasting pan and continue roasting the duck for one hour. Pour off the fat from the pan.

12. Increase the oven heat to 375 degrees and continue roasting 15 minutes. (If, on the other hand, the duck seems too dark and about to burn, do not increase the oven heat.) Turn the duck breast side down and continue roasting fifteen minutes. Remove the duck from the oven. It is now ready to serve. Ideally the duck should be served piping hot, but even under the best of conditions this is almost impossible. It is excellent, nonetheless, lukewarm.

13. Slit the skin top to bottom and pull it from the duck. Cut the skin into bite-sized morsels and arrange them on a hot platter. Cut the meat into bite-sized pieces and arrange them on another platter. Sprinkle the duck with fresh coriander sprigs.

14. Open a steamed pancake onto a plate and smear two or three teaspoons of duck sauce in the center. Top this with one or two green onion flowers, then add a few pieces of duck skin and flesh.

15. Roll the pancake so that the filling is enclosed and eat it with the fingers.

STEAMED PANCAKES:

12 to 16 pancakes

2 cups sifted all-purpose flour
1 cup boiling water
2 tablespoons sesame oil, approximately

1. The pancakes may be made in advance, cooked in a skillet, and steamed just before serving. To prepare them, spoon the flour into a mixing bowl. Bring the water to a vigorous boil and add it gradually to the flour while stirring all around with a wooden spoon. Add all but about three tablespoons to the dough. Knead the dough well until it is smooth and elastic, about ten minutes. If it needs more water to make it manageable,

add it. Wrap the dough in waxed paper and let stand ten minutes.

2. Shape the dough with the hands into a sausagelike roll, one and one-half inches in diameter. Slice the dough into half-inch pieces, then flatten and shape with floured fingers or rolling pin into "biscuits" about one-quarter inch thick. When all the dough has been shaped, lightly brush the tops of each biscuit with sesame oil. Top half the biscuits with the remaining biscuits, sandwich like, with the oiled surfaces together.

3. Roll these out, one at a time, on a lightly floured surface. Roll from the center to make a circle. The thinner you roll them, the better. When the pancakes are all rolled, heat a skillet or griddle and cook them briefly without browning, first on one side, then on the other. As each one is cooked and while still warm, pull it apart at the center. Fold each pancake at the center with the oiled side inside.

4. When ready to serve, place a rack in a steamer (see note page 40) and cover the rack with a damp cloth. Arrange the pancakes on it (they may overlap slightly) and steam the pancakes ten minutes. Serve hot.

PEKING DUCK SAUCE:

About 1 cup

¾ cup hoi sin deung (sweet bean sauce)
¼ cup finely minced green onion
1 teaspoon finely grated orange rind
¼ cup granulated sugar

Combine all the ingredients and let stand until ready to serve.

GREEN ONION FLOWERS:

24 flowers

Trim off the roots and green ends of 12 green onions and cut the white part of each into two-inch lengths. Cross-split the ends of each of these pieces and drop into ice water. The ends will open up. Let stand one hour, then drain.

Cantonese Roast Duck

4 to 6 servings

1 duck (5 to 6 pounds), cleaned
  Salt to taste
1 tablespoon peanut oil
1 clove garlic, finely minced
½ cup finely chopped onion
1 green onion, trimmed and chopped
2 teaspoons star anise
2 teaspoons Szechwan peppercorns
4 cups water
2 tablespoons crushed fresh Chinese parsley (coriander or cilantro)
2 tablespoons dry sherry
¼ cup soy sauce
1 teaspoon granulated sugar
¼ cup honey
1 tablespoon cider vinegar
  Fresh coriander sprigs for garnish
¼ cup chopped green onion for garnish

1. Sew up the neck of the duck securely with string. This must be done carefully, to prevent liquid from running through when the duck roasts. Tie another string onto the duck's neck and hang the duck in a dry place for an hour or longer.

2. Preheat the oven to 400 degrees.

3. Rub the duck generously inside and out with salt.

4. Heat the oil in a saucepan and cook the garlic, onion, and green onion until the onion is translucent. Crush the star anise and peppercorns and add. Add half the water, the crushed Chinese parsley, sherry, soy sauce, and sugar. Bring to a boil and simmer ten minutes. Holding the duck neck side down, pour this mixture into the cavity of the duck. Carefully sew up the opening with string so that no liquid can run out. Place the duck, breast up, on a rack in a roasting pan and put it in the oven.

5. Combine the remaining water, honey, and vinegar and baste the duck. Roast, basting occasionally, twenty minutes, then reduce the oven heat to 350 degrees. Roast one hour, basting, and reduce the heat to 300 degrees. Roast thirty minutes longer, basting. Remove the strings and carve the duck. Arrange the pieces on a platter and serve garnished with coriander and chopped green onion.

Five-Spice Duck

4 servings

1 duck (4 to 6 pounds)
2 cups leeks cut into 2-inch lengths and rinsed well
¼ cup sherry
¼ cup soy sauce
1 tablespoon honey
2 cups water
1 teaspoon five spices powder (buy a very small quantity; see note)

1. Preheat the oven to 350 degrees.
2. Roast the duck for one hour, discarding the fat as it accumulates.
3. In a large saucepan or a small roaster with a cover, place half of the leeks and lay the duck over them. Add the sherry, soy sauce, and honey. Bring to a boil over a high flame. Add the water and again bring to a boil. Cover and cook over medium heat for one-half hour, basting a few times.
4. Sprinkle the remaining leeks over the duck, cover, and cook for another half hour. Sprinkle the five spices powder over the duck, baste a few more times, and cook another fifteen minutes. There should be about one-quarter cup juice left when it is time to serve.

Note: Five spices powder—a combination of ground star anise, anise pepper, fennel, cloves, and cinnamon—is available in oriental and Chinese markets.

Soya Duck

4 servings

1 duck (4 to 5 pounds), at room temperature
½ cup soy sauce
½ cup honey
2 tablespoons dry sherry
2 teaspoons grated fresh ginger or 1 teaspoon ground ginger
1 clove garlic, crushed
Salt and freshly ground black pepper
1 onion, peeled
1 rib celery

1. The duck may be cooked in the oven or on a revolving spit. If an oven is to be used, preheat it to 350 degrees.
2. Combine the soy sauce, honey, sherry, ginger, and garlic in a saucepan. Simmer the mixture briefly until the ingredients are well blended.
3. Dry the cavity of the duck with paper towels. Sprinkle the inside with salt and pepper and add the onion and celery. Skewer the body opening or sew it closed with a needle and thread.
4. If the duck is to be oven roasted, put it on a rack in a roasting pan and place in the oven. If the duck is to be cooked on a spit, adjust the duck on a roasting spit. The coals to be used in cooking should not be directly below the duck; they should be banked slightly on either side of the duck so that the drippings from the duck do not fall into the coals.
5. Roast the duck, basting occasionally with the sauce, for one to one and one-half hours, or until the duck is well done. When done, the duck should be covered with a well-blackened though unburned glaze.

Foh Opp

(Chinese Roast Duck)

4 servings

1 Long Island duckling (4 to 5 pounds), cleaned and drawn
2 tablespoons honey
1 teaspoon red vegetable coloring (optional)
2 teaspoons granulated sugar
½ teaspoon salt
¼ cup mein sin deung (yellow bean paste)
¼ cup hoi sin deung (sweet bean paste)
2 tablespoons gin
Rind of ½ orange, finely shredded
2 green onions or ½ leek, cut into 2-inch lengths
1 clove garlic, finely chopped
2 tablespoons dark soy sauce

1. There are two ways to prepare this duck, on a barbecue grill or roasted in the oven. Generally speaking, the oven is preferable.

2. Add enough water to a large kettle to cover the duck, when it is added, halfway. Bring the water to a boil and add the honey. Using large tongs or a sling made of cheesecloth, dip the duck first on one side, then the other. Repeat several times, making certain the duck's back in particular is well scalded. If a reddish color is desired in the duck skin, add one teaspoon of red vegetable color to the water.

3. Drain the duck. Place it on a rack and let drain in a place where air freely circulates. Let stand one hour.

4. Combine the remaining ingredients and spoon the mixture into the cavity of the duck. Let stand two hours longer. Do not refrigerate. Keep at room temperature.

5. If the duck is to be cooked in the oven, preheat the oven to 400 degrees. If the duck is to be cooked over coals, roast it, turning frequently, until done.

6. If the oven method is used, place the duck on a rack in a roasting pan, breast side up, and roast thirty minutes. Pour off the fat as it accumulates. Reduce the oven heat to 350 degrees and continue to roast thirty to forty minutes, depending on the size of the duck.

7. To serve the duck Chinese style, disjoint the duck, split the body into halves, and cut, through both flesh and bones, into one-inch pieces, using a cleaver. Serve with duck sauce or plum sauce (available in bottles at Chinese groceries) as a dip.

Ginger and Pork Fried Rice

4 servings

6 tablespoons peanut oil
2 eggs, lightly beaten
⅓ pound (about 1 cup) pork or beef, ground
1 teaspoon freshly grated ginger or ½ teaspoon ground ginger
2 cups cooked rice
Salt and freshly ground pepper to taste
¼ cup chopped green onion
12 lettuce leaves

1. Heat two tablespoons of the oil, add the eggs and scramble to the soft stage.

2. Heat two additional tablespoons of oil in a wok (Chinese cooking utensil) or large skillet and add the pork. Cook, stirring, until the meat is thoroughly cooked. Add the ginger and stir. Add the rice, salt, and pepper and cook, stirring rapidly to blend all the ingredients. When the rice is piping hot, mix in the remaining oil, the green onion, and the egg, broken up roughly. Spoon portions of the hot fried rice into the lettuce leaves, roll with the fingers, and serve immediately.

Young Jewel Fried Rice

4 servings

Lettuce in the average American household is strictly for the salad bowl, but it has other, fascinating uses. Europeans braise it and serve it as a vegetable; they sometimes cook it in soup. The Chinese use the fresh leaves sandwich-style—finger food, as it were— with fillings like hot minced squab or hot fried rice. Below is a recipe for Young Jewel fried rice, in which shredded lettuce is mixed with chicken, pork, and shrimp. ("Young Jewel" is a corruption of Yeung Chau, a province of ancient China famous for its fried-rice dishes.)

¼ cup soy sauce
¼ teaspoon ground pepper
1 teaspoon monosodium glutamate (optional)
¼ cup vegetable oil
2 eggs, lightly beaten
1 cup diced roast pork
1 cup diced cooked shrimp
1 cup diced cooked chicken
2 cups fresh bean sprouts (see note)
2 green onions, chopped, green part and all
4 cups hot cooked rice
1 cup shredded lettuce

1. Combine the soy sauce, pepper, and monosodium glutamate.

2. Heat half the oil in a wok (Chinese cooking utensil) or frying pan and scramble the eggs lightly. Remove from pan.

3. Increase the heat and add the remaining oil. Add the pork, shrimp, chicken, bean sprouts, and green onions. Cook, stirring, two minutes. Add the rice and soy sauce mixture, mix thoroughly, and stir in the eggs. Stir in the lettuce and serve immediately.

Note: Fresh bean sprouts are available in many Chinese markets. Canned bean sprouts may be used if rinsed in cold water and drained.

Har-Gow

(Steamed Shrimp Dumplings)

About 3 dozen

¼ pound pork, ground
1 pound fresh shrimp, shelled, deveined, and chopped
¼ cup chopped bamboo shoots
2 green onions, white part only, finely chopped
1 teaspoon soy sauce
1 teaspoon salt
Freshly ground black pepper
Vegetable oil
1½ cups wheat starch
½ cup tapioca flour
1½ cups boiling water

1. Place the pork, shrimp, bamboo shoots, green onions, soy sauce, salt, pepper to taste, and one tablespoon oil in a large bowl and mix thoroughly. Refrigerate at least one hour.

2. Sift together the wheat starch and tapioca flour in a large bowl. Add the boiling water gradually, stirring. Knead the dough with a little oil until firm. Let stand ten minutes.

3. Lightly oil a board or table. Break off the dough into small pieces and roll into balls about one inch in diameter. Brush one side of a flat cleaver with a little oil, place each ball on the oiled surface, and flatten very thin. Put one teaspoonful or so of the filling in the center of each piece of dough. Gather up the sides of the dough and squeeze together to seal tightly. Repeat until all the filling is used. Arrange a damp cloth or damp paper towel over a steaming rack (see note page 40) and place the dumplings on it. Cover and steam ten minutes. Serve hot.

Chinese Fried Dumplings

40 or more dumplings, depending on size

1 cup dried shrimp (optional)
10 dried Chinese mushrooms
3½ cups finely chopped Chinese cabbage
3 cups ground pork (part lean, part fat)
3½ tablespoons cornstarch
Salt to taste
½ teaspoon monosodium glutamate (optional)
1 egg white
1 tablespoon dry sherry
2 tablespoons soy sauce, preferably dark
½ teaspoon granulated sugar
3 green onions, trimmed and chopped
1 tablespoon vegetable oil
3 cups sifted all-purpose flour
⅔ to 1 cup hot, almost boiling water
Vegetable oil for frying
Water

1. Place the shrimp in a mixing bowl and add boiling water to cover. Let stand overnight.

2. Place the mushrooms in another bowl and add boiling water to cover. Let stand overnight.

3. When ready to make the dumplings, drain the shrimp and chop them. Put them in a large mixing bowl.

4. Drain the mushrooms but reserve the liquid. Cut away and discard the hard stems. Chop the mushroom caps and add them to the shrimp. Add the cabbage, pork, cornstarch, salt, monosodium glutamate, egg white, dry sherry, soy sauce, sugar, green onions, and one tablespoon oil, then add most of the reserved mushroom liquid and stir. The filling should be moist but not wet. Set aside.

5. Place the flour in a mixing bowl and add the hot water, a little at a time, while stirring with chopsticks or a spoon. Add only enough water to make a very firm, nonsticky dough. If too much liquid is added, you may have to add more flour. Work the dough in the bowl with the fingers until all the flour has been incorporated. Turn the dough out onto a lightly floured board and knead about fifteen minutes, or until smooth and elastic. Cover loosely with a damp towel and set aside. Let stand at least thirty minutes.

6. Roll the dough with the hands on a lightly floured surface. Shape and pull it into a sausage shape about two inches thick. Divide the dough in half and keep one half covered. Continue rolling the other half of the dough into a sausage shape slightly less than one inch thick. Using a knife, cut the dough into three-quarter-inch lengths. With lightly floured fingers shape each piece into a small, round "pillow." Roll each pillow into a very thin oval. Spoon from one to one and one-half tablespoons of the filling into the center of each oval and fold one long end over to touch the other. Pinch the edges of the dough to enclose the filling, like ravioli. As each dumpling is made, place it on a lightly floured tray. Keep covered with a damp cloth so the dumplings do not dry out.

7. To fry, heat one and one-half tablespoons oil in a heavy, twelve-inch skillet. Add a few dumplings, flat side down, to fill the skillet. Let cook over medium-high heat until golden brown on the bottom side only. Pour in three-quarters cup of water and cover with a close-fitting lid. Reduce the heat, but do not remove the cover until all the water is evaporated, about seven to nine minutes. Sprinkle with about two and one-half tablespoons of oil and continue to cook, uncovered, about four minutes, twirling the skillet this way and that to distribute the oil. Use a spatula or pancake turner to scoop under the dumplings and remove them from the skillet. Keep them warm while preparing the others. Continue to fry the remaining dumplings, adding more oil to the skillet and more water when they are browned. Serve hot with vinegar and hot oil, Dumpling and Hor Gwo Sauce (page 64), or Szechwan Sauce for Dumplings (page 64).

Shrimp and Pork Egg Rolls

20 egg rolls

10 egg roll wrappers (see note)
 1 small head Chinese cabbage
¼ pound raw shrimp, shelled and deveined
 2 teaspoons dry sherry
    Salt to taste
½ teaspoon monosodium glutamate
½ teaspoon cornstarch
¼ pound Chinese Roast Pork (page 50), or roast pork may be purchased
 3 tablespoons peanut oil
½ teaspoon granulated sugar
½ pound fresh bean sprouts, rinsed and drained
⅓ cup shredded fresh mushrooms
 1 egg, lightly beaten
    Vegetable oil for deep frying

1. Place the ten egg roll wrappers in one stack on a flat surface and slice them diagonally to make triangles. Cover and set aside.

2. Chop the tender leaves of the cabbage to make three cups, loosely packed.

3. Cut the shrimp into bite-sized pieces and place in a mixing bowl. Add the sherry, salt, half the monosodium glutamate, and the cornstarch. Stir to blend and let stand.

4. Cut the roast pork into fine shreds. Set aside.

5. Heat one tablespoon peanut oil in a small skillet and cook the shrimp until they turn pink, stirring constantly. Pour the shrimp into a colander.

6. Heat the remaining two tablespoons oil and cook the cabbage quickly for about one minute. Add salt, sugar, and the remaining monosodium glutamate. Cook, stirring, about five minutes. Add the bean sprouts, mushrooms, shrimp, and pork and stir. Let the mixture stand until cool.

7. Spoon a small row of filling across the base of one egg roll triangle. Bring the left and right corners of the triangle toward the center, then roll, envelope fashion, to enclose the filling. Brush the top pointed corner with egg and seal. Continue until all the filling and triangles are used. Fry in hot oil until golden brown all over. Serve hot, with plum sauce and hot mustard, if desired.

Note: Egg roll wrappers may be purchased in two-pound packages in Chinese grocery stores; unused wrappers may be frozen.

Szechwan Sauce for Dumplings

About ¾ cup

½ cup soy sauce
2 tablespoons finely chopped green onion
1 clove garlic, finely minced
1 to 8 drops hot salad oil (see note)
2½ teaspoons white vinegar
2 teaspoons sesame oil
½ teaspoon shredded fresh ginger
1 teaspoon granulated sugar

Combine all the ingredients and serve with steamed or fried Chinese dumplings, such as Chinese Fried Dumplings (page 62) or Har-Gow (page 61).
Note: Hot salad oil is available in Chinese groceries.

Dumpling and Hor Gwo Sauce for One

About ⅓ cup

2 teaspoons sesame paste or peanut butter
1 tablespoon chopped green onion
1 tablespoon chopped Chinese parsley (coriander or cilantro)
1 tablespoon soy sauce, preferably dark
1½ teaspoons white vinegar
1 tablespoon dry sherry
⅛ teaspoon monosodium glutamate (optional)
¼ teaspoon chili pepper with garlic or finely chopped garlic and hot pepper sauce to taste
1 teaspoon lan chi (shrimp roe soya sauce)

Combine all the ingredients and stir to blend.

Peking duck (China

Colombia

Cocido Bogotano

(Colombian Beef and Vegetable Stew)

6 to 8 servings

2 pounds boneless lean beef stew meat, cut into 1½-inch cubes
1 bay leaf
½ teaspoon ground cumin
6 peppercorns
1 clove garlic, halved
1 teaspoon cider vinegar
2 teaspoons salt
3 cups plus 1 teaspoon cold water
2 medium potatoes, peeled and cubed
2 large carrots, peeled and cubed
4 long ribs celery, sliced
4 ears of corn, cut into 2-inch lengths
½ cup chopped onion
½ cup diced fresh tomato
¼ teaspoon ground saffron
½ teaspoon dried orégano
1 cup fresh or frozen peas

1. Place the meat in a saucepan with the bay leaf, cumin, peppercorns, garlic, vinegar, salt, and three cups water. Cover and cook slowly for about one hour, until the meat is almost tender.

2. Add the potatoes, carrots, celery, corn, onion, and tomato. Cover and cook for fifteen to twenty minutes, until the vegetables are almost tender.

3. Dissolve the saffron in the one teaspoon water and add to the stew, along with the orégano and peas. Cover and cook for two to ten minutes, until the vegetables are done. Stick food picks or corn holders into the ends of each piece of corn and serve two or three pieces with each serving of stew.

Chicken Colombiana

6 servings

1 chicken (3 pounds), cut into serving pieces
⅔ cup all-purpose flour
2 tablespoons butter
2 tablespoons shortening
¾ cup chopped onion
1 clove garlic, finely minced
½ cup chopped green pepper
½ cup finely diced carrot
½ cup diced celery
1 tablespoon salt or to taste
½ teaspoon coarsely ground black pepper
1 teaspoon crushed cumin
2 cups Italian plum tomatoes
¾ cup chopped stuffed olives
¾ cup raw corn kernels cut off the cob

1. Preheat the oven to 325 degrees.

2. Dredge the chicken in flour and brown on all sides in the butter and shortening, then transfer to a casserole or Dutch oven. Add the onion, garlic, green pepper, carrot, and celery to the skillet in which the chicken cooked. Cook briefly, stirring. Spoon the vegetables over the chicken and add the salt, pepper, cumin, and tomatoes.

3. Cover the casserole and bake one hour, or until the chicken is fork tender. Ten minutes before the chicken is done, add the olives and corn.

Cuba

Black Bean Soup I

6 servings

1 pound dried black beans
6 cups water
¼ pound salt pork
2 cloves garlic, finely minced
1 teaspoon cumin seed
1 teaspoon orégano
½ teaspoon dry mustard
2 tablespoons peanut oil
2 cups finely chopped onion
1 green pepper, cored, seeded, and chopped
  Juice of ½ lemon
6 slices lemon
1 hard-cooked egg, chopped

1. Combine beans and water in a large saucepan and soak overnight. Add salt pork and simmer, partly covered, until almost tender.

2. Combine the garlic, cumin, orégano, and mustard in a mixing bowl and mash with a wooden or large kitchen spoon until well blended.

3. Heat the oil and cook the onion and green pepper, stirring, until wilted. Add the garlic mixture, lemon juice, and one-half cup of the bean liquid. Cover and simmer about ten minutes. Spoon this into the beans, partly cover, and simmer one hour longer, or until the beans are thoroughly tender.

4. Pour two cups of beans with liquid into the container of an electric blender and blend well. Return this to the saucepan and stir.

5. Serve in hot soup bowls. Garnish with lemon slices and sprinkle with chopped egg. Serve with a cruet of olive oil.

Black Bean Soup II

6 generous servings

1 pound dried black beans
2 quarts cold water
1 medium onion, chopped
1 rib celery, chopped
1 ham bone or 1 cup small pieces of ham
1½ tablespoons lemon juice
  Salt and coarsely ground black pepper
¼ teaspoon dry mustard
  Cayenne pepper
  Garlic salt
½ cup dry sherry, approximately
1 cup cooked fluffy rice
6 teaspoons coarsely grated onion

1. Wash the beans and soak them overnight in water to cover. Drain and add the two quarts of cold water, chopped onion, celery, and ham bone. Simmer until the beans are very soft, three to four hours.

2. Remove the bone and put the soup through a strainer. Add the lemon juice, salt, pepper, mustard, cayenne pepper to taste, and a dash of garlic salt. Simmer thirty minutes.

3. Just before serving, add four tablespoons of sherry to each quart of soup. Place one heaping tablespoon of fluffy rice in the center of each serving and top the rice with one teaspoon of coarsely grated onion.

Carne Mechada

(Cuban Stuffed Beef)

10 to 12 servings

1 boliche (see note) or other boneless beef roast (6 to 8 pounds)
2 chorizos (dried Spanish or Portuguese sausages)
¼ pound lean boneless ham, cut into small cubes
3 slices bacon, each cut into 3 pieces
2 thin slices American cheese, cut into small cubes
1 hard-cooked egg, cut into 6 pieces
20 pimento-stuffed olives
20 raisins
6 prunes, pitted and soaked in warm water until soft.
   Salt and freshly ground pepper to taste
3 cups olive oil
1 large onion, finely chopped
1 large green pepper, cored, seeded, and finely chopped
4 cloves garlic, finely minced
¼ teaspoon orégano
¼ teaspoon cumin seed
¼ teaspoon paprika
1 teaspoon freshly chopped parsley
1 bay leaf
1 teaspoon ground ginger
½ cup orange juice
½ bottle dry sherry
3 quarts water, approximately

1. For this dish, the roast has to be stuffed in six places. Insert a long, sharp, narrow knife into one end near the center of the roast and twist it around and around to make a hole about the size of the knife blade. Bore the hole almost to the middle of the meat. Make two more holes in the same end. Turn the roast and make three similar holes in the other end, making the first near the center of the meat.

2. Stuff one chorizo into the center hole at each end.

3. Using the fingers, stuff alternate pieces of ham, bacon, cheese, egg, and some of the olives, raisins, and prunes. Finish stuffing the holes with a piece of ham or bacon. Sprinkle the roast all over with salt and pepper.

4. In a large oval or oblong heatproof cooking utensil, brown the meat on all sides in six tablespoons of the olive oil. The meat should have a fine mahogany color.

5. Remove the meat and wash the cooking utensil. Place the utensil back on the heat and add one-quarter cup oil. When hot, add the onion, green pepper, and garlic. Cook, stirring, until the onion is translucent. Add the roast, orégano, cumin, paprika, parsley, bay leaf, ginger, and the remaining olives, raisins, and prunes.

6. Pour the orange juice over the meat, then turn the meat and add the remaining olive oil and half the sherry. Add enough water to cover the meat halfway. Cover the roaster and simmer until the meat is thoroughly tender, about two hours. If the sauce becomes too thick, add more sherry and water.

7. Remove the meat from the pan and let it cool slightly. Cut the meat into slices and arrange the slices on a platter. Put the sauce with the solids through a food mill, then heat the sauce, which should be somewhat thickened, and pour it over the meat.

Note: Boliche is a typical Spanish cut of meat, which comes from the thigh. Potatoes are sometimes cooked with this dish, about ten or fifteen added during the last hour of cooking.

Santiago Pork Roast

8 to 10 servings

1 loin of pork (6 to 7 pounds)
1 large onion, thinly sliced in rings
2 bay leaves
2 teaspoons salt
½ cup lime or lemon juice
¾ cup soy sauce
¾ cup granulated sugar
1 teaspoon grated fresh ginger or ½ teaspoon dried ginger
2 cloves garlic, finely minced

1. Place the loin of pork in a roasting pan and scatter the onion rings over it. Combine the remaining ingredients and stir until the sugar dissolves. Pour this over the meat and cover with plastic wrap. Refrigerate twelve hours or so, turning the meat once in a while.
2. Preheat the oven to 325 degrees.
3. Place the meat in the oven and bake, basting frequently, about three and one-half hours, or until the meat is thoroughly cooked.

Cuban Black Beans

8 to 10 servings

1 pound black beans, soaked overnight
1 large green pepper, cored, seeded, and quartered
1 medium onion, quartered
8 sprigs fresh coriander leaves
1 teaspoon orégano
1 bay leaf
¼ pound salt pork, quartered
1½ cups Sofrito (see below)
¼ cup vinegar
1 teaspoon granulated sugar

1. Drain the beans and add water to cover to a depth of one and one-half inches.

2. Add the green pepper, onion, coriander leaves, orégano, bay leaf, and salt pork. If a pressure cooker is used, cook the beans forty-five minutes. If they are cooked on top of the stove, simmer them one and one-half hours, or until tender, adding more water as necessary. When the beans are cooked, they should be somewhat liquidy without being soupy. Add the sofrito.
3. Using a wooden spoon, break up a few of the beans, crushing them against the side of the cooking utensil. This will thicken the beans. Add the vinegar and sugar and bring to a boil. Serve with rice.

SOFRITO:

About 1½ cups

1 cup coarsely chopped onion
1 cup coarsely chopped green pepper
1 clove garlic, finely minced
½ cup olive oil

Combine all the ingredients in a skillet and cook until the vegetables are tender.

Fried Plantains

12 servings

6 plantains
1 cup peanut or vegetable oil
Salt to taste

1. Peel the plantains and cut each into one-inch lengths.
2. Heat the oil, and when it is hot fry the pieces of plantain until half browned, three to five minutes. Remove from the pan, sprinkle with salt, and drain on brown paper.
3. Place another sheet of brown paper on top and flatten the pieces of plantain slightly. Heat the oil again and cook the pieces of plantain until browned, about one minute. Serve sprinkled with salt.

Czechoslovakia

Sauerkraut Soup

8 to 10 servings

2 pounds short ribs of beef
2 pounds beef bones
1 cup chopped onion
3 carrots, coarsely chopped
2 cloves garlic, peeled
1 teaspoon dried thyme
1 bay leaf
2 quarts water
2½ cups (1 20-ounce can) tomatoes
8 cups shredded cabbage
  Salt and freshly ground black pepper
3 tablespoons lemon juice
3 tablespoons granulated sugar
1 pound sauerkraut, washed and squeezed dry

1. Preheat the oven to 450 degrees.
2. Place the short ribs, beef bones, onion, carrots, garlic, thyme, and bay leaf in a roasting pan. Bake for about twenty minutes, until the meat is brown.
3. Transfer the mixture to a kettle. Place the roasting pan over heat and add a little of the water. Stir to dissolve the brown particles, then pour this into the kettle. Add the remaining water, tomatoes, cabbage, and salt and pepper to taste.
4. Bring the mixture to a boil and skim the fat from the top. Simmer for one and one-half hours. Add the lemon juice, sugar, sauerkraut, and more water, if necessary. Cook for one hour longer. Serve with sour cream.

Paprika Meat Balls

6 servings

1 clove garlic, minced
1 small onion, chopped
1 tablespoon butter
1 pound lean beef, ground
1½ teaspoons salt
  Dash of cayenne pepper
2 tablespoons finely chopped parsley
⅓ cup fine dry bread crumbs
1 tablespoon shortening
1 beef bouillon cube
½ cup tomato juice
1 tablespoon paprika
1 cup sour cream

1. Cook the garlic and onion in the butter until the onion is wilted.
2. Combine with the beef, one teaspoon of the salt, the cayenne, parsley, and bread crumbs. Shape into one-inch balls.
3. Brown on all sides in the shortening for twelve to fifteen minutes. Drain off the fat, reserving one-quarter cup.
4. Add the bouillon cube, tomato juice, and the reserved fat to the meat balls. Cook for five to six minutes. Combine the paprika, remaining salt, and the sour cream and add. Heat only until hot. Serve over noodles.

Sauerbraten, Czechoslovakian Style

6 or more servings

  1 bottom round roast (3½ pounds)
  ½ cup pickling spices
  2 lemons
  5 slices bacon
  5 carrots, diced
  2 parsley roots, diced, or 8 sprigs fresh parsley
  2 celery roots (knob celery), peeled and diced, or 5 ribs celery, diced
  2 cups finely chopped onion
    Salt and freshly ground pepper
  3 tablespoons peanut or vegetable oil
1½ tablespoons cornstarch
  ¼ cup water
  1 cup heavy cream

1. Trim all the fat from the meat.

2. Pick over the pickling spices and remove all but four or five of the hot red peppers and all but four or five of the cardamom seeds (see note). Tie in a cheesecloth bag and set aside.

3. Carefully peel the yellow skin from one of the lemons. Chop it finely and set aside. Squeeze the juice from both lemons and set aside.

4. Cook the bacon in a skillet or casserole until crisp. Remove the bacon and use it for another purpose.

5. To the fat in the skillet add the carrots, parsley, celery, and onions. Cook, stirring, until the vegetables are brown. Add the pickling spices, lemon juice, and chopped rind. Add enough boiling water (four to five cups) to completely cover the meat. Let this mixture cool.

6. Place the meat in a deep glass, stainless steel, or enamel dish and pour the liquid and vegetable mixture over it. Cover and refrigerate three to four days, turning the meat occasionally.

7. When ready to cook, preheat the oven to 325 degrees.

8. Remove the meat from the marinade. Strain the marinade, reserving both the vegetables and the liquid.

9. Sprinkle the meat with salt and pepper. Heat the oil in a heavy casserole and brown the meat on all sides. Add approximately two cups of the reserved liquid and salt and pepper to taste. Cover and bake, basting frequently, about two hours. Add the vegetables and, if necessary, more liquid. Continue baking and basting about forty-five minutes longer, or until the meat is quite tender. Remove the cheesecloth bag.

10. Remove the meat and keep it warm. Put the liquid and vegetables through a sieve or food mill, then put in a saucepan and bring to a simmer. Blend the cornstarch with the water and stir it into the sauce. Simmer about five minutes, then add salt and pepper to taste. Stir in the cream and bring to a boil. Serve the sauce with the sliced meat, with dumplings on the side.

Note: Pickling spices vary from packager to packager. The hot red peppers may be long or shaped like small red balls. Some may not contain cardamom seeds, and these may have to be added. Use your judgment and individual taste.

Stuffed Pork Chops in Sour Cream

6 servings

5 tablespoons butter
¾ cup finely chopped mushrooms
3 tablespoons finely chopped shallots or onion
¾ cup soft fresh bread crumbs
1 egg, lightly beaten
   Salt and freshly ground black pepper
½ teaspoon dried thyme
6 double loin pork chops, with pockets
   Chicken Stock (page 115)
¼ cup Cognac
1 cup sour cream

1. Melt two tablespoons of the butter in a skillet. In it cook the mushrooms and shallots until the liquid is evaporated. Add the bread crumbs and continue to cook for five minutes, stirring occasionally.

2. Cool the mixture slightly. Add the egg, salt and pepper to taste, and the thyme. Stuff the pork chops with this mixture and fasten with small skewers or food picks.

3. Melt the remaining butter in a skillet and quickly cook the pork chops in it on both sides. When browned, season with salt and pepper and enough stock barely to cover the bottom of the skillet. Cover the skillet, lower the heat, and cook the chops for forty-five minutes, turning once during the cooking.

4. When the chops are tender, add the Cognac and ignite it. Remove the chops to a warm platter and add the sour cream to the skillet. Heat thoroughly, but do not boil or the cream will curdle. To serve, pour the sauce over the pork chops.

Baked Veal Stew

6 servings

5 pounds shoulder of veal, cut into 2-inch pieces
   All-purpose flour
   Salt and freshly ground black pepper
3 tablespoons butter
8 small spring onions, tops chopped and bottoms left whole
3 ribs celery, cut into 1-inch pieces and leaves chopped
½ pound fresh mushrooms, sliced
6 small carrots, scraped and cut into 1-inch pieces
3 cups Beef Stock (page 115)
¼ cup white wine
2 egg yolks

1. Preheat the oven to 350 degrees.

2. Sprinkle the veal with flour, salt, and pepper. Melt the butter in a deep casserole and add the veal and the onion tops. Sauté very slowly until delicately browned. Add the celery pieces and leaves, mushrooms, carrots, onion bottoms, stock, wine, and salt and pepper to taste. Simmer, covered, for two hours.

3. Remove the casserole from the oven. Mix the egg yolks with some of the slightly cooled cooking liquid, then stir the egg yolk mixture into the casserole. Serve in the casserole.

Stuffed Veal Steak with Onions

4 to 6 servings

12 small white onions
 2 slices of day-old bread
   Milk
¾ cup chicken livers
½ cup Chicken Stock (page 115)
½ pound fresh mushrooms
 2 egg yolks
 2 tablespoons finely chopped parsley
 2 tablespoons finely chopped shallots or green onion
½ teaspoon finely grated lemon rind
   Salt and freshly ground black pepper
   Cayenne pepper
¼ teaspoon ground thyme
¼ cup port or Madeira
 1 boneless veal steak (2 pounds), cut from the leg
   All-purpose flour
¼ cup butter
 2 cups sour cream
 1 bay leaf
 1 leek, trimmed and well rinsed
 1 rib celery
 2 sprigs parsley

1. Preheat the oven to 325 degrees.
2. Cook the onions in a small amount of boiling water until they are nearly tender. Drain and reserve.
3. Soak the bread in a small amount of milk and squeeze dry. Simmer the chicken livers in the stock until barely done.
4. Grind the bread, chicken livers, and mushrooms. Add the egg yolks, parsley, shallots, and lemon rind. Season with salt, pepper, and cayenne to taste and the thyme. Beat the mixture with a wooden spoon and stir in the wine. Cool.
5. Pound the steak with a mallet until thin. Spread out the steak and dredge with flour. Spoon the cooled stuffing over the center. Bring the ends of the meat over in envelope fashion and tie with a string at several places.
6. Melt the butter in an ovenproof casserole, add the veal roll, and brown on all sides. Pour the sour cream over the roll and add the parboiled onions. Tie the bay leaf, leek, celery, and parsley together in a cheesecloth bag and add to the casserole. Cover the casserole tightly. Bring the liquid in the casserole to a boil over medium heat, then immediately put the casserole in the oven.
7. After thirty minutes, turn the veal roll once. Replace the cover and continue to bake for thirty minutes longer. Remove the strings from the roll and place the roll on a serving platter. Arrange the onions around it. Bring the sauce to a boil, strain some of it over the meat, and serve the remainder, strained, in a sauceboat.

Spatzle

4 to 6 servings

3 eggs
3 cups sifted all-purpose flour
  Salt to taste
¼ teaspoon nutmeg or to taste
1 cup milk
3 tablespoons butter

1. Place the eggs in the bowl of an electric beater and beat until frothy. Gradually beat in the flour and add the salt and nutmeg. Gradually beat in the milk and beat until thoroughly blended, about five minutes.
2. Place a spatzle maker over a basin of boiling salted water and scrape the mixture into it, turning the handle of the spatzle machine. Stir. The spatzle are done when they float on the top. Drain well. The spatzle may be made in advance.
3. To finish the spatzle, heat the butter in a skillet and toss the spatzle quickly in it. Spatzle are especially good with roast veal, and they may also be used in soups.

CZECHOSLOVAKIA 73

Dahomey

African Fish Stew

4 servings

2 porgies (1½ pounds each), cleaned but
with heads and tails left on
All-purpose flour
Salt and freshly ground black pepper
¼ cup palm oil or salad oil
2 cups finely chopped onions
2 tomatoes, peeled and chopped
1 cup Fish Stock (page 116) or water
Coarsely ground red pepper flakes

1. Cut the fish crosswise, chopping it
through the backbone into two-inch lengths.
2. Dredge the fish pieces with flour seasoned with salt and pepper.
3. Heat the oil in a skillet and cook the
fish pieces in it until golden on all sides. Remove the fish from the skillet and add the
onions and tomatoes. Cook, stirring, for
about ten minutes, then add the stock and
simmer for ten minutes. Return the fried fish
to the skillet, season with salt and red pepper
to taste, and continue to cook for about
twenty-five minutes.

Shrimp Dahomienne

4 to 6 servings

1 cup finely chopped onion
½ cup peanut oil
1 cup raw shrimp, cut into ½-inch cubes
1 clove garlic, finely minced
¾ cup ham, cut into ½-inch cubes
Salt and freshly ground pepper to taste
1 bay leaf
1 cup Fresh Tomato Sauce (page 279), or
canned tomato sauce
1 hot red pepper, seeded and chopped (optional but recommended), or Tabasco to
taste

1. Cook the onion in the peanut oil until
it just starts to brown. Add the shrimp and
cook, stirring constantly, about five minutes.
Add the garlic and ham and cook five minutes longer, stirring.
2. Add the remaining ingredients and
cook about fifteen minutes longer, stirring
frequently. Serve in a ring of Pureed Peas
(page 75), made either by spooning the peas
into a ring and filling it with the shrimp or
by putting the peas into a ring mold.

Rice Bujambura

6 to 8 servings

5 cups Chicken Stock
2 cups uncooked converted rice
1 tablespoon salt
¼ teaspoon freshly ground black pepper
4 bay leaves
¼ cup chopped pimento-stuffed olives

1. Bring the chicken stock to a boil in a three-quart saucepan and add the rice, salt, pepper, and bay leaves. Cover and cook over low heat until the stock is absorbed and the rice is fluffy and stands in separate grains.
2. Before serving, remove the bay leaves and add the olives.

Pureed Peas

4 to 6 servings

1½ cups dried black-eyed peas
Salt and freshly ground pepper to taste
¼ cup butter

1. Place the black-eyed peas in a mixing bowl and add cold water to a depth of one inch. Let stand overnight.
2. Drain the peas and pick them over to remove the outer skin, which should slip off easily. When peeled, the peas should be stark white.
3. Place the peeled peas in a kettle and add water to cover. Add salt and pepper and simmer until the peas are tender and most of the water is absorbed, twenty minutes or longer. If any liquid remains, drain it off.
4. Put the peas through a food mill or sieve. Heat thoroughly over low heat, while beating in the butter with a wooden spoon.

Peas and Shrimp

4 to 6 servings

1½ cups black-eyed peas
Salt and freshly ground pepper to taste
¾ cup palm oil or salad oil
½ cup finely minced onion
2 cloves garlic, coarsely chopped
¾ cup raw shrimp, cut into ½-inch cubes
1 cup ham, cut into ½-inch cubes
¼ cup Fresh Tomato Sauce (page 279), or canned tomato sauce
2 tablespoons finely chopped hot red pepper, or to taste (optional)
2½ tablespoons shrimp powder

1. Place the peas in a mixing bowl and add cold water to reach one inch over the top of the peas. Let stand overnight.
2. Drain the peas and add more cold water to cover. Add salt and pepper and simmer until the peas are tender, forty-five minutes to an hour. They should be moist but not too liquid.
3. While the peas cook, heat the oil in a skillet and add the onion and garlic. Cook briefly, stirring, until the onion is translucent.
4. Add the shrimp and cook, stirring, ten minutes. Add the ham and tomato sauce and cook, stirring, about ten more minutes. Stir in the remaining ingredients.
5. Add the sauce to the peas. If the dish seems too dry, add enough boiling water to bring it to the desired consistency.

Denmark

Danish Fish Pudding

4 to 6 servings

3 tablespoons fine bread crumbs
2 eggs
  Salt and freshly ground white pepper
¼ teaspoon nutmeg
¼ cup milk, approximately
1 pound fresh haddock, salmon, or pike fillets, picked over to remove bits of bone and skin
¾ cup heavy cream
  All-purpose flour, if necessary
½ cup melted butter
  Juice of 1 lemon, or to taste

1. Preheat the oven to 300 degrees. Butter a one-quart ring mold and sprinkle with the bread crumbs, shaking out the excess.

2. Beat the eggs with salt and pepper to taste, nutmeg, and one-quarter cup milk.

3. Chop the fish and spoon it into the container of an electric blender. Blend while adding the egg mixture. Scrape the puree into a mixing bowl. Add the cream slowly, while beating rapidly with a wooden spoon.

4. The mixture should be smooth but not liquid. If in doubt, test it by dropping a teaspoonful of the mousse into boiling water. Let cook briefly. If it seems too liquid, blend a little flour into the mousse; if too firm, add a little milk. Pour this mixture into the prepared ring mold.

5. Cover the mold with aluminum foil and set in a larger pan. Pour simmering water around the mold to a depth of one inch and bake one to one and one-half hours, or until a knife inserted in the mousse comes out clean. Add more water to the pan if the original water evaporates.

6. Serve the pudding with hot melted butter blended with lemon juice. Serve hot asparagus separately.

Note: If a steamer is available, the mold may be steamed instead of baked. Fish pudding is often served with Hollandaise sauce and fish or lobster as garnish.

Danish Colors Jellied Soup

4 to 6 servings

1 envelope unflavored gelatin
¼ cup dry vermouth
½ cup boiling water
2 cans (12½ ounces each) jellied madrilène soup
½ pint sour cream
½ tablespoon freshly grated horseradish, or to taste

1. Soften the gelatin in vermouth and add the boiling water. Stir to dissolve, then pour into the soup. Chill eight hours. Spoon into chilled cups.

2. Combine the sour cream with horseradish and push through a pastry tube to garnish the soup.

Scandinavia's contribution to gastronomy is enormous—roast reindeer; liver patés; Jansson's temptation, that hearty combination of anchovies and potatoes in cream; open-faced, butter-smeared sandwiches. Possibly its most delectable gift is an incredible variety of ways to prepare herring. The most impressive herring table in this country is that of Manhattan's Copenhagen Restaurant. It offers herring in mustard sauce, herring with dill, herring in sour cream, curried herring, herring salad, and a host of other herring triumphs. Several of the Copenhagen's herring secrets are disclosed herewith. Most of the recipes start with a basic preparation of marinated herring and go on from there. And the beverage to go with herring—aquavit or beer, of course. Danish, of course.

Marinated Herring

56 or more servings

24 herring fillets in brine
 2 whole herring in brine
 2 cups imported Swedish vinegar or cider vinegar
 2 cups water
 1 cup superfine granulated sugar
½ teaspoon ground allspice
 1 teaspoon white pepper
 8 bay leaves
 1 cup chopped Bermuda onion

1. Place the herring fillets and the whole herring in a large enamel or stainless steel container. Add cold water to cover. Change the water occasionally, always using freshly drawn cold water. You may prepare smaller quantities of herring and reduce the marinating liquid accordingly. Soak the herring overnight.

2. Drain the herring fillets. Cut each fillet crosswise into one-inch pieces. Place the pieces in a large stainless steel, enamel, or glazed earthenware mixing bowl.

3. Prepare the whole herring similarly. Cut each herring crosswise into one-inch pieces and place in a mixing bowl as described in step 2 above.

4. To prepare the marinade, combine the vinegar, water, sugar, allspice, white pepper, bay leaves, and onion and bring to a boil. Simmer one minute, then remove from the heat and let stand until cool.

5. Pour most of the cooled marinade over the pieces of herring fillets and pour the remainder over the whole herring pieces. Let the herring marinate in a cool place for six hours or longer. When ready to prepare the recipes that follow, drain the herring but save the marinade. Press the herring gently between the hands. Divide the herring into seven batches.

Note: Leftover herring will keep for several weeks in the refrigerator.

Herring in Curry Sauce

8 or more servings

    5 shallots, coarsely chopped
    2 green apples, unpeeled, cut into eighths
    3 pieces dried ginger
    4 bay leaves
    3 tablespoons Curry Powder (page 33)
    3 tablespoons chopped Major Grey chutney in syrup
    ⅓ cup imported Swedish vinegar or cider vinegar
    1⅓ cups water
    ⅓ cup marinated herring liquid (from recipe on page 77)
       Salt to taste
    ½ cup chopped Bermuda onion
    4 marinated herring fillets (page 77), cut into 1-inch pieces
       Onion rings
       Parsley sprigs

1. In a stainless steel or enamel saucepan, combine the shallots, apples, ginger, bay leaves, curry, chutney in syrup, vinegar, and water. Bring to a boil and simmer, stirring frequently and turning the apple pieces. Cook ten minutes. Let stand until thoroughly cool.

2. Place a sieve over a mixing bowl and pour the cooled mixture into the sieve. Press the liquid and soft ingredients through the sieve, using a wooden spoon. Discard the solids.

3. Add the marinated herring liquid, salt, and onion to the curry sauce and stir in the herring. Refrigerate until ready to use, then pour the herring and sauce into a serving dish and garnish with onion rings and parsley sprigs.

Herring in Dill

8 or more servings

    4 marinated herring fillets (page 77), cut into 1-inch pieces
    ¾ cup chopped Bermuda onion
    ⅔ cup marinated herring liquid (from recipe on page 77), approximately
    ⅔ cup beet juice from Pickled Beets (page 83)
       Onion rings
    ⅓ cup finely chopped fresh dill

1. Arrange the fillet pieces neatly in two rows in an oblong serving dish. Spoon the chopped onion between the rows. Combine the reserved marinade and the beet juice and pour over.

2. Garnish with onion rings and sprinkle with dill.

Herring in Mustard Sauce

8 or more servings

    ½ cup Mayonnaise (page 265)
    ⅓ cup sour cream
    ¼ cup commercially prepared mustard
    3½ tablespoons Danish Mustard (page 83)
    ⅓ cup finely chopped dill, preferably fresh
    4 marinated herring fillets (page 77), cut into 1-inch pieces
       Fresh dill sprigs

1. Combine the mayonnaise, sour cream, the two mustards, and chopped dill in a mixing bowl. Stir in the herring pieces. Chill.

2. Spoon the herring and sauce into a serving dish and garnish with dill sprigs.

Herring in Sour Cream

8 or more servings

2 cups sour cream
1 medium Bermuda onion, quartered and thinly sliced
¼ cup chopped green onion (green part only)
Coarsely ground pepper
Salt, if desired (Remember that the herring will add salt)
4 marinated herring fillets (page 77), cut into 1-inch pieces
Onion rings
Chopped chives

1. Combine the sour cream, sliced onion, green onion, pepper, and salt and blend. Stir in the herring. Chill.
2. Pour the herring into a serving dish and garnish with onion rings and chopped chives.

Herring in Tomato Sauce

8 or more servings

1 cup catsup
1½ tablespoons Danish Mustard (page 83)
6 tablespoons light brown sugar
⅓ cup imported Swedish vinegar or cider vinegar
Tabasco to taste
⅓ teaspoon coarsely ground black pepper
⅔ cup chopped white onion
4 marinated herring fillets (page 77), cut into 1-inch pieces
Onion rings

1. Combine the catsup and mustard and stir to blend.
2. Combine the brown sugar, vinegar, Tabasco, and pepper and stir until the sugar dissolves. Stir this into the catsup mixture. Blend the sauce with the onion and herring, then pour into a serving dish and garnish with onion rings.

Herring Salad

12 to 18 servings

4 marinated herring fillets (page 77), cut into 1-inch pieces
½ recipe Pickled Beets (page 83)
1 pound cold, cooked potatoes, peeled
1 raw apple, peeled, quartered, and cored
½ cup canned, sliced pie apples
1 cup Pickled Cucumbers (page 83) or canned senfgurken (German cucumber)
3 tablespoons Major Grey chutney
Salt and freshly ground pepper to taste
2 tablespoons Danish Mustard (page 83)
1½ cups sour cream
Dash of red food coloring
2 hard-cooked eggs, chopped

1. Put the herring, beets, potatoes, raw apple, sliced pie apples, cucumbers, and chutney through the food grinder, using the fine blade.
2. Drain the mixture briefly in a large sieve and return to a mixing bowl. Add the remaining ingredients except the eggs and stir. Chill. Pour into a serving dish and garnish with chopped hard-cooked egg.

Note: Leftover herring salad will keep for weeks in the refrigerator.

Chef's Herring

8 or more servings

10 thin slices (circles) fresh horseradish
15 thin raw carrot rings
 1 red onion, sliced into rings
¾ cup marinated herring liquid (from recipe on page 77)
   Freshly ground pepper
 2 whole marinated herring (page 77), cut into 1-inch pieces
   Chopped green onion

1. Combine the horseradish circles, carrot rings, sliced onion, marinade, pepper, and herring. Cover the mixture well and refrigerate for several days.
2. Pour the mixture into a serving dish and garnish with chopped green onion.

Matjes Herring in Horseradish Sauce

6 or more servings

10 tablespoons sour cream
 3 to 4 tablespoons horseradish bottled in vinegar
 1 tablespoon granulated sugar
   Salt (optional)
2½ tablespoons freshly grated horseradish
 3 large whole matjes herring fillets
 1 sprig parsley

1. Place the sour cream in a mixing bowl.
2. Place the commercial horseradish between sheets of paper toweling and press to remove most of the vinegar. Add this to the mixing bowl, then add the sugar, salt, if desired (remember that the herring will add salt as it stands), and freshly grated horseradish.

3. Do not rinse or soak the matjes herring fillets. Add them to the sour cream sauce and chill until ready to serve. Before serving, cut the herring crosswise into one-inch pieces. Rinse off and pat dry two pieces of herring fillet and garnish with the parsley sprig.

Matjes Herring in Sherry

6 or more servings

1 cup medium-dry sherry
1 medium red onion, cut lengthwise into sixteenths
2 shallots, quartered
2 whole bay leaves
2 tablespoons granulated sugar
3 matjes herring fillets
  Bay leaf for garnish
  Onion ring for garnish

1. Combine the sherry, onion, shallots, bay leaves, and sugar in a saucepan. Bring to a boil and remove from the heat. Cool.
2. Rinse the herring fillets under cold running water and drain. Pat dry on absorbent paper toweling. Cut the herring crosswise into halves before mixing with the sauce. Serve garnished with a bay leaf and a small onion ring.

Roast Pig with Danish Fruit Stuffing

About 20 servings

1 suckling pig (15 pounds), prepared for the oven
1½ cups butter, at room temperature
2 cups finely chopped onion
1 pound pork liver, cubed
1 pound pork, cubed
½ pound veal, cubed
4 eggs, lightly beaten
3 cups heavy cream
1 cup Cognac
½ cup all-purpose flour
1 teaspoon chopped fresh thyme
¼ cup finely chopped parsley
½ teaspoon rubbed sage
   Salt and freshly ground black pepper
1 1-pound, 9-ounce can pie apples, drained
2 cups canned whole prunes, drained
1 cup walnut meats
½ cup raisins
1 large pimento-stuffed olive
1 red apple
   Whole cranberries

1. Wash the pig well inside and outside and dry with paper towels.

2. Heat one-half cup of the butter in a large skillet and add the onions. Cook, stirring, until wilted. Add the liver, pork, and veal and cook, stirring occasionally, until the meats are very lightly browned. Put this mixture through a food grinder and stir in the eggs, two cups of the cream, the Cognac, flour, thyme, parsley, sage, and salt and pepper to taste. Let cool.

3. Stir in the apple slices, prunes, walnuts, and raisins.

4. Preheat the oven to 325 degrees.

5. Stuff the pig with the filling and sew up with string. Place a wooden block in the mouth to hold it open during cooking. Cover the ears and tail with foil to prevent scorching, and place the pig in a kneeling position on a rack in a shallow pan.

6. Melt the remaining butter and brush the pig with it. Roast the pig six to eight hours (about thirty to thirty-five minutes a pound), or until the internal temperature of the thickest lean part registers 185 degrees. Baste frequently with butter and cover with a tent of aluminum foil if the pig starts to brown too rapidly. During the last hour of cooking, pour the remaining heavy cream over the pig and continue basting until done.

7. When fully cooked, remove to a board or warm platter. Place a slice of olive in the eye sockets, remove the wooden block and replace with the apple, and hang a cranberry necklace around the pig's neck.

Short Ribs of Beef with Caraway

4 servings

2 tablespoons butter
1 tablespoon salad oil
3 pounds lean short ribs of beef
  Salt and freshly ground black pepper
1 cup finely chopped onion
1 teaspoon caraway seeds
2 sprigs fresh thyme or 1 teaspoon dried thyme
1 bay leaf
1½ cups Beef Stock (page 115) or canned beef broth

1. Melt the butter and salad oil in a Dutch oven and cook the short ribs of beef on all sides until well browned. Sprinkle with salt and pepper and cover. Cook over low heat for one hour.

2. Pour off the fat from Dutch oven and add the onion. Cook, stirring, until the onion is wilted, then add the caraway, thyme, bay leaf, and stock. Cover and simmer one to two hours longer, or until the meat is fork tender.

Danish Stuffed Cabbage

6 to 8 servings

1 large, firm green cabbage
1 pound boneless veal
½ pound boneless pork
2½ cups soft fresh bread crumbs, without crusts
1 cup milk
2 eggs
1 teaspoon salt
¼ teaspoon freshly ground black pepper
½ teaspoon ground sage
⅓ cup butter

1. Remove the loose outer leaves of the cabbage. Cut a deep slice from the stem end (save this slice for a lid) and hollow out the head, leaving a wall about the thickness of five leaves.

2. Grind the veal and pork together twice, using the finest blade of the grinder. Add half of the crumbs to the milk and soak until soft. Add the eggs, salt, pepper, and sage to the soaked crumbs. Mix well with the ground meats and turn the stuffing into the cabbage shell. Leave enough room for the meat to expand.

3. Place the reserved cabbage slice over the meat and tie in place. Stand the cabbage in a saucepan and surround with boiling water about halfway up the head. Cover and simmer for about two hours.

4. Remove the cabbage lid. Brown the remaining bread crumbs in the butter and pour crumbs and butter over the top of the cabbage. Cut the cabbage with its stuffing into wedges. Serve with additional melted butter, if desired.

Cabbage in Caraway Cream

4 servings

2 tablespoons butter
1 small head of firm cabbage, coarsely shredded
1 teaspoon salt
1 clove garlic, minced
1 teaspoon caraway seeds
1 teaspoon granulated sugar
1½ tablespoons vinegar
½ cup sour cream

1. Heat the butter in a skillet. Add the cabbage, salt, and garlic and stir well. Cover tightly and steam ten minutes.

2. Add the caraway seeds, sugar, and vinegar and mix well. Stir in the sour cream and serve immediately.

Danish Cucumber Salad

4 to 6 servings

2 cucumbers, peeled and sliced thin
5 green onions, trimmed and chopped
2 tablespoons vinegar
¼ cup sour cream
1 teaspoon granulated sugar (optional)
   Salt and freshly ground black pepper to
   taste

1. Combine the cucumbers and green onions in a mixing bowl.
2. Blend the remaining ingredients, pour over the vegetables, and toss lightly. Chill before serving.

Pickled Cucumbers

2 pints

3 large cucumbers
   Salt
4 sprigs dried dill or 1 tablespoon dill seeds
¾ cup water
¾ cup white vinegar
2 pieces dried ginger
¼ cup superfine granulated sugar

1. Peel the cucumbers and slice each one into eighths. Scrape away and discard the seeds. Cut the cucumber strips in half and place in a bowl.
2. Sprinkle the strips liberally with salt and let stand several hours to extract much of the moisture. Drain, then wrap in cheesecloth and squeeze gently. Stuff the strips into sterilized pint jars with pieces of dill sprigs or dill seeds.
3. Bring the remaining ingredients to a boil and stir until the sugar dissolves. Pour the hot liquid over the strips, then seal the jars and let stand until cool. Refrigerate.

Pickled Beets

About 2 pounds

2 pounds beets
¾ cup cider vinegar
½ teaspoon salt
2 tablespoons granulated sugar
½ teaspoon pickling spices

1. Cook the beets in water to cover until tender. Drain, reserving one cup of the cooking water. Slip off the skins and slice.
2. Heat the vinegar and reserved cooking water to a boil. Mix the salt and sugar. Add to the vinegar and let boil again.
3. Place the sliced beets in a mixing bowl. Add the pickling spices and cover with the hot vinegar mixture. Cover and chill. Drain before using in Herring Salad (page 79), but reserve the beet liquid.

Danish Mustard

About 1 cup

½ cup dry mustard
7 tablespoons granulated sugar
¼ cup boiling water
3 tablespoons vegetable oil
2 teaspoons Worcestershire sauce
¼ teaspoon salt
½ teaspoon imported Swedish vinegar or
   cider vinegar

1. Combine the mustard and sugar in a bowl. Beat in the boiling water to make a paste.
2. Beat in the remaining ingredients. Let cool and refrigerate.

Red Fruit Pudding with Frozen Berries

4 to 6 servings

2 packages (10 ounces each) frozen raspberries, thawed
2 packages (10 ounces each) frozen strawberries, thawed
⅓ cup cornstarch
½ cup water
1 tablespoon lemon juice
  Granulated sugar
⅓ cup blanched, slivered almonds

1. Combine the berries in a saucepan. Bring to a boil, stirring occasionally. Strain through a fine sieve or puree in an electric blender.

2. Combine the cornstarch and water to make a smooth paste. Bring the fruit back to the boiling point. Stir the cornstarch into the fruit, then bring to a boil and cook three minutes, stirring constantly.

3. Remove the mixture from the heat and blend in the lemon juice. Pour into a glass serving dish and sprinkle the top with a little sugar. Chill. Before serving, decorate with slivered almonds. Serve with cream.

Danish Loaf Cakes

2 loaves (6 to 8 servings each)

¾ cup blanched almonds, finely chopped, not ground
3 cups sifted all-purpose flour
1 tablespoon plus 1 teaspoon baking powder
½ teaspoon salt
2 cups heavy cream
2 teaspoons vanilla extract
½ teaspoon almond flavoring
2⅓ cups granulated sugar
4 eggs
¾ cup pignoli (pine nuts)
⅓ cup kirsch, warmed

1. Preheat the oven to 350 degrees.

2. Heavily butter two loaf pans, each measuring nine by five inches across the top. Coat the sides and bottom of each pan with the finely chopped almonds.

3. Sift together the flour, baking powder, and salt and set aside.

4. Whip the cream in the large bowl of an electric mixer until it holds a shape. Add the vanilla, almond flavoring, and, gradually, two cups of the sugar. Beat in the eggs one at a time, then, at the lowest speed, beat in the dry ingredients.

5. Pour about one-quarter of the batter into each pan. Sprinkle each with about two tablespoons of pine nuts and cover evenly with the remaining batter. Smooth the tops. Sprinkle with the remaining nuts.

6. Bake one hour, or until the cakes rebound to the touch when pressed gently in the center. Remove from the oven and brush on the glaze made by mixing the kirsch and one-third cup sugar together. Let the cakes cool in the pans.

Cheese-Filled Danish Pastries

40 pastries

DOUGH:

1 cup milk, scalded
¼ cup granulated sugar
1 teaspoon salt
1¾ cups butter
½ cup warm water (105 to 115 degrees)
2 packages active dry yeast
3 eggs, beaten
2 teaspoons grated orange rind
¼ teaspoon vanilla extract
¼ teaspoon lemon extract
4 to 6 cups sifted all-purpose flour

FILLING:

1 pound cream cheese
6 tablespoons granulated sugar
2 tablespoons orange juice
2 teaspoons grated orange rind

GLAZE:

2 egg yolks
¼ cup water
Chopped nuts (optional)

1. Combine the milk, sugar, salt, and one-quarter cup of the butter and cool to lukewarm. Chill the remaining butter.

2. Place the warm water in a large, warm bowl and sprinkle with the yeast. Stir to dissolve.

3. Stir in the cooled milk mixture, the eggs, orange rind, extracts, and enough flour to make a soft dough. Turn onto a board and knead for about ten minutes, until smooth and elastic. Place in a greased bowl and grease the top of the dough. Cover and let rise in a warm place, free from draft, for about one hour, until doubled in bulk.

4. Roll out the chilled butter between two pieces of floured waxed paper into two rectangles (12 x 9 inches). Flour lightly; cover with wax paper and chill again.

5. Punch the dough down. Roll out to a rectangle (18 x 24 inches) on a cloth or lightly floured board. Mark off the dough into thirds. Place one rectangle of chilled butter over the middle third and fold one end of the dough over it. Place the remaining butter on top and fold the second end of dough over it. Press the edges together.

6. Turn the dough so that one short end is nearest you. Roll the dough into a rectangle (18 x 24 inches). Turn both ends in to meet at the middle, then fold in half to make four layers. Place on a cookie sheet and cover with aluminum foil. Chill for thirty minutes.

7. Repeat the rolling and folding three times, chilling dough for twenty minutes between foldings. After the final folding, chill for two hours.

8. While the dough is chilling, beat together the cream cheese, sugar, orange juice, and rind to make the filling. Reserve.

9. Halve the chilled dough. Take one half and roll it out to a rectangle (⅛ x 18 x 24 inches). Divide into twenty three-inch squares. Place one teaspoon of the filling in each square. Bring two diagonal corners of the square together, overlap lightly and pinch to secure. Place on a greased cookie sheet. Cover and chill for twenty minutes. Repeat with the remaining dough.

10. Preheat the oven to 450 degrees.

11. Combine the egg yolks with water to make the glaze. Brush over the pastries. Sprinkle with nuts, if desired.

12. Bake for eight minutes. Reduce the oven heat to 375 degrees and bake for about ten minutes longer, until golden brown.

Danish Cones with Whipped Cream

About 15 cones

¼ cup butter
½ cup granulated sugar
2 eggs
¾ cup sifted all-purpose flour
1 cup heavy cream
　Strawberry jam

1. Preheat the oven to 300 degrees.
2. Melt the butter and stir in the sugar. Beat in the eggs, one at a time, and then the flour. Drop spoonfuls of the batter about four inches apart onto a well-buttered baking sheet. Smooth the batter into ovals. Bake about six minutes.
3. Remove the cookies with a spatula and quickly roll into cone shapes while the cookies are still hot and flexible. (Gloves may be handy in doing this.) Let the cones cool. Rebutter the baking sheet before spooning out more batter.
4. At serving time, whip the cream and fill the cones with it. Add a little strawberry jam in the center of the cream.

England

Broiled Kippered Herring

6 servings

Although there are those who would deny it, there is much to be said for the first meal of the day—and a plague on coffee and Danish! A real breakfast can have style and offer solace to family and guests on Sundays and holidays. Perhaps the best breakfast of all (or call it "brunch" and serve it at one o'clock) would include, along with any number of other dishes with an English flavor, kippered herring. And, as long as we are being British, serve lashings of tea. Or coffee. Or imported brut champagne, if that's your kind of budget.

3 cans kippered herring or 2 pair wrapped
    Canadian kippered herring
½ cup butter
    Lemon juice
    Lemon wedges
    Parsley

1. Preheat the broiler.
2. If canned kippers are used, drain them. Line one or two large baking sheets with foil. Arrange the kippers in one layer on the foil and dot generously with butter. Broil about four inches from the heat until the butter is golden and the kippers are thoroughly hot.
3. Carefully transfer the kippers to a hot serving dish and sprinkle liberally with lemon juice. Garnish with lemon wedges and parsley.

Curried Kidneys, English Style

4 servings

2 veal kidneys
¼ cup butter
2 tablespoons freshly chopped shallots or
    green onion
2 teaspoons Curry Powder (page 33)
    All-purpose flour
1 cup strong Chicken Stock (page 115)
    Salt and freshly ground pepper to taste
1 ounce vodka, gin, or Cognac

1. Carefully trim the kidneys to remove the membranes and tubes. Cut into small, bite-sized pieces.
2. Heat the butter in a skillet or chafing dish and add the shallots. Cook until soft, then add the curry powder and cook over low heat, stirring, about five minutes.
3. Dredge the kidney pieces lightly in flour and add to the skillet. Cook, stirring, just until they lose color. Add the chicken stock, salt and pepper to taste, and vodka and simmer until tender, about ten minutes. Serve, if desired, with crisp bacon.

Steak and Kidney Pie I

8 or more servings

2½ pounds fillet of beef or boneless top sirloin
 Salt and freshly ground black pepper
 Nutmeg
4 veal kidneys, trimmed of fat
¼ cup butter
½ pound mushrooms, washed and thinly sliced
¼ cup chopped shallots
1 tablespoon finely minced garlic
1 tablespoon dried tarragon
1 cup drained canned tomatoes
1 cup dry white wine
1½ cups Brown Sauce (page 268) or 1 10¾-ounce can beef gravy
1 teaspoon finely chopped thyme
5 hard-cooked eggs
 Flaky or rich pastry for 1 crust
1 egg, beaten
1 tablespoon water

1. Cut the fillet into twelve equal slices like filet mignon, or cut the top sirloin into one-inch cubes. Sprinkle lightly with salt, pepper, and nutmeg.

2. Cut the kidneys into approximately twenty-four bite-sized pieces. Sprinkle lightly with salt and pepper.

3. Heat half the butter in a large skillet and cook the meat on both sides until browned. Remove the meat and reserve it in a warm place.

4. Add the kidneys to the skillet in which meat was cooked and brown on all sides. Remove the kidneys to a separate dish to drain.

5. Add the mushrooms and remaining butter to the skillet and cook until wilted. When the mushrooms are limp, add the shallots, garlic, tarragon, tomatoes, and wine. Stir in the brown sauce and thyme. Bring to a boil, stirring. Add the steak and kidneys and cover. Simmer ten minutes, or until the meat is tender.

6. Pour into a two-and-one-half- to three-quart casserole or deep pie dish, preferably one with a rim around the edge. Let cool to lukewarm. The meat should protrude slightly above the gravy. If there is too much gravy, spoon out and reserve.

7. Preheat the oven to 450 degrees.

8. Cut the hard-cooked eggs in quarters and arrange lengthwise over the meat.

9. A metal or glass funnel placed in the middle of the dish will help to hold the pastry up and provide an escape for the steam. Cover the pie with the pastry, allowing a double thickness around the rim. Do not stretch the pastry. Decorate around the funnel opening (or a slash made) with pastry leaves cut from the trimmings. Brush with beaten egg and water.

10. Bake fifteen minutes, or until the pastry is set and lightly browned. Reduce the oven heat to 350 degrees and bake about thirty minutes longer, or until the pastry is cooked. Serve with the reserved gravy.

Steak and Kidney Pie II

5 or 6 servings

2 pounds lean beef chuck, cut into 1-inch cubes
  All-purpose flour
  Salt and freshly ground black pepper
3 tablespoons bacon fat or butter
2 cups boiling Beef Stock (page 115)
  Cayenne pepper
2 tablespoons chopped fresh basil or 1 teaspoon dried basil
1 veal kidney or 2 lamb kidneys
2 tablespoons butter
  Rich unbaked pastry for 1 crust

1. Dredge the beef cubes with flour seasoned with salt and pepper. Brown well in the bacon fat, a few pieces at a time, and transfer the pieces to a large saucepan. Add the stock, cayenne pepper to taste, and the basil. Cover and bring to a boil. Simmer slowly for one hour or longer, until the meat is tender. Cool, then refrigerate.

2. When the meat is cold, skim off and discard the congealed fat from the surface. Bring the meat and sauce to a boil.

3. Preheat the oven to 425 degrees.

4. Trim the kidney well, removing the hard center core and white fibers. Slice the kidney and brown it quickly in the butter. Add to the beef. Pour the meat and liquid into a deep casserole or deep pie dish.

5. Roll out the pastry into a circle and prick it with a fork. Fit the pastry over the casserole and flute the edges. Bake for thirty to forty minutes, or until the pastry is golden brown. Serve immediately.

Note: This dish may be flavored with Worcestershire sauce or Madeira, if desired. A touch of Madeira may be poured onto each hot portion as it is served.

English Lamb Chops

6 servings

To the average cook, a lamb chop is only a lamb chop, a trifle to be grilled or broiled or browned in a skillet. Actually, this most interesting of chops is excellent when breaded and cooked—as the French say—à l'anglaise. Such a recipe is given here.

12 rib lamb chops, prepared French style (the lower part of the rib trimmed of meat and scraped)
¾ cup all-purpose flour
2 eggs, lightly beaten
  Salt and freshly ground pepper to taste
1 teaspoon oil
1 teaspoon water
2 cups fresh bread crumbs
½ cup butter, approximately

1. All traces of fat and skin should be pared away from the chops. Pound them or have them pounded with a mallet or the bottom of a skillet. Dredge them in the flour.

2. Blend the eggs, salt, pepper, oil, and water in a pie plate. Dip the floured chops in this, then in the bread crumbs to coat well. Pat lightly with hand or mallet to help the crumbs adhere.

3. Heat half the butter in a skillet and brown a few of the chops at a time on both sides. Heat the remaining butter and brown the remaining chops. (This may also be done at the same time, in two skillets.)

Melton Mowbray Pie

8 servings

Traditionally, every farmhouse, inn, and hunting lodge in the English shires produced its own special pork pie. Below is one from Melton Mowbray; please note that one of the special touches here is the use of anchovy paste, which, amazingly, serves to keep the pork filling pink.

MEAT FILLING:
- 1 pork shoulder (4 pounds) but with bones reserved
- 1 veal knuckle, cracked
- 2 quarts cold water, approximately
- 1 onion, peeled and quartered
- 2 carrots, scraped and cut in half
- 6 sprigs parsley
- 1 bay leaf
- 1 teaspoon peppercorns
- 3 teaspoons salt
- ½ teaspoon white pepper
- ¼ to ½ teaspoon sage
- 2 teaspoons anchovy paste
- 1 ¼-ounce envelope unflavored gelatin

HOT-WATER PASTRY:
- 4 cups sifted all-purpose flour
- ¾ teaspoon salt
- ½ cup plus 2 tablespoons water
- ½ pound lard

GLAZE:
- 1 egg, lightly beaten
- 1 tablespoon milk

1. Place the bones from pork shoulder and the veal knuckle in a large kettle. Pour in the two quarts cold water, adding additional water, if necessary, to cover the bones. Bring to a boil and continue to boil for ten minutes, skimming if necessary. Add the onion, carrots, parsley, bay leaf, peppercorns, and two teaspoons of the salt. Simmer for two hours.

2. Cut the pork into inch cubes. Remove and discard the excess fat and skin. Toss the meat in a bowl with the remaining teaspoon salt, the white pepper, and sage, then set aside.

3. Strain the stock and measure off two and one-half cups. When cool, pour one cup of stock into the meat in the bowl, add the anchovy paste, and toss the meat mixture lightly. Reserve the other one and one-half cups of stock.

4. To prepare the hot-water pastry, measure the flour into a mixing bowl and stir in the salt. In a small saucepan, boil water with the lard, then immediately pour the hot liquid into the flour. Stir quickly together, gather into a ball, and knead for two or three minutes on a lightly floured board until smooth. Cover the pastry with a damp cloth and let rest for thirty minutes before rolling out.

5. Preheat the oven to 350 degrees. Butter and flour a leaf pan (9 x 5 x 3).

6. Roll out two-thirds of the pastry into a rectangle approximately eighteen inches long by ten inches wide and one-quarter inch thick. Gently fit the pastry into the loaf pan, covering the entire interior. Leave a small edge of pastry slightly overhanging the sides of the pan.

7. Fill the pastry-lined pan with the pork mixture. Roll out the top crust, cover the pie, and trim away any excess pastry. Crimp the two layers of pastry securely together, raising the fluted edges so that they rise straight above the pan. Cut a half-inch circle out of the center and make a pastry "rose," if desired, by arranging pastry petals around

the circle. Then replace the cut-out circle or rose of dough, letting it rest lightly over the hole.

8. Bake the pie for two to two and one-half hours, covering the pastry with foil if it shows sign of browning too deeply. Half an hour before the pie is thoroughly baked, brush the crust with a glaze made from combining the egg and milk.

9. Remove the pie from the oven and cool for fifteen minutes. In a small saucepan combine the remaining one and one-half cups stock with the gelatin and bring to a boil. Remove cut-out circle or rose from the top crust, insert a funnel into the opening, and pour in as much hot stock as the pie will hold. Tilt the pan from side to side several times to help distribute the liquid throughout.

10. Cool the pie to room temperature, then refrigerate for at least six hours, until the aspic is quite firm.

11. Unmold by running the blade of a knife around the inside of the loaf pan, then dipping the bottom of the pan into hot water. Wipe the pan dry and gently turn the pie out onto a serving plate. To serve, cut into slices about one-quarter to one-half inch thick.

Bread Sauce for Poultry

2 servings

1 small onion, studded with 2 cloves
1 cup milk
3 to 5 slices white bread, grated or cut into cubes
  Cream (optional)
  Salt (optional)
  Freshly ground black pepper
2 tablespoons butter

1. Put the onion in a saucepan and add the milk. Bring to a boil and simmer ten minutes.

2. Add the bread crumbs or cubes and cook, stirring, until soft and creamy. If the sauce is too thin, add more bread. If the sauce is too thick, add a little cream. The sauce should be medium thick and creamy.

3. Remove the onion and add salt, if desired. Add a touch of black pepper and simmer a little longer. When ready to serve, stir in the butter. Serve with roast poultry.

Hot Cross Buns

30 to 36 large buns

There are as many legends about hot cross buns as about any bread in Christendom. They are said to have originated in pagan England; they figure in nursery rhymes; and, even today, hot cross buns baked on Good Friday are supposed to have miraculous curative powers. The fact is that they are part and parcel of the Easter season and turn a late breakfast or brunch into a festive meal.

1 cup granulated sugar
½ cup plus 2 tablespoons melted butter
5 egg yolks
2¼ cups milk, scalded and cooled to lukewarm
1 envelope dry active yeast
¼ cup warm water
7 to 8 cups sifted all-purpose flour
1½ teaspoons salt
1 teaspoon nutmeg
¼ teaspoon powdered cloves
4 egg whites
1 cup currants
½ cup chopped candied fruits (optional)
1 cup confectioners' sugar
2 tablespoons lemon juice
2 tablespoons water

1. The day before the buns are to be baked, mix the sugar with the one-half cup melted butter in a large bowl. Add four of the egg yolks, well beaten, and the milk.

2. Soften the yeast in the warm water and add to the bowl. Sift half the flour with the salt, nutmeg, and cloves and beat into the batter.

3. Beat the egg whites until frothy but not stiff and incorporate into the batter. Add the currants and fruits, then add enough flour to make a soft dough.

4. Place the dough in an oiled bowl. Oil the top of the dough, cover with plastic wrap and a damp cloth, and let stand in a warm place two to three hours. Store in the refrigerator overnight.

5. Remove the bowl from the refrigerator and let stand at room temperature for thirty minutes to an hour. Knead the dough on a lightly floured board until smooth and elastic, about ten minutes. Shape into thirty to thirty-six balls.

6. Place the balls about one inch apart on a greased baking sheet. Brush with the remaining melted butter. Cover with a towel and let rise in a warm place until doubled, about one and one-half hours.

7. Preheat the oven to 375 degrees.

8. Brush the buns with the remaining egg yolk mixed with the water. Cut with scissors to form a cross, if desired. Bake twenty-five minutes, or until browned and done.

9. Cool and frost with the confectioners' sugar mixed with the lemon juice and water.

Almond Curd

10 servings

½ cup uncooked rice
4 ounces sweet almonds, blanched
1 ounce bitter almonds or 1 more ounce sweet almonds, blanched
8⅓ cups water
1½ cups granulated sugar
2 envelopes unflavored gelatin
1 teaspoon almond extract (1½ teaspoons if all sweet almonds are used)
Ice cubes
10 maraschino cherries

1. Soak the rice and all the almonds overnight in two cups of the water. Puree in a blender or pound in a mortar until pastelike. Strain in a flannel bag or four thicknesses of cheesecloth, squeezing out all possible almond milk. Discard the solids in the bag.

2. Bring four cups of the water, one-half cup of the sugar, and the almond milk to a boil. Meanwhile, soften the gelatin in one-third cup water. Add the softened gelatin to the almond milk mixture and stir until the sugar and gelatin have dissolved. Boil for ten minutes, then add the almond extract.

3. Pour the curd into a flat pan to make a layer about one-half inch deep. Chill until firm.

4. Make a thin sugar syrup by boiling the remaining cup sugar and two cups water until the sugar has dissolved. Chill the syrup.

5. To serve the dessert, cut the almond curd into small diamonds. Cover the bottom of a serving bowl with ice cubes and arrange the diamonds over the ice. Garnish with the maraschino cherries and pour the sugar syrup over all.

English Trifle

10 to 12 servings

1 Sponge Jelly Roll (page 285)
2 tablespoons Madeira
4 eggs, separated
¼ cup superfine granulated sugar
½ tablespoon unflavored gelatin
1¼ cups light cream
2 cups heavy cream
2 tablespoons light rum
1 tablespoon confectioners' sugar
1 teaspoon vanilla extract

1. Cut the jelly roll into half-inch thick slices. Use the slices to line the bottom and sides of a large crystal bowl, reserving a few slices for the top of the trifle. Sprinkle with the Madeira and refrigerate.

2. Place the egg yolks in the bowl of an electric mixer and add the sugar. Beat thoroughly and add the gelatin. Bring the light cream to a boil and add it to the yolk mixture, stirring constantly with a whisk. Use a rubber spatula to scrape the mixture into a large saucepan. Cook and stir the custard over low heat until it coats the back of a wooden spoon. Immediately remove the saucepan from the fire and place in a bowl with ice cubes to cool. Stir until cool.

3. Clean the mixing bowl thoroughly and dry it. Add the egg whites and beat them until they stand in soft peaks. Fold the whites into the cooled custard.

4. Beat half the heavy cream until stiff and fold into the custard, then fold in the rum. Spoon the custard into the chilled bowl lined with jelly roll slices. Place briefly in the freezer only until set; do not let the trifle freeze. Cover the top with the reserved slices of jelly roll.

5. Beat the remaining cream and sweeten it with the confectioners' sugar and vanilla extract. Using a pastry tube or spoon, garnish the top of the trifle with the sweetened cream.

Fiji

Kokoda

(The Fijian Version of Seviche)

4 or more servings

2 cups skinned and boned kingfish, mackerel, or salmon fillets, cut into bite-sized pieces
   Salt to taste
¾ cup lemon juice
½ carrot, scraped and grated
3 green onions, trimmed and chopped
½ cup Heavy Coconut Cream (see below)

1. Place the fish pieces in a mixing bowl and add a generous amount of salt. Add the lemon juice and cover. Refrigerate for one and one-half hours. Once in a while, press the fish pieces gently in the liquid with the back of a spoon. Turn the fish occasionally in the marinade.

2. Drain the fish well and add the carrot and onion, then add the coconut cream and blend gently. Refrigerate thirty minutes. Most of the liquid will be absorbed by the fish. Serve chilled, as an appetizer.

HEAVY COCONUT CREAM:

About ¼ cup

For each quarter cup of coconut cream desired, split one coconut in half and discard the coconut water. Remove the coconut meat and pare away the dark skin. Grate the coconut on a grater or blend the pieces in a blender. Do not add any liquid, but put the grated coconut in cheesecloth and squeeze as tightly as possible to extract as much liquid as possible. This is coconut cream.

Baked Cod in Cream Sauce

4 servings

2 cups boneless cod fillet, cut into 1-inch cubes
1½ cups Fiji Cream Sauce (page 95)
½ cup freshly grated Cheddar cheese

1. Preheat the oven to 350 degrees.

2. Arrange the cod pieces in one layer in a baking dish and pour the sauce over all. Sprinkle with the grated cheese and bake about thirty minutes, or until the cheese is melted and lightly browned.

Baked Shrimp in Cream Sauce

4 servings

2 cups raw shrimp, shelled, deveined, rinsed, and patted dry
1½ cups Fiji Cream Sauce (below)
⅓ cup fine bread crumbs

1. Preheat the oven to 350 degrees.
2. Place the shrimp in one layer in a small, flat baking dish and spoon the sauce over them. Sprinkle with the bread crumbs and bake thirty to forty-five minutes, or until browned on top.

Fiji Cream Sauce

About 1½ cups

1 tablespoon butter
3 tablespoons finely chopped onion
3 tablespoons finely chopped green pepper
1½ cups Coconut Milk Made in a Blender (page 34)
Salt to taste
1½ tablespoons cornstarch

1. Melt the butter in a saucepan and cook the onion and green pepper, stirring, until the onion is wilted. Add one and one-quarter cups of the coconut milk and bring to a boil.
2. Blend the remaining one-quarter cup coconut milk with the cornstarch and stir it into the simmering sauce. Simmer three minutes, stirring.

Palusami

(Fijian Stuffed Cabbage)

6 servings

1 head white cabbage
1 pound shrimp, cooked, shelled, and deveined
1 cup finely chopped onion
Salt and freshly ground pepper to taste
¾ cup Heavy Coconut Cream (page 94)

1. Preheat the oven to 350 degrees.
2. Core the cabbage, then separate the leaves. Rinse the leaves well and drain.
3. Cut out six rectangles (8 x 10 each) of heavy-duty aluminum foil and place them on a flat surface.
4. Arrange a large cabbage leaf, cup side up, on each rectangle.
5. Finely chop two or three of the remaining leaves to make about three cups loosely packed chopped cabbage. Place the cabbage in a mixing bowl.
6. Chop the shrimp and add them to the chopped cabbage. Add the chopped onion, salt, and pepper. Spoon equal parts of this mixture inside each of the cabbage leaves.
7. Spoon two tablespoons of heavy coconut cream over each portion of filling. Fold the leaves to enclose the filling, then seal each stuffed leaf in foil. Arrange the packages in a baking dish and bake one hour. Serve hot.

France

Clams au Beurre Blanc

4 servings

2 dozen clams
½ cup butter, at room temperature
2 tablespoons lemon juice
2 tablespoons finely chopped parsley
2 tablespoons finely chopped chives
⅓ cup dry white wine
1 tablespoon finely chopped shallots or green onion
½ clove garlic, finely chopped

1. Have the clams opened at the fish store, or open them by hand with a knife or patented clam opener. Reserve the clam liquor. Prepare the clams on the half shell by running a knife around the clams to loosen them. Arrange the clams close together on a jelly-roll pan or any other suitable pan with sides. Pour the reserved clam liquor over them and chill until ready to use.

2. Preheat the oven to 350 degrees.

3. Place the butter in a saucepan in a warm place near the stove and beat with a wooden spoon or wire whisk until the butter is soft but not melted. Add the lemon juice, parsley, and chives and beat until well blended. Set aside, but do not allow the butter to melt.

4. Combine the wine, shallots, and garlic in a saucepan. Bring the mixture to a boil and simmer for one minute. Gradually beat this mixture into the butter mixture. The mixture should then take on the consistency of a sauce.

5. Place the clams on the half shell in the oven. Heat thoroughly for five to ten minutes, but do not overcook or the clams will toughen. Arrange the clams in piping hot soup bowls, pour the sauce over them, and serve immediately, as an appetizer, with a crusty loaf of French or Italian bread and chilled dry white wine.

Ingredients for a seafood stew Méditerranée (Franc

Stuffed Clams Florentine

50 to 60 appetizers

3½ quarts cherrystone clams
 ½ cup water or dry white wine
 1 10-ounce package fresh spinach
12 tablespoons butter
 3 tablespoons finely chopped shallots
 1 clove garlic, finely minced
 ½ cup finely chopped heart of celery
 3 tablespoons dry white wine
 2 tablespoons finely chopped parsley
 1 tablespoon finely chopped tarragon
 1 tablespoon finely chopped chives
 1 cup fresh bread crumbs
 2 tablespoons Pernod, Ricard, or other anise-flavored liqueur (optional)
 1 egg yolk
    Salt and freshly ground black pepper
 ½ cup freshly grated Parmesan cheese
    Lemon wedges

1. Preheat the oven to 425 degrees.
2. Rinse the clams well under cold running water to remove all traces of sand. Place them in a four-quart kettle or saucepan and add the water or wine. Cover closely, bring to a boil, and cook until clams open, five minutes or longer. Let the clams cool.

3. While the clams cook, rinse the spinach with cold water, shake to remove excess moisture, and place in a saucepan. Do not add additional water. Cover and cook until the spinach is wilted, eight to ten minutes. Stir, cover again, and cook about two minutes longer. Drain in a colander and cool.
4. Melt one-quarter cup of the butter in a skillet and cook the shallots, garlic, and celery, stirring. Cook about five minutes. Add the three tablespoons wine and simmer until almost all the wine evaporates.
5. Squeeze the spinach carefully but tightly to remove all the excess moisture. Chop the spinach, then add to the skillet and stir.
6. Remove the clams from the shells and reserve fifty to sixty clam shells. Strain the clam juice through cheesecloth and reserve one-half cup. The remainder may be used for another purpose.
7. Using a butcher knife, chop the clams until they are very fine. This should yield about one and one-half cups chopped clams. Add the clams to the skillet and stir.
8. Add the remaining butter, the parsley, tarragon, chives, bread crumbs, reserved clam juice, and Pernod. Add the egg yolk and mix well with a wooden spoon, then season with salt and pepper to taste. Cook briefly in the skillet. Use the mixture to fill the reserved clam shells. Sprinkle with Parmesan cheese and place, on baking sheets, in the oven. Bake ten minutes, or until the clams are piping hot and golden brown. If not brown, the clams may be run briefly under the broiler. Serve hot, with lemon wedges.

rinated herring variations surround a bottle of chilled aquavit (Denmark)

Coquilles Saint-Jacques

6 or more servings

One of our most delicate shellfish is the ocean or bay scallop. And the most delicate preparation for the sweet-fleshed morsels is known as coquilles Saint-Jacques. *Too often, however, this turns out to be scallops in a mucilaginous cream sauce. Genuine* coquilles Saint-Jacques *are prepared with a little white wine in sauce thickened merely with butter, flour, and egg yolks. The recipe below is for the genuine article.*

1½ pounds bay or sea scallops
2 sprigs fresh thyme or ½ teaspoon dried thyme
1 bay leaf
1 sprig parsley
8 peppercorns
    Salt to taste
½ cup water
½ cup dry white wine
7 tablespoons butter
3 tablespoons all-purpose flour
2 egg yolks
1 teaspoon lemon juice
    Cayenne pepper
    Parmesan cheese

1. Preheat the oven to 400 degrees.
2. Combine the scallops, thyme, bay leaf, parsley, peppercorns, salt, water, and wine in a small saucepan and bring to a boil. Cover and simmer exactly two minutes. Remove the parsley, bay leaf, and thyme sprigs and drain, but reserve the cooking liquid. Let the scallops cool. If bay scallops are used, cut them in half and set aside. If sea scallops are used, cut them into thin slices and set aside.
3. Melt two tablespoons of butter and stir in the flour with a wire whisk. When blended, add the scallop liquid (about one and one-half cups), stirring vigorously.
4. Remove the sauce from the heat and beat vigorously with an electric beater. Add the remaining butter, a little at a time, very gradually. Beat in the egg yolks, lemon juice and cayenne; continue beating until cool.
5. Spoon a little of the mixture into twelve to sixteen small scallop shells or six to eight large scallop shells or ramekins. Top with equal parts of scallops. Cover with the remaining sauce and sprinkle with Parmesan.
6. Bake five to ten minutes, or until bubbling and golden brown. If necessary, glaze under the broiler. Serve as a first course.

Coquilles Saint-Jacques Provençale

4 servings

1 large tomato
3 tablespoons butter
2 shallots, finely chopped
1 or 2 cloves garlic, finely minced
3 tablespoons dry white wine
1 teaspoon finely chopped mixed herbs, such as dried thyme, rosemary, and orégano
    Salt and freshly ground pepper to taste
12 sea scallops or 24 bay scallops
¼ cup all-purpose flour
3 tablespoons olive or peanut oil
    Finely chopped parsley

1. Peel the tomato and cut it into small cubes.
2. Heat the butter in a skillet and add the tomato cubes, shallots, garlic, wine, and dried mixed herbs. Simmer five minutes. Add salt and pepper to taste.
3. Meanwhile, dredge the scallops in the flour seasoned with salt and pepper.
4. Heat the oil in another skillet and cook the scallops until golden brown all over, three to six minutes.
5. Spoon the scallops into scallop shells, if available, or into individual ramekins. Spoon the sauce over each serving and sprinkle each with chopped parsley. Serve as a first course.

Shrimp and Artichokes aux Câpres

30 servings

5 pounds raw, unpeeled shrimp
  Salt
18 peppercorns
1 rib celery, quartered
1 bay leaf
2 cloves garlic, peeled
5 packages (9 ounces each) frozen artichoke hearts
  Juice of 1 lemon
¼ cup capers
¼ cup freshly chopped basil leaves
¼ cup finely chopped onion
  Freshly ground black pepper
2½ cups Mayonnaise (page 265)
  Tabasco

1. Place the shrimp in a kettle and add water to cover. Add salt to taste, the peppercorns, celery, bay leaf, and garlic and bring to a boil. Simmer exactly five minutes and let cool without draining. When cool enough to handle, peel and devein the shrimp, using a paring knife.

2. Meanwhile, cook the artichoke hearts according to package directions. Drain in a colander and let cool.

3. Place the shrimp in a large mixing bowl and add the lemon juice, capers, basil, onion, pepper to taste, mayonnaise, and Tabasco to taste. Toss until well coated. Add the artichokes and toss gently. Serve as an appetizer.

Shrimp aux Câpres

4 to 6 servings

1½ pounds medium raw shrimp
  Water to cover
1 bay leaf
12 peppercorns
  Salt
1 sprig parsley
1 cup Mayonnaise (page 265)
  Juice of 1 lemon
1 onion, sliced into wafer-thin rings
3 tablespoons capers

1. Place the shrimp in a saucepan and add water to cover. Add the bay leaf, peppercorns, salt to taste, and the parsley and bring to a boil. Simmer one minute, then remove from the heat and drain.

2. Combine the shrimp with the remaining ingredients and let stand overnight or longer to develop the flavor. Serve as an appetizer, with buttered toast.

Shrimp Baratin

4 or more servings

¼ cup butter
 3 dozen medium raw shrimp or 18 raw extra-jumbo shrimp, shelled and deveined
   Salt
 2 tablespoons finely minced shallots
   Freshly ground black pepper
 1 teaspoon lemon juice
 3 tablespoons warm Cognac

1. Melt the butter in a chafing dish and, when hot, add the shrimp in one layer. Sprinkle with salt. Cook the shrimp until pink on one side, then turn to cook the other side, a total of about four minutes.

2. Sprinkle the shrimp with the shallots, pepper, and lemon juice and continue cooking, stirring. Sprinkle with warm Cognac and ignite. Spoon the sauce over and over the shrimp as the flame burns. Serve immediately on warm plates as a first course.

Shrimp Tarragon

4 or more servings

To the recipe for Shrimp Baratin (see above), add one-half teaspoon dried tarragon or one teaspoon chopped fresh tarragon leaves with the shallots. When the shrimp are done, pour three-quarters cup hot cream over them and bring to a boil. Using a whisk, immediately stir in a beurre manié made by blending one tablespoon flour and one tablespoon butter, stirring until thickened. Serve hot, as an appetizer.

Boiled Shrimp with Anchovy Butter

4 servings

24 to 36 raw, unpeeled shrimp
 1 bay leaf
 1 rib celery, cut in half
   Salt
12 peppercorns
 1 cup butter
1½ tablespoons anchovy paste
 1 teaspoon Worcestershire sauce
   Juice of ½ lemon
   Tabasco to taste

1. Rinse the shrimp under cold running water, drain, and set aside.

2. Add enough water to a kettle to cover the shrimp, but do not add the shrimp. Add the bay leaf, celery, salt to taste, and peppercorns and bring to a boil. Add the shrimp and return to a boil. Simmer five minutes, then drain the shrimp and place in a bowl. The shrimp are to be served hot in the shell.

3. Meanwhile, melt the butter in a saucepan and add the remaining ingredients. Stir to blend.

4. Divide the sauce into four warm bowls and serve the hot shrimp separately, as an appetizer, with hot, buttered French bread. Let each guest peel his own shrimp and dip them into the sauce. Serve with finger bowls or pass damp napkins.

Escargots à la Bourguignonne

8 appetizer servings

1 cup soft butter
¼ cup finely chopped parsley
2 shallots, finely chopped
1 clove garlic, finely chopped
2 tablespoons brandy
32 canned French snails
32 snail shells

1. Preheat the oven to 350 degrees.

2. Combine the butter, parsley, shallots, garlic, and brandy in a bowl and blend well.

3. Place a snail in each shell and fill the cavity with the seasoned butter. Place on a baking pan and bake for twelve minutes. Serve hot, as an appetizer, on individual snail dishes or on small folded napkins on plates, to keep the shells from sliding about.

Fruits de Mer Caprice

6 to 8 servings

1¾ pounds (35 to 40 small) mussels
½ cup dry white wine
16 small raw shrimp, peeled and deveined
   Salt and freshly ground black pepper
¼ cup butter
¾ pound bay scallops
2 tablespoons finely chopped shallots
1 cup sliced mushrooms
1⅓ cups heavy cream
2 egg yolks
1 teaspoon lemon juice
   Cayenne pepper or Tabasco

1. Scrub the mussels well and place them in a kettle or large saucepan. Add the wine and cover. Bring to a boil and steam just until the shells open, five to ten minutes.

2. Remove the mussels from the shells and peel off the small peripheral edge that resembles a rubber band. Place the mussels in a small mixing bowl and strain the kettle liquid over them.

3. Sprinkle the shrimp with salt and pepper. Heat half the butter in a skillet and add the shrimp. Cook, turning once, until the shrimp turn red all over. Remove with a slotted spoon and keep warm.

4. Melt the remaining butter in the same skillet and add the scallops. Cook briefly to barely cook through, tossing and stirring, about one minute. Add the shallots, mushrooms, and shrimp and cook briefly, about one minute longer, tossing and stirring.

5. Using a slotted spoon, remove the seafood to a warm place, leaving the cooking liquid in the skillet. Add the mussels to the seafood and add the mussel liquid to the cooking liquid in the skillet.

6. Reduce the liquid in the skillet to about half the original volume. Add one cup heavy cream and simmer ten minutes to reduce.

7. Combine the egg yolks with the remaining cream and add to the hot sauce. Add the lemon juice and cayenne to taste and bring just below the boil, stirring constantly. Add the seafood and continue cooking and stirring just until thick. Do not cook over high heat or the sauce may curdle. Spoon the creamed seafood into hot scallop shells or individual ramekins and serve immediately, as an appetizer.

Beef Périgourdine

12 servings

It is, admittedly, a luxury item, but a cold roast fillet of beef in aspic is one of the most beautiful dishes in all of French cooking—and one of the handsomest dishes for any buffet. The beef, which really should be cooked rare, is arranged on a bed of jellied périgourdine *sauce containing truffles, and then coated with a clear aspic. As a final fillip, the ensemble is garnished with a tomato rose. A fine claret goes well with beef* périgourdine.

    1 fillet of beef (4 pounds)
    ¼ cup butter
      Salt and freshly ground pepper to taste
    ¼ cup Madeira
    ¼ cup Cognac
    3 cups Brown Sauce (page 268) or two
      cans (10¾ ounces each) brown beef
      gravy
    3 black truffles, finely chopped
    2 tablespoons unflavored gelatin
 1½ cups Clear Aspic (page 264), cool but
      not firm

1. Preheat the oven to 450 degrees.
2. Tie the fillet of beef with string. Melt the butter in a roasting pan and roll the fillet in it until well coated on all sides.
3. Sprinkle the fillet on all sides with salt and pepper. Bake 15 minutes, basting occasionally. Reduce the heat to 375 degrees and bake one to two minutes longer. It is best

rare, but if you wish it more well done, continue cooking and use your judgment.
4. Transfer the meat from the pan. Let cool, then refrigerate.
5. Place the roasting pan on the stove and add the wine and Cognac. Ignite the spirits and let burn until the flame dies. Stir in the brown sauce and truffles. Stir in the gelatin and blend well.
6. Spoon the sauce from the roasting pan into a skillet or large saucepan and bring to a boil. Simmer three minutes, skimming the surface to remove the scum and foam as necessary. Spoon the sauce over the bottom of an oval serving dish and chill.
7. Slice the fillet of beef and arrange the slices over the sauce so they overlap symmetrically. Then chill the platter once more.
8. Brush the meat with the cool, liquid aspic and apply two or three coats of the aspic, chilling the meat after each application. If the aspic starts to set, reheat it gently. If kept properly chilled, this dish can be made several hours in advance. Serve as a first course.

Note: Imported black truffles in cans are available in fine food shops throughout America, and are among the most expensive delicacies on earth. Truffles cost between three and four dollars an ounce. The liquid in which truffles are packed should not be discarded because it has a truffle flavor and may be used in sauces.

If a can of truffles is opened and all the truffles are not used, the leftover truffles may be kept in the refrigerator. To do this, it is best to transfer the truffles to a glass jar and cover them with cognac, sherry, port, or Madeira. Seal with a cap and leave in the refrigerator until ready to use. They will remain in good condition for several weeks, and the liquid in which they are kept may also be used in sauces. They may also be frozen.

Boeuf à la Mode en Gelée

About 30 servings

Although a daube *of beef is nothing more than a jellied and glorified pot roast, it is an elegant dish, at home on the most sumptuous buffet. It pairs well with several dozen other cold offerings that come to mind, including salads of shrimp or crab or lobster in mayonnaise, tomato salads, cucumber salads. Or cold, sliced baked ham. Or smoked salmon. Or foie gras. Or caviar. And it is also the kind of dish that goes with fine dry wine, white or red. Not to mention brut champagne.*

3 calves' feet, if available
¼ pound salt pork, thinly sliced
1 boneless knuckle of beef or other boneless stewing beef (5 pounds)
Salt and freshly ground black pepper
2 ribs celery, coarsely chopped
2 cloves garlic, coarsely chopped
2 carrots, coarsely chopped
1 large onion, peeled and chopped
4 sprigs fresh thyme or ½ teaspoon dried thyme
1 sprig fresh rosemary or ½ teaspoon dried rosemary
6 sprigs parsley
1 bay leaf
2 tomatoes, peeled and chopped
1 1-pound 1-ounce can Italian plum tomatoes
6 cups cold water
3 cups dry white wine
2 carrots, scraped and cut into neat ½-inch cubes
1 cup neatly sliced celery
19 small white onions, peeled
1 tablespoon Cognac (optional)

1. Preheat the oven to 275 degrees.
2. Have the butcher trim the meat from the calves' feet and reserve both meat and bones.
3. Heat the salt pork in a Dutch oven and cook, stirring occasionally, until rendered of fat.
4. Sprinkle the meat with salt and pepper and brown well on all sides in the fat from the salt pork. Add the coarsely chopped celery, garlic, carrots, onion, thyme, rosemary, parsley, bay leaf, fresh tomatoes, canned tomatoes, water, and wine. Add the meat and bones from the calves' feet. Bring to a boil, then cover and bake until meat is fork tender, two to four hours.
5. Remove the beef to a platter and reserve. Remove the cooked meat from the calves' feet and chop.
6. Strain the cooking liquid and simmer it thirty minutes. Add the chopped calves' feet meat, the cubed carrots, sliced celery, and small onions and cook until the onions are tender, about forty-five minutes. Cool thoroughly.
7. Cut the beef into large slabs and arrange over the bottom of an earthenware casserole or deep dish. Sprinkle with Cognac and pour the sauce over. Refrigerate until the liquid is set. Serve sliced, as an appetizer.

Pâté à l'Auberge

15 to 20 servings

1½ pounds salt pork
1¼ pounds pork or lamb liver
 ½ pound lean pork
 ¼ pound lean veal
 ½ cup heavy cream
  2 egg yolks
 ⅓ cup dry sherry
  2 tablespoons Armagnac or Cognac
 ½ teaspoon poultry seasoning
    Salt and freshly ground black pepper to
    taste
  1 bay leaf, chopped and ground to a pow-
    der
  2 shallots, finely chopped
  1 teaspoon chopped parsley
 ½ teaspoon dried thyme

1. Cut one pound of the salt pork into thin slices and line the bottom and sides of a mold (8½ x 4½ x 2½), leaving enough slices to cover the top of the mold. Cube the remaining half pound of salt pork.

2. Preheat the oven to 350 degrees.

3. Put the cubed salt pork, liver, pork, and veal through a food grinder equipped with a coarse blade. Blend the meats with the remaining ingredients.

4. Pour the pâté mixture into the mold lined with salt pork and cover with the remaining salt pork. Set the mold in a pan of hot water and place over high heat. When the water in the pan starts to boil, transfer the pan to the oven. Bake one to one and one-half hours, or until a skewer inserted in the center of the pâté comes out clean. Do not overcook. Remove the mold from the pan in which it baked and place a weight on the top. Let cool, then chill. Slice and serve as an appetizer, with sour pickles.

Pâté Barbara

1 loaf

 ½ pound salt pork, sliced
  3 pounds fresh shoulder of pork
  5 medium onions, quartered
  2 pounds calves' liver, cut into 2 pieces and
    trimmed
  2 eggs
    Salt and freshly ground black pepper
  1 teaspoon marjoram
 ½ teaspoon nutmeg
    Pinch of allspice
  1 tablespoon Maggi seasoning
 ½ pound sliced bacon

1. Preheat the oven to 300 degrees.

2. Arrange the salt pork in an open roasting pan, add the shoulder of pork and roast one and one-half hours.

3. Add the onion. Roast one and one-half hours more, or until the pork is well done. When done, remove the pork and add the liver to the onions in the pan. Raise the oven temperature to 350 degrees and roast fifteen to twenty minutes. Cool.

4. Lower the oven temperature to 300 degrees.

5. Remove the meat from the pork bones and grind the meat and liver twice. Sieve the onions and pan juices into the meats.

6. Add the eggs, salt and pepper to taste, marjoram, nutmeg, allspice, and Maggi seasoning. Mix well.

7. Line a bread pan with the bacon and fill the pan three-quarters full with the pâté mixture. Bake thirty minutes, then cool and chill. Serve as an appetizer.

Liver Pâté

12 servings

1 pound chicken livers or pork liver
¼ cup butter
1 pound pork, ground
2 pounds veal, ground
1 cup dry white wine
¼ cup Cognac
3 cloves garlic, finely chopped
12 black peppercorns, roughly crushed with a pestle and mortar
12 juniper berries, roughly crushed
1½ tablespoons salt
½ teaspoon ground mace
¼ teaspoon ground allspice
½ pound fresh pork fatback, diced except for three thin strips
Truffles
Sour pickles
Salad greens

1. Preheat the oven to 350 degrees.
2. Sauté the livers in the butter until browned on the outside but still pink on the inside, three to five minutes. Chop or grind all but twelve one-inch pieces of the liver.

3. Combine the pork, veal, ground liver, wine, Cognac, garlic, peppercorns, juniper berries, salt, mace, and allspice. Thoroughly beat the mixture until smooth. Stir in the diced pork fat.
4. Pack half of the mixture into a two-quart terrine or casserole. Arrange the liver pieces in two rows down the length of the terrine and place the truffles down the center in between. Add the remaining meat mixture and pack down well. Place the strips of pork fat over the top.
5. Cover tightly with a lid or foil and place in a pan with boiling water extending two-thirds of the way up the terrine. Bake about two hours, or until the internal temperature is 185 degrees. Remove the terrine from the oven and the pan it was baked in and place weights on top. Cool, then chill before unmolding onto a platter. Garnish with sour pickles and salad greens and serve as an appetizer.

Terrine of Pheasant

10 servings

1 dozen slices bacon, approximately
1 whole pheasant breast, boned
3 pounds pheasant meat, boned and cubed (two birds are needed to supply the whole breast above plus the additional meat)
¾ pound lean boneless pork from the loin or shoulder
½ pound unsalted fatback with streaks of lean
½ pound prosciutto, fat included
1 tablespoon salt
1 teaspoon seasoned salt
1 teaspoon freshly ground black pepper
Quatre épices (see note) to taste
1 teaspoon chopped fresh tarragon or ½ teaspoon dried tarragon
⅓ cup Cognac
3 eggs

1. Preheat the oven to 325 degrees.
2. Place the bacon strips in a saucepan and add cold water to cover. Bring to a boil and simmer thirty seconds. Drain well.
3. Butter a terrine and line it with the bacon strips, letting the slices overlap the rim so they may be brought over to cover the top of the meat when it is added.
4. Cut the whole breast into strips half the thickness of a man's thumb.
5. Put the cubed pheasant meat, the lean pork, fatback, and prosciutto through the fine blade of a meat grinder. Spoon the mixture into a mixing bowl and add the salt, seasoned salt, pepper, quatre épices, tarragon, Cognac, and eggs. Blend well with the hands.
6. Make a half-inch layer of the ground mixture in the prepared terrine, then arrange three strips of breast meat over it. Add another layer of the ground mixture, three more strips of breast, and so on, ending with the ground mixture. Fold the loose ends of bacon strips over the top.
7. Cover the terrine closely with two sheets of aluminum foil and set the terrine in a larger pan. Add boiling water to the larger pan and bake two hours. Remove the terrine from the pan and let the meat cool. Place a weight in the center of the terrine, over the foil, to weight down the meat. Refrigerate overnight. Serve sliced, accompanied by cornichons (French gherkins) and hot French bread.

Note: Quatre épices, which means "four spices," is a French blend available in specialty shops. It is a blend of one cup plus two tablespoons white pepper, one and one-half tablespoons powdered cloves, one-quarter cup grated nutmeg and three and one-half tablespoons ground ginger.

Terrine Sauvage

(Terrine of Game)

*About 12 first-course servings or
20 cocktail servings*

1 medium pheasant or 1 wild hare (2 pounds)
12 chicken livers, gristle removed and halved
   Cognac
3 bay leaves
6 sprigs parsley
½ teaspoon dried thyme
1 teaspoon salt
¼ teaspoon ground mace
4 shallots, chopped, or 1 small onion, minced
2 tablespoons butter
½ pound lean pork, ground twice
1 pound veal, ground twice
½ pound pork fat (not salt pork), ground
2 egg yolks, beaten
   Freshly ground black pepper
½ clove garlic, finely minced
½ pound wafer-thin sliced bacon, preheated in boiling water 1 minute
1 large or 2 small truffles, chopped (optional)

1. Slice the meat from the breast of the game. Put the meat and chicken livers in a bowl with Cognac to cover, one of the bay leaves, the parsley, thyme, one-half teaspoon of the salt, and the ground mace. Cover closely and marinate overnight.

2. Drain the meat and livers, and reserve one-quarter cup of the marinade. Sauté the shallots and livers in the butter a few minutes, or to the point at which the livers are still pink inside. Remove the livers and reserve.

3. Preheat the oven to 375 degrees.

4. Cut the remaining meat from the game, grind, and add to the pork, veal, and pork fat. Add the egg yolks, pepper, remaining salt, and garlic.

5. Add the reserved Cognac marinade to the skillet with the shallots and stir to dissolve the particles that cling to the pan. Add to the ground meat mixture and mix well. Fry a bit of the mixture to taste the seasoning, and adjust if necessary.

6. Line the bottom and sides of a terrine or dish with a close-fitting cover with blanched strips of bacon. Spread one-third of the ground meat on the bottom. Add a layer of sliced game. Sprinkle the chopped truffles over the game layer, then add a layer of chicken livers. Add another layer of ground meat, another layer of sliced game, of truffles, and of chicken livers, and a final layer of ground meat. Top with blanched bacon and the remaining bay leaves. Cover closely. Seal with flour-and-water-paste dough if the top does not fit tightly.

7. Place the terrine on top of a folded cloth (to prevent breaking) in a pan of hot water. Bake two hours, adding boiling water as needed.

8. Uncover and pour off the melted fat. Place a piece of aluminum foil over the terrine. Add a weighted plate (use heavy cans of fruit or fruit juice) and let stand overnight, refrigerated.

9. Unmold. Serve bottom side up on a platter or return bottom side up to the terrine dish.

Note: Clear Aspic (page 264) may be poured over the whole platter or in the terrine, or it may be served as is.

Galantine of Duck

24 servings

In the world of cold buffets, there are few things more elegant and more sumptuous than an aspic-coated, truffle-and-cognac-perfumed galantine of duck. It can take its place with the finest pâtés and terrines or molded fish mousses. A galantine is made with boned poultry—generally chicken, turkey, or duck—that is stuffed with meats and nuts, cooked, then chilled and coated with aspic. It does take patience and a certain skill, but the result is well worth the effort.

1 duck (5 pounds), boned (page 109), giblets reserved
1¼ pounds boneless loin of pork, including fat
3 shallots
1 egg yolk
Salt and freshly ground pepper
6 tablespoons Cognac
½ teaspoon nutmeg
⅓ cup heavy cream
2 teaspoons Parisienne spice (optional)
¼ pound lean ham, cut into ½-inch cubes
2 large truffles, cut into ¼-inch cubes
1 bay leaf, broken in half
2 sprigs parsley
1 sprig rosemary
½ cup fresh pistachio nuts, shelled
2 cups Duck Stock (page 109)
2 envelopes unflavored gelatin
2 egg whites, lightly beaten
2 egg shells, crushed

1. You may bone the duck yourself or have it boned by the butcher or poultry man. Reserve all the scraps of meat and the solid fat inside the duck. Place the scraps in a mixing bowl.

2. When boned, turn the duck inside out and very carefully slice away the breast meat in two large pieces. Set aside.

3. Carefully pare away the remaining flesh that clings to the skin. Reverse the skin to its natural state and refrigerate until ready to use.

4. Using the fine or medium blade, put the pork, fat and all, through a meat grinder. Continue grinding while adding the duck liver, gizzard, heart, and all the meaty scraps and trimmings. Do not grind the breast meat. Grind in the shallots, then, using a wooden spoon, beat in the egg yolk, salt and pepper to taste, four tablespoons of the Cognac, half the nutmeg, the cream, and half the Parisienne spice.

5. Meanwhile, heat the reserved duck fat in a skillet and cook until it becomes liquid. Beat one-third cup of the liquid fat into the ground mixture, cover with plastic wrap, and refrigerate about six hours. Pour the remaining duck fat into a roasting pan and set aside.

6. Cut the breast meat into half-inch cubes and place it in a mixing bowl. Add the ham, truffles, and remaining two tablespoons Cognac. Add salt and pepper to taste and the remaining nutmeg. Add the bay leaf, parsley, rosemary, and remaining Parisienne spice.

7. Pour boiling water over the pistachios and let stand ten minutes, then peel and add to the breast mixture. Cover and refrigerate six hours.

8. Six hours later, preheat the oven to 400 degrees.

9. Remove the boned duck from the refrigerator and turn it inside out. Sprinkle the interior with salt and pepper, then return the duck to skin side out.

10. Combine the meat mixtures and use them to stuff the duck. Tuck the wing pieces inside. Sew the openings with string, then tie the string at intervals around the duck to help retain its shape.

11. Place the duck, breast side up, in the roasting pan containing the fat. Roast two hours, basting frequently and pouring off the fat as it accumulates around the duck.

12. Remove the duck to a platter. When it is cool, place the duck and platter in the

refrigerator along with another oval serving platter.

13. Put the duck stock in a saucepan and stir in the gelatin. Add the egg whites and shells. Bring to a simmer slowly and simmer five minutes. Strain through damp flannel.

14. Let the gelatin mixture, or aspic, cool slightly, but do not let it set. (If it does set, however, it may be reheated.) Spoon about one-third of the aspic over the bottom of the chilled oval platter; chill.

15. Remove all the strings from the duck and cut almost half the duck into neat slices. Place the unsliced duck on the aspic and arrange the slices around it. Brush a little of the cool but still liquid aspic over the unsliced duck and also over the slices. Refrigerate.

16. Chill the remaining aspic, then turn it onto a damp chopping board. Chop the aspic and use it to decorate the duck and the platter. Refrigerate until served. Serve as an appetizer.

HOW TO BONE A DUCK:

Boning a duck or other poultry is not so difficult as it may seem. The important thing is to avoid piercing the skin. Be sure to reserve all scraps of meat for later use.

To start, use a boning knife or a small sharp paring knife. Start at the neck and work down toward the tail section. Scrape and carve carefully around the bones, pushing with the fingers to loosen the flesh as necessary. Work always as close to the bones as possible. If the flesh seems to get somewhat mangled in the process, don't be concerned, although the breast meat should be left as whole as possible. The only danger area is at the cartilage-like point of the breastbone. Use a little ingenuity and your sharp knife to leave a bit of this cartilage intact so as not to rip the skin. If worse comes to worst, however, you may sew up the spots where the skin has been slit. Cut off the wing tips and the wings' second joints.

As the boning progresses and after the thigh is boned, use poultry shears or knife to cut between the drumstick and thigh. Bone each drumstick only halfway down, then use poultry shears to cut the bone in half. Leave the tips of each drumstick unboned and intact. When all the boning is done, reserve the carcass for stock. Turn the duck inside out and proceed with the recipe for galantine of duck.

DUCK STOCK:

2 cups

1 carcass from a 5-pound duck
1 onion, peeled
2 sprigs parsley
1 carrot, peeled and quartered
1 rib celery with leaves
  Salt to taste
12 peppercorns

Break up the carcass and place it in a large saucepan. Add the remaining ingredients and water to cover. Bring to a boil and simmer, partly covered, one hour. Strain. Reduce to two cups by boiling.

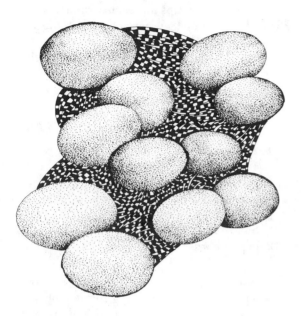

Eggs in Aspic

8 servings

1 tablespoon white vinegar
8 eggs
1½ cups Quick Aspic (page 264)
¾ cup shredded crabmeat, chopped tongue, and/or ham
1 tablespoon chopped parsley
8 pieces of pimento, cut out to resemble flowers
16 tarragon leaves or pieces of green onion, cut out to resemble leaves

1. Use a stainless steel, enameled cast iron, or aluminum skillet and add enough water to almost fill it. Add the vinegar and bring to a simmer.

2. Break the eggs into the water and let the water return to a simmer. Poach the eggs (see below) to the desired degree of doneness. Using a slotted spoon, transfer the eggs to a basin of cold water. When cool, transfer the eggs to absorbent paper towels to drain thoroughly. Trim the eggs neatly with a knife. Arrange them on a rack and refrigerate.

3. Prepare the aspic and let it cool slightly (see note).

4. Sprinkle the shredded crab and/or meat and parsley neatly over the bottom of a round or oval platter. Spoon a thin layer of the cool but still liquid aspic over the crab layer. Refrigerate to allow the aspic to become firm.

5. Meanwhile, remove the cold eggs from the refrigerator. Dip each of the pimento and tarragon cutouts and leaves into the cool but still liquid aspic and apply in a decorative pattern on the tops of the eggs. Refrigerate until the aspic cutouts are firm.

6. Spoon thin layers of the cool but still liquid aspic over the eggs, chilling between each layer. Do not add more than two or three layers. When the last layer has been chilled, arrange the eggs in a neat fashion over the prepared platter. Refrigerate until ready to serve. Chop some of the remaining aspic and use as a garnish for the dish. Serve as an appetizer.

Note: The aspic should not be allowed to become too firm. It may, however, be reheated to melt it, then cooled again.

POACHED EGGS:

8 poached eggs

Fill a stainless steel, aluminum, or enamel skillet with water to the depth of one inch. The water should be deep enough to cover the eggs when they are added. Add one teaspoon of salt to the water and bring to a boil. When the water is simmering, gently break eight fresh eggs into it. Poach gently until the whites are firm and the yolks retain a runny center. Remove the eggs gently with a slotted spoon and drain on paper towels. Trim neatly with a cookie cutter or paring knife. Allow to cool before adding to the aspic.

Eggs with Sauce Gribiche

6 servings

1 teaspoon finely chopped parsley
1 teaspoon finely chopped onion
1 teaspoon finely chopped fresh thyme or
  ½ teaspoon dried thyme
1 clove garlic, finely minced
2 teaspoons Dijon or Düsseldorf mustard
1 egg yolk
  Salt and freshly ground black pepper
2 tablespoons wine vinegar
1½ cups oil (olive or salad oil or a combination of both)
¾ cup diced, seeded, peeled tomatoes
6 hard-cooked eggs, peeled and halved horizontally
2 tablespoons finely chopped chives

1. Place the parsley, onion, thyme, garlic, mustard, egg yolk, salt and pepper to taste, and vinegar in a mixing bowl. Begin beating with a whisk and gradually start adding the oil. Add it a little at a time, beating rapidly, until the sauce begins to thicken. The oil may then be added in a thicker stream. When mixture is thickened and smooth, it is ready.

2. Stir in the tomatoes. Spoon the sauce over the egg halves and sprinkle with chopped chives. Serve as an appetizer.

Caviar Eggs in Aspic

12 servings

12 hard-cooked eggs, chilled
 1 jar (2 ounces) caviar
½ small onion, grated
  Juice of ½ lemon
  Mayonnaise (page 265)
  Quick Aspic (page 264)
  Lemon wedges

1. Remove a small lengthwise slice from each of the eggs and reserve the slice. Carefully scoop out the yolks and press through a fine sieve.

2. Reserve some of the caviar for garnishing and add the remaining to the yolks. Add the onion, lemon juice, and enough mayonnaise to make a smooth paste.

3. Spoon the yolk mixture into a pastry bag fitted with a plain tube. Place the tube in the cavity of the egg white and gently fill it, then replace the reserved slice. Chill while preparing the aspic.

4. Spoon a layer of chilled aspic into twelve egg molds or small ramekins. Chill. Decorate with a few grains of reserved caviar, spoon a thin layer of aspic over, and chill. Place an egg, sliced side up, into each mold. Fill the mold with chilled but still liquid aspic. Chill.

5. To unmold, dip the outside of the mold quickly into a bowl of warm water and turn out onto a serving dish. Garnish with chopped aspic and wedges of lemon and serve as an appetizer.

Celery Root Rémoulade

8 to 12 servings

4 or more celery roots, enough to make 3 cups when shredded
2 egg yolks
1 tablespoon white vinegar
2 tablespoons Dijon or Düsseldorf mustard
¼ teaspoon Tabasco
   Salt and freshly ground pepper to taste
1½ cups olive oil (may be part salad oil)
   Lemon juice to taste
   Water
1 teaspoon chopped parsley

1. Peel the celery roots and drop them into cold water.

2. Place the egg yolks in a mixing bowl and add the vinegar, mustard, Tabasco, and salt and pepper to taste. Start beating with a wire whisk or an electric beater, gradually adding the oil. Continue beating until all the oil is used and the mayonnaise is thick. Add the lemon juice to taste. If necessary, thin the sauce with a little water, adding it a little at a time.

3. Drain the celery roots. Cut them into the thinnest possible slices, then cut the slices into the thinnest possible shreds (julienne). Place the shreds in a mixing bowl and add enough mayonnaise to bind thoroughly. Season to taste with salt and pepper. Chill. Serve cold, sprinkled with parsley, as an appetizer or first course.

Deep-Fried Mushrooms

4 servings

32 medium fresh white mushrooms
   All-purpose flour
   Salt and freshly ground black pepper
2 eggs
1 teaspoon water
1 teaspoon peanut or vegetable oil
1½ cups fresh bread crumbs
   Fat for deep frying

1. Trim off the tips of the mushroom stems but leave the stems on. Rinse the mushrooms under cold running water and drain. Do not dry.

2. Dredge the mushrooms in flour seasoned with salt and pepper.

3. Beat the eggs with the water and oil and place in a pie dish.

4. Toss or turn the mushrooms in the egg mixture until well coated, then coat the mushrooms on all sides with bread crumbs. Let stand until ready to cook.

5. Heat the fat in a large skillet and, when hot (375 degrees), add the mushrooms. Cook until golden brown all over. Drain on paper towels and serve hot, as an appetizer, with Tartar Sauce I (page 277).

Potatoes and Anchovies au Vin Blanc

6 servings

6 large or 12 medium potatoes, scrubbed
  Chicken Stock (page 115) or water to
  cover
¼ cup dry white wine
2 tablespoons wine vinegar, or to taste
⅓ cup olive oil
18 flat or rolled anchovy fillets

1. Cook the potatoes in the chicken stock until tender, then drain. While still warm, peel and slice into thick slices. Sprinkle with wine and let cool to room temperature.

2. Sprinkle with vinegar and oil and garnish with anchovies. Serve as an appetizer.

Cheese Crisps

About 4 dozen squares

1 cup sifted all-purpose flour
  Salt
¼ teaspoon cayenne pepper
⅔ cup grated Parmesan cheese
½ cup butter, at room temperature
¼ cup milk or cream

1. Preheat the oven to 350 degrees.

2. Place the flour in a mixing bowl and add salt to taste, the cayenne, and cheese.

3. Add the butter, and with the fingers work the dough until it just holds together. Gather it into a ball and roll out on a lightly floured board to a thickness of one-half inch. Brush the dough lightly with milk or cream and slice into one-inch squares. With a spatula, transfer the squares to a baking dish and bake twelve to fifteen minutes, or until lightly browned. Serve warm, as an appetizer.

French Onion Tart

4 to 6 servings

PÂTE BRISÉE PASTRY:
2 cups sifted all-purpose flour
1 tablespoon confectioners' sugar
  Pinch of salt
⅔ cup softened butter

ONION FILLING:
2 Bermuda onions, finely chopped
⅔ cup butter
2 tablespoons all-purpose flour
3 eggs
¾ cup cream
½ cup milk
  Salt and freshly ground black pepper
  Nutmeg

1. To prepare the pastry, sift the flour, sugar, and salt into a mixing bowl. Rub in the softened butter with the tips of the fingers or cut it in with a pastry blender until the mixture resembles fine bread crumbs. Do this very gently and lightly or the mixture will be greasy and heavy. Roll into a ball and chill one-half hour or longer.

2. Preheat the oven to 450 degrees.

3. When ready to use the pastry, turn onto a floured board and knead or pat lightly into a round. Place in a ten-inch pie pan and press out with the fingertips to line the pan (no rolling is necessary). Finish the edge of the pastry by fluting as usual and prick the bottom with a fork to avoid air bubbles while cooking. Bake ten minutes. Cool slightly before pouring in the onion filling.

4. To prepare the onion filling, sauté the onions in the butter until transparent. Cool.

5. Preheat the oven to 375 degrees.

6. Add the flour, eggs, cream, and milk to the onions and mix well. Season with salt, pepper, and nutmeg to taste.

7. Pour the mixture into the prepared pie shell and bake twenty-five to thirty minutes. Serve very hot, as an appetizer.

Pissaladière

4 servings

What is the name of a European pastry that is flat like a pie and has an onion and anchovy and frequently a tomato filling? Pizza, yes—but there is a French creation that also fits that description, the pissaladière of France's southern coast around the Italian border.

"This dish," Elizabeth David *wrote in* A Book of Mediterranean Food *(Penguin, 95 cents),* *"is one of the delights of Marseilles, Toulon and the Var country, where it is sold in the market places and the bakeries in the early morning and can be bought, piping hot, by the slice, off big iron trays."*

A pissaladière or pissaladina, as it is also called, would make an excellent accompaniment for cocktails or would be an interesting dish for a luncheon menu.

1 package active dry yeast
¾ cup lukewarm water
1½ tablespoons salad oil
2 cups sifted all-purpose flour, approximately
Salt
2 pounds Bermuda or Spanish onions, cut into rings
1 clove garlic, finely chopped
Olive oil
6 ripe tomatoes, peeled, seeded, and chopped
1 cup freshly grated Parmesan cheese
Freshly ground black pepper
½ teaspoon rosemary
3 cans flat anchovy fillets
Pitted black olives (preferably French, Greek, or Italian)

1. Add the yeast to the lukewarm water and salad oil and stir to dissolve.

2. Place the flour and three-quarters teaspoon salt in a bowl and stir in the yeast mixture to form a medium-soft dough. Turn onto a lightly floured board and knead until smooth and satiny, about ten minutes. Place in a greased bowl, cover with a towel, and let rise in a warm place until doubled in bulk, about forty-five minutes.

3. Meanwhile, place the onions, garlic, and two tablespoons of olive oil in a large heavy skillet. Cover and cook slowly until the onions are tender and golden but not brown, about forty minutes.

4. Place the tomatoes in a heavy pan and boil, uncovered, until they are thick, twenty to twenty-five minutes. Stir occasionally.

5. Preheat the oven to 400 degrees.

6. Punch the dough down, then place on a lightly floured board and let rest, covered with a towel, for about five minutes. Roll the dough out to make a circle fifteen inches in diameter and lift onto a fifteen-inch pizza pan.

7. Sprinkle the dough with the Parmesan cheese.

8. Season the onion mixture with salt and pepper to taste, then spoon over the cheese-topped pastry.

9. Season the tomato mixture with the rosemary and salt and pepper to taste. Spoon the tomato sauce over the onion mixture.

10. Crisscross the entire pie with anchovies and place an olive in each space.

11. Brush the olives with olive oil and bake until the crust is browned and the filling bubbly and hot, fifteen to twenty minutes. Serve sliced.

Seafood Quiche

4 to 6 servings

Unbaked 9-inch Pastry Shell (page 289)
1 egg white
2 tablespoons finely chopped shallots or green onion
2 tablespoons butter
½ pound lump crabmeat, picked over to remove bits of bone and cartilage
½ pound shrimp, cooked and shelled
2 tablespoons Cognac
1 teaspoon chopped fresh tarragon or ½ teaspoon dried tarragon
2 cups heavy cream
4 eggs, well beaten
1 teaspoon finely chopped chives
1 black truffle, chopped (optional)
4 drops Tabasco
Salt and freshly ground black pepper

1. Preheat the oven to 450 degrees.
2. Line a deep pie plate with the pastry, flute the edges, and prick the bottom and sides well with a fork. Brush with the egg white and bake five minutes.
3. Cook the shallots in butter until wilted and add the seafood. Heat through and sprinkle with the Cognac and chopped tarragon. If dried tarragon is used, let it stand in the Cognac for twenty minutes before using.
4. Heat the cream, but do not boil it. Blend the cream and eggs. Add the chives, truffle, Tabasco, and salt and pepper to taste. Stir the mixture into the seafood and pour all of it into the prepared pie shell. Bake fifteen minutes, then reduce the oven temperature to 350 degrees and bake until a knife inserted one inch from the pastry edge comes out clean, about ten minutes longer. Serve as an appetizer, with a well-chilled bottle of dry white Burgundy wine.

Beef Stock

2 to 3 quarts

4 to 5 pounds short ribs of beef or other beef with bones, such as shin of beef
2 leeks, trimmed, split, and washed well
2 carrots, trimmed and scraped
2 ribs celery, cut in half
1 onion stuck with 2 cloves
2 sprigs fresh thyme or ½ teaspoon dried thyme
Salt to taste
1 teaspoon peppercorns

1. Place the beef in a kettle and cover with cold water. Bring to a boil and blanch about five minutes, then drain and run under cold water.
2. Return the bones to the kettle and add the remaining ingredients. Add more cold water to cover and simmer, uncovered, about three hours. Skim the surface as the stock cooks to remove scum and fat. Strain.

Chicken Stock

About 1¾ quarts

3 pounds chicken necks, wings, and backs
10 cups water
1 onion, peeled
2 ribs celery
2 sprigs parsley
Salt to taste
10 peppercorns

Place all the ingredients in a large kettle and bring to a boil. Simmer, uncovered, for an hour and a half, skimming the surface as necessary. Strain through cheesecloth and boil rapidly, uncovered, to reduce the stock to about seven cups. Skim off all the fat and chill.

Fish Stock

8 to 10 cups

2½ pounds fish bones (may include head of fish)
2 cups coarsely chopped celery
2 cups thinly sliced onions
1 whole clove garlic, unpeeled, sliced in half
2 cups chopped, well-washed green part of leeks
3 sprigs fresh thyme
1 bay leaf
2 quarts water
½ bottle dry white wine
¼ teaspoon peppercorns
¼ teaspoon anise seeds, crushed
   Salt to taste

Combine all the ingredients in a large pot. Bring to a boil and simmer about twenty minutes. Strain.

Note: Leftover stock may be frozen.

Consommé with Marrow

4 servings

One of the great mystifications of the American table is its neglect of soups. Whether clear or cream or vegetable, soups have been a mainstay of classic menus since the days of Lucullus and before. Yea, unto Esau. And on wintry days in particular, there are few things that better assuage the chill and offer the body that glorious sense of well-being. Below is a soup tailored to the season—an elegant consommé with beef marrow.

4 marrow bones, each about 3 inches long
   Salt and freshly ground black pepper
4 cups consommé (see note)
4 teaspoons chopped chives

1. Have the butcher split the marrow bones and remove the marrow. Cut the marrow into one-quarter- to one-half-inch lengths and place in a bowl. Add cold water to cover and let stand overnight in the refrigerator.

2. Drain the marrow and place it in a saucepan. Add fresh water to cover and salt and pepper to taste. Bring to a boil and simmer briefly, just until the marrow is heated through and changes color. Do not simmer too long or the marrow will dissolve. With a slotted spoon, scoop out the pieces of marrow and add equal amounts to each of four cups of consommé. Serve sprinkled with chopped chives.

Note: To make consommé, reduce Beef Stock (page 115) by simmering, uncovered, until it reaches the desired flavor.

Fish Soup

6 servings

3½ pounds fresh fish bones
2 quarts water
1 onion, sliced
4 cloves garlic, sliced
2 ribs celery without leaves
6 sprigs fresh thyme or 1 teaspoon dried thyme
2 bay leaves, broken in half
15 peppercorns
1 cup dry white wine
1 dozen cherrystone clams
3 tablespoons olive oil
2 onions, coarsely chopped
1 small sprig rosemary
2 tomatoes, cored and quartered
1 quart potatoes, peeled and quartered (about 6 whole potatoes)
¼ cup heavy cream
2 tablespoons Pernod, Ricard, or other anise-flavored liqueur
2 tablespoons finely chopped parsley

1. Place the fish bones, water, sliced onion, one clove garlic, celery, half the thyme, one bay leaf, peppercorns, wine, and clams into a kettle.

2. Bring to a boil and cook twenty minutes. Strain through a colander, pushing to extract as much liquid as possible from the solids. Reserve the liquid.

3. Heat the oil and add the remaining garlic, thyme, bay leaf, and the chopped onions. Add the rosemary, tomatoes, potatoes and reserved stock. Bring to a boil and cook forty-five minutes. Strain through a sieve or food mill equipped with a fine blade to puree some of the solids. Beat well with a wire whisk and bring to a boil. Add the cream and simmer five minutes. Add the liqueur, stir in the chopped parsley, and serve hot.

Fish Soup au Cognac

8 or more servings

For the cold tag end of winter, fish soups should make a welcome choice for a dish that is hot and hearty. This fish soup with Cognac is an excellent preface to a meal.

3 tablespoons olive oil
1 tablespoon minced garlic
1 cup finely chopped onion
2 teaspoons crumbled leaf saffron, or to taste
½ teaspoon chopped fresh or dried thyme
1½ pounds fish fillets, such as flounder, striped bass, etc.
Salt and freshly ground pepper to taste
Tabasco to taste
1 cup dry white wine
4 cups water
⅓ cup tomato puree
1 teaspoon crushed fennel seeds
3 tablespoons Cognac
2 cups heavy cream

1. Heat the oil in a kettle and add the garlic, onion, saffron, and thyme. Cook, stirring, until the onion is wilted. Add the fish, salt and pepper to taste, and Tabasco. Cook briefly, stirring to break up the fish.

2. Add the wine, water, tomato puree, and fennel seeds. Bring to a boil and simmer fifteen minutes, stirring occasionally.

3. Add salt and pepper to taste, then add the Cognac. Stir in the cream and bring to a boil. Reduce the heat and simmer ten minutes.

Food as well as weather gives each season its special character. In autumn, there are game and oysters; in winter, turnips and leeks. Spring brings shad and asparagus, and summer is the time for things of the sea. There are clams and lobsters and mussels, stripers and black bass, all ready for steaming, broiling, or grilling, or for turning into fish soups, such as the splendid bouillabaisses that follow.

Bouillabaisse I

About 10 servings

 1 whole striped bass, black bass, or other white, fleshy, non-oily fish (3½ pounds)
¼ cup olive oil
 2 cups finely chopped onion
 2 cups well-washed, finely chopped white part of leeks
½ cup finely chopped celery
½ tablespoon minced leaf saffron
 Salt and freshly ground pepper
 1 1-pound can heavy-concentrate tomato puree
 1 teaspoon finely chopped fresh thyme or ½ teaspoon dried thyme
 1 tablespoon minced garlic
 3 ripe tomatoes, chopped
 Tabasco to taste
 8 to 10 cups Fish Stock (page 116)
 2 live lobsters (3 pounds each)
 2 eels, cleaned and cut into 2-inch lengths
20 mussels, well scrubbed
20 littleneck clams, well scrubbed
 2 tablespoons Pernod, Ricard, or other anise liqueur

1. Cut the fish crosswise into "steaks" like salmon steaks, about one and one-half inches thick. Refrigerate until ready to use.

2. Heat the oil in a very large, heavy skillet and add the chopped onion, leeks, and celery, along with the saffron, salt, and pepper. Bring to a boil and add the tomato puree, thyme, garlic, tomatoes, and Tabasco. Simmer one-half hour, stirring frequently. Bring to a boil and add the fish stock.

3. Meanwhile, plunge a knife into the lobsters where the body and tail meet. This will kill them instantly. Cut the tail off, then cut it crosswise into two-inch segments and arrange in a large skillet. Crack the claws and add them to the tail pieces. Split the bodies in half and, after discarding the tough sacs near the eyes, add to the tail pieces. Pour one-third of the tomato sauce over the lobsters and cover closely. Bring to a boil and cook until done, ten to fifteen minutes.

4. Arrange a single layer of the fish and eels in a large, flat skillet. Pour the remaining sauce over all. This may stand for an hour or so before cooking. When ready to cook, add the mussels and clams. Cover and simmer about ten minutes, until the mussels and clams open. Add the lobsters or serve separately. Season with Pernod and serve.

Bouillabaisse II

4 servings

3 tablespoons olive oil
1 cup chopped leeks
3 cloves garlic, finely minced
1 cup chopped onion
1¾ cups chopped tomatoes
2 sprigs fresh thyme or ½ teaspoon dried thyme
2 sprigs fresh parsley
1 bay leaf
1 cup dry white wine
2 cups water
1 large teaspoon leaf saffron, crumbled
Salt and freshly ground black pepper
¼ teaspoon Tabasco, or to taste
1 lobster (1½ pounds)
3 tablespoons butter
1½ teaspoons all-purpose flour
1 pound fresh red snapper, striped bass, sea bass, porgy, or other white fish, cut into serving pieces
1 quart fresh mussels, scrubbed well
2 dozen cherrystone clams
12 raw shrimp, peeled, shelled, and deveined
1 tablespoon anisette, Pernod, Ricard, or other anise-flavored liqueur (optional)
Garlic Croutons (see below)

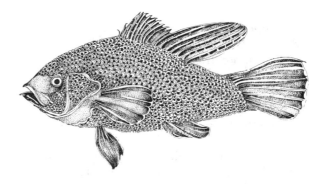

1. Heat the olive oil in a large saucepan and add the leeks, garlic, and onion. Cook until the vegetables are wilted. Add the tomatoes, thyme, parsley, bay leaf, wine, water, saffron, salt and pepper to taste, and the Tabasco. Simmer ten minutes.

2. Plunge a knife into the place where tail and carcass meet on the lobster. This will kill the lobster immediately. Split the tail and carcass and cut the carcass in half lengthwise. Scoop out the liver and coral from the carcass and place in a small mixing bowl. Cut the tail section into four crosswise pieces and set aside.

3. Add the carcass and any scraps of lobster to the tomato mixture. Cover and simmer thirty minutes.

4. Meanwhile, blend the butter and flour with the fingers and mix with the reserved coral and liver.

5. Strain the tomato mixture through a sieve, pushing through as many solids as possible. Bring to a boil and add the red snapper, mussels, clams, shrimp, and reserved lobster tail. Simmer fifteen minutes. Stir in the coral mixture, and when the mixture boils add the anisette. Scoop into hot soup plates and serve with garlic croutons on top.

GARLIC CROUTONS:
Bake eight thin slices of bread in a 400-degree oven until crisp and brown, but do not burn. Rub with garlic and brush with melted butter or olive oil.

Potage Crème Normande
(Creamed Fish Soup)

4 servings

½ pound cod, haddock, or sole
1 onion, quartered
½ rib celery, chopped
2 tomatoes, peeled and seeded
½ cup dry white wine
1 bay leaf
2 sprigs fresh thyme or ½ teaspoon dried thyme
Salt
12 peppercorns
3 cups water
1 tablespoon fresh white bread crumbs
1 cup cooked, shelled, deveined shrimp
½ cup heavy cream
Nutmeg
1 teaspoon chopped parsley

1. Place the fish in a saucepan and add the onion, celery, tomatoes, wine, bay leaf, thyme, salt to taste, peppercorns, and water. Bring to a boil and simmer thirty minutes.

2. Strain the soup into another saucepan. Transfer the fish and vegetables to the container of an electric blender, taking care to remove and discard any bones. Discard the bay leaf, thyme, and peppercorns. Add the bread crumbs, shrimp, and one-half cup of the soup stock and blend well. Bring to a boil and add the cream. Heat thoroughly and season with nutmeg to taste and the parsley.

Seafood Soup

6 servings

⅓ cup olive oil
3 tablespoons finely chopped shallots
3 cloves garlic, minced
½ cup finely chopped parsley
1 tablespoon crushed leaf saffron
3 cups tomato puree
3½ cups Fish Stock (page 116) or water
1 cup dry white wine
Salt and freshly ground black pepper
1 teaspoon crushed dried mint
1 teaspoon crushed dried basil
Cayenne pepper
½ pound fresh bay scallops or quartered sea scallops
12 raw shrimp, shelled and deveined
1 pound cod, preferably the tail section, cut into 6 pieces
3 small lobsters, cut into serving pieces (tails split in half, claws cracked)
12 littleneck clams, the smaller the better
2 tablespoons Pernod or Ricard

1. Heat the oil in a large kettle and add the shallots. Cook briefly, stirring, then add the garlic and cook briefly without browning. Add the parsley, saffron, tomato puree, fish stock, wine, salt and pepper to taste, mint, basil, and cayenne pepper to taste. Simmer fifteen minutes. Add the scallops, shrimp, cod, and lobsters and simmer fifteen minutes more.

2. Add the clams and simmer just until they open. Stir in the liqueur. Serve hot, with toasted French bread rubbed with garlic.

Soupe de Poissons

10 to 12 servings

¼ cup vegetable or olive oil
2 cups finely chopped onion
3 garlic cloves, finely minced
1 green pepper, cored, seeded, and chopped
4 ripe tomatoes, cored and quartered
3½ pounds fresh fish, cleaned and gills removed
2 leeks or green onions
½ teaspoon dried thyme
1 bay leaf
4 sprigs parsley
4 quarts water
2 tablespoons anise-flavored liqueur
French bread croûtes

1. Heat the oil in a large saucepan or kettle and add the onions. Cook, stirring, until the onions are golden. Add the garlic and green pepper and stir briefly, then add the tomatoes and simmer for ten minutes, stirring frequently.

2. Cut the fish into one-inch lengths and add to the vegetables. Stir thoroughly. Cook for five minutes, stirring.

3. If the leeks are used, split them and wash well. Tie them, or the green onions, into a bundle with the thyme, bay leaf, and parsley. Add the herb bundle and the water to the fish. Boil vigorously, skimming the surface as necessary, for forty-five minutes.

4. Strain, forcing as much of the solid matter through the colander or sieve as possible.

5. Return the strained soup to the kettle and simmer for fifteen minutes longer. Add the liqueur.

6. Place one croûte in the bottom of each hot soup bowl. Ladle the soup on top and serve immediately.

Tuna Soup Martinique

6 or more servings

3 pounds fish bones
2½ cups water
3 sprigs parsley
1 small rib celery with leaves
3 tablespoons butter
¾ cup finely minced green pepper
1 cup finely minced onion
1 cup finely minced celery
2 cloves garlic, finely minced
¼ cup all-purpose flour
1 pound boneless fish such as flounder, cod, or red snapper, cubed
1 sprig fresh thyme or ½ teaspoon dried thyme
  Salt and freshly ground black pepper
  Cayenne pepper
2 cans (7 ounces each) water-packed tuna
⅓ cup drained capers

1. Combine the fish bones, water, parsley, and celery rib in a saucepan. Simmer fifteen minutes. Drain and reserve the stock.

2. In a one-and-one-half-quart saucepan, heat the butter and add the green pepper, onion, minced celery, and garlic. Cook, stirring occasionally, until the vegetables wilt. Sprinkle with the flour. Add the fish and fish stock, stirring. Add the thyme and salt, pepper, and cayenne to taste and simmer until the fish flakes easily. Beat the soup briskly with a whisk to break up the fish.

3. Flake and mash the tuna and add it. Add the capers. Bring to a boil and simmer five minutes. Serve hot.

Clam Bisque

12 or more servings

Back in the old days, the thick cream soup we call bisque was usually made with craw-fish or other shellfish. Later, the repertory of bisques came to include game, both furred and feathered—quail and pheasant and rabbit and the like. The name bisque is in all probability not unrelated to bisquit, for the original bisque contained bread made into a sort of mush. Modern-day bisques are a blessing of the electric blender, easily made either of vegetables or of shellfish, such as lobster and clams. The clam bisque below is rich and elegant. And delicious.

24 large cherrystone clams
¼ cup butter
2 cups chopped onion
1 teaspoon chopped stem saffron (optional)
2 teaspoons finely chopped garlic
2 teaspoons chopped fresh thyme or 1 teaspoon dried thyme
2½ cups chopped ripe fresh or canned tomatoes
 Salt (very little) and freshly ground pepper
1 cup uncooked rice
2 cups dry white wine
 Tabasco to taste
1 cup heavy cream
2 cups milk

1. Open the clams or have them opened, but reserve all the meat and all the juice. There should be about one and one-half cups of raw clam meat and three cups of clam juice. If fresh clams are not available, use that quantity of canned clams, but add them where indicated in the recipe.

2. Melt the butter in a large saucepan and add the onion, saffron, garlic, and thyme. Cook until the onions are wilted and add the fresh clams. If canned clams are used, do not add until later. Cook, stirring, about five minutes, then add the tomatoes and salt and pepper to taste.

3. Add the rice, fresh or canned clam juice, wine, and Tabasco to taste. Simmer forty-five minutes. If canned clams are used, add them now and bring to a boil.

4. Put the mixture through a food mill, pressing through as much of the solids as possible.

5. Transfer the soup, a little at a time, to an electric blender and blend until smooth. When the soup is blended, return to a saucepan and add the remaining ingredients and salt to taste. Serve piping hot or very cold. Thin the soup, if desired, with more milk or cream. Serve with a peppermill.

Lobster Bisque

12 or more servings

2 to 4 live lobsters (about 4 pounds)
2 tablespoons oil
3 tablespoons butter
1 cup finely chopped celery
1 cup finely chopped carrots
1 cup finely chopped onion
1 sprig thyme or ½ teaspoon dried thyme
1 bay leaf
3 cloves garlic, chopped
2 cups tomatoes, cored and quartered
1 cup dry white wine
4 cups Chicken Stock (page 115)
1 cup uncooked rice
 Cognac
1 6-ounce can tomato paste
 Salt and freshly ground pepper to taste
 Tabasco or cayenne pepper to taste
2 cups heavy cream

1. Kill each lobster by plunging a knife into the place where body and tail meet. Break off the tail and leave it whole, with the shell on. Cut the carcass (the main body) into quarters, discarding the tough sac near the eyes. Reserve the coral and liver for later use. Crack the claws.

2. Heat the oil and butter in a large kettle and add the lobster tails, claws, and carcasses.

3. Add the celery, carrots, onion, thyme, bay leaf, garlic, tomatoes, wine, stock, and rice. Bring to a boil and add three tablespoons Cognac. Stir in the tomato paste and cook forty-five minutes.

4. Remove the claws and tail sections from the soup. Set aside one of the tails. (Refrigerate the claws and other tails for salads or sandwiches.)

5. Put the stew mixture, with the carcasses, into a food mill. Do not use a blender. Push through the soup liquid, as much of the soft ingredients and as much liquid as can be extracted from the solids.

6. Put the extracted material, a little at a time, into an electric blender and blend until smooth, then pour into a kettle or large saucepan and season to taste with salt and pepper and Tabasco. Put the coral and liver through a sieve and add to the soup. Add the cream and bring to a boil.

7. Remove the shell from the reserved tail and cut the tail meat into tiny cubes. Add to the bisque. Add another tablespoon of Cognac, if desired. Serve very hot or cold.

Clam Soup French Style

8 or more servings

80 littleneck clams, the smaller the better
¼ cup butter
1 large onion, finely chopped
4 shallots, finely chopped
1 clove garlic, finely minced
1 teaspoon finely chopped fresh thyme or ½ teaspoon dried thyme
1 tablespoon finely chopped fresh tarragon or 1 teaspoon dried tarragon
2 tablespoons all-purpose flour
1 bottle dry white wine
2 cups heavy cream
2 egg yolks
 Salt and freshly ground black pepper to taste
 Tabasco to taste
 Chopped chives

1. Rinse the clams under cold running water to remove all traces of sand from the shells.

2. Heat the butter in a large soup kettle and simmer the onion, shallots, and garlic, stirring, until the onion is wilted. Sprinkle with the thyme, tarragon, and flour.

3. Add the wine, stirring constantly with a whisk. Simmer five minutes and add the clams. Cover and cook, stirring with a wooden spoon and shaking the kettle occasionally, until the clams open, five to ten minutes.

4. Add half the cream and stir. Blend the remaining cream with the egg yolks and stir into the soup. Cook over low heat almost to the boiling point; do not let the soup boil or it may curdle. Taste to determine if the soup needs salt. If so, add it to taste, and add pepper and Tabasco to taste. Serve in hot soup bowls, with a sprinkling of chopped chives on top of each serving.

Billi Bi

(Cream of Mussel Soup)

About 6 servings

Strain the cooking liquid from Moules Marinière (page 154) into a saucepan and cook until it is reduced by half. When reduced, measure the liquid. For each quart of cooking liquid add one cup of heavy cream and bring to a boil. Meanwhile, beat five egg yolks and stir in a little of the hot soup. Return this mixture to the soup, stirring constantly without boiling. Bring just to a boil, but do not boil or the soup will curdle. Add a teaspoon of lemon juice and salt and pepper to taste.

Cream of Turtle Soup

6 servings

1 can (1 pound 4 ounces) turtle soup
1½ cups heavy cream
4 egg yolks, lightly beaten
   Nutmeg

1. Empty the turtle soup into a saucepan and bring to a boil.
2. Blend the cream and egg yolks and beat lightly. Stir a little of the hot soup into the yolk mixture, then add to the soup, stirring constantly with a wooden spoon. Cook over very low heat, without boiling, until the soup coats the spoon. Do not boil or the soup will curdle. Serve sprinkled with nutmeg to taste.

Cream of Carrot Soup

4 to 6 servings

8 carrots, scraped and sliced
2 ribs celery, chopped
1 small bay leaf
3 cups Chicken Stock (page 115)
  Salt and freshly ground black pepper
½ cup heavy cream
1 egg yolk, beaten

1. Combine the carrots, celery, bay leaf, chicken stock, and salt and pepper to taste in a saucepan. Bring to a boil and simmer until the carrots are tender. Do not overcook. Remove the bay leaf.

2. Force the mixture through a food mill or puree in an electric blender. Return the mixture to the saucepan and bring to a boil. Remove from the heat and add the heavy cream and egg yolk. Reheat, but do not boil. Serve immediately.

Crème Saint-Jacques

4 to 6 servings

1 pound fresh bay or sea scallops
2 cups dry white wine
2 tablespoons finely chopped shallots
4 sprigs parsley
3 tablespoons butter
¼ teaspoon cayenne pepper
6 mushrooms, coarsely chopped
  Salt and freshly ground black pepper
1 cup heavy cream
3 egg yolks, lightly beaten

1. If bay scallops are used, leave them whole. If sea scallops are used, cut them in half or quarters.

2. Combine the scallops with the wine, shallots, parsley, butter, cayenne, mushrooms, and salt and pepper to taste. Bring to a boil and simmer five minutes. Strain and reserve both the liquid and the scallops. If desired, the scallops may be chilled and mixed with mayonnaise and capers to make a first course. Return the liquid to the simmer.

3. Combine the cream and egg yolks. Add to the liquid in the pan and stir rapidly with a whisk. Do not boil but cook slowly until the soup is thickened slightly. Serve piping hot.

Leek and Potato Soup

4 or more servings

2 large leeks
1 medium onion, finely chopped
3 tablespoons butter
2 medium potatoes, peeled and cut into ½-inch cubes
3 cups Chicken Stock (page 115)
1 cup heavy cream
  Salt and freshly ground black pepper
  Chopped chives (optional)

1. Trim the root end of the leeks, then cut off and discard approximately half of the green stems. Slit the leeks several times lengthwise from the stem and rinse well under cold water. Some leeks are rather sandy. Chop the leeks and cook them with the onion in the butter. Cook three minutes, stirring.

2. Add the potatoes and stock and bring to a boil. Simmer about fifteen minutes, or until the potatoes are tender. Add the cream and bring just to a boil. Season with salt and pepper to taste and serve hot, sprinkled with chopped chives, if desired.

Onion Soup Gratinée

4 to 6 servings

2 large Bermuda onions
3 tablespoons butter
1 clove garlic, finely minced
  Salt and freshly ground black pepper
1 tablespoon all-purpose flour
6 cups Chicken Stock (page 115) or Beef Stock (page 115)
¼ bay leaf
¼ teaspoon dried thyme
10 to 12 slices French bread, each ¾- to 1-inch thick
½ cup grated Gruyère or Swiss cheese

1. Peel the onions, cut each in half, and slice thinly.

2. Heat the butter in a kettle and add the onions and garlic. Sprinkle with salt and pepper to taste and cook, stirring, about fifteen minutes, or until the onions are golden brown.

3. Sprinkle the onions with the flour and cook, stirring, three minutes. Pour in the liquid and add the bay leaf and thyme. Cover and simmer thirty to forty minutes.

4. Meanwhile, preheat the oven to 500 degrees. Arrange the bread on a baking sheet and bake, turning the slices once or twice so that they toast evenly.

5. Pour the hot soup into a one-and-one-half-quart ovenproof earthenware casserole or into four individual casseroles. The soup should come nearly to the top of the utensils. Float the toast on the soup and sprinkle with the cheese.

6. Place the casseroles in the oven in a foil-lined baking dish to catch the drippings. Bake until the soup is piping hot and the cheese is melted and golden brown on top.

Onion Soup Chablisienne

6 to 8 servings

5 tablespoons butter
1 clove garlic, finely minced
4 cups finely chopped onion
⅓ cup all-purpose flour
4 cups Chicken Stock (page 115) or Beef Stock (page 115)
1 cup dry white wine
  Salt and freshly ground black pepper

1. Melt three tablespoons of the butter in a saucepan and add the garlic and onion. Cook, stirring, until the onion is golden brown and starts to darken.

2. Sprinkle with the flour and stir in the stock, using a wire whisk. Add the wine and simmer fifteen minutes, stirring occasionally. Add salt and pepper to taste. Remove the soup from the heat and swirl in the remaining butter by rotating the pan gently. Serve immediately.

Onion Soup, Lyonnaise Style

4 to 6 servings

This soup, specifically from the Lyonnais region, is a marvelous winter dish that is served in France when you go out at night— "on the town," as Americans say. Around four or five o'clock in the morning, it is a sort of custom for everybody to eat la gratinée.

2 tablespoons butter
1 large onion, sliced very thin
3 cups Beef Stock (page 115) or Chicken Stock (page 115)
    Salt and freshly ground white pepper
4 slices of firm-textured bread, toasted
¾ cup grated Gruyère cheese
3 egg yolks
¾ cup port wine

1. Preheat the oven to 400 degrees.

2. Melt the butter in a large saucepan, add the onion, and sauté for ten to fifteen minutes, or until lightly browned. Add the broth and salt and pepper to taste and bring to a boil; cook for ten minutes.

3. Meanwhile, cut each slice of toasted bread into eight squares. Place one-third of the toast squares in the bottom of a soup tureen (any capacious, ovenproof casserole handsome enough to go to the table will do). Sprinkle with some of the cheese, add more toast, then more cheese, saving enough to sprinkle over the top of the soup.

4. Fill the tureen with the hot soup, then sprinkle the remaining cheese on top. Place in the oven for twenty-five minutes.

5. Bring the gratinée to the table. In front of the guests, combine the yolks with the port wine in a deep soup plate and whip very hard with a fork. With a ladle, make a "hole" in the gratinée, pour in the port mixture, and fold with a ladle into the soup.

Pumpkin Soup

About 8 servings

7 tablespoons butter
6 green onions, chopped
1 onion, sliced
2½ pounds diced pumpkin or 3 cups pumpkin puree, homemade or canned
6 cups Chicken Stock (page 115)
½ teaspoon salt
3 tablespoons all-purpose flour
1 cup light cream
    Croutons (page 129)
    Lightly salted whipped cream

1. Melt four tablespoons of the butter in a large saucepan. Sauté the green onions and onion until soft and golden.

2. Add the pumpkin, chicken stock, and salt. Bring to a boil, stirring, then simmer until the pumpkin is soft, or ten minutes if the puree is used. Rub the soup through a fine sieve, or strain, if the puree has been used. Return the soup to the pan.

3. Knead the flour with two tablespoons of the butter and gradually add to the soup while beating with a whisk. Bring the soup to a boil, whisking until it thickens. Correct the seasoning, then add the light cream and remaining tablespoon of butter.

4. Serve garnished with the croutons and whipped cream.

Cream of Spinach Soup I

8 servings

½ pound fresh spinach, stems removed
6 tablespoons butter
1 cup chopped onion
4 medium potatoes, peeled and quartered (about 3 cups)
2 cups Chicken Stock (page 115)
2 cups water
Salt and freshly ground black pepper
1 cup heavy cream

1. Rinse the spinach and shred it with a knife.
2. Heat four tablespoons of the butter in a large saucepan and cook the onion until wilted. Add the spinach, potatoes, stock, and water and cook until the potatoes are tender, about twenty-five minutes.
3. Put the soup through a sieve; season with salt and pepper to taste and stir in the cream. Bring to a boil. Remove the sauce from heat and swirl in the remaining butter by rotating the pan gently. Serve immediately.

Cream of Spinach Soup II

4 to 6 servings

2 tablespoons butter
½ cup chopped onion
2 tablespoons all-purpose flour
3 cups Chicken Stock (page 115)
2 cups coarsely chopped, well-rinsed fresh spinach
⅓ cup heavy cream
Salt and freshly ground black pepper
3 egg yolks

1. Melt the butter in a saucepan and add the onion. Cook until the onion is translucent.

Stir in the flour, using a wire whisk. When blended, add the chicken stock, stirring vigorously with the whisk. Bring to a boil.
2. When the soup is thickened and smooth, add the spinach and cook briefly. Stir in the cream and add salt and pepper to taste.
3. Beat the yolks lightly in a mixing bowl. Add a little of the hot mixture to the yolks, then return to the saucepan while stirring. Cook briefly but do not let the soup boil, or the yolks might curdle. Serve hot.

Cream of Sorrel or Watercress Soup

8 servings

¼ pound fresh sorrel or 1 bunch watercress
6 tablespoons butter
1 cup chopped onion
4 medium potatoes, peeled and quartered (about 3 cups)
2 cups Chicken Stock (page 115) or canned chicken broth
2 cups water
1 cup heavy cream

1. Rinse the sorrel or watercress. Reserve about twenty leaves without stems for garnish. Shred with a knife and set aside.
2. Pick over the remaining sorrel or watercress and chop off any tough stems.
3. Heat four tablespoons of the butter in a large saucepan and cook the onion until wilted. Add the whole sorrel or watercress and the potatoes. Add the chicken stock and water and bring to a boil. Cook until the potatoes are quite tender. Put the soup through a sieve or food mill, return to the saucepan, and stir in the cream. Bring to a boil, then remove from the heat and add the shredded leaves and the remaining butter. Serve immediately.

Galantine of duck (France

Tomato Soup

8 servings

Within the past two decades there has been an outbreak of fascinating foreign soups to tempt native palates—everything from gazpacho (cold chopped vegetables with oil and garlic) to senegalese (cold curried chicken). But there is probably nothing more tempting than a plate of old-fashioned, homemade tomato soup. It's good hot. It's good cold. And with or without croutons.

¾ cup butter
2 tablespoons olive oil
1 large onion, thinly sliced (about 2 cups)
2 sprigs fresh thyme or ½ teaspoon dried thyme
4 basil leaves, chopped, or ½ teaspoon dried basil
Salt and freshly ground pepper to taste
2½ pounds fresh, ripe tomatoes, cored, or 1 2-pound 3-ounce can tomatoes, preferably the imported Italian style
3 tablespoons tomato paste
¼ cup all-purpose flour
3¾ cups Chicken Stock (page 115) or canned chicken broth
1 teaspoon granulated sugar
1 cup heavy cream
Croutons (see below) for garnish (optional)

1. Heat one-half cup of the butter in a kettle and add the olive oil. Add the onion, thyme, basil, salt, and pepper. Cook, stirring occasionally, until the onion is wilted.

2. Add the tomatoes and tomato paste and stir to blend. Simmer ten minutes.

3. Place the flour in a small mixing bowl and add about five tablespoons of the stock, stirring to blend. Stir this into the tomato mixture. Add the remaining chicken stock and simmer thirty minutes, stirring frequently all over the bottom of the kettle to make certain that the soup does not stick, scorch, or burn.

4. Put the soup through the finest sieve or food mill possible. Return it to the heat and add the sugar and cream. Simmer, stirring occasionally, about five minutes. Add the remaining butter, swirling it around in the soup. Top each portion with a crouton, if desired, and serve.

CROUTONS:

8 servings

8 slices crusty, day-old French or Italian bread
1 large clove garlic, split
8 teaspoons olive oil, approximately

1. Preheat the oven to 400 degrees.

2. Rub the bread slices on both sides with the garlic, then brush generously with the olive oil. Place the bread on a rack or baking sheet and bake until golden, turning once if necessary.

ïoli, the famous garlic dish of Provence

Curried Tomato Bisque

About 12 servings

2 tablespoons butter
1½ cups chopped onion
1½ cloves garlic, finely minced
2 tablespoons Curry Powder (page 33)
5 cups cored, quartered ripe tomatoes (or 10 cups cherry tomatoes)
½ bay leaf
1 sprig fresh thyme or ½ teaspoon dried thyme
½ cup uncooked rice
2 cups Chicken Stock (page 115)
Tabasco to taste
Salt and freshly ground pepper to taste
2 cups cold milk
1 cup heavy cream

1. Heat the butter in a kettle and add the onion and garlic. Cook, stirring frequently, until the onion wilts. Sprinkle with the curry powder and cook about three minutes longer, stirring.

2. Add the tomatoes, bay leaf, thyme, rice, chicken stock, Tabasco to taste, and salt and pepper. Partly cover and simmer forty-five minutes.

3. Put the mixture through a food mill, extracting as many solids as possible, then put in the container of an electric blender and blend. Pour the soup into a bowl, add the milk and cream, and stir to blend well. Heat to a boil and serve hot, or chill thoroughly and serve cold.

Striped Bass Mayonnaise

40 to 60 servings

3 striped bass (about 5 pounds each)
4 leeks, trimmed, split, well rinsed, and cut into 1-inch cubes
4 onions, coarsely chopped
6 carrots, scraped and cut into rounds
4 bay leaves
4 sprigs fresh thyme or ½ teaspoon dried thyme
2 tablespoons peppercorns
4 whole cloves garlic, peeled
2 bottles dry white wine
Salt
4 cups Mayonnaise (page 265)
2 cloves garlic, finely minced
¾ cup finely chopped shallots or green onion
2 tablespoons finely chopped parsley
1 tablespoon chopped thyme
Freshly ground black pepper
Tabasco
1 tablespoon vinegar, or to taste
1 quart steamed, diced potatoes

1. Wipe the bass inside and out with a damp cloth.

2. In a fish cooker or other utensil large enough to hold the fish, place the leeks, chopped onions, carrots, bay leaves, thyme sprigs, peppercorns, whole garlic cloves, wine, and salt to taste. Add enough water to cover the fish, but do not add the fish. Bring the liquid to a boil and simmer the court bouillon ten minutes.

3. Place the three fish on the rack of a fish cooker or in a cheesecloth sling. Lower them into the court bouillon and simmer exactly twenty minutes. Let the fish cool in the broth. Remove the fish; remove the skin and bones and flake the flesh.

4. Combine the flaked fish with the remaining ingredients and pile the mixture on a platter.

Striped Bass au Vin Blanc

6 servings

Although cooking fish in red wine is by no means a rarity in French cuisine (many sole and eel dishes rely on red wine), fish and white wine enjoy a natural affinity. One of the classic combinations of the two is in striped bass au vin blanc, for which a recipe is given below.

    1   striped bass (5 pounds)
    1¼ cups Fish Stock (page 116)
    9   tablespoons butter
    2   tablespoons finely chopped shallots or
        white onion
        Salt and freshly ground pepper
    ½   cup dry white wine
    2   tablespoons all-purpose flour
    1   cup heavy cream
    2   egg yolks
    ¼   cup water
        Juice of ½ lemon
        Cayenne pepper

1. Have the fish cut into two fillets. Reserve both the fillets, plus the bones, head, and tail.

2. Prepare the fish stock, using the reserved bones, head, and tail.

3. Preheat the oven to 450 degrees.

4. Generously butter (using about two tablespoons of butter) a baking dish large enough to hold the fish fillets. Sprinkle the dish with the shallots, salt, and pepper.

5. Arrange the fish fillets, skin side down, on the prepared dish and dot with two tablespoons butter. Pour half a cup of fish stock and the wine over the fish. Cover with aluminum foil and bake ten to fifteen minutes, or until the fish flakes easily when tested with a fork. Do not overcook.

6. Meanwhile, melt two tablespoons of butter in a saucepan and stir in the flour. When blended, add the remaining fish stock, stirring vigorously with a whisk. When blended and smooth, continue simmering, stirring occasionally, about ten minutes longer.

7. Carefully and gently pour the cooking liquid from the fish into a saucepan. Keep the fish warm and covered. Boil the liquid over high heat until it is reduced about half. Add this to the sauce in the other saucepan, stirring to blend. Stir in the cream and bring to a boil. Keep hot.

8. Place the egg yolks in a small saucepan and start beating vigorously with a whisk. Add the water and cook over very low heat, beating constantly as if making a Hollandaise. Beat in the lemon juice and, when the mixture is saucelike, remove from the heat. Do not overcook or the egg yolks will curdle. Off the heat, beat in three tablespoons butter. Beat in the fish sauce and add cayenne pepper to taste. Pour this over the fish and run the dish under the broiler until it is golden and lightly glazed.

132   FRANCE

Striped Bass with White Wine

3 or 4 servings

  6 tablespoons butter
½ cup finely chopped onion
  1 carrot, cut into rounds
  2 sprigs parsley
½ bay leaf
½ teaspoon dried thyme
  1 clove garlic, peeled
    Salt
 12 peppercorns
1½ cups dry white wine
½ cup water
  1 striped bass (3 to 4 pounds), cleaned
    and scaled but left whole
  3 tablespoons all-purpose flour
    Juice of 1 lemon or to taste

1. Use three tablespoons of the butter to grease a large fish cooker or Dutch oven. Add the vegetables, parsley, bay leaf, thyme, garlic, salt to taste, peppercorns, wine, and water. Bring the liquid to a boil and place the fish in it. Cover and simmer fifteen to eighteen minutes, or until the fish flakes easily when tested with a fork.

2. Very gently transfer the fish to a serving platter. Strain the cooking liquid into a saucepan and knead together the remaining butter and the flour. Bring the liquid to a boil and add the butter-flour mixture bit by bit, stirring constantly. When thickened and smooth, add the lemon juice. Serve the sauce with the fish.

Baked Bluefish with Rosemary

6 servings

  1 bluefish (4 pounds)
    Salt and freshly ground black pepper
  1 teaspoon chopped fresh rosemary
½ cup butter
  1 tablespoon wine vinegar
    Lemon slices

1. Preheat the oven to 400 degrees.

2. Thoroughly clean and scale the fish, but leave the head and tail intact. Rinse the fish under cold water and pat dry with paper towels. Sprinkle the fish inside and out with salt and pepper.

3. Place the fish in a baking dish and sprinkle the rosemary around the fish. Dot the fish generously with butter.

4. Bake the fish, basting every three minutes or so. When the fish flakes easily when tested with a fork, transfer to a hot serving platter.

5. Add the vinegar to the baking dish, heat thoroughly, and pour the pan drippings over the fish. Garnish with lemon slices and serve with boiled potatoes.

Aïoli

More than one sage has noted that where people eat garlic, happiness abounds. No region is better known for its garlic specialties than that sun-filled area of France called Provence. There, in the heart of the Midi, the most famous garlic dish is aïoli (*pronounced approximately* eye-oh-LEE, *and sometimes spelled* ailloli) *which is also the name of the sauce that accompanies it. Sauce* aïoli *is much like a mayonnaise except for the garlic essence—it contains from six to twelve cloves. Or more. A complete* aïoli *consists of an assortment of good things—such as poached cod, cauliflower, potatoes, artichokes, tomatoes, chick-peas, hard-cooked eggs, carrots, maybe even snails—arranged on a large platter, with the sauce on the side.*

AÏOLI SAUCE:

About 2½ cups

- 6 to 12 cloves garlic, peeled and finely minced
- 4 egg yolks
- 1 tablespoon rapidly boiling water
- ½ tablespoon or more salt
  Freshly ground pepper to taste
- 1¼ cups peanut oil
- 1 cup olive oil
- 1 tablespoon or more lemon juice

Place the garlic in a large mixing bowl and add the egg yolks. Start beating with a wire whisk, a rotary beater, or an electric mixer. Add the rapidly boiling water, salt, and pepper, then add the peanut oil, drop by drop, until more than half of it is added. The peanut oil and olive oil may then be added in increasing quantities. Beat in the lemon juice. Serve with the cod, vegetables, and other components of the dish (see the following recipes).

COD FOR AÏOLI:

6 servings

2½ pounds salt cod, cut into 6 serving pieces
4 cloves

1. Place the cod in a large mixing bowl and add cold water to cover. Drain the cod frequently and add more water to cover. Soak for at least twenty-four hours.
2. When ready to cook, drain the cod. Place it in one layer, skin side down, in a large stainless steel or aluminum skillet and add cold water to cover. Add the cloves and bring to a boil. Simmer ten to fifteen minutes, depending on the thickness. Do not overcook. Turn off the heat and let stand until ready to serve (immediately or within half an hour). Drain before serving and arrange on a platter surrounded by the vegetables and other components of the dish. Serve with the aïoli sauce.

ARTICHOKES FOR AÏOLI:

6 servings

3 large artichokes
  Lemon
  Salt
¼ cup all-purpose flour

1. Using sharp scissors, cut off the upper parts of the artichoke leaves. Cut off the stems of the artichokes. Cut the artichokes into quarters with a heavy knife and quickly rub all cut surfaces with lemon to prevent discoloration.
2. Drop the artichoke quarters into cold water to cover and add salt to taste. To retain the color of the artichokes, place the flour in a sieve and run cold water through it into the artichoke water. Bring to a boil and simmer thirty minutes, or until the artichokes are crisp and tender. Arrange on the platter with the other components of the dish. Serve hot or lukewarm with the aïoli sauce.

CARROTS FOR AÏOLI:

6 servings

Scrape carrots and trim them. Cut them into quarters or olive shapes or leave them whole. Cook in boiling salted water until tender but still firm. Drain and arrange on the platter with the other components of the dish. Serve with the aïoli sauce.

CAULIFLOWER FOR AÏOLI:

6 servings

1 firm, unblemished cauliflower
  Salt
¼ cup all-purpose flour

1. Break the cauliflower into flowerets (individual segments).
2. Place the flowerets in a large saucepan and add salted water to cover. Put the flour in a sieve and let cold water run through it into the saucepan. This will keep the cauliflower white.
3. Bring to a boil and simmer until the cauliflower is crisp and tender, about fifteen minutes. Drain and arrange on a platter with the other components of the dish. Serve hot or lukewarm, with the aïoli sauce.

CHICK-PEAS FOR AÏOLI:

About 1½ cups

½ pound dried chick-peas
1 bay leaf
  Salt to taste

1. Place the chick-peas in a bowl and add cold water to cover. Soak overnight.
2. Drain the chick-peas and put them in a saucepan. Add cold water to cover them to a depth of one inch. Add the bay leaf and salt and bring to a boil. Simmer one and one-half hours, or until tender. Drain and arrange on a platter with the other components of the dish. Serve hot or lukewarm, with the aïoli sauce.

POTATOES FOR AÏOLI:

6 servings

Peel six small potatoes and cook them until tender in boiling salted water. Drain and arrange them while still hot on the platter with the other components of the dish. Serve with the aïoli sauce.

TOMATOES FOR AÏOLI:

6 servings

Remove the core from three medium tomatoes. Cut them into quarters and arrange them on the platter with the other components of the dish. Serve with the aïoli sauce.

HARD-COOKED EGGS FOR AÏOLI:

6 servings

Place six eggs in a saucepan and add cold water to cover. Bring to a boil, then reduce the heat and simmer twelve to fifteen minutes. Immediately plunge the eggs into cold water to facilitate peeling. Chill the eggs and peel them. Halve or quarter the eggs and arrange them on the platter with the other components of the dish. Serve with the aïoli sauce.

SNAILS FOR AÏOLI:

6 servings

1 can snails (about 18 snails) with their liquid
1 bay leaf
2 sprigs fresh thyme or ¼ teaspoon dried thyme

Combine all the ingredients in a saucepan and simmer about two minutes. Drain and arrange on the platter with the other components of the dish. Serve with the aïoli sauce.

Brandade de Morue

About 6 cups or 10 to 12 buffet servings

"Tell me what you eat," Brillat-Savarin advised, "and I shall tell you what you are." He might have added, "And where you come from." New Yorkers consume thousands of pounds of salt cod each year, but those who really dote on it are generally from Latin countries, especially those that border the Mediterranean. One of the best salt cod dishes is a specialty of Provence, brandade de morue. *It has the robust taste of the salt cod and the pungency of garlic. Serve it with a cold white wine, a chilled rosé, champagne, or beer.*

  1 Idaho potato (½ pound, approximately)
1½ pounds salt cod, soaked 24 hours in cold
      water to cover
  ½ cup milk
  1 small onion, sliced
  2 cloves
1½ cups salad oil (or olive oil, if you prefer
      a stronger flavor)
  1 cup heavy cream
  3 large cloves garlic, finely minced
      Freshly ground pepper to taste
      Cayenne pepper to taste
      Crouton Triangles (see below, optional)
      Chopped truffles (optional)

1. Preheat the oven to 400 degrees and bake the potato until tender, forty-five minutes or longer.

2. Cut the soaked cod into three or four large pieces and place it in a skillet. Add the milk, onion, cloves, and enough water to cover the cod generously. Bring the liquid just to a boil, then simmer gently about ten minutes. Drain the cod and flake it. There should be about four cups.

3. Place the oil in one small saucepan and the cream in another. Heat both thoroughly without boiling.

4. Meanwhile, heat the bowl of an electric mixer with hot water. Drain and wipe dry.

5. Scoop out the flesh of the hot potato and add it to the mixer bowl. Start beating and gradually add the flaked cod and garlic. Continue beating and add the hot oil and hot cream simultaneously. These may be added in fairly generous amounts.

6. When all the oil and cream have been beaten, season to taste with pepper and cayenne. To serve, mound the brandade in the center of a serving plate. Arrange the crouton triangles around the base of the cod and sprinkle the chopped truffles over all. Serve lukewarm or cold, as a buffet course or appetizer.

CROUTON TRIANGLES:

Preheat the oven to 350 degrees. Trim the crusts from several slices of bread and cut the slices into small triangles, about one and one-half inches to each side. Generously brush the triangles with butter and place them, buttered side up, on a baking dish. Bake until golden brown on top. Turn the triangles over and bake until golden brown. Take care that the triangles do not become too brown or burn.

Finnan Haddie à la Crème

4 servings

1½ pounds thick, boneless finnan haddie
2 cups milk
2 sprigs fresh thyme or ½ teaspoon dried thyme
1 bay leaf
1 small onion, thinly sliced
3 tablespoons butter
¼ cup all-purpose flour
¼ cup heavy cream
¼ teaspoon nutmeg
Salt to taste
2 hard-cooked eggs, sliced
Freshly made toast
Freshly ground pepper

1. Place the fish in a flameproof baking dish and add the milk, thyme, bay leaf, and onion. Let stand one hour, then place the dish on the stove. Simmer over low heat about ten minutes, or until the fish flakes easily. Drain the fish, reserving the cooking liquid.

2. Flake the fish and set it aside.

3. Heat the butter in a saucepan and stir in the flour. When blended, add the cream and reserved cooking liquid, stirring vigorously with a wire whisk. When thickened and smooth, add the nutmeg and salt. Stir in the flaked fish and fold in the eggs. Serve on toast, with a pepper mill or freshly ground pepper on the side.

Mackerel au Vin Blanc

5 to 10 servings

3 cups thinly sliced onions
2 cloves garlic, thinly sliced
3 sprigs fresh thyme or ½ teaspoon dried thyme
1 teaspoon whole peppercorns
1 teaspoon salt
1 teaspoon vegetable oil
¼ cup white vinegar
Dry white wine
2 bay leaves
2 sprigs parsley
2 large carrots, scraped and cut into ¼-inch rounds
5 large mackerel, filleted
1 large lemon, thinly sliced (slices should be almost transparent)
4 small, dried hot red peppers

1. Preheat the oven to 350 degrees.

2. Combine the onions, garlic, thyme, peppercorns, salt, and vegetable oil in a large saucepan. Cook, stirring occasionally, about five minutes. Add the vinegar, one-half cup wine, bay leaves, parsley, and carrots and cook twenty minutes.

3. Carefully remove any bones that may remain in the fish fillets. Lightly oil a pan large enough to hold the fillets in a single layer and place the fillets in the pan, skin side down. Neatly arrange the lemon slices and the cooked carrot rounds over the fish. Pour the hot wine and vinegar mixture, including the vegetables, over the fish.

4. Add enough additional white wine so that the fish is lightly covered with liquid. Scatter the hot red peppers over the fish and cover the pan with aluminum foil. Place the pan on top of the stove and bring the liquid to a boil. Transfer the pan to the oven and bake twenty minutes. Let cool before serving.

Soused Mackerel

4 to 6 servings

1 carrot, thinly sliced
1 onion, thinly sliced
1 sprig parsley
1 strip of lemon peel
1 bay leaf
12 peppercorns
1 blade of mace
    Salt and freshly ground black pepper to taste
    Equal parts of white wine and vinegar, or 1 part water and 3 parts vinegar (enough to cover the fish)
1 large or 2 small mackerel, split and cleaned, boned or left whole

1. Combine the carrot, onion, parsley, lemon peel, bay leaf, peppercorns, mace, salt and pepper, and the liquid. Bring to a boil, then simmer for ten minutes and let cool.

2. Arrange the mackerel in an enamelware or stainless steel skillet and pour the liquid over. Bring to a boil, then cook the fish as gently as possible for ten to fifteen minutes, or until done.

3. Let cool in the liquid, then refrigerate until ready to serve.

Quenelles de Brochet

8 quenelles

The American palate has come a long, long way since World War II, when "something different" for dinner almost invariably meant a curry of chicken or shrimp with peanuts and chutney on the side. The public has explored the pleasures of paella (now a bit passé), sukiyaki, cassoulet and various quiches (principally quiche Lorraine) and beef Wellington. One of the most sophisticated of these delights and one that has become increasingly popular within the last few years is quenelles (pronounced kuh-nelles) of pike. These are poached morsels of ground fish similar in texture to a mousse and served with various sauces. Below is a recently devised blender version of this elegant dish of classic French cookery.

2 pike (about 1½ pounds each)
2 eggs, separated
½ cup all-purpose flour
¼ teaspoon nutmeg
    Salt and freshly ground pepper to taste
3 tablespoons melted butter
½ cup milk
1 cup heavy cream
4 cups boiling salted water

1. In making this dish it is important that all the ingredients be quite cold before they are put together.

2. Have the fish man bone and fillet the pike. (Reserve the bones and skin for stock.) Keep the fish, bones, and skin refrigerated until ready to use. There should be about one and one-half pounds of fish fillets.

3. Combine the egg yolks, flour, half the nutmeg, salt, and pepper in a saucepan and stir rapidly with a whisk. While stirring, add

the melted butter. Bring the milk just to a boil and beat it in with the whisk. Continue stirring and cooking rapidly until the mixture pulls away from the sides of the saucepan. Let cool. This mixture is called a "panade." Cover and refrigerate until quite cold, or put the mixture in the freezer, but do not let it freeze.

4. Place each fish fillet on a flat surface. Trim away and discard the tiny fish line down the center of each. Cut the remainder of the fillets into two-inch lengths and add, a few at a time, to the container of an electric blender. Continue blending, stirring down with a rubber spatula until all the fish is blended. As the fish is blended, transfer it to the bowl of an electric mixer.

5. Season the fish with salt, pepper, and the remaining nutmeg and beat well on medium-low speed. Continue beating while adding the panade, a little at a time. When this is well blended, add the egg whites, a little at a time. Beat the cream in gradually.

6. Butter a large, deep pan (about 17¼ x 11¾ x 2¼ inches). Using two large dessert spoons dipped into the hot water, shape the quenelles into oval, rounded shapes. They should resemble large duck eggs. As they are shaped, arrange them neatly on the buttered pan. Dip the spoons into the hot water between shaping each quenelle.

7. Butter a large length of waxed paper and place it, buttered side down, over the quenelles. Pour the water on top of the waxed paper, letting the water flow outward into the pan. Bring to a boil on top of the stove and simmer five to ten minutes. Drain and serve with hot Mushroom Sauce (see below), or serve gratinéed (see note).

Note: To gratinée the quenelles, cover with the mushroom sauce and sprinkle with equal parts of grated Parmesan and Swiss cheese. Bake fifteen minutes in a 400-degree oven, or until hot through, then run under the broiler until brown.

MUSHROOM SAUCE:

About 2 cups

3 tablespoons butter
¼ cup all-purpose flour
1½ cups Fish Stock (page 116)
¼ pound mushrooms, thinly sliced
   Salt and freshly ground pepper to taste
1 tablespoon finely chopped shallots
½ cup dry white wine
¾ cup heavy cream

1. Heat two tablespoons of the butter in a saucepan and stir in the flour with a whisk. When blended, add the fish stock, stirring rapidly with the whisk. When the mixture is blended and smooth, cook over low heat, stirring frequently, about twenty minutes.

2. Heat the remaining butter in a skillet and add the mushrooms, salt, and pepper. When the mushrooms are wilted, add the shallots and wine. Simmer over medium-high heat until the wine is almost evaporated. Stir in the fish sauce and cook, stirring frequently, over medium heat about thirty minutes. Stir in the heavy cream and bring to a boil. Cook about five minutes longer.

Sole Judic

8 servings

The French tend to view lettuce as a nice bit of trivia to be dressed with oil and vinegar or braised or—sometimes—used in a dish with a difference like sole Judic, the recipe given here. (No one knows the origin of the name, but gastronomists speculate that it may —for some inexplicable reason—be related to judicial reform.)

1 large head Boston lettuce
8 small fillets of sole or flounder
1 pound fresh mushrooms
15 tablespoons butter
2 tablespoons finely chopped shallots
1 lemon
　Salt and freshly ground pepper to taste
1 cup dry white wine
2 cups heavy cream
1 tablespoon all-purpose flour

1. Preheat the oven to 375 degrees.

2. Place the lettuce in a large saucepan and soak it about fifteen minutes in cold water to cover. Drain. Return the lettuce, core up, to the saucepan and add water barely to cover. Bring to a boil, then simmer about five minutes. Drain and squeeze the lettuce lightly between the hands. Carefully pull off sixteen of the largest leaves for wrapping the fish fillets.

3. Place the fish fillets on a flat surface. You will note that there is a small line of tiny bones down the center of each. Run a knife along either side and remove it. Push the two halves of each fillet back together to reshape them as they were.

4. Put the mushrooms through a meat grinder, using the fine blade. Put the ground mushrooms in a length of cheesecloth and squeeze to extract most of the mushroom liquid.

5. Melt two tablespoons of the butter in a saucepan and add half of the chopped shallots and the squeezed-out mushrooms. Cook, stirring, and add the juice of half a lemon and salt and pepper to taste. Cook, stirring, until the mixture is fairly dry. This is called a "duxelles." Chill thoroughly.

6. Sprinkle the fish fillets with salt and pepper. Spoon equal portions of the duxelles onto the center of each fillet and roll the fillets lengthwise, jelly-roll fashion, to form "paupiettes."

7. Place a leaf of lettuce on a flat surface and cover with another leaf (with the stem ends facing out in opposite directions). Add a rolled fillet of sole. Pull up the edges of the lettuce to enclose the fish. Continue until all the rolls of sole are enclosed in lettuce.

8. Use two tablespoons butter to grease the bottom of a metal baking dish. Sprinkle with the remaining shallots, salt, and pepper. Arrange the lettuce-enclosed fish on the baking dish and dot the top of each serving with a tablespoon of butter. Add the wine and bring to a boil on top of the stove. Immediately place the baking dish in the oven and bake fifteen minutes.

9. Remove the baking dish and carefully pour off the liquid from it into a saucepan. Cover the lettuce-enclosed fish with foil to keep warm.

10. Reduce the sauce by cooking over high heat, about five minutes. Add the other juice that has then accumulated in the baking pan. Add the heavy cream and cook five minutes.

11. Blend one tablespoon butter with the flour and add this, bit by bit, to the sauce, stirring. Remove the sauce from the heat, add the juice of half a lemon, and swirl in the remaining butter by rotating the pan gently. Spoon part of the sauce over the fish and serve the remainder separately. Serve with rice.

Sole Monte Carlo

4 servings

It must have taken considerable thought on the part of the chef who created sole Monte Carlo to give it a name. It is the essence of French cooking but with a foundation—pasta —that is Italian. The French have never been much moved by the varieties of pasta except for noodles or a little vermicelli as a garnish for soups. In any event, sole Monte Carlo, which consists of paupiettes or turbans of fish on a bed of spaghetti with a delicate white wine sauce, is a classic.

¼ pound large spaghetti (perciatelloni no. 14, if available)
4 fillets of lemon sole or flounder
    Salt and freshly ground pepper
8 thin slices of raw salmon (about 2 x 4 inches each)
6½ tablespoons butter
1 tablespoon minced shallots
⅓ cup dry white wine
1½ tablespoons all-purpose flour
¾ cup Fish Stock (page 116)
1 cup heavy cream
½ teaspoon lemon juice
2 tablespoons thinly slivered black truffles (optional)

1. Preheat the oven to 425 degrees.

2. Place the spaghetti in a clean cloth and break it into one-and-one-half-inch lengths. There should be about one and one-half cups. Cook according to package directions and rinse under hot water.

3. Place the sole or flounder fillets on a flat surface. Note that there is a line of tiny bones running lengthwise down each. Run a sharp knife down each side of this bone line to remove it and to divide the sole in half. Discard the bone line.

4. Sprinkle the fillets with salt and pepper to taste. Lay one salmon slice on each fillet and roll jelly-roll fashion. Skewer with toothpicks.

5. Grease a heavy skillet or baking dish with one tablespoon of the butter and sprinkle with the shallots. Arrange the rolled fillets in the skillet and dot with two tablespoons of butter. Sprinkle lightly with salt and pepper and pour in the wine. Cover with a greased circle of waxed paper. Bring to a boil on top of the stove, then bake for ten to fifteen minutes. Do not overcook or the fish will become dry.

6. Meanwhile, melt one and one-half tablespoons of butter in a small saucepan and stir in the flour, using a wire whisk. When blended, add the fish stock, stirring rapidly with the whisk. When thickened and smooth, simmer, stirring occasionally, over low heat while the fish cooks.

7. When the fish is done, carefully pour off the cooking liquid from the skillet into a saucepan. Keep the fish warm. Cook the liquid over high heat until the liquid is reduced by half. Stir in the fish sauce, beating with the whisk until smooth. Stir in the cup of cream and simmer briefly. Add salt and pepper to taste, then remove from the heat and swirl in the remaining butter and the lemon juice by rotating the pan gently.

8. Place the spaghetti in a skillet. Note that more liquid will have accumulated around the fish rolls. Pour this into the spaghetti. Heat the spaghetti briefly in the liquid, then add one-quarter cup of sauce. Heat just to a boil, stirring. Spoon the spaghetti into an oval or round dish and arrange the sole over it. Spoon the sauce over the fish and sprinkle with truffle strips. Serve immediately.

Sole with Mushrooms I

6 servings

6 sole fillets
  Salt and freshly ground black pepper
½ pound button mushrooms
⅔ cup butter
  Juice of ½ lemon
3 shallots or green onions, finely chopped
3 tablespoons finely chopped parsley
2 tablespoons finely chopped chives
⅓ cup dry white wine
1½ cups clam juice or Fish Stock (page 116)
3 tablespoons all-purpose flour
1 cup heavy cream

1. Preheat the oven to 400 degrees.
2. Split each sole fillet lengthwise, at the same time removing the line of tiny bones down the center. Sprinkle the fillets on all sides with salt and pepper and roll each like a jelly roll. Secure with food picks.
3. Place the mushrooms in a small saucepan and add two tablespoons of the butter. Add the lemon juice, cover tightly, and steam for five minutes.
4. Rub three tablespoons of the butter over the bottom of a deep skillet with an ovenproof handle. Sprinkle with salt and pepper to taste and the shallots. Arrange the fillets on top. Sprinkle with the parsley and chives and pour the wine and one-half cup of the clam juice over all. Cover tightly with aluminum foil and bring to a boil on top of the stove. Place the skillet in the oven and bake for twenty minutes.
5. Meanwhile, melt three tablespoons of the butter in a saucepan, stir in the flour with a wire whisk, and blend well. Add the remaining clam juice, stirring vigorously with the whisk. When the sauce is thickened and smooth, cook for ten minutes, stirring frequently. Add the mushrooms and mushroom juices.
6. Remove the fish from the oven and immediately turn off the oven heat. Leave the oven door open. Transfer the fish to an oven-proof serving platter, cover with foil and keep warm in the oven.
7. Place the skillet over high heat and reduce the cooking liquids by one third. Add the sauce and the heavy cream, stirring rapidly with a wire whisk. Remove the skillet from the heat and stir in the remaining cold butter. Pour the sauce over the fish and serve immediately.

Sole with Mushrooms II

6 servings

8 small fillets of sole
  Salt and freshly ground pepper to taste
3 cups thinly sliced mushrooms
  Juice of ½ lemon
5 tablespoons butter
4 tablespoons chopped parsley
1 cup dry white wine
1 tablespoon all-purpose flour
½ cup heavy cream

1. Preheat the oven to 400 degrees.
2. Place each fillet of sole on a flat surface. Note that there is a line of tiny bones running down the center of each fillet. Trim this away, and divide the fillets in half, by running a sharp knife along either side of the bones. Sprinkle with salt and pepper.
3. Roll the fillet halves jelly-roll fashion and arrange on a heatproof baking dish. Scatter the mushrooms over and around them and sprinkle with lemon juice. Dot with four tablespoons of the butter and sprinkle with parsley. Pour the wine over all and cover with foil. Bring to a boil on top of the stove, then place in the oven and bake ten to fifteen minutes.
4. Carefully remove the fish to a hot serving dish. Blend the remaining tablespoon of butter with the flour and stir this into the baking juices left in the pan. Add the cream, then bring to a boil and simmer briefly. Season to taste with salt and pepper. Pour the sauce over the fish and serve hot.

Fillets of Sole in Shrimp Sauce

6 servings

2 pounds sole or flounder fillets
6 tablespoons butter
1 tablespoon chopped shallots
  Salt and freshly ground black pepper
3 cups water or equal parts water and dry white wine
¼ cup all-purpose flour
  Juice of 1 lemon
2 egg yolks
¾ cup heavy cream
1½ cups cooked shrimp, shelled and deveined
  Chopped parsley

1. Remove the line of tiny bones down the center of each fillet by running a sharp knife along either side of the bones.

2. Spread the bottom of a large skillet with two tablespoons of the butter. Sprinkle with the chopped shallots and arrange the sole fillets on top. Sprinkle the fish with salt and pepper and add the liquid. Cover with a round of buttered aluminum foil and bring to a boil. Simmer for ten minutes, or until the fish flakes easily when tested with a fork.

3. Remove the fish to a warm platter. Strain the liquid from the skillet and reserve two cups for the sauce.

4. Melt the remaining butter in a saucepan and stir in the flour. Bring the reserved liquid to a boil and add it all at once to the butter-flour mixture, stirring vigorously with a wire whisk. When the mixture is thickened and smooth, stir in the lemon juice.

5. Lightly beat the egg yolks and add them to the cream. Stir the mixture into the sauce and cook over low heat for five minutes, stirring constantly. Add the shrimp and season to taste. Heat and pour over the fish. Serve sprinkled with parsley.

Red Snapper Antiboise

6 servings

1 red snapper, mackerel, bluefish, or similar firm-fleshed fish (3½ to 4 pounds), filleted
2 tablespoons peanut oil
  Salt and freshly ground black pepper
1 onion, finely chopped
2 shallots, finely chopped
1 clove garlic, finely chopped
1 cup peeled, chopped fresh tomatoes
1 teaspoon chopped fresh thyme or ½ teaspoon dried thyme
1 bay leaf, broken in half
1 cup dry white wine
2 tablespoons freshly chopped parsley
  Juice of 1 lemon

1. Preheat the oven to 400 degrees.

2. Wipe the fish with a damp cloth.

3. Rub the bottom of a metal baking dish with oil and arrange the fillets on it. Sprinkle with salt and pepper. Scatter the onion, shallots, and garlic over the fish and cover with the tomatoes. Add the thyme, bay leaf, and white wine. Add more salt and pepper to taste and bring the dish to a boil on top of the stove. Place in the oven and bake thirty minutes.

4. Carefully transfer the fish to a serving dish and let cool. Pour the sauce into a saucepan and cook over high heat until the sauce is quite thick and almost completely reduced. Let cool. Spoon the sauce over the fish and let stand until ready to serve. Serve sprinkled with parsley and lemon juice.

Trout Meunière

6 servings

James M. Barrie in The Little Minister *called trout "God's critters tempting decent men"— on the theory that trout bite best on Sunday. Whenever they bite best, there is no gainsaying the fact that a trout in the pan is among the most covetable of dishes. Delicate in texture and in flavor, trout are quickly cooked* meunière, *or "miller's wife" style—that is, coated in flour and sautéed.*

6 fresh trout
1 cup milk, approximately
⅓ cup all-purpose flour, approximately
1 teaspoon salt
¼ teaspoon freshly ground black pepper
   Vegetable oil
¼ cup butter
   Lemon wedges
   Parsley sprigs

1. Clean the fish and rinse well inside and out under cold running water.
2. Arrange the trout in a pan and pour over them enough cold milk to cover. Let the fish stand thirty minutes or longer.
3. Drain the fish but do not dry them. Coat the fish, one at a time, in the flour seasoned with the salt and pepper.
4. Add enough oil to a large skillet to cover the bottom to the depth of one-quarter inch.
5. Heat the oil and cook the trout until they are golden brown on one side. Carefully turn and brown the other side.
6. Transfer the trout to a warm serving platter and keep warm.
7. Quickly pour off the oil from the skillet and wipe the skillet with paper towels. Add the butter and cook until nut brown. Do not burn. Immediately pour the butter over the fish and serve, garnished with lemon wedges and parsley.

Trout Amandine

6 servings

Cook the trout in the oil as indicated in the recipe for Trout Meunière (see above). When the fish are transferred to a warm platter, pour the oil from the skillet and wipe the skillet with paper towels. Add the butter to the skillet, along with one-third cup slivered blanched almonds, and cook until the butter is brown. Do not burn. Pour the almonds and butter over the fish and serve.

Trout Grenobloise

6 servings

Peel two large lemons and pare away all the white undercovering. Section the fruit and discard the membrane and seeds. Cut the juicy flesh into tiny cubes. Cook the trout in the oil as indicated in the recipe for Trout Meunière (see above). When the fish are transferred to a warm platter, pour the oil from the skillet and wipe the skillet with paper towels. Scatter the lemon and one-quarter cup capers over the fish. Add the butter to the skillet and cook until the butter is brown. Do not burn. Pour the butter over the fish and serve.

Stuffed Trout with Fish Mousse

6 servings

If Americans eat more than six million pounds of domestic rainbow trout every year, there's a good reason. It is one of the most delicate of the fish that swim in our streams and is delicious simply broiled or pan-fried. And when stuffed with a rich, creamy fish mousse and served with a white wine sauce, it makes a meal for the angels.

6 trout (about ¾ pound each) or 12 frozen trout fillets
½ pound flounder or sole fillets
1 egg white
3 cups heavy cream
¼ teaspoon cayenne pepper
Salt and freshly ground pepper
10 tablespoons butter
¼ cup finely chopped shallots
6 sprigs parsley
6 large mushrooms, rinsed, drained, and sliced thin
1 cup dry white wine
12 raw shrimp, peeled and deveined
Juice of ½ lemon
2 tablespoons all-purpose flour

1. Unless you are an expert at boning fish, have the fish dealer fillet the trout, leaving the skin intact. If frozen trout fillets are used, defrost them.

2. Preheat the oven to 400 degrees.

3. There is a line of tiny fish bones down the length of flounder or sole fillets. Trim this away and discard. Cut the flounder or sole into small pieces and place in the container of an electric blender. Add the egg white and blend on high speed. Stir the mixture down with a rubber spatula, taking care that the spatula does not touch the blades. Add one cup of the cream, the cayenne, and salt and pepper to taste and continue blending and stirring down until the mixture is smooth and well blended. Spoon this mousse mixture into a bowl.

4. Lay six of the trout fillets, skin side down, on a flat surface and spoon equal parts of the mousse mixture over them. Top each of these with one trout fillet, skin side up.

5. Butter a baking dish large enough to hold the trout, using four tablespoons of the butter. Sprinkle with shallots, salt, and pepper. Carefully lay the fillets in the dish and sprinkle with salt and pepper. Dot the fish with two tablespoons butter. Sprinkle the parsley sprigs and mushrooms over the trout and add the wine. Cover closely with heavy-duty aluminum foil and bring to a boil on top of the stove. Immediately place the dish in the oven and bake twenty minutes. Turn off the oven heat.

6. Meanwhile, butter a serving platter with two tablespoons of butter. Carefully transfer the trout to this dish, discarding the parsley. Pour the liquid and mushrooms from the baking dish into a large saucepan. Remove the skin from the top fillets.

7. Cover the trout in the serving platter with foil and place them in the oven with the door open. They should not cook further, but they should be kept warm.

8. To the saucepan with the mushrooms, add the shrimp. Simmer five minutes, then remove the shrimp and mushrooms with a slotted spoon. Keep the shrimp and mushrooms covered in a warm mixing bowl.

9. Cook the sauce down over high heat for about three minutes. Add the remaining cream to the sauce and cook over moderately high heat about ten minutes. When the sauce is nearly ready, pour in the liquid that may have accumulated around the trout in the oven. Add the lemon juice.

10. Meanwhile, knead together two tablespoons of butter with the flour. Stir this into the sauce bit by bit, using a wire whisk. Garnish the trout with the mushrooms and shrimp and spoon the sauce over. Serve with hot rice.

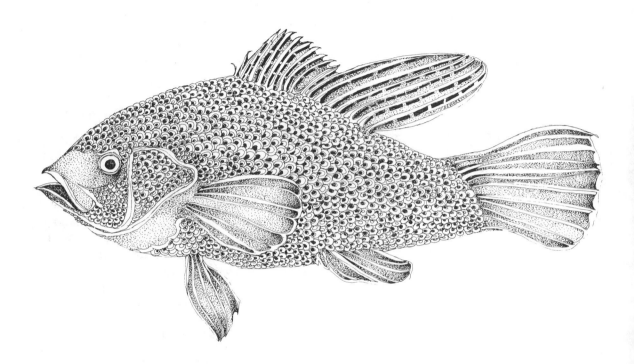

Truites au Bleu

2 servings

  4 cups water
  6 tablespoons olive oil
½ cup lemon juice
  4 tablespoons minced green onion
12 sprigs parsley
  2 ribs celery with leaves
¼ teaspoon dried thyme
    Salt to taste
24 peppercorns
  2 live trout (½ pound or less each) (see note)
    White vinegar
    Melted butter

1. Combine the water, olive oil, lemon juice, green onions, parsley, celery, thyme, salt, and peppercorns in a deep saucepan or kettle and simmer the court bouillon, uncovered, for fifteen minutes.

2. Meanwhile, kill the trout with a blow on the head and clean them. Put the fish in vinegar barely to cover for five minutes.

3. Bring the court bouillon to a boil and add the fish. Cook rapidly for ten minutes, then drain and transfer to a warm platter. Serve with melted butter.

Note: This dish can be made only if you are fortunate enough to get the trout alive.

Fish or Seafood Orly

8 to 12 servings

To most people, Orly is an airport. Only a few recognize it as the name of a capital fish creation. Fish or seafood Orly is deep-fried fish or seafood served with a lightly spiced tomato sauce. The name has absolutely no connection with the Paris airport, but is credited to the sixteenth-century Flemish painter, Bernard van Orley. The "e" has been lost over the centuries, and so has the reason for the honor. One can only suppose that van Orley's interest in good food was the equal of his interest in art. Almost any fish or seafood can be cooked in the Orly style—flounder, sole, shrimp, whiting, all are typical.

2 pounds flounder or other fish fillets or 50 medium raw shrimp
  Salt and freshly ground black pepper
  Fritter Batter Orly (see below)
  Vegetable oil for deep frying

1. If fish fillets are used, cut away the line of tiny bones running lengthwise down the center of the fillets. Cut the fillets diagonally into strips measuring four inches long and three-quarters inch wide. Sprinkle the strips with salt and pepper. If shrimp are used, shell and devein them.

2. Prepare the fritter batter and add the fish strips or shrimp.

3. Heat the oil and, using a fork, drop the batter-coated strips, one at a time, into the hot fat. Do not crowd the strips in the fat. When the fish strips are brown on one side, turn and brown on the other. Drain on absorbent toweling. Continue cooking until all the fish has been cooked. If the fish is not to be served immediately, keep hot in a warm oven, but for no longer than five or ten minutes.

4. Serve with Sauce Orly (below).

FRITTER BATTER ORLY:

Enough batter to coat 50 pieces of fish or shellfish

1 cup all-purpose flour
¼ teaspoon grated nutmeg
⅛ teaspoon cayenne pepper
2 eggs, separated
  Salt and freshly ground black pepper
⅔ cup milk

1. Place the flour, nutmeg, and cayenne in a mixing bowl and make a well in the center. Add the egg yolks and salt and pepper to taste and gradually add the milk, stirring.

2. Beat the egg whites until stiff and fold into the batter mixture. Use the batter for dipping strips of flounder, sole or other fish.

SAUCE ORLY:

About 2 cups

2 tablespoons olive oil
6 tablespoons butter
1½ cups finely chopped onion
2 cloves garlic, finely minced
3 sprigs fresh thyme or ½ teaspoon dried
1 bay leaf
1 teaspoon granulated sugar
2 cups chopped fresh tomatoes or canned Italian plum tomatoes
6 tablespoons tomato paste
  Salt and freshly ground black pepper

1. Heat the oil and two tablespoons of the butter in a saucepan and cook the onion and garlic, stirring occasionally, until the onion is wilted. Add the thyme, bay leaf, sugar, tomatoes, tomato paste, and salt and pepper to taste and simmer, stirring occasionally, twenty minutes.

2. Strain the sauce through a sieve or food mill into another saucepan. Return to a boil, then remove the sauce from the heat and swirl in the remaining butter by rotating the pan gently.

Seafood Crêpes

8 to 10 servings

Filled with lobster, shrimp, and crab meat lightly seasoned with herbs, the seafood crêpes below are served lightly covered—or masqué, as the French say—with two sauces, one deviled, one curried. The recipe here is from Jean Vergnes, who was chef at the Colony Restaurant for many years.

16 Crêpes with Fines Herbes (see below)
1½ cups Curry Sauce (page 270), approximately
1½ cups Sauce Piquante (page 274)
    Butter
  2 tablespoons finely chopped shallots
⅓ cup dry white wine
  1 tablespoon each finely chopped chives, parsley, and tarragon
  1 cup finely diced, cooked lobster meat
  1 cup finely diced, cooked shrimp
  1 cup cooked lump crabmeat
    Salt and freshly ground pepper to taste

1. Prepare the crêpes.

2. Start the sauces. While they are simmering, prepare the filling.

3. Place three tablespoons of butter in a saucepan and add the shallots. Cook briefly, stirring, then add the wine. Cook to reduce by half. Add the herbs and seafood and stir to blend. Sprinkle with salt and pepper to taste and cook briefly, stirring, until heated through.

4. Preheat the oven to warm.

5. Spoon equal portions of the mixture into the center of each crêpe and roll. Arrange the crêpes on a platter and brush with melted butter. Butter a sheet of waxed paper and place it, buttered side down, over the crêpes. Cover and place in the oven. Bake briefly, just until heated through, but not until piping hot.

6. Serve on hot plates, spooning a little of the curry sauce on half of each crêpe, a little of the sauce piquante on the other half.

CRÊPES WITH FINES HERBES:

About 20 crêpes

1½ cups sifted all-purpose flour
  2 eggs
¼ teaspoon salt
2½ cups milk
  1 tablespoon each chopped fresh tarragon, parsley, and chives
  3 tablespoons melted butter

1. Combine the flour, eggs, and salt in a mixing bowl. Gradually add the milk, stirring constantly with a wire whisk.

2. Strain the batter into a mixing bowl, then add the herbs and melted butter.

3. Heat a six- to seven-inch seasoned crêpe pan and brush it lightly with butter. Ladle a little of the batter in, swirling the pan around until the bottom is thoroughly covered with a thin coating. Cook until lightly browned on one side. Flip and cook briefly on the other side. The crêpe should not be brown on the second side. Repeat the procedure until the batter is used up.

Seafood Stew Méditerranée

4 to 6 servings

There is no such thing as a bad fish stew, provided—and it's an important proviso— that only the freshest ingredients are used and that liquids and herbs are added judiciously. The seafood stew here, with a hot loaf of crusty, buttery garlic bread, is a meal sufficient unto itself. It is given body with cubed potatoes and dash with cloves, saffron, and dry white vermouth. And, that final fillip —the least touch of anise-flavored liqueur.

1½ pounds raw shrimp
1 medium Idaho potato (about ½ pound)
¼ cup olive oil
1 cup chopped onion
2 cloves garlic, finely chopped
½ teaspoon hot pepper flakes
1 teaspoon dried thyme
2 teaspoons dried basil
1 teaspoon leaf saffron, crumbled
2 whole cloves
   Salt and freshly ground pepper to taste
4 cups peeled tomatoes, fresh or canned
1 cup dry white vermouth
1 live lobster, cut into serving pieces (see note)
1 pound white-fleshed fish such as cod or striped bass, cut into large pieces (see note)
1 tablespoon Pernod or Ricard

1. Clean and shell the shrimp and set aside.

2. Peel the potato and split in half lengthwise. Cut each half into slices about half an inch thick. Drop the slices immediately into cold water and set aside.

3. Heat the oil in a deep skillet or saucepan. Add the onion and cook until translucent.

4. Add the garlic, hot pepper flakes, thyme, basil, saffron, cloves, and salt and pepper to taste. Add the tomatoes and vermouth and bring to a boil. Put through a food mill, then return to the skillet. Add the potato, cover, and cook fifteen minutes. Add the shrimp, lobster, and fish and simmer, partly covered, thirty minutes longer. Just before serving, add the Pernod and serve piping hot in hot soup plates.

Note: If lobster or white fish are not available, increase the quantity of shrimp to four pounds.

To kill and dismember a lobster, plunge a knife into the place on the lobster where the tail and body meet. This will kill the lobster instantly. Break off the claws and crack them with a knife. Cut the tail into three sections crosswise. Split the body in half lengthwise, then remove and discard the tough sac near the eyes.

Lobster Américaine

About 4 cups (4 servings)

2 live lobsters (1½ pounds each)
¼ cup peanut or salad oil
Salt and freshly ground black pepper to taste
½ cup finely chopped onion
½ cup finely chopped carrot
6 tablespoons finely chopped celery
4 shallots, finely chopped
¼ cup warm Cognac
2 cloves garlic, minced
3 sprigs fresh thyme or ½ teaspoon dried thyme
2 whole cloves
12 peppercorns
2 teaspoons minced tarragon
½ cup tomato paste
1 cup chopped tomatoes
1 cup dry white wine
1 cup Fish Stock (page 116), or ½ cup clam juice and ½ cup water
4 sprigs parsley
2 tablespoons butter
1½ tablespoons all-purpose flour
Cayenne pepper to taste

1. Plunge a knife into the place on each lobster where tail and body meet. This will kill them instantly. Break off the claws and crack them with a knife. Cut each tail into three sections crosswise. Split the bodies in half, then remove and discard the tough sac near the eyes. Remove the liver and coral and chill until ready to use.

2. Heat the oil in a large, heavy skillet and add the lobster, including the body and claws. Cook, stirring, until the shell is red, then sprinkle with salt and pepper. Add the onion, carrot, celery, and shallots. Cook, stirring, until the moisture evaporates and the vegetables start to brown. Add the Cognac, garlic, thyme, cloves, peppercorns, tarragon, tomato paste, chopped tomatoes, wine, stock, and parsley. Cover and simmer fifteen minutes.

3. Remove the lobster and, when it is cool enough to handle, remove the meat from the claws and tail and set aside. Discard the shell. Leave the sauce in the skillet.

4. Blend the butter and flour with the fingers, then, using a wire whisk, blend in the reserved coral and liver. Stir this into the sauce and bring just to a boil, stirring well. Put the sauce through a food mill or sieve. Taste for seasonings and add the cayenne pepper and, if desired, more salt and pepper. Add the lobster to the sauce and serve hot. (If the lobster is to be used in Cheese Soufflé with Lobster [page 239], pour off one cup of sauce to serve hot with the soufflé and add the lobster to the remaining sauce.)

Note: This dish may be prepared several hours in advance.

Lobster Marseillaise

4 servings

6 tablespoons butter
⅓ cup finely chopped carrots
⅓ cup finely chopped shallots
¾ cup finely chopped onion
¾ cup finely chopped leeks (if not available, increase the chopped onion by ½ cup)
6 live lobsters (1½ pounds each)
1 sprig fresh thyme
1 bay leaf
Salt and freshly ground pepper to taste
⅓ cup plus 1 tablespoon Pernod or Ricard
2 cups Fish Stock (page 116) or Chicken Stock (page 115)
½ cup tomato paste
Tabasco to taste
1 cup heavy cream

1. Melt four tablespoons of the butter in a deep casserole and add the chopped carrots, shallots, onion, and leeks and sauté until the vegetables are tender.

2. Plunge a knife into the place on each lobster where the body and tail meet. This will kill them instantly. Do not split the lobsters but leave them whole. Add them to the kettle. Add the thyme, bay leaf, salt and pepper to taste, Pernod, fish stock, tomato paste, and Tabasco. Cover closely and simmer about twenty minutes.

3. Remove the lobsters. When they are cool enough to handle, remove the claw and tail meat (a knife or kitchen scissors are good for cutting the carcass to get at the meat). Set the meat aside. Return the shells to the sauce and simmer about five minutes.

4. Put the sauce through a food mill, pressing through as many solids as possible. Add the lobster shells, except the heads and thorax, to the food mill and try to extract as much liquid from the shell pieces as possible.

5. Boil the sauce about five minutes, skimming the surface as necessary.

6. Simmer the cream about ten minutes and add it to the sauce. Cut the tail meat into thirds. Add all the lobster meat to the sauce. Off the heat, swirl in the remaining butter and the additional tablespoon of Pernod by rotating the pan gently. Serve piping hot, with rice garnished with the lobster heads.

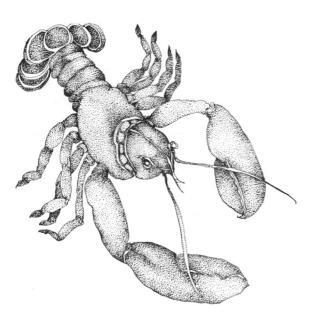

Lobsters Cooked in Seawater

8 servings

Seawater to cover
8 chicken lobsters (about 1 pound each)

1. Add enough seawater to a kettle to cover the lobsters completely when they are added. Do not add other seasoning.

2. If the lobsters have rubber bands on their claws, remove them. Add the lobsters, one at a time, to the boiling water. Cover and let the water return to a boil. When the water is boiling, cook the lobsters exactly twenty minutes. If larger lobsters are used, simmer them twenty minutes to the pound. Prepare for serving as described below, and serve with Sauce Nantaise (page 274), Mayonnaise (page 265), or other seafood sauces.

AN ELEGANT WAY TO SERVE WHOLE LOBSTERS IN THE SHELL:

First stick a paring knife between the eyes of the cooked lobsters and hang them head side down to let the water drain out. Do not tear off either the lobsters' claws or tails.

When the lobsters are cool enough to handle, grasp the hard, curved tail of the shell in the palm of the hand. Squeeze gently; this will break the shell. Using the fingers, break the under part of the shell. Carefully pull away the shell, leaving the tail itself intact and attached to the body.

Now prepare the claws. Tear off the small pincer from each claw, then, using a sharp heavy knife, crack the tips of each of the large main claws, taking care not to chop off the claw meat. Crack the claws but leave them intact. Serve.

Lobster Thermidor

4 to 8 servings

Created and first served to the public on the evening of Jan. 24, 1894, by the owner of Chez Maire, a once-famous Paris restaurant, now defunct, lobster thermidor was named for the drama Thermidor, *by Victorien Sardou. Sardou's play, a highly controversial work, opened and closed the same evening; lobster thermidor is a still-running hit.*

- 4 live lobsters (1 to 1½ pounds each)
  Salt and freshly ground pepper to taste
  Vegetable oil
- 3 tablespoons finely chopped shallots
- 1 tablespoon chopped fresh tarragon
- 1 tablespoon chopped fresh chervil or parsley
- ½ cup dry white wine
- 5 tablespoons butter
- 5½ tablespoons all-purpose flour
- 1 cup milk
- 1 cup heavy cream
  Cayenne pepper
- 1 egg yolk, lightly beaten
- 2 tablespoons imported mustard, such as Dijon or Düsseldorf (not the baseball-park variety)
- 3 to 4 tablespoons grated Parmesan cheese

1. Preheat the oven to 400 degrees.
2. Kill the lobsters by plunging a knife into each where tail and body meet. Split them lengthwise and cut off the claws, then remove and discard the tough sac near the eyes of each. Place the lobster halves, split side up, on one or two baking dishes. Sprinkle each lobster half with salt and pepper and brush lightly with oil. Bake twenty minutes.
3. Meanwhile, place the shallots, tarragon, chervil, and wine in a small saucepan and bring to a boil. Simmer until most of the liquid evaporates.
4. Melt four tablespoons of the butter in another saucepan and stir in the flour, using a wire whisk. When blended, add the milk and cream, stirring rapidly with the whisk. Add the cayenne pepper and salt and pepper to taste. Spoon the herb mixture into the sauce and remove it from the heat. Add the egg yolk and stir to blend. Add the mustard and set aside.
5. When the lobster is cooked, remove the tail meat and cut it into bite-sized pieces. Crack the claws and cut the meat into bite-sized pieces. Melt the remaining tablespoon of butter and toss the meat in it quickly. Add half the sauce to the lobster meat and use this mixture to fill the tail sections of the lobsters. Spoon equal portions of the remaining sauce over the lobsters (into the upper part as well as the tail). Sprinkle with Parmesan cheese and bake fifteen minutes. Serve immediately.

Mussels Vinaigrette

8 to 12 servings

- Moules Marinière (page 154)
- 1 tablespoon mustard, preferably Dijon or Düsseldorf
- 6 tablespoons wine vinegar
- 1 cup vegetable oil
  Salt and freshly ground pepper to taste
- ¼ cup finely chopped parsley

1. Prepare the mussels and drain them, reserving the cooking liquid for Billi Bi (page 124).
2. Remove and discard one shell of each mussel, leaving the remaining mussels on the half shell. Pile these into two oval casseroles or other serving dishes.
3. Add the mustard to a mixing bowl and beat in the vinegar. Gradually beat in the oil, salt, and pepper and pour equal amounts of this over the mussels. Serve, without chilling, sprinkled with chopped parsley and accompanied by French bread.

Pilaf of Mussels

4 to 6 servings

3 pounds mussels, well scrubbed
2 tablespoons finely chopped onion
1 tablespoon chopped shallots
5 tablespoons chopped parsley
6½ tablespoons butter
½ cup dry white wine
3 tablespoons all-purpose flour
1½ cups thinly sliced mushrooms
½ teaspoon minced onion
½ teaspoon minced shallot
½ cup heavy cream
    Salt and freshly ground black pepper
    Rice for Pilaf of Mussels (see below)

1. Place the mussels in a kettle and add the chopped onion, chopped shallots, three tablespoons of the parsley, one tablespoon of the butter, and the white wine. Cover and bring to a boil. Cook for five to ten minutes, or until the mussels open.

2. Strain the cooking liquid and reserve. Open each mussel and take from the shell. Pull off and discard the tough, stringlike band attached to each mussel. Reserve the mussels in a small covered container.

3. Melt two and one-half tablespoons of the remaining butter in a small saucepan and add the flour. Stir with a wire whisk until blended. Add one and three-quarters cup of the liquid from the mussels, stirring vigorously with the whisk until the mixture boils.

4. In a skillet, heat two tablespoons of the remaining butter and cook the mushrooms until they are wilted. Add the minced onion and minced shallot and stir. Cook briefly and add this, liquid and all, to the sauce. Simmer over very low heat for forty-five minutes. Add the cream and continue cooking about ten minutes. Add salt and pepper to taste.

5. Preheat the oven to 300 degrees.

6. Butter a curved, one-quart ovenproof bowl and add two cups of the cooked rice. With the fingers or a spoon, press the rice against the bowl, leaving a well in the center to receive the mussels.

7. Spoon one-half cup of the sauce and one tablespoon of the remaining parsley onto the mussels and blend. Heat thoroughly and spoon the mussels into the rice-lined bowl. Top with the remaining rice and press down to enclose the mussels.

8. Cover with aluminum foil and place in the oven just to heat through, about five minutes. Discard the foil and unmold onto a round, warm serving platter.

9. Add the remaining parsley to the sauce and bring to a boil. Remove from the heat and swirl in the remaining butter. Spoon a little sauce around the rice mold and serve the remainder separately.

RICE FOR PILAF OF MUSSELS:

3 to 4 cups cooked rice

2 tablespoons finely chopped onion
2 tablespoons butter
1½ cups uncooked rice
2¼ cups Chicken Stock (page 115) or canned chicken broth
½ bay leaf
2 parsley stems
    Salt to taste

1. Preheat the oven to 400 degrees.

2. In a one-quart casserole with a lid, cook the onion in the butter until wilted. Add the rice and continue cooking without browning. Stir with a wooden spoon until all the grains are coated.

3. Add the remaining ingredients and bring to a boil. Cover and bake until the rice is tender but still firm, twenty to thirty minutes. Uncover and let cool.

Scallops au Citron

4 servings

½ cup fine bread crumbs
1 teaspoon salt
1 pound scallops
1 egg, well beaten
2 tablespoons lemon juice
¼ cup butter
   Buttered toast triangles
   Chopped fresh parsley
   Lemon wedges

1. Mix the bread crumbs and salt. Roll the scallops in the crumbs and dip them into the beaten egg, which has been mixed with the lemon juice. Roll the scallops in the crumbs again.
2. Heat the butter in a skillet and sauté the scallops until they are golden brown and tender. Heap the scallops on buttered toast triangles and sprinkle with parsley. Serve with lemon wedges.

Moules Marinière

8 to 12 servings

8 tablespoons butter
1½ cups finely chopped shallots
½ cup finely chopped white onion
½ cup finely chopped parsley
8 quarts mussels, scrubbed and debearded
3 cups dry white wine
1 teaspoon salt
2 teaspoons freshly ground black pepper

1. In a large, heavy kettle, melt the butter and add the shallots, onion, and parsley. Cook, stirring, without browning, until the onions are wilted and cooked.
2. Add the mussels, wine, salt, and pepper. Cover closely and cook, shaking the kettle and stirring occasionally, about fifteen minutes.
3. The mussels and their broth are now ready to be eaten. The mussels may be served hot, sprinkled with parsley, with the broth. Or the broth may be strained and reserved for the cream of mussel soup, Billi Bi (page 124). The mussels may be served at room temperature with a vinaigrette sauce (page 152).

Breaded Scallops

4 servings

32 bay scallops or 16 ocean scallops
   Salt and freshly ground pepper to taste
   All-purpose flour for dredging
1 large or 2 small eggs, lightly beaten
1½ to 2 cups fresh bread crumbs
   Fat for deep frying
   Lemon wedges and parsley

1. If bay scallops are used, leave them whole; if ocean scallops are used, cut them in half.

2. Season the scallops with salt and pepper, then dredge in flour and coat with egg. Dredge them in the bread crumbs and deep-fry for two to three minutes at 360 degrees, depending on size. Garnish with lemon wedges and parsley and serve with Tartar Sauce I (page 277).

Broiled Scallops with Lemon

6 to 8 servings

2 pounds scallops
　Salt and freshly ground black pepper to taste
6 fresh basil leaves, chopped, or 1 teaspoon dried basil
2 fresh rosemary sprigs or ½ teaspoon dried rosemary
1 lemon, thinly sliced
　Tabasco to taste
¼ cup salad oil

1. If bay scallops are used, leave them whole. If large sea scallops are used, cut them in half. Put them in a bowl with the remaining ingredients and cover. Refrigerate two hours or longer.

2. Remove the scallops from the marinade and arrange in one layer in a baking dish. Broil about three minutes, then turn and broil about three minutes longer, or until barely cooked through. Do not overcook the scallops or they will toughen. Serve immediately.

Shrimp Marseillaise

4 to 6 servings

20 large raw shrimp (about 1¾ pounds)
¾ teaspoon salt
¼ teaspoon freshly ground black pepper
½ teaspoon leaf saffron or ¼ teaspoon powdered saffron
1 large shallot, chopped
2 small cloves garlic, finely chopped
½ teaspoon chopped fresh thyme or ¼ teaspoon dried thyme
3 tablespoons olive oil
　Juice of 2 lemons
½ cup butter
1 tablespoon chopped parsley

1. Peel the shrimp but leave on the tail segment. Devein, rinse under cold running water, and dry on paper towels.

2. In a bowl, mix the salt, pepper, saffron, shallot, garlic, thyme, oil, and lemon juice. Cover the shrimp with the marinade and let stand in the refrigerator an hour or two, turning once or twice.

3. Melt the butter in a small saucepan and set aside.

4. Place the shrimp on a broiler rack and broil two to three minutes a side until pink, turning once. The marinade will drip through into pan. Arrange the shrimp on a warm platter and sprinkle with parsley. Pour the pan drippings and extra marinade into the butter. Heat the sauce just to boiling and serve separately with the shrimp.

Stuffed Shrimp

4 servings

The American appetite for shrimp can only be described as insatiable. They come to the port of New York from forty-five countries, and they range in size from two and three shrimp to the pound to 200 and 300 to the pound. Some of the tiniest are from Iceland, some of the largest from Panama and Spain. The nation's favorite preparation for the shellfish is undoubtedly a simple shrimp cocktail, but it is also deserving of more elaborate treatment. Below is an excellent recipe for shrimp stuffed with mushrooms, bread crumbs and herbs. With a green salad and a wedge of ripe cheese, it would make a splendid luncheon or supper.

12 extra-jumbo raw shrimp (about 1¼ pounds) or 1 pound medium raw shrimp
Salt and freshly ground black pepper
 6 tablespoons butter
½ cup finely chopped onion
½ cup finely minced mushrooms (optional)
¼ bay leaf
 1 clove garlic
 2 sprigs fresh thyme or ½ teaspoon dried thyme
 1 teaspoon finely chopped fresh tarragon or ½ teaspoon dried tarragon
 1 hard-cooked egg, finely chopped
½ cup heavy cream
 1 cup fine soft bread crumbs
 1 egg yolk
 2 tablespoons finely chopped parsley
 4 tablespoons freshly grated Parmesan cheese

1. Using a pair of kitchen scissors, cut through the upper shell of each shrimp but leave the tail segment intact. Peel the shrimp, leaving the tail intact. Devein the shrimp, rinse under cold running water, and pat dry. Using a paring knife, split the underside of the shrimp to "butterfly" them. Do not cut all the way through. Carefully pound the butterfly shrimp to flatten the split portion.

2. Butter a baking dish or four individual scallop shells. Arrange the shrimp, with tails up, over the dish or shells. Sprinkle with salt and pepper.

3. Melt three tablespoons of the butter in a skillet and add the onion and, if used, the mushrooms.

4. Chop together the bay leaf, garlic, and thyme until all are pureed. (If dried, crumble the bay leaf and add with the thyme.) Add to the skillet. Add the tarragon and cook slowly about twenty minutes. Add the hard-cooked egg and cook, stirring occasionally, five minutes longer.

5. Add salt and pepper to taste and the cream. Simmer fifteen minutes. Stir in the bread crumbs, egg yolk, and parsley. Spoon equal dabs of filling into each shrimp and refrigerate until ready to use.

6. Preheat the broiler.

7. Melt the remaining butter and pour over the shrimp. Sprinkle with the Parmesan, then place the baking dish under the broiler and broil until golden brown and cooked through, eight to ten minutes for large shrimp. Serve hot.

Snails Provençale on Toast

4 servings

Purists in the food world frown on most things canned, but there is one outstanding exception: snails, those meaty, delectable inhabitants of France's vineyards. The preparation of fresh snails is a tedious exercise involving soaking, boiling, and simmering in broth prior to a final dressing with butter, garlic, or whatever. Snails have become so popular in America that they can be found ready to bake in a number of frozen-food outlets. They are usually stuffed in the shell with a herb butter. The recipe on this page is an interesting change. The snails, cooked with tomatoes, garlic, and shallots, are served out of the shell on hot, buttered toast.

2 cans imported snails (each containing 18 snails)
Dry white wine
4 dozen cherry tomatoes or 2 medium ripe tomatoes
½ cup butter
Salt and freshly ground pepper
4 teaspoons finely chopped garlic
6 tablespoons chopped shallots
4 slices buttered toast (may be made from French bread)

1. Drain the snails and place them in a saucepan. Add the wine to cover and bring to a boil. Simmer ten minutes, then drain.

2. Meanwhile, drop the tomatoes into boiling water to cover. Cook exactly twelve seconds, no longer, and drain quickly. Peel the tomatoes, using a paring knife to pull away the skin. Put the tomatoes in a saucepan and add six tablespoons of the butter and salt and pepper to taste. Simmer ten minutes, then add three teaspoons of the garlic and four tablespoons of the chopped shallots and simmer three minutes longer.

3. Heat the remaining butter in a skillet and add the snails. Cook briskly about three minutes, stirring frequently, then add the remaining garlic and shallots.

4. Arrange the toast on each of four hot plates and spoon half the sauce over the toast. Dividing the snails equally, place on the toast and top with the remaining sauce. Serve immediately.

158   FRANCE

Frogs' legs, one of the rarer delicacies of the world, are becoming more difficult to find in the markets every year. Once upon a time this country was almost self-sufficient as far as frogs' legs were concerned. Today the picture is quite different. Florida and Louisiana still supply a good number, but cannot meet the demand. If it were not for imports from Japan, frogs' legs fanciers would feel deprived indeed. The two recipes given here—one with a tomato sauce, the other with a cream sauce—make the most of this tender white meat.

Frogs' Legs à la Crème

6 servings

12 large pairs or 24 small pairs frogs' legs
1 cup milk
1 cup all-purpose flour, approximately
  Salt and freshly ground pepper to taste
6 tablespoons butter
2 tablespoons finely chopped shallots or green onion, white part only
¼ cup dry white wine
1 cup heavy cream
1 teaspoon lemon juice
  Freshly ground nutmeg to taste

1. Prepare one pair of frogs' legs at a time. Slip one leg in between the two muscles of the lower part of the other leg. The muscles can be easily separated to form a hole without detaching them from the bone. This is not essential in preparing this recipe, but it keeps the frogs' legs flat and they brown more evenly on all sides.

2. Dip the frogs' legs first in milk, removing them without patting dry. Dredge the legs in flour seasoned with salt and pepper.

3. Melt four tablespoons of the butter in a large skillet and lightly brown the frogs' legs on all sides. Remove to a warm platter and keep warm.

4. Add the shallots to the skillet and stir briefly. Add the wine and cook over high heat until most of the wine evaporates. Add the cream and cook to reduce slightly. Season to taste with salt and pepper and add the frogs' legs, then stir in the lemon juice and nutmeg. Off the heat, swirl in the remaining butter by rotating the pan gently. Serve piping hot with rice.

Frogs' Legs Provençale

4 to 6 servings

12 large pairs or 24 small pairs frogs' legs
1 cup milk
1 cup all-purpose flour, approximately
  Salt and freshly ground pepper to taste
2 cups peeled tomatoes, fresh or canned
½ cup vegetable or salad oil
1 cup butter
1 tablespoon finely chopped garlic
¼ cup finely chopped parsley

1. Prepare one pair of frogs' legs at a time. Slip one leg in between the two muscles of the lower part of the other leg to keep the frogs' legs flat.

2. Soak the legs briefly in the milk.

3. Drain the legs but do not dry, then dredge each pair in flour seasoned with salt and pepper.

4. Meanwhile, pour the tomatoes into a saucepan and simmer until thickened, about twenty to thirty minutes. Season to taste.

5. In a large skillet, heat the oil and four tablespoons of the butter. Cook the legs until golden on one side, then turn and cook the other side until golden.

6. Butter a heatproof serving dish lightly and arrange the frogs' legs on it in a symmetrical fashion. Spoon the tomato sauce neatly over the centers of the frogs' legs.

7. Pour the fat from the skillet and wipe out the skillet with paper toweling. Melt the remaining butter in the skillet and add the garlic. When the butter is hot and foaming, pour it over the frogs' legs. Sprinkle with parsley.

Beef au Madère

6 or more servings

2 pounds fillet or lean sirloin of beef
½ cup all-purpose flour
  Salt and freshly ground black pepper
3 tablespoons butter
1 tablespoon vegetable oil
¾ cup finely minced onion
1 tablespoon finely minced shallots
2 cups sliced fresh mushrooms
2 cups Beef Stock (page 115) or canned beef broth
1 cup chopped fresh tomatoes
⅓ cup Madeira
½ cup sour cream

1. Preheat the oven to 350 degrees.
2. Cut the meat into thin strips.
3. Season the flour with salt and pepper to taste and dredge the meat in the mixture.
4. Heat the butter and oil in a skillet and cook the meat quickly over high heat until brown. Do not burn. Reduce the heat, and, using a slotted spoon, transfer the meat to a two-quart casserole.
5. Add the onion and shallots to the skillet and cook until wilted. Add the mushrooms and cook, stirring, about five minutes. Spoon the mushroom mixture over the meat and add the beef stock. Strain the tomatoes through a sieve and add, then add the Madeira and salt and pepper to taste. Cover and bake forty-five minutes. Spoon into hot plates and top each serving with sour cream.

Beef Fillet with Madeira Sauce

About 12 servings

A fillet of beef is to many people the nearest thing to manna. Since it is also the most expensive cut of beef, it is usually reserved for festive occasions. Not the least of its virtues is simplicity of preparation. Cooking time (for rare beef, which is best) is half an hour, more or less.

6 tablespoons butter
1 fillet of beef (8 to 10 pounds), well trimmed
  Salt and freshly ground pepper
2 cups Madeira Sauce (page 273), approximately

1. Preheat the oven to 450 degrees.
2. Heat four tablespoons of the butter in a shallow roasting pan. When it is just melted, turn the fillet in it until the meat is coated with butter. Sprinkle with salt and pepper to taste.
3. Bake, twenty-five to thirty-five minutes, basting frequently. This will yield a rare interior, which most connoisseurs prefer. Cook the meat longer if you wish it well done. Transfer the meat to a large serving dish and keep warm.
4. Pour off most of the fat from the pan and pour in the Madeira sauce. Stir to dissolve the brown particles that cling to the bottom and sides of the pan. Swirl in the remaining two tablespoons butter by rotating the pan gently.
5. Slice the fillet (slice only the amount to be served immediately and leave the rest of the fillet whole, to be sliced later). Spoon the sauce over the beef or spoon part of it over the beef and serve the rest in a sauceboat.

Beef périgourdine (France)

Pot Roast Provençale

8 servings

One man's passion for anchovies, olives, or herring is another man's crise de foie. There are some dishes, however, that seem to give universal pleasure. One of these is pot roast. It may be a simple, braised, homely affair with a bit of onion and herbs, or a more elaborate Provençale concoction, like the one on this page. Some claim that it is even more delicious served cold the next day.

1	bottom round of beef (4 pounds), well trimmed
	Salt pork
	Salt and freshly ground pepper
1	onion, coarsely chopped
1	clove garlic, coarsely sliced
2	carrots, scraped and chopped
10	sprigs fresh parsley
1	bay leaf
2	branches fresh thyme or 1 teaspoon dried thyme
1½	cups water
1	cup dry white wine
3	cups Chicken Stock (page 115)
6	tablespoons tomato paste
2	teaspoons cornstarch
2	tablespoons cold water
1	3-ounce jar imported pitted Spanish olives
16	cherry tomatoes
3	tablespoons butter

1. If possible, lard the meat with strips of salt pork (page 164) or have it larded by the butcher.

2. Preheat the oven to 350 degrees.

3. Cut one-quarter pound salt pork into small cubes and cook in a skillet until rendered of fat. Remove the bits of pork.

4. Sprinkle the meat with salt and pepper and cook it in the skillet on all sides until rich brown. Do not burn. Transfer the meat to a Dutch oven and surround with the onion, garlic, and carrots. Cook the meat and vegetables, stirring around occasionally, until the onions start to color.

5. Combine the parsley sprigs, bay leaf, and thyme and tie them into a bundle with string. Add to the Dutch oven.

6. Pour off the fat from the skillet in which the meat browned and add the water. Bring to a boil, stirring to dissolve the brown particles that cling to the bottom and sides of the skillet. Add to the Dutch oven along with the wine and stock. Bring to a boil and stir in the tomato paste.

7. Cover closely and bake two and one-half to three hours, or until the meat is tender. Remove the meat; cover it with foil to keep warm. Skim off and discard the fat from the cooking liquid. Bring the liquid to a boil and simmer fifteen minutes.

8. Strain the cooking liquid into a large saucepan and return to a boil. Simmer forty-five minutes, uncovered, to reduce.

9. Blend the cornstarch and cold water and add to the liquid, stirring constantly with a whisk.

10. Return the beef to the Dutch oven.

11. Drain the olives and place in a small saucepan. Cover with cold water. Bring just to a boil, then drain and scatter around the beef.

12. Drop the tomatoes into boiling water and let stand nine to twelve seconds, no longer, or they will become mushy. Drain immediately and peel. The skin will slip off easily when pulled with a paring knife.

13. Heat the butter in a skillet and add the tomatoes. Sprinkle with salt and pepper. Toss the tomatoes gently in the butter, just to heat through. Do not overcook.

14. Add the tomatoes to the Dutch oven. Pour the boiling sauce over the meat.

15. To serve, carve the meat, pour half the sauce over it and garnish with olives and tomatoes. Serve the remaining sauce separately, if desired.

œuf à la mode en gelée (France)

Squid Vinaigrette

10 to 12 servings

5 quarts boiling salted water
3 pounds squid
½ cup chopped fresh dill or 1 tablespoon dried dill
¾ cup finely chopped fresh parsley
1½ cups coarsely chopped onion
¼ cup chopped fresh basil or 1 teaspoon dried basil
1½ teaspoons coarsely ground black pepper or to taste
3 cloves garlic, peeled
1½ cups olive oil
½ cup wine vinegar
2 lemons
   Salt

1. Have the water boiling furiously in a large kettle. Add the squid, return to a boil, and cook fifteen minutes.

2. Drain the squid in a colander. When they are cool enough to handle, remove the slivers of translucent cartilage from each squid. Cut the squid into one-half-inch lengths and place in a large bowl.

3. Add the dill, parsley, onion, basil, pepper, and garlic to the squid. Add the oil and vinegar and toss.

4. Slice the ends off the lemons. Cut the lemons into thin slices and remove the seeds. Cut each lemon slice into eight wedges and add to the squid. Toss the ingredients and add salt to taste.

5. Place in a glass or enamel container, cover closely, and let stand in the refrigerator for two days. Serve with mayonnaise on the side and toast or French bread, if desired.

Ribs of Beef au Vin Rouge

40 to 60 servings

1 25-pound standing rib roast (about 7 ribs)
2 bottles plus ½ cup dry red wine
   Salt
1 tablespoon peppercorns
3 cloves garlic, minced
3 bay leaves
6 sprigs fresh thyme or 1 teaspoon dried thyme
4 whole cloves
6 sprigs fresh parsley
2 leeks, trimmed, split, rinsed well, and chopped
2 large onions, coarsely chopped
2 ribs celery, quartered
6 carrots, scraped and coarsely chopped
¼ cup Cognac
¼ cup vegetable oil
1 quart Brown Stock (page 163)
¼ cup butter
1 quart mushrooms, finely chopped or cubed
   Freshly ground pepper
⅔ cup cornstarch
   Glazed Onions (page 163)
   Chopped parsley

1. Have the butcher carefully separate the meat in one whole piece from the ribs. Have the ribs cracked and use them to make the brown stock.

2. Cut the meat crosswise into three large pieces, each approximately the same size. Place the pieces in a large container and add the two bottles of wine, salt to taste, peppercorns, and garlic. Tie the bay leaves, thyme, cloves, and parsley sprigs in a piece of cheesecloth and add, along with the leeks, chopped onions, celery, carrots, and Cognac. Cover and let stand overnight.

3. When ready to cook the meat, preheat the oven to 400 degrees.

4. Drain the meat, reserving the marinade and vegetables. Wipe the meat with a clean cloth.

5. Heat the oil in a large skillet and brown the meat well on all sides. The meat should be dark brown but not burned. Transfer the meat to a large casserole or kettle and add the marinade and vegetables. Add the brown stock.

6. Melt the butter and cook the mushrooms until they are wilted. Add them to the meat. Bring to a boil on top of the stove, then place in the oven. Cover and bake two and one-half to three hours, or until the meat is tender.

7. Remove the meat and strain the liquid into a large saucepan. Cook the liquid over high heat 15 minutes. Add salt and pepper to taste. Blend the remaining wine with the cornstarch and stir into the simmering sauce. Cook five minutes longer. Add the glazed onions to the sauce.

8. Slice the meat and arrange it on a platter. Spoon a little of the sauce over it and sprinkle with parsley. Serve the remaining sauce separately.

BROWN STOCK:

About 2 quarts

¼ cup vegetable oil
   Ribs from a 25-pound standing rib roast (about 7 ribs)
3 pounds bony chicken parts (necks, backs, and wings)
2 cloves garlic, unpeeled
4 carrots, scraped and chopped
   Salt
12 peppercorns
1 rib celery, quartered
1 bay leaf
3 sprigs fresh thyme or ½ teaspoon dried thyme
2 cups coarsely chopped mushrooms
1 onion
1 gallon water

1. Preheat the oven to 450 degrees.

2. Heat the oil on top of the stove in an open roasting pan and brown the bones on all sides. Add all the remaining ingredients except the gallon of water. Place the pan in the oven and bake 45 minutes to one hour, stirring the bones and vegetables around. The ingredients should be well browned but not burned.

3. Transfer the ingredients to a kettle and add the water. Bring to a boil and cook six hours, skimming the surface as necessary. Strain the stock through cheesecloth and reserve.

Note: Leftover stock may be frozen.

GLAZED ONIONS:

48 glazed onions

48 small white onions, peeled
   Salt to taste
1 teaspoon granulated sugar
2 tablespoons butter
1½ cups water, approximately

1. Preheat the oven to 450 degrees.

2. Place the onions in a large skillet. There should be only one layer and the onions should fit closely. Add the remaining ingredients and bring to a boil. Simmer until almost all the water has evaporated.

3. Bake, uncovered, until the onions are browned and nicely glazed.

Daube de Boeuf en Gelée

About 12 servings

 1 bottom round roast (4 pounds)
 ¼ pound larding pork, cut into long strips
   Salt and freshly ground pepper to taste
 3 tablespoons butter
 1 tablespoon peanut or vegetable oil
 1 large onion, coarsely chopped
 2 large carrots, scraped and quartered
 3 tomatoes, cored and quartered
 6 cloves garlic, unpeeled but crushed
10 sprigs fresh thyme or 1 teaspoon dried thyme
 1 bay leaf
 6 sprigs fresh parsley
 3 cups dry red wine
 5 cups Brown Sauce (page 268) or 4 cans (10¾ ounces each) beef gravy
 4 envelopes unflavored gelatin
1¾ cups Beef Stock (page 115) or canned beef broth
 2 tablespoons arrowroot or cornstarch
 ½ cup plus 2 tablespoons water
 1 tablespoon Cognac
40 small white onions, cooked and peeled, or use drained contents of 1 no. 303 can of onions
 1 tablespoon granulated sugar
 ½ cup cooked green peas
24 separately cooked carrot rounds
 1 cup cooked green beans, cut into 1-inch lengths
   Clear Aspic (page 264)

1. Preheat the oven to 400 degrees.

2. Lard the roast (see below) or have it larded with the strips of larding pork. Sprinkle the meat with salt and pepper to taste.

3. Heat one tablespoon of the butter and the oil in a skillet and brown the meat well on all sides. It should be mahogany colored.

4. Place the chopped onion, quartered carrots, tomatoes, garlic, thyme, bay leaf, and parsley in the bottom of a heavy kettle and add the meat. Do not add liquid and do not cover. Bake for one and one-half hours.

5. Add the wine and brown sauce or beef gravy and stir. Bring to a boil on top of the stove and cover.

6. Reduce the oven heat to 350 degrees and bake the daube for two and one-half hours longer. The meat, when cooked, should be fork tender.

7. Remove the meat from the kettle and scrape it with a knife to remove any fat from the outside. Place the meat in a crock, terrine, or other container in which it fits nicely. Bring the sauce in the kettle to a boil.

8. Place the gelatin in a mixing bowl and add the beef stock. When softened, stir the mixture into the boiling sauce. Combine the arrowroot or cornstarch with one-half cup of the water and add to the sauce. Simmer five minutes, then strain through a fine sieve. Season the sauce rather highly with salt and pepper and stir in the Cognac. Pour the sauce over the meat. The meat should be covered with sauce. If not, transfer the meat to a smaller container.

9. Meanwhile, add the white onions, remaining butter, and remaining water to a skillet. Sprinkle with sugar and cook, shaking the skillet, until the onions are caramelized all over. Set aside.

10. Add half the onions, peas, carrot rounds, and green beans to the sauce-covered meat, pushing the vegetables into the sauce. Chill the daube until it is firm.

11. Decorate the top of the daube with the remaining onions, peas, carrot rounds, and green beans and spoon the clear aspic over all. Chill until firm. Serve the meat thinly sliced directly from the mold.

TO LARD MEAT:

Thread a larding needle by placing a long, thin strip of larding pork in the open end. Insert the pointed end of the needle into the roast at right angles to the grain. Push, then pull the needle through the meat. Trim the larding pork off flush with the meat.

Boiled Beef

6 servings

1 brisket of beef (3 to 4 pounds)
1 shank bone
8 leeks, trimmed and rinsed well
7 carrots
1 onion studded with 4 cloves
2 ribs celery with leaves
12 peppercorns, bruised slightly with a mortar and pestle or the back of a knife
Salt
1 bay leaf
1 teaspoon dried thyme
12 white onions

1. Place the meat and shank bone in a deep kettle or Dutch oven. Cover with boiling water.

2. Add two leeks halved, one carrot quartered, the onion, celery, peppercorns, salt to taste, bay leaf, and thyme. Bring to a boil, cover, and simmer three hours, or until the meat is tender.

3. During the last half hour of cooking, add the remaining vegetables and cook until tender. Serve on a warm platter surrounded by the vegetables, with any or all of the following accompaniments.

THE CLASSIC ACCOMPANIMENTS FOR BOILED BEEF:

Prepared mustard, preferably Dijon or Düsseldorf (not the baseball-park variety)

Cornichons (French gherkins), available in specialty food shops

Hot mustard made by combining dry mustard with enough white wine to make a paste. Season with salt to taste and let stand ten minutes to develop the flavor.

Grated fresh horseradish

Tomato Sauce I (page 278)

Caper Sauce (page 268) or Sour Cream and Horseradish Sauce (page 276)

Coarse salt, such as kosher or Maldon

Steaks à la Crème

4 servings

4 filets mignons or other individual cuts of steak
2 tablespoons fresh peppercorns
Salt to taste
Oil
3 tablespoons butter
1 tablespoon finely chopped shallots or green onion
2 tablespoons Cognac
1 cup heavy cream
2 tablespoons finely chopped parsley

1. Have the meat at room temperature.

2. Preheat the oven to 350 degrees.

3. Crush the peppercorns with a mortar and pestle or with the bottom of a heavy skillet. Press the crushed pepper into the bottom and sides of the steaks and sprinkle with salt.

4. Lightly oil the bottom of a heavy skillet and brown the meat on all sides. Continue cooking to the desired degree of doneness. (The length of time will depend on the thickness of the steaks. The steaks will also cook briefly in the oven.) Transfer the steaks to a warm serving platter and place in the oven.

5. Wipe the skillet in which the steaks cooked with paper towels and add the butter. When it is hot, add the shallots. Cook briefly, stirring. Add the Cognac and ignite. When the flame dies, add the cream and cook over moderate heat, stirring briefly, until slightly thickened. Pour the sauce over the steak and sprinkle with parsley. Serve hot.

The dish called steak au poivre (which translates limply as pepper steak) is an oddity in French cuisine. Its essence depends on a large quantity of crushed peppercorns applied with near abandon to both sides of a steak before cooking. The result is eminently delicious but perhaps not for all palates. There are two kinds of steak au poivre, one with a dark sauce and the other made with cream. The perfect accompaniment is Ciro Potatoes.

Steak au Poivre

4 to 8 servings

4 boneless sirloin steaks (1 pound each, and each about 1 inch thick)
¼ to ⅓ cup peppercorns
  Salt
5 tablespoons butter
3 tablespoons finely chopped shallots
3 tablespoons finely chopped onion
2 tablespoons Cognac
1 cup dry red wine
1¼ cups Brown Sauce (page 268) or 1 can (10¾ ounces) brown gravy
  Chopped parsley

1. Trim the steaks of all but a quarter-inch rim of fat.

2. Crush the peppercorns with a mortar and pestle or crush on a flat surface with the bottom of a heavy skillet. The peppercorns must not be too coarse nor too fine. Dip the steaks, one at a time on both sides, into the crushed peppercorns. Press the pepper into the steaks with the heel of the hand. Sprinkle lightly on both sides with salt.

3. Heat three tablespoons of the butter in a skillet large enough to hold the steaks or divide the butter between two smaller skillets. Brown the steaks on one side, then turn and brown on the other. Cook to the desired degree of doneness.

4. Remove the steaks to a warm platter and add the shallots and onion to the skillet. Stir quickly and add the Cognac and wine. Bring to a boil, then stir in the brown sauce. Cook briefly, stirring. Add salt to taste. Pour in any drippings from the steak platter. Swirl the remaining butter into the sauce by rotating the pan gently and pour the sauce over the steak. The whole steaks may be served or they may be cut in half for eight servings. Dot the center of each steak with a generous pinch of chopped parsley. Serve with Ciro Potatoes (page 252).

Steak au Poivre à la Crème

4 to 6 servings

2 boneless shell steaks or sirloin steaks (about 1½ pounds each)
2 tablespoons or more black peppercorns
  Salt
  Vegetable oil
¼ cup butter
2 tablespoons finely chopped shallots or green onions
3 tablespoons warm Cognac
2 cups heavy cream
1 tablespoon Dijon or Düsseldorf mustard

1. Trim the steaks of most of their fat.

2. Using a mortar and pestle or bottom of a heavy skillet, pound the peppercorns until coarsely crushed. Pour the crushed pepper onto a piece of waxed paper and dredge the steaks on both sides in the pepper. Press the pepper into the steaks with the heel of the hand. Sprinkle lightly on both sides with salt.

3. Place a heavy skillet on the stove and brush the bottom lightly with oil. When hot, add the steaks and cook over medium-high heat until brown on one side, about seven minutes. Turn the steaks and brown on the other side. Continue cooking the steaks, turning occasionally, to the desired degree of doneness.

4. Remove the steaks to a warm platter and pour off any fat that accumulated in the pan. Cover the steaks with aluminum foil and keep warm. Wipe out the pan with paper towels and add the butter and shallots. Cook, stirring, about three minutes. Do not brown. Add the Cognac and ignite. Add the cream and cook, stirring frequently, about ten minutes. Remove the skillet from the heat and stir in the mustard. Do not cook further. Pour the hot sauce over the steaks and serve immediately with Ciro Potatoes (page 252).

Steak aux Échalotes

6 servings

There is certainly small doubt that steak is America's favorite meat, but the sameness with which most steaks are grilled or broiled and sauced testifies to a shameful lack of imagination. One of the tastiest of steaks is one cooked quickly in butter and seasoned with shallots and vinegar. A French idea and a good one, the recipe for which is given below.

6 shell steaks (5 to 6 ounces each)
  Salt and freshly ground black pepper
9 tablespoons butter
¼ cup finely chopped shallots or 2 cloves garlic, finely chopped
¼ cup red wine vinegar
2 tablespoons finely chopped parsley

1. Sprinkle the steaks with salt and pepper.

2. Heat three tablespoons of the butter in a large skillet. When it is quite hot and starting to brown, cook the steaks on one side until brown, then turn and brown on the other side. The total cooking time should be from about five to ten minutes, unless you want them well done.

3. Remove the steaks to a hot platter and add the shallots or garlic and the wine vinegar to the skillet. Let the vinegar reduce slightly, then remove the skillet from the heat.

4. Add the remaining butter, swirling it around in the pan. Stir in the parsley and pour the sauce over the steaks.

Note: Although shell steaks are called for in this recipe, almost any good, tender, well-marbled cut of beef will do. The important thing about preparing this dish is to cook the meat to a proper degree of doneness and to prepare the sauce as rapidly as possible after the meat is transferred to a platter.

Potted Steak Burgundy Style

6 servings

- 1 chuck steak (2 pounds), 1½ inches thick
- 1 teaspoon salt
  Freshly ground black pepper
  All-purpose flour
- ½ cup finely chopped onion
- 2 to 4 tablespoons bacon drippings
- ½ pound fresh mushrooms, sliced
- 1¼ cups Beef Stock (page 115)
- ½ cup dry red wine
- ¼ teaspoon ground thyme
- 1 bay leaf

1. Preheat the oven to 275 degrees.
2. Cut the steak into six serving pieces. Sprinkle with the salt and pepper to taste and pound with a mallet or the rim of a plate. Dredge heavily with flour and pound the flour into the steak.
3. Cook the onion in half of the bacon drippings until golden. Add the mushrooms and cook briefly.
4. Remove the vegetables from the skillet and add the remaining bacon drippings. Brown the steak well on all sides.
5. Heat an ovenproof casserole and arrange the steak pieces over the bottom. Sprinkle with the onion and mushrooms. Heat the beef stock, wine, thyme, and bay leaf in the skillet in which the steak was cooked and pour over the meat in the casserole. Cover the casserole with a tight-fitting lid and bake for about two hours, until the meat is fork tender. Remove the bay leaf and serve.

Tournedos Rossini

6 servings

- 6 center slices filet mignon, each about 2 inches thick
  Salt and freshly ground black pepper
- 6 tablespoons butter
- 6 slices French bread
- 6 slices foie gras
- ¼ cup port wine
- 1¼ cups Brown Sauce (page 268) or canned beef gravy
- ¼ to ½ cup finely chopped truffles
- 3 tablespoons truffle juice

1. Preheat the oven to 350 degrees.
2. Place the filets mignons between pieces of waxed paper and pound lightly with a flat mallet. Sprinkle the meat on all sides with salt and pepper.
3. Heat four tablespoons of the butter in a large skillet and cook the filets mignons on all sides until browned, about twelve to fifteen minutes.
4. Meanwhile, place the bread slices on a rack and bake until golden brown. When the bread is done, lower the oven heat to 200 degrees.
5. Arrange the bread slices on an ovenproof serving dish and place one cooked filet mignon on top of each bread slice. Top with slices of foie gras. Place in the oven while making the sauce.
6. To the skillet in which the beef was cooked, add the wine and brown sauce and stir. Add the truffles and truffle juice and bring to a boil. Swirl in the remaining butter by rotating the pan gently. Serve the sauce separately, or spoon it over and around the filets mignons.

Tournedos Ismal Bayeldi

4 servings

The virtues of a fillet of beef are too obvious to dwell on. It may still be pointed out, however, that the fillet is one of the most versatile of foods, a luxury whose value extends far beyond the charcoal grill. It is, to be sure, excellent with a simple sauce of butter and lemon with a sprinkling, perhaps, of parsley, but it can be far more interesting if it is elaborated on. Take, for example, the recipe outlined here, tournedos Ismal Bayeldi.

  4 Sautéed Eggplant Slices (see below)
 12 Sautéed Cherry Tomatoes (see below)
  4 tournedos (small filets mignons), each
     about 1½ inches thick
     Salt and freshly ground black pepper
3½ tablespoons butter
  2 tablespoons chopped shallots
 ⅓ cup Madeira
  1 cup Brown Sauce (page 268) or canned
     beef gravy
 ⅓ cup water

1. Prepare the eggplant slices and tomatoes and set aside.
2. Sprinkle the beef with salt and pepper to taste.
3. Heat one and one-half tablespoons of the butter in a large skillet, and when the butter is golden brown cook the filets mignons on all sides until browned. Cooking time will depend on individual preferences, but about five minutes to the side should be sufficient. Transfer the steaks to a warm platter.
4. Add the shallots to the skillet and cook briefly, then pour in the wine. Add the brown sauce or beef gravy and water. Stir to blend and simmer five minutes. Add salt and pepper to taste and remove the sauce from the heat. Swirl in the remaining butter by rotating the pan gently.
5. Top each tournedos with a cooked eggplant slice and three cherry tomatoes. Pour the sauce over or around the meat or serve the sauce separately.

SAUTÉED EGGPLANT SLICES:

4 slices

  4 eggplant slices, peeled, each about ¾ inch
     thick
     Salt and freshly ground black pepper
 ¼ cup all-purpose flour
     Vegetable oil

1. Sprinkle the eggplant slices with salt and pepper and dredge with flour.
2. Add oil to the depth of one-quarter inch to a skillet large enough to hold the eggplant slices. Cook the slices on all sides until they are golden brown. Transfer to paper towels to drain. Keep warm.

SAUTÉED CHERRY TOMATOES:

12 tomatoes

12 cherry tomatoes
 3 tablespoons butter
 1 small clove garlic, finely minced
    Salt and freshly ground black pepper

1. Drop the cherry tomatoes into boiling water and let stand no longer than twelve seconds. Drain immediately. Using a paring knife, pull away the peel of each tomato. Set aside.
2. Heat the butter in a skillet and add the garlic. Cook briefly, but do not brown. Add the tomatoes and sprinkle with salt and pepper to taste. Just before serving, heat the tomatoes, but do not overcook. If they are overcooked, they will fall apart.

Roulades de Boeuf

4 servings

2 pounds top round of beef, ¼ inch thick
⅓ cup finely chopped onion
1 clove garlic, finely minced
2 tablespoons butter
½ pound veal, ground
¼ pound lean pork, ground
½ cup bread crumbs
¼ teaspoon salt
⅛ teaspoon freshly ground black pepper
2 tablespoons chopped parsley
¼ teaspoon dried marjoram
1 egg, lightly beaten
2 tablespoons olive oil
1 carrot, quartered
1 onion, quartered
2 tablespoons all-purpose flour
1 cup dry vermouth
1 cup Beef Stock (page 115)
1 bay leaf

1. Pound the beef with the edge of a plate or a mallet until the beef is one-eighth inch thick. Cut the meat into eight rectangles (about 4 x 3 inches).

2. Sauté the chopped onion and the garlic in the butter until tender. Remove from the heat and add the veal, pork, bread crumbs, salt, pepper, parsley, marjoram, and egg. Mix to combine.

3. Divide the stuffing among the pieces of meat and roll each rectangle to enclose the stuffing, tucking in the sides where possible. Tie with string or secure with food picks.

4. Brown the rolls, a few at a time, in the oil. Add the carrot and onion to the fat remaining in the pan and sauté until browned. Sprinkle with the flour and stir over medium heat for one minute.

5. Stir in the vermouth and stock, bring to a boil, add the bay leaf, and season with additional salt and pepper to taste. Replace the beef rolls, cover tightly, and simmer slowly for about one and one-quarter hours,

until the beef is tender. Turn the rolls or baste with the sauce several times.

6. Transfer the rolls to a warm platter and remove the strings or picks. Strain the sauce and pour some of it over the rolls. Serve the remainder separately.

Grilled Steak Sandwiches with Tartar Sauce

8 sandwiches

8 thin slices filet mignon or other steak for grilling
  Salt and freshly ground pepper to taste
  Vegetable oil or butter
8 hamburger buns
16 tablespoons Tartar Sauce II (page 277)

1. The meat should be sandwich size, about half an inch thick. Place it on a flat surface and pound it with a flat mallet or the bottom of a clean skillet.

2. Sprinkle the meat on both sides with salt and pepper. If the meat is to be grilled, dip it in or brush it with oil, then grill on both sides to the desired degree of doneness. Or to cook it in a skillet, heat the butter and cook the meat on both sides.

3. Split the buns and spread each split side with one tablespoon tartar sauce. Serve the meat in between.

Beef Ragoût

6 servings

3 pounds lean beef, cut into 2-inch cubes
2 teaspoons salt
¼ teaspoon freshly ground black pepper
2 tablespoons salad oil, approximately
2 tablespoons butter
1 medium onion, chopped
1 carrot, scraped and chopped
2 ribs celery, chopped
2 cloves garlic, minced
½ cup all-purpose flour
2 cups Beef Stock (page 115)
2 cups dry red wine
2 fresh tomatoes, chopped, or 1 cup canned
  Italian plum tomatoes
4 sprigs parsley
2 bay leaves
¼ teaspoon dried thyme
12 small white onions
6 carrots, scraped and halved
12 small potatoes, peeled
1 tablespoon chopped parsley

1. Sprinkle the meat with the salt and pepper. Heat the oil and butter in a skillet and brown the meat on all sides over high heat, adding more oil if necessary. Lower the heat to medium. Add the chopped onion, chopped carrot, celery, and garlic and cook until the onion is lightly browned.

2. Stir in the flour and cook until the flour is blended. Gradually stir in the beef stock and wine and bring to a boil. Add the tomatoes, parsley sprigs, bay leaves, and thyme. Cover and cook over low heat for one and one-half hours.

3. Add the onions, carrots, and potatoes, cover again, and continue cooking for one hour longer. Before serving, sprinkle with parsley.

Short Ribs à la Française

About 12 servings

9 pounds short ribs of beef
2 sprigs parsley
  Pinch of dried thyme
1 bay leaf
2 whole cloves
1 clove garlic
  Salt and freshly ground black pepper
4 carrots, scraped and cut into quarters
3 turnips, peeled and cut into quarters
6 leeks, trimmed, split to the root end, and
  washed well
6 small onions, peeled and halved
1 small cabbage, cut into quarters
1 rib celery, trimmed and cut into quarters
6 small potatoes, peeled and halved
  Grated fresh horseradish
  Coarse salt

1. Place the short ribs in a kettle. Add enough cold water to cover the meat and, later, the vegetables. Bring to a boil, then reduce the heat.

2. Tie the parsley, thyme, bay leaf, cloves, and garlic in cheesecloth and add to the kettle. Simmer slowly for one hour. Add salt and pepper to taste, the carrots, turnips, leeks, and onions; simmer for one hour longer. Add the cabbage, celery, and potatoes. Cook for about forty-five minutes, until the cabbage and potatoes are tender but not mushy.

3. Serve the meat and vegetables on a large platter, along with fresh horseradish and coarse salt.

Note: Reserve the broth for another meal and serve with broken vermicelli.

Boeuf en Daube Provençale

8 to 10 servings

There is no apparent end to dishes made with beef in the repertory of French cooking. The uses of the fillet alone number in the hundreds and range from Alexandra (sautéed and garnished with truffles and quartered artichokes) to Zingara (sautéed and garnished with mushrooms, truffles, ham, and tongue). Some of the most ambitious and gratifying beef dishes, however, are those made with the lesser cuts such as chuck or plate of beef, and this would include the dish below, boeuf en daube provençale. *It is a country dish, easily made and delicately spiced in the style of Provence with rosemary and thyme.*

5 pounds chuck or plate of beef, cut into 2-inch cubes
   Salt and freshly ground black pepper
4 cloves garlic, coarsely chopped
2 carrots, scraped and sliced
2 medium onions, sliced
1 bay leaf, broken
3 sprigs fresh thyme or 1 teaspoon dried thyme
3 sprigs parsley
1 sprig fresh rosemary or 1 teaspoon dried thyme
1 bottle dry red wine
1 pound salt pork, cubed
⅓ cup all-purpose flour
½ pound mushrooms, quartered
5 tablespoons butter
¾ cup pitted green olives
1 pint cherry tomatoes
1 tablespoon chopped shallots

1. Place the beef cubes in a large mixing bowl and sprinkle with salt and pepper. Add the garlic, carrots, onions, bay leaf, thyme, parsley, rosemary, and red wine. Cover and let stand six hours or longer.

2. Preheat the oven to 350 degrees.

3. Place the salt pork in a saucepan and add water to cover. Bring to a boil and simmer five minutes. Drain.

4. Cook the salt pork in a large casserole until crisp. Remove with a slotted spoon and reserve.

5. Drain the meat, reserving the marinade and vegetables.

6. Add the cubes of beef to the casserole and cook, stirring, about ten minutes. Add the vegetables and herbs from the marinade and continue cooking and stirring about ten minutes longer. Sprinkle with the flour and stir to coat the meat.

7. Place in the oven and bake, uncovered, about twenty minutes, stirring once or twice. Add the marinade and water, if necessary, to barely cover the meat. Cover and bring to a boil on top of the stove. Return the casserole to the oven and bake one and one-half hours.

8. Remove the meat from the sauce. Strain the sauce through a colander, pressing to extract as much liquid as possible from the solids. Return the sauce to the meat. Bring to a boil on top of the stove and return to the oven.

9. Meanwhile, cook the mushrooms in two tablespoons of the butter until they have a nutty smell. Add the mushrooms to the beef and continue cooking about thirty minutes, or until the meat is fork tender.

10. Place the olives in a saucepan and add water. Bring to a boil, then drain. Place the tomatoes in boiling water for nine seconds. Drain immediately and pull off the skins with a paring knife. They will peel easily.

11. Toss the shallots in the remaining butter and cook briefly. Add the tomatoes and cook just to heat through. Do not overcook or the tomatoes will disintegrate. Add the olives and keep warm.

12. Pour the daube into a large heated platter and surround it with the tomato and olive mixture. Sprinkle with the crisp pork bits and serve.

Petite Marmite

6 servings

The French creation known as petite marmite *("little kettle"), a savory combination of chicken, beef, and vegetables in a clear broth, is one of the most adaptable of dishes. With its precisely cut morsels of meat and vegetables, it makes an appetizing and attractive preface to luncheon or dinner. Served in more generous quantities,* petite marmite *can be the mainstay of a simple family meal. Crusty French bread and a tossed green salad are the only accompaniments needed. For a light supper, the broth and meats may be served as separate courses. In this case, noodles or rice may be added to the broth.* Petite marmite *is also a dish for all seasons, as appetizing in warm weather as in cold.*

1 pound beef top round, eye round, or chuck steak
1 chicken (3½ pounds), cut into serving pieces
2 ribs celery
2 carrots
3 small or 2 large leeks
1 white turnip, peeled and cut into ½-inch cubes (optional)
1 large onion, cut into ½-inch pieces
7 cups Chicken Stock (page 115)
Salt and freshly ground pepper to taste
Chopped parsley

1. The important thing about this recipe is the cutting of the various ingredients. The pieces of meat and vegetable must be pleasing to the eye, and their size affects the cooking time.

2. Cut the beef into one-inch cubes.

3. Do not bone the chicken parts. Cut each leg into three pieces and each thigh into three pieces. Cut each wing bone into two pieces. Split the breast in half and cut each half into four pieces.

4. Combine the raw beef and chicken in a large kettle or saucepan and add cold water to cover. Bring to a boil and simmer five minutes. Immediately place the saucepan under the faucet and run cold water into the saucepan. Continue until the water runs clear and the meats are chilled. Drain well.

5. Trim the celery ribs and cut them into two-inch lengths. Then cut each length into matchlike strips. Trim and scrape the carrots and cut them into two-inch lengths. Cut each length into strips the same size as the celery strips. Trim the leeks and rinse them well to remove all sand. Cut the leeks into two-inch lengths and then cut these also into matchlike bits. Combine the celery, carrots, leeks, turnip, and onion in a saucepan and add cold water to cover. Bring to a boil and simmer fifteen minutes. Drain.

6. Combine the blanched beef, chicken, and vegetables in a large saucepan or kettle and add the chicken stock. Bring to a boil and add salt and pepper to taste, then simmer, skimming the surface as necessary, one hour or longer. Some maintain that the longer a petite marmite is cooked over low heat the better it gets. Serve, sprinkled with chopped parsley, in hot soup plates.

Note: Cooked rice or noodles may be added to the broth before serving. A good accompaniment is crisp, buttered toast. Petite marmite, incidentally, is very good when reheated.

Fondue Bourguignonne

6 servings

One of the food phenomena of the decade of the sixties was the zoom to popularity of fondue bourguignonne. *Despite its name, it is probably not a Burgundian dish; exactly where it originated is a matter of conjecture, although the Swiss, perhaps because of their cheese fondue, are generally given credit for it. A natural for informal entertaining, it consists of meat cubes cooked at the table and served with a variety of sauces.*

3 pounds fillet of beef
1 large veal kidney (about ½ pound, optional)
¾ pound chicken livers
1 cup salad oil
2 cups clarified butter (see note)
  Sour Cream and Horseradish Sauce (page 276)
  Tartar Sauce II (page 277)
  Béarnaise Sauce (page 266)
  Bordelaise Sauce (page 267)
  Paprika Sauce (page 274)

1. Cut the beef into neat, bite-sized cubes, slightly less than one inch. Pile it in a mound or mounds on a plate.

2. Remove and discard the core from the kidney. Cut the kidney into bite-sized pieces. Arrange the pieces on a plate.

3. Cut each chicken liver in half and cut away any veinlike pieces. Arrange the pieces on a plate.

4. To serve, combine the oil and butter in one or two, preferably two, utensils the sides of which slope in to prevent splattering. Heat to the bubbling point and keep bubbling throughout the meal.

5. Furnish each guest with a fondue fork. The procedure is to spear one cube of beef, kidney, or liver and drop it into the boiling fat, then cook to the desired degree of doneness. The meat should be transferred quickly from the fondue fork to a dinner fork. Let each guest help himself to the sauces used for dipping the hot morsels of meat.

Note: To clarify butter, place about three-quarters of a pound of butter in a one-quart, heatproof, glass measuring cup and let it melt slowly. Do not stir the butter. Pour off the clear, golden liquid on top, leaving the white milky substance at the bottom. The clear liquid is clarified butter.

Beef Salade Vinaigrette

6 to 8 servings

4 cups tender, thinly sliced Boiled Beef (page 165)
1 cup finely chopped onion
½ cup finely sliced sour pickles, preferably the imported French cornichons
1 tablespoon finely chopped chives
2 tablespoons mustard, preferably Dijon or Düsseldorf
⅓ cup wine vinegar
1½ cups peanut oil
  Salt and freshly ground black pepper to taste

Combine all the ingredients and serve at room temperature.

Charcoal-Grilled Lamb Provençale

8 to 10 servings

1 leg of lamb (6 pounds), boned or butter-
   flied
1 cup olive oil
⅔ cup lemon juice
3 cloves garlic, crushed
2 bay leaves
6 sprigs parsley
2 teaspoons salt
½ teaspoon freshly ground pepper
1 tablespoon dried sage
1 tablespoon rosemary
1 tablespoon dried thyme
½ cup Beef Stock (page 115)
¼ cup red wine
2 tablespoons chopped shallots
3 tablespoons butter, at room temperature
3 tablespoons chopped parsley

1. Remove all the fat and skin from the lamb. Combine the oil, lemon juice, garlic, bay leaves, parsley sprigs, salt, pepper, and half the sage, rosemary, and thyme. Marinate the lamb in the mixture about twenty-four hours, turning occasionally.

2. Drain the meat and reserve the marinade. Place the meat flat on a hot grill and sear each side. Lower the heat and cook the meat forty-five minutes to one hour, brushing with the reserved marinade from time to time. The outside should be crusty and the inside pink. Do not overcook.

3. To make the sauce, combine the stock, wine, shallots, and remaining sage, rosemary, and thyme. Boil the sauce rapidly to reduce to about one-half cup. Remove from the heat and add the butter and chopped parsley. Pour over the sliced meat.

Roast Lamb à la Française

8 or more servings

1 leg of lamb (6 pounds)
3 cloves garlic
   Salt and freshly ground black pepper
1 carrot, scraped and left whole
1 onion, peeled
½ cup water

1. Preheat the oven to 450 degrees.

2. Make small incisions in the lamb with a paring knife. Cut the garlic into thin slivers and insert the slivers into the incisions. Place the lamb, skin side down, on a baking dish and sprinkle with salt and pepper. Add the carrot and onion and bake for one hour, basting occasionally with the pan drippings. Continue cooking until the lamb is cooked to the desired degree of doneness, eighteen minutes per pound for well done (175 degrees F. on a meat thermometer), twelve for rare (140 degrees F.).

3. Pour off the fat and remove the carrot and onion. Add the water to the pan and stir to dissolve the brown particles that cling to the bottom and sides of the pan. Let the lamb stand twenty minutes before carving. Serve with the natural pan juices.

Parsleyed Rack of Lamb

4 servings

Great cooking doesn't necessarily imply long or complicated hours in the kitchen. For instance, a roast rack of lamb should—indeed, must—be done with a certain celerity. Of course, the lamb must be tender, of first quality, to begin with. When you have lamb of such quality, it can be prepared excellently and quickly, using the recipe below. Note well that this lamb is best cooked rare.

- 1 rack of lamb (2½ pounds)
- 6 tablespoons butter
   Salt and freshly ground pepper to taste
- ½ cup fresh bread crumbs
- 2 tablespoons chopped parsley
- 1 clove garlic, finely minced
- 1 shallot, finely minced
   Parsley for garnish

1. Using the fingers, pull away as much as possible of the top fat and top skin from the lamb. Cut away the remaining fat (this may be done by the butcher). Prepare the tip ends of the lamb bones French style, scraping all the meat away from the bottom inch or two of the lamb bones to expose them.

2. Preheat the oven to 500 degrees.

3. Rub a baking dish (large enough to hold the lamb) with butter. Rub three tablespoons of the butter all over the rack of lamb, then sprinkle all over with salt and pepper.

4. Meanwhile, combine the bread crumbs, chopped parsley, garlic, and shallot and set aside.

5. Arrange the lamb, meaty side down, in the baking dish. Place under the broiler and cook about eight minutes.

6. As the lamb cooks, melt the remaining three tablespoons of butter.

7. Remove the lamb and turn it meat side up. Sprinkle generously with the bread crumb mixture, then pour the melted butter over. Put the lamb in the oven and bake five to ten minutes, depending on how well done you

want the lamb to be. Ideally, it should be served on the rare side. If you want a more golden crust, run it briefly under the broiler.

8. Transfer the lamb to a serving platter and garnish with parsley. Slice and serve while still hot.

Noisettes d' Agneau à l' Estragon

4 servings

- 8 lamb chops, each about 1½ inches thick
   Salt and freshly ground black pepper
- 3 tablespoons butter
- 3 tablespoons finely chopped shallots
- ⅓ cup dry white wine
- 1 tablespoon chopped fresh tarragon or 1 teaspoon dried tarragon
- 1⅓ cups Brown Sauce (page 268) or 1 10¾-ounce can beef gravy
- 16 fresh tarragon leaves (optional)

1. Carefully remove the bones from the lamb chops but leave a thin layer of fat on. Sprinkle with salt and pepper. Roll each chop and secure with food picks.

2. Melt two tablespoons of butter in a heavy skillet and brown the noisettes on all sides, eight minutes or longer, depending on the doneness desired.

3. Remove the noisettes to a hot platter, arrange neatly, and keep warm in a slow oven. Pour off the fat from the skillet and add the shallots. Cook, stirring, one to two minutes. Add the wine and cook, stirring, until the wine is almost totally evaporated. Add the chopped tarragon. Stir in the brown sauce and, when blended, remove from the heat. Off the heat, swirl in the remaining butter by rotating the pan gently.

4. Drop the tarragon leaves into boiling water and drain immediately, then plunge into cold water. Carefully unfold the leaves onto paper towels. Arrange two crossed leaves on each noisette and serve with the sauce.

Lamb Chops Rouennaise

4 or 8 servings

3 tablespoons butter
1 carrot, scraped and finely diced
1 rib celery, finely chopped
1 cup plus 2 tablespoons finely chopped onion
1½ tablespoons all-purpose flour
1 cup Chicken Stock (page 115)
1 bay leaf
2 sprigs fresh thyme or ½ teaspoon dried
3 chicken livers, trimmed
8 rib lamb chops, each about 2 inches thick
1 tablespoon vegetable oil
2 tablespoons Calvados or applejack
Bread croutons (see note)

1. Heat the butter in a saucepan and add the carrot, celery, and one cup of chopped onion. Cook, stirring, until the onion is wilted. Stir in the flour and cook, stirring frequently, until the flour is brown. Do not burn. Add the stock, stirring rapidly with a whisk. When the mixture is thickened and smooth, add the bay leaf and thyme. Strain the sauce into another saucepan and keep hot.

2. Puree the chicken livers in an electric blender and set aside.

3. Neatly trim the chops to remove excess fat. Heat the oil in a large skillet and brown the chops on both sides. Add the remaining two tablespoons of onion and continue to cook the chops to the desired degree of doneness.

4. Arrange the chops on a warm serving platter and keep warm. Add the sauce to the skillet and bring to a boil. Add the Calvados and pureed livers, bring to a boil, and cook briefly. Spoon the sauce over the chops and garnish the platter with bread croutons.

Note: To make the croutons, use a biscuit cutter to cut rounds from eight slices of white bread. Brown the rounds in hot oil on both sides and drain on paper towels.

Lamb Shanks au Vin Rouge

4 servings

4 lamb shanks
3 tablespoons all-purpose flour
Salt and freshly ground pepper to taste
2 tablespoons butter
2 tablespoons peanut or vegetable oil
1½ cups finely chopped onion
1 cup finely chopped celery
1 cup finely chopped carrot
1 clove garlic, finely minced
1 cup dry red wine
2 sprigs parsley
1 teaspoon dried thyme or 1 sprig fresh thyme
1 bay leaf
1 teaspoon dried marjoram

1. Preheat the oven to 350 degrees.

2. Rub the lamb shanks with flour seasoned with salt and pepper.

3. Heat the butter and oil in a skillet. Brown the lamb on all sides, then transfer to a casserole. To the same skillet add the onion and cook, stirring, until wilted. Add the celery, carrot, and garlic and cook briefly. Stir in the wine and pour the mixture over the shanks. Add the remaining ingredients and salt and pepper to taste. Cover closely and bake one and one-half to two hours, or until the meat is fork tender.

Lamb Shanks Côte d' Azur

4 servings

The choicest cuts of lamb and veal—rack, loin, saddle, and chops—are not one whit more delectable than those less esteemed parts, the shanks. Meaty and bony, shanks may be roasted, braised, or turned into a stew. They are worthy of the cook's attention as the recipe below will testify.

4   lamb shanks (about 1¼ pounds each)
    Salt and freshly ground pepper
¼   cup salad or vegetable oil
1   large onion, finely minced
2   carrots, scraped and diced
1   clove garlic, finely minced
2   ribs celery, finely diced
3   sprigs parsley
2   sprigs thyme
1   bay leaf
½   cup plus 2 teaspoons water
1   cup dry white wine
1½ cups Chicken Stock (page 115)
1   cup Tomato Sauce I (page 278)
3   tablespoons tomato paste
1   teaspoon dried mint
2   tablespoons cornstarch
    Chopped parsley

1. Sprinkle the lamb shanks with salt and pepper to taste. Heat the oil in a large skillet and brown the shanks on all sides. As they are browned, transfer them to a kettle with a heavy lid and add the onion, carrots, garlic, and celery. Tie the parsley, thyme, and bay leaf into a bundle with string and add to the kettle.

2. Add the one-half cup water to the skillet in which the shanks were browned and scrape and stir to dissolve the brown particles that cling to the bottom and sides. Add the wine, chicken stock, tomato sauce, tomato paste, and salt and pepper to taste. Stir briefly and pour over the meat. Sprinkle with the mint and cover.

3. Cook one and one-half hours, or until the shanks are fork tender. Remove the shanks to a hot platter. Discard the herbs.

4. Blend the two teaspoons water with the cornstarch and stir into the sauce over medium heat, to thicken it. Sprinkle the meat with parsley and serve with the sauce and pureed potatoes.

Lamb Stew Forestière

6 servings

2   tablespoons butter, approximately
2   tablespoons vegetable oil, approximately
12 small white onions, peeled
½   pound mushrooms, thinly sliced
2   pounds lamb, cut into 1-inch cubes
1   tablespoon tomato paste
2   tablespoons all-purpose flour
½   cup dry vermouth
1½ cups Beef Stock (page 115) or Chicken Stock (page 115)
½   teaspoon dried thyme
1   bay leaf
    Salt and freshly ground black pepper
½   cup heavy cream
    Freshly chopped parsley

1. Preheat the oven to 350 degrees.

2. Heat the butter and oil in a heavy skillet and cook the onions and mushrooms, stirring, until the mushrooms are wilted and the onions just start to take on color. Transfer the onions and mushrooms to a baking dish.

3. Brown the lamb in the same skillet, adding more butter and oil if necessary. When the lamb is browned, add it to the baking dish.

4. Add the tomato paste and flour to the skillet in which the lamb cooked. Cook briefly, stirring, then stir in the vermouth and stock and bring to a boil.

5. Pour the mixture over the lamb. Add the thyme, bay leaf, and salt and pepper to taste; cover. Bake for one hour or longer, until the meat is quite tender. Stir in the cream and serve sprinkled with parsley.

Haricot de Mouton

6 to 8 servings

*A bourgeois but excellent French concoction
called* haricot de mouton *is a lamb stew that
in its classic form is made without beans. Its
name has been the occasion for much dis-
cussion. Haricot means bean, but this particular* haricot, *some authorities hold, is a
corruption of* harigoter, *meaning to cut. The
lamb (or* mouton) *in the recipe is cut up.
Linguistics aside, it is an excellent dish for
a buffet—and our version includes beans.
Appropriately enough for such a garbled
delicacy, they are Italian white beans.*

     1 pound pea beans or Italian white beans
    ½ pound salt pork
     1 onion, studded with 2 cloves
     1 whole carrot, scraped
     2 sprigs parsley
       Salt
    12 peppercorns, tied in a small cheesecloth
       bag
     3 pounds lamb, cut into cubes
     1 tablespoon peanut oil, approximately
     1 carrot, scraped and chopped
     2 cloves garlic, finely chopped
     1 bay leaf
     1 large onion, chopped
     2 sprigs fresh thyme or ½ teaspoon dried
       thyme
       Freshly ground black pepper
    ¼ cup all-purpose flour
     4 cups water
     2 large ripe tomatoes, peeled, or 1 1-pound-
       1-ounce can Italian plum tomatoes

1. Pick over the beans and add cold water
to cover to a depth of two inches. Add the
salt pork and let soak overnight.

2. Drain the beans and salt pork and place
in a large saucepan. Add water to cover to a
depth of one inch and add the onion studded
with the cloves, the whole carrot, parsley,
salt to taste, and peppercorns. Simmer one
hour or longer or until the beans are tender
but not mushy.

3. When cooked, drain the beans and discard the onion, salt pork, carrot, parsley, and
peppercorns.

4. Meanwhile, preheat the oven to 400
degrees.

5. In a large skillet with a lid, brown the
lamb on all sides in the oil. If the lamb is
very lean, it may be necessary to add a little
more oil. When the lamb is quite brown, add
the chopped carrot, garlic, bay leaf, chopped
onion, thyme, and salt and pepper to taste.
Place in the oven, uncovered, and bake for
ten minutes.

6. Sprinkle the meat with flour and return
to the oven. Reduce the heat to 375 degrees.
Shake the pan occasionally and bake, uncovered, for thirty minutes.

7. Pour off any fat that may have accumulated in the skillet. Add the four cups water,
the tomatoes, and salt and pepper to taste.
Bring to a boil on top of the stove, cover,
and bake one hour, or until the meat is tender.

8. Remove the cubes of lamb and put the
remaining sauce and solids through a sieve or
food mill. Add the lamb and the beans. Stir
to distribute the meat and beans evenly.
Cover and bake fifteen minutes longer.

Curried Lamb à la Française

8 to 10 servings

Curry was among the first of the foreign dishes to invade America's kitchens twenty years or so ago. It was followed by shish kebab, beef in Burgundy wine, paella, quiche Lorraine and other now-familiar examples of international cuisine. In recent years, curry has become less common, but it is still an excellent dish for entertaining. On this page we give a French version. There are many differences between it and an authentic Indian or Pakistani curry, particularly the use of heavy cream.

1 leg of lamb (5 pounds), boned and trimmed of fat
2 tablespoons butter
1 cup finely chopped onion
¾ cup finely chopped celery
1 cup chopped apple
2 firm, ripe bananas, cubed
1 clove garlic, finely minced
¼ cup Curry Powder (page 33), or to taste
2 tablespoons all-purpose flour
1 cup diced, peeled tomatoes
½ cup Chicken Stock (page 115)
1 cup water
Salt and freshly ground pepper to taste
1 cup heavy cream

1. Preheat the oven to 375 degrees.
2. Cut the lamb into one-and-one-half-inch cubes. Heat the butter in a large, ovenproof skillet, Dutch oven, or casserole and add the lamb. Cook, turning the pieces, until they lose color. Add the onion, celery, apple, bananas, and garlic and cook, stirring, until most of the moisture evaporates.
3. Sprinkle with the curry powder and flour and stir until the meat is coated. Add the tomatoes, chicken stock, water, salt, and pepper and bring to a boil. Cover and bake in the oven for one and one-half hours, or until the meat is thoroughly tender.

4. Return to the top of the stove and bring to a boil. Spoon off the fat. Stir in the heavy cream and season, if desired, with more salt and pepper. Serve with hot rice and such curry garnishes as chutney, plumped currants or raisins, chopped cashews or peanuts, Coconut Side Dish (see below), and Tomato Sambal (page 181).

COCONUT SIDE DISH:

2 cups coconut sauce, 1 cup toasted coconut

1 large coconut
2½ cups Chicken Stock
1 tablespoon coriander seeds
1 tablespoon mustard seeds
1 teaspoon chopped fresh ginger
½ teaspoon leaf saffron
1 tablespoon butter
1 onion, chopped
¾ cup blanched almonds, grated or ground

1. Crack the coconut, and drain off and discard the coconut water in the center. Remove the meat from the shell and pare away the dark outer coating of the meat. Grate three tablespoons of coconut and set aside. Cut the remaining coconut into cubes and add to the container of an electric blender. Add the stock, coriander, mustard, ginger, and saffron and blend at high speed.
2. Heat the butter in a skillet and cook the onion until translucent. Add the coconut mixture and cook, uncovered, thirty minutes. Strain through cheesecloth to extract as much of the liquid as possible. Reserve the coconut pulp.
3. Return the sauce to the skillet and add the grated almonds and the three tablespoons fresh grated coconut. Cook until thickened, about ten minutes. Use as a side dish for curry.
4. Put the reserved coconut pulp in a skillet and cook, stirring, over moderate heat. Cook until golden brown. Use as a garnish.

TOMATO SAMBAL:

About 2 cups

1 large, firm tomato, peeled and cut into small cubes
3 green onions, including green part, chopped
   Salt to taste
½ clove garlic, finely minced
1 or more canned serrano or jalapena chilies, seeded and chopped
1 tablespoon salad oil
1 teaspoon chopped fresh coriander

Combine the ingredients and refrigerate until ready to serve. Use as a side dish for curry.

Roast Loin of Pork au Vin Blanc

6 to 8 servings

To the purists in cooking, most dishes made with pork are a little too earthy, a touch too peasantlike to be accorded real status. And yet, no meat is better suited to the winter table and none more versatile. One of the most hackneyed sayings in the world of cuisine is that all the pig is edible except the squeal and that went into the Model T. Elegant or not, a roast of pork is a lovely dish for fall and winter feasting. A recipe for pork roasted with white wine is given here.

1 loin of pork (6 to 8 pounds)
4 cloves garlic
   Salt and freshly ground black pepper
3 sprigs parsley
3 sprigs fresh thyme or 1 teaspoon dried thyme
1 bay leaf, crumbled
¼ cup olive oil
½ bottle dry white wine
¾ cup water

1. Wipe the pork with a damp cloth.
2. Cut the garlic into thin slivers. Make small incisions around the ribs and bones of the loin and insert the garlic slivers inside. Sprinkle the loin liberally with salt and pepper and place in a baking dish. Add the parsley, thyme, and bay leaf. Rub the loin with the oil and pour the wine over all. Cover with aluminum foil and refrigerate twelve hours or longer. Turn the pork occasionally in the wine marinade.
3. Preheat the oven to 325 degrees.
4. Roast the pork forty minutes to the pound, basting occasionally with the marinade. When cooked, the roast should be mahogany brown. Remove the pork from the oven and keep warm about twenty minutes.
5. Strain the drippings in the pan into a large glass measuring cup. Pour off or skim off most of the fat. Return the drippings to the roasting pan and add the water. Cook on top of the stove, stirring to dissolve the brown particles that cling to the bottom and sides of the pan. Pour the sauce into a sauceboat and serve separately.

Oven-Roasted Pork Loin

10 or more servings

1 loin of pork (8 pounds)
3 cloves garlic
  Salt and freshly ground black pepper
½ cup water

1. Preheat the oven to 400 degrees.
2. Using a sharp paring knife, cut small incisions in the pork flesh next to the bone. Also cut vertical incisions in the fat.
3. Cut the garlic into thin slivers and insert one small sliver in each incision. Salt and pepper the meat on all sides and ends. Use a generous amount of salt and pepper.
4. Place the pork roast, fat side up, on a rack in a baking pan. Bake and baste with the natural drippings for forty-five minutes. Turn the pork fat side down and reduce the oven heat to 350 degrees. Continue baking and basting two hours longer. Pour off the fat from the pan and add the water, stirring to dissolve the brown particles that cling to the bottom and sides of the pan. Place the loin fat side up once more and continue baking and basting thirty minutes longer, or until thoroughly cooked and the internal temperature registers 185 degrees.

Note: To cook loin of pork on a spit, slash and season with salt, pepper, and garlic as in the recipe above and then insert the skewer, following the line of the backbone. A drip pan should be fashioned out of heavy-duty foil and placed under the turning meat. The coals should be placed to one side of the meat and continually replenished throughout the cooking. Length of cooking time over charcoal varies with weather conditions and the distance of the meat from the fire, but at least thirty minutes a pound should be allowed. The meat should be well done and the internal temperature should register 185 degrees.

Ragoût of Pork au Vin Rouge

About 12 servings

A ragoût by any name (and it goes by many, such as stew, casserole, and fricassee) is a dish to warm the inner man and thus particularly appropriate for the frosty season. A savory choice for a winter menu is the ragoût of pork outlined below—unusual because it is cooked with red wine rather than the customary white wine. And of course a basic red wine goes well with it.

1 loin of pork (8 pounds)
  Salt and freshly ground pepper to taste
1 large onion, coarsely chopped
1 clove garlic, finely chopped
2 carrots, scraped and cut into rounds
2 ribs celery, chopped
2 sprigs fresh thyme or ½ teaspoon dried thyme
1 sprig fresh rosemary or ½ teaspoon dried thyme
1 bay leaf
8 cups dry red wine, approximately
½ cup vegetable oil, approximately
½ cup all-purpose flour
1 pound fresh mushrooms, sliced
2 tablespoons butter

1. Have the loin of pork boned. Have the meat cut into two-inch cubes and the bones cut into rib and back sections.
2. Rub the meat and bones with salt and pepper and put in a deep bowl. Add the onion, garlic, carrots, celery, thyme, rosemary, bay leaf, and wine. The wine should barely cover the pork. Let stand overnight.
3. Preheat the oven to 400 degrees.
4. When ready to cook, remove the meat and bones from the marinade and pat dry with paper towels. Drain the vegetables, reserving both the vegetables and the liquid in separate bowls.

5. Heat the oil in two or three large skillets and brown the meat and bones on all sides. As the meat and bones are browned, transfer them to a Dutch oven. Add the vegetables and bake, uncovered, ten minutes. Sprinkle with flour and stir to distribute the flour evenly. Bake twenty minutes and pour off the fat that accumulates. Add the marinade and bring to a boil on top of the stove, then simmer ten minutes, skimming the surface as necessary. Partly cover and bake one hour, or until the meat is quite tender. Remove the meat to a hot serving dish. Strain the sauce and cook it over high heat about ten minutes, skimming off any fat on the surface.

6. Meanwhile, cook the mushrooms in the butter until wilted. Sprinkle with salt and pepper, then combine with the pork, the bones, and the sauce. Season with salt and pepper and serve hot, with mashed potatoes or noodles.

Grilled Pork Chops

6 servings

Cooking over hot embers is one of the oldest methods of preparing food—and one of the best. It is easy to imagine that the shish kebab gnawed by forkless nomads thousands of years ago had much to recommend it. Here the ancient technique of charcoal or charred wood cookery is used for pork chops.

6 pork chops, each about 1½ inches thick
Salt and freshly ground black pepper

1. Have the butcher pare away and chop off the upper bone of each chop, but leave about two inches of the main rib bone attached. Have the fat trimmed, but leave a one-half-inch rim of fat. Pound the chops with a mallet to flatten them slightly. Sprinkle with salt and pepper to taste.

2. Prepare a charcoal fire or preheat the broiler. Grill or broil the chops, turning once or twice. They should be well cooked over a hot fire, ten to fifteen minutes to a side. Serve with Sauce Robert I (page 276).

Pork Chops with Mustard

4 servings

There is a certain amount of theater in flaming a dish with Cognac or other spirits, and maîtres d'hôtel have long been aware that a dish flamed one brief moment at the table can command a higher price than the same delicacy flamed in the kitchen. A dash of Cognac—and a bit of heavy cream—can give tone even to such a commonplace item as pork chops. What really gives the chops here a fillip, however, is the tang of mustard in the sauce.

2 tablespoons butter
4 pork chops, each 1½ inches thick
  Salt and freshly ground black pepper to taste
1 tablespoon chopped shallots or green onion
1 tablespoon all-purpose flour
1 cup Chicken Stock (page 115) or canned chicken broth
2 tablespoons Brown Sauce (page 268) or canned beef gravy
2 teaspoons prepared mustard, preferably Dijon or Düsseldorf
2 tablespoons chopped sour gherkins or sweet pickles

1. Melt one tablespoon of the butter in a skillet and cook the chops on both sides over relatively high heat. Sprinkle the chops with salt and pepper, then reduce the heat and continue cooking over very low heat until the chops are tender. Cook thoroughly until the chops are well done, turning occasionally.

2. Transfer the chops to a warm platter and keep warm.

3. Pour off all but one tablespoon of fat from the skillet and add the shallots. Cook, stirring, until the shallots are wilted. Sprinkle with the flour and stir. Gradually add the stock, stirring with a whisk until blended and smooth. Return the chops to the sauce and continue to cook, about five minutes to a side.

4. Return the chops to the platter. Add the brown sauce, mustard, gherkins or pickles, and the remaining tablespoon of butter. Swirl the sauce around but do not boil. Spoon the sauce over the chops and serve hot.

Stuffed Cabbage

16 to 18 cabbage balls

The cabbage was known to Romans in days of yore and the Greeks had a word for it. The residents of Mittel-europa dote on it, and it is a substantial part of the diet of Poles and Russians. Almost all the countries of Europe prepare stuffed cabbage in one form or another for the reason pure and simple that it is not only one of the least expensive dishes in the world, but it is also one of the most versatile and delicious. A properly stuffed cabbage is fit food for princes and paupers as well. Stuffed cabbage is another of those dishes that the master chefs of France delight in creating as a trompe-l'oeil, something designed to fool the eye. That is the way with the stuffed cabbage recipe below. The cabbage leaves are pulled apart, filled with a savory stuffing, and then brought together to resemble a whole cabbage.

1 large or 2 small heads cabbage, preferably savoy
¼ pound salt pork
1 cup finely chopped onion
1 clove garlic, chopped
½ teaspoon chopped fresh thyme
1 cup cooked rice
1 pound lean pork, ground
2 chicken livers
1 egg
Salt and freshly ground pepper to taste
1 teaspoon chopped fresh dill
2 teaspoons chopped fresh parsley
2 tablespoons bacon fat
½ cup chopped carrot
½ bay leaf
2 cups canned tomatoes
1 sprig parsley
1 cup sauerkraut

1. Pull off the tough outer leaves from the head of cabbage. Use a knife to cut away the tough white center core. Drop the cabbage into boiling salted water to cover and let cook about five minutes, or until the leaves separate easily. Invert the cabbage in a colander and let stand until cool and thoroughly drained.

2. Cook the salt pork in a skillet until rendered of fat. Add one-half cup of the chopped onion and the garlic and cook until the onion is wilted. Add the thyme and cooked rice. Stir to blend. Place the ground pork in a mixing bowl and add the rice mixture. Stir lightly until blended.

3. Finely chop the chicken livers on a flat surface or put them through the fine blade of a grinder. Add them to the pork and rice mixture. Add the egg, lightly beaten, salt and pepper to taste, chopped dill, and parsley. Mix lightly with a fork or with the fingers.

4. Separate the leaves of cabbage and pat dry. Use a sharp knife to make a V cut at the tough center end of each large leaf. Leave the tender smaller leaves intact. Rinse out a large square of cheesecloth in cold water, then squeeze dry and place on a flat surface. In the center place a large cabbage leaf, curly edge up. Arrange a smaller cabbage leaf in the center of the large leaf. Spoon one or two tablespoons of the filling into the center of the small leaf.

5. Bring the four corners of cheesecloth together and twist the ends together over a bowl. This will shape the leaves into a compact round. Remove the cabbage ball from the cheesecloth. It will not be necessary to use any string. Continue making the balls until all the cabbage leaves and filling are used.

6. Preheat the oven to 400 degrees.

7. Heat the bacon fat in a skillet and add the chopped carrot, bay leaf, and remaining one-half cup chopped onion. Cook until the onion is wilted. Add the tomatoes and parsley sprig. Sprinkle the sauce with salt and pepper to taste and stir in the sauerkraut.

8. Arrange the stuffed cabbage in a neat pattern on top of all and cover with aluminum foil. Bring to a boil on top of the stove, then place in the oven. Bake the stuffed cabbage from one to one and one-half hours, basting frequently with the pan juices, or until the cabbage is thoroughly tender. The finished dish may be served with sour cream. It is also good when reheated.

Chou Farci

6 to 8 servings

1 large head cabbage, savoy if available
1 pound boneless loin of pork with a little fat left on, bones reserved
2 slices white bread, chopped
1 tablespoon butter
1 cup chopped onion
2 large cloves garlic, sliced
½ pound fresh mushrooms, washed and finely chopped
1 teaspoon chopped fresh thyme or ½ teaspoon dried thyme
Salt and freshly ground black pepper to taste
1 egg, lightly beaten
1 tablespoon finely chopped parsley
¼ cup heavy cream
¼ teaspoon nutmeg
2 pounds chicken necks or wings
¼ pound salt pork
2 carrots, sliced
2 small onions, sliced
1 rib celery with leaves, chopped
3 sprigs fresh thyme
1 bay leaf
2 whole cloves
½ cup dry white wine
1¼ cups Brown Sauce (page 268) or 1 10¾-ounce can beef gravy
2 cups Chicken Stock (page 115) or canned chicken broth
½ cup chopped tomatoes, fresh or canned

1. Preheat the oven to 375 degrees.
2. Peel off the tough outer leaves from the cabbage. Drop the cabbage head into boiling water to cover. Simmer ten to fifteen minutes, turning occasionally. Drain the cabbage and plunge it into cold water, then turn upside down to drain in a colander. Set aside while preparing the stuffing.
3. Grind the pork, then add half the bread to the grinder. Grind it through. Heat the butter and cook the onion, garlic, mushrooms, thyme, salt, and pepper. Cook, stirring, until the onions wilt. Cool slightly and add to the pork. Add the remaining bread, the egg, parsley, cream, and nutmeg. Add salt and pepper and beat well with a wooden spoon.

4. Spread a flat surface with a double thickness of cheesecloth. Pull off six or seven large outer cabbage leaves and arrange them, slightly overlapping, in a semicircular fan shape, the stem ends to the outside. If necessary, slice through the stem ends to make the leaves lie flat. Place one large leaf in the center.

5. Spoon about one-quarter of the pork stuffing into the center of the leaves. With the back of a wooden spoon, smooth it from the center almost but not quite to the ends of the leaves. Now make a smaller circle of overlapping cabbage leaves on top of the stuffing and add the same amount of filling. Spread it over the leaves as before.

6. Continue making layers as indicated above. There should be four layers of filled leaves, each smaller than the previous layer. Bring the edges of the cheesecloth together and pull them to reshape the stuffed leaves in the form of a whole cabbage. Tie securely with string and snip off the excess cheesecloth with scissors.

7. Cook the chicken necks and salt pork in a large, heavy casserole until well browned. Add salt, pepper, the reserved bones, and the remaining ingredients. Add the cabbage, tied side down, and cover. Bring to a boil, then bake two hours. Remove the cabbage from the cheesecloth and slice like a pie. Strain the sauce and serve hot with the cabbage.

Stuffed Lettuce Balls

About 12 balls

½ pound pork sausage meat
¼ cup finely chopped onion
3 medium mushrooms, sliced
¾ cup cooked rice
¼ cup finely chopped celery
¼ teaspoon salt
⅛ teaspoon freshly ground black pepper
¼ teaspoon ground sage
2 or 3 tablespoons Brown Sauce (page 268)
2 or 3 heads Boston lettuce
3 cups Tomato Sauce I (page 278), approximately

1. Sauté the sausage meat slowly in a saucepan until the meat is lightly browned. Remove all but two tablespoons of the fat.

2. Add the onion and cook for three to five minutes longer. Add the mushrooms and sauté the mixture for two minutes. Add the rice, celery, salt, pepper, sage, and brown sauce. Mix well.

3. Cut the lettuce into leaves and wash well. Blanch the leaves by holding them with tongs and dipping them, a few at a time, into a pan of boiling water and removing immediately. Drain.

4. Overlap six or eight leaves, to make a bed of lettuce leaves about four inches in diameter, atop a six-inch square of muslin. Place a heaping tablespoon of the filling on top of the leaves and cover with one more blanched leaf. Gather the corners of the muslin together and gently squeeze the stuffed lettuce leaves to form a ball. Remove the ball from the muslin and place in a shallow baking dish. Continue making balls until all the filling is used. Place the balls side by side in the baking dish.

5. Preheat the oven to 350 degrees.

6. Pour the tomato sauce over the lettuce balls. Bake for fifteen to twenty minutes, or until well heated.

Ham Braised in Cider

15 servings

2 carrots, coarsely chopped
2 medium onions, coarsely chopped
2 ribs celery, coarsely chopped
1 uncooked ham (10 to 12 pounds)
1 bay leaf
1 teaspoon dried thyme
2 or 3 whole cloves
1 quart cider
¼ cup fine granulated sugar
¾ teaspoon Parisienne spice
3 tablespoons arrowroot
2 tablespoons cold water
½ cup Calvados
3 tablespoons soft butter

1. Preheat the oven to 325 degrees.

2. Place the carrots, onions, and celery in the bottom of a large roasting pan with a cover. Place the ham, fat side up, on the vegetables. Add the bay leaf, thyme, cloves, and cider and bring to a boil on top of the stove. Cover and place in the oven. Bake for two and one-half to three hours, basting occasionally.

3. Drain the liquid from the pan and reserve. Place the ham on a rack in the roaster and dust the top and sides of the ham with sugar that has been mixed with the Parisienne spice. Increase the oven temperature to 400 degrees and return the ham to the oven for about thirty minutes, or until nicely glazed.

4. Meanwhile, skim the grease off the reserved liquid from the ham and heat the liquid in a saucepan. Dissolve the arrowroot in the cold water and beat into the hot liquid. Simmer for five minutes. Stir in the Calvados and simmer two to three minutes longer. Add the butter bit by bit until just melted and remove from the heat. Serve the ham sliced in thin slices, with a little of the sauce spooned over and the remainder on the side.

Ham and Endive Mornay

6 servings

6 large heads endive
1 teaspoon granulated sugar
¼ cup Chicken Stock (page 115) or water
  Salt and freshly ground black pepper
7 tablespoons butter
5 tablespoons all-purpose flour
3 cups milk
1 cup heavy cream
¼ teaspoon grated nutmeg or to taste
  Cayenne pepper
6 large thin slices of boiled ham
2 egg yolks
¾ cup grated Swiss, Gruyère, Fontina, or Danish Esrom cheese

1. Trim off a very thin slice from the bottom of each endive. Place the endives in one layer in an ovenproof casserole and sprinkle with sugar. Add the stock, salt and pepper to taste, and one tablespoon of the butter. Cover, bring to a boil, and simmer for forty-five minutes. Turn the endives, cover, and simmer for fifteen minutes longer. Drain well.

2. Preheat the oven to 400 degrees.

3. Melt three tablespoons of butter in a saucepan and stir in the flour. When blended, add the milk, stirring vigorously with a wire whisk. When blended and smooth, add salt and pepper to taste and cook, stirring frequently, for fifteen minutes or longer. Add the cream, nutmeg, and cayenne to taste. Bring to a boil, then remove the sauce from the heat.

4. While the sauce is cooking, melt the remaining butter in a skillet, and when hot and bubbling add the drained endives. Cook until nicely browned on one side. Turn and cook until browned all over.

5. Wrap one slice of ham around each endive.

6. Spoon a little sauce into a casserole and arrange the ham-wrapped endives over the bottom. Pour half the sauce over the ham. Beat the egg yolks into the remaining sauce and spoon this over all. Sprinkle with cheese and bake for ten to fifteen minutes, until boiling. Run the casserole under the broiler until the top is nicely browned. Serve immediately.

Veal Bordelaise

4 servings

2 tablespoons butter
1 boneless veal roast (2 pounds)
2½ cups celery cut into 1-inch pieces
12 small white onions
1 cup sliced mushrooms
6 medium carrots, cut into 1-inch pieces
½ cup veal or Chicken Stock (page 115)
½ cup dry white Bordeaux wine
½ teaspoon salt
⅛ teaspoon freshly ground black pepper

1. In a Dutch oven heat the butter and brown the meat well on all sides. Add the remaining ingredients. Bring to a boil, cover, and simmer for about two hours, until the meat is tender.

2. Cut the meat into thin slices. Serve it surrounded by the vegetables and with the gravy in a sauceboat.

Roast Veal Ménagère

6 servings

Take the whitest of veal, stuff it with herbs, and roast until golden and brown. That dish, called veal ménagère, *is food for the palate and soul, an elegant dish for fall and winter dining.*

1 leg of veal (3½ pounds), rolled and boned, with bones reserved
½ cup fresh bread crumbs
1 teaspoon rubbed sage
2 tablespoons chopped fresh parsley
1 teaspoon finely minced garlic
1 egg yolk
3 tablespoons heavy cream
   Salt and freshly ground black pepper
1 onion, cut into eighths
1 bay leaf
6 carrots, scraped and cut in half
3 tablespoons tomato paste
½ cup dry white wine
½ cup water

1. Preheat the oven to 400 degrees.
2. Untie the rolled roast and lay it on a flat surface.
3. Combine the bread crumbs, sage, parsley, garlic, egg yolk, cream, and salt and pepper to taste and mix well with a rubber spatula. Spread the mixture in one thin layer over the veal or tuck into pockets made in the flesh. Reshape the veal and tie it securely with fresh string and skewers, if necessary. Sprinkle the meat with salt and pepper and lay, seam side down, in an ovenproof skillet or heavy shallow roasting pan. Arrange the reserved veal bones around the roast and add the onion, bay leaf, and carrots. Bake, uncovered, thirty minutes. Turn the roast seam side up and bake thirty minutes longer.
4. Turn the meat seam side down again and pour the tomato paste mixed with the wine and water over the meat. Continue baking, basting frequently, for one hour and fifteen minutes, for a total cooking time of about two hours and fifteen minutes. If the roast begins to brown too fast, cover with an aluminum foil tent.
5. Transfer the meat to a warm serving platter and cut into one-quarter-inch slices. Garnish with the cooked carrots, if desired, or use freshly cooked carrots. Strain the sauce and serve it with the meat.

Roast of Veal à la Française

About 6 servings

1 veal roast (3 pounds)
   Salt and freshly ground white pepper
6 tablespoons butter
2 tablespoons peanut oil
2 carrots, thinly sliced
2 onions, thinly sliced
3 sprigs parsley
1 bay leaf
½ teaspoon dried thyme

1. Preheat the oven to 325 degrees.
2. Sprinkle the meat with salt and pepper. Heat three tablespoons of the butter and the oil in a Dutch oven large enough to hold the veal comfortably. Brown the veal until golden all over, turning frequently in the fat. This should take about fifteen minutes.
3. Remove the veal and add the remaining butter, carrots, and onions and cook, stirring, about five minutes. Return the veal to the Dutch oven and add the parsley, bay leaf, and thyme.
4. Cover the meat with aluminum foil and place in the oven. Bake one to one and one-half hours. If a meat thermometer is used, the meat should register 175 degrees when done.
5. Transfer the meat to a hot platter and strain the juice. Skim off most of the fat and reduce the sauce, if desired, over high heat. Serve the sauce separately. Vegetables such as small cooked onions and baby carrots are frequent garnishes for this dish.

Stuffed Veal or Pork Chops aux Pistaches

8 servings

8 veal or pork rib chops (about ½ pound each and each about 1 inch thick)
½ pound pork, twice ground
3 tablespoons finely chopped shallots
½ cup finely chopped onion
1 clove garlic, finely minced
¼ pound raw chicken livers, chopped
¾ cup finely chopped cooked ham
¼ cup shelled pistachios
½ cup fresh bread crumbs
2 tablespoons chopped parsley
  Salt and freshly ground pepper to taste
1 egg, lightly beaten
1 tablespoon Cognac
2 tablespoons butter
2 cups Tomato Sauce II (page 278)
½ cup dry white wine
1 tablespoon chopped fresh tarragon or 1 teaspoon dried tarragon

1. Prepare the chops for stuffing. To do this, slice each chop through the center down to the bone, butterfly fashion. Place each chop on a flat surface, lift up the upper half and lightly pound the lower half with a small flat mallet or rolling pin. Reverse the chop and pound the other half in the same fashion. Scrape the meat and fat from the upper bone. Continue until all the chops are ready.

2. Place the ground pork in a skillet and cook, breaking up the meat with the side of a kitchen spoon. Add the shallots, onion, and garlic and cook until the meat loses its color. It should not be dry. Add the chicken livers, stir, then remove the mixture from the heat.

3. Stir in the ham, pistachios, bread crumbs, parsley, salt and pepper to taste, egg, and Cognac. Let cool.

4. Preheat the oven to 350 degrees.

5. Spoon equal portions of the mixture inside each split chop. Sew the chops with string to keep the filling in.

Anchovy-Stuffed Breast of Veal

5 servings

1 boneless breast of veal (3 to 4 pounds), with a pocket for stuffing
  Salt and freshly ground black pepper
2 cloves garlic
1 cup dry bread crumbs
2 tablespoons chopped parsley
10 anchovy fillets with oil
10 ripe olives, preferably imported, pitted and diced
  All-purpose flour
2 tablespoons butter
¼ cup Chicken Stock (page 115)
¼ cup sour cream (optional)

1. Sprinkle the inside of the veal pocket with salt and pepper.

2. Combine the garlic, bread crumbs, parsley, anchovy fillets in oil, and olives. Stuff the pocket with the mixture and fasten the edges together with skewers or by sewing.

3. Dredge the meat with flour and brown on all sides in the butter in a Dutch oven.

4. Add the chicken stock, cover, and simmer until tender, about two hours.

5. Place the meat on a warm platter and remove the skewers or string. Thicken the drippings in the pan, allowing one tablespoon of flour for each cup. Bring to a boil and simmer gently two minutes.

6. Stir in the sour cream, if desired, and reheat but do not boil. Serve the sauce with the meat.

6. Heat the butter in a very large skillet or use two large skillets, using half the butter in each. Brown the chops first on one side, then the other. Cover and put the chops in the oven. Bake thirty minutes.

7. Return the chops to the top of the stove and skim or pour off the fat. Add the tomato sauce, diluted with the white wine, and the tarragon and cover. Return to the oven and bake ten to fifteen minutes longer, until the sauce is boiling and the chops are tender. Remove the string before serving and serve the chops with the sauce, accompanied by hot, buttered noodles or parsley potatoes.

Veal Chops Beau Séjour

6 servings

In French cooking, beau séjour (literally, "beautiful sojourn") means a garnish for sautéed dishes. Its characteristic ingredients are garlic and bay leaf, but neither seasoning comes on strong. A typical, and excellent, dish with this name is veal chops beau séjour. The recipe—which, incidentally, could also be used with chicken breasts—is given below.

    6 veal chops (preferably cut from the veal
       rack), each 1½ inches thick and frenched
       All-purpose flour
    ¼ cup salad oil
    ¼ cup butter
    6 whole cloves garlic, peeled
    1 large or 2 medium bay leaves
    ½ teaspoon dried thyme
       Salt and freshly ground black pepper
    2 tablespoons wine vinegar
    ½ cup Chicken Stock (page 115)
    ¼ cup water

1. Dredge the chops lightly on all sides in flour. Heat the oil and three tablespoons of the butter in a skillet large enough to hold the chops. Brown the chops on all sides.

2. Scatter the garlic cloves around the meat. Cut the large bay leaf into six pieces or cut each medium bay leaf into three pieces. Place one piece of bay leaf on each chop. Add the thyme and salt and pepper to taste. Cook the chops, tightly covered, over moderate to low heat about thirty minutes, or until the chops are cooked through and the natural sauce in the skillet is syrupy. Transfer the chops to a hot serving dish and keep warm in the oven. Let the garlic and bay leaf stay in the skillet.

3. Add the vinegar to the skillet and cook, stirring, until the vinegar has evaporated. Add the stock and water and cook, stirring, about five minutes. Check the seasoning. Turn off the heat and swirl in the remaining butter by rotating the pan gently. Pour the sauce over the chops and garnish each with one clove of garlic and a piece of bay leaf. Serve immediately.

Braised Veal Shanks

6 servings

Take a loaf of bread, a jug of wine, and a braised shank of veal, and for those who like to dine well it can be paradise enough. A veal shank has virtues that few other cuts possess. It is meaty, incredibly tender when cooked properly, and the natural gelatin in the bones gives substance galore to a stew or ragout. The shanks on this page are braised in the classic French style by browning and cooking with a liquid, vegetables, spices, and herbs.

6 veal shanks
3 tablespoons olive oil
  Salt and freshly ground black pepper
4 large carrots
1 cup dry white wine
12 small white onions, peeled
1 cup celery cut into thin, short, matchlike strips (julienne)
2 cloves garlic, finely chopped
¼ cup all-purpose flour
3 cups water
2 cups chopped tomatoes
6 sprigs fresh thyme or 1 teaspoon dried thyme
2 bay leaves
6 potatoes, peeled and quartered
3 turnips, peeled and quartered

1. Preheat the oven to 500 degrees.
2. Place the shanks with the oil in a large, heavy kettle and sprinkle with salt and pepper. Place in the oven and bake, uncovered, for thirty minutes. Turn the shanks occasionally, so that they brown well all over.
3. Scrape the carrots and cut them into one-inch lengths. Add to the veal. Add the wine, onions, celery, and garlic and sprinkle with the flour. Cover and bake fifteen minutes, then remove from the oven.
4. Add the remaining ingredients and salt and pepper to taste. Cover and bring to a boil on top of the stove.

5. Reduce the oven heat to 350 degrees. Place the kettle in the oven and continue baking one to one and one-half hours, or until the meat is fork tender. When ready to serve, strain the kettle liquid, and, if it seems too thin, reduce it over high heat on top of the stove. Serve the shanks with the vegetables, if desired, and with the sauce on the side.

Veal Cutlets Provençale

4 servings

4 veal cutlets, each ⅓- to ½-inch thick
1 egg
1 tablespoon water
  All-purpose flour
½ teaspoon salt
¼ teaspoon freshly ground black pepper
⅓ cup butter
1 clove garlic, minced
2 medium tomatoes, peeled and chopped
½ cup Chicken Stock (page 115) or tomato juice
  Chopped parsley

1. Dip the cutlets into the egg beaten with the water, then into flour seasoned with salt and pepper.
2. Heat the butter in a skillet and brown the cutlets on both sides. Add the garlic, tomatoes, and chicken stock. Cover and simmer for thirty minutes, or until tender. Sprinkle with parsley and serve.

Veal Scallops Chasseur

4 servings

1½ pounds leg of veal, cut into ½-inch-thick slices
    Salt and freshly ground pepper
    All-purpose flour for dredging
¼ cup butter
½ pound mushrooms, sliced
1 tablespoon finely chopped onion
¼ cup each Chicken Stock (page 115) and dry white wine
3 tablespoons Fresh Tomato Sauce (page 279) or canned
3 tablespoons Brown Sauce (page 268) or canned beef gravy
1 tablespoon chopped parsley

1. Put the veal slices between pieces of waxed paper and flatten with a wooden mallet, or have the butcher flatten the slices.

2. Season the meat with salt and pepper to taste and dredge it lightly with flour.

3. In a large skillet, melt the butter and sauté the veal in it for about six to seven minutes, or until brown on both sides.

4. Transfer the meat to a warm serving platter and add the mushroom slices to the skillet. Cook until the mushrooms are soft. Add the onion, chicken stock, and wine and cook until the liquid is reduced by half. Add the tomato sauce and brown sauce and simmer for four minutes. Return the meat to the sauce, sprinkle with parsley, and serve immediately.

Oiseaux sans Tête
(Paupiettes de Veau)

6 servings

½ pound pork, ground
    Salt and freshly ground pepper to taste
1 cup finely chopped onion
2 teaspoons minced garlic
2 tablespoons chopped shallots
1 teaspoon chopped fresh thyme or ½ teaspoon dried thyme
1 cup fresh bread crumbs
2 eggs, lightly beaten
¼ cup chopped parsley
¼ cup butter
1 cup chopped, peeled tomatoes
1 cup finely chopped mushrooms
1½ cups Brown Sauce (page 268) or canned beef gravy
1 bay leaf
6 veal scallops (about ¼ pound each), pounded thin
3 tablespoons dry white wine

1. Preheat the oven to 350 degrees.

2. Cook the pork in a saucepan until it loses its color and sprinkle with salt and pepper. Stir to break up the pieces. Add half the onion, half the garlic, half the shallots, half the thyme, the bread crumbs, eggs, and one tablespoon of the parsley. Mix well and set aside.

3. Heat two tablespoons of the butter and add the remaining onions, garlic, shallots, thyme, and one tablespoon of parsley. Add the tomatoes, mushrooms, brown sauce, and bay leaf and simmer ten minutes.

4. Meanwhile, place the veal scallops on a flat surface and add equal parts of filling to the center of each. Roll and fold envelope fashion, tucking in the edges. Tie neatly with string.

5. Heat the remaining butter and brown the scallops on all sides. Add the wine and sauce, cover, and bake one hour. Serve sprinkled with the remaining parsley. Serve with rice.

Paupiettes de Veau

(Stuffed Veal Birds)

4 to 8 servings

8 boneless slices veal (4 ounces each)
6 tablespoons butter
1 tablespoon finely chopped shallots or green onion
1 tablespoon finely chopped onion
½ clove garlic, finely minced
¼ pound sausage meat
½ cup finely minced mushrooms
¼ teaspoon ground thyme
¼ cup fine white bread crumbs
1 tablespoon finely chopped parsley
1 egg yolk lightly beaten
1 carrot, sliced
1 small onion, sliced
½ bay leaf
1 clove garlic, peeled
2 sprigs parsley
2 cups Chicken Stock (page 115) or 1 cup dry white wine and 1 cup stock

1. Place the veal slices between pieces of waxed paper and pound thin with a mallet or rolling pin.

2. Heat two tablespoons of the butter in a skillet and add the shallots, onion, and minced garlic, cooking until the onion is translucent. Add the sausage meat and cook for ten to fifteen minutes, until the sausage is heated through but not browned. Add the mushrooms and cook, stirring, until their juices evaporate. Stir in the thyme, bread crumbs, and chopped parsley. Let the mixture cool slightly, then stir in the egg yolk.

3. Preheat the oven to 375 degrees.

4. Lay the veal slices on a flat surface and spoon two tablespoons of stuffing into the center of each. Roll the slices and tie each with string or secure with food picks.

5. Rub the bottom and sides of a baking pan with two tablespoons of the butter. Sprinkle with the sliced carrot and onion, then add the bay leaf, peeled garlic clove, and parsley sprigs.

6. Brown the veal rolls lightly in the remaining butter. Arrange the rolls in the baking pan over the sliced vegetables and pour the stock over them. Cover with aluminum foil and bake for thirty to forty-five minutes, or until tender, basting occasionally with the stock. Remove the foil and strings or food picks during the last fifteen minutes of cooking.

7. Arrange the veal birds on a serving platter. Strain the sauce remaining in the baking pan and pour over the veal.

Blanquette de Veau

12 servings

Veal may never attain the popularity of beef and chicken in this country (it is far more highly regarded in France and Italy, where the quality is generally better), but it is still a versatile and delectable meat. The best veal, rarely available here except in the finest restaurants and luxury meat markets, is white and tender when it is cooked. Supermarket veal is very good, however, in such dishes as the blanquette *of veal—a creamy stew—outlined below.*

  4 pounds boned shoulder of veal, cut into 1-inch cubes
  4 pounds breast of veal, cut into 1-inch cubes
  2 tablespoons butter
    Salt and freshly ground black pepper
24 small white onions, peeled
  1 clove garlic, finely minced
  1 pound fresh mushrooms, preferably small
  ½ cup all-purpose flour
  1 cup dry white wine
1½ cups Chicken Stock (page 115) or canned chicken broth
  2 cups water
  3 small carrots or 1 large carrot, scraped
  3 ribs celery, trimmed
  2 sprigs parsley
  2 sprigs fresh thyme or ½ teaspoon dried thyme
  1 bay leaf
  1 clove
  2 egg yolks
  1 cup heavy cream
    Juice of ½ lemon

1. Preheat the oven to 400 degrees.
2. Place the meat in a large kettle and add cold water to cover. Bring to a boil and skim the foam and scum off the surface. To "refresh" the meat, place the kettle under cold running water and let the water run until the meat is chilled. Drain well and set aside.
3. Rinse the kettle well and add the butter. Add the meat and cook, stirring very gently with a wooden spoon. Do not let the meat brown. Add salt and pepper to taste and the onions, garlic, and mushrooms. Cook for about ten minutes, stirring gently, without letting any of the ingredients brown.
4. Sprinkle with the flour and stir gently until most of the ingredients are coated with flour. Add the wine, stock, water, carrot, and celery. Cover and bring to a boil.
5. Meanwhile, tie the parsley, thyme, bay leaf, and clove in a cheesecloth bag and add. Cover and place the kettle in the oven. Cook one to one and one-half hours, or until the meat is quite tender. The stew should boil gently. If necessary, lower the heat.
6. When the meat is tender, remove the kettle from the oven. Using a large, slotted spoon, transfer the meat and vegetables to a large bowl. Cover and keep warm. Discard the celery, carrot, and cheesecloth bag. Bring the cooking liquid to a boil.
7. Beat the egg yolks and cream together gently. Add a little of the hot stock, then add the cream mixture to the kettle, stirring vigorously. Cook just until sauce is thickened, without letting it boil. Add the lemon juice, then add the meat and onions and heat through. Serve hot, with rice.

Veal Blanquette with Dill

8 servings

½ cup butter
4½ pounds veal, cut into 1½-inch cubes
   Salt and freshly ground pepper
1 clove garlic, minced
1 cup finely chopped onion
4 tablespoons chopped fresh dill
½ cup all-purpose flour
½ teaspoon nutmeg
1½ cups Chicken Stock (page 115)
1½ cups water
3 carrots
2 leeks
1 cup heavy cream

1. Preheat the oven to 375 degrees.
2. Heat half the butter in a large, deep casserole and add the veal. Sprinkle with salt and pepper to taste and add the garlic, onion, and half the dill. Cook, stirring, without browning for five minutes. Sprinkle with flour and nutmeg and add the chicken stock and water. Bring to a boil. Cover and bake one hour.
3. Meanwhile, scrape the carrots and trim the leeks. Split the leeks down the center and rinse thoroughly under cold running water to remove all trace of sand. Cut the carrots and leeks crosswise into two-inch pieces and then lengthwise into the thinnest possible strips or shreds (julienne). Set aside.
4. Heat the remaining butter in a skillet and cook the leeks and carrots until wilted. Stir half this mixture into the veal. Stir in the cream and bring to a boil.
5. Spoon the veal mixture onto a hot serving platter and garnish the top with the remaining leeks, carrots, and chopped dill. Serve with Baked Rice (page 240).

Veal Bon Appetit

6 servings

½ cup butter
1 teaspoon vegetable oil
1 onion, chopped
2 cloves garlic, minced
2 pounds boneless veal shoulder, cubed
2 cups Chicken Stock (page 115)
1 teaspoon tomato paste
   Salt and freshly ground black pepper
1½ cups heavy cream
1 pound mushrooms, halved
¼ cup Cognac
2 tablespoons chopped parsley

1. Heat four tablespoons of the butter and the oil in a heavy skillet. Add the onion and garlic and cook, stirring, until wilted.
2. Add the veal and cook, stirring, until the meat loses its pink color. Do not brown. Add the stock, tomato paste, and salt and pepper to taste. Cover and simmer gently one and one-half hours. Add the cream and simmer, uncovered, one-half hour.
3. Melt the remaining butter and sauté the mushrooms two to three minutes. Add the mushrooms to the meat mixture and cook fifteen minutes longer. Add the Cognac and serve garnished with parsley.

Veal Marengo

4 servings

2 pounds veal, from the leg, cut into 1½-inch cubes
1 teaspoon salt
¼ teaspoon freshly ground black pepper
¼ cup butter
2 onions, chopped
1 clove garlic, minced
¼ cup all-purpose flour
1½ cups Chicken Stock (page 115)
½ cup white wine
1 cup canned tomatoes
2 sprigs parsley
1 rib celery, chopped
1 bay leaf
12 small onions or 3 medium onions, quartered
2 tablespoons chopped parsley

1. Sprinkle the meat with the salt and pepper. Heat the butter in a skillet and fry the veal, a few pieces at a time, over high heat until well browned on all sides.

2. When all the veal has been browned, return all of it to the skillet and lower the heat to medium. Add the chopped onions and garlic and cook until the vegetables are lightly browned. Stir in the flour and cook until the flour is lightly browned. Gradually stir in the chicken stock and white wine and bring to a boil. Add the tomatoes, parsley sprigs, celery, and bay leaf. Cover and cook over low heat for one hour.

3. Add the onions, cover, and cook for forty-five minutes longer. Sprinkle with chopped parsley and serve with buttered noodles.

Veal Sauté with Mushrooms

4 to 6 servings

2 pounds shoulder of veal, cut into 1½-inch cubes
2 tablespoons vegetable oil
5 tablespoons butter
1 tablespoon finely chopped shallots
1 clove garlic, finely minced
2 cups Chicken Stock (page 115), approximately
1 tablespoon tomato paste
   Salt and freshly ground pepper to taste
2 sprigs fresh thyme or ½ teaspoon dried thyme
1 bay leaf
½ teaspoon powdered sage
½ pound mushrooms, thinly sliced
¼ cup finely chopped parsley

1. Preheat the oven to 300 degrees.

2. In a skillet brown the veal cubes in a mixture of oil and two tablespoons of the butter.

3. Remove the meat to a casserole with a tight-fitting lid.

4. To the skillet add the shallots and garlic and cook briefly, stirring. Add the stock (there should be enough to barely cover the veal) and tomato paste and cook, stirring, until the mixture boils. Pour this over the veal and add the salt, pepper, thyme, bay leaf, and sage. Bring to a boil and cover closely. Place in the oven and bake about forty-five minutes.

5. Meanwhile, cook the mushrooms in the remaining butter, then add the mushrooms and their juices to the casserole. Cover again and bake fifteen minutes longer. Serve sprinkled with chopped parsley.

Calves' Feet Poulette

4 servings

3 calves' feet
1 onion studded with 3 cloves
1 large carrot, scraped
1 rib celery
4 sprigs parsley
2 sprigs fresh thyme or ½ teaspoon dried thyme
20 peppercorns
5 tablespoons all-purpose flour
¼ cup cold water
   Salt and freshly ground black pepper
2 tablespoons butter
2 tablespoons finely chopped shallots or green onion
¼ cup dry white wine
½ cup heavy cream
1 egg yolk
¼ teaspoon nutmeg
1 tablespoon finely chopped parsley
1 teaspoon lemon juice

1. Have the butcher remove and discard the main leg bones, about five inches long, attached to the calves' feet. Reserve all the skin and flesh and, naturally, the tip of the feet.

2. Rinse the reserved portions in cold water. Place in a large saucepan and add water to cover. Bring to a boil and simmer for about three minutes. Drain and rinse once more under cold running water.

3. Return the calves' feet to the saucepan and add the onion, carrot, celery, parsley, thyme, and peppercorns. Add cold water to cover.

4. Blend three tablespoons of the flour with the cold water and pour through a sieve into the saucepan. Add salt and pepper to taste and bring to a boil. Simmer three hours. Strain the stock, reserve it, and let the meat cool.

5. Melt the butter in a saucepan and add the remaining flour. When blended, add the stock, stirring rapidly with a wire whisk.

6. When the meat is cool enough to handle, remove it from the bones.

7. Combine the shallots and wine in a saucepan and simmer until the wine is reduced to about half. Add the sauce and the meat and continue to cook briefly.

8. Blend the cream, egg yolk, nutmeg, and parsley. Beat lightly and stir into the sauce. Heat thoroughly and add the lemon juice. Season with salt and pepper to taste. Serve hot with rice and a peppermill.

Oxtail Ragoût

8 servings

4 oxtails
All-purpose flour
Salt and freshly ground black pepper
¼ cup peanut oil
1 bay leaf
½ teaspoon dried thyme
2 ribs celery, chopped
1 carrot, scraped and chopped
1 large onion, peeled and chopped
2 cloves garlic, crushed
1½ cups dry red wine
2½ cups Beef Stock (page 115)
1 whole tomato, cored and coarsely chopped
2 carrots, cut into strips
1½ cups peeled, quartered small turnips (optional)
3 tablespoons butter

1. Cut the oxtails into two-inch lengths or have them cut by the butcher.
2. Preheat the oven to 350 degrees.
3. Dredge the oxtails in flour seasoned with salt and pepper.
4. Heat the oil in a large heavy skillet and brown the oxtails well. As the oxtails are browned, arrange in a baking dish.
5. Add the bay leaf, thyme, celery, chopped carrot, onion, and garlic. Add the wine and beef stock and bring to a boil on top of the stove. Add the chopped tomato. Cover and bake two hours.
6. When the oxtails are fork tender, remove them and keep warm. Strain the sauce.
7. Place the carrot strips and turnips in salted water to cover. Cook, covered, about ten minutes. Do not overcook. Melt the butter, then drain and toss the carrots and turnips in the hot butter. Add the vegetables to the sauce and simmer fifteen to twenty minutes, or until the vegetables are tender. Add the oxtails and heat. Serve hot, with noodles.

Pigs' Feet Sainte-Menehould

4 servings

4 large pigs' feet, preferably with the knuckles, or 4 pigs' feet and 4 pigs' knuckles
2 ribs celery
1 tablespoon salt
Coarsely ground black pepper
1 onion, peeled and studded with 2 cloves
1 carrot, scraped and quartered
1 piece French bread about 5 inches long, or about 3 slices ordinary bread
¼ cup mustard, preferably Dijon or Düsseldorf
Vegetable oil

1. Put the pigs' feet in a large saucepan and add water to cover. Add the celery, salt, pepper to taste, onion, and carrot. Bring to a boil and simmer for two hours. Remove the meat from the broth and cool. Reserve one-half cup of the cooking liquid.
2. Bake the bread in a hot oven until dried out and browned. Do not let the bread burn. To make crumbs, grate the bread on an ordinary cheese grater or put in a blender. Put the crumbs in a sieve and shake them to obtain crumbs of a uniform size.
3. When the pigs' feet are cool, preheat the oven to 425 degrees.
4. Blend the reserved cooking liquid with the mustard and dip the pigs' feet in it. Coat well and chill. Coat the pigs' feet with crumbs.
5. Oil a baking dish and place the pigs' feet on it. Bake thirty minutes. If the pigs' feet start to burn, reduce the oven heat. At the end of thirty minutes, turn the pigs' feet and continue to cook five to ten minutes longer or until crisp on the outside and tender within. Serve with Sauce Diable (page 270).

Pot au Feu

8 to 12 servings

6 corned pigs' knuckles (if not available, use 1 5-pound piece of brisket of beef)
1 cabbage (3 pounds), cored but left whole
8 small white onions, peeled
2 whole cloves garlic, peeled
2 small carrots, scraped and quartered
3 leeks, split, rinsed well, and tied with string
6 cloves
2 bay leaves
  Salt
15 peppercorns
1 Stuffed Chicken (see below)
10 potatoes, peeled
1 or 2 Polish sausages

1. Place the pigs' knuckles or brisket and cabbage in a kettle large enough to hold all the ingredients. Add water to cover and bring to a boil. Cover and simmer thirty minutes, skimming the surface as necessary.

2. Add the onions, garlic, carrots, leeks, cloves, bay leaves, salt to taste, and peppercorns. Cover again and continue to simmer thirty to forty-five minutes.

3. Add the stuffed chicken, potatoes, and sausage and continue to simmer, covered, one hour. Carve the meats and serve, accompanied by the vegetables, Tomato Sauce I (page 278), coarse salt (such as kosher salt), a peppermill, a good imported mustard, and horseradish, preferably fresh. Cornichons, the French sour pickles available in specialty food markets, are a traditional accompaniment. The stock from the dish may also be served.

Note: The stock makes a good base for soups and may be frozen indefinitely.

STUFFED CHICKEN:

1 stuffed chicken

1/3 pound pork or sausage, ground
1/4 cup finely chopped onion
1/2 clove garlic, finely minced
3 fresh chicken livers, ground
3/4 cup fresh bread crumbs
1/4 cup milk
1 egg yolk
1/4 cup finely chopped fresh herbs, mixed if possible (parsley, tarragon, thyme, rosemary, basil) or use about 1 tablespoon chopped dried herbs
  Salt and freshly ground pepper to taste
1 chicken (2½ to 3 pounds)

Cook the pork or sausage in a skillet briefly and add the onion and garlic. When the meat loses its color, add the ground chicken livers and cook briefly. Stir in the bread crumbs, milk and egg yolk. Cook briefly, stirring. Stir in the herbs and salt and pepper to taste. Stuff the chicken and truss it (page 217).

Sweetbreads Florentine

6 servings

2 pairs calves' sweetbreads
  Salt
2 carrots, scraped and cut into rounds
½ onion, cut into thin slices
2 ribs celery, coarsely chopped
2 sprigs fresh thyme or ½ teaspoon dried thyme
1 bay leaf
2 sprigs fresh parsley
  Freshly ground pepper
1¾ cups Chicken Stock (page 115) or canned chicken broth
6 tablespoons butter
3 tablespoons all-purpose flour
2 pounds fresh spinach
¼ cup heavy cream
2 egg yolks
  Juice of ½ lemon
¼ teaspoon cayenne pepper
½ cup grated Gruyère cheese
2 tablespoons grated Parmesan cheese

1. Generally speaking, there is one large and one small portion to each sweetbread. Cut the sweetbreads in half where these portions join. Place them in a basin and add very cold water to cover. Let stand at least one hour. Drain.

2. Place the sweetbreads in a saucepan and add water to cover and salt to taste. Bring to a boil and simmer ten minutes. Drain well, then run them immediately under cold running water to chill. Trim the sweetbreads by cutting away the connective tissue and cartilage. Place the sweetbreads between cloths and put a weight on them for two hours to flatten them well before cooking. The bottom of a skillet or casserole filled with heavy objects will do.

3. Preheat the oven to 400 degrees.

4. Generously butter a baking dish just large enough to hold the sweetbreads. Sprinkle the bottom with the carrots, onion, celery, thyme, bay leaf, parsley, and salt and pepper to taste. Add the sweetbreads and sprinkle with salt and pepper. Pour in the chicken stock. Cover the sweetbreads with a round of buttered waxed paper and a cover. Bake forty-five minutes.

5. Melt three tablespoons of the butter and stir in the flour. Strain the liquid from the sweetbreads (there should be about two cups) and stir into the butter and flour mixture. When blended and smooth, simmer the sauce thirty minutes, stirring frequently.

6. Meanwhile, pick over the spinach and rinse it well in cold water. Remove and discard any tough stems. Place the spinach in a saucepan, using only the water that clings to the leaves, and cover closely. Cook, stirring occasionally, until the spinach is wilted and slightly cooked. Drain the spinach and let cool. When cool enough to handle, press the spinach between the hands to remove excess moisture.

7. Heat the remaining three tablespoons of butter in a skillet and toss the spinach briefly to heat thoroughly. Sprinkle with salt and pepper. Spread the spinach in a buttered baking dish.

8. Cut the sweetbreads into half-inch slices and arrange them symmetrically over the spinach.

9. Add the heavy cream and egg yolks to the sauce, stirring rapidly. Let thicken slightly, but do not boil or the sauce may curdle. Add the lemon juice and cayenne.

10. Spoon the sauce over the sweetbreads and sprinkle with the Gruyère and Parmesan. Bake until piping hot throughout. Run the dish briefly under the broiler to glaze the surface. Serve immediately.

Sweetbreads Périgourdine

4 to 6 servings

One of the ironies of the American diet is that a delicacy with the flavor and elegance of sweetbreads is so uncommonly found on the American dining table. Ironic because sweetbreads, or ris de veau, *have an undeniable appeal. They appear on the menu of all French restaurants of substance. They are also available in the best of the nation's meat markets. Sweetbreads are, of course, the thymus gland of calf or lamb, and calves' sweetbreads are the more popular of the two. They are easily prepared, have a splendid texture when cooked, and lend themselves to several hundred dishes. An excellent sweetbread dish is given here, à la périgourdine, which is to say with truffles.*

 2 pairs calves' sweetbreads
   Salt to taste
¼ cup butter
10 small white onions, peeled
 1 cup sliced mushrooms or an equal quantity of very small mushrooms
   Freshly ground pepper to taste
 2 tablespoons all-purpose flour
½ cup dry white wine
½ cup Chicken Stock (page 115)
½ bay leaf
 2 sprigs fresh thyme or ½ teaspoon dried thyme
 1 ½-ounce can truffles
½ cup heavy cream
 1 egg yolk

1. Generally speaking, there is one large and one small portion to each sweetbread. Cut them in half where these portions join. Place the sweetbreads in a basin and add very cold water to cover. Let stand at least one hour, then drain.

2. Place the sweetbreads in a saucepan and add water to cover and salt to taste. Bring to a boil and simmer ten minutes. Drain well, then run immediately under cold water to chill. Trim the sweetbreads by cutting away connective tissue and cartilage. Place the sweetbreads between cloths and lay a heavy weight on them to flatten them well before cooking. The bottom of a stainless steel skillet or casserole filled with heavy objects is good for this. Remove the weights and cloths and cut the sweetbreads into one-inch cubes.

3. Melt the butter in a large saucepan and add the sweetbreads, onions, mushrooms, salt, and pepper. Let simmer over moderate heat, stirring occasionally and gently, until most of the moisture in the bottom of the saucepan evaporates, about five minutes. Do not brown. Sprinkle with the flour and stir until the foods are evenly coated. Add the wine, stock, bay leaf, and thyme, stirring with a spoon until the sauce is blended and smooth. Pour in the juice from the can of truffles and simmer ten minutes. Chop the truffles from the can and add. Cover and simmer five minutes.

4. Blend the cream with the egg yolk. When thoroughly blended, stir this into the sweetbread mixture. Stir constantly and bring almost to a boil, but do not boil. Serve with hot, fluffy rice.

Sweetbreads Maréchale

6 servings

3 pairs calves' sweetbreads
   Salt and freshly ground pepper to taste
2 eggs, lightly beaten
1 tablespoon salad oil
2 tablespoons water
   All-purpose flour
2 to 3 cups fresh bread crumbs
1 cup butter
   Truffle slices for garnish

1. Generally speaking, there is one large and one small portion to each sweetbread. Cut them in half where these portions join. Place the sweetbreads in a basin and add very cold water to cover. Let stand at least one hour. Drain.

2. Place the sweetbreads in a saucepan and add water to cover and salt to taste. Bring to a boil and simmer ten minutes. Drain well, then run immediately under cold running water to chill. Trim the sweetbreads by cutting away connective tissue and cartilage. Place the sweetbreads between cloths and lay a weight on them to flatten them well before cooking. The bottom of a stainless steel skillet or casserole filled with heavy objects will do. This will produce six oval-shaped pieces. Slice each piece horizontally into two or three thin oval-shaped pieces. Sprinkle lightly with salt and pepper.

3. Combine the eggs, oil, and water in a shallow dish. Stir in salt and pepper to taste.

4. Dip the sweetbread slices first in flour, then in egg and finally in bread crumbs until well coated. Tap lightly with the flat side of a knife so that the crumbs adhere.

5. Heat all but four tablespoons of the butter in a large skillet and cook the breaded sweetbreads on all sides until golden brown. Drain quickly on paper towels and transfer to a hot serving dish. Garnish each slice with a truffle slice.

6. Heat the remaining butter to bubbling and quickly pour over the sweetbreads. Serve with hot, buttered asparagus.

Ragoût des Pauvres

(Poor People's Stew)

6 servings

3 tablespoons vegetable oil
1 lamb's lung, cut into cubes
1 lamb's liver, cut into cubes
1 lamb's heart, cut into cubes
   Salt and freshly ground pepper to taste
1 cup finely chopped onion
3 small carrots, scraped and cut into 1-inch
   lengths
2 ribs celery, cut into 1-inch lengths
2 cloves garlic, finely minced
½ teaspoon thyme, chopped
1 bay leaf
1 tablespoon all-purpose flour
1 tablespoon tomato paste
2 cups water

1. Preheat the oven to 375 degrees.

2. Heat the oil in a large skillet and cook the lamb's lung, liver, and heart until brown on all sides. Sprinkle with salt and pepper and add the onion, carrots, celery, garlic, thyme, and bay leaf. Continue cooking until the onion is wilted. Pour off the fat from the skillet, using a lid to keep the meat and vegetables in the skillet. Discard the fat.

3. Sprinkle the ingredients in the skillet with the flour and stir to distribute the flour evenly. Stir in the tomato paste, then the water. Bring to a boil, stirring, then empty the mixture into a casserole with a tight-fitting lid. Cover and bake one hour and forty-five minutes.

204   FRANCE

Lapin Gibelotte
(French Rabbit Stew)

8 servings

America's food patterns and preferences can be fascinating. On the West Coast, there is an abundance of rabbit in the frozen-food counters of many supermarkets. In the East, the same product is a rarity. In New York, however, there are several sources for fresh rabbit, which is a delicacy that seems widely admired only by people of European ancestry. That in itself is curious, for rabbit is as tender, choice, white-fleshed and succulent as chicken. The recipe below is a case in point.

½ pound salt pork, cut into thin slices or small cubes
2 young rabbits (3 to 3½ pounds each), cut into serving pieces
Salt and freshly ground black pepper to taste
12 small white onions, peeled
1 pound fresh mushrooms, sliced
3 cloves garlic
1 teaspoon chopped fresh thyme or ½ teaspoon dried thyme
¼ cup all-purpose flour
2 cups dry white wine
1 6-ounce can tomato paste
1 13¼-ounce can chicken broth
2 bay leaves
Butter
3 tablespoons mustard, preferably Dijon or Düsseldorf

1. Preheat the oven to 400 degrees.
2. Place the salt pork in a saucepan and add water to cover. Bring to a boil and simmer five minutes. Drain and reserve.
3. Place the drained pork in a Dutch oven or heavy casserole and cook over moderate heat, turning to brown all sides. Remove the pork pieces and reserve.
4. Sprinkle the rabbit pieces with salt and pepper. Reserve the rabbit livers. Brown the rabbit pieces, a few at a time, in the Dutch oven. When all the pieces are browned, add the onions and mushrooms and cook briefly. Return the rabbit to the Dutch oven and continue to cook while preparing the remainder of the recipe.
5. Chop together the garlic and thyme and add to the meat. Stir gently with a wooden spoon to distribute the seasonings. Sprinkle with the flour, stirring with the spoon to distribute the flour evenly. Bake for fifteen minutes, uncovered. Add the wine, tomato paste, chicken broth, and bay leaves. Stir to distribute the liquid. Cover and bake for one hour. Add the bits of salt pork.
6. Cook the rabbit livers on both sides in a little butter. Add the livers to the Dutch oven, cover, and continue to bake for thirty minutes or longer.
7. Scoop out a cup of the sauce and stir the mustard into it. Blend well, then return the mustard mixture to the sauce. Stir to blend. Simmer briefly and serve piping hot with freshly cooked, buttered noodles.

Rabbit with Wine

4 servings

¼ pound salt pork, cut into cubes
1 rabbit (3½ pounds), cut into serving pieces
1 teaspoon salt
¼ teaspoon freshly ground black pepper
2 onions, chopped
1 clove garlic, minced
¼ cup all-purpose flour
1½ cups Chicken Stock (page 115)
½ cup white wine
1 cup canned tomatoes
2 sprigs parsley
1 rib celery, chopped
1 bay leaf
12 small white onions or 3 medium onions, quartered
2 tablespoons chopped parsley

1. Cook the salt pork in water to cover about five minutes. Drain. Brown in a skillet, then remove and reserve.

2. Sprinkle the rabbit pieces with salt and pepper and cook, a few pieces at a time, in the drippings until well browned on all sides. Lower the heat to medium, add the onions and garlic and cook until the vegetables are lightly browned. Stir in the flour and cook until the flour is lightly browned.

3. Gradually stir in the chicken stock and wine and bring to a boil. Add the salt pork cubes, tomatoes, parsley sprigs, celery, and bay leaf. Cover and cook over low heat for one hour. Add the onions; cover and cook for forty-five minutes longer. Sprinkle with chopped parsley and serve with buttered noodles.

Chicken in Champagne Sauce au Pavillon

2 servings

1 roasting chicken (3½ pounds)
  Salt and freshly ground white pepper
¼ cup butter
1 tablespoon peanut or vegetable oil
½ cup finely chopped mushrooms
2 tablespoons chopped shallots
2 cups Béchamel Sauce (page 267)
1 split of imported dry champagne
2 hearts celery, neatly trimmed
  Chicken Stock (page 115)

1. Preheat the oven to 350 degrees.

2. Sprinkle the chicken inside and out with salt and pepper and place in a roasting pan with the butter and oil. Roast, basting occasionally with the pan fat, for about forty minutes, or until done.

3. Meanwhile, add the mushrooms and shallots to the Béchamel sauce and simmer for twenty minutes.

4. Remove the chicken from the roasting pan and pour off the fat from the pan. Place the pan over medium heat and add the champagne. Bring to a boil and reduce slightly, stirring to dissolve all the brown particles on the bottom and sides of the pan.

5. Add the pan juices to the Béchamel sauce and bring to a boil. Strain the sauce twice through a double thickness of cheese-cloth. Correct the seasonings.

6. Meanwhile, cook the celery hearts in chicken stock until tender. Place the celery and chicken on a hot serving platter and pour the sauce over. Serve hot.

Chicken with Champagne Sauce

40 to 60 servings

9 chickens (3½ pounds each), cut into serving pieces
¾ cup butter
   Salt and freshly ground pepper
2 cups finely chopped onion
½ teaspoon nutmeg
2 cups all-purpose flour
½ cup Cognac
2 bay leaves
12 cups chicken broth (made, if desired, with backbones and giblets of the chickens; or use canned chicken broth)
1 bottle dry champagne or other dry white wine
6 sprigs fresh thyme or 1 teaspoon dried thyme
1 quart quartered mushrooms
1 quart plus 1 cup heavy cream
   Chopped or sliced truffles (optional)

1. Preheat the oven to 475 degrees.
2. In a kettle large enough to hold them, toss the chicken pieces in four tablespoons of the butter over medium heat. Stir with a wooden spoon until the pieces are well coated, but do not brown. Sprinkle with salt and pepper to taste and stir in the onions and nutmeg. Continue cooking and stirring lightly about five minutes.
3. Place the kettle in the oven and bake, uncovered, about twenty minutes, stirring occasionally.
4. Sprinkle with the flour and stir to coat the pieces. Bake twenty minutes more, stirring once in a while, then add the Cognac, bay leaves, chicken broth, champagne, salt and pepper (if necessary), and thyme. Place the kettle on top of the stove and bring to a boil, then reduce the heat, cover, and simmer gently.
5. Place the mushrooms in a large skillet and add the one cup cream. Bring to a boil, then simmer two minutes. Season with salt and add to the chicken. Cover the kettle and bake forty-five minutes.
6. Carefully remove the chicken pieces and keep warm while making the sauce.
7. Boil down the sauce in the kettle by about one-third. Add the quart of cream and continue cooking, stirring frequently, one hour. Strain the sauce and return it to a boil, then remove from the heat and swirl in the remaining eight tablespoons butter.
8. Arrange the chicken on one or two large serving dishes and pour part of the sauce over the chicken. Serve the remaining sauce in a sauceboat. Garnish the chicken, if desired, with truffles and serve immediately with rice.

Chicken Chasseur

4 servings

½ cup all-purpose flour
2 teaspoons salt
½ teaspoon freshly ground black pepper
1 frying chicken (2½ to 3 pounds), cut into serving pieces
¼ cup butter
2 tablespoons finely chopped shallots or green onion
1 clove garlic, finely minced
¼ pound fresh mushrooms, sliced
½ cup dry white wine
¾ cup chopped, canned Italian plum tomatoes
½ teaspoon or more dried tarragon or thyme
1 tablespoon chopped parsley

1. Combine the flour, half the salt, and half the pepper. Dredge the chicken in the seasoned flour.

2. Heat three tablespoons of the butter in a large, heavy skillet; do not let the butter brown or burn. When the butter is hot, add the chicken pieces and cook until brown on one side. Using kitchen tongs, turn the pieces as they brown and let them brown on the other side. Cook, turning, until the pieces are browned all over. Transfer the chicken pieces to a warm dish.

3. Put the remaining butter in the skillet and add the shallots, garlic, and mushrooms. Cook about three minutes over low heat, stirring, without browning. Pour in the wine and cook, stirring, until the brown particles are dissolved. Continue to cook until most of the liquid evaporates. Return the chicken to the skillet and add the tomatoes. Sprinkle with the remaining salt and pepper or, if desired, add salt and pepper to taste. Sprinkle with the tarragon or thyme. Cover and cook over low heat thirty to forty-five minutes, or until the chicken is tender. Sprinkle with the chopped parsley and serve hot with rice or noodles.

Chickens Demi-Deuil

(Chickens in Half-Mourning)

8 servings

One of the most bizarrely named dishes in French cuisine is poularde *or* poulet demi-deuil. *That translates as chicken in half mourning, a Gallic attempt at black humor, kitchen division. The name comes from the sliced black truffles inserted between the skin and flesh of the fowl. Chicken demi-deuil, however, is far from somber. Served with a rich cream sauce and, traditionally, a side dish of rice, it is a delight to the palate. P.S. If you omit the truffles, it is still a good dish. Just call it chicken with cream sauce.*

2 chickens (3 pounds each), cleaned and left whole
3 or 4 black truffles, cut into ⅛-inch slices
1 tablespoon butter or chicken fat
½ cup finely chopped onion
½ clove garlic, finely minced
½ cup finely diced celery
1 cup diced green beans
1 cup diced white turnips (optional)
1 cup finely diced carrots
  Salt and freshly ground pepper
¼ teaspoon finely chopped fresh or dried thyme
1 large chicken breast, skinned and boned
1 egg white
  Freshly ground nutmeg
½ cup heavy cream
  Chicken Stock (page 115)
4 cups Cream Sauce (page 209)

1. Starting at the neck opening, loosen the skin of each chicken by carefully running the fingers between the skin and meat. Loosen the skin around the breast and down the chicken thighs and legs. This is not difficult, since the skin is very lightly attached to the flesh, but try to avoid breaking the skin.

2. Arrange the truffle slices polka-dot fashion between the skin and meat. Place them on the thighs, over the breast, and so on. Refrigerate until ready to stuff.

3. To prepare the stuffing, melt the butter and add the onion, garlic, celery, beans, turnips, carrots, salt and pepper to taste, and thyme. Do not add the liquid. Cover and cook over low heat, stirring occasionally, about ten minutes or until the vegetables are tender. Let this mixture cool.

4. Carefully trim the boned chicken breast to remove the white nerve fibers, if any. Cut the meat into cubes. There should be about one packed cup of meat.

5. Place the egg white in the container of an electric blender and add the raw cubed chicken breast gradually. Blend, stirring down as necessary with a rubber spatula. Season with salt, pepper, and nutmeg. When blended, pour in the cream, stirring down as necessary. Add this to the cooled, cooked vegetables and mix well. Divide the mixture evenly between the chickens, stuffing the cavity of each. Truss the chickens neatly and put them in a kettle.

6. Add chicken stock to cover and bring to a boil. Simmer gently, with the kettle partly covered, one hour. Keep the chicken hot while preparing the cream sauce. Serve the chickens carved, with the stuffing, and serve the cream sauce spooned over or in a separate bowl. The ideal accompaniment for this dish is rice.

CREAM SAUCE:

4 cups

¼ cup butter
4 tablespoons all-purpose flour
3 cups broth in which chicken cooked
1 cup heavy cream
 Salt and freshly ground pepper

Melt the butter in a saucepan and add the flour. Stir until blended, then add the broth, stirring rapidly with a whisk. Stir until the sauce boils. Simmer, stirring occasionally, twenty minutes. Add the cream and cook, stirring occasionally, fifteen minutes. Add salt and pepper to taste.

Chicken in Cream with Tomatoes

4 to 6 servings

2 chickens (2½ pounds each), cut into serving pieces
  Salt and freshly ground pepper to taste
6 tablespoons butter
1 cup sliced fresh mushrooms
¼ cup finely chopped shallots
1½ cups cubed, peeled tomatoes
½ cup dry white wine
1 teaspoon chopped fresh thyme or ½ teaspoon dried thyme
1 tablespoon chopped fresh tarragon or 1½ teaspoons dried tarragon
1½ cups heavy cream

1. Sprinkle the chicken with salt and pepper.

2. Heat four tablespoons of the butter and brown the chicken on all sides. Cook slowly about thirty minutes, or until done.

3. Meanwhile, in a separate skillet, cook the mushrooms in the remaining butter until wilted. Set aside.

4. Remove the chicken and keep it warm. To the skillet add the shallots and cook briefly, stirring. Add the tomatoes, wine, mushrooms, thyme, and tarragon. Cook ten to fifteen minutes, then add the cream and season to taste with salt and pepper. Return the chicken to the skillet and cook until the chicken and sauce are piping hot.

Chicken and Noodles with Wine Sauce

4 to 6 servings

2 broiling chickens, quartered
  All-purpose flour
½ cup butter
½ cup finely chopped onion
1 clove garlic, minced
¼ teaspoon crushed rosemary leaves
¼ teaspoon marjoram
4 cups Chicken Stock (page 115)
1½ cups chopped tomatoes, fresh or canned
2 teaspoons salt
½ teaspoon freshly ground white pepper
1 small bay leaf
1 small carrot
3 ribs celery
½ pound fresh mushrooms, sliced
½ cup dry white wine
12 ounces medium noodles

1. Wipe the chicken pieces and coat them with flour. Sauté in the butter until golden brown. Remove from the pan and set aside.

2. Add the onion to the pan and sauté. Add the garlic, rosemary, and marjoram and cook until the onion is wilted. Blend in one-half cup flour. Using a whisk, gradually add the chicken stock, stirring constantly, and cook until thickened. Add the tomatoes, salt, and pepper.

3. Add the chicken to the sauce. Add the bay leaf, carrot, and celery and simmer slowly fifteen minutes.

4. Add the mushrooms and wine. Bring to a boil, cover, then reduce the heat and simmer slowly until the chicken is tender, about thirty minutes.

5. Meanwhile, cook the noodles according to package directions. Drain, place on a serving plate, and top with the chicken. Pour the wine sauce over the chicken and serve immediately.

Chicken Paysanne

4 servings

There is a dish called chicken paysanne, something of a fantasy with French pretensions, that is a testament to summer, although with the ready availability of fresh vegetables all year round it is excellent in winter as well. It is a rewarding blend of good things from the garden including fresh corn and luscious ripe tomatoes. To give the dish a fillip, there is also a goodly helping of horseradish, although this ingredient is optional. The horseradish should be freshly grated, because the commercial preparation is generally pickled in vinegar.

1 fat chicken (4 pounds)
1 onion, studded with 2 cloves
2 carrots, scraped and quartered
3 sprigs parsley
1 bay leaf
  Salt
15 peppercorns
3 tablespoons butter
4 tablespoons all-purpose flour
⅓ cup chopped onion
4 ears corn, approximately
2 large tomatoes, approximately
5 tablespoons or more freshly grated horseradish (optional)
1 cup heavy cream
  Freshly ground black pepper
  Chopped parsley or chives

1. Place the chicken in a kettle and add the onion studded with cloves, the carrots, parsley sprigs, bay leaf, salt to taste, and peppercorns. Add water to cover and bring to a boil. Simmer gently until the chicken is tender, about one hour. Skim off the chicken fat and reserve. Strain two cups of broth and reserve. Leave the chicken in the remaining broth.

2. Melt the butter and stir in the flour with a wire whisk. When blended, add the reserved two cups of hot chicken broth, stirring rapidly with the whisk. Simmer, stirring frequently, about thirty minutes.

3. Heat three tablespoons of the reserved chicken fat and add the chopped onion. Cook, stirring, until wilted.

4. Cut and scrape the corn from the cob. There should be two cups of scraped kernels and pulp.

5. Peel the tomatoes by dipping each one into boiling water for nine seconds and pulling off the skin with a paring knife. Cut them into small cubes. There should be about one and one-half cups.

6. Add the corn and tomatoes to the stewed onion in the saucepan. Simmer about three minutes, then add to the sauce. Add the horseradish and heavy cream. Season with salt and pepper to taste and bring to a boil while preparing the chicken.

7. Remove the skin from the chicken. Cut the chicken into serving pieces and arrange it on a warm platter. Spoon half the sauce over the chicken and sprinkle with chopped parsley or chives. Serve with buttered noodles, with the remaining hot sauce on the side.

Chicken Sauté au Parmesan

4 servings

1 chicken (2½ to 3 pounds), cut into serving pieces
Salt and freshly ground black pepper
4½ tablespoons butter
1½ tablespoons all-purpose flour
¾ cup milk
¼ cup heavy cream
¼ teaspoon nutmeg
½ cup grated Swiss or Gruyère cheese
½ cup grated Parmesan cheese
2 tablespoons bread crumbs

1. Sprinkle the chicken with salt and pepper and brown on all sides in three tablespoons of the butter. This should require about twenty minutes.

2. Preheat the oven to 350 degrees.

3. Melt the remaining butter in a saucepan and stir in the flour. When blended, add the milk and cream, stirring rapidly with a whisk. When the mixture is boiling, thickened, and smooth, remove from the heat and stir in the nutmeg and Swiss or Gruyère cheese.

4. Sprinkle a baking dish with half the Parmesan cheese and arrange the chicken pieces over it. Spoon the sauce over the chicken and sprinkle with the remaining Parmesan and the bread crumbs. Bake until golden brown.

Chicken with Tarragon and Sour Cream

4 servings

1 frying chicken (2 to 3 pounds), cut into serving pieces
3 tablespoons butter
¼ cup chopped onion
1 clove garlic, finely chopped
2 tablespoons all-purpose flour
2 tablespoons tomato paste
1½ cups Chicken Stock (page 115)
1 teaspoon salt
½ teaspoon freshly ground black pepper
1 tablespoon chopped fresh tarragon leaves or 1½ teaspoons dried tarragon
¾ cup sour cream
2 tablespoons grated Parmesan cheese

1. Brown the chicken pieces in the butter in a large heavy skillet, turning to brown all sides. Remove the chicken and keep warm.

2. Add the onion and garlic to the pan and cook until tender, stirring occasionally. Stir in the flour and tomato paste and then add the stock slowly. Bring to a boil, stirring until the mixture thickens. Return the chicken to the pan.

3. Add the salt, pepper, and tarragon. Cover and simmer gently for about forty-five minutes, or until the chicken is tender.

4. Remove the chicken to a warm platter. Gradually stir the sour cream into the sauce and heat, stirring, but do not boil. Pour over the chicken and sprinkle with Parmesan cheese.

Chicken Vallée d' Auge

8 servings

The Auge Valley in Normandy is noted for its pasturelands and cheeses (Pont l'Evêque and Camembert), but it is with a delicate entrée that the valley is associated in gourmets' minds. This is chicken Vallée d'Auge. The chicken is roasted or sautéed and served with a cream sauce lightly perfumed with another Norman specialty, the famed applejack known as Calvados. One version of the dish is outlined here. If Calvados is not available, domestic applejack may be used.

2 chickens (3 pounds each)
   Salt and freshly ground pepper to taste
3 tablespoons butter
1 cup finely chopped onion
3 or 4 carrots
1 medium white turnip
1 cup fresh green beans, cut into 1-inch lengths
1 cup shelled fresh green peas
5 tablespoons Calvados or applejack
2 cups heavy cream

1. Preheat the oven to 400 degrees.
2. Sprinkle the insides of the chickens with salt and pepper. Truss the chickens (page 217) and rub all over with butter, then place on their sides in a shallow roasting pan and roast fifteen to twenty minutes, basting occasionally with the pan drippings. Turn the chickens and continue roasting, basting occasionally.
3. When the chickens have cooked thirty minutes, add the onion.
4. Place the chickens on their backs and continue roasting and basting until they are golden brown all over.
5. Meanwhile, prepare the vegetables. Scrape the carrots and cut into one-inch lengths, then cut each length into quarters or sixths (the pieces should be about the size of the green beans).
6. Peel the turnip and cut it into one-inch pieces about the same size as the carrot pieces.
7. Cook each vegetable separately in boiling salted water to barely cover. Cook each until crisp but tender and almost done. They will cook briefly in the sauce. When the vegetables are cooked, drain them and set aside.
8. When the chickens are golden brown all over, remove them. Cover with foil and keep warm. Add the carrots and turnip to the pan drippings and bring to a boil. Add four tablespoons of the Calvados and cook about two minutes. Stir in the cream and boil five minutes. Add the green beans and peas and heat thoroughly. Stir in the remaining Calvados and, if necessary, add salt and pepper to taste.
9. Quarter the chickens and serve the hot sauce over the pieces.

Chicken in Velouté

6 servings

1 stewing chicken (5 pounds), cut up
1 onion, quartered
2 ribs celery with leaves, cut up
1 carrot, cut up
  Salt and freshly ground black pepper
1 bay leaf
3 cups water
6 tablespoons butter or chicken fat
6 tablespoons all-purpose flour
1 cup heavy cream
⅓ cup dry white wine
1 teaspoon lemon juice
½ pound small mushroom caps, washed
3 tablespoons Blender Hollandaise Sauce
  (page 271)

1. Place the chicken in a heavy kettle with the onion, celery, carrot, one tablespoon salt, one-quarter teaspoon pepper, the bay leaf, and water. Cover and simmer gently for three hours, or until the chicken is tender.

2. Strain the broth and reserve. Discard vegetables. Remove the chicken from the bones in large pieces and reserve. Skim the fat off the broth; this is done most easily if the broth is chilled for several hours.

3. Melt the butter or chicken fat in the top of a double boiler and blend in the flour. Stir in one and one-half cups of the reserved chicken broth and the cream. Bring to a boil, stirring. Cover and cook over hot water, stirring occasionally, for thirty minutes.

4. Place the white wine, lemon juice, and mushrooms in a small skillet; cover and poach gently for five minutes. Stir into the cooked sauce.

5. Add three cups of the cooked chicken. Stir in the Hollandaise Sauce and serve immediately in a rice ring or molded spinach ring.

Chicken with Velouté Sauce

6 to 8 servings

1 dressed capon (6 pounds), trussed
2 ribs celery with leaves
12 peppercorns
1 leek, trimmed
4 sprigs parsley
1 bay leaf
3 sprigs fresh thyme or ½ teaspoon dried thyme
  Salt
1 onion, peeled
5 tablespoons butter
½ cup all-purpose flour
1 cup cream
1 teaspoon lemon juice

1. Place the capon in a large saucepan or kettle and add the celery and peppercorns.

2. Trim the root end of the leek and trim off part of the green leaves. Split the leek almost to the root end and rinse between the leek leaves with cold running water, taking care to remove all sand or grit. Drain.

3. Enclose the parsley, bay leaf, and thyme inside the leaves of the leek, then tie the leaves together with string. Add this bunch to the kettle. Add salt to taste, the onion, and water to cover. Bring slowly to a boil and skim the surface as necessary.

4. Partially cover and simmer two hours or longer, or until the joint between the thigh and drumstick runs clear when pricked. Remove the chicken and keep covered and warm. Boil the cooking stock over brisk heat to reduce, about five minutes. Strain the stock.

5. Melt four tablespoons of the butter in a saucepan and stir in the flour. When it is blended, add four cups of the stock, stirring the sauce vigorously with a whisk. Simmer one hour, stirring frequently.

6. Meanwhile, return the chicken to the kettle with any remaining stock. Do not heat, but keep warm.

7. When the sauce is ready, stir in the cream and, if it is thought necessary, thin the sauce with a little of the remaining stock. Check the seasoning. Add the lemon juice and swirl in the remaining butter by rotating the pan gently.

8. When ready to serve, remove the trussing from the chicken. Cut the chicken into serving pieces or remove the meat from the bones. Serve with rice, and with the hot sauce on the side.

Truffled Steamed Chicken

6 servings

¼ cup butter
1 pound chicken livers
  Salt and freshly ground black pepper
3 black truffles, peeled and thinly sliced, reserving the peelings
½ cup heavy cream
2 tablespoons Cognac
2 frying chickens (3 pounds each)
  Juice of 1 lemon
1 carrot, finely chopped
2 ribs celery, finely chopped
3 shallots or 1 onion, finely chopped
1 tablespoon chopped parsley
1 tablespoon chopped chervil
2 whole cloves
1 cup Chicken Stock (page 115)
2 cups dry white wine
2 egg yolks

1. Melt half the butter in a skillet. Sauté the chicken livers in it, then chop them very fine. Add salt and pepper to taste, the remaining butter, one of the sliced truffles, just enough of the cream to moisten, and the Cognac. Set aside.

2. Rub the skin of the chickens with the lemon juice. Using the fingers carefully, loosen the skin of the breast, legs, and thighs and insert the remaining truffle slices between the skin and flesh. Replace the skin carefully. Stuff the birds with the liver mixture and truss them (page 217). Wrap each in cheesecloth.

3. Place the carrot, celery, shallots, parsley, chervil, truffle peelings, and cloves in a large kettle. Pour in the stock and wine. Place the chickens on a rack in the kettle, cover tightly, and steam for about forty-five minutes, until the chicken is done.

4. Remove the chickens from the kettle and keep them warm while preparing the sauce.

5. Take two cups of the liquid from the kettle and cook in a separate saucepan until reduced by one third. Combine the egg yolks with the remaining cream and add to the saucepan, stirring. Cook until the sauce thickens enough to coat a metal spoon. Place the chickens on a deep serving platter and spoon the sauce over.

Chicken Vieille France

4 to 6 servings

All things considered—flavor, versatility, universal appeal, and economy—chicken may be the choicest of entrées. It marries well with a multitude of herbs (garlic, sage, rosemary, parsley, bay leaf, thyme); vegetables (tomatoes, artichokes, peas, even spinach and potatoes), and liquids (both white and red wines and even water). Chicken Vieille France—a splendid old French recipe—embraces white wine, mushrooms, cream, and Cognac.

1 cup Brown Chicken Sauce (see below)
2 chickens (2½ pounds), cut into serving pieces, necks, backbones, and wing tips reserved
Salt and freshly ground pepper
¼ cup butter
2 tablespoons finely chopped shallots
3 tablespoons Cognac
⅓ cup dry white wine
1 cup heavy cream
2 cups sliced fresh mushrooms

1. Start the brown sauce and let it cook while preparing the chicken.
2. Preheat the oven to 300 degrees.
3. Sprinkle the chicken with salt and pepper. Heat three tablespoons of butter in a heavy skillet and brown the chicken slowly, on all sides, for about twenty minutes.
4. Remove the chicken to a warm serving dish and cover with aluminum foil. Place in the oven while preparing the remaining steps. Do not let the chicken bake more than fifteen minutes or it will dry out.
5. Add the shallots to the skillet and stir with a wooden spoon, scraping the bottom and sides. Add two tablespoons of the Cognac and ignite. Add the wine and bring to a boil, still scraping with the wooden spoon. Let this almost evaporate, then add the cream. Boil five minutes.
6. Meanwhile, in another skillet, cook the mushrooms in the remaining tablespoon of butter and sprinkle with salt and pepper to taste. Cook until the mushrooms give up their juices, then let most of this moisture evaporate. Add the mushrooms to the skillet containing the shallots and cream, then stir in the brown sauce and add the remaining tablespoon of Cognac. Add the chicken and serve with hot, fluffy rice or buttered noodles.

BROWN CHICKEN SAUCE:

About 1 cup

2 necks, 2 backbones, and 4 wing tips from chickens
¾ cup finely chopped onion
2 tablespoons chopped celery
2 tablespoons finely diced carrots
½ clove garlic, finely minced
3 sprigs parsley
2 sprigs fresh thyme or ½ teaspoon dried thyme
1 bay leaf
Salt and freshly ground pepper

1. Cut the necks and backbones into small pieces and place them, along with the wing tips, in a heavy saucepan without fat. (The necks and backbones will give up their own fat.) Cook, stirring occasionally, until browned.
2. Add the remaining ingredients, but use very little salt. Add water to barely cover, then simmer one hour and strain. Continue simmering the sauce until it is reduced to about one cup.

Cold Tarragon Chicken

12 servings

>   3 chickens (3 pounds each)
>   Salt and freshly ground black pepper
>   6 sprigs fresh tarragon
>   3 cloves garlic, peeled
>   1½ bay leaves
>   ½ cup butter
>   6 small white onions, peeled
>   3 carrots, coarsely chopped

1. Preheat the oven to 450 degrees.

2. Sprinkle the chickens inside and outside with salt and pepper.

3. Place two sprigs of tarragon, one clove garlic, half a bay leaf, and approximately one teaspoon of butter in the cavity of each chicken. Truss the chickens neatly with string (see below).

4. On top of the stove, heat the remaining butter in a large, open skillet and place the chickens in it, laying each chicken on its side. Turn the chickens in the butter without browning.

5. Scatter the onions and carrots around the chickens, then place the skillet in the oven and bake for fifteen minutes, using a large spoon to baste the chickens occasionally. Turn the chickens to the other side and continue to bake and baste for fifteen minutes. Turn the chickens on their backs and continue to bake and baste until the chickens are golden brown, about thirty minutes. The entire cooking time should be about one hour. When cooked, the chickens should be nicely browned, and, when the thigh is pierced with a fork, the liquid should run clear. Let the chickens stand at room temperature until cool, then chill until ready to serve.

TO TRUSS POULTRY:

Using one hand, hold both legs and press them down toward the bird's tail. Push a threaded trussing needle through the fleshy part of one thigh, then through the cavity and out the other thigh. Pull the thread through, leaving about three inches extending from the place where the needle was first inserted. Weave the needle through all the bones of the wing—second, main, and wing tip—then go across to the other wing and thread the bones in reverse. Pull the thread through. Cut the thread, leaving enough thread to tie the two ends together. The thread should be fairly taut, but not enough to tear the flesh.

Truss the tail opening by pushing the needle through the tail bone on both sides of the bird, about halfway down the cavity. Cut the thread, leaving about six inches on either side. Bring the thread up and around the legs, tying securely to enclose both legs and cavity. Snip off the loose ends.

Cold Roast Chicken

6 or more servings

3 frying chickens (3 pounds each)
 Salt and freshly ground black pepper
3 cloves garlic, peeled
3 bay leaves
 Dried thyme
¼ cup butter

1. Preheat the oven to 450 degrees.
2. Sprinkle the chicken inside and out with salt and pepper.
3. Place one garlic clove, one bay leaf, and a pinch of thyme in the cavity of each chicken. Truss the chickens (page 217).
4. Heat the butter in a large ovenproof skillet and turn the chickens around in the butter to coat them. When the chickens start to brown, arrange them on their sides and place the skillet in the oven. Cook, uncovered, for fifteen minutes, basting frequently.
5. Turn the chickens to the other side and continue to baste and cook for fifteen minutes longer.
6. Place the chickens on their backs and continue to cook and baste until the chickens are done, about thirty minutes. When done, the chickens should be golden brown. When the thighs are pierced with a fork, the liquid should run clear, and so should the liquid in the cavities. Let the chickens stand at room temperature until cool, then chill until ready to serve.

Fricassee of Chicken I

6 servings

3 cups water
1 ready-to-cook chicken (3 pounds), cut into serving pieces
2 whole onions, studded with 4 cloves
1 carrot, sliced
1 tablespoon salt
½ teaspoon thyme leaves
½ teaspoon marjoram
½ teaspoon rosemary
½ teaspoon freshly ground black pepper
1 bay leaf
5 tablespoons butter
¼ cup all-purpose flour
3 egg yolks, beaten
¼ pound (1¼ cups) sliced fresh mushrooms
8 whole fresh mushrooms
 Paprika
 Hot, cooked rice

1. Place the water, chicken, onions, carrot, salt, thyme, marjoram, rosemary, pepper, and bay leaf in a three-quart saucepan. Cover and cook slowly, until the chicken is tender, about one hour.
2. Melt four tablespoons of the butter in a saucepan. Blend in the flour. Using a whisk, stir in three cups of the broth in which the chicken cooked and cook until the mixture begins to thicken.
3. Mix a little of the sauce with the beaten egg yolks and gradually stir into the mixture. Cook over low heat one minute, stirring constantly.
4. Sauté the sliced and whole mushrooms in the remaining butter. Add the sliced mushrooms to the sauce. Arrange the chicken in a serving dish and pour the sauce over it. Garnish with the sautéed whole mushrooms and paprika. Serve over rice.

Fricassee of Chicken II

4 to 6 servings

½ cup all-purpose flour
2 teaspoons salt
¼ teaspoon freshly ground black pepper
1 teaspoon paprika
1 roasting chicken (4 pounds), cut into serving pieces
¼ cup butter
3 cups water or Chicken Stock (page 115)
1 cup dry white wine
2 onions, coarsely chopped
1 large carrot, cut into ½-inch rounds
1 rib celery, cut into 1-inch lengths
1 clove garlic, peeled
½ bay leaf
Pinch of dried thyme
6 tablespoons cold water
Chopped parsley

1. Combine the flour, salt, pepper, and paprika in a brown paper bag. Add the chicken pieces, a few at a time, and shake well until the pieces are coated. Reserve any leftover flour. Melt the butter in a skillet and brown the chicken pieces on all sides.

2. Add the water, wine, onions, carrot, celery, garlic, bay leaf, and thyme and simmer over low heat until the chicken is tender, one to one and one-half hours. Transfer the chicken to a covered dish and strain the pot broth into a saucepan. Bring to a boil.

3. Combine the reserved flour with the cold water and stir into the boiling broth. Cook, stirring, about five minutes. Pour the sauce over the chicken and sprinkle with parsley.

Fricasseed Chicken

6 servings

1 roasting chicken (4 pounds), cut into serving pieces
1 medium onion studded with 2 cloves
4 peppercorns
½ bay leaf
1 tablespoon salt
7 tablespoons butter (optional)
7 tablespoons all-purpose flour
2 to 3 tablespoons white wine
½ teaspoon grated lemon rind
¼ teaspoon freshly ground black pepper
1 egg yolk
¼ cup heavy cream

1. Place the chicken in a kettle and barely cover with boiling water. Add the onion, peppercorns, bay leaf, and salt. Simmer gently until the chicken is tender, one and one-half to two hours.

2. Remove the chicken from the kettle and strain the broth. Cook the broth over high heat until reduced to three cups.

3. Skim off seven tablespoons of fat from the broth, or use an equal amount of butter, and heat in a saucepan. Stir in the flour; when it is blended, stir in the broth.

4. Stir constantly until the sauce is thickened. Add the wine, lemon rind, and pepper. Taste the sauce and adjust the seasoning, if necessary.

5. Blend the egg yolk with the cream and add a little of the hot sauce to it. Pour the egg mixture into the sauce and cook without boiling for two to three minutes, stirring constantly.

Fricassee of Chicken with Tarragon

6 or more servings

Some dishes are as fundamental to French cooking as fresh butter, heavy cream, wine, and shallots, and one of these is a delectable creation called fricassee. It is a dish that lends itself to many variations (one calls for chicken and crayfish) and it is incredibly easy to prepare. Most dishes similar to a fricassee call for browning the meat first before adding a liquid and stewing. In this one, however, the meat is "stewed" in butter before finishing with flour, stock, and cream.

¼ cup butter
2 cups finely chopped onion
2 chickens (3 pounds each), cut into serving pieces
   Salt and freshly ground black pepper
1 clove garlic, finely chopped
1 bay leaf
1 teaspoon chopped fresh thyme or ½ teaspoon dried thyme
½ teaspoon grated nutmeg
3 tablespoons chopped fresh tarragon or 2 teaspoons dried tarragon
1 bundle tarragon stems, if available, tied
   Cayenne pepper
½ cup all-purpose flour
1 cup Chicken Stock (page 115)
1 cup dry white wine
2 cups heavy cream
2 egg yolks
   Juice of ½ lemon
   Chopped parsley or tarragon

1. Preheat the oven to 400 degrees.
2. Heat the butter in a large casserole and add the onion, chicken, salt and pepper to taste, garlic, bay leaf, thyme, nutmeg, tarragon, tarragon stems, and cayenne to taste. Cook, stirring occasionally, on top of the stove for about five minutes. Do not brown the chicken.

3. Sprinkle the chicken with the flour and stir until all the pieces are well coated. Add the chicken stock and wine and stir well. Bring to a boil on top of the stove. Cover and bake one hour, or until the chicken is fork tender. Place the casserole on top of the stove and add half the cream. Bring to a boil. Blend the remaining cream with the egg yolks and stir into the sauce. Bring just to a boil, but do not boil. Season the sauce with the lemon juice and salt and pepper to taste, and sprinkle with parsley or tarragon. Serve with rice.

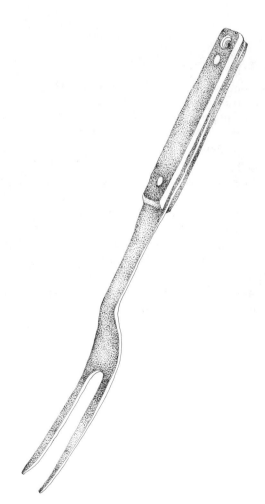

Poulet au Riesling

4 servings

2 tablespoons butter
2 broiling chickens (2½ pounds each), quartered
½ teaspoon salt
¼ teaspoon white pepper
4 shallots, chopped
½ pound mushrooms, sliced
1 bay leaf
 Pinch of dried thyme
⅔ cup Alsatian Riesling
⅓ cup heavy cream
1 egg yolk

1. Heat the butter in a heavy skillet. Add the chicken and sprinkle with the salt and pepper. Cook over low heat until the chicken is lightly browned on all sides.

2. Add the shallots, mushrooms, bay leaf, thyme, and wine. Bring to a boil, then cover and simmer for about thirty minutes, or until the chicken is tender.

3. Remove the chicken to a heated serving dish and keep warm. Continue to cook the sauce until it is reduced to about one third of its volume.

4. Combine the cream and egg yolk in a bowl. Stir the egg mixture into the sauce in the pan and cook over low heat for two minutes, stirring constantly. Do not allow the sauce to boil. Pour the sauce over the chicken and serve hot.

Poulet au Riz

4 servings

2 chickens (2½ pounds each), trussed
½ lemon (optional)
2 leeks, trimmed, split to the root end, and washed well
4 ribs celery, trimmed and cut into quarters
2 carrots, scraped and cut into quarters
2 sprigs parsley
1 medium onion, peeled
2 bay leaves
 Pinch of dried thyme
10 whole peppercorns
 Salt
5 tablespoons butter
5 tablespoons all-purpose flour
2 cups heavy cream

1. Rinse the chickens well under cold water and rub them with half a lemon, if desired. Place the chickens in a kettle and cover with cold water.

2. Tie the leeks, celery, carrots, and parsley with a string and add them to the kettle. Add the onion. Tie the bay leaves, thyme, and peppercorns in a small piece of cheesecloth and add to the kettle. Add salt to taste, bring to a boil, and skim the surface. Cook until the chickens are tender, about thirty minutes.

3. Remove the chickens from the broth and keep them warm while preparing the sauce. Reserve the broth.

4. Melt three tablespoons of the butter in a saucepan and stir in the flour. When blended, add two cups of hot chicken broth, stirring vigorously with a wire whisk. Cook the sauce slowly, stirring occasionally, for thirty minutes. (The sauce should be fairly thick from the beginning.)

5. Strain the sauce through a sieve, if necessary, and stir in the cream. Bring to a boil, reduce the heat and stir in the remaining butter. Spoon a little of the sauce over the chickens and serve the remainder in a sauceboat. Serve with rice.

Chicken Breasts Albuféra

6 servings

The semantics of cookery can sometimes be as baffling as that of political doctrine. Take chicken Albuféra, for example, the classic and jewel-like dish below. A bufera *is a storm in Italian;* Albufeira *is the name of a port in Portugal, and* Albufera *is a lagoon in Spain known for its abundance of waterfowl. Still, most authorities agree that chicken Albuféra is a French creation, and it has been ascribed by* Larousse Gastronomique *to the great nineteenth-century French chef, Antonin Carême. It is conceivable that he created the dish for, and named it in honor of, France's Marshal Suchet who, after various victories in Spain, was named the Duke d'Albuféra in 1812. Whatever its origin, chicken Albuféra is a creation to acclaim.*

    5 tablespoons butter
    3 large chicken breasts, split in half, skinned, and boned
        Salt and freshly ground pepper to taste
    1 tablespoon finely chopped shallots
    3 tablespoons Cognac
  2½ cups heavy cream
        Albuféra Rice (see below)
        Pimento and truffle cutouts from Albuféra Rice

1. Heat three tablespoons of the butter in a large skillet and add the chicken breasts seasoned with salt and pepper. Cook over moderate heat. Let the breasts brown very lightly, if at all. Turn them and, letting them "stew" in the butter and natural juices, cover and cook ten to fifteen minutes. Do not overcook.

2. Remove the chicken to a warm mixing bowl and cover with aluminum foil. Keep warm while making the sauce. Add the shallots to the skillet and cook briefly. Add the Cognac and cook about thirty seconds. Stir in the cream and cook, stirring frequently, until thickened slightly, about ten minutes. Season to taste with salt and pepper and swirl the remaining butter around in the skillet.

3. Quickly spoon the hot rice onto a round or oval serving platter. Shape it with a rubber spatula to make a "bed" for the chicken pieces. Arrange the chicken pieces on the rice, spoon some of the hot sauce over them, and garnish each piece with cutouts of pimento and truffles. Serve the remaining sauce separately.

ALBUFÉRA RICE:

6 servings

   ¼ cup butter
   1 tablespoon finely chopped onion
   ½ teaspoon minced garlic
   1 cup uncooked rice
   ½ bay leaf
  1½ cups Chicken Stock (page 115)
     Salt to taste
   ¼ pound chicken livers, picked over and cubed
  1½ cups diced raw mushrooms
   4 pimentos
   2 black truffles (optional)

1. Preheat the oven to 350 degrees.

2. Melt two tablespoons of the butter in an ovenproof saucepan or casserole with lid. Add the onion and garlic and cook briefly without browning.

3. Add the rice and bay leaf and cook, stirring, about two minutes. Add the stock and salt to taste and bring to a boil. Cover closely and bake exactly seventeen minutes.

4. Meanwhile, melt the remaining butter in a skillet and add the chicken livers. Cook, stirring, over moderate heat until the livers lose their red color. Add the mushrooms and cook until most of the liquid evaporates. Do not overcook or the livers will become too dry.

5. Prepare the garnish for the finished dish by cutting out six diamond-shaped pieces from the pimentos and six thin slices or cutouts from the truffles. Chop the remaining pimentos and truffles.

6. When the rice is cooked, stir in the liver and mushroom mixture, chopped pimentos and truffles. Set aside but keep warm.

Chicken Breasts à l' Empereur

8 servings

4 large chicken breasts, boned
5 tablespoons butter
½ cup chopped onion
2 cloves garlic, finely minced
1 shallot, finely chopped
¼ pound mushrooms, sliced
2 tablespoons chopped parsley
½ pound lean, boneless pork
4 chicken livers
2 slices day-old bread, crumbled
1 egg, lightly beaten
  Salt and freshly ground black pepper
½ cup dry white wine
⅓ cup finely chopped carrots
½ cup finely chopped onion
¼ cup finely chopped celery
1 cup finely diced mushrooms
1 cup canned Italian plum tomatoes
1 bay leaf
2 sprigs fresh thyme or ½ teaspoon dried thyme
½ cup Chicken Stock (page 115)
½ cup Brown Sauce (page 268) or canned beef gravy

1. When the chicken breasts are boned, there will or should be eight halves plus eight small, tender strips known as "fillets." Have the butcher make a "pocket" in each large piece for stuffing. Have him flatten the fillets, which will also be used.

2. Melt two tablespoons of the butter in a skillet and cook the onion, one minced garlic clove, and the shallot until the onion is wilted. Add the sliced mushrooms and cook, stirring, until mushrooms give up their juices, about five minutes. Add the parsley.

3. Put the pork, chicken livers, and bread through a food grinder, using the fine blade. Add to the onion mixture. Cook, stirring, until the pork and chicken livers lose their red color. Let cool slightly, then add the egg and salt and pepper to taste.

4. Spoon equal portions of the stuffing inside the chicken breasts. Flatten the chicken fillets and use to cover the opening. It is not necessary to sew or skewer the opening. Refrigerate one hour or longer.

5. Preheat the oven to 425 degrees.

6. Melt the remaining butter in a large ovenproof skillet and place the breasts, skin side up, in the skillet. Sprinkle with salt and pepper. Bake, uncovered, fifteen minutes.

7. Transfer the skillet to the top of the stove and reduce the oven heat to 375 degrees. Sprinkle the chicken with the wine, and around it scatter the finely chopped carrots, onion, celery, mushrooms, and the remaining garlic. Add the tomatoes, bay leaf, thyme, chicken stock, and brown sauce. Bring the sauce and chicken to a boil and return the skillet to the oven. Bake thirty to forty-five minutes, or until tender and done.

8. Pour the sauce into a pan and cover with a lid. Bring the sauce to a boil and simmer over high heat about ten minutes, or until the sauce is reduced by one-third. Strain. Arrange the breasts on a serving dish and serve the sauce separately.

Chicken with Noodles Parisien

4 to 6 servings

Take chicken and spice, noodles and cream and conjure up a dish for a real feast— Chicken with noodles Parisien, subtly seasoned with tomatoes and glazed in the oven with Parmesan cheese. Although the time element isn't essential, this is a casserole that may be assembled for the sake of convenience several hours before baking.

  1 chicken (3½ to 4 pounds)
     Chicken Stock (page 115) or water
  1 carrot, scraped and sliced
  2 ribs celery, broken in half
  1 onion, studded with 2 cloves
 12 peppercorns
     Salt
1½ cups Tomato Sauce I (page 278)
 ¼ cup butter
 ¼ cup all-purpose flour
     Freshly ground black pepper
 ¾ cup heavy cream
     Few drops Tabasco
 ½ pound broad noodles
  3 tablespoons chopped chives
  1 egg yolk
 ¾ cup grated Parmesan cheese

1. Place the chicken in a kettle and add the chicken stock or water to cover, carrot, celery, onion, and peppercorns. If water is used instead of stock, season with salt. Bring to a boil and simmer until the chicken is tender, about forty-five minutes.

2. Meanwhile, prepare the tomato sauce.

3. Remove the chicken and continue to boil the broth until it is reduced to about two cups. Strain the broth and reserve. When the chicken is cool enough to handle, remove and discard the skin and bones. Pull or cut the chicken meat into strips and reserve.

4. Melt two tablespoons of the butter and add the flour. When it is blended, add the reserved chicken broth, stirring vigorously with a wire whisk. When blended and smooth, simmer over low heat, stirring occasionally, for about thirty minutes. This is called a "velouté."

5. Preheat the oven to 350 degrees.

6. Melt one tablespoon of butter in a skillet and add the reserved chicken meat. Sprinkle with salt and pepper to taste. Blend one-half cup of the cream with one cup of the velouté. Add a touch of Tabasco and stir this sauce into the chicken. Remove from the heat.

7. Cook the noodles in boiling salted water until they are tender, but do not overcook. Drain and rinse in cold water. Heat the remaining tablespoon of butter and toss the noodles in it just long enough to warm them.

8. Generously butter a baking dish and add a layer of noodles and a layer of tomato sauce. Sprinkle with chives and spread the chicken in cream sauce over all.

9. Blend the remaining velouté with the remaining cream and the egg yolk. Heat but do not boil. Spread this over the chicken layer and sprinkle with the cheese. Bake thirty to forty-five minutes, or until golden brown. Serve immediately.

Ragoût de Poulet

4 servings

4 strips bacon

5 tablespoons butter

1 chicken (3 pounds), cut into serving
  pieces
  Salt and freshly ground pepper to taste

3 tablespoons Cognac

2 tablespoons chopped shallots

3 tablespoons all-purpose flour

1 cup dry white wine

1 cup Chicken Stock (page 115)

8 small white onions, peeled

2 potatoes, peeled and cut into 1-inch cubes

2 carrots, scraped and cut into 1-inch
  lengths

2 ribs celery

4 sprigs parsley

2 sprigs fresh thyme or ½ teaspoon dried
  thyme

1 bay leaf

½ pound mushrooms, sliced

1. Preheat the oven to 400 degrees.

2. Cut the bacon into cubes or small strips
and place it in a small saucepan. Add cold
water to cover and bring to a boil. Simmer
about half a minute, then drain.

3. Heat three tablespoons of the butter in
a skillet and add the bacon. Cook, stirring,
over low heat until the bacon is crisp, then
remove with a slotted spoon and reserve.

4. Sprinkle the chicken with salt and pepper and brown on all sides in the skillet.
When brown, sprinkle with Cognac and
ignite. Transfer the chicken pieces to a casserole with a tight-fitting cover.

5. Add the shallots to the skillet and cook,
stirring with a wire whisk. Sprinkle with
flour and cook for a brief while longer, stirring with the whisk. Add the wine, stirring
rapidly with the whisk. When the sauce is
thickened and smooth, add the chicken stock

and pour over the chicken. Add the onions,
potatoes, and carrots. Tie the celery, parsley,
thyme, and bay leaf together with string and
add to the casserole.

6. Meanwhile, heat the remaining butter
in a skillet and cook the mushrooms until
wilted. Add them to the casserole along with
the reserved bacon, salt, and pepper, and
cover closely. Bring the liquid in the casserole to a boil on top of the stove, then place
the casserole in the oven. Bake fifteen minutes, then reduce the heat to 350 degrees and
bake fifteen minutes longer, or until the
chicken and vegetables are tender. Remove
the celery and herb bundle and serve.

Ragoût Toulousaine

4 to 6 servings

Of all the refinements in classic French cookery, there are few more elegant than a ragoût Toulousaine, *that extraordinary marriage of white-wine sauce with cubes of poached sweetbreads and poached chicken, mushrooms, truffles, and cream, garnished with a few spheres of chicken forcemeat known as quenelles, and perfumed with a dash of Cognac. Taken altogether, it is feasting at its best. This creation demands both patience and time, but it deserves it.*

 4 pairs veal sweetbreads
   Salt to taste
 3 tablespoons butter
 1 onion, sliced
 1 carrot, sliced
 1 rib celery, sliced
 1 bay leaf, broken
¼ teaspoon thyme
   Freshly ground pepper to taste
½ cup dry white wine
1¼ cups chicken broth from Poached Chicken Breast (page 227), plus canned broth if necessary
½ pound small mushrooms, quartered
 1 to 1½ cups cubed Poached Chicken Breast (page 227)
 1 cup cold Chicken Velouté (page 227)
1½ cups heavy cream
 1 truffle, cut into thinnest possible (julienne) strips
¼ teaspoon nutmeg
⅛ teaspoon cayenne pepper
14 to 16 Chicken Quenelles (page 227)
 1 teaspoon lemon juice
 1 teaspoon Cognac

1. Generally speaking, there is one large and one small portion to each sweetbread. Cut the sweetbreads in half where these portions join. Place them in a basin, add very cold water to cover, and let stand at least one hour. Drain.

2. Place the sweetbreads in a saucepan and add water to cover and salt to taste. Bring to a boil and simmer ten minutes. Drain well and run immediately under cold running water to chill, then trim by cutting away connective tissue and cartilage. Place the sweetbreads between cloths and put a weight on them for two hours so they will be well flattened before cooking. The bottom of a skillet filled with heavy objects will do.

3. Preheat the oven to 400 degrees.

4. Use two tablespoons of the butter to grease a large skillet. Sprinkle with the onion slices, carrot slices, celery, bay leaf, thyme, salt, and pepper. Arrange the sweetbreads on this bed and sprinkle with salt and pepper. Cook briefly, without browning, about three minutes. Cover and steam ten minutes. Add the wine and one-half cup of the chicken broth and bake forty-five minutes.

5. Place the mushrooms in a small skillet, add enough of the remaining chicken broth barely to cover, and simmer five minutes.

6. Using a slotted spoon, transfer the mushrooms to the cubed, poached chicken breast.

7. Boiling rapidly, reduce the mushroom cooking liquid by half and set aside.

8. Prepare the chicken quenelles, using one tablespoon of the cold velouté, and set aside. Place the remaining velouté on the stove and add the mushroom liquid, stirring vigorously with a whisk until blended and smooth. Add the cream, stirring rapidly. Simmer five minutes. Add the truffle strips and season the sauce with nutmeg and cayenne pepper.

9. Gently stir in the chicken cubes, mushrooms, and the chicken quenelles. Heat thoroughly, then remove from the heat and swirl the remaining tablespoon of butter into the sauce by rotating the pan gently. At the

last minute, add the lemon juice and Cognac.

10. Arrange the hot sweetbreads on a hot platter and pour the sauce over them. Serve immediately.

POACHED CHICKEN BREAST:

½ poached chicken breast
About 1¼ cups chicken broth

1 whole chicken breast, split
  Water or slightly salted Chicken Stock (page 115) to cover
1 rib celery, chopped
1 bay leaf
1 small onion, peeled and quartered
1 clove garlic, split
1 sprig parsley
1 carrot, scraped and chopped
12 peppercorns
  Salt to taste
½ teaspoon dried thyme

1. Place half the chicken breast in a saucepan. Carefully skin and bone the remaining half, reserving the meat to make Chicken Quenelles (see below). Add the skin and bones to the saucepan.

2. Add the remaining ingredients to the saucepan and simmer, skimming the surface as necessary, thirty minutes or longer, until the breast meat is tender. Strain and reserve the broth. Skin and bone the cooked half breast, then cut the meat into cubes and reserve, covered.

CHICKEN VELOUTÉ:

About 1 cup

2 tablespoons butter
2 tablespoons all-purpose flour
1 cup Chicken Stock (page 115)

Melt the butter in a small saucepan and add the flour, stirring with a whisk. Add the stock, stirring rapidly with the whisk, until the mixture is thickened and smooth. Chill in the saucepan.

CHICKEN QUENELLES:

14 to 16 quenelles

½ chicken breast, skinned and boned and trimmed to remove white fibers
1 tablespoon Chicken Velouté (see above)
  Nutmeg to taste
½ egg white, approximately
  Salt and freshly ground pepper to taste
⅓ cup heavy cream
  Chicken Stock (page 115)

1. Cut the chicken breast into cubes. There should be about one-half cup. Place the meat in the container of an electric blender.

2. Add the chicken velouté, nutmeg, egg white, salt, and pepper. Blend about thirty seconds on high speed, stirring down as necessary with a rubber spatula. Add the cream while blending. This should produce a mousselike mixture.

3. Butter a small enamel-coated or stainless steel skillet. Using two teaspoons, shape the quenelles into small ovals. To do this, pick up a teaspoonful of the mixture. Wet the other spoon and use it to round off the mixture, then spoon into the buttered skillet. Continue making quenelles until all the mixture is used.

4. Carefully add chicken stock to the skillet until the quenelles are barely covered. Cover gently with buttered waxed paper and bring to a boil. Cook, shaking the skillet gently, until the quenelles are firm, three to five minutes.

Chicken and Mushroom Crêpes Florentine

6 servings

1 chicken breast (¾ pound)
2½ cups Chicken Stock (page 115)
10 ounces fresh spinach
½ pound mushrooms
7 tablespoons butter
2 shallots, finely chopped
5 tablespoons all-purpose flour
2 cups milk
1 cup heavy cream
  Salt and freshly ground pepper to taste
⅛ teaspoon cayenne pepper
¼ teaspoon nutmeg
1½ cups finely grated Gruyère, Fontina, or Swiss cheese
12 to 16 Savory Crêpes (see below)
½ cup grated Parmesan cheese

1. Place the chicken breast in a saucepan and add chicken stock to cover. Bring to a boil and simmer, partly covered, about 20 minutes. Let the chicken cool in the liquid.

2. When the chicken has cooled, remove and discard the skin and bones. Chop the chicken meat, then cover and set aside.

3. Meanwhile, pick over the spinach and wash it in cold water. Cook the spinach, covered, in the water that clings to the leaves, only until wilted, stirring once or twice. Drain well. When cool enough, press the spinach between the hands to extract most of the liquid. Chop and set aside.

4. Rinse the mushrooms in cold running water and drain. Dry with paper towels, then chop fine.

5. Heat two tablespoons of butter in a skillet. Add the shallots and cook briefly. Add the mushrooms and cook until they give up their liquid. Continue to cook, stirring frequently, until all the liquid evaporates.

6. Heat the remaining butter and stir in the flour, using a wire whisk. Add the milk, stirring rapidly with the whisk. When the mixture is thickened and smooth, stir in the cream, salt and pepper to taste, cayenne, and nutmeg.

7. Combine the chicken, spinach, and mushrooms. Add one-half cup of the sauce or enough to make the mixture hold together.

8. Heat the oven to 350 degrees.

9. Add the Gruyère cheese to the remaining sauce. Spoon a thin layer of sauce over the bottom of an ovenproof baking dish.

10. Spoon a little of the chicken and mushroom mixture onto each of the crêpes, then roll the crêpes. Arrange the rolled crêpes close together in the baking dish. Spoon the remaining sauce on top. Sprinkle with the Parmesan cheese and bake thirty to forty minutes.

SAVORY CRÊPES

12 to 16 6- or 7-inch crêpes

¾ cup sifted all-purpose flour
1 egg, lightly beaten
  Salt
1 to 1¼ cups milk
3 tablespoons melted butter

1. Place the flour in a mixing bowl.

2. Beat together the egg, a dash of salt, and milk. Add to the flour, stirring with a wire whisk. Whisk in the melted butter and strain.

3. Brush a seasoned crêpe pan with a cloth dipped in melted butter. Heat the crêpe pan and spoon in two tablespoons, more or less, of the batter, turning the pan this way and that, in a circular pattern, so that the batter neatly covers the bottom of the pan. Cook briefly until brown on the bottom, then turn the crêpe with a spatula and cook briefly on the other side. Continue until all the batter is used.

Chicken Croquettes

4 to 6 servings

1 Boiled Chicken (see below)
½ cup finely chopped celery
2 tablespoons finely chopped onion
  Butter
  All-purpose flour
2 tablespoons chopped chives
1 tablespoon finely chopped black truffle (optional)
¼ teaspoon nutmeg, or to taste
2 drops Tabasco, or to taste
3 egg yolks
  Salt and freshly ground pepper to taste
1 cup plus 6 tablespoons fine, soft bread crumbs
1 cup heavy cream
2 eggs
6 tablespoons water
1 teaspoon salad oil
16 truffle slices for garnish

1. Preheat the oven to 425 degrees.

2. Pull the skin off the chicken and place it on a small baking dish or in a skillet. Bake, watching closely, until it is crisp, about twenty minutes. Set aside to cool.

3. Remove the meat from the chicken and cut into very small cubes. Do not grind. Set aside in a skillet.

4. Combine the celery, onion, and one tablespoon butter in a small saucepan and add enough of the reserved stock to cover. Bring to a boil, cover, and simmer about ten minutes. Drain and add to the chicken.

5. Heat three tablespoons of the reserved chicken fat or butter in a one-quart saucepan and add five tablespoons of flour. Stir with a whisk, and when blended stir in two and one-half cups of the reserved chicken stock. When blended and smooth, cook over low heat, stirring frequently, about thirty minutes. This sauce is a velouté.

6. To the chicken add the chives and three-quarters cup of the sauce. Reserve the remaining sauce.

7. Chop the crisp chicken skin finely and add to the chicken. Simmer five minutes, stirring, then add the chopped truffle, nutmeg, and Tabasco. Off the heat add the egg yolks, stirring rapidly. Return the chicken to the heat and cook briefly, stirring, until the chicken mixture thickens. Add salt and pepper to taste.

8. Stir in the six tablespoons bread crumbs and chill the mixture thoroughly.

9. Meanwhile, add the cream to the reserved velouté and simmer about ten minutes.

10. Shape the chicken mixture into eight to twelve flat cakes of uniform size.

11. Beat the eggs with the water, oil, and salt and pepper to taste. Dip the cakes first into the flour, then into the egg mixture, and then into the remaining bread crumbs. Coat well all over.

12. Heat butter to a depth of one-quarter inch in one or two skillets and cook the cakes until golden brown on all sides. Transfer to a hot platter, garnish each cake with a truffle slice, and serve with the remaining hot sauce.

BOILED CHICKEN:

1 chicken

1 chicken (3½ pounds)
  Chicken Stock (page 115) or water to cover the chicken (approximately 8 cups)
1 onion stuck with 2 cloves
2 carrots, scraped and quartered
1 large or 2 small ribs celery with leaves
1 bay leaf
10 peppercorns
1 sprig fresh thyme or ½ teaspoon dried
  Salt to taste

Combine all the ingredients in a kettle and bring to a boil. Simmer about thirty minutes, or until the chicken is tender. Skim the surface as the chicken cooks to remove the scum and foam. Let the chicken cool in the stock, then remove when ready to use, reserving both the stock and the fat.

Chicken Mousse

8 servings

Perhaps the most remarkable kitchen utensil introduced in the present century is the electric blender. Aside from its obvious uses in preparing daiquiris and pureeing soups and sauces, it is great for making bread crumbs and grating peppercorns and hard cheeses of the Parmesan type. The blender is also a real aid in the preparation of dishes like the elegant chicken mousse below, which, traditionally, was made by pounding meat with a pestle or forcing it through a sieve.

1½ pounds boneless, skinless chicken breasts, with cartilage and pieces of nerve removed
2 cups heavy cream
Salt and freshly ground pepper to taste
¼ teaspoon nutmeg
⅛ to ¼ teaspoon cayenne pepper
1 egg white, lightly beaten
Sauce Aurore (page 266)
1 teaspoon chopped parsley

1. Preheat the oven to 400 degrees.
2. Cut the chicken meat into cubes. There should be about three cups.
3. Place a few of the cubes in a blender and blend until smooth; scrape out into a bowl and repeat with a few more cubes until all the chicken has been blended. If necessary, a small amount of the cream can be added to facilitate blending.
4. Add the salt and pepper to taste, nutmeg, and cayenne, then mix and chill the mixture well. Set the bowl in a larger bowl of ice cubes and gradually beat in the remaining cream. Beat in the egg white and chill again.
5. Butter a one-and-one-half-quart turk's head mold or savarin mold. Scrape the mixture into it and smooth the top. Cover with a buttered circle or ring of paper, buttered side down. Place in a baking dish and pour about one inch of boiling water into the baking dish.
6. Bake twenty-five to thirty-five minutes. Unmold and serve with sauce aurore poured over and sprinkled with the parsley.

Duck Fermière

4 servings

1 duck (4½ to 5 pounds)
  Salt and freshly ground pepper to taste
3 leeks
2 tablespoons all-purpose flour
2 large carrots, peeled and cut into rounds
  (about 1½ cups)
2 large white turnips, peeled and cut into
  cubes (about 2 cups)
1 clove garlic, minced
½ cup dry white wine
1 cup peeled tomatoes, fresh or canned
½ cup fresh or frozen green peas
¼ cup finely chopped parsley

1. Preheat the oven to 500 degrees.
2. Cut the duck or have it cut into serving pieces. Set aside the neck and gizzard. Place the duck pieces, fat side down, on a flat surface and cut away much of the fat around the edges. Sprinkle with salt and pepper.

3. Heat a large skillet and add the duck pieces, fat side down. Sear over moderately high heat until the fat side is well browned. Pour off the fat from the skillet and turn the pieces to brown the other side. Transfer the duck to a flameproof casserole and add the neck and gizzard. Bake, uncovered, twenty minutes, pouring off the fat as it accumulates.

4. Split the leeks lengthwise and rinse well under cold running water. Pull the leaves apart while rinsing to make certain there is no grit between the leaves. Dry lightly and chop. Add to the duck.

5. Place the casserole over moderate heat and cook, stirring, until most of the moisture disappears. Sprinkle with the flour and stir well. Add the carrots, turnips, and garlic and sprinkle with more salt and pepper, if necessary.

6. Add the wine and tomatoes. Bring to a boil, then cover and simmer about forty minutes, or until the duck is thoroughly tender. Add the peas, cover, and cook briefly until the peas are done. Serve sprinkled with chopped parsley.

Duck Montmorency

(Duck with Cherries)

6 to 8 servings

A plump young duck, whether simply roasted or graced with a sauce of oranges or cherries, is excellent fare for winter. Duck with cherries is known in French cookery as Montmorency. A recipe for that dish is given below.

3 fully dressed ducks (5 pounds each), giblets and wing tips reserved
  Salt and freshly ground black pepper
1 onion, coarsely chopped
2 cloves garlic, chopped or thinly sliced
1 carrot, scraped and sliced
2 sprigs fresh thyme or ½ teaspoon dried thyme
1 bay leaf
2 ribs celery, chopped
2 sprigs fresh parsley
  Water
2½ cups Brown Sauce (page 268) or canned beef gravy
2 pounds fresh black cherries, if available, or 1 no. 2 can (1 pound 14 ounces) Bing cherries
  Granulated sugar
¼ cup white vinegar

1. Preheat the oven to 350 degrees.
2. Sprinkle the ducks inside and outside with salt and pepper and truss the ducks (page 217). Place them on their sides in a roasting pan and put the pan in the oven.
3. Assemble the duck gizzards, necks, and wing tips in a large, heavy skillet. Do not add additional fat but cook the duck parts slowly until rendered of fat and golden brown.
4. Add the onion, garlic, carrot, thyme, bay leaf, celery, parsley, and duck livers and sprinkle with salt and pepper. Cook briefly, stirring, and add four cups of water and the brown sauce. Simmer, uncovered, skimming the top of scum and fat as it accumulates, about one and one-half hours.
5. When the ducks have roasted for thirty minutes on one side, pour off the fat from the roasting pan and turn the ducks to the other side. Continue roasting, pouring off fat as it accumulates, thirty minutes longer. Turn the ducks onto their backs and continue roasting and pouring off the fat for one and one-half hours. The total cooking time is about two and one-half hours.
6. While the sauce cooks and the ducks roast, prepare the cherries. If fresh cherries are used, pit them and put them in a skillet with one-half cup water and one-half cup sugar. Cover and simmer five minutes, then uncover and cook ten to fifteen minutes, or until the cherry liquid is syrupy and the cherries are lightly glazed. If fresh cherries are not available, drain the liquid from the canned cherries into a saucepan. Simmer fifteen minutes, then add the cherries without boiling.
7. Combine the vinegar and one-quarter cup sugar in a saucepan. Bring to a boil and simmer until the liquid is caramelized. Do not burn. When caramelized, remove the saucepan from the heat.
8. Strain the giblet sauce into the caramel mixture and stir. Add the cherries and their syrup and bring to a boil.
9. Carve the duck, arrange it on a platter, and serve the sauce separately.

Duck Nivernaise

4 servings

1 duck (5 pounds), cut into serving pieces and liver and fat from cavity reserved
  Salt and freshly ground pepper to taste
¾ cup chopped onion
4 carrots, scraped and cut into 1-inch lengths
¼ teaspoon dried thyme
¼ bay leaf
3 tablespoons all-purpose flour
¾ cup dry white wine
1¾ cups Chicken Stock (page 115), or stock made from the neck and giblets of the duck (see note)
1 sprig parsley
3 tender white turnips, peeled and quartered
3 tablespoons butter (optional)
1 10-ounce package frozen peas, cooked according to package directions, or 1 pound fresh peas, shelled and cooked

1. Preheat the oven to 450 degrees.
2. Sprinkle the duck with salt and pepper. Cut the duck fat into cubes. Render some of the fat in a large heatproof skillet and brown the pieces of duck in it. Place the skillet in the oven and cook twenty minutes.
3. Pour off most of the fat from the skillet and add the onion, carrots, thyme, and bay leaf. Sprinkle with flour. Turn the pieces of duck over in the skillet and bake five minutes.
4. Reduce the oven heat to 400 degrees.
5. Add the wine, chicken stock, and parsley. Stir the liquid and duck pieces around in the skillet and bake twenty minutes, covered. Add the turnips, cover the skillet, and bake twenty minutes longer, or until the turnips are tender. If the skillet does not have a cover, use aluminum foil.
6. Meanwhile, if desired, heat the butter and cook the duck liver in it, cooking on all sides until done, about 10 minutes. Cut the liver into bite-sized pieces. (Duck liver does not appeal to all palates, and its use is optional.)
7. When the duck is done, transfer the pieces and the vegetables to a hot serving platter. Strain the gravy and skim off as much fat as possible. Add the peas and cubed liver to the gravy. Heat thoroughly and pour over the duck and turnips.

Note: This duck dish may be prepared as much as half an hour before serving. It should be kept warm in a 200-degree oven.

To make duck stock, put the neck and giblets in two cups of water with one-half teaspoon salt, a few peppercorns, and a sprig of parsley. Cook, covered, until tender, then remove the cooked giblets and strain the stock.

Duck and Rutabaga Stew

5 or 6 servings

½ cup finely chopped onion
1 tablespoon rendered duck fat
1 duck (4 to 5 pounds), cut into serving pieces
¼ cup chopped ham or luncheon meat
4 cups hot water or Chicken Stock (page 115)
3 teaspoons salt
⅛ teaspoon freshly ground black pepper
3 sprigs parsley, tied together
1 ¾-pound rutabaga (yellow turnip), diced
12 small white onions
½ teaspoon crumbled dried thyme
1 clove garlic, split
3½ tablespoons all-purpose flour

1. Sauté the chopped onion in the duck fat in a heavy Dutch oven or saucepan. Add the duck pieces and brown on all sides.

2. Add the ham, three cups of the hot water, the salt, pepper, and parsley. Simmer, covered, for thirty minutes, or until the duck is almost tender.

3. Add the rutabaga, whole onions, thyme, and garlic to the duck mixture. Cook, covered, for twenty-five to thirty minutes, or until the duck is tender. Remove excess grease.

4. Brown the flour in a skillet over medium heat. Mix the browned flour with the remaining water, add to the stew, and cook until slightly thickened. Serve hot.

Rock Cornish Hens Ménagère

6 to 12 servings

There is nothing more versatile than poultry, be it chicken, squab or Cornish game hen. In one form or another, it suits menus for all seasons. Rock Cornish hen ménagère, *which is to say stuffed lightly with cubes of bread and herbs, is food proper for a banquet.*

6 Rock Cornish hens or 6 chickens (1 pound each), giblets reserved
  Salt and freshly ground black pepper
½ cup chopped parsley
6 large cubes (about 2 inches square) of day-old French or Italian bread with crusts
1 clove garlic, peeled
½ cup butter
2 small onions, peeled and sliced
2 sprigs fresh thyme or ½ teaspoon dried
¾ cup cold water

1. Preheat the oven to 425 degrees.

2. Sprinkle the inside of each hen with salt and pepper.

3. Cut the livers in half and sprinkle with salt and pepper. Toss with the parsley.

4. Rub the cubes of bread on all sides with the garlic clove. Stuff each hen cavity with equal portions of the livers and a cube of bread. Truss the birds (page 217).

5. Melt the butter in an ovenproof shallow baking dish and turn the birds around in the butter until coated on all sides. Add the gizzards and necks, onions, and thyme. Lay the birds on one side and cook, basting, ten minutes. Turn to the other side and continue to cook and baste for ten minutes. Lay the birds on their backs and cook, basting, ten minutes longer, or until done.

6. Remove the trussing from the hens and spoon some of the cooking fat into the interiors. Add the water to the pan and return the hens to the oven for five minutes. Serve split in half.

Stuffed Squab

4 servings

¼ pound larding fat, cut into small cubes
4 whole chicken livers
¼ pound calves' liver, cut into cubes
¼ pound mushrooms, thinly sliced
½ cup chopped onion
½ bay leaf, crumbled
2 sprigs fresh thyme or ¼ teaspoon dried thyme
  Salt and freshly ground black pepper
3 tablespoons Cognac
4 squabs (1 to 1¼ pounds each), necks and gizzards reserved
7 tablespoons butter
⅓ cup fresh bread crumbs

1. Place the larding fat in a skillet and cook until most of the fat is rendered. Add the chicken livers, calves' liver, mushrooms, onion, bay leaf, thyme, and salt and pepper to taste and cook over moderately high heat, stirring, until the liver is just cooked through. Add the Cognac and ignite it. Put the entire mixture through the finest blade of a food grinder. Do not use a blender or the mixture will become too liquid.

2. Place the stuffing in a cold place, a refrigerator or freezer, and chill thoroughly.

3. Preheat the oven to 450 degrees.

4. Spoon equal amounts of the chilled mixture inside each squab and truss the squabs neatly (page 217) to contain the filling.

5. Melt four tablespoons of the butter in an ovenproof skillet and add the squabs. Scatter the necks and gizzards around them. Sprinkle the squabs with salt and pepper, then turn until they are coated all over with butter. Lay the squabs on one side and place them in the oven. Roast ten minutes, basting occasionally. Turn the squabs on their other sides and roast ten minutes, basting. Turn the squabs on their backs and continue to roast and baste ten minutes longer. The squabs should cook thirty to forty minutes in all, depending on doneness desired. When cooked, remove them to a hot platter and keep warm.

6. Melt the remaining butter in a skillet, and when the butter starts to turn nut brown add the bread crumbs. Cook, stirring, until the crumbs are brown. Immediately spoon the crumbs and butter over the squabs and serve.

Stuffed Squab with Madeira Sauce

8 servings

8 squabs
Salt
7 tablespoons butter
¾ pound sausage meat
3 small onions, finely chopped
3 medium apples, very finely chopped
⅓ cup raisins, cooked in boiling water for 8 minutes
⅓ cup shelled pistachio nuts
Freshly ground black pepper
¼ cup melted butter
1 tablespoon vegetable oil
8 strips bacon, simmered in water for 10 minutes, drained, and patted dry
1 tablespoon minced shallots
2 cups Chicken Stock (page 115)
⅓ cup Madeira or port wine

1. Preheat the oven to 400 degrees.

2. Season the cavities of the squabs with one and one-half teaspoons salt and five tablespoons of the butter.

3. In a skillet, cook the sausage meat until it starts to turn brown, breaking it up as it cooks. Add the onions and cook until they wilt and turn yellow. Pour off most of the fat and add the apples, raisins, and nuts. Turn off the heat after seasoning with salt and pepper to taste.

4. Fill the cavities of the squabs with the sausage meat stuffing; truss (page 217). Dry and rub the skin with combined melted butter and oil.

5. Cut the bacon in half lengthwise and tie the strips over the thighs and breast of each bird. Bake the birds in a roasting pan thirty to forty minutes, basting and turning the birds every seven minutes.

6. Transfer the squabs to a warm platter and remove the trussing. Pour off the fat from the roasting pan and add the minced shallots. Stir in the chicken stock and wine

and boil the sauce until it has reduced to three-quarters cup. Correct the seasoning, turn off the heat, and swirl in the remaining two tablespoons butter by rotating the pan gently. Serve the sauce separately.

Note: The squabs may be served with sautéed mushroom caps and sautéed potatoes.

Turkey with Noodles Florentine

About 24 servings

1 uncooked turkey breast (12 pounds) or 2 breasts (5 to 6 pounds each) or 1 whole bird (15 to 16 pounds), cut up
Salt to taste
¼ cup peppercorns
4 carrots, scraped and trimmed
6 ribs celery
3 to 4 pounds fresh spinach
½ cup plus 5 tablespoons butter
Freshly ground pepper
¼ teaspoon nutmeg
¾ cup all-purpose flour
8 cups strained stock in which turkey cooked
2 cups heavy cream
2 8-ounce packages medium noodles
2 egg yolks, lightly beaten
1 cup freshly grated Parmesan cheese

1. Place the entire turkey breast in a large kettle. Add cold water to cover, salt, the peppercorns, carrots, and celery. Bring to a boil and simmer two hours for a thawed twelve-pound breast (two thawed five-pound breasts, each cooked in a separate pot, should be simmered for one hour; a thawed sixteen-pound, cut-up bird will take three and one-half hours for legs, one and one-half hours for breasts),

or until the turkey is cooked and tender. Do not overcook or the meat will be dry. Remove the turkey and then remove the meat from the bones. Cut the meat into one-inch or bite-sized cubes. Strain the stock and set aside.

2. Meanwhile, rinse the spinach and cook it briefly, covered, in the water that clings to the leaves. No further liquid is needed, but stir the spinach while cooking. Drain, then run the leaves under cold running water and press between the hands to remove most of the moisture. Toss the spinach in two table-spoons of hot butter and season with salt, pepper, and nutmeg.

3. Melt the one-half cup butter in a large saucepan and add the flour, stirring with a whisk. When it is blended, add the eight cups of stock, stirring rapidly with the whisk. Cook, stirring frequently, about forty-five minutes. Stir in the cream. Continue cooking and stirring about 10 minutes.

4. Meanwhile, cook the noodles in boiling salted water. Cook only until barely tender (al dente). Do not overcook, since the noodles will be reheated in the sauce. Drain the noodles and run them under cold running water. Drain well.

5. Using a large casserole or two smaller ones, total capacity about ten quarts, make layers of noodles, spinach, turkey. Continue making layers until all the ingredients are used. Pour half the sauce over the layers and stir with a two-pronged fork.

6. Combine the egg yolks with the remaining sauce and pour this over all. Sprinkle with grated cheese and dot with the remaining butter.

7. Before serving, preheat the oven to 400 degrees. Add the casserole and heat until the mixture is heated through. Run the casserole under the broiler just until the cheese is golden brown.

Note: For a more economical or heavier dish, three eight-ounce packages of noodles may be used.

Eggs in Tomato Shells

4 servings

4 firm, ripe, medium tomatoes
  Salt and freshly ground black pepper
4 teaspoons finely chopped fresh basil or 2 teaspoons finely chopped tarragon
4 teaspoons butter
4 large eggs
2 tablespoons freshly grated Parmesan cheese
4 large toast rounds, buttered
  Watercress

1. Preheat the oven to 350 degrees.

2. Cut off a small slice from the top of each tomato. Run a paring knife around the inner rim of the tomato and carefully scoop out the pulp to make a hollow shell or case. Discard the pulp. Sprinkle the inside of the cases with salt and turn upside down on a rack to drain.

3. Place the tomatoes right side up and sprinkle with salt and pepper to taste. Add equal quantities of basil or tarragon and equal parts of butter to each case and break one egg inside each. Place the tomatoes on a buttered ovenproof dish and bake twenty to twenty-five minutes. Do not let the yolks become too firm. Sprinkle with Parmesan cheese and run the tomatoes quickly under the broiler. Serve on warm buttered toast rounds, garnished with watercress.

Mushroom and Fines Herbes Omelet

4 servings

1 pound fresh mushrooms, thinly sliced
7 tablespoons butter
2 tablespoons all-purpose flour
¾ cup sour cream
   Salt and freshly ground black pepper
6 eggs
¼ cup Chicken Stock (page 115)
1 teaspoon chopped fresh parsley
1 teaspoon chopped fresh chives
½ teaspoon chopped fresh thyme or ½ teaspoon dried thyme
½ teaspoon chopped fresh tarragon or ½ teaspoon dried tarragon
   Parsley for garnish

1. Cook the mushrooms in four tablespoons of the butter, stirring until mushrooms are softened and lightly browned. Sprinkle with the flour, stirring constantly. Remove the saucepan from the heat and add the sour cream. Stir to blend and season with salt and pepper to taste. Bring just to a boil, then remove from the heat.

2. Beat the eggs lightly with the stock and add the chopped parsley, chives, thyme, and tarragon. Season with a little salt and pepper. Heat the remaining butter in a skillet and add the egg mixture. As the eggs cook, lift them up with a spatula to let the liquid egg flow under. The eggs should remain moist. Spoon the mushroom filling into the center, fold the omelet over and slide onto a hot platter. Garnish with parsley and serve.

Pipérade with Ham

6 servings

¼ cup ham fat cut into cubes, if available, or use 2 tablespoons bacon fat or butter
2 medium onions
3 to 5 cloves garlic
½ bay leaf
2 large tomatoes, peeled and chopped
2 sprigs fresh thyme, chopped, or ½ teaspoon dried thyme
   Salt and freshly ground black pepper
7 tablespoons butter
12 thin slices ham
12 eggs
   Parsley sprigs (optional)

1. Place the ham fat in a large skillet and cook until rendered of liquid fat.

2. Meanwhile, peel the onions and slice in half. Place each onion half sliced side down. Slice each onion half into paper-thin slices and add to the skillet.

3. Chop the garlic cloves. Top the chopped garlic cloves with the bay leaf and continue to chop until the bay leaf is finely chopped. Add to the skillet.

4. Add the tomatoes, thyme, and salt and pepper to taste. Cook, stirring occasionally, until the sauce becomes thick, about fifteen minutes.

5. Heat three tablespoons of butter in a large skillet and add the ham slices. Cook briefly.

6. Beat the eggs and season with salt and pepper to taste. Add to the sauce. Cook, stirring, until thickened, then stir in the remaining butter. Arrange two slices of ham on each of six plates. Spoon the pipérade over the ham. Garnish, if desired, with parsley sprigs.

Soufflé Laurette

6 servings

¼ cup butter
¼ cup sifted all-purpose flour
1 cup milk
1 teaspoon salt
½ teaspoon freshly ground black pepper
½ cup grated Parmesan cheese
8 egg yolks
10 egg whites
6 whole eggs

1. Preheat the oven to 375 degrees.
2. Melt the butter in a saucepan and stir in the flour. When the mixture is blended and smooth, add the milk, stirring vigorously with a wire whisk. Season with the salt and pepper. When the mixture is thickened, remove from the heat and cool slightly.
3. Stir the grated cheese into the sauce. Beat the eight egg yolks lightly and stir them into the sauce. Return to the heat briefly but do not boil.
4. Beat the ten egg whites until stiff. Stir half of the egg whites into the sauce with a wire whisk. Fold the mixture into the remaining egg whites with a rubber spatula or wooden spoon.
5. Pour half of the soufflé mixture into a well-buttered two-quart soufflé dish and over it break the six whole eggs. Spoon the remaining soufflé mixture over the eggs and smooth the top surface.
6. Bake the soufflé for thirty to thirty-five minutes, until well puffed and browned.

Cheese Soufflé with Lobster

6 servings

A cheese soufflé is delectable. And so is lobster américaine, *that celestial, delicate blend of lobster, tomato, tarragon, and wine. Baked together—as they are in the recipe below—the result is Lucullan. Such a dish would be elegant for a very special luncheon or as a fish course at dinner.*

3 tablespoons butter
3 tablespoons all-purpose flour
1 cup milk
   Salt to taste
   Cayenne pepper to taste
¼ teaspoon nutmeg
2 teaspoons cornstarch
3 tablespoons water
6 eggs, separated
1 cup coarsely grated Swiss or Gruyère cheese
¼ cup grated Parmesan cheese
   Lobster Américaine (page 150)

1. Preheat the oven to 375 degrees.
2. Melt the butter in a saucepan and stir in the flour. Add the milk gradually, stirring with a wire whisk until the mixture is thick and smooth. Add the seasonings. Combine the cornstarch and water and add.
3. Beat the egg yolks into the sauce. Cook thirty seconds over low heat, then remove and stir in the Swiss cheese and half the Parmesan cheese.
4. Beat the egg whites until they stand in peaks. Add half the whites to the sauce and stir quickly. Gently fold in the remaining whites.
5. Generously butter a two-and-one-half-quart soufflé dish. Sprinkle the bottom of the dish with the remaining Parmesan cheese. Chill. Pour in the lobster américaine and top with the soufflé mixture. Bake until puffed and browned, thirty to forty minutes. Serve at once.

Eggplant Soufflé

6 servings

2 medium eggplants
  Oil
  Salt and freshly ground pepper to taste
3 tablespoons butter
5 tablespoons all-purpose flour
1½ cups milk
  Pinch of ground cloves
8 ounces Swiss or Gruyère cheese, finely chopped
6 eggs, separated
  Tabasco to taste

1. Preheat the oven to 450 degrees.
2. Cut the eggplants in half and make crisscross incisions through the flesh without penetrating the skin. Place them, cut side up, on a baking dish, brush liberally with oil, and sprinkle with salt and pepper. Bake thirty minutes. When cool enough to handle, scoop out the flesh and chop thoroughly.
3. Reduce the oven heat to 300 degrees.
4. Meanwhile, heat the butter in a saucepan and stir in the flour with a wire whisk. When blended, add the milk, stirring rapidly with the whisk. When smooth, add the cloves, salt, and pepper and simmer, stirring, about one minute. Remove from the heat and stir in the eggplant and cheese.
5. Beat in the egg yolks and return the mixture to the heat. Bring just to the boiling point, stirring rapidly, and remove from the heat. Add Tabasco. Scrape the mixture into a mixing bowl.
6. Beat the egg whites until stiff and fold them into the sauce. Spoon into a buttered soufflé dish. Bake twenty to thirty minutes, until puffed and browned. Serve immediately.

Baked Rice

8 to 12 servings

5 tablespoons butter
¼ cup minced onion
½ teaspoon minced garlic
2 cups uncooked rice
3 cups Chicken Stock (page 115)
3 sprigs parsley
2 sprigs thyme or ½ teaspoon dried thyme
1 bay leaf
¼ teaspoon cayenne pepper or Tabasco to taste

1. Preheat the oven to 400 degrees.
2. Melt two tablespoons of the butter in a heavy saucepan and cook the onion and garlic, stirring with a wooden spoon, until the onion is translucent. Add the rice and stir briefly over low heat until all the grains are coated with butter.
3. Stir in the stock, making sure there are no lumps in the rice. Add the parsley, thyme, bay leaf, and cayenne. Cover with a close-fitting lid and place in the oven.
4. Bake the rice exactly seventeen minutes. Remove the cover and discard the parsley and thyme sprigs. Using a two-pronged fork, stir in the remaining butter. If the rice is not to be served immediately, keep covered in a warm place.
Note: Like most dishes, this rice is best if served as soon as it is baked, but it may be made as much as half an hour in advance as long as it is kept tightly covered and warm.

Flageolets Bretonne

6 to 8 servings

2 cups flageolets (French dried beans) or dried white beans
1 onion, studded with 1 clove
¼ pound salt pork
1 large carrot, scraped and cut in half
2 sprigs fresh thyme or ½ teaspoon dried
1 bay leaf
  Salt
2 tablespoons butter
1¼ cups chopped onion
1 shallot, finely chopped
1 teaspoon finely chopped garlic
1 teaspoon finely chopped thyme
3 cups peeled fresh or drained canned tomatoes, coarsely chopped
2 tablespoons chopped parsley

1. Place the flageolets in a kettle and add water to cover to the depth of about one inch. Soak overnight.

2. Drain the beans and return them to the kettle. Add two quarts of water, the whole onion, salt pork, carrot, thyme, bay leaf, and salt to taste. Bring to a boil and simmer forty-five minutes to one hour.

3. Remove the salt pork and cut it into small cubes; reserve. Continue to cook the beans thirty minutes longer, or until tender. Different varieties require different lengths of cooking time.

4. Heat the butter in a skillet and cook the salt pork cubes until golden brown, stirring occasionally. Add the chopped onion, shallot, garlic, and thyme. When the onions are wilted, add the tomatoes and cook, stirring frequently, until the mixture is thickened.

5. Remove the carrot and whole onion and drain the beans, but reserve the bean liquid. Add the beans to the tomato sauce and stir gently. Let simmer about ten minutes. If the beans seem too dry, use a little of the reserved bean liquid to moisten. Serve the beans hot, sprinkled with chopped parsley.

Green Beans with Shallots

6 to 8 servings

1½ pounds green beans, trimmed
  Salt
¼ cup butter
3 large shallots, chopped
  Freshly ground black pepper
  Juice of 1 lemon
3 tablespoons chopped parsley

1. Cook the beans in six to eight quarts of rapidly boiling salted water for about eight minutes, or until barely tender. Drain the beans in a sieve and run a generous amount of cold water over them.

2. Put the beans in a skillet over medium heat and shake the pan for a minute or two to dry them out. Add the butter and shallots and continue to shake the pan until the beans are very hot and well coated with the butter and shallots. Season with salt and pepper to taste. Turn the beans out into a hot serving dish and sprinkle with the lemon juice and parsley.

Cassoulet

About 12 servings

5 cups white flageolets (French dried beans), white haricots, or other white beans
4 ounces salt pork
½ pound pork butt, cubed
1 bay leaf
3 sprigs parsley
1 teaspoon dried thyme
4 peppercorns
2 carrots, scraped and halved
1 whole onion studded with 8 cloves
2 teaspoons salt
2 pounds pork loin, boned and cubed, with bones reserved
1½ pounds shoulder of lamb, boned and cubed, with bones reserved
2 onions, chopped
2 cloves garlic, chopped
1 cup tomato puree
Beef Stock (page 115)
1 pound garlic sausages, French style, or hot Italian sausages (about 3)
1 cup fresh bread crumbs
Freshly ground black pepper

1. Pick over the beans, wash, and place in a deep, heavy, four-quart casserole. Add water to cover and let soak overnight.

2. Cover the salt pork with water, bring to a boil, and simmer five minutes. Drain and dice, including the rind.

3. To the soaked beans in the casserole, add enough water to cover. Add the diced salt pork and pork butt. Add the bay leaf, parsley, thyme, and peppercorns, all tied in a muslin or cheesecloth bag. Add the carrots, the onion studded with the cloves, and the salt.

4. Bring to a boil and simmer gently until the beans are tender, about one to one and one-half hours. Remove the muslin bag, carrots, and onion.

5. Meanwhile, render a piece of the fat from the pork loin in a large skillet. Brown the pork loin cubes, lamb cubes, and bones very well in the fat.

6. Add the chopped onions, garlic, and tomato puree to the meat. Cover and cook until the meat is tender, about one hour. Add beef broth if needed.

7. Remove the bones and add the meat mixture to the bean mixture. Test for seasoning. Add beef stock if the mixture is too stiff.

8. Prick the garlic sausages all over, cover with water, bring to a boil, and simmer one hour. Drain and slice.

9. Preheat the oven to 375 degrees.

10. In a deep earthenware or porcelainized ironware casserole or deep oval baking dish, place layers of the bean and meat mixture with slices of sausage between. Top with sausage slices and bread crumbs mixed with pepper to taste. Bring to a boil on top of the stove, then bake about one hour.

Chilled White Bean Casserole

6 to 8 servings

2 cups pea beans
1 clove garlic, peeled
Salt and freshly ground black pepper
2 cups chopped onion
¾ cup olive oil
2 tomatoes, peeled, seeded, and chopped
¼ cup chopped parsley
2 tablespoons wine vinegar
½ cup chopped green onion, including green part

1. Soak the beans overnight in water to cover or bring them to a boil in water to cover, cook two minutes, and let stand one hour. Add the garlic, two teaspoons salt,

and pepper to taste and simmer the beans and liquid until the beans are tender, one hour or longer.

2. Cook the onion in one-half cup of the oil until tender. Add the tomatoes and parsley and cook, stirring, ten minutes.

3. Drain the beans and blend with the tomato mixture. Chill. Just before serving, stir in the remaining oil and vinegar and add salt and pepper to taste. Sprinkle with the chopped green onions and serve cold.

Cabbage Mornay

4 to 6 servings

1 small head of cabbage
  Salt
3 tablespoons butter
3 tablespoons all-purpose flour
1½ cups milk
  Salt and freshly ground black pepper
½ cup shredded sharp Cheddar cheese
  Cayenne pepper
½ cup buttered fresh bread crumbs

1. Preheat the oven to 350 degrees.

2. Remove the tough outer leaves and pare away the core of the cabbage. Cut the cabbage into shreds to yield about three cups. Place the cabbage shreds in a saucepan and add boiling salted water to cover. Bring to a boil and simmer for two minutes. Drain.

3. Heat the butter and stir in the flour with a wire whisk. When the mixture is blended, add the milk, stirring rapidly with the whisk. Season with salt and pepper to taste. Remove the sauce from the heat, stir in the cheese, and add cayenne pepper to taste.

4. Combine the cabbage and sauce and spoon into a buttered six-cup casserole. Sprinkle with bread crumbs and bake until the crumbs are browned and the cabbage mixture bubbles, about twenty minutes.

Sauerkraut with Pork Balls

6 to 8 servings

½ pound bacon, sliced
3 pounds sauerkraut
1 onion, studded with four cloves
2½ cups Chicken Stock (page 115) or canned chicken broth
2 cups dry white wine
  Salt and freshly ground pepper to taste
3 cloves garlic, finely minced
10 juniper berries tied in cheesecloth
½ pound lean pork, ground
1 teaspoon caraway seeds, crushed or pounded fine
1 kielbasa (Polish ring sausage, optional)
6 to 8 frankfurters (optional)
6 to 8 slices smoked pork

1. Preheat the oven to 350 degrees.

2. Place the bacon slices in a saucepan and add cold water to cover. Bring to a boil, simmer one minute, then drain. Use the slices to line the bottom and sides of a three-quart saucepan with a heavy lid.

3. Drain the sauerkraut and squeeze it to extract more of the moisture. Place in the saucepan, make a "nest" in the center and add the onion. Add the stock, wine, salt, pepper, garlic, and juniper berries. Bring to a boil on top of the stove, then put in the oven. Bake thirty minutes, then reduce the heat to 300 degrees and cook two and one-half hours.

4. Combine the ground pork with salt and the caraway seeds and mix well. Shape into twelve or more marble-sized balls and add to the sauerkraut one to one and one-half hours before serving.

5. Prick the Polish sausage all over and add to the sauerkraut.

6. Add the frankfurters and smoked pork slices and bake five minutes longer, or until thoroughly heated.

Choucroute Garnie

8 to 12 servings

Not the least virtue of sauerkraut, that admirable and aromatic creation of peasant origin, is its compatibility. Kraut has a natural affinity with dry white wines, it was created to complement sausages, and its rapport with spareribs is legendary. Sauerkraut is an excellent dish for quantity cookery. The traditional accompaniment for choucroute garnie is plain boiled potatoes and, as far as beverages go, beer, a dry white wine, or champagne. The recipe here has a novel addition —caraway-flavored pork balls, or boulettes, *as they are called in France.*

  8 pounds sauerkraut
  3 tablespoons lard
  1 onion, cut into ¼-inch slices
  1 carrot, scraped and cut into rounds
  6 sprigs fresh thyme or ½ teaspoon dried thyme
20 juniper berries
  4 cloves garlic, finely minced
  1 bay leaf
     Salt
10 peppercorns
 ½ pound bacon, sliced, or 1 ham rind
  2 small racks of spareribs
  1 bottle dry white wine
  2 cups Chicken Stock (page 115)
     Pork Boulettes (see below, optional)
  8 to 12 frankfurters or knockwurst (optional)
  2 Cervelas (page 245, optional)

1. If desired, soak the sauerkraut in cold water to cover. This will make a milder dish at the end. In any event, drain the sauerkraut and press it with the hands to extract most of the liquid.

2. Preheat the oven to 450 degrees.

3. Heat the lard in a large casserole or kettle and over it spread the onion, carrot, thyme, juniper berries, garlic, bay leaf, salt to taste, and peppercorns. Cover with the bacon or ham rind and spareribs. Sprinkle with salt and bake forty minutes. Turn the spareribs occasionally as they cook.

4. Loosen the sauerkraut with the fingers and spread it over the meat. Add the wine and chicken stock. Bring the liquid to a boil on top of the stove, then return the casserole to the oven. Cover and reduce the oven heat to 350 degrees. Bake thirty minutes.

5. If the boulettes are to be used, prepare them and arrange them over the sauerkraut. Bake one to one and one-half hours longer. If the frankfurters or knockwurst are to be used, add them for the last twenty minutes of cooking. Serve the cervelas, which are cooked separately, sliced. Serve the sauerkraut with boiled potatoes and mustard on the side.

PORK BOULETTES:

24 boulettes

1½ pounds ground pork
     Salt and freshly ground black pepper
  1 teaspoon caraway seeds
 ¼ cup white wine

1. Place the pork in a mixing bowl and add salt and pepper to taste. Grind the caraway seeds with a mortar and pestle or blend them briefly in an electric blender. Add to the pork and beat in the wine, using a wooden spoon.

2. Wet the hands and shape the mixture into twenty-four small meat balls.

3. Cook as directed in Choucroute Garnie recipe, above.

CERVELAS (garlic sausage):

2 cervelas

2 cervelas (1 pound each)
2 sprigs fresh thyme or ½ teaspoon dried thyme
1 small onion, sliced
1 carrot, scraped and sliced

1. Prick the cervelas with a fork and place them in a large saucepan or casserole. Add water to cover and the remaining ingredients.
2. Bring to a boil and simmer exactly one hour. Let stand in the cooking liquid until ready to use. To serve, peel and slice while hot or lukewarm.

Carrot Puree

4 to 6 servings

12 medium carrots, scraped and left whole
Salt
Freshly ground black pepper
½ to 1 teaspoon granulated sugar
¼ cup heavy cream

1. Preheat the oven to 400 degrees.
2. Place the carrots in a kettle and add water to cover and salt to taste. Bring to a boil and simmer until tender. Length of cooking time will depend on the size and age of the carrots.
3. Put the carrots through a fine sieve or food mill and add salt and pepper to taste, sugar, and cream. Pour into a small buttered baking dish. Bake until lightly browned on top.

Three-Day Sauerkraut with Champagne

6 servings

3 pounds sauerkraut
½ pound bacon, cut into 1-inch cubes
2 tablespoons goose or chicken fat
1 pound short ribs of beef, cracked
10 juniper berries, crushed
Freshly ground pepper to taste
1½ bottles dry champagne or dry white wine
1 kielbasa (Polish sausage), 12 garlic frankfurters, or 6 wienerwurst

1. Rinse the sauerkraut well and drain it. Squeeze to remove excess moisture.
2. Place the bacon and goose fat in a heavy kettle and add the beef ribs, sauerkraut, and juniper berries. Sprinkle with pepper. Add half a bottle of champagne (about one and one-half cups).
3. Cover and cook over low heat from early morning until bedtime. Remove the kettle from the heat and refrigerate overnight.
4. Place the kettle back on the heat and add another half bottle of champagne. Cook all day. Remove from the heat and refrigerate overnight.
5. Return the kettle to the heat and add the remaining half bottle of champagne. Continue cooking all day. If kielbasa is used, add it about forty-five minutes before serving. Add garlic frankfurters about twenty minutes before serving. Add wienerwurst about ten minutes before serving.
6. Serve hot, with boiled new potatoes and, if desired, roast tenderloin of pork.

Puree of Chestnuts

4 servings

1 pound chestnuts
  Salt to taste
1 rib celery, quartered
1 small bulb fennel, halved
2 tablespoons butter
½ cup heavy cream

1. With a sharp paring knife, cut a small cross in the side of each chestnut. Place them in a saucepan and add water to cover and salt. Bring to a boil and simmer fifteen to thirty minutes, or until the shells can be removed. Drain.

2. When the chestnuts are cool enough to handle, peel them. Remove both the outer shell and inner peel.

3. Return the chestnuts to the saucepan and add water to cover, salt, celery, and fennel. Simmer, covered, thirty minutes, or until the chestnuts are tender.

4. Put the chestnuts through a food mill and, while they are still hot, beat in the butter and cream. Serve hot, as an accompaniment to turkey, goose, venison, or other game dishes.

Eggplant Arlésienne

6 to 8 servings

1 green pepper, diced
1 clove garlic, peeled
½ cup finely chopped onion
2 tablespoons olive or cooking oil
1 eggplant (1 pound)
1 cup coarsely diced tomatoes
1 teaspoon salt
½ teaspoon freshly ground black pepper
½ teaspoon dried orégano
1 tablespoon capers
  Pimentos, rolled anchovies, and sliced stuffed olives

1. Sauté the green pepper, garlic, and onion in the oil for ten minutes, or until the vegetables are tender.

2. Wash, peel, and dice the eggplant. Add to the sautéed vegetables along with the tomatoes and salt. Cover and cook slowly for fifteen minutes, or until the eggplant is tender.

3. Add the black pepper, orégano, and capers. Increase the heat, cover, and cook until almost all the liquid has evaporated.

4. Cool and turn into a serving dish. Garnish, in lattice fashion, with quarter-inch pimento strips. Insert rolled anchovies and sliced olives in the spaces between the pimento strips. Serve chilled, with cold meats, sandwiches, or salads.

Eggplant and Rice Provençale

8 servings

The English food chronicler, P. Morton Shand (author of A Book of Food, *1927), once wrote that eggplants—or aubergines, as they are known in Britain—represent in certain forms the very zenith of vegetable cookery. While some may speak with more restraint, it is true that eggplants are exceptional in their adaptability and flavor. That adaptability is apparent here in an eggplant and rice dish from Provence.*

2 large eggplants (about 2 pounds)
¼ cup olive oil
3 cups finely chopped onion
1 green pepper, cored, seeded, and cut into 1-inch cubes
2 cloves garlic, finely minced
1 teaspoon chopped fresh thyme or ½ teaspoon dried thyme
1 bay leaf
3 tomatoes, peeled, cored, and chopped
1 cup uncooked rice
3¼ cups Chicken Stock (page 115) or canned chicken broth
Salt and freshly ground black pepper
½ cup grated Parmesan cheese
2 tablespoons butter

1. Preheat the oven to 400 degrees.
2. Trim the ends off the eggplants. Do not peel. Slice the eggplants and then cut into one-inch cubes.
3. Heat the oil in a large skillet and add the eggplants. Cook over a high flame, shaking the skillet occasionally, until lightly browned. Add the onion, green pepper, garlic, thyme, and bay leaf, stirring. Stir in the tomatoes and reduce the heat. Simmer five minutes, or until most of the liquid in the skillet has evaporated. This is important—the ingredients must be stewed until fairly thickened.

4. Stir in the rice and chicken stock. Season with salt and pepper to taste, then spoon into a baking dish and sprinkle with cheese. Dot with butter and bake, uncovered, thirty minutes.

Eggplant with Cumin Rice

6 or more servings

1 medium eggplant
¼ cup butter
Salt and freshly ground black pepper
1 green pepper, cored, seeded, and cut into 1-inch cubes
1 large onion, chopped
1 cup peeled, chopped fresh tomatoes or canned Italian plum tomatoes
2 cups uncooked rice
1 tablespoon ground cumin
2 cups Chicken Stock (page 115) or canned chicken broth
1 cup water

1. Preheat the oven to 375 degrees.
2. Pare off the ends of the eggplant. Do not peel. Cut the eggplant into slices, then into half-inch cubes. There should be about three cups.
3. Heat the butter in a large casserole and cook the eggplant, stirring. Sprinkle with salt and pepper. Add the green pepper and onion and cook, stirring occasionally. When the eggplant is soft but not mushy, add the tomatoes, rice, cumin, chicken broth, and water. Bring to a boil on top of the stove, then cover closely and put in the oven.
4. Bake exactly twenty to twenty-five minutes. Fluff the rice with a two-pronged fork and serve hot.

Braised Endive I

6 servings

6 heads endive
1 tablespoon lemon juice
2 tablespoons butter
½ tablespoon salt
6 tablespoons water
½ teaspoon granulated sugar

1. Trim off and discard any discolored leaves from the endives. Place the heads in a kettle and add the lemon juice, butter, salt, water, and sugar. Cover and bring to a boil, then reduce the heat to moderate and cook for thirty to forty minutes, until tender.
2. Drain the endives and press gently to remove the excess moisture. Serve hot.

Braised Endive II

6 servings

12 heads endive
   Juice of 1 lemon
3 tablespoons granulated sugar
   Salt and freshly ground black pepper
1 cup water
3 tablespoons butter

1. Preheat the oven to 400 degrees.
2. Generously butter a large skillet.
3. Sprinkle the endives with the lemon juice, sugar, and salt and pepper to taste. Add the water and bring to a boil on top of the stove. Cover and bake in the oven one and one-half hours, then remove and drain well.
4. Melt the butter in a large skillet and add the endive in one layer. Brown well on both sides, then cook, uncovered, over low heat for thirty minutes.

Braised Lettuce

6 servings

6 heads Boston lettuce
2 slices bacon, each cut into quarters
1 onion, sliced and broken into rings
1 carrot, scraped and thinly sliced
½ bay leaf
2 sprigs thyme or ½ teaspoon dried thyme
½ rib celery, thinly sliced
   Salt and freshly ground pepper
¾ cup Chicken Stock (page 115) or canned chicken broth
¾ cup Brown Sauce (page 268) or canned beef gravy
2 tablespoons butter

1. Preheat the oven to 350 degrees.
2. Place the lettuce in a large basin of cold water and shake briefly. Drain and pull off one layer of large outer leaves. Trim off a thin slice from the stem ends but do not remove the core.
3. Place the lettuce in a large kettle or casserole and add water to cover. Bring to a boil, then reduce the heat and simmer about five minutes. Place the kettle under cold running water. When the lettuce has been chilled by the water, take one head at a time and squeeze, stem to top, to extract most of the moisture.
4. Place the bacon in a ten-inch skillet with cover and add the onion, carrot, bay leaf, thyme, and celery. Cook briefly, until the bacon gives up most of its fat, but do not brown. Arrange the six lettuce heads over all and sprinkle with salt and pepper to taste. Cook briefly, then add the stock and brown sauce and bring to a boil. Cover and bake one and one-half hours.
5. Remove the lettuce. Split each head in half and arrange on a hot platter. Strain the pan sauce over the lettuce and top with butter.

Mushroom Puree

4 servings

1 pound mushrooms
5 tablespoons butter
  Juice of ½ lemon
¾ cup heavy cream
  Salt and freshly ground black pepper to
  taste
3 tablespoons all-purpose flour

1. Wash and drain the mushrooms.
2. Line a mixing bowl with cheesecloth. Grind the mushrooms directly into the bowl. Bring the edges of the cloth together and squeeze to extract the liquid. Do not let the mushrooms stand.
3. Immediately melt three tablespoons of the butter and add the mushrooms. Squeeze the lemon juice over them. (The lemon juice keeps the mushrooms from darkening.)
4. Cook, stirring, about three minutes. Add the cream, salt, and pepper.
5. Blend the remaining butter with the flour to make a beurre manié. Add it, bit by bit, to the simmering mushroom mixture, stirring constantly. When the puree is thickened, serve hot.

Baked Mushrooms in Cream

4 servings

1 pound large white mushroom caps
¼ cup melted butter
¾ cup heavy cream
  Salt and freshly ground black pepper
1 tablespoon freshly grated Parmesan cheese, or to taste
  Toast

1. Preheat the oven to 450 degrees.
2. Rinse the mushrooms in cold water and drain.
3. Slice off the stem of each mushroom, flush with the base. Arrange the mushrooms, stem side down, in a buttered baking dish. Brush the tops of the mushrooms with butter and pour the cream over them. Sprinkle with salt and pepper to taste and the Parmesan cheese. Bake fifteen minutes. Serve on toast.

Fried Parsley

About 6 cups

6 cups loosely packed parsley, approximately
  Oil for deep frying
  Salt

1. If the parsley has any trace of sand or soil, it should be washed. To do this, rinse in several changes of cold water and shake off the excess moisture, using a salad basket. Pat dry with a clean cloth or paper toweling.
2. Heat the oil and fry the parsley, a handful at a time, using a slotted spoon to see that the parsley cooks evenly in the oil. When done, it will be dark green, or greenish black, and crisp. Drain on absorbent toweling. Sprinkle with salt before serving.

Green Peas à la Française

6 to 8 servings

3 pounds green peas
6 tablespoons butter
¼ cup chopped onion
½ cup chopped lettuce
   Salt and freshly ground black pepper to taste
½ to 1 teaspoon granulated sugar, depending on the age of the peas

1. Shell the peas. If the peas are young and tender, add a pod or two.

2. Cut the butter into squares or cubes and add to the peas. Add the remaining ingredients. Using the fingers, knead all the ingredients together, including the peas. Knead gently, however, so as not to crush the peas. Spoon the mixture into a saucepan with lid, cover, and bring to a boil. Simmer until the peas are tender, five to ten minutes. Do not lift the lid any more than necessary, however.

Petits Pois à la Française I

4 servings

¼ pound salt pork, cut into tiny cubes
1 cup finely chopped onion
1½ cups shredded or chopped lettuce
1 tablespoon butter
2 to 3 cups shelled green peas (3 to 4 pounds fresh or 2 packages [10 ounces each] frozen)
   Salt and freshly ground black pepper to taste
1 teaspoon granulated sugar
⅓ cup water

1. Place the pork in a saucepan and add water to cover. Cook the pork in the sauce-

pan, stirring, until it is rendered of fat and lightly browned. Add the onion and cook briefly, stirring.

2. Add the lettuce and cook, stirring, until wilted. Cover and cook five minutes. Add the remaining ingredients, cover, and cook until the peas are tender, ten to twenty minutes or longer, if necessary. If frozen peas are used, cook all the ingredients except the peas for ten minutes. Stir in the peas, cover, and cook five minutes.

Petits Pois à la Française II

8 servings

3 cups loosely packed Boston lettuce leaves
½ cup coarsely chopped onion
¾ cup water
   Salt
3 cups freshly shelled green peas
3 tablespoons butter
   Freshly ground black pepper

1. Rinse the lettuce well and shake it out in a French salad basket to remove most of the moisture. Put the lettuce into a saucepan and add the onion, water, and salt to taste. Bring to a boil and simmer, covered, fifteen minutes.

2. Add the peas, cover closely, and simmer until the peas are tender. The peas should be barely covered with liquid as they cook. If necessary, add a little boiling water during the cooking. Cooking time will depend on the age and size of the peas. Do not drain. Stir in the butter, more salt to taste, if desired, and pepper to taste.

Potatoes Grandmère

6 servings

1½ pounds potatoes in their skins
 2 cups heavy cream
 1 clove garlic, unpeeled
 2 tablespoons butter
 1 tablespoon mustard, preferably Dijon or Düsseldorf
    Salt and freshly ground pepper to taste
 1 tablespoon chopped chives or parsley

1. Wash the potatoes and place them in a saucepan. Cover with water and bring to a boil, then simmer until tender. Drain and let cool, then peel and slice.

2. Place the cream, garlic, butter, mustard, salt, and pepper in a skillet and bring to a boil. Add the potato slices and cook slowly twenty minutes. Serve sprinkled with chopped chives.

Potatoes Toupinel

6 servings

 6 large Idaho potatoes
 7 tablespoons butter
 2 tablespoons all-purpose flour
2½ cups milk
 ½ cup heavy cream
    Salt and freshly ground pepper
 ½ cup grated Gruyère cheese
 2 egg yolks
 6 eggs
 2 or more tablespoons grated Parmesan cheese

1. Preheat the oven to 400 degrees.

2. Bake the potatoes forty-five minutes to one hour, depending on size.

3. Heat three tablespoons of butter and stir in the flour. When blended, add one and one-half cups of the milk and the cream gradually, stirring rapidly. Season with salt and pepper. Off the heat, add the Gruyère cheese and egg yolks, stirring rapidly.

4. When the potatoes are done and still hot, cut off a slice from the top. The slice should be about a quarter-inch thick but large enough to remove the potato pulp for the stuffing. Scoop out the pulp, leaving the shell for stuffing. Put the pulp through a sieve or ricer into a saucepan.

5. Heat the remaining cup of milk, then, over low heat, beat the remaining four table-spoons of butter and the hot milk into the sieved potato. Season with salt and pepper.

6. Preheat the oven to 500 degrees.

7. Poach the eggs, drain them, and trim neatly.

8. Spoon the potato mixture into the shells, but do not fill them completely. Make a cavity in each one for the poached eggs. Add one poached egg to each cavity, cover with the sauce, and sprinkle with the Parmesan cheese. Bake until heated through and golden brown. Do not overcook or the poached eggs will become too firm.

Ciro Potatoes

6 or more servings

6 medium Idaho potatoes
½ cup butter
  Salt and freshly ground black pepper
  Chopped parsley

1. Peel the potatoes and, using a vegetable slicer, cut into wafer-thin slices. There should be about four cups of sliced potatoes. As the potatoes are sliced, drop them into cold water.

2. Drain the potatoes and pat them dry.

3. Heat half the butter in a seasoned ten-inch iron skillet and add the potatoes. Add salt and pepper to taste. Cook over relatively high heat while shaking the skillet, tossing the potatoes in the skillet without breaking the slices. When the potatoes are more or less limp, press them down with a pancake turner or spatula. Reduce the heat and cook until the potatoes are golden brown on one side. Carefully flip the potatoes over (they should now be like a pancake) and brown on the other side. The total cooking time should be about thirty minutes.

4. Heat the remaining butter until it is almost brown. Pour over the potatoes and serve sprinkled with chopped parsley.

Fondant Potatoes

4 to 6 servings

12 medium red-skinned new potatoes
  Salt to taste
½ cup butter
  Freshly ground pepper
½ cup Chicken Stock (page 115)

1. Using a swivel-bladed vegetable peeler, peel the potatoes. As they are peeled, drop them into cold water. Drain the potatoes and put them in a saucepan. Add enough water to cover and salt to taste. Simmer ten minutes, then drain well.

2. Place the potatoes in a single layer in a heavy iron skillet and add the butter. Sprinkle liberally with pepper and cover with a close-fitting lid. Cook over moderately low heat for about twenty minutes. As the potatoes cook, turn them once or twice without breaking the skin. Add the chicken stock, cover again, and cook until tender, about fifteen minutes.

Macaire Potatoes

6 to 8 servings

5 medium Idaho potatoes
  Vegetable oil
½ cup butter
¼ to ½ teaspoon nutmeg
  Salt and freshly ground black pepper

1. Preheat the oven to 375 degrees.

2. Lightly rub the skin of the potatoes with oil. Lay a sheet of aluminum foil on a rack in the oven and place the potatoes on the foil. Bake forty-five minutes to one hour, or until tender clear through. To test for doneness, take up one potato, using a towel to protect the hands from heat, and squeeze the outside to see if it is soft inside.

3. When cooked, remove the potatoes from the oven and split them in half while still hot. Using a spoon, scoop out the insides into a mixing bowl. Using a heavy fork, start mashing the potatoes while adding the butter, a little at a time. Add the nutmeg and salt and pepper to taste. When all is blended, turn the mixture into a nine- or ten-inch black iron skillet.

4. Bake the potatoes forty-five minutes to one hour or until golden brown top and bottom. With care, it should be possible to unmold the potatoes onto a hot round serving dish.

Tomatoes Provençale

4 servings

4 ripe tomatoes
  Salt and freshly ground black pepper
⅓ cup fresh bread crumbs
1 clove garlic, finely minced
2 tablespoons finely chopped green onion
3 tablespoons minced parsley
  Pinch of dried thyme
3 tablespoons olive oil
  Butter

1. Halve the tomatoes horizontally; remove and discard the seeds. Sprinkle the insides of the tomatoes with salt and pepper and invert to drain.

2. Preheat the oven to 400 degrees.

3. Combine the bread crumbs, garlic, green onion, parsley, thyme, and olive oil. Season with salt and pepper to taste. Stuff the tomatoes and dot with butter. Bake in an oiled pan until hot and the crumbs are golden, about fifteen minutes.

Grilled Tomatoes with Rosemary

4 servings

2 large or 4 small tomatoes, as red and ripe
  as possible
2 or more cloves garlic
2 teaspoons fresh or dried rosemary
  Salt and freshly ground pepper to taste
  Olive oil

1. Preheat the broiler to high.
2. Rinse and dry the tomatoes carefully.
Do not core or peel them. Split the tomatoes
in half as close to the center as possible and
arrange the halves on a baking dish.
3. Cut the garlic into thin slivers. Insert
the slivers at various points over the cut surface of the tomato halves.
4. Chop the rosemary coarsely and sprinkle
the cut surface of the tomatoes with it.
Sprinkle with salt and pepper and dribble the
olive oil over all.
5. Run the tomatoes under the broiler,
four or five inches away from the flame, and
let them broil three minutes or longer, until
the garlic is browned and the tomatoes are
soft but firm.
6. Remove the pieces of garlic and serve
the tomatoes hot.

Tomatoes Vinaigrette

6 to 8 servings

6 large, ripe tomatoes
  Salt and freshly ground black pepper
6 tablespoons wine vinegar
½ cup olive oil
¼ cup freshly chopped parsley

1. Pare away the core of each tomato and
a thin slice from the bottom.
2. Cut the tomatoes into slices one-half
inch thick and arrange the slices on a serving
platter. Sprinkle generously with salt and
pepper to taste, the vinegar, oil, and parsley.

Zucchini au Gratin

4 to 6 servings

2 tablespoons olive or corn oil
3 or 4 tender zucchini, washed, peeled and
  cut into thin rounds
½ pound mozzarella cheese, cut in small
  cubes
¼ cup grated Parmesan cheese
  Salt
1 sprig fresh parsley, chopped
½ cup bread crumbs
2 tablespoons butter

1. Preheat the oven to 350 degrees.
2. Pour the oil into an eight-inch baking
dish and add about one third of the zucchini,
mozzarella cubes, Parmesan cheese, salt to
taste and parsley. Make layers in this manner
until all the ingredients are used. Cover with
the bread crumbs and dot with butter. Bake,
uncovered, until golden brown, about forty-
five to fifty minutes.

Gratin Sydney I

4 to 6 servings

6 medium zucchini, thinly sliced
1 medium eggplant, thinly sliced
½ cup peanut oil
   Salt and freshly ground black pepper
3 shallots, chopped
¼ teaspoon dried thyme
1 bay leaf
6 tomatoes, cored, peeled, and stewed until thickened
   Freshly grated Parmesan cheese

1. Preheat the oven to 350 degrees.
2. Cook the zucchini and eggplant in half the oil until wilted and browned. Sprinkle with salt and pepper, then pour into a colander to drain.
3. Cook the shallots in the remaining oil until wilted and add the drained zucchini and eggplant.
4. Add the thyme and bay leaf, then bake twenty minutes. Remove from the oven and increase the oven heat to 400 degrees.
5. Put half the tomatoes into a baking dish, then add the zucchini and eggplant. Add the remaining tomatoes and sprinkle with cheese. Place in the oven until the cheese is browned.

Gratin Sydney II

10 to 12 servings

4 zucchini
1 cup olive oil, approximately
   Salt and freshly ground pepper
1 medium onion
2 green peppers, cored and sliced
3 cloves garlic, finely minced
1 sprig thyme, chopped, or ½ teaspoon dried thyme
½ bay leaf
4 cups peeled, chopped tomatoes, fresh or canned
12 ½-inch slices unpeeled eggplant
½ cup grated Parmesan cheese

1. Preheat the oven to 400 degrees.
2. Trim off and discard the ends of the zucchini. Cut the zucchini into slices about one-eighth inch thick. Heat two tablespoons of the oil in a skillet and cook the zucchini until wilted. Sprinkle with salt and pepper, then set aside.
3. Cut the onion in half, then cut each half into wafer-thin slices. Heat two tablespoons of oil in another skillet and cook the onion and green pepper until wilted. Let brown slightly, then add the garlic, thyme, and bay leaf and stir. Add the tomatoes and simmer about ten minutes. Add salt and pepper to taste.
4. Cook the eggplant slices until golden in the remaining olive oil, using a little oil at a time and adding more as necessary. It will take considerable oil to cook the eggplant, but it will be poured off later. Sprinkle the eggplant with salt and pepper.
5. Arrange layers of eggplant, the tomato mixture, and zucchini in a baking dish. Sprinkle with Parmesan cheese and bake twenty to thirty minutes. Before serving, pour off the oil that will have accumulated in the dish.

Ratatouille

6 or more servings

6 tablespoons olive oil
1 medium eggplant, unpeeled and cut into 1½-inch cubes
3 medium zucchini, quartered and cut into 1-inch lengths
  Salt and freshly ground black pepper
3 onions, coarsely chopped
2 green peppers, cored, seeded, and coarsely chopped
4 cloves garlic, finely minced
1 bay leaf
2 pounds fresh tomatoes, peeled and cut into 1-inch cubes
½ cup finely chopped parsley
2 teaspoons finely chopped fresh thyme or ½ teaspoon dried thyme
1 tablespoon finely chopped basil or 1 teaspoon dried basil
  Lemon wedges (optional)

1. Preheat the oven to 350 degrees.
2. Heat half the oil in a large skillet and add the eggplant, zucchini, and salt and pepper to taste. Cook, stirring, about five minutes.
3. In another skillet, heat the remaining oil and add the onions and green peppers. Chop the garlic and bay leaf together to make a fine paste. Add this to the onion mixture. Add the tomatoes and simmer, stirring occasionally, about ten minutes. Add the eggplant and zucchini, then stir in the parsley, thyme, and basil. Spoon the mixture into a casserole, cover, and bake twenty minutes, or until the vegetables are tender. Serve hot or cold. If cold, serve with lemon wedges.

Asparagus Vinaigrette Salad

4 servings

6 tablespoons olive oil
2 tablespoons lemon juice
¾ teaspoon salt
¼ teaspoon freshly ground black pepper
1 clove garlic, finely minced
2 tablespoons minced sweet pickles
1 tablespoon minced onion
2 tablespoons minced green pepper
1 tablespoon chopped capers
1 tablespoon chopped parsley
2 pounds fresh asparagus, trimmed, washed, cooked, and chilled
  Boston lettuce leaves

1. Combine the oil, lemon juice, salt, pepper, garlic, pickles, onion, green pepper, capers, and parsley. Mix well and chill.
2. Arrange the asparagus spears on the lettuce leaves and pour the chilled dressing over all.

Vegetables for a ratatouille (Franc

Beet and Onion Salad

12 servings

12 fresh, new beets
   Salt and freshly ground black pepper
1 or 2 Bermuda onions
¾ cup wine vinegar
1 tablespoon granulated sugar
6 sprigs fresh dill or ground coriander to taste

1. Cut off the leaves of the beets but leave a one-inch length of stem. Do not trim the beets or cut off their root ends. Rinse under cold water and place in a kettle or large saucepan with water to cover. Add salt to taste. Bring to a boil and simmer, partially covered, until tender, about forty-five minutes to one hour or longer, depending on the age and size of the beets. When tender, drain and let cool. Pare the leaf and stem ends off the beets and slip off the skin. Cut the beets into thin slices and place in a bowl. Chill.

2. Sprinkle the beets with salt and pepper to taste. Cut the onions into thin slices, then break into rings and add to the beets. Add the vinegar and sugar and toss. Pour into a serving dish and garnish with dill. Or, if desired, sprinkle with coriander.

Lentil Salad

6 servings

2 cups lentils
1 onion studded with 2 cloves
1 bay leaf
   Salt
1 tablespoon finely cubed green pepper
1 tablespoon finely chopped shallots or green onion, including green part
1 tablespoon chopped parsley
2 tablespoons cider vinegar
3 tablespoons olive oil
¼ cup peanut oil
   Freshly ground black pepper

1. Soak the lentils overnight and pick them over to remove bits of rock. If processed, "quick-cooking" lentils are used, presoaking is not necessary.

2. Drain the lentils and put them in a kettle with water to cover. Add the onion, bay leaf, and salt to taste. Bring to a boil and simmer until the lentils are tender but not mushy. Quick-cooking lentils require twenty-five to thirty minutes.

3. Drain the lentils and discard the onion and bay leaf. Let cool, then chill.

4. Sprinkle the lentils with the green pepper, shallots, and parsley and dress with the vinegar, olive oil, and peanut oil. Sprinkle with coarsely ground black pepper. Let marinate overnight and serve sprinkled with additional freshly chopped parsley.

Potato and Anchovy Salad

6 to 8 servings

3 pounds waxy new potatoes
1 cup finely chopped onion or green onion
3 hard-cooked eggs, chopped
2 cans (2 ounces each) anchovy fillets, chopped
¼ cup lemon juice
2 tablespoons wine vinegar
3 tablespoons olive oil
1 teaspoon salt
¼ teaspoon freshly ground black pepper
1 cup finely chopped celery
⅓ cup Mayonnaise (page 265)
1 can rolled stuffed anchovies
Whole jumbo green stuffed olives

1. Cover the potatoes with hot water and bring to a boil, then cover and cook about twenty minutes, or until barely tender.

2. Drain the potatoes and peel them as soon as they are cool enough to handle. Slice into a bowl.

3. Add the onions or green onions, chopped eggs, and chopped anchovies to the potatoes.

4. Mix together the lemon juice, vinegar, and oil with the salt and pepper. Add to the potato mixture, toss, and chill.

5. Just before serving, add the celery and mayonnaise and toss to mix. Pile into a serving dish and garnish with stuffed anchovies and stuffed olives.

Herbed Potato Salad

About 30 servings

6 pounds white or red-skinned potatoes
Salt
¾ cup finely chopped white onion
1 tablespoon finely chopped parsley
2 teaspoons finely chopped tarragon
2 teaspoons finely chopped fresh basil
1 teaspoon finely chopped fresh thyme or ½ teaspoon dried thyme
1 tablespoon finely chopped chives
½ cup dry white wine
½ cup Chicken Stock (page 115) or broth in which a sausage was cooked
¼ cup wine vinegar
⅓ cup peanut or olive oil
Freshly ground black pepper

1. Place the potatoes in a large kettle and add water to cover and salt to taste. Bring to a boil and cook until the potatoes are tender, twenty to twenty-five minutes, depending on size. Drain, then let the potatoes cool in their skins.

2. Peel the potatoes and cut them into slices about one-quarter inch thick. Put them in a mixing bowl, and while they are still warm sprinkle with the onions, parsley, tarragon, basil, thyme, chives, wine, stock, vinegar, and oil. Toss gently to mix. Add salt and pepper to taste and, if desired, more vinegar or oil. Let stand until lukewarm or cool.

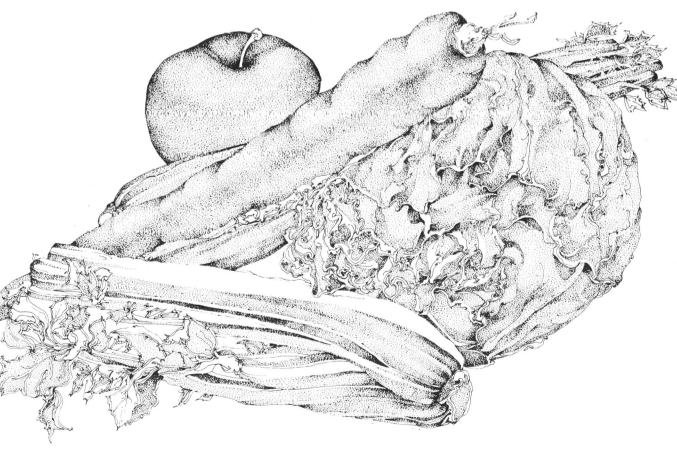

Francillon Salad

4 servings

4 medium potatoes, scrubbed
2 cups Chicken Stock (page 115)
1½ teaspoons salt
1 cup steamed and shelled mussels (16 to 20 mussels, see note)
4 or 5 truffles
1 cup champagne
¼ teaspoon freshly ground black pepper
¼ teaspoon dried tarragon
2 tablespoons wine vinegar
½ cup Sauterne
¼ cup olive oil
1 tablespoon chopped parsley

1. Simmer the potatoes in the stock with one teaspoon of the salt for about twenty-five minutes, until tender. Peel the potatoes and slice into a large bowl. Add the mussels.

2. Very gently, simmer the truffles in the champagne for ten minutes, then drain and cut into very thin slices. If desired, strain the stock and the champagne and reserve for other uses.

3. Combine the remaining salt with the pepper, tarragon, vinegar, Sauterne, oil, and parsley. Mix well and pour over the potato mixture. Toss gently. Chill for at least two hours, then garnish with the truffles and serve.

Note: To steam mussels, scrub them well and place in a kettle with about one cup water. Bring the water to a boil and steam the mussels about ten minutes. Discard any mussels that do not open. Remove the mussels from the shells with a knife.

Rice Salad

6 servings

1 cup uncooked rice
2 tomatoes, peeled
1½ cups cooked, unbuttered peas
1 green pepper, cored, seeded, and chopped fine
¼ cup finely chopped green onion, including green part
½ cup Mayonnaise (page 265), approximately
1 tablespoon chopped fresh basil
1 teaspoon chopped fresh mint
Salt and freshly ground black pepper

1. Cook the rice according to package directions and chill. The grains should be tender yet firm and dry.

2. Gently squeeze the liquid and seeds from the nonfirm sections of the tomatoes into a mixing bowl. Reserve this liquid, discarding the seeds. Cut the tomatoes into small cubes.

3. Combine the rice, tomatoes, peas, green pepper, and green onion in a mixing bowl.

4. Stir the mayonnaise into the reserved tomato juice and mix well. Add the mayonnaise mixture to the rice and toss together with the herbs and salt and pepper to taste.

Tomatoes with Salad Russe

4 servings

4 medium ripe tomatoes
  Salt
½ cup cooked green peas
½ cup cooked, cubed carrots
½ cup cooked, cubed potatoes
¼ cup Mayonnaise (page 265)
¼ cup sour cream
  Freshly ground black pepper
1 teaspoon capers
1 tablespoon finely chopped parsley
1 teaspoon finely minced onion
  Lemon juice
  Parsley sprigs (optional)

1. Pare away the top of each tomato, then pare around the inside of the tomato to remove most of the pulp and seeds. Sprinkle the inside of the tomatoes with salt and turn them upside down to drain.

2. Place the other vegetables in a mixing bowl and add the mayonnaise, sour cream, salt and pepper to taste, capers, parsley, onion, and lemon juice to taste. Toss until the vegetables are coated with the mayonnaise mixture. Fill the tomato shells with the mixture and garnish, if desired, with parsley sprigs.

Charcutier Salad

6 servings

1 7-ounce jar pickled pigs' feet, drained
1 15-ounce jar pickled lambs' tongues, drained
¼ cup peanut oil
¼ cup olive oil
3 tablespoons wine vinegar
1 clove garlic, minced
1 tablespoon finely chopped shallots or onion
  Salt and freshly ground black pepper
1 tablespoon chopped parsley
1 teaspoon chopped fresh tarragon
1 hard-cooked egg, chopped

1. Trim the bones, if any, from the pigs' feet. Cut the feet and the tongues into small bite-sized pieces.

2. Combine the oils, vinegar, garlic, shallots, and salt and pepper to taste. Whip with a fork until well blended, then stir in the parsley, tarragon, and egg. Toss the sauce with the meats. Chill until serving time.

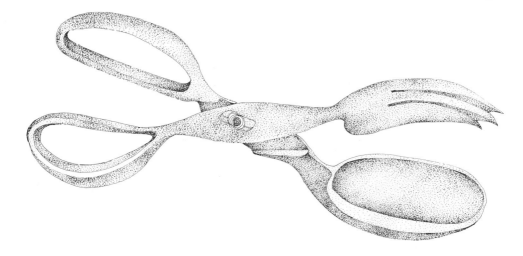

When a Parisian speaks of salad, he usually has one thing in mind—a few leaves of laitue, *or Boston lettuce, tossed with oil and vinegar, salt and pepper. But the pride of the Riviera is that substantial and delicious blend of tuna, anchovies, and olives called* salade Niçoise. *It is an ideal dish for a midsummer day served with a crusty loaf of bread and a glass of chilled rosé wine. Note that in the recipe here imported black olives are specified. All ingredients may be prepared in advance and refrigerated before assembling.*

Salade Niçoise I

6 to 10 servings

- 2 teaspoons mustard, preferably Dijon or Düsseldorf
- 2 tablespoons wine vinegar
- 1½ teaspoons salt
- 1 or 2 cloves garlic, finely minced
- 6 tablespoons peanut or vegetable oil
- 6 tablespoons olive oil
  Freshly ground black pepper
- 1 teaspoon chopped fresh thyme or ½ teaspoon dried thyme
- 2 pounds green beans
- 2 green peppers
- 4 ribs celery, approximately
- 1 pint cherry tomatoes
- 5 medium, red-skinned potatoes, cooked, peeled, and sliced
- 3 cans (7 ounces each) tuna
- 1 2-ounce can flat anchovies
- 10 stuffed olives
- 10 black olives, preferably imported Greek or Italian
- 2 small or 1 large red onion, if available, or use Bermuda onions
- 2 tablespoons chopped fresh basil or 1 teaspoon dried basil
- ⅓ cup finely chopped fresh parsley
- ¼ cup finely chopped green onion
- 6 hard-cooked eggs, quartered

1. In a mixing bowl, combine the mustard, vinegar, salt, garlic, peanut oil, olive oil, pepper to taste, and thyme. Beat with a fork until well blended and set aside.

2. Pick over the beans and break them into one-and-one-half-inch lengths. Place in a saucepan and cook in salted water to cover until tender but crisp. Drain and run under cold water, then drain in a colander and set aside.

3. Remove the cores, seeds, and white membranes from the green peppers. Cut the peppers into thin rounds and set aside.

4. Trim the celery ribs and cut crosswise into thin slices. There should be about two cups of sliced celery. Set aside.

5. Bring a quart of water to a boil. Drop in the cherry tomatoes and let stand for exactly fifteen seconds, no longer, or they will become mushy. Drain immediately. Using a paring knife, pull off the tomato skins. Set the tomatoes aside.

6. In a large salad bowl, make a more or less symmetrical pattern of the green beans, peppers, celery, tomatoes, and potatoes. Flake the tuna and add to the bowl. Arrange the anchovies on top and scatter the olives over all.

7. Peel the onions and cut into thin, almost transparent slices. Scatter the onion rings over all. Sprinkle with basil, parsley, and green onion. Garnish with hard-cooked eggs.

8. Toss the salad with the dressing after the garnished bowl has been presented to the guests for their enjoyment. Serve with a crusty loaf of French or Italian bread.

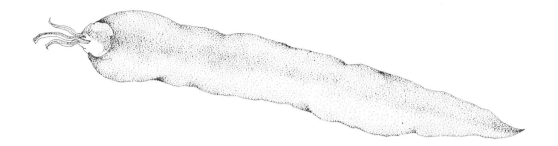

Salade Niçoise II

8 servings

1 2-ounce can flat anchovy fillets, chopped
3 cans (7 ounces each) tuna, drained and cut into chunks
¾ cup finely chopped celery
1 clove garlic, finely minced
¼ cup finely chopped onion
⅓ cup chopped green pepper
½ teaspoon dried thyme
1 bay leaf, crumbled
½ teaspoon dried rosemary
2 tablespoons wine vinegar
7 tablespoons olive oil
  Salt and freshly ground black pepper
3 ripe tomatoes, skinned and cut into wedges
12 pitted black olives, quartered
3 hard-cooked eggs, quartered
  Onion rings

1. Combine the anchovies, tuna, celery, garlic, onion, green pepper, thyme, bay leaf, and rosemary in a mixing bowl. Toss gently.

2. Add the vinegar, oil, and salt and pepper to taste. Toss again. Gently fold in the tomatoes, olives, and eggs. Chill well, then garnish with onion rings before serving.

Provençal Salad

6 to 8 servings

½ cup olive oil
⅓ cup lemon juice
  Salt
1 clove garlic, crushed
  Grated rind of 2 oranges
¾ cup cured black olives, pitted
¾ cup celery root cut in finest possible strips (julienne)
½ cup chopped fresh parsley
3 bunches watercress, stems removed
  Freshly ground black pepper

1. Combine the oil, lemon juice, and one-half teaspoon salt. Let the garlic stand in the mixture for an hour or two.

2. Place the orange rind, olives, celery root, and parsley in the bottom of a large china bowl. Cover with watercress and chill, covered, in the refrigerator.

3. At serving time, remove the garlic from the oil mixture. Toss the watercress mixture with the oil mixture. Add salt and pepper to taste.

Clear Aspic

About 1 quart

3 cups Chicken Stock (page 115)
1 cup tomato juice (the juice becomes clear when the aspic is made)
4 envelopes unflavored gelatin
  Salt and freshly ground black pepper
1 teaspoon granulated sugar
1 sprig fresh tarragon or 1 teaspoon dried tarragon
2 egg shells, crushed
2 egg whites, lightly beaten
2 tablespoons dry sherry

1. In a saucepan combine the chicken stock with the tomato juice, gelatin, salt and pepper to taste, sugar, tarragon, egg shells, and egg whites. Heat slowly, stirring constantly, until the mixture boils up in the pan.
2. Remove the pan from the heat and stir in the sherry.
3. Strain the mixture through a sieve lined with a flannel cloth that has been rinsed in cold water and wrung out. If the aspic starts to set or becomes too firm, it may be reheated, then brought to any desired temperature.

Quick Aspic

About 2 quarts

6 cups Chicken Stock (page 115)
2 cups tomato juice
8 envelopes unflavored gelatin
  Salt and freshly ground black pepper
2 teaspoons granulated sugar
4 egg shells, crushed
4 egg whites, lightly beaten
¼ cup Cognac

1. In a saucepan combine the chicken stock with the tomato juice, gelatin, salt,

pepper, sugar, egg shells, and egg whites and heat slowly, stirring constantly, until the mixture boils up in the pan.
2. Remove the pan from the heat and stir in the Cognac.
3. Strain the mixture through a sieve lined with a flannel cloth that has been rinsed in cold water and wrung out. If the aspic starts to set or becomes too firm, it may be reheated, then brought to any desired temperature.

Herb and Cream Salad Sauce

About ½ cup

½ egg yolk
1 teaspoon chopped fresh thyme, marjoram, orégano, or parsley, or a combination
1 clove garlic, finely minced
2 teaspoons Dijon or Düsseldorf mustard
2 tablespoons wine vinegar
6 tablespoons olive oil
1 drop Tabasco
2 tablespoons heavy cream
  Salt and freshly ground pepper to taste
1 teaspoon lemon juice, or more to taste

1. Add the egg yolk, thyme or other herbs, garlic, mustard, and vinegar to a salad bowl and blend with a wire whisk. Gradually add the oil, while stirring, until homogenous.
2. Stir in the remaining ingredients and chill well before adding chilled salad greens.

Mayonnaise

About 1½ cups

1 egg yolk
1 teaspoon prepared mustard, preferably Dijon or Düsseldorf
  Salt and freshly ground black pepper
  Pinch of cayenne pepper
1½ teaspoons white vinegar
1 cup peanut oil
  Lemon juice

1. Place the egg yolk in a mixing bowl.

2. Add the mustard, salt and pepper to taste, the cayenne, and vinegar. Start beating with a whisk, rotary beater or electric beater, gradually adding the peanut oil. Continue beating, adding the oil gradually. Beat in lemon juice to taste. Taste for seasoning and beat in more salt, cayenne, or lemon juice, if desired.

Tarragon Mayonnaise

About 1 cup

1 egg yolk
1 teaspoon Dijon or Düsseldorf mustard
2 teaspoons white vinegar
  Salt and freshly ground black pepper
¾ cup peanut oil
  Lemon juice
2 teaspoons freshly chopped tarragon or ½ teaspoon dried tarragon

1. Place the egg yolk in a small bowl and add the mustard, vinegar, and salt and pepper to taste. Beat lightly with a whisk or rotary beater.

2. Gradually add the oil, pouring in a small, steady stream until the mayonnaise starts to thicken; then the oil may be added in a larger stream. Beat vigorously until thoroughly thickened. Add lemon juice to taste, tarragon, and, if desired, more salt. Serve with eggs, fish, and vegetables.

Allemande Sauce

About 2 quarts

¼ cup butter
¼ cup all-purpose flour
5 cups hot milk
6 egg yolks
1 cup heavy cream
  Salt

1. In a saucepan, melt the butter and stir in the flour, using a wire whisk. When blended add the milk all at once, stirring vigorously with the whisk. When the mixture is blended and smooth let the sauce simmer fifteen to twenty minutes, stirring frequently with the whisk. Remove the sauce from the heat and cool slightly.

2. Beat the egg yolks lightly and blend with the cream. Add a little of the hot sauce to the egg-yolk mixture, then return this mixture to the sauce. Stir rapidly and season with salt to taste. Serve with poached chicken or vegetables.

Sauce Aurore

About 3 cups

¼ cup butter
3 tablespoons finely chopped onion
3 tablespoons finely chopped shallots or green onion
2 cups tomatoes, chopped and put through a food mill
Salt and freshly ground pepper to taste
½ bay leaf
½ teaspoon dried tarragon
½ teaspoon dried thyme
1½ tablespoons all-purpose flour
1 cup Chicken Stock (page 115)
½ cup heavy cream

1. Melt one tablespoon of the butter in a saucepan and add the onion and shallots. Cook, stirring, until the onion is wilted. Add the tomatoes, salt, pepper, bay leaf, tarragon, and thyme. Cook, stirring frequently, about thirty minutes.

2. Meanwhile, melt another tablespoon of butter and stir in the flour. When blended, add the chicken stock and simmer, stirring occasionally, about half an hour. Add the tomato sauce and cook about fifteen minutes longer. Strain and stir in the cream, salt, and pepper. Bring to a boil again, then remove from the heat and swirl in the remaining butter by rotating the pan gently. Serve spooned over Chicken Mousse (page 230) or with fish.

Béarnaise Sauce

About 2 cups

1 cup butter
1 tablespoon finely chopped onion
2 tablespoons finely chopped shallots
½ teaspoon crushed peppercorns
1 tablespoon finely chopped fresh tarragon or 1½ teaspoons dried tarragon
3 tablespoons tarragon vinegar
2 tablespoons water
3 egg yolks
Salt to taste
Cayenne pepper to taste

1. Place the butter in a measuring cup and heat in a very warm place or in a slow oven until melted. Pour the clear golden liquid on top into a small saucepan. Discard the white milky substance at the bottom. Heat the clear golden liquid, which is clarified butter, but do not cook it.

2. Meanwhile, combine the onion, shallots, peppercorns, tarragon, and vinegar in a saucepan and cook over moderately high heat until the liquid is almost completely reduced. Remove the saucepan from the heat and let it cool slightly. Beat the water and egg yolks together and add to the saucepan. Cook the mixture, whisking rapidly, over hot water or on top of an asbestos pad.

3. When the egg yolks start to thicken, remove the saucepan from the heat and gradually pour in the butter, beating rapidly with the whisk. Season to taste with salt and cayenne pepper. Do not cook this sauce, or it will curdle. Serve with Fondue Bourguignonne (page 174), broiled meat dishes, fish, or eggs.

Béchamel Sauce

About 2 cups

¼ cup butter
¼ cup flour
2 cups milk
Salt and freshly ground pepper
Pinch of nutmeg

1. Melt the butter in a saucepan over moderate heat without letting it brown. Add the flour and stir with a wire whisk until well blended.

2. Meanwhile, heat the milk, bringing it almost to the boiling point. Add to the butter-flour mixture, stirring vigorously. Cook, stirring, until the mixture comes to a boil. Reduce the heat and simmer for five minutes. Season to taste with salt, pepper, and nutmeg.

Sauce Belle Aurore

About 4 cups

6 tablespoons butter
3 tablespoons all-purpose flour
1¾ cups Chicken Stock (page 115) or canned chicken broth
¾ cup cooking stock from a boiled ham (or use an equal and additional quantity of Chicken Stock , page 115)
2 cups Fresh Tomato Sauce (page 279)
1 cup heavy cream
¼ cup port wine

1. Melt half the butter in a saucepan and stir in the flour, using a wire whisk. Add the chicken stock and ham stock, stirring vigorously with the whisk. When the mixture is thickened and smooth, continue cooking about one hour, stirring occasionally.

2. Add the tomato sauce and stir. Cook five minutes. Stir in the heavy cream and strain through a sieve or food mill. Return the sauce to a saucepan, bring to a boil, and swirl in the remaining butter by rotating the pan gently. Add the port, heat thoroughly, and serve hot, with ham.

Bordelaise Sauce

About 1¾ cups

4 shallots, finely chopped
6 peppercorns, crushed
2 sprigs parsley
½ teaspoon dried thyme
1 bay leaf
1 teaspoon finely chopped garlic
1 cup dry red wine
1¼ cups Brown Sauce (page 268) or canned beef gravy
Salt and freshly ground pepper to taste
Juice of 1 lemon
2 tablespoons butter

1. Combine the shallots, peppercorns, parsley, thyme, bay leaf, garlic, and wine in a saucepan. Cook over moderately high heat until reduced by half.

2. Stir in the brown sauce and simmer about ten minutes. Add salt and pepper, then strain through a sieve and bring just to a boil again. Stir in the lemon juice. Remove from the heat and swirl in the butter. Serve hot. Serve with Fondue Bourguignonne (page 174), grilled meats, broiled meats, or sweetbreads.

Brown Sauce

About 2 quarts

5 pounds veal bones, cracked
1 onion, quartered
4 ribs celery, chopped
4 carrots, scraped and quartered
½ teaspoon dried thyme
2 bay leaves
1 teaspoon coarsely cracked black peppercorns
3 cloves garlic, unpeeled
1 tablespoon salt
½ cup all-purpose flour
3 quarts water
1 10½-ounce can tomato puree
3 sprigs parsley

1. Preheat the oven to 475 degrees.
2. Combine the bones, onion, celery, carrots, and seasonings in a large roasting pan. Bake forty-five minutes. If the bones start to burn, reduce the heat to 400 degrees. When cooked, the bones should be dark brown.
3. Sprinkle the bones with flour and stir with a fork. Return the pan to the oven. Bake fifteen minutes longer.
4. Spoon the ingredients into a large heavy kettle with at least a seven-quart capacity. Add three cups of the water to the roasting pan and place the pan over moderate heat. Stir to dissolve all brown particles that cling to the pan.
5. Pour the liquid from the pan into the kettle and add the tomato puree. Add the parsley and remaining water and bring to a boil. Simmer two hours skimming occasionally to remove fat and foam as it rises to the surface. Strain. The sauce may be used immediately or it may be frozen and defrosted as needed.

Caper Sauce

About 1 cup

¾ cup peanut or vegetable oil
3 tablespoons wine vinegar
1 tablespoon lemon juice
Salt and freshly ground black pepper to taste
½ clove garlic, finely minced
½ teaspoon grated lemon rind
2 tablespoons chopped parsley
2 to 3 tablespoons capers

Combine all the ingredients in a mixing bowl and beat with a fork until well blended. Let stand at room temperature until ready to serve. Serve with chilled poached salmon.

Cardinal Sauce

5 cups

5 tablespoons butter
5 tablespoons all-purpose flour
3 cups hot, strong Fish Stock (page 116)
1 cup heavy cream
1 tablespoon tomato paste
Salt and freshly ground white pepper
Juice of ½ lemon
3 tablespoons cream (optional)
¾ cup chopped cooked lobster
4 tablespoons Lobster Butter (optional, see below)

1. Melt the butter in a saucepan, add the flour, and stir for three minutes over medium heat. Do not allow to brown.
2. Add the fish stock, stirring with a whisk until the stock comes to a boil. Add the one cup cream and tomato paste and simmer over low heat for about fifteen minutes.

3. Season with salt and pepper to taste and add the lemon juice. If desired, the sauce may be refrigerated for several hours or overnight and reheated. Spread three tablespoons of cream on the top to prevent a skim from forming on the surface.

4. Just before serving, reheat the sauce to the boiling point, add the finely chopped lobster, and, off the heat, swirl in the lobster butter. Serve with fish.

LOBSTER BUTTER:

5 tablespoons

Shell and body of 1 cooked lobster
5 tablespoons butter

1. Pound the shell pieces in a mortar until they are thoroughly crushed.
2. Place the pieces of shell and body in a saucepan with the butter. Add water to cover and boil over medium heat for one-half hour.
3. Strain through several thicknesses of cheesecloth into a bowl and chill until butter is formed on the surface of the liquid. Pour off the liquid and allow the butter to soften at room temperature before using.

Sauce Charcutière

About 2 cups

2 cups Sauce Robert II (page 276)
¼ cup finely slivered or chopped sour gherkins

Prepare the sauce and add the strips of gherkins along with the mustard. Serve with grilled pork dishes.

Sauce Chasseur

About 2 cups

5 tablespoons butter
½ cup chopped mushrooms
1 tablespoon chopped shallots
¾ cup dry white wine
½ cup Tomato Sauce I (page 278)
½ cup chopped, peeled, and seeded tomato
¾ cup Brown Sauce (page 268)
½ teaspoon each chopped fresh tarragon and chervil or ¼ teaspoon each dried tarragon and chervil

1. Melt two tablespoons of the butter in a saucepan and cook the mushrooms. When they start to wilt, add the shallots. Cook, stirring occasionally, for about five minutes, or until the mushroom liquid nearly evaporates.
2. Add the wine and cook until it is reduced by half. Add the tomato sauce, tomato, and brown sauce. Simmer for ten minutes, then remove from the heat.
3. Stir in the remaining cold butter and add the herbs. Serve immediately with game dishes.

Curry Sauce

About 1½ cups

4½ tablespoons butter
1 clove garlic, finely minced
⅓ cup finely chopped onion
⅓ cup finely chopped celery
3 tablespoons chopped carrot
2 tablespoons all-purpose flour
2 tablespoons Curry Powder (page 33)
½ bay leaf
2 sprigs parsley
2 sprigs fresh thyme or ½ teaspoon dried thyme
1¾ cups Chicken Stock (page 115)
   Salt and freshly ground pepper to taste

1. Heat three tablespoons of the butter in a saucepan and add the garlic, onion, celery, and carrot. Cook, stirring, until the onion is wilted. Add the flour and cook, stirring, about three minutes. Stir in the curry powder, bay leaf, parsley, and thyme.

2. Using a wire whisk, continue to stir briskly while adding the stock. Simmer, covered, stirring occasionally, about thirty minutes. Put the mixture, including the soft vegetables, through a fine sieve, using a wooden spoon. Swirl in the remaining butter by rotating the pan gently and add salt and pepper to taste. Serve with Seafood Crêpes (page 148).

Sauce Diable

About 1 cup

2 tablespoons coarsely chopped onion
2 shallots, finely chopped
1 clove garlic, finely chopped
15 peppercorns, crushed
   Pinch of dried thyme
½ bay leaf
¼ cup wine vinegar
1 cup Beef Stock (page 115)
1 tablespoon cornstarch
1 tablespoon water
1 tablespoon butter
2 teaspoons imported mustard, such as Dijon or Düsseldorf

1. Cook the onion, shallots, garlic, peppercorns, thyme, bay leaf, and wine vinegar in a small saucepan until almost all the liquid has evaporated. Add the beef stock and simmer ten minutes. Blend the cornstarch and water and stir it into the simmering liquid.

2. Strain the mixture through a sieve, pushing as much of the solids through as possible. Return to the heat and bring to a boil.

3. Remove the sauce from the heat and stir in the butter. Stir in the mustard; do not boil after the mustard is added. Serve with grilled pork and veal dishes.

Sauce Diane

About 3 cups

1 pound venison bones, preferably breast-
   bones
¼ pound salt pork, cut into small cubes
1 teaspoon freshly ground black pepper
   Salt
1 carrot, scraped and coarsely chopped
1 onion, finely chopped
1 clove garlic, coarsely chopped
2 sprigs parsley
1 sprig rosemary
1 bay leaf
1 sage leaf
2 tablespoons all-purpose flour
1 cup dry red wine
1 cup water
1 10¾-ounce can beef gravy
1 cup heavy cream
2 tablespoons cold butter
1 tablespoon Cognac (optional)

1. Combine the bones and salt pork in a
large saucepan or ovenproof casserole and
cook, stirring occasionally, until brown. Add
the pepper, salt to taste, carrot, onion, garlic,
parsley, rosemary, and bay and sage leaves.
Sprinkle with the flour and continue to cook,
stirring, about three minutes longer.

2. Add the wine, water, and beef gravy.
Simmer, stirring occasionally, forty-five minutes.

3. Strain the sauce and add the cream.
Return to a boil, then simmer fifteen minutes.

4. Remove the sauce from the heat and
swirl in the butter by rotating the pan gently.
Add the Cognac and serve immediately with
grilled or broiled venison or other game.

Note: Up to the addition of the cream, the
sauce may be made well in advance. It may
also be frozen.

Herb Sauce

About 2 cups

1 egg yolk
   Salt and freshly ground black pepper
1 teaspoon prepared mustard, preferably
   Dijon or Düsseldorf
3 tablespoons wine vinegar
½ cup olive oil
½ cup vegetable oil
3 tablespoons chopped chives
¼ cup finely chopped parsley
2 tablespoons finely chopped shallots
1 teaspoon chopped tarragon

1. This sauce is made like a mayonnaise.
Place the egg yolk in a mixing bowl and add
salt and pepper to taste, mustard, and vinegar. Immediately begin whipping the mixture
with a wire whisk or rotary beater.

2. Add the oils, at first only a few drops
at a time, then continuously in a steady
stream, beating constantly. The sauce should
become increasingly thick.

3. Stir in the chives, parsley, shallots, and
tarragon. Serve with cold egg dishes.

Blender Hollandaise Sauce

Enough for 4 servings

Heat one-half cup butter to bubbling, but
do not brown. Into the container of an
electric blender put two egg yolks, two
tablespoons lemon juice, one-quarter teaspoon salt and a pinch of cayenne. Flick
motor quickly on and off twice at high speed.
Remove cover, turn motor on high and add
butter gradually until mixture thickens. If
too thick, add cold water. Serve with vegetables, fish, or eggs.

Chive Hollandaise Sauce

1 cup

¾ cup butter
2½ teaspoons lemon juice
3 egg yolks, well beaten
Dash of salt
Dash of cayenne pepper
1½ teaspoons finely chopped chives

1. Place one third of the butter in the top part of a double boiler. Add the lemon juice and egg yolks and place over hot, not boiling, water. Cook slowly, beating constantly with a rotary beater or wire whisk.

2. Add another third of the butter when the first butter has completely melted. Cook, beating, until the mixture begins to thicken.

3. Add the remaining butter and cook until the sauce has the consistency of mayonnaise, beating constantly. Remove from the hot water immediately and add the salt, cayenne, and chives. Serve over hot asparagus.

Martinique Sauce Chien

About 1 cup

If, as many travelers aver, the island of Martinique has the finest food in all the Caribbean, it may be because it is a French département. *French foods, including the famed butter of Isigny, fine cheeses and, in season, oysters and* sanglier *(wild boar), as well as French wines, are flown to the island. Some of the best-known dishes are stuffed crab; a soup made with tuna and capers; pineapple tarts, and an unusual sauce of lime, oil, and peppers called* sauce chien, *which is served with grilled foods like chicken, fish, and pork. A recipe for the sauce follows.*

⅓ cup lime juice
¼ cup peanut or vegetable oil
½ clove garlic, finely minced
Salt and freshly ground black pepper to taste
3 tablespoons finely chopped parsley
1 tablespoon finely chopped green onion
1 teaspoon thinly sliced fresh or canned hot green peppers
Cayenne pepper

Combine all the ingredients and beat with a fork or whisk to blend. Serve with hot grilled foods such as chicken, fish, or pork.

Madeira Sauce

About 2 cups

1 tablespoon butter
4 large mushrooms, sliced
　Salt and freshly ground pepper
2 tablespoons finely chopped shallots
⅓ cup Madeira
1½ cups Brown Sauce (page 268) or 1 can
　(10¾-ounce) beef gravy

1. Heat the butter in a skillet and add the mushrooms. Sprinkle with salt and pepper to taste and cook until the mushrooms give up their liquid. Add the shallots and cook, stirring, until most of the liquid evaporates.

2. Add the wine and cook one minute, then add the brown sauce and simmer fifteen minutes longer. Serve hot, with roasted and sautéed meat dishes.

Mustard-Egg Sauce

4 cups

1 teaspoon dry mustard
1 teaspoon cold water
6 tablespoons butter
1 onion, sliced wafer thin
6 tablespoons all-purpose flour
3 cups milk
1 teaspoon salt
½ teaspoon freshly ground black pepper
4 hard-cooked eggs, diced
1 teaspoon fresh lemon juice

1. Combine the mustard and water and let stand for ten minutes to develop the flavor.

2. Melt the butter in a saucepan. Add the onion and cook until translucent, then blend in the flour. Add the milk, stirring constantly, and continue to cook and stir until the mixture is thickened and smooth.

3. Add the salt, pepper, eggs, lemon juice, and the mustard mixture. Serve over cauliflower.

Mushroom Sauce

6 to 8 servings

4½ tablespoons butter
3 tablespoons all-purpose flour
¾ cup milk
¾ cup heavy cream
　Salt and freshly ground black pepper
⅛ teaspoon grated nutmeg
1 cup grated Gruyère or Swiss cheese
1 egg yolk
¼ cup dry white wine
½ pound mushrooms, sliced

1. Melt two and one-half tablespoons of the butter, blend in the flour, and gradually stir in the milk and cream. Bring to a boil.

2. Season with salt and pepper to taste and the nutmeg. Stir in the cheese until it is melted.

3. Beat the egg yolk with the wine, add a little of the hot mixture, return to the pan, and cook one minute.

4. Cook the mushrooms separately in the remaining butter three to five minutes. Add to the pan and reheat. Serve with roast meat or chicken.

Sauce Nantaise

About 1½ cups

2 tablespoons whole peppercorns
⅔ cup dry white wine
⅔ cup white vinegar
⅓ cup finely chopped shallots
⅔ cup heavy cream
   Salt to taste
½ cup butter, at room temperature
   Juice of ½ lemon

1. If you have a sturdy surface to crush the peppercorns, place them on that surface and crush with the bottom of a heavy skillet. Otherwise, place the peppercorns in a napkin or towel and crush them coarsely with a hammer or mallet.

2. Combine the peppercorns with the wine, vinegar, and shallots and bring to a boil. Simmer over moderate heat until the liquid is almost completely reduced, about ten or fifteen minutes, stirring frequently. The ingredients must not, however, become dry.

3. Add the cream and salt and cook, stirring almost constantly, eight to ten minutes, or until the sauce is reduced and thickened. The sauce is ready at the point when small pools that look like melted butter form on top of the sauce. Remove the saucepan from the fire and let stand about three minutes, until partly cool. Add the butter gradually, off the heat, about a tablespoon at a time, stirring rapidly with a wire whisk. Beat in the lemon juice.

4. When the sauce is ready, put it through a very fine sieve or line a sieve with cheesecloth and squeeze the sauce through. Keep the sauce warm until ready to serve. Do not bring to a boil, or the sauce will curdle. Serve with lobster and other seafood.

Paprika Sauce

About 3 cups

3 tablespoons butter
3 tablespoons finely chopped onion
¼ cup all-purpose flour
1 tablespoon paprika
3 medium tomatoes, coarsely chopped
   (about 3½ cups)
   Salt and freshly ground pepper to taste
2 tablespoons sour cream

1. Melt two tablespoons of butter in a skillet. Add the onion and simmer until wilted. Stir in the flour and paprika, then stir in the tomatoes and add salt and pepper. Simmer fifteen minutes, stirring frequently.

2. Put the sauce through the finest strainer possible or use a food mill. Stir in the sour cream. Swirl in the remaining butter by rotating the pan gently and serve hot. Serve with Fondue Bourguignonne (page 174).

Sauce Piquante

About 1½ cups

2 tablespoons mustard, preferably Dijon
   or Düsseldorf
3 tablespoons Sauce Robert I (page 276)
4 tablespoons Sauce Diable (page 270)
¼ teaspoon Worcestershire sauce
¼ teaspoon Tabasco
1¼ cups heavy cream
   Salt and freshly ground pepper to taste

In a saucepan, combine all the ingredients. Simmer, stirring occasionally, about ten minutes. Serve with Seafood Crêpes (page 148).

Sauce Portugaise

About 2 cups

¼ cup butter
¼ cup finely chopped onion
1 clove garlic, finely minced
1¼ cups canned tomatoes
½ teaspoon dried thyme
½ bay leaf
Salt and freshly ground black pepper
2 pounds fresh fish bones
10 peppercorns
1 sprig parsley
1 rib celery with leaves, cut in half
1 small onion, cut in half
1½ tablespoons all-purpose flour
½ cup heavy cream
1 tablespoon dry Madeira
1 teaspoon Cognac (optional)

1. Melt one tablespoon of the butter in a saucepan. Add the chopped onion and garlic and cook until the onion is translucent. Add the tomatoes, thyme, bay leaf, and salt and pepper to taste and simmer, stirring occasionally, fifteen minutes.

2. Meanwhile, combine the fish bones, water to cover, peppercorns, parsley, celery, onion, and salt and pepper to taste in a small kettle. Bring to a boil and simmer, skimming the surface as necessary, for twenty minutes. Strain the stock and reserve.

3. Melt one and one-half tablespoons of butter in a saucepan and stir in the flour, using a wire whisk. Add one and one-quarter cups of the reserved fish stock, stirring vigorously with the whisk. (Leftover fish stock may be frozen.) When the mixture is thickened and smooth, continue cooking about one hour, stirring occasionally.

4. Add the tomato mixture and stir. Simmer five minutes.

5. Stir in the heavy cream and strain the sauce through a sieve or food mill. Return the sauce to a saucepan, bring to a boil, and swirl in the remaining butter by rotating the pan gently. Add the Madeira and Cognac and heat thoroughly. Serve hot, with poached fish.

Poulette Sauce

About 1½ cups

1½ tablespoons butter
1 tablespoon all-purpose flour
1 cup Chicken Stock (page 115)
⅓ cup heavy cream
1 egg yolk
Salt
Paprika
2 teaspoons dry white wine or lemon juice
2 teaspoons chopped parsley

1. Melt the butter and blend in the flour, then stir in the stock slowly. Bring to a boil, stirring.

2. Mix the cream and egg yolk. Add some of the hot liquid to the cream mixture. Return to the pan and cook until the egg yolk thickens, but do not boil.

3. Season with salt and paprika to taste, then stir in the wine or lemon juice and the parsley. Serve hot, with vegetables.

Sauce Robert I

About 1 cup

¼ cup dry white wine
1 bay leaf
2 tablespoons finely chopped shallots or green onion
1½ teaspoons chopped onion
1 small clove garlic, finely minced
2 sprigs fresh thyme or ½ teaspoon dried thyme
½ cup tomato puree
½ cup Chicken Stock (page 115)
½ cup Brown Sauce (page 268) or canned beef gravy
½ cup thinly sliced cornichons (French gherkins)
2 tablespoons finely chopped parsley
Beef Stock (optional; see page 115)
1 tablespoon Dijon or Düsseldorf mustard
2 tablespoons butter

1. Combine the wine, bay leaf, shallots, onion, garlic, and thyme in a saucepan and simmer until the wine is reduced to about two tablespoons. Add the tomato puree, chicken stock, and brown sauce and cook twenty minutes, stirring occasionally.

2. Remove the thyme and bay leaf and add the cornichons and parsley. If the sauce seems too thick, thin it with a little beef stock. Bring the sauce to a boil and remove it from the heat.

3. Stir in the mustard and swirl in the butter by rotating the pan gently. Do not cook further but serve hot. Serve with grilled pork dishes.

Sauce Robert II

About 2 cups

⅓ cup finely chopped shallots
⅓ cup finely chopped onion
¼ cup butter
¾ cup dry white wine
1½ cups Brown Sauce (page 268)
1 to 2 tablespoons prepared mustard, preferably Dijon

1. Cook the shallots and onion in two tablespoons of the butter until golden brown. Add the wine and cook until it is reduced by half.

2. Add the brown sauce and cook for ten minutes. Turn off the heat and stir in the remaining cold butter.

3. Add the mustard; do not cook after the mustard is added. Serve hot, with grilled pork dishes.

Sour Cream and Horseradish Sauce

About ¾ cup

¾ cup sour cream
1 tablespoon or more freshly grated horseradish (see note)
1 tablespoon finely chopped onion
Salt to taste

Place the ingredients in a mixing bowl and stir to blend.

Note: If fresh horseradish is not available, use the bottled variety. But place the horseradish in a square of cheesecloth and squeeze to extract most of the vinegar in which it is packed. Serve with Fondue Bourguignonne (page 174) and fish.

Tartar Sauce I

About 2 cups

1½ cups Mayonnaise (page 265)
  2 tablespoons chopped sour pickle
  1 teaspoon finely minced onion
  2 tablespoons finely chopped parsley
  2 tablespoons coarsely chopped capers
  1 teaspoon chopped chives
  1 teaspoon mustard, preferably Dijon or Düsseldorf (not the baseball-park variety)
  ½ teaspoon finely chopped tarragon
    Lemon juice to taste
  1 hard-cooked egg, sieved (optional)

Combine all the ingredients and chill. Serve with fish and shellfish.

Tartar Sauce II

About 1 cup

  ¼ cup wine vinegar
  1 egg yolk
  2 teaspoons imported mustard, preferably Dijon or Düsseldorf
    Salt and freshly ground pepper to taste
  ¾ to 1 cup vegetable oil
  ¼ cup finely chopped parsley
  1 tablespoon finely chopped chives
  2 tablespoons capers
  5 small cornichons (French gherkins) or other small sour pickles

1. Place the vinegar in a small saucepan and bring just to a boil.

2. Place the egg yolk in a mixing bowl and add the mustard, salt, pepper, and one and one-half teaspoons of the hot vinegar. Start beating vigorously with a whisk. Add the oil in a small, steady stream, beating constantly with the whisk. Stir in about one and one-half teaspoons of vinegar, or to taste. Pour the remaining vinegar back into the bottle. Add the parsley and chives.

3. Chop the capers and pickles together and add to the sauce. Serve with fish.

French Sardine Butter

1 cup

1 6½-ounce can spiced, truffled sardines
½ cup butter, softened
2 tablespoons lemon juice
½ teaspoon salt
Dash of cayenne pepper

Mash the sardines with the oil in the can. Blend with the remaining ingredients and serve as a spread for canapes or sandwiches.

Tomato Sauce I

About 3 cups

1 onion, chopped
2 tablespoons salad oil
½ cup tomato paste
2 teaspoons all-purpose flour
2 cups Beef Stock (page 115) or Chicken Stock (page 115)
3 medium tomatoes, cored and chopped
Salt and freshly ground black pepper to taste
1 sprig fresh thyme or ½ teaspoon dried thyme

1. Cook the onion in oil until wilted. Add the tomato paste and cook, stirring. Sprinkle with flour and stir.

2. Using a wire whisk, stir in the broth and add the remaining ingredients. Simmer one hour. Pass through a sieve or food mill, reheat and serve.

Note: This sauce may be seasoned with grated horseradish, if desired, and if no other horseradish sauce is served.

Tomato Sauce II

About 3 cups

3 tablespoons olive oil
½ pound mushrooms, sliced
2 tablespoons butter
1 cup finely chopped onion
1 clove garlic, finely minced
½ cup chopped, seeded, and cored green pepper
1 1-pound-1-ounce can Italian peeled tomatoes
Salt and freshly ground black pepper to taste
¼ teaspoon or more granulated sugar
2 tablespoons chopped fresh basil or ½ teaspoon dried basil
1 sprig fresh thyme or ½ teaspoon dried thyme
1 bay leaf
2 tablespoons tomato paste
½ cup Beef Stock (page 115) or water

1. Add the olive oil to a skillet and cook the mushrooms until they give up their moisture. Continue cooking, stirring occasionally, until the liquid evaporates.

2. Heat the butter in a heavy saucepan and cook the onion, garlic, and green pepper until the onion is wilted but not brown.

3. Add the mushrooms, tomatoes, salt and pepper to taste, one-quarter teaspoon sugar or to taste, basil, thyme, bay leaf, tomato paste, and stock and stir well. Simmer over low heat for about forty-five minutes, stirring occasionally. Before serving, remove the bay leaf.

Fresh Tomato Sauce

About 2 cups

- 1 tablespoon butter
- ½ cup finely chopped onion
- 1 clove garlic, finely minced
- 2 cups chopped fresh tomatoes
- 2 sprigs fresh thyme or ½ teaspoon dried thyme
- 1 bay leaf
  Salt and freshly ground black pepper to taste

1. Heat the butter in a saucepan and cook the onion and garlic until onion is translucent.

2. Add the remaining ingredients and cook, stirring occasionally, about fifteen minutes (see note).

Note: If this is to be used as a tomato sauce per se, strain it. For use in Sauce Belle Aurore (page 267) it will be strained later.

Homemade Hot Mustard

About ¼ cup

- 3 tablespoons dry mustard
  Dry white wine
- ¼ teaspoon salt

1. Place the mustard in a small mixing bowl. Gradually add the wine, stirring with a fork. Add enough wine to make a thin paste. Season with the salt.

2. Let the mustard stand ten minutes to develop its flavor.

Note: Mustard tends to lose its strength and become bitter if it stands too long, so it is best to make a fresh batch each time it is to be used. Beer, water, or milk may be used as a substitute for the wine.

Cherries Jubilee

6 servings

- 1½ pounds pitted cherries, poached (see note)
- 1 tablespoon cornstarch
- ½ cup Cognac
  French Vanilla Ice Cream (page 307)

1. Drain the cherries and reserve one cup of the juice.

2 Combine the cornstarch with the juice, a little at a time, and simmer three minutes, stirring constantly. Add the cherries. Warm the Cognac slightly and pour it into the cherries. Immediately ignite with a match. Spoon the juices over the cherries and serve flaming over French vanilla ice cream.

Note: To poach cherries, combine one cup sugar, two cups water, and one-eighth teaspoon salt in a saucepan. Bring to a boil, then add the cherries. Reduce the heat and simmer till tender.

Les Oranges aux Liqueurs

8 large seedless oranges
½ cup confectioners' sugar
2 tablespoons Cognac
3 tablespoons Grand Marnier
3 tablespoons kirsch

1. Peel the oranges, removing all the white membrane. Section them by running a sharp knife on either side of the connecting tissues between the golden, juicy flesh. Keep the sections intact. Squeeze the juice from the connecting tissues onto the orange sections.
2. Sprinkle the juicy sections with confectioners' sugar and refrigerate for an hour or longer.
3. Sprinkle with the liqueurs and toss lightly with a fork and spoon. Serve on chilled dessert plates.

Note: Other fruits and berries, such as peaches, strawberries and raspberries—alone or in combination—may be prepared the same way.

Oranges with Glazed Peel in Grand Marnier Syrup

6 servings

6 large navel oranges
½ cup water, approximately
2 tablespoons honey
1½ cups granulated sugar
¼ cup orange juice
¼ cup Grand Marnier

1. Remove the thin orange part of the peel from three of the oranges and cut into very thin julienne strips.
2. Place the peel in a small saucepan, barely cover with water, bring to a boil, then simmer ten minutes. Drain and run cold water over the peel.
3. Place the water, honey, and sugar in another saucepan. Heat, stirring, until the sugar dissolves. Continue to boil until the syrup registers 230 degrees on a candy thermometer. Immediately remove from the heat, add the blanched peel, and stir gently.
4. Let the peel stand in the syrup for thirty minutes, then add the orange juice and Grand Marnier.
5. Remove the remainder of the peel and pith from all of the oranges. Slice each orange into three or more slices and place in a shallow serving dish. Top with the glazed peel and spoon the syrup over the oranges.
6. Chill the oranges well before serving, spooning the syrup over occasionally.

Strawberries in Liqueur

6 servings

1 quart strawberries
½ cup confectioners' sugar
1 tablespoon Cointreau
1 tablespoon kirsch
2 tablespoons brandy or Cognac
6 slices spongecake

1. Wash, hull, and drain the strawberries. Slice them, then sprinkle the sugar over them and mix gently.
2. Pour the liqueurs over the berries and mix carefully. Cover and let stand at room temperature one hour, then refrigerate three to four hours. Serve over slices of spongecake.

Pears in Port Wine

8 servings

8 firm but ripe pears
  Juice of ½ lemon
4 cups water
1 cup port wine
1¼ cups granulated sugar
1 piece cinnamon
  Rind of ½ orange
1 strip lemon peel

1. Peel the pears and drop them into a basin of cold water with the lemon juice. This will keep them from darkening.
2. Combine the four cups of water with the remaining ingredients and bring to a boil. Stir until the sugar is dissolved.
3. Add the pears and simmer until the fruit is tender. Do not overcook. Let the pears cool in the syrup, then chill before serving.

Poached Pears with Chestnuts

6 servings

2 cups water
2 tablespoons lemon juice
¾ cup granulated sugar
1 1-inch length of cinnamon stick
6 firm, ripe pears
6 bottled chestnuts in syrup
2 cups English Custard with Chestnuts (page 295)

1. Combine the water, lemon juice, sugar, and cinnamon stick in a saucepan and bring to a boil. Reduce the heat to a simmer.

2. Peel the pears and split each in half. Use a melon ball cutter to remove the center core of each half. Drop the halves into the simmering liquid and cover. Simmer about eight minutes, or until the pears are tender yet firm. They must not become mushy. Let the pears stand in the liquid until cool. Drain the pears and chill.
3. Place one chestnut in a pear half, then add another pear half to reshape the pear. Arrange the reshaped, stuffed pears in a serving dish and pour the custard over all.

Pineapple Flambée

6 servings

1 ripe pineapple
¼ cup granulated sugar
½ cup sherry
½ cup water
1½ cups currant jelly
½ cup Cognac or kirsch
  French Vanilla Ice Cream (page 307)
  Macaroon crumbs

1. Prepare the pineapple by removing the hull, eyes, and core and cutting the flesh into paper-thin half slices.
2. Combine the sugar, sherry, and water and bring to a boil. Poach the pineapple slices in the mixture for about five minutes.
3. Melt the currant jelly over low heat. Add the drained pineapple slices and simmer, spooning the syrup over the fruit. Cook for five minutes. Add the Cognac directly in the center of the fruit mixture and let it heat for several minutes without stirring.
4. When well warmed, light the Cognac and spoon over the fruit while flaming. Serve the fruit sauce over the French vanilla ice cream and topped with macaroon crumbs.

Cheesecake with Genoise

10 to 12 servings

1 recipe Genoise (page 283), unfrosted, or use a store-bought sponge cake

PASTRY:
1 cup sifted all-purpose flour
⅛ teaspoon salt
1 tablespoon granulated sugar
1 teaspoon grated lemon rind
5 tablespoons butter
1 egg yolk
¼ teaspoon vanilla extract

FILLING:
1 pound farmer's cheese
1 pound cream cheese
1½ cups granulated sugar
½ cup sour cream
½ teaspoon vanilla extract
4 whole eggs
3 egg yolks
Grated rind of one lemon
2 tablespoons lemon juice

FRUIT GLAZE:
¼ cup fruit jelly, such as apple or currant
1 tablespoon water

TOPPING:
Fresh or canned fruit (peaches, blueberries, strawberries)

1. To prepare the genoise or store-bought sponge cake, use a long, sharp knife and slice off a layer one-half inch thick. Reserve this as a base for the cheesecake. (Serve the remaining genoise or cake cut into wedges with sweetened fruit, whipped cream, and so forth.)

2. To prepare the pastry, place the flour, salt, sugar, and lemon rind in a bowl. With the fingertips or a pastry blender, work in the butter until the mixture has the consistency of coarse oatmeal. Add the egg yolk and vanilla extract and stir to make a dough.

3. On a lightly floured board, roll out the dough into a long sausage. Place the sausage around the outside perimeter of the bottom of a buttered nine-inch spring-form pan. With the fingers, work the dough up the sides of the pan in an even layer until it almost reaches the top of the pan. Chill while preparing the filling.

4. Preheat the oven to 425 degrees.

5. To prepare the filling, beat the cheeses together in an electric mixer until creamy smooth. Gradually beat in the sugar.

6. Beat in the sour cream, vanilla extract, and then the eggs and egg yolks, one at a time, very well. Add the lemon rind and juice.

7. Place the layer of genoise in the bottom of the spring-form pan and fill in any space around with pieces cut from the remaining genoise. Pour in the cheese filling.

8. Bake twenty-five to thirty minutes, or until the cake is well browned. Remove from the oven and let stand thirty minutes at room temperature. Reduce the oven heat to 400 degrees and bake twenty-five to thirty minutes longer, covering the top with foil if it starts to overbrown. The center should feel partly firm but not set. Turn off the oven, leave the door ajar, and allow the cake to cool in the oven one hour. Cool on a rack, then chill.

9. Meanwhile, make the fruit glaze by combining the jelly with the water in the top of a double boiler, letting stand over hot water until melted. Use currant jelly for dark fruits such as blueberries, apple jelly for light fruits such as peaches.

10. Decorate the top with the fruit and spoon over the glaze. Chill again.

Genoise

10 to 12 servings

6 eggs, lightly beaten
1 cup granulated sugar
1 teaspoon vanilla extract
1 cup sifted cake flour
½ cup butter, melted, clarified, and cooled
(see note page 174)
1 teaspoon grated lemon or orange rind
Buttercream Filling (page 285)
Mocha Frosting (page 286)
1 cup chopped walnuts or pecans

1. Preheat the oven to 350 degrees.

2. Mix the eggs and sugar in a warm four-quart electric mixer bowl. Cover and let stand in a warm place (similar to yeast-rising conditions) until the mixture feels lukewarm to the fingers. Stir occasionally, taking care that the egg does not harden around the sides or on the bottom of the bowl because of too intense heat or evaporation.

3. When the egg and sugar mixture is lukewarm, beat at high speed until the mixture is very thick and pale in color and stands in stiff peaks. The volume achieved varies according to the efficiency of the mixer but should, under ideal conditions, almost fill a four-quart mixer bowl.

4. Remove the bowl from the mixer. Using a rubber spatula, fold in the vanilla extract. Very gently, in three installments, fold in the sifted flour. Add the butter gradually, folding gently, until no streaks show in the batter. Fold in the rind.

5. Pour the batter into four eight-inch layer pans or three nine-inch pans that have been greased, lined on the bottom with waxed paper, and greased again. The pans should be about two-thirds full of the batter. (Beaten to maximum volume, the batter will fill four eight-inch layer pans, but if less volume is achieved, there will only be sufficient batter for three eight-inch pans.

6. Bake the layers about twenty-five minutes, or until done and springy to the touch. Release the sides of the cooling genoise from the pans with the aid of a small spatula because the cake layers do shrink slightly as they cool.

7. After cooling the layers in the pans five to ten minutes, turn onto cooling racks to finish cooling. Fill in between the layers with the buttercream filling and frost the top with the mocha frosting. Pat the nuts around the sides. Refrigerate until serving time.

Note: If the oven to be used cannot bake more than two layers at a time, it is suggested that the recipe be halved, as the butter tends to separate on standing. A half recipe would also be ideal if the genoise is to be used in Cheesecake with Genoise (page 282).

If desired, the mocha frosting may be used as filling as well as frosting.

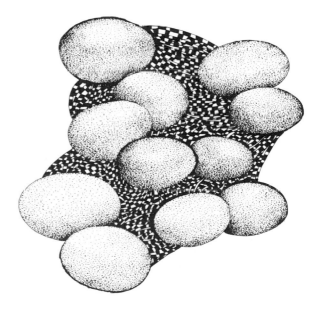

Gâteau Bretonne

8 servings

Orange juice is one of the most healthful of beverages and certainly one of the most delicious. But it has still other virtues. One is to enhance scores of desserts, including the one described here, a gâteau Bretonne or Brittany cake.

1 cup butter, at room temperature (the temperature is essential)
1 whole egg
3 egg yolks
½ cup granulated sugar
¼ teaspoon almond flavoring
1 tablespoon grated orange rind
⅓ teaspoon baking powder
1¾ cups sifted all-purpose flour
¼ cup ground almonds
3 tablespoons orange juice

1. Preheat the oven to 375 degrees.
2. Cream together the butter, whole egg, two of the egg yolks, sugar, and almond flavoring. Stir in the orange rind.
3. Sift together the baking powder and flour. Fold the flour mixture and ground almonds into the dough, then fold in one tablespoon of the orange juice.
4. Spoon the dough into a well-buttered nine-inch layer pan and brush the top with the remaining egg yolk beaten with the remaining orange juice. Bake twenty-five to thirty minutes. Wrap in foil and keep twenty-four hours before serving.

Sponge Roll

6 servings

Although sponge roll, burdened too frequently with the prosaic name jelly roll, is of European origin (in French it is called biscuit roulé), *it is common enough in this country to seem indigenous. But whatever its ancestry, properly made, sponge roll is one of the most excellent of desserts. The recipe below is for a sponge roll lightly flavored with almond and filled with pistachios mixed with red currant jelly. It goes well with champagne.*

4 eggs, at room temperature
¾ teaspoon baking powder
1 teaspoon salt
¾ cup granulated sugar
½ teaspoon almond extract
¾ cup sifted cake flour
Confectioners' sugar
1 12-ounce jar red currant jelly
⅓ cup shelled, skinned pistachios

1. Preheat the oven to 400 degrees.
2. Beat the eggs, preferably in an electric mixer, with the baking powder and salt until thick and light colored, gradually adding the granulated sugar. Add the almond extract and fold in the flour.
3. Turn into a jelly roll pan (15½ x 10½) that has been greased and lined with greased waxed paper. Bake fifteen minutes.
4. Turn from the pan onto a clean dish towel that has been dusted with confectioners' sugar. Quickly remove the paper and cut off the crisp edges of the cake. Roll, jelly-roll fashion, with the towel inside and enwrapping the cake. Chill.
5. Combine the jelly and pistachios. Unroll the cake, spread with the jelly-nut mixture, then roll up again.

Sponge Jelly Roll

6 servings

3 tablespoons butter, melted
4 eggs
¼ teaspoon salt
¾ cup plus 2 tablespoons granulated sugar
¾ cup sifted all-purpose flour
1 teaspoon vanilla extract
2 tablespoons confectioners' sugar
¾ cup tart currant jelly

1. Preheat the oven to 350 degrees.
2. Brush a jelly-roll pan (8 x 12) with half the melted butter. Line the pan with a large sheet of waxed paper, letting a little of the paper hang over the sides. Brush the waxed paper with the remaining melted butter and set aside.
3. Break the eggs into the bowl of an electric mixer. Add the salt and the three-quarters cup sugar. Beat until stiff or until the mixture forms a ribbon and falls back on itself when the mixer is lifted from the bowl. Carefully fold in the flour and the vanilla. Pour this into the prepared pan and spread it smooth with a rubber spatula. Bake fifteen minutes.
4. Sift together the remaining two tablespoons of granulated sugar with the confectioners' sugar. Lay out a clean dish towel and sprinkle it with the sugar mixture. When the cake is done, loosen the cake from the pan very quickly. If the edges look as though they may crack, trim them off with a knife. Turn the cake out onto the cloth and carefully peel away the waxed paper. Sprinkle the cake with a little more granulated sugar, then quickly but gently roll up like a jelly roll, with the towel inside, and let stand fifteen minutes enclosed in the cloth. Unroll and spread with a thin coating of the jelly. Roll the cake once more.

Buttercream Filling

Enough filling for 4 8-inch layers

⅔ cup granulated sugar
⅛ teaspoon cream of tartar
⅓ cup water
5 egg yolks, well beaten
1 cup soft butter
1 tablespoon Cognac

1. Combine the sugar, cream of tartar, and water in a small pan. Heat to boiling, stirring only until the sugar dissolves. Continue boiling, without stirring, until the syrup forms a soft ball and registers 240 degrees on a candy thermometer. Cool about one minute.
2. Pour the syrup onto the egg yolks while beating vigorously, and continue beating until the mixture is cool.
3. Add the butter gradually, one tablespoon at a time, until the mixture is very thick and creamy. Add the Cognac. Chill until the filling is firm enough to spread.

Buttercream Mousseline

Enough frosting for a 3-layer cake

1½ cups granulated sugar
¾ cup very strong, black espresso coffee
10 egg yolks, at room temperature
2¼ cups butter

1. Combine the sugar and coffee in a saucepan and bring to a boil. Simmer until the soft ball stage (234 to 240 degrees on a thermometer). The soft ball stage is reached when a small quantity of the liquid is dropped into ice water and does not disintegrate. The liquid flattens when picked up with the fingers.
2. Beat the egg yolks until they are quite thick and lemon colored. Gradually add the hot syrup, beating vigorously.
3. Cream the butter and pour the egg mixture into it while beating on low speed. Chill until the buttercream is of spreading consistency. If the buttercream becomes too solid, it may be left to stand at room temperature until it is spreadable.

Mocha Frosting

*Enough frosting to frost the top
and sides of a 4-layer cake and
for 1 layer of filling, if desired*

6 ounces (6 squares) semisweet chocolate
¼ cup extra-strong hot coffee
4 egg yolks
3 tablespoons confectioners' sugar, approximately
⅓ cup soft butter
⅓ cup half-firm butter
1 teaspoon vanilla extract
1 tablespoon Cognac or rum

1. Melt the chocolate in the coffee in the top part of a double boiler.
2. In an electric blender, or using an electric beater, beat the remaining ingredients until the mixture is smooth.
3. Chill until of spreading consistency. If time is a factor, a small quantity of confectioners' sugar may be added to attain spreading consistency.

Cream Cornets

2 to 3 dozen

2 egg whites
½ cup granulated sugar
3 tablespoons sifted all-purpose flour
2 tablespoons finely ground almonds
2 tablespoons melted butter
   Sweetened whipped cream

1. Preheat the oven to 450 degrees.
2. Beat the egg whites until stiff but not dry. Gradually add the sugar, beating constantly until stiff but not dry. Beat in the flour and almonds. Gradually stir in the melted butter.
3. Spoon heaping teaspoonfuls of the batter onto a well-greased cookie sheet. Spread to make rounds two inches in diameter. Prepare only six at a time. Bake until lightly browned, three to four minutes.
4. Cool a few seconds and carefully remove from the cookie sheet with a spatula. If the cookies stick, return to the oven for a minute or two. Roll to form cones. Press the overlapped ends at the wide end to seal and hold the shape.
5. Cool and, just before serving, fill with sweetened whipped cream.

Florentines

About 2 dozen cookies

½ cup heavy cream
3 tablespoons butter
½ cup granulated sugar
⅛ teaspoon salt
1¼ cups very finely chopped almonds
⅓ cup sifted enriched flour
¾ cup finely chopped Candied Orange Peel (see below)
  Chocolate Frosting (see below)

1. Preheat the oven to 350 degrees.

2. In a saucepan combine the cream, butter, sugar, and salt and bring to a boil. Remove from the heat and add the almonds, flour, and candied orange peel.

3. Drop the batter from a teaspoon onto a buttered baking sheet, leaving at least two inches between the cookies. Only bake four to six cookies at a time. Bake eight to ten minutes and watch to make certain they do not burn.

4. Using a buttered knife, remove the cookies from the baking sheet while hot. Leave them flat or bend them slightly around the greased handle of a wooden spoon. Let cool on a cake rack before frosting.

CANDIED ORANGE PEEL:

About 1 cup

4 large oranges
  Granulated sugar
1 cup water
1 teaspoon Grand Marnier

1. Carefully cut the peeling from the oranges (a swivel-bladed vegetable peeler is easiest). Cut the peel into slices and eliminate as much of the white pith as possible. Cut each slice of peel into the thinnest possible (julienne) strips.

2. Combine two cups of sugar, the water, and Grand Marnier and cook until the syrup

forms a soft ball in cold water (238 degrees on a candy thermometer). Add the orange peel and simmer ten minutes longer, or until most of the water has evaporated. Drain in a coarse sieve.

3. Drop the strips, a few at a time, in a pan containing a layer of granulated sugar. Separate the pieces with a fork. Roll until each strip is completely covered with sugar. Shake off the excess sugar and place on a rack or waxed paper to dry.

Note: Leftover candied orange peel keeps indefinitely in a tightly covered glass jar.

CHOCOLATE FROSTING:

About 1 cup

2 tablespoons sweet butter
8 ounces fine-quality sweet chocolate
1 tablespoon Grand Marnier

Melt the butter and chocolate together and stir in the Grand Marnier. Use while still hot or warm.

Tarte Tatin

6 to 8 servings

14 tablespoons sweet butter
⅔ cup white granulated sugar
7 tablespoons dark brown sugar
6 large Red Delicious apples
1 Short Crust Pastry (see below)
1 tablespoon water
   Sweetened whipped cream

1. Preheat the oven to 450 degrees.

2. The ideal dish for making this tart is a metal dish ten inches in diameter and about two inches deep. In the dish, place twelve tablespoons of the butter, one-third cup of the white sugar, and half the dark brown sugar. Blend thoroughly with the fingers and pat this mixture around the sides and bottom of the dish.

3. Peel and core the apples and slice them one-eighth to one-quarter inch thick. Arrange them in an overlapping, symmetrical, petal-like fashion over the butter and sugar base. When finished, the apples should come just to the rim of the dish and no higher.

5. Melt the remaining two tablespoons of butter and add the remaining dark brown sugar. Stir this mixture, then sprinkle it over the apples.

6. Roll out the pastry into a circle one-eighth inch thick and cut it to fit as precisely as possible over the apples. Fit the pastry over the apples, making sure it does not overlap the rim of the dish. Cut a small slit in the center of the pastry to allow the steam to escape.

7. Bake the tart for thirty minutes, or until the pastry is lightly browned.

8. Remove the dish from the oven and increase the oven heat to 550 degrees. Make a round of foil to fit over the dish to prevent the pastry from burning. Bake, covered, for forty-five minutes to one hour, until the liquid that forms around the apples has changed from a runny yellow to a dark,

oozing, sticky amber. This can be noted by carefully tilting the pan and looking under the crust. Note that oven thermostats in homes vary and it may be necessary to adjust the oven heat if the tart starts to burn. On the other hand, the oven must be hot enough to caramelize the filling.

9. When the tart is done, place a serving plate over the top of the dish, then quickly invert the tart. The apples should be dark and caramelized.

10. Melt the remaining sugar, with the water, in a thick-bottomed saucepan. When the sugar has melted and is dark amber, remove it from the heat. Using a pastry brush and working as quickly as you can, paint a thin layer of caramel over the surface of the apples. Let cool. Serve warm with sweetened whipped cream.

SHORT CRUST PASTRY:

1 10-inch pie crust

2 cups sifted all-purpose flour
1 teaspoon salt
5 tablespoons very cold shortening
5 to 7 tablespoons ice-cold water

1. Sift the flour and salt twice into a chilled bowl. Using a pastry cutter, cut in the shortening until the mixture resembles crumbs.

2. Sprinkle in the water, tossing the pastry with a two-pronged fork. Add only as much water as is necessary to hold the pastry together.

3. Do not knead, but gather the mixture into a ball, pressing lightly. Place the ball on a lightly floured board and roll out to an eighth-inch thickness.

Pots de crème, an elegant French desser

Pastry Shell

1 9-inch pastry shell

1½ cups sifted all-purpose flour
½ teaspoon salt
½ cup shortening or lard
3 tablespoons cold water

1. Place the flour and salt in a mixing bowl. With a pastry blender or two knives, cut in the shortening until the mixture has the consistency of coarse cornmeal.

2. Using a two-pronged fork, toss the mixture lightly but thoroughly while adding the water, a little at a time. When blended, gather the dough into a ball.

3. Roll the dough on a lightly floured board to a circle about one inch larger in diameter than a nine-inch pie plate. Line the plate and trim off the excess pastry, leaving a neat rim. Fold the pastry rim over and flute with the fingers.

Note: After the pie plate has been lined with pastry it may be chilled until ready for use. Or, if desired, the pastry-lined pie plate may be covered and frozen until ready for use.

For a two-crust pie, double the recipe.

Martinique Pineapple Tart

6 servings

1 large, ripe pineapple, peeled, cored, and cut into ½-inch-thick slices, or 2 no. 2 cans sliced pineapple, drained
⅓ cup kirsch
1½ cups all-purpose flour
1 tablespoon granulated sugar
¼ teaspoon salt
¼ cup butter
¼ cup shortening
1 egg yolk
Ice water
¼ cup confectioners' sugar

1. Preheat the oven to 425 degrees.

2. Soak the pineapple in the kirsch.

3. Combine the flour, granulated sugar, and salt in a bowl. Blend in the butter and shortening with a pastry blender or the fingertips. Add the egg yolk and, using a fork, mix to a dough with a tablespoon or two of ice water. Roll out on a lightly floured board or pastry cloth into a rectangle (about 12 x 4 inches).

4. Decorate the edges by crimping them with the fingers as you would a pie crust and chill twenty minutes. Prick all over with a fork and bake fifteen minutes, or until cooked and lightly browned.

5. Drain the pineapple, reserving the marinade. Pat the pineapple dry and place overlapping slices along the length of the pastry. Sprinkle with the confectioners' sugar and broil under the broiler until lightly browned.

6. Cool to room temperature and, just before serving, sprinkle with some of the kirsch marinade.

trio of orange desserts from France. Clockwise from left: bavarois à l'orange,
âteau Bretonne, soufflés à l'orange in individual shells

Chestnut-Chocolate Tarts

6 tarts

6 cold, baked tart shells, each 5 inches in
    diameter
    Chestnut-Chocolate Filling (see below)
    Rich Vanilla Cream Filling (see below)
⅓ cup heavy cream, whipped

Fill the left half of each tart shell with the
chestnut-chocolate filling and the right half
with the rich vanilla cream filling. Garnish
with a row of whipped cream down the middle of each tart.

CHESTNUT-CHOCOLATE FILLING:
¾ cup crème de marrons glacés (chestnut
    cream)
3 tablespoons butter, softened
1 square (1 ounce) unsweetened chocolate
1 teaspoon vanilla extract

Mix the chestnut cream with the softened
butter. Melt the chocolate over hot water,
cool slightly, and add. Stir in the vanilla extract. Cool.
Note: Chestnut cream is available in gourmet food stores.

RICH VANILLA CREAM FILLING:
¼ cup granulated sugar
    Dash of salt
3 tablespoons all-purpose flour
1 cup milk
1 egg, beaten
½ teaspoon vanilla extract

1. Combine the sugar, salt, and flour in a
saucepan. Gradually stir in the milk and
cook over low heat, stirring constantly, until
thickened.
2. Remove from the heat. Stir a little of
the mixture into the beaten egg and then
blend into the hot mixture. Cook over low
heat until very thick, one to two minutes.
Cool.
3. Stir in the vanilla extract.

Dessert Crêpes

12 to 18 crêpes

4 whole eggs
4 egg yolks
1 cup plus 2 tablespoons sifted all-purpose
    flour
1 cup milk
1 tablespoon melted butter
1 teaspoon granulated sugar
¼ teaspoon salt

1. Combine all the ingredients except the
sauce in a mixing bowl and beat until thoroughly smooth. The batter should have the
consistency of heavy cream. Refrigerate one
hour or longer.
2. Heat a seven-inch (size 18) crêpe pan
over moderate heat. Now is the time to test
the texture of the batter. Spoon a little batter
into the pan and quickly tilt the pan to all
sides to coat it evenly. If the batter is too
thick, stir in a little more milk. Cook the
crêpes until golden on one side, then turn
with a spatula and cook the other side until
light brown. As each crêpe is cooked, transfer to a clean dish towel and fold the towel
over it. Continue cooking until all the batter
is used. Serve the crêpes with Crêpe Sauce
(see below).

CRÊPE SAUCE:

About 1¼ cups

½ cup butter
    Juice of 2 oranges
1 cup confectioners' sugar
    Grated rind of 1 orange
2 to 4 tablespoons bourbon whisky, Cognac,
    Cointreau, or other liqueur

Combine all the ingredients in a skillet and
stir over low heat until slightly thickened.

Dessert Crêpes with Pears

24 to 30 crêpes, or 6 to 8 servings

The French pancake or crêpe has had a surge of popularity within the past decade that borders on the awesome. Ten years or so ago, we were all familiar with crêpes Suzette —and not much else. Today we serve crêpes as a first course, a main course, and a dessert. Dessert crêpes range far and wide from the old standard crêpes Suzette. One of the best, the recipe for which follows, is filled with a fresh pear conserve and served with an English custard sauce.

Crêpes are not really difficult to make. The prime necessity is a good crêpe pan that has been properly cured. This is done by pouring oil in the pan and heating it to the smoking point. Then let the oil stand overnight, pour it out, and wipe the pan carefully.

1½ cups sifted all-purpose flour
2 eggs
½ cup granulated sugar
1 teaspoon vanilla extract
¼ teaspoon salt
2½ cups milk
3 tablespoons melted butter
   Pear Conserve (see below)
2 cups Crème Anglaise (page 308)

1. Combine the flour, eggs, sugar, vanilla extract, and salt in a mixing bowl. Gradually add the milk, stirring constantly with a wire whisk. Stir in the melted butter.

2. Strain the batter into a mixing bowl.

3. Heat a seasoned six- to seven-inch crêpe pan and brush it lightly with butter. Ladle a little of the batter in at a time, swirling the pan around until the bottom is thoroughly covered with a thin coating. Cook until lightly browned on one side. Flip or turn the crêpe in the pan and cook briefly on the other side. It will not or should not be brown on the second side. Continue making crêpes until all the batter is used.

4. Place one crêpe on a hot dessert plate, spoon a little hot pear conserve down the center and roll the crêpe quickly. Place another on the plate, fill, and roll. Repeat with a third crêpe. Spoon the hot sauce over and serve immediately.

5. Continue until all the crêpes are served.

PEAR CONSERVE:

Stuffing for 24 to 30 crêpes

10 ripe but firm pears
1 cup granulated sugar
¼ cup water
½ teaspoon vanilla extract
½ cup chopped crystallized ginger

1. Peel the pears and drop them into cold water. This will prevent them from darkening. Slice each pear in half and, using a melon ball cutter, scoop away the tough, round seed portion. Using a knife, cut away the small stringy part from the seed section to the stem. Turn each pear half cut side down and slice very thin.

2. Combine the sugar and water in a skillet and cook until the syrup is caramel colored. Do not burn. Add the pear slices, vanilla extract, and crystallized ginger and simmer until the pears are tender and thickened, twenty to thirty minutes. Use as a filling for crêpes.

Bavarian Cream

12 to 14 servings

2 packages unflavored gelatin
¾ cup orange juice
8 egg yolks
1 cup plus 3 tablespoons granulated sugar
1 tablespoon cornstarch
1½ cups boiling milk
6 egg whites
⅛ teaspoon salt
¾ cup heavy cream, whipped
¾ cup finely chopped mixed glacé fruit soaked in ¼ cup dark rum

1. Soak the gelatin in the juice.

2. Beat the egg yolks, one cup of the sugar, and the cornstarch together until well mixed.

3. Beat in the milk. Place the mixture in a heavy pan and heat, stirring, over medium heat until the mixture thickens and coats the back of the spoon. Do not boil.

4. Add the softened gelatin to the hot custard and stir to dissolve the gelatin. Allow to cool to room temperature.

5. Beat the egg whites and salt until frothy. Add the remaining sugar and beat until stiff but not dry. Fold into the cooled custard.

6. Fold in the cream and the fruit soaked in the rum. Pour into one large mold (ten to twelve cups) or two that stack one on top of the other (with similar combined capacity). The molds should be rinsed with cold water or very lightly oiled. Any leftover mixture can be poured into custard cups.

7. Refrigerate four to five hours or overnight.

Chocolate Bavarian Cream

8 servings

It may be a shaggy play on words but one wit, in speaking of gelatin desserts, stated that many are cold but few are frozen. Among the best of the gelatin desserts are the Bavarian creams, and not the least of their virtues is their infinite variety. They range from basic vanilla to the novelty of Nesselrode to chocolate, which is choice. A Bavarian cream —or bavarois, *as it is known in French—is not difficult to make and is an excellent dessert for summer.*

5 egg yolks
½ cup granulated sugar
1 cup milk
3 squares (3 ounces) semisweet chocolate
1 square (1 ounce) unsweetened chocolate
1½ tablespoons (1½ envelopes) unflavored gelatin
1 tablespoon cold water
1 cup heavy cream
Whipped cream

1. Place the egg yolks and sugar in the bowl of an electric mixer and beat until light and lemon colored.

2. Heat the milk in a saucepan and add the semisweet and unsweetened chocolate squares. Stir until dissolved, blended, and smooth.

3. Soften the gelatin in the cold water, then add it to the hot chocolate mixture. Stir until dissolved.

4. Start beating the yolk mixture once more and gradually pour and scrape it into the chocolate mixture. When the two are thoroughly blended, pour the mixture into a round-bottomed mixing bowl. Place this bowl in a larger bowl containing ice. Stir with a rubber spatula, over and around the bottom of the bowl, until the mixture starts

to thicken. Take care, because the mixture will seem quite liquid for several minutes and suddenly start to thicken.

5. Beat the cream until it stands in soft, firm peaks, but do not beat until stiff.

6. Using the rubber spatula, fold the cream into the Bavarian mixture. Rinse a six-cup mold with cold water. Pour the mixture into the mold and refrigerate until set. Unmold by dipping the mold briefly in warm water and decorate with whipped cream.

Coffee Charlotte

8 servings

12 ladyfingers, split
2 tablespoons instant coffee
¼ teaspoon salt
⅔ cup granulated sugar
2 envelopes unflavored gelatin
3 cups milk
¼ cup Cognac
2 cups heavy cream, whipped
   Shaved chocolate

1. Line a spring-form pan with the ladyfingers.

2. Combine the instant coffee, salt, sugar, and gelatin in a saucepan. Add the milk and stir over low heat until the sugar and gelatin are dissolved. Remove from the heat and add the Cognac. Chill until the mixture mounds slightly, then fold in the whipped cream.

3. Pour the mixture into the lined pan and chill until firm. To serve, unmold and garnish with shaved chocolate.

Bavarois à l' Orange

8 servings

4 egg yolks
½ cup granulated sugar
⅛ teaspoon salt
1¾ cups milk
1 envelope unflavored gelatin
¼ cup cold orange juice
2 tablespoons Grand Marnier or Cointreau
1 cup heavy cream
   Sweetened orange sections

1. Place a small, heavy saucepan on an asbestos pad or Flame Tamer over medium heat. Add the egg yolks, sugar, and salt. Beat with a wire whisk or rotary beater until lemon colored and fluffy.

2. Meanwhile, heat the milk without boiling. Gradually pour the milk into the egg yolk mixture, beating with the whisk. Start stirring with a wooden spoon and stir continuously until the custard coats the spoon. Do not overcook or the mixture will curdle. To test for doneness, remove the spoon from the sauce and run a finger down the center. When done, the finger will leave a clear space with a custard coating on either side.

3. Soften the gelatin in the orange juice and add to the hot custard. Stir until the gelatin is thoroughly dissolved. Stir in the Grand Marnier and pour the mixture into a mixing bowl. Chill.

4. Whip the cream and fold it into the custard with a rubber spatula. Rinse out a one-quart ring mold with cold water and pour in the custard. Chill four hours or longer. To unmold, dip in warm water. Serve filled with sweetened orange sections.

Spiced Apple Charlotte

6 servings

4 cups finely diced apples
¾ cup granulated sugar
¼ teaspoon salt
½ teaspoon ground cloves
¼ teaspoon grated lemon rind
½ cup orange juice
3 tablespoons medium dry sherry
¼ cup butter, melted
3 cups soft fresh bread crumbs

1. Preheat the oven to 350 degrees.
2. Mix the apples with the sugar, salt, cloves, lemon rind, orange juice, and sherry. Set aside.
3. Combine the melted butter and the bread crumbs, mixing well. Fill a buttered one-quart casserole with alternating layers of bread crumbs and the apple mixture, beginning and ending with bread crumbs.
4. Cover the pudding and bake for thirty minutes. Remove the cover and bake for about fifteen minutes longer, or until the crumbs are brown and the apples are tender. Serve warm, with cream.

Crème Brûlée

8 to 10 servings

4 cups heavy cream
¼ cup granulated sugar
8 egg yolks
¼ teaspoon salt
2 teaspoons vanilla extract
1 cup sifted light brown sugar

1. Preheat the oven to 275 degrees.
2. Place the cream in a double boiler and heat but do not boil. Add the sugar and stir until dissolved.
3. Beat the egg yolks well and add the salt and vanilla extract. Stir the hot cream into the egg mixture. Pour the mixture into an oblong baking dish (10 x 6). The custard should be about one and one-half inches thick. Place the dish in a larger dish and pour boiling water around it.
4. Place in the oven and bake about one hour, or until set. Remove from the oven and let stand until cool, then refrigerate until thoroughly chilled. Remove the custard from the refrigerator and sprinkle with an even, one-quarter-inch layer of light brown sugar.
5. Place the sugar-topped custard under the broiler. Cook quickly, just until the sugar melts and runs together. Return to the refrigerator until thoroughly chilled. Just before serving, shatter the glaze by tapping lightly with a knife.

Almond Crème Brûlée

6 servings

3 cups heavy cream
6 tablespoons granulated sugar
6 egg yolks
1 teaspoon vanilla extract
½ teaspoon almond extract
½ cup blanched almonds
½ cup light brown sugar

1. Preheat the oven to 300 degrees.

2. Heat the cream over boiling water and stir in the sugar.

3. Beat the egg yolks until light in color and pour the hot cream gradually over them, stirring rapidly. Stir in the vanilla and almond extracts and strain the mixture into a one-quart baking dish. Stir in the almonds. Put the dish in a pan containing one inch of hot water and bake for thirty-five minutes, or until a silver knife blade inserted in the center comes out clean. Do not overbake. Chill thoroughly.

4. Before serving, cover the surface of the cream with the brown sugar. Set the dish on a bed of cracked ice and put under a broiler flame until the sugar is brown and melted. Serve immediately or chill again and serve cold.

Bread-and-Butter Custard

4 to 6 servings

3 eggs
⅔ cup granulated sugar
⅓ teaspoon grated nutmeg
¼ teaspoon salt
3 cups half-and-half or milk
4 slices of white bread, crusts trimmed
¼ cup butter, at room temperature

1. Preheat the oven to 350 degrees.

2. Beat the eggs with the sugar, nutmeg, and salt until light. Add the half-and-half slowly, while stirring. Strain the mixture into a medium-sized baking dish.

3. Spread one side of the slices of bread with the butter and arrange them, slightly overlapping, buttered side up, on the custard mixture. Bake forty-five minutes, or until a knife inserted in the center comes out clean. Serve warm.

English Custard with Chestnuts

About 3 cups

1 cup milk
1 cup heavy cream
6 egg yolks
½ cup granulated sugar
⅛ teaspoon salt
1 teaspoon vanilla extract
½ cup coarsely chopped bottled chestnuts in syrup
¼ cup liquid from bottled chestnuts in syrup

1. Combine the milk and cream in a saucepan and bring just to a boil.

2. Meanwhile, combine the egg yolks and sugar in a mixing bowl and beat thoroughly until light yellow and thickened. Gradually pour the milk and cream into the egg yolk mixture, stirring vigorously with a whisk. Add the salt and vanilla.

3. Transfer the mixture to a saucepan and stir over very low heat (preferably with the saucepan on an asbestos pad or Flame Tamer). Use a wooden spoon to stir, taking care that it covers the entire bottom of the saucepan. Cook, stirring, without boiling until the sauce coats the spoon with an obvious creamy layer. Do not overcook, or the sauce will curdle. Let cool, then chill. Stir in the chestnuts and chestnut liquid.

Rum Custard

6 servings

1 cup milk
2 tablespoons granulated sugar
6 egg yolks
2 tablespoons heavy cream
3 tablespoons rum
24 ladyfingers, split

1. Combine the milk and sugar in the top of a double boiler. Stir until the sugar dissolves and milk is quite hot.
2. Beat the egg yolks with the cream until light and creamy, then pour into the hot milk mixture, stirring constantly. Continue stirring until the mixture coats the spoon. Stir in the rum.
3. Line six sherbet glasses with four ladyfingers each and pour the custard into them. Serve warm or cold.

Lemon Sponge Custard

4 to 6 servings

¾ cup granulated sugar
2 tablespoons butter, at room temperature
2 teaspoons grated lemon peel
3 eggs, separated
3 tablespoons all-purpose flour
¼ cup lemon juice
1 cup light cream or milk
⅛ teaspoon salt
  Whipped cream (optional)

1. Preheat the oven to 350 degrees.
2. Cream the sugar, butter and lemon peel together. Add the egg yolks and beat well with a wooden spoon.
3. Stir in alternately the flour, lemon juice, and cream.
4. Beat the egg whites with the salt until stiff, then fold them into the egg yolk mixture. Pour the batter into a seven-inch ovenproof dish and set the dish in a larger pan filled with one inch of hot water. Bake the custard one hour, or until set. Serve hot or cold, with whipped cream, if desired.

Mont Blanc with Chestnut Puree

6 or more servings

1 15½-ounce can unsweetened chestnut puree
1½ cups whipped cream, sweetened
  Candied violets

1. Spoon the chestnut puree into a ricer and hold the ricer over a serving dish. Squeeze the ricer and allow the puree to fall into a high-piled mound.
2. Garnish the top with whipped cream and decorate with candied violets.

Oeufs à la Neige

(Eggs in the Snow)

10 or more servings

4 cups milk
1¼ cups granulated sugar
1 vanilla bean or 1 teaspoon vanilla extract
6 eggs, separated
½ teaspoon cornstarch
Pinch of salt
Kirsch or rum (optional)
¼ cup water

1. Bring the milk to a boil in a skillet. Add six tablespoons of the sugar and the vanilla bean or vanilla extract. Stir to dissolve the sugar.

2. Beat the egg whites until stiff. While beating, gradually add six more tablespoons sugar, the cornstarch, and the salt.

3. When the meringue is stiff, use two large spoons to shape it into egg-shaped ovals. Drop a few at a time into the simmering milk.

4. Cook about thirty seconds on one side, then, using a slotted spoon, gently turn the "eggs" over. Poach the other sides thirty seconds.

5. Drain the "eggs," which should be quite firm by now, on paper toweling. Let cool while preparing the remainder of the recipe.

6. Strain the milk in which the "eggs" cooked. If a vanilla bean was used, remove it, rinse, and wipe dry, then store in sugar for another use.

7. Beat the egg yolks until light and lemon colored. Gradually pour into the strained milk. Stir over low heat just until the custard coats the spoon.

8. The custard may be flavored with kirsch or rum. In any event, strain the custard into a wide, shallow serving dish and cover with the "eggs." Chill.

9. Combine the remaining sugar with the quarter cup water in a saucepan. Cook until the caramel is dark amber in color, but do not let it burn.

10. Before the caramel has a chance to set, pour it in a thin thread all over the tops of the "eggs."

Pots de Crème

6 to 8 servings

A pot de crème—which is, precisely as the name implies, a cream dessert served in a small pot—is one of the most elegant dishes in the French repertory. It is also easy to prepare.

2 cups heavy cream
4 egg yolks
5 tablespoons granulated sugar
⅛ teaspoon salt
1 tablespoon grated orange rind
2 tablespoons Grand Marnier
Candied violets (optional)

1. Place the cream in a saucepan and bring it almost but not quite to a boil.

2. Meanwhile, beat the egg yolks, sugar, and salt until light and lemon colored. Gradually add the cream to the egg yolks, stirring with a wire whisk.

3. Place the saucepan over low heat (using an asbestos pad or double boiler) and stir with a wooden spoon until the custard thickens and coats the spoon. Immediately set it in a basin of cold water to stop the cooking action.

4. Stir in the grated rind and Grand Marnier. Pour the custard into individual crème pots or custard cups and chill thoroughly. Garnish each, if desired, with a candied violet.

Coeurs à la Crème with Sauce

6 servings

5 ounces cream cheese, at room temperature
1 1½-inch piece vanilla bean or ½ teaspoon pure vanilla extract
¼ cup confectioners' sugar
1 cup heavy cream
1 pint strawberries
¼ cup sherry
¾ cup currant jelly

1. Soften the cream cheese and beat with an electric beater.
2. Split the vanilla bean and scrape the seeds into the cheese. Continue beating, adding the sugar gradually.
3. Whip the cream until stiff and fold it into the cheese.
4. Rinse out six pieces of cheesecloth in cold water and use them to line six small coeur à la crème molds. Spoon equal portions of the cream mixture into the molds. Bring up the overlapping ends of the cheesecloth and fold lightly over the top of each portion of cheese. Chill thoroughly.
5. Meanwhile, trim and rinse the strawberries. Drain. Blend the wine and jelly and cook over low heat, stirring, until blended and smooth. Combine with the strawberries.
6. Unmold the cheese onto chilled dessert plates and serve the strawberries and Crème Fraîche (see below) on the side. Pass a sugar bowl for those who wish it.

CRÈME FRAÎCHE:

About 1 cup

1 cup heavy cream
1 tablespoon buttermilk

1. Combine the cream and buttermilk in a jar with a screw top. Secure the top and shake the mixture for a second or two.
2. Let the mixture stand eight to twelve hours, or until the cream is lightly thickened.

Marquise de Chocolat

About 12 servings

8 ounces semisweet chocolate bits
1 cup sweet butter
¼ cup superfine granulated sugar
6 eggs, separated
2 tablespoons Grand Marnier
   Finely shaved chocolate or crushed macaroons

1. Melt the chocolate with the butter and three tablespoons of the sugar over low heat.
2. Place the egg yolks in the bowl of an electric mixer. Add the chocolate mixture gradually and beat on high speed ten minutes.
3. Beat the egg whites until stiff and add the remaining tablespoon sugar. Add to the egg yolk mixture. Add the Grand Marnier and beat on high speed another ten minutes. Pour the mixture into a buttered two-quart soufflé dish. Refrigerate twelve hours.
4. Unmold two hours before serving by dipping the bottom and sides of the soufflé dish in hot water. Run a sharp knife around the sides of the mold to loosen and invert the mold onto a serving plate. Smooth the surface of the chocolate mold with a knife and cover with shaved chocolate or crushed macaroons. Refrigerate again until serving time.

French Bread-and-Butter Pudding

6 to 8 servings

It is at once the most naive and the most sophisticated of desserts. British and Americans call it "bread-and-butter pudding"; French menus list it as "bread-and-butter pouding." It is reputedly the favorite dessert of the Duchess of Windsor, who in years past ate it frequently when dining at Le Pavillon in New York. This version is made with candied fruits, French bread, a generous splash of kirsch, and heavy cream. A glass of sauterne is an excellent accompaniment.

½ cup mixed candied fruit
¼ cup kirsch
½ cup dried raisins
   Butter
10 small thin slices French bread
1 quart milk
1 cup cream
1 cup granulated sugar
5 eggs
4 egg yolks
1 teaspoon vanilla extract
   Confectioners' sugar

1. Combine the candied fruit and kirsch in a small mixing bowl and set aside.
2. Place the raisins in another small bowl and add boiling water to cover. Let stand five minutes, then drain.
3. Generously butter one side of the bread and set aside.
4. Preheat the oven to 375 degrees.
5. Combine the milk and cream and bring just to a boil, then remove from the heat. Add the sugar and stir until dissolved. Combine the eggs and egg yolks, beat lightly, and add to the liquid. Stir in the vanilla extract.
6. Butter a two-quart oval baking dish. Drain the candied fruits and sprinkle over the bottom of the baking dish. Sprinkle with raisins.
7. Arrange the bread slices, buttered side up, over the fruit. Strain the custard over the bread and fruit. Place the baking dish in a larger dish and pour boiling water around it. Set in the oven and bake about forty minutes, or just until set. If desired, sprinkle lightly with confectioners' sugar and run briefly under the broiler to glaze.

Farina Pudding Mold

6 servings

⅓ cup quick-cooking farina
1 envelope unflavored gelatin
¼ teaspoon salt
⅓ cup granulated sugar
2 cups milk
2 eggs, separated
1 cup heavy cream
2 tablespoons kirsch or 1½ teaspoons vanilla extract
   Bing cherries flamed with orange liqueur

1. Place the farina, gelatin, salt, and sugar in a pan. Gradually stir in the milk. Bring to a boil, stirring.
2. Add a small amount of the hot mixture to the beaten egg yolks, then return to the pan and bring the mixture to a boil, but do not boil. Remove from the heat and cool.
3. Stir in half of the cream. Beat the egg whites until stiff but not dry, then whip the remaining cream. Gently fold the whipped cream, the kirsch or vanilla, and the egg whites into the farina mixture. Pour into a lightly oiled three-cup mold and chill.
4. Unmold and serve with Bing cherries, flamed with orange liqueur.

Rice Pudding à la Française

8 servings

PUDDING:

½ cup uncooked rice
3 cups milk
½ teaspoon grated lemon rind
½ teaspoon grated orange rind
½ envelope unflavored gelatin
2 tablespoons cold water
½ cup mixed candied fruits or citron
⅓ cup kirsch or rum
3 egg yolks
¾ cup granulated sugar
¼ teaspoon pure vanilla extract
1 cup heavy cream

SAUCE:

1 cup seedless red raspberry jam or apricot nectar
  Kirsch (if apricot nectar is used)
¾ cup granulated sugar (if apricot nectar is used)
2 teaspoons lemon juice (if apricot nectar is used)
½ cup dark rum (if apricot nectar is used)

1. Combine the rice and milk in a saucepan and bring to a boil. Add the grated lemon and orange rinds. Simmer about twenty minutes, then cover and cook over low heat twenty minutes longer, or until the rice is tender. Soak the gelatin in the cold water and stir into the cooked, hot rice mixture.

2. Meanwhile, place the mixed candied fruits or citron in a mixing bowl and add the kirsch or rum. Let stand.

3. Beat the egg yolks with the sugar until light and lemon colored. Add the vanilla and beat.

4. Beat the rice mixture into the egg yolk mixture, then return this to the saucepan and bring to a boil, but only for one second. Do not let it boil for more than a second or it will curdle. Let the mixture cool, then stir in the candied fruits and the marinating liqueur. Chill until it starts to thicken slightly.

5. Lightly oil the inside of a one-and-one-half-quart ring mold.

6. Beat the cream until it stands in soft peaks (about three-quarters the usual beating for whipped cream) and fold into the rice mixture. Pour into the mold. Refrigerate overnight.

7. To unmold, dip in warm water. Serve with a sauce made of raspberry jam thinned with kirsch and a little water. Or make an apricot sauce by cooking the apricot nectar and sugar for five minutes. Remove from the heat and stir in the lemon juice and one-half cup dark rum.

Papuan Rice Pudding

8 to 10 servings

⅔ cup uncooked rice
5 cups milk
3 eggs, separated
1⅔ cups granulated sugar
½ teaspoon salt
1½ teaspoons grated lemon rind
2½ teaspoons vanilla extract
2 tablespoons butter
¾ teaspoon nutmeg

1. Simmer the rice in the milk for one and one-half hours, until very tender.

2. Preheat the oven to 325 degrees.

3. Beat the egg yolks lightly and add them to the cooked rice. Add one and one-third cups of the sugar, the salt, lemon rind, one and one-half teaspoons of the vanilla extract, and the butter. Turn into a buttered two-quart casserole and sprinkle with the ground nutmeg.

4. Set the casserole in a pan of hot water and bake for two and one-half to three hours, until a knife inserted in the center comes out clean.

5. Top the pudding with a meringue made from the three egg whites beaten until stiff with the remaining teaspoon of vanilla and one-third cup sugar. Bake for fifteen minutes more and serve warm.

Riz à l' Impératrice

8 to 10 servings

Puddings are a little like olives or snails. Either you like them or you don't. For those who dote on such dishes, there are few desserts more sublime than a creamy, rich ring of rice lightly laced with a liqueur or just a trace of vanilla. Rice puddings span the range from naive to sophisticated. Below is a sophisticated, classically elegant dessert.

  4 ounces finely chopped mixed glacé fruits
  ¼ cup kirsch or orange liqueur
1½ envelopes unflavored gelatin
  ½ cup uncooked rice
3⅙ cups milk
  1 cup granulated sugar
  2 tablespoons butter
  2 teaspoons vanilla extract
  5 egg yolks
  1 teaspoon cornstarch
  3 tablespoons apricot preserves, sieved
  1 cup heavy cream, whipped

1. Preheat the oven to 300 degrees.
2. Combine the fruits, kirsch, and gelatin and set aside.
3. Add the rice to a large kettle of boiling water and cook for five minutes. Drain well.

4. Combine one and two-thirds cups of the milk with one-quarter cup of the sugar and the butter in a saucepan and bring to a boil. Stir in the drained rice and one teaspoon of the vanilla extract. Pour the mixture into a one-quart casserole, cover with aluminum foil, and bake for forty minutes, or until the rice is tender and the milk absorbed.

5. Beat the egg yolks until thick. Gradually add the remaining sugar slowly, continuing to beat, until the mixture is thick and lemon colored. Bring the remaining milk to a boil and beat in along with the cornstarch. Pour the mixture into a heavy pan and heat, stirring, until the custard coats the back of a spoon. Do not allow the custard to boil or the eggs will curdle.

6. Remove from the heat and stir in the fruit mixture until the gelatin is dissolved. Add the remaining vanilla and the apricot preserves.

7. Gradually stir in the rice. Cool, then chill until cold but not set. Fold in the whipped cream. Pour into an oiled mold or basin and cover with oiled waxed paper. Chill for at least four hours or overnight.

8. Unmold onto a chilled platter and surround with a strawberry sauce.

Soufflé Sarah Bernhardt

6 servings

½ cup Curaçao
12 macaroons
3 tablespoons butter
3 tablespoons all-purpose flour
1 cup milk
⅓ cup granulated sugar
5 egg yolks
1½ teaspoons vanilla extract
7 egg whites
¼ teaspoon salt

1. Preheat the oven to 375 degrees.
2. Pour Curaçao over the macaroons and allow them to soak up the liquor.
3. Melt the butter in a saucepan, add the flour, and cook until bubbling. Remove from the heat and add the milk and sugar. Return to the heat and cook, stirring constantly, until thick and smooth. Set aside to cool slightly.
4. Beat the egg yolks and add to the custard. Add the vanilla. The mixture should be the consistency of mayonnaise. If too thin, return to the fire and cook over low heat, stirring vigorously until thickened.
5. Beat the egg whites with the salt until stiff but not dry. Mix about one-third of the egg whites into the egg yolk mixture, then fold in the remaining egg whites very lightly. Pour half the mixture into a buttered and sugared one-and-one-half-quart soufflé dish. Add half the macaroons and then add the remaining soufflé mixture. Place the remaining macaroons around the edge of dish. Bake twenty-five minutes. Do not overcook; the soufflé should be very moist in the center.
Note: You may bake the soufflé on the bottom shelf at 350 degrees for one-half hour.

Chocolate Soufflé

4 servings

Cake flour
3½ ounces (3½ squares) semisweet baking chocolate
2 tablespoons strong coffee
3 tablespoons cornstarch
1 cup milk
⅓ cup plus 1 tablespoon granulated sugar
2 tablespoons softened butter
5 egg whites
⅛ teaspoon salt
3 egg yolks
Confectioners' sugar

1. Preheat the oven to 375 degrees.
2. Grease a one and one-half-quart soufflé dish and dust lightly with cake flour.
3. Put the chocolate and coffee in the top part of a double boiler and heat over hot water until the chocolate is melted.
4. Blend the cornstarch with a little milk. Beat in the remaining milk and one-third cup of the sugar.
5. Bring the milk to a boil, stirring. Simmer for three or four seconds, then remove from heat and beat in the chocolate. Divide the butter over the surface of the mixture. Cool to lukewarm.
6. Beat the egg whites and salt together until soft peaks form. Sprinkle with the remaining sugar and beat until stiff.
7. Beat the egg yolks into chocolate mixture, then gently fold in the egg whites, adding gradually. Pour into the prepared soufflé dish.
8. Bake for forty-five minutes, or until a straw plunged into the soufflé comes out clean. Sprinkle with confectioners' sugar and serve immediately.

Cold Chocolate Soufflé

6 to 8 servings

1 tablespoon unflavored gelatin
¼ cup cold water
3 ounces dark sweet chocolate
1 cup milk
½ cup confectioners' sugar
Pinch of salt
1 teaspoon vanilla extract or 1 tablespoon strong coffee or 1 tablespoon brandy or rum
2 cups heavy cream
Sweetened whipped cream (optional)
Shaved chocolate (optional)

1. Soften the gelatin in the cold water.
2. Melt the chocolate in a double boiler over simmering water and add the milk. Beat with a rotary beater until smooth. Remove from the heat and stir in the gelatin. Add the sugar and salt and stir until the gelatin is dissolved. Let cool slightly, then add the flavoring. Let cool until just beginning to set.
3. Whip the cream until stiff. Beat chocolate mixture until smooth, then add, a little at a time, to the whipped cream, beating each time until smooth. Pour into a one-and-one-half-quart soufflé dish and chill. The soufflé may be garnished with sweetened whipped cream and a little shaved chocolate.

Lemon Soufflé

6 servings

3 tablespoons butter
3 tablespoons all-purpose flour
1 cup milk
½ cup granulated sugar
1 teaspoon grated lemon rind
3 tablespoons lemon juice
4 eggs, separated
½ teaspoon cream of tartar

1. Preheat the oven to 325 degrees.
2. Melt the butter in a saucepan over low heat. Stir in the flour. Add the milk and sugar and cook over low heat, stirring constantly, until thickened; do not boil.
3. Stir in the lemon rind and juice and remove from the heat.
4. Beat the egg yolks until thick and lemon colored. Stir in a little of the hot mixture and return to the saucepan, blending.
5. Beat the egg whites until foamy. Sprinkle with the cream of tartar and continue beating until stiff. Blend about one quarter of the beaten egg whites into the lemon mixture, then fold in the remaining egg whites.
6. Pour the mixture into an ungreased one-and-one-half-quart soufflé dish. Bake for fifty to sixty minutes, or until puffed and lightly browned. Serve at once, with thawed frozen raspberries or whipped cream.

Soufflés à l' Orange

6 servings

A dessert with a difference is individual orange soufflés, an idea adopted from a small country inn in Burgundy. They are easy enough to make, the important thing being to prepare the orange shells without breaking them. The best oranges for the soufflés are the largest available in the markets.

6 hostess sugar dots or 1½ hostess sugar
 tablets
7 very large navel oranges
2 teaspoons orange juice
3 tablespoons butter
3 tablespoons all-purpose flour
¾ cup milk
3 eggs, separated
6 tablespoons granulated sugar
6 tablespoons Curaçao

1. Rub the hostess dots or tablets all over one of the oranges until the dots are covered with the zest, oil, and color of the orange skin. Place the dots in a small bowl and add the orange juice.

2. Prepare the remaining oranges for filling. To do this, cut off a slice from three-quarters inch to one inch off the navel end of each. Using a spoon, carefully scoop out the insides of the oranges, leaving the natural shell. Save the scooped-out part for another use. It will not be used in this recipe.

3. Cut off the thinnest possible slice from the stem end of each prepared orange to make a base on which the orange will stand upright. (If a hole is punctured in the bottom of an orange, it may be patched with a small slice from the top.)

4. Preheat the oven to 450 degrees.

5. Melt the butter in a saucepan and stir in the flour, using a wire whisk. When blended, add the milk, stirring rapidly with the whisk. Cook, stirring constantly, until the sauce is thickened and smooth. Remove the sauce from the heat and add the egg yolks, beating rapidly with the whisk. Return the sauce to the heat and bring just to a boil, stirring rapidly with the whisk. Do not cook for more than a split second or the sauce will curdle.

6. Remove the saucepan from the heat and stir in the granulated sugar. Add the softened hostess dots and beat well. Let cool twenty minutes. Stir in the liqueur.

7. Place the empty orange shells on a baking sheet and bake about five minutes.

8. Meanwhile, beat the whites until stiff and stir half of them into the sauce. Fold in the remaining whites, using a wooden spatula. Divide the soufflé mixture among the six orange shells and bake about ten minutes, or until the soufflés are puffed and browned.

Chestnut Mousse

6 to 8 servings

The French chef who first dubbed a mousse a mousse had a felicitous way with words as well as food. Mousse means froth, and that's all it is—a bit of fluff made stable with a touch of gelatin. Mousses come in many flavors, but few are the equal of the delicacy on this page, a chestnut mousse lightly laced with rum and served with a rich English custard. It is the recipe of chef Marcel Gosselin, the former owner of Manhattan's L'Armorique restaurant.

1 15½-ounce can unsweetened chestnut puree
2 cups milk
9 tablespoons granulated sugar
2 envelopes unflavored gelatin
½ teaspoon vanilla extract
6 egg yolks
2 tablespoons dark rum or Grand Marnier
1 cup heavy cream

1. Blend the chestnut puree with the milk and stir in the sugar. Beat with a wire whisk until smooth. Add the gelatin and bring to a boil, then stir in the vanilla.
2. Beat the egg yolks in a mixing bowl and beat in a little of the hot sauce. Add the egg yolk mixture to the hot sauce, stirring rapidly. Cook, stirring, until the mixture thickens slightly. Do not boil. Stir in the rum or Grand Marnier and strain the mixture through a sieve into a mixing bowl. Let cool, but do not let it start to jell.
3. Whip the cream and fold it into the chestnut mixture. Pour into a lightly oiled one-and-one-half-quart mold and refrigerate several hours until firm. Unmold and serve, with two cups of English Custard with Chestnuts (page 295) as a sauce on the side.

Lemon Mousse

6 servings

2 lemons
4 eggs, separated
¼ cup granulated sugar
1 tablespoon gelatin
¾ cup heavy cream
Sweetened whipped cream
Toasted slivered almonds

1. Grate the rind of the lemons and reserve. Squeeze the juice and reserve.
2. Combine the egg yolks with the rind and sugar and beat vigorously until the mixture is light and lemon colored.
3. Combine the lemon juice and gelatin and let stand ten minutes. Heat the mixture over low heat or hot water until the gelatin dissolves, then stir it into the egg yolk mixture.
4. Whisk the cream until thick and fold it into the mousse mixture. Whip the egg whites and fold them in.
5. Attach a buttered paper collar around the top of a one-quart soufflé dish and pour in the mousse mixture. Chill at least two hours. Before serving, remove the collar and decorate the top of the mousse with whipped cream and toasted almonds.

It may very well melt, but it surely won't fall, this frozen soufflé, another caprice in the repertoire of French pastry chefs. And it is altogether delicious, a frozen cream with a hundred variations. There is a distinct advantage that the frozen version has over the baked soufflé. A frozen soufflé will keep in the refrigerator for hours before serving, and properly cared for it could keep for days.

Soufflé Glacé with Candied Fruit

8 servings

- 5 egg yolks
- 5 whole eggs
- 1½ cups granulated sugar
- ¾ cup chopped candied fruit
- ¼ cup kirsch or Cognac
- 2 cups heavy cream

1. To make this dessert it is best to have a portable electric beater and a standard electric beater with a sound motor. Put the egg yolks and eggs in the mixing bowl of an electric beater. Set the bowl in a kettle containing hot water and set the kettle over low heat. Start beating with the portable beater and gradually add the sugar. The egg yolk mixture should become thick and like a soft meringue, several times the original volume. The beating time should be ten to fifteen minutes.

2. Remove the mixing bowl from the kettle and set the bowl in place in the standard beater. Start beating and continue until the egg yolk mixture reaches room temperature.

3. Meanwhile, soak the fruit in the kirsch. Fold the fruit and kirsch into the egg yolk mixture.

4. Whip the cream until stiff and fold it into the egg yolk mixture.

5. Arrange an aluminum foil or waxed paper collar around the top of a one-and-one-half-quart soufflé dish. Pour the soufflé mixture into the dish and place in the freezer. Freeze until fairly solid.

Vanilla Soufflé Glacé

6 servings

- 1 cup milk
- 1 cup light cream
- 1 length (1 inch) of vanilla bean
- 4 egg yolks
- ½ cup granulated sugar
- 2 cups heavy cream, whipped
- 1 tablespoon cocoa

1. Heat the milk, light cream, and pulp from the vanilla bean to boiling.

2. Meanwhile, beat the egg yolks with the sugar until thick and light colored.

3. Beat some of the hot liquid into the egg mixture. Return to the pan and heat, stirring, until the mixture coats the back of the spoon. Strain through a fine sieve. Cool to room temperature.

4. Fold in the cream and pour into a one-quart soufflé dish fitted with a two-inch-high, lightly greased waxed paper collar. Freeze until firm. Before serving, remove the paper collar and sprinkle with cocoa through a sieve.

SOUFFLÉ GLACÉ VARIATIONS:

There are a hundred ways to vary the composition of a soufflé glacé. The basic mixture may be seasoned with very strong coffee, with numerous spirits and liqueurs, such as rum, Cognac, or Grand Marnier, and with melted chocolate. Toasted almonds or pistachio nuts are delicious folded into the basic mixture.

Banana Ice Cream

1¼ quarts or 6 to 8 servings

Peel and mash four sweet, ripe but firm bananas. Put them through a sieve or food mill. Prepare the recipe for French Vanilla Ice Cream (see below), but omit the vanilla. Stir the banana pulp into the custard mixture and add one and one-third tablespoons lemon juice. Freeze according to standard freezer instructions.

French Vanilla Ice Cream

1¼ quarts or 6 to 8 servings

2 cups milk
½ cup granulated sugar
⅛ teaspoon salt
4 egg yolks, lightly beaten
1 cup heavy cream
2 teaspoons pure vanilla extract

1. Bring the milk almost but not quite to a boil.
2. Combine the sugar, salt, and egg yolks in the top of a double boiler. Beat the mixture lightly with a wire whisk.
3. Continue stirring over hot water, but with a wooden spoon. Cook until the mixture coats the spoon, then cool and strain into a mixing bowl.
4. Stir in the milk, cream, and vanilla. Freeze according to standard freezer instructions.

Strawberry Ice Cream

18 or more servings

3 quarts whole strawberries
1¾ cups granulated sugar, approximately
8 egg yolks
¼ teaspoon salt
4 cups milk
2 2-inch lengths of vanilla bean or ½ teaspoon pure vanilla extract
4 cups heavy cream

1. Remove the stems from the strawberries, then pick over the berries to remove any overripe or bruised ones. Crush the berries and add one-quarter cup of the sugar. Blend and set aside.
2. In the bowl of an electric mixer combine the egg yolks with one and one-half cups sugar and beat until thick and lemon colored. Add the salt.
3. Meanwhile, bring the milk almost but not quite to a boil.
4. Add the milk gradually, while beating, to the beaten egg yolks. Pour the mixture into a large saucepan and add the vanilla bean or vanilla extract. Cook over very low heat (preferably over an asbestos pad), stirring constantly with a wooden spoon. Do not boil, but continue cooking and stirring until the mixture coats the spoon. Take care not to overcook the custard, or it will curdle. When the custard is ready, cool it.
5. Remove the vanilla bean pieces. Split them, squeeze out the seeds, and add them to the custard. Stir in the strawberries and cream. Now taste the mixture and, if desired, add more sugar to taste. It should be on the sweet side, since freezing tends to diminish the sweetness. Freeze according to standard freezer instructions.

Frozen Lemon Cream

6 servings

1 cup milk
1 cup heavy cream
1 cup granulated sugar
   Grated rind and juice of 2 lemons
6 whole large lemons

1. Combine the milk, cream, and sugar, stirring until the sugar is thoroughly dissolved. Pour the mixture into a refrigerator tray and freeze until mushy.

2. Add the lemon rind and juice, beat the mixture well with a rotary beater, and freeze again for two hours. Beat the mixture again thoroughly, return to the freezer, and freeze until solid.

3. Slice off the tops of the lemons and remove all the pulp. (Discard the pulp or save it for another use.) Cut a thin slice from the bottom of each lemon shell so that it will stand upright. Fill the shells with the frozen mixture, piling it high. Serve garnished with a lemon leaf or other green leaf.

Sherbet with Liqueur

With a spoon or an ice cream scoop, place individual servings of lemon, orange, or raspberry sherbet in chilled sherbet cups or serving dishes. Pour over each serving one tablespoon or so of a suitable liqueur. Crème de menthe goes well with lemon sherbet; an orange-flavored liqueur such as Cointreau or Grand Marnier with orange sherbet; and cassis, a currant liqueur, with raspberry.

Crème Anglaise

(Custard Sauce)

About 2 cups

1 cup milk
1 cup heavy cream
5 egg yolks
½ cup granulated sugar
1 tablespoon Grand Marnier, Cognac, or kirsch

1. Combine the milk and cream in a saucepan and bring just to a boil.

2. Meanwhile, combine the egg yolks and sugar in a mixing bowl and beat thoroughly until light yellow and thickened. Gradually pour the milk and cream into the yolk mixture, stirring vigorously with a whisk.

3. Transfer the mixture to a saucepan and stir over very low heat (preferably with the saucepan on an asbestos pad or Flame Tamer). Use a wooden spoon to stir, taking care that it moves over the entire bottom of the saucepan. Cook, stirring, without boiling until the sauce coats the spoon with an obvious creamy layer. Do not overcook or the sauce will curdle. Stir in the Grand Marnier. Use warm as a sauce for Dessert Crêpes (page 290), or warm or cold on fruit desserts, puddings, or ice cream.

Sauce Amandine

About 3 cups

3 egg yolks
¾ cup confectioners' sugar
1 cup heavy cream
2 tablespoons Cognac, kirsch, or Grand Marnier or any orange liqueur
10 shelled nut meats, such as walnuts or blanched almonds
Candied violets (optional)

1. Place the egg yolks in the top part of a double boiler. Beat with a rotary beater, gradually adding the sugar. Beat until it forms a ribbon when it falls back upon itself, or until thick and pale yellow.

2. Beat the cream until stiff and fold into the egg yolk mixture. Fold in the flavoring, spoon the mixture into a silver or glass serving bowl, and chill one hour.

3. Garnish with walnuts or almonds and, if desired, with candied violets. Serve with fresh fruit.

French Rum Punch

40 to 50 servings

1½ cups granulated sugar
2 tablespoons peppercorns
1 piece dried ginger
2 bay leaves
2 cardamom seeds
3 pieces mace
1 teaspoon shaved nutmeg or ¼ teaspoon grated nutmeg
1 cinnamon stick
1 1-inch piece vanilla bean or 1 teaspoon vanilla extract
3 strips lemon peel, yellow part only
3 strips orange peel, orange part only
2 cups water
3 cups orange juice
1 cup lemon juice
2 bottles light rum
1 cup Cognac
1 cup Cointreau
3½ to 4 quarts ice cubes
2 orange wedges, seeded
1 pint strawberries, washed and drained, sliced or left whole

1. Combine the sugar, peppercorns, ginger, bay leaves, cardamom seeds, mace, nutmeg, cinnamon, vanilla, lemon and orange peels, and water in a saucepan. Bring to a boil and simmer twenty-five minutes. Let the infusion stand until cool, then chill, if desired. Strain.

2. Combine the infusion with the orange and lemon juices, rum, Cognac, and Cointreau and stir to blend. When ready to serve, pour the punch into a bowl and add the ice. There should be about one and one-half times as much ice as there is punch. Immediately garnish the bowl with the orange wedges and strawberries and serve.

Germany

Sauerbraten

6 servings

3 pounds bottom round of beef
3 tablespoons whole peppercorns
1 tablespoon mustard seeds
25 whole cloves
25 bay leaves
3 large onions, peeled and sliced
2 cups wine vinegar
¼ cup butter
  Salt to taste
6 slices bacon
  Beef Stock (page 115)
2 tablespoons all-purpose flour
¼ cup cold water
2 to 3 tablespoons heavy cream

1. The meat must be marinated three days in advance. Trim off most of the fat from the beef, then cut the beef into six large chunks. Select a glass, enamel, or stainless-steel bowl large enough to hold the meat comfortably. Combine the peppercorns, mustard seeds, cloves, bay leaves, onions, and vinegar and pour all of it over the beef. Cover and let stand in a very cool place or the refrigerator for three days.

2. When ready to cook, preheat the oven to 400 degrees.

3. Melt the butter in a casserole.

4. Drain the meat and reserve both the meat and half the marinade with the seasonings.

5. Place the meat in the casserole and add the reserved liquid and seasonings. Add salt to taste. Place the casserole, uncovered, in the oven. Cook about one hour, then reduce the heat to 300 degrees.

6. Turn the meat in the liquid and cover each piece of meat with bacon. Continue cooking about one hour, or until the meat is tender. Remove the bacon and discard it. Cook the meat about ten minutes longer, then transfer to a warm platter and strain the cooking liquid. Discard the solids. To the cooking liquid add enough beef stock to make four cups.

7. Return the meat to a clean casserole and add the liquid. Bring to a boil. Blend the flour with the cold water and add it to the boiling liquid, stirring. Simmer about five minutes, adding more salt, if desired. Stir in the cream. Serve hot, with noodles, dumplings, or potatoes.

Rolladen

4 servings

4 large, thin slices top round of beef (each about ¼ inch thick and about 12 x 6 inches)
  Salt and freshly ground pepper to taste
6 teaspoons prepared mustard
2¼ cups finely chopped onion
4 strips bacon
4 dill pickle spears
¼ cup butter
1 tablespoon paprika
2 cups Beef Stock (page 115)

1. Place the pieces of meat on a flat surface and sprinkle with salt and pepper. Spread each piece with approximately one and one-half teaspoons of mustard, then sprinkle each piece with three tablespoons of chopped onion.

2. Cut each piece of bacon in half, then cut each piece in half lengthwise. Arrange four pieces of bacon, ladder fashion, on the beef, top to bottom.

3. Split each dill spear in half lengthwise and arrange two dill halves between two bacon slices.

4. Roll the beef top to bottom, enclosing the filling. Tie each roll securely with string.

5. Heat the butter in a skillet and add the remaining onion. Cook, stirring, until golden, then sprinkle with paprika. Cook, stirring, about seven seconds, no longer. Add the beef rolls and turn them in the paprika mixture until well coated on all sides. Add one cup of the beef stock and cover. Cook over medium-high heat about thirty minutes, taking care that the meat does not burn or stick. Turn the meat and add half a cup of stock. Cover and cook thirty minutes longer. Add the remaining stock, turn the meat, and continue cooking fifteen to thirty minutes, or until the meat is fork tender.

Bavarian Pork and Veal Roast

6 to 8 servings

2 pounds boned shoulder of pork, cut into 4 equal-sized pieces
1 pound loin of veal, cut into 2 equal-sized pieces
  Freshly ground pepper to taste
¼ cup butter
3½ cups coarsely chopped onion
6 or 7 cloves garlic, peeled and thinly sliced
1½ tablespoons caraway seeds
  Salt to taste
1 tablespoon marjoram, crushed
1 cup water, approximately

1. Preheat the oven to 400 degrees.

2. Sprinkle the veal and pork with pepper on all sides.

3. Heat the butter in a roasting pan large enough to hold the meat in one layer. Scatter the onion and garlic around the pieces of meat. Sprinkle the caraway seeds, salt, and marjoram over all. Add half the water and place in the oven. Bake one hour and fifteen minutes without basting, adding more water as necessary. Turn the meat pieces and stir around them. Let cook an hour longer. When the meat is browned on this side, reduce the oven heat to 350 degrees. Turn the meat and let cook fifteen minutes or longer, until the meat is quite tender.

4. Serve the meat pieces whole or cut in half. Serve with buttered noodles or dumplings.

Pork with Sauerkraut

4 servings

No dish was ever better suited to winter weather than sauerkraut. It is warming, invigorating, and delicious. The name is Teutonic, of course, sauer *meaning "sour" in the pickled sense and* kraut *meaning "cabbage." Sauerkraut has a natural affinity for dry white wine, juniper berries, and pork. It relates well, too, to caraway seeds. The dish below, pork with sauerkraut, resembles to some degree the Polish hunter's stew called* bigos. *It is good when made—and excellent warmed over.*

2 pounds sauerkraut
¼ pound bacon, sliced
1 clove garlic, finely minced
6 juniper berries
12 peppercorns
1 onion studded with 4 cloves
1½ to 2 cups dry white wine
1½ to 2 cups Chicken Stock (page 115)
2 pounds boneless shoulder of pork, cut into 2-inch cubes
Salt and freshly ground black pepper to taste
2 tablespoons oil
2 cups coarsely chopped onion
1 bay leaf
2 sprigs fresh thyme or ½ teaspoon dried thyme
2 cups peeled, chopped fresh tomatoes or canned Italian plum tomatoes

1. Preheat the oven to 375 degrees.

2. Squeeze the sauerkraut between the hands to extract much of the liquid. If desired, the kraut may be washed in cold water and squeezed. This will make a blander and, to some tastes, a less interesting dish.

3. Line a two-quart flameproof casserole with the bacon and add the kraut. Add the garlic, juniper berries, peppercorns, and the onion studded with the cloves. Using equal parts of wine and chicken stock, add just enough liquid to cover the sauerkraut.

4. Bring to a boil on top of the stove, then place the casserole, covered, in the oven. Bake for an hour or so.

5. Meanwhile, sprinkle the pork cubes with salt and pepper. Heat the oil in a large casserole and cook the pork cubes, stirring and turning the pieces in the fat, until they are golden. Place in the oven and bake for fifteen minutes. Add the chopped onion, bay leaf, and thyme and cook, stirring occasionally, until the onion is wilted. Add the tomatoes and season with salt and pepper. Bake one hour.

6. Using a slotted spoon, add the sauerkraut to the pork, stirring to blend. Continue baking, uncovered, for fifteen minutes or longer, until the pork is fork tender. Serve with boiled potatoes.

GERMANY   *313*

Roast Venison

8 to 10 servings

Venison used to be a sometime thing, available only during hunting season, but since the advent of the freezer, venison fanciers can enjoy it whenever the fancy moves them. It is, of course, one of the choicest of meats and never better than when served with poivrade (*black pepper*) *sauce. Here are recipes for the roast venison and the sauce.*

1 boneless venison roast (4½ pounds), tied with string, with part of the bone from the roast reserved for Poivrade Sauce (see below)
  Salt and freshly ground pepper to taste
¼ cup butter
¼ cup Cognac

1. Preheat the oven to 450 degrees. Remember that the venison will be served with a poivrade sauce, and the sauce should cook while the venison roasts.

2. Sprinkle the meat with salt and pepper to taste. Melt the butter in an open skillet and turn the roast in the butter, without browning, until coated.

3. Place the roast, uncovered, in the oven and bake, basting frequently and turning the meat occasionally, thirty minutes.

4. Reduce the oven heat to 400 degrees and continue basting and roasting, fifteen minutes for medium-rare meat or longer for well done.

5. Remove the meat, cover with foil, and keep warm.

6. Add the Cognac to the skillet and ignite it. Stir. This liquid will be added to the poivrade sauce.

7. Serve the meat sliced, with the poivrade sauce.

POIVRADE SAUCE:

8 to 10 servings

1 tablespoon crushed peppercorns
3 tablespoons finely chopped shallots
½ bay leaf
½ teaspoon dried thyme or 3 small sprigs fresh thyme
1 cup dry red wine
  A few venison bones, cracked into small pieces
1 cup heavy cream
  Salt and freshly ground pepper to taste
1 tablespoon butter

1. Place the peppercorns, shallots, bay leaf, thyme, wine, and venison bones in a small, heavy saucepan and bring to a boil. Simmer, covered, about one hour.

2. Strain the sauce through a sieve, discarding the bones but pressing any other solids through the sieve. Add the cream and bring to a boil. Simmer about fifteen minutes. Add the drippings from the skillet in which the venison cooked. Add salt and pepper, and at the last minute remove from the heat and swirl in the butter by rotating the pan gently. Serve hot, with the sliced venison.

Sweet and Sour Cabbage

6 to 8 servings

 1 red cabbage (4½ to 5 pounds)
½ cup butter
   Salt and freshly ground pepper to taste
 1 teaspoon or more grated nutmeg
 3 tablespoons white vinegar
 3 tablespoons or more brown sugar
 1 cup raisins
 2 cooking apples, peeled, cored and cut into small dice (about 2 cups)

1. Preheat the oven to 400 degrees.

2. Cut away and discard the core of the cabbage. Shred the cabbage finely.

3. Heat the butter in a large, heavy casserole and add the cabbage. Sprinkle with salt and pepper to taste and nutmeg. Add the vinegar, brown sugar, raisins, and diced apples. Do not add any more liquid. Cover, bring to a boil, and cook about ten minutes, stirring once in a while. Place in the oven and bake, covered, one and one-half hours, stirring occasionally.

4. If desired, add more nutmeg and brown sugar to taste.

Note: Nutmeg is a natural complement to this dish.

Sauerkraut with Sherry Wine

4 to 6 servings

 ½ pound bacon, sliced
 1 pound sauerkraut
 1 onion stuck with 4 cloves
10 juniper berries
 2 cloves garlic, finely chopped
 ½ teaspoon caraway seeds
   Salt and freshly ground pepper to taste
 ¼ cup dry sherry
2½ cups Chicken Stock (page 115)

1. Preheat the oven to 300 degrees.

2. Place the bacon in a saucepan and add cold water to cover. Bring to a boil and simmer one minute. Drain and set aside.

3. Drain the sauerkraut in a colander but do not press it.

4. Line a casserole with the bacon slices and add the sauerkraut to the center. Place the onion in the middle of the sauerkraut and add the juniper berries, garlic, caraway seeds, salt, pepper, sherry, and chicken stock. Cover and bring to a boil on top of the stove. Place the casserole in the oven and bake two and one-half hours.

5. Increase the oven heat to 400 degrees. Uncover the casserole and continue baking twenty minutes, or until lightly brown on top. Serve with mustard and boiled, buttered potatoes.

German Cabbage Salad

8 or more servings

1 firm head green cabbage
  Salt to taste
1½ to 2 tablespoons wine vinegar (see note), or to taste
  Freshly ground pepper to taste
⅓ cup finely chopped onion
8 slices bacon, cut into very fine dice

1. Pull off and discard the loose outside leaves of the cabbage, then cut out and discard the core of the cabbage. Cut the cabbage into quarters.

2. Meanwhile, bring enough water to a boil to cover the cabbage when it is added. Add salt to taste and the quartered cabbage. Cook the cabbage, uncovered, for about twenty minutes, or until crisp tender.

3. Drain the cabbage well and chill under cold running water. Drain well.

4. Shred the cabbage, then chop, but not too fine. Add vinegar, pepper, and the onion.

5. Meanwhile, cook the bacon in a small skillet, stirring, until it is crisp. Do not let it burn. Immediately remove it from the heat and pour the bacon bits and the fat over the cabbage. Toss well and serve.

Note: Seasoned vinegar such as tarragon vinegar may also be used.

Cucumber and Sour Cream Salad

8 servings

4 firm, unblemished cucumbers
  Salt and freshly ground pepper to taste
¼ cup finely chopped fresh dill
2 tablespoons wine vinegar
1 cup sour cream

1. Peel the cucumbers and slice them thin. Sprinkle with salt, pepper, dill, and vinegar.

2. Stir the sour cream rapidly to thin it and add to the cucumbers. Stir gently to blend. Let stand one hour, then serve.

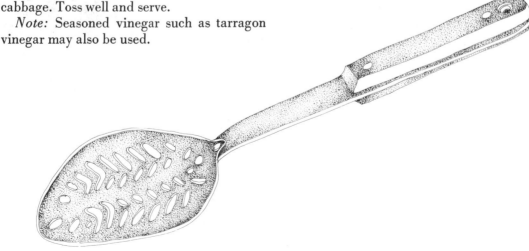

Christmas Stollen

1 stollen

To many Austrians and Germans, a stollen *is as much a part of the Christmas scene as Yule logs and evergreens. A* stollen *is a very special, eminently delicious bread full of good things that smell like Christmas—yeast and cinnamon and cardamom and mace. Candied fruits and a frosting crowned with pecan halves give texture and add to its goodness. One of America's chief* stollen *bakers is David Dugan of North Caldwell, New Jersey, a retired professional baker. He bakes 200 pounds of fruitcake every year for Christmas gifts, but his* stollen *is reserved for family only. Here is his* stollen *recipe.*

⅔ cup milk, scalded
⅔ cup granulated sugar
¾ teaspoon salt
  Butter
2 tablespoons vegetable shortening
2 packages dry active yeast
¼ cup warm water
2 eggs, lightly beaten
½ teaspoon ground cinnamon
⅛ teaspoon ground mace
⅛ teaspoon ground cardamom
3½ cups sifted all-purpose flour, approximately
1 cup diced mixed candied fruits
¼ cup raisins
½ cup chopped pecans
  Frosting (see below)
  Pecan halves

1. Pour the milk into a large bowl. Add the sugar, salt, one-half cup butter, and shortening and stir to melt the butter and dissolve the sugar. Let cool to lukewarm.

2. Soften the yeast in the warm water and add to the cooled mixture. Beat in the eggs, cinnamon, mace, and cardamom and enough flour to make a soft dough that can be kneaded.

3. Turn onto a lightly floured board and knead until smooth. Knead in the fruits (first tossed in a little flour), raisins, and chopped nuts until evenly distributed.

4. Place the dough in a greased bowl. Cover and let rise in a warm place until doubled in bulk, about two and one-half to three hours.

5. Punch down and roll into an oval (12 x 8). Fold over lengthwise so that the two edges do not quite meet.

6. Place on a greased baking sheet, cover, and let rise in a warm place until doubled in bulk, about one and one-half to two hours.

7. Preheat the oven to 400 degrees. Bake the stollen ten minutes. Reduce the oven temperature to 350 degrees and bake 25 minutes longer, or until the loaf sounds hollow when tapped on the bottom.

8. Brush with butter and let cool on a rack. When cool, spread with the frosting and decorate with pecan halves.

FROSTING:
1½ tablespoons butter
1 cup confectioners' sugar, approximately
½ tablespoon light corn syrup
¼ teaspoon vanilla extract

Cream the butter and sugar together until light and fluffy, then beat in the corn syrup and vanilla extract.

Marzipan Cake

9 to 12 servings

2 whole eggs
3 egg yolks
¼ cup almond paste
2 tablespoons milk
½ teaspoon vanilla extract
1 cup sifted all-purpose flour
1 teaspoon baking powder
¼ teaspoon salt
1 cup granulated sugar
⅓ cup melted butter
  Frosting
  Red and yellow marzipan for decoration
  Red candy sprinkles for decoration

1. Place the eggs and egg yolks in the bowl of an electric mixer and stand the bowl in warm water.

2. Preheat the oven to 350 degrees. Grease a baking pan (9 x 9 x 1¾).

3. Blend the almond paste with the milk and vanilla. Sift together the flour, baking powder, and salt.

4. Remove the bowl with the eggs from the water and beat the eggs on moderately high speed, adding the sugar gradually, until the mixture stands in stiff peaks. Add about one-half cup to the almond paste mixture, then add this mixture to the rest of the eggs and blend.

5. Fold in the dry ingredients, one quarter at a time. Cool the butter, add it to the batter, and fold in lightly and quickly. Turn the batter into the prepared pan.

6. Bake for thirty to thirty-five minutes, or until the cake begins to shrink from sides of pan and rebounds when touched gently in the center.

7. Frost with a standard vanilla butter frosting. Decorate with a red marzipan poinsettia and ruffle, made according to the directions below.

POINSETTIA:

Draw a poinsettia. Place strips of red marzipan over the drawing, shape into leaves, and place on the cake. Fill center with tiny yellow marzipan balls and press a red candy sprinkle into each.

RUFFLE:

Mix enough egg white with red marzipan to soften it. Force through a pastry tube around the edge of the cake.

Apple Nut Torte

6 or more servings

1 egg
¾ cup granulated sugar
½ cup all-purpose flour
1 teaspoon baking powder
½ teaspoon salt
1 cup chopped, peeled, cored apples, preferably on the tart side
½ cup chopped walnuts
1 teaspoon vanilla extract
  Sweetened whipped cream

1. Preheat the oven to 350 degrees.

2. Beat the egg with an electric beater until light and lemon colored. Gradually beat in the sugar.

3. Sift together the flour, baking powder, and salt and fold into the egg mixture. Stir in the apples, walnuts, and vanilla.

4. Butter the inside of an eight-inch-square pan and pour in the batter. Bake thirty-five to forty minutes. Serve warm, with sweetened whipped cream.

Filled Marzipan Cookies

16 to 18 large diamonds

½ cup butter
¼ cup granulated sugar
1 egg yolk
½ cup plus 3 tablespoons almond paste
1½ cups sifted cake flour
1 egg white, approximately
Raspberry Jam

1. Cream the butter; add the sugar, egg yolk, and the three tablespoons almond paste. Add the flour, blend well, and chill.

2. Preheat the oven to 350 degrees. Grease cookie sheets.

3. Work the half cup of almond paste with the fingers until smooth. Add the egg white gradually, using enough to soften the paste so it can be forced through a pastry tube. Set aside.

4. Roll the chilled cookie dough on a lightly floured cloth to a thickness of one-quarter inch. Cut into diamond or other shapes. Arrange the cookies one inch apart on the cookie sheets.

5. Force the almond paste and egg white mixture through a small tube to form a one-inch circle in the center of each cookie. Fill the circle with jam. Bake for fifteen minutes.

Pfeffernüsse

8 to 9 dozen

½ cup light corn syrup
¼ cup shortening
2 tablespoons butter, at room temperature
½ cup unsulfured molasses
⅓ cup light brown sugar, firmly packed
2 large eggs, separated
Juice of 1 lemon
Grated rind of 1 lemon
3 cups unsifted unbleached flour
¼ teaspoon salt
¼ teaspoon baking soda
¼ teaspoon ground ginger
½ teaspoon ground cinnamon
⅛ teaspoon ground cloves
¼ teaspoon cream of tartar
3 tablespoons granulated sugar
1 pound confectioners' sugar

1. Preheat the oven to 350 degrees.

2. Heat the corn syrup to lukewarm. Stir in the shortening and butter, then add the molasses and brown sugar. Beat in the egg yolks, lemon juice, and lemon rind.

3. Blend the flour, salt, baking soda, ginger, cinnamon, and cloves. Stir the dry ingredients into the corn syrup mixture. The dough will be sticky. Use a one-inch melon ball cutter or a spoon to drop the dough in balls onto ungreased Teflon cookie sheets. Bake eleven minutes, then let cool.

4. Meanwhile, prepare a meringue with the egg whites. Beat the egg whites lightly and add the cream of tartar. Beat thoroughly until soft peaks form, then add the granulated sugar. Continue beating until stiff peaks form.

5. Dip each of the spice drops into the meringue, then into the confectioners' sugar to coat thoroughly.

White Spritz Cookies

About 5 dozen

1 cup butter
⅔ cup granulated sugar
1 teaspoon vanilla extract
3 egg whites
2 to 2⅓ cups sifted all-purpose flour
¼ teaspoon salt

1. Preheat the oven to 375 degrees.
2. Cream the butter and sugar together. Add the vanilla extract and the egg whites, beating vigorously and thoroughly. Gently stir in the flour and salt. Using a pastry tube or cookie press, push out small shapes, such as stars or rings. Bake eight to ten minutes, or until the edges of the cookies are golden brown.

Christmas stollen (Germany)

Greece

Stuffed Grape Leaves with Avgolemono Sauce

15 to 20 servings

2 onions, finely chopped
¼ cup finely chopped heart of celery
2 tablespoons butter
½ pound round steak, ground
½ pound lamb, ground
¼ cup uncooked rice
1 tablespoon finely chopped mint
¼ cup finely chopped parsley
    Salt and freshly ground black pepper
1 jar (1 pound) grape leaves
1 cup Beef Stock (page 115) or water, approximately
    Juice of 1 lemon
½ cup dry white wine
    Avgolemono Sauce (see below)

1. Cook the onion and celery in one tablespoon of the butter until tender but not brown.
2. Place the meat in a bowl and add the onion and celery. Add the rice, mint, parsley, and salt and pepper to taste. Blend well.
3. Turn the grape leaves into a colander and rinse them gently under cold running water, separating the leaves. Dry gently and place them one at a time on a flat surface, shiny side down. Place a small amount of filling in the center of each leaf and roll each tightly from the stem end toward the point of the leaf. Arrange the leaves in layers in a heavy saucepan.
4. Add the stock, lemon juice, and remaining butter. Pour in the wine and cover with a heavy plate to prevent the leaves from opening. Cook over low heat one hour. When done, there should be some liquid remaining in the pan for making the sauce. If not, add a little more stock and bring to a boil.
5. Transfer the leaves to a hot platter and keep warm while making the sauce, then pour the sauce over and serve immediately, as an appetizer.

AVGOLEMONO SAUCE:

About 1½ cups

4 egg yolks
    Juice of 1 lemon
    Cooking liquid from Stuffed Grape Leaves (see above)

Beat the egg yolks well with a rotary beater. Add the lemon juice, then add the cooking liquid to the egg yolks, still beating.

Dolmadakia

(Stuffed Grape Leaves)

About 2 dozen

There is an Arabic saying, "Al akl 'ala kadd el mahabeh"—"The food equals the affection," or "The more a guest eats, the more he shows his love for the host." The glorious savories that comprise the beginning of a meal in the Middle East offer a guest unlimited opportunities to prove his affection. There are dishes made with sesame paste and chick-peas, eggplant and lamb, grape leaves and yogurt. If they are accompanied by sun-ripened olives, vinegar peppers, and crusty bread, so much the better. Below is a recipe for stuffed grape leaves.

 1 cup olive oil
 3 large onions, chopped
 1 clove garlic, finely chopped
 1 teaspoon salt
 ¼ teaspoon freshly ground black pepper
 1 cup uncooked rice
 2 tablespoons fresh snipped dill
 ¼ cup finely chopped Italian parsley
 2 tablespoons pignoli (pine nuts)
 6 green onions, finely chopped
 1 cup lemon juice
 3 cups water
 1 8-ounce jar grape leaves in brine
   Parsley stems (optional)
   Lemon wedges

1. Heat one-half cup of the oil in a skillet and sauté the onions and garlic until tender but not browned.

2. Add the salt, pepper, and rice and cook slowly for ten minutes, stirring frequently. Add the dill, parsley, nuts, green onions, one-half cup of the lemon juice and one cup of the water. Stir to mix, cover, and simmer gently until all the liquid has been absorbed, about fifteen minutes.

3. Rinse the grape leaves under running water, separate, and place, shiny side down, on a board. If the leaves are small, put two together.

4. Place one teaspoon of the rice filling near the stem end of the leaves and roll up jelly-roll fashion toward the tip, tucking in the edges to make a neat roll.

5. Place the remaining oil, lemon juice, and one cup of water in a large skillet. Arrange the rolls in the pan, separating the layers with parsley stems if more than one layer is prepared. Place a heavy plate, or plate and weight, on top and simmer twenty-five minutes. Add the remaining water and cook about ten minutes longer, or until the rice is tender. Cool and serve at room temperature with lemon wedges.

Dolmadakia Yialandji
(Stuffed Grape Leaves)

3 dozen

4 medium onions, finely chopped
Salt
⅔ cup uncooked rice
¾ cup olive oil
1 teaspoon chopped fresh mint
1 teaspoon chopped fresh dill
½ cup chopped parsley
3 large bunches green onions, chopped, green part and all
Freshly ground black pepper
Lemon juice
1 12-ounce jar grape leaves
Parsley stalks
1 cup boiling water

1. Steam the onions, covered, with one teaspoon salt five to ten minutes over very low heat, stirring occasionally.

2. Remove from the heat. Add the rice and one-half cup of the olive oil, then the herbs and green onions. Mix well. Add salt and pepper to taste and the juice of half a lemon.

3. Wash the grape leaves thoroughly to remove all brine. Separate the leaves carefully and remove the thick portions. Cut large leaves in half. Place one tablespoon filling on the underside of each leaf. Starting at the base, fold over and fold in the sides, rolling tightly toward the point.

4. Interlace parsley stalks on the bottom of a saucepan. Arrange the stuffed leaves in layers over the parsley stalks. Add the remaining oil and the juice of half a lemon. Weigh down the leaves with a heavy plate, cover the saucepan, and simmer twenty minutes over low heat. Add the boiling water and simmer twenty-five minutes longer. Serve cold, sprinkled with additional lemon juice.

Cucumbers with Yogurt, Greek Style

6 small servings

1 pint Yogurt (page 554)
2 cucumbers, peeled, seeded, and cubed
1 or more cloves garlic, finely minced
1 tablespoon olive oil
Lemon juice to taste
Salt and freshly ground black pepper to taste
Chilled cucumber strips

1. Line a bowl with cheesecloth and spoon the yogurt into it. Gather up the ends of the cheesecloth and tie to make a bag for letting the yogurt drain. Tie the bag with a long string and suspend it over a bowl to drain. Let stand in a cool place or the refrigerator about two hours. This will yield about one cup drained yogurt.

2. Pour the drained yogurt into a mixing bowl and add all the remaining ingredients except the cucumber strips. Let stand until ready to serve. Serve, with the chilled cucumber strips, as an appetizer.

Crabmeat Wrapped in Phyllo

About 6 dozen squares

       1 small onion, chopped
       5 tablespoons butter
       2 tablespoons all-purpose flour
       2 cups or more lukewarm milk
       1 tablespoon chopped parsley
       1 tablespoon chopped dill
   ½ cup chopped mushrooms
       1 tablespoon chopped pimento
       2 hard-cooked eggs, chopped
       1 dash Tabasco
       1 tablespoon A-1 Sauce
       1 dash Maggi seasoning
       1 teaspoon sherry
       1 dash dried basil
          Salt to taste
 1½ pounds lump crabmeat, picked over
   ½ cup or more fine bread crumbs
   ½ pound phyllo pastry
   ¾ cup melted butter

1. Sauté the onion in the five tablespoons butter until brown, then stir in the flour. Add the milk slowly and mix until creamy. Remove from the heat and add the remaining ingredients except the phyllo pastry and melted butter. If the consistency is too loose, add more bread crumbs. If too thick, add more milk.

2. Preheat the oven to 350 degrees.

3. Cut the sheets of pastry into strips three inches wide. Keep the strips wrapped in waxed paper and work with a single strip at a time to prevent it from drying. Brush the strip with melted butter. Place one full teaspoon of the crabmeat mixture in the center of the strip, one inch from the bottom. Fold the strip upwards over the mixture two times. Fold the left side one-third over and turn two times. Fold the right side one-third over and turn two times until the entire strip is folded into a square. Bake on an ungreased cookie sheet until golden. Serve as an appetizer.

Kotopita

(A Greek Pastry Made with Chicken)

8 servings

       1 chicken (3 pounds), cut into serving pieces
          Salt
   10 tablespoons butter
       1 tablespoon vegetable oil
   ½ cup finely chopped onion
   ½ cup finely diced carrot
   ½ cup finely chopped leek
   ½ cup finely chopped celery
       2 cloves garlic, unpeeled
       1 bay leaf
       1 tablespoon finely chopped parsley
   ½ teaspoon orégano
 1½ cups dry white wine
          Freshly ground black pepper
       4 egg yolks
       1 cup heavy cream
       1 teaspoon lemon juice
       8 sheets phyllo pastry

1. Preheat the oven to 350 degrees.

2. Dry each piece of chicken and season with salt.

3. Place a heavy flameproof casserole over moderate heat and add three tablespoons of the butter. Add the oil. When fat is hot, add the chicken parts. Cook gently, turning, without browning, for about fifteen minutes. Remove the chicken pieces and cover to keep warm.

4. Add the onion, carrot, leek, celery, and remaining butter. Cook, stirring occasionally, without browning.

5. Smash the garlic with the flat side of a knife and add. Add the bay leaf, parsley, orégano, and wine and return the chicken to the casserole. Sprinkle with salt and pepper to taste and cover with a piece of buttered waxed paper, then with the lid of the casserole. Bring to a boil. Place the casserole in the oven and bake twenty-five to thirty minutes, or until the drumsticks are tender and

the liquid runs clear when the drumsticks are pierced with a fork.

6. Remove the chicken. Strain the cooking liquid and reserve both liquid and vegetables. Discard the garlic and bay leaf. Let the liquid cool, then skim to remove the fat. Bring the liquid to a boil.

7. Meanwhile, remove and discard the skin and bones from the chicken. Put the chicken and reserved vegetables through the coarse blade of a food chopper or grinder.

8. Beat the egg yolks lightly and blend with the cream. Gradually add one-half cup of the boiling chicken liquid, beating constantly. Stir in the remaining chicken liquid and lemon juice. Heat slowly, stirring with a wooden spoon, until thickened. Do not boil or the sauce will curdle. Cool slightly, then add the mixture to the chopped chicken.

9. Generously butter the bottom and sides of a baking dish (11 x 8). Place one sheet of pastry over the pan, pressing the pastry to fit the bottom and sides. The pastry should overlap the rim. Trim the pastry neatly so that approximately one inch overlaps the rim. Generously brush the bottom and sides with butter and add another sheet of pastry, trimming so that only one inch overlaps. Continue adding pastry, brushing with butter and trimming, until four layers have been used. Pour in the chicken mixture, spreading it evenly.

10. Cover with another layer of phyllo, trim it and brush with butter. Add another layer, trim, brush with butter, and so on until all the layers are used. Roll the overlapping edges of pastry over and over themselves to seal the pie and make a pastry border just inside the pan. Cover loosely with aluminum foil and bake thirty minutes, or until thoroughly heated and the pastry is golden brown.

Spanakopetes
(Spinach Cheese Puffs)

About 4 dozen

1 medium onion, minced
2 tablespoons butter
1 pound fresh spinach, washed and chopped
½ pound feta cheese, crumbled
6 ounces pot cheese
3 eggs, lightly beaten
　Salt and freshly ground black pepper
　Nutmeg
¼ cup fresh bread crumbs
½ pound phyllo pastry sheets
1 cup melted butter

1. Preheat the oven to 425 degrees.

2. Sauté the onion in the two tablespoons butter until golden. Add the spinach and cook over low heat, stirring occasionally, until the spinach is wilted and most of the moisture has evaporated. Stir in the feta cheese, pot cheese, eggs, salt, pepper, and nutmeg to taste, and the bread crumbs.

3. Cut the phyllo pastry sheets into long strips two inches wide. Brush one strip at a time with melted butter. Keep the phyllo not being used covered at all times with waxed paper and a lightly dampened towel. Put one teaspoon of the spinach mixture at one end of each strip and fold over and over into a small triangle. With each fold, make sure that the bottom edge is parallel with the alternate edge.

4. After all the filling is used, arrange the triangles on a baking sheet and brush with melted butter. Bake fifteen to twenty minutes, or until golden. Serve hot.

Tiropetes

(Cheese Pastries)

4 dozen

3 tablespoons butter
3 tablespoons all-purpose flour
1½ cups hot milk
2 eggs
1 egg yolk
⅛ teaspoon freshly ground black pepper
¾ pound feta cheese, finely crumbled
½ pound phyllo pastry sheets
1 cup melted butter

1. Preheat the oven to 425 degrees.
2. In a saucepan, melt the three tablespoons butter. Add the flour and cook, stirring, until well blended. Remove from the heat and add the hot milk. Mix with a wire whisk until blended, return to the heat, and cook, stirring with the whisk, until the sauce is smooth and thickened.
3. Beat the eggs and egg yolk with a little of the hot sauce, stir into the sauce, and cook over low heat, whisking constantly, two minutes. Remove from the heat and stir in the pepper and cheese.
4. Cut the phyllo pastry sheets into long strips two inches wide. Brush one strip at a time with melted butter. Keep the phyllo not being used covered at all times with waxed paper and a lightly dampened towel. Put one teaspoon of the cheese mixture at one end of each strip and fold over and over into a small triangle. With each fold, make sure that the bottom edge is parallel with the alternate edge.
5. When all the filling is used, arrange the triangles on a baking sheet and brush with butter. Bake the pastries ten to fifteen minutes, or until golden. Serve hot.

VARIATION:

To prepare another easy filling, combine one-half pound each pot cheese and crumbled feta cheese, one egg, one egg yolk, two tablespoons chopped fresh dill, and one-quarter teaspoon freshly ground black pepper.

Mayeritsa Avgolemono

(Greek Easter Soup)

8 servings

1 lamb's head, split in half but tied together to keep the brains intact
1 small bunch green onions, trimmed
2 cups diced celery root
4 sprigs fresh parsley
1 sprig fresh dill
10 cups water
Salt and freshly ground pepper to taste
½ cup lamb's intestines
½ pound lamb's liver
½ pound lamb's heart
½ pound lamb's spleen
¼ cup finely chopped parsley
2 tablespoons finely chopped dill
6 egg yolks
Juice of 1 lemon

1. Soak the lamb's head in cold water two to three hours.
2. Place the tied lamb's head in a kettle. Tie the bunch of onions, celery root, parsley, and dill sprigs in cheesecloth and add to the kettle. Add the water, salt, and pepper and bring to a boil.

3. Meanwhile, clean the intestines. Rinse them well, then turn them inside out. To do this, use a small stick about the size of a pencil. Tie one end of one length of intestine. Fit this onto the tip of the stick, then reverse the intestine down the stick much as you would a stocking, pushing the inside out with the fingers. Rinse well and add the intestines to the kettle. Bring to a boil and cook about one hour.

4. While the lamb's head cooks, place the liver, heart, and spleen in a saucepan and add cold water to cover. Add salt and pepper and simmer until tender, twenty minutes or longer.

5. Remove the lamb's head and intestines from the stock. Discard the cheesecloth bag. Remove the brains from the head and chop them, discarding the head. Chop the intestines. Dice the heart, liver, and spleen. Add all this to the stock, then add the chopped parsley and dill. Let simmer.

6. Heat the mixing bowl of an electric beater. Add the yolks and beat them well. Add the lemon juice, bit by bit, beating rapidly. Beat in two cups strained hot stock, beating rapidly. Beat the remaining stock, strained, and serve immediately in hot soup bowls.

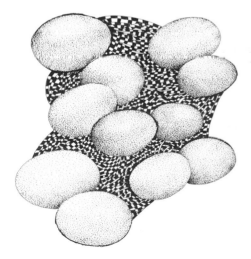

Shrimp Scorpio

4 servings

One of the staples of the Greek table is feta, a cheese that is becoming increasingly popular in America. It is a chalk-white product, somewhat salty because it is preserved in brine. It can be mild, medium, or sharp. In Greek kitchens feta is used as a table cheese to eat with fruit or in salads, or in cooking, as in the recipe here for shrimp.

3 tablespoons olive oil
2 cups finely chopped onion
1 clove garlic
¼ cup finely chopped parsley
1 tablespoon finely chopped dill (optional)
⅛ teaspoon dry mustard
¼ teaspoon granulated sugar
2 cups chopped, peeled tomatoes, fresh or canned
½ cup Tomato Sauce I (page 278)
1 pound (about 24) raw shrimp in the shell
½ pound feta cheese, crumbled (see note)

1. Preheat the oven to 425 degrees.

2. Heat the oil in a saucepan and add the onion. Cook, stirring, until the onion starts to brown.

3. Add the garlic, parsley, and dill. Stir in the mustard and sugar. Do not add salt at any time. Add the tomatoes and tomato sauce and simmer thirty minutes.

4. Peel and devein the shrimp, then rinse and drain. Add the shrimp to the sauce and cook briefly.

5. Pour the mixture into a one-and-one-half-quart casserole and sprinkle with the cheese. Bake ten to fifteen minutes, or until the cheese is melted. Serve immediately.

Note: Cubed mozzarella cheese may be substituted for the feta cheese. If so, season the tomato sauce with salt before adding the shrimp.

Greek-Style Shrimp

4 to 6 servings

By no means the least virtue of shrimp is that they are among the most versatile of shellfish. They marry well with tomatoes and are equally at home with cream. Here is a shrimp dish that is Greek to the core, with its use of feta cheese and ouzo, an anise-flavored liqueur, as a seasoning. Ricard or Pernod could be substituted for the ouzo with no real loss of character.

6 tablespoons olive oil
1 medium yellow onion, chopped
1 clove garlic, peeled
1 no. 2½ can tomatoes, or 6 to 8 medium fresh tomatoes, put through a sieve or food mill
   Salt and freshly ground pepper to taste
¼ teaspoon granulated sugar
2 tablespoons butter
2 pounds raw shrimp, shelled and deveined
2 tablespoons Cognac
2 tablespoons ouzo (an anise-flavored Greek liqueur; if not available, use Pernod or Ricard)
¼ pound feta cheese, sliced or diced
2 tablespoons finely chopped parsley

1. Heat four tablespoons of the oil in a heavy saucepan. Cook the onion and garlic until very lightly browned. Add the tomatoes, salt, pepper, and sugar and cook over moderate heat until thick, about thirty minutes. Remove the garlic from the sauce.

2. Preheat the oven to 425 degrees.

3. Melt the butter and remaining oil in a large, heavy skillet. Sauté the shrimp over a brisk fire until they turn pink. Add the Cognac and ouzo; heat and flame the shrimp.

4. Place the shrimp in a casserole. Cover with the tomato sauce, then with the cheese. Sprinkle with the parsley and bake until well heated, about ten minutes.

Baked Fresh Shrimp with Feta Cheese

3 or 4 servings

12 fresh raw jumbo shrimp, shelled and deveined
2 tablespoons butter
1 egg
¼ cup heavy cream
¼ cup finely crumbled feta cheese
   Tabasco
1 large tomato, peeled and sliced
   Juice of ½ lemon
1 tablespoon chopped parsley
   Freshly ground black pepper

1. Preheat the oven to 400 degrees.

2. Cook the shrimp in the butter on both sides just until the shrimp turn pink. Transfer them to a small baking dish and discard the butter.

3. Combine the egg and cream and beat with a fork until blended. Add the cheese and continue mixing. Add Tabasco to taste and pour the mixture over the shrimp. Arrange the tomato slices on top and bake until the cheese mixture starts to bubble, about ten minutes. Squeeze the lemon juice on top and sprinkle with parsley. Serve immediately with pepper to taste.

Beef Stew with Quinces

6 to 8 servings

5 pounds center-cut chuck or plate of beef, cut into 2-inch cubes
Flour seasoned with salt and pepper for dredging
8 shallots, finely chopped
5 tablespoons butter
2 carrots, scraped and sliced
1 bay leaf
1 teaspoon dried thyme
3 sprigs parsley
1 cup Tomato Sauce I (page 278)
1 cup Beef Stock (page 115)
3 cups dry red wine
Salt and freshly ground pepper to taste
1 teaspoon granulated sugar
½ pound fresh mushrooms, quartered
3 quinces, peeled, cored, and each cut into 8 equal slices

1. Preheat the oven to 375 degrees.
2. Dredge the meat in the flour and set aside.
3. In a large, heavy skillet, cook the shallots in three tablespoons of the butter, stirring, about two minutes. Add the floured meat and cook, stirring, about two minutes longer. Add the carrots, bay leaf, thyme, parsley, tomato sauce, stock, wine, salt, pepper, and sugar. Simmer, uncovered, on top of the stove fifteen minutes.
4. Cover and place the stew in the oven. Bake one and one-half hours.
5. Transfer the meat from the sauce and set aside. Strain the sauce through a sieve, pressing to extract as much liquid as possible from the solids. Combine the strained sauce and meat and return to a boil.
6. Meanwhile, cook the mushrooms in the remaining butter until they have a nutlike odor and are golden brown. Add the mushrooms and the quince slices to the meat; cover and bake forty minutes longer, or until the meat and quinces are fork tender.

Roast Baby Lamb

8 to 10 servings

1 baby lamb (14 to 18 pounds)
½ cup butter, at room temperature
Salt and freshly ground pepper
Juice of 1½ lemons
Chopped parsley and parsley sprigs for garnish

1. Preheat the oven to 500 degrees.
2. Wipe the lamb with a damp cloth. Rub it all over with the butter and sprinkle with salt and pepper.
3. Place the lamb in a large, shallow roasting pan. The pan may be lined with aluminum foil. Put the lamb in the oven and reduce the oven temperature to 350 degrees. Bake, basting frequently, three to three and one-half hours, or until the leg moves freely from the body. If any portion starts to burn, cover it with a piece of foil.
4. About ten minutes before the lamb is done, sprinkle with lemon juice. Cut the meat into serving portions and garnish with chopped parsley and parsley sprigs. Serve with Artichokes for Roast Lamb (page 332).

Braised Lamb with Eggplant

4 to 6 servings

- 1 shoulder of lamb (3 pounds), boned
  Salt and freshly ground black pepper
- 1 clove garlic, slivered
- ¼ cup olive or vegetable oil
- 2½ cups (1 1-pound 4-ounce can) Italian plum tomatoes
- ½ bay leaf
- ½ teaspoon dried thyme
- 10 small white onions, peeled
- 6 wafer-thin slices of lemon
- 1 large eggplant, peeled and cut into 1-inch cubes
- 3 tablespoons melted butter
- ¼ cup finely chopped parsley

1. Sprinkle the meat with salt and pepper and cut small gashes in the flesh. Insert garlic slivers into the gashes.

2. Heat the oil in a heavy kettle or Dutch oven and brown the meat in it on all sides. Pour the tomatoes around the lamb and add the bay leaf, thyme, and onions. Arrange the lemon slices in a single layer on top of the meat. Cover and cook over moderate heat for one hour and fifteen minutes.

3. Arrange the eggplant cubes over the tomatoes and pour the butter over all. Add salt and pepper to taste. Replace the cover and continue to cook until eggplant and meat are tender.

4. Transfer the lamb to a hot platter. Cook the sauce over high heat for three minutes, then pour the sauce over the meat and sprinkle with parsley. Serve with rice.

Podarakia Arniou

(Baked Lamb Shanks)

4 servings

- 4 lamb shanks
  Salt and freshly ground pepper to taste
- 2 cloves garlic, finely minced
- 2 small carrots, cut in thin strips
- 1 large onion, thinly sliced
- 2 ribs celery, cut into 2-inch pieces and thinly sliced lengthwise
- 2 bay leaves, broken
- 1 teaspoon orégano
- ½ teaspoon dried thyme
- 1 cup Tomato Sauce I (page 278)
- 1 cup water
- ½ cup olive oil
- 8 or more new potatoes, peeled

1. Preheat the oven to 375 degrees.

2. Sprinkle the lamb shanks with salt and pepper and rub with garlic.

3. Sprinkle the bottom of a roasting pan large enough to hold the shanks with the carrots, onion, celery, and bay leaves. Add the lamb shanks and sprinkle with orégano and thyme. Add the tomato sauce, diluted in the water, and the olive oil. Cover closely and bake one and one-half to two and one-half hours, depending on the size of the shanks (see note).

4. During the last half hour of cooking raise the temperature of the oven to 400 degrees and uncover the roasting pan. Add the potatoes and continue cooking, uncovered, basting the potatoes and meat with the pan drippings. Serve the shanks surrounded by the potatoes. Skim the fat off the strained sauce and serve the sauce separately.

Note: If the shanks seem to be cooking too quickly, reduce the oven heat to 350 degrees at the end of the first hour of cooking.

Veal Shanks, Greek Style

4 servings

4 veal shanks
  Salt and freshly ground black pepper
  All-purpose flour
½ cup olive oil
4 cups tomatoes, preferably Italian plum style
1 teaspoon orégano
1 clove garlic, finely minced
1 eggplant
4 cups Chicken Stock (page 115) or canned chicken broth, approximately

1. Preheat the oven to 450 degrees.
2. Wipe the veal shanks with a damp cloth and sprinkle them with salt and pepper. Dredge in flour.
3. Pour half the oil into a heavy skillet large enough to hold the shanks. Add the shanks and place in the oven. Bake, basting frequently with the oil, about twenty minutes, or until the meat is golden brown.
4. Pour off the fat from the skillet and reduce the oven heat to 350 degrees.
5. Pour the tomatoes around the shanks and add the orégano, garlic, and remaining oil. Return to the oven and continue baking and basting fifteen minutes.
6. Meanwhile, pare the ends off the eggplant but leave the skin on. Cut the eggplant into cubes and scatter these around the meat. Add one cup of the chicken stock and continue cooking and basting. Add more chicken stock as the original broth boils away. The total cooking time for this dish is about one and one-half to two hours, depending on the size and tenderness of the veal.

Macaroni with Greek Lamb Sauce

4 servings

1½ pounds cubed shoulder of lamb
1 tablespoon salad oil
1 medium onion, chopped
1 clove garlic, finely minced
1 6-ounce can tomato paste
1¾ cups water
4 teaspoons salt
¼ teaspoon dry mustard
¼ teaspoon whole allspice
¼ teaspoon freshly ground pepper
½ cinnamon stick
2 teaspoons lemon juice
½ pound elbow macaroni
  Grated Parmesan cheese

1. In a Dutch oven or heavy saucepan, brown the lamb thoroughly in the oil; drain off the fat. Add the onion and garlic to the meat and cook one minute.
2. Mix in the tomato paste, one and three-quarters cups of water, one teaspoon of the salt, the mustard, allspice, pepper, cinnamon stick, and lemon juice. Simmer, covered, one and one-half hours, or until the meat is tender.
3. Meanwhile, add the remaining salt to two to four quarts rapidly boiling water. Add the macaroni gradually, so that the water continues to boil. Cook uncovered, stirring occasionally, until tender. Drain in a colander. Turn into a serving dish and sprinkle with cheese. Serve with the lamb sauce.

Pastitsio
(Greek Macaroni with Meat)

24 servings

Pasta is one of the most versatile ingredients in cookery. Its character depends on what goes with it, whether it's a simple sauce of butter and cheese, a silky tomato creation, or something more substantial with mushrooms and meat. A recipe for an exceptionally good dish is given here, for a Greek pastitsio.

   2   pounds elbow macaroni
 10   tablespoons butter
   2   cups finely chopped onion
   3   pounds round steak, ground
   2   cups tomato puree
        Salt and freshly ground black pepper
 ½   teaspoon cinnamon
 ½   teaspoon orégano
 ¼   teaspoon nutmeg
   6   tablespoons all-purpose flour
   6   cups milk
 1½   cups cream
   5   egg yolks, lightly beaten
 1½   cups freshly grated Parmesan cheese

1. Preheat the oven to 375 degrees.
2. Cook the macaroni in boiling salted water until tender but still firm, about eight minutes. Do not overcook because the macaroni will be baked. Drain the macaroni in a colander and rinse under cold running water; set aside.
3. Heat four tablespoons of the butter in a skillet and add the onion. Cook, stirring, until the onion is wilted. Add the meat and cook, breaking up the lumps of meat with a slotted spoon. Cook about ten minutes and add the tomato puree, salt and pepper to taste, cinnamon, orégano, and nutmeg.
4. Melt the remaining butter in a saucepan and stir in the flour. Add the milk and cook, stirring, until the mixture is thickened and smooth. Combine the cream with the egg yolks and blend. Stir this into the sauce and heat thoroughly, but do not boil or the mixture will curdle.
5. Using a large buttered baking pan (18 x 12 x 2) (a six-quart or two three-quart shallow pans may be substituted), make a layer of macaroni, a layer of meat, another layer of macaroni, and another layer of meat. Pour the cream sauce over all and sprinkle with the cheese. Bake forty-five minutes.
6. Remove the macaroni from the oven and let stand until warm. Slice into large squares and serve lukewarm.

Artichokes for Roast Lamb

16 servings

   8   artichokes
   2   lemons, cut in half
 ¼   cup all-purpose flour
   1   tablespoon salt
        Chopped fresh dill

1. Trim the artichokes at the base but leave one inch of stem. Peel away the tough outside leaves. Cut off the leafy part of the artichokes about one inch from the top, holding the knife parallel to the base. Cut each artichoke in half lengthwise and scrape away the fuzzy choke. Pare around the stem. Rub the cut portions with lemon juice.
2. Meanwhile, prepare the liquid to cook the artichokes. Add enough water to a large saucepan to cover the artichokes when they are added. Blend the flour with one-half cup of water, stir to blend, and strain into the water. Add the salt. Drop the artichokes into the liquid as they are prepared. Bring to a boil and cover with cheesecloth and a plate. Simmer about twenty minutes, or until slightly tender when touched with a fork. Drain and arrange around the lamb twenty minutes before the lamb is done. Serve sprinkled with chopped dill.

Moussaka

12 to 14 servings

3 large eggplants
2 quarts water
  Salt
  All-purpose flour
1 cup olive oil
6 tablespoons butter
3 cups finely chopped onion
2 cloves garlic, finely minced
1½ pounds beef round steak, ground
1½ pounds lean lamb, ground
2 cups Tomato Sauce I (page 278)
2 bay leaves
  Pinch of dried orégano
  Freshly ground black pepper
2 cups dry red wine
½ teaspoon ground cinnamon
2 tablespoons chopped parsley
10 fresh mushrooms
2 quarts Béchamel Sauce (page 267)
1 cup freshly grated Romano or Parmesan
  cheese

1. Preheat the oven to 400 degrees.

2. Cut the eggplant into one-quarter-inch slices (rounds) and cover the slices with the water and one-half cup salt. Let stand for twenty minutes, then drain. Rinse the slices under cold water and dry on paper towels.

3. Dredge the slices with flour and brown quickly on both sides in the hot oil. Drain again on paper towels.

4. Heat four tablespoons of the butter in a large skillet and cook the onion and garlic in it until golden. Add the ground meats and cook, stirring, for about ten minutes. Break up any lumps that form. Add the tomato sauce, bay leaves, orégano, salt and pepper to taste, the wine, cinnamon, and parsley; blend well. Cook until almost all liquid is absorbed.

5. Meanwhile, trim the mushrooms and slice them. Cook them in the remaining butter until golden brown. Add them to the meat mixture.

6. Butter or oil a roasting pan (12 x 16 x 2) and arrange half of the eggplant slices on the bottom. Add the chopped meat mixture and cover with the remaining eggplant slices. Pour the béchamel sauce over all and sprinkle with the cheese. Bake for about one hour, or until the top is golden. It may be best to line the bottom of the oven with aluminum foil to catch drippings.

7. Remove the moussaka from the oven and let stand for at least forty minutes before serving. The moussaka may be reheated the next day and be even better.

Greek Eggplant

8 to 10 servings

- 3 large or 4 medium green peppers
- 2 large eggplants
- 1 tablespoon dried coriander
- 1 tablespoon dried dill weed
- 1 tablespoon dried dill seed
- 1 tablespoon leaf sage
- 1 tablespoon caraway seeds
- 3 sprigs fresh thyme or 1 teaspoon dried thyme
- 1 sprig fresh rosemary or 1 teaspoon dried rosemary
- 5 cloves garlic, coarsely chopped
- 3 cups water
- 1 cup white vinegar
- 1⅓ cups olive oil
  Salt and freshly ground pepper to taste
  Juice of 1 lemon
- 3 cups peeled, chopped red-ripe tomatoes
- 1 tablespoon granulated sugar
- 24 pitted Greek or Italian black olives (optional)

1. Core and seed the peppers and split them in half. Cut them lengthwise into twenty or thirty strips.

2. Trim the ends off the eggplants, but do not peel. Cut into one-inch cubes.

3. Place the coriander, dill weed, dill seed, sage, caraway, thyme, rosemary, and garlic on an eight-inch square of cheesecloth. Gather up the corners and tie with string to make a sachet.

4. Combine the water, vinegar, oil, sachet, salt, pepper, and lemon juice in a large kettle or casserole. Add the eggplant, green pepper, tomatoes, and sugar. Cover and cook over high heat about thirty minutes. Add the black olives and cook five minutes longer.

Spanakopitta

10 to 12 servings

One of the best Greek cooks in town is Mrs. Christos Bastis, whose husband owns the Sea Fare of the Aegean. At Greek Easter, she serves an incredibly good spinach pie baked in layers of leafy thin phyllo pastry. We give her recipe for the pie below.

- 1 bunch green onions, chopped
- 1 cup plus 2 tablespoons butter
- 2 pounds spinach, washed and drained
- 6 eggs, lightly beaten
- ½ pound feta cheese, crumbled
- 8 ounces cottage cheese
- 2 tablespoons farina
- ½ cup chopped parsley
- ½ cup fresh snipped dill
  Salt and freshly ground pepper to taste
- ¾ to 1 pound phyllo pastry

1. Sauté the green onions in the two tablespoons butter until tender.

2. Chop the spinach and place it in a large pan. Cover and cook until wilted. Drain, pressing out as much moisture as possible.

3. Preheat the oven to 375 degrees. Place a small cookie sheet with edge or the bottom round from a ten-inch spring-form pan on the oven shelf.

4. Butter a two-quart decorated ring mold.

5. Mix together the green onions, eggs, feta, cottage cheese, farina, parsley, dill, and spinach. Season lightly with salt and pepper.

6. Melt the remaining butter.

7. Unfold the phyllo pastry and place it under a damp towel. Remove one sheet of the pastry at a time, brush it with melted butter, cut into two, lengthwise, and place diagonally across the mold. Allowing it to extend about one and one-half inches over the sides of the pan, fit it down into the pan and over the center opening. Press against the sides of the mold.

8. Repeat with the other sheets of pastry, working around and around the mold with the strips to make even layers. Use a total of one-half to three-quarters of the pastry in successive layers.

9. Fill with the spinach mixture. Cut out and discard the disk of pastry covering the center hole. Brush another sheet of pastry with butter and cut into half moons to fit over the filling. Repeat with several layers. Draw up the overhanging pieces of dough over the covered filling.

10. Place on the cookie sheet (to catch the butter drips) and reduce the oven temperature to 350 degrees. Bake one and one-quarter hours, or until golden brown and puffed. Let stand in the mold five to fifteen minutes before unmolding onto a warm platter.

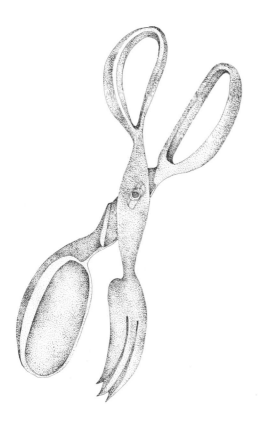

Greek Salad

4 to 6 servings

4 cups salad greens (escarole, romaine, chicory, or other greens), cut or torn into bite-sized pieces
4 to 8 radishes, cut into "roses"
8 black olives, preferably imported, such as Calamata or Alonso
1 red onion, peeled and cut into rings (use according to taste)
1 small green pepper, cored, seeded, and cut into thin rings or strips
4 to 8 tomato wedges or cherry tomatoes
4 to 8 flat anchovy fillets
  Coarse salt to taste
1 clove garlic, peeled and split
  Freshly ground pepper to taste
2 tablespoons lemon juice or vinegar, according to taste
9 to 11 tablespoons imported olive oil, preferably Greek

1. Have ready the salad greens, radishes, olives, onion, green pepper, tomatoes, and anchovies.

2. Pour a little coarse salt into a salad bowl and rub the salt around the surface of the bowl with the garlic clove. Add the salad greens and other salad ingredients. Sprinkle with pepper and the lemon juice or vinegar and toss lightly. Add the oil and toss again. Add more lemon juice or vinegar and oil to taste. Serve immediately.

Quince Compote

About 8 servings

6 large quinces
3 cups water
2 cups granulated sugar
1 stick cinnamon
2 whole cloves
1 tablespoon lemon juice

1. Pare, quarter, and core the quinces.
2. Cut each quarter into three slices.
3. Combine the water and sugar and add the quince slices. Add the remaining ingredients and simmer gently about one hour, or until the fruit is tender and has turned an orange color. Cool and serve. This is good with roast poultry and meats.

Quince Jelly

About 3½ pints

6 large quinces
3 quarts water
   Granulated sugar
1 stick cinnamon
2 whole cloves
1 tablespoon lemon juice

1. Scrub the quinces with a towel or brush so that the skin contains no fuzz. Wash well, but do not peel. Quarter, but do not core or remove the seeds.
2. Place the quinces in a large enamel or stainless steel pot. Add the water and cook until the fruit is very soft, about one and one-half hours. Strain the juice through cheesecloth until the juice is very clear. Discard the fruit.
3. Measure the strained fruit juice and simmer about ten minutes, skimming off any foam or scum.
4. Add one-half cup sugar for each cup of fruit juice.

5. Add the cinnamon, cloves, and lemon juice. Stir until the sugar is completely dissolved. Keep the flame low and simmer about two hours, stirring occasionally to prevent scorching, or until the syrup heavily coats the spoon.
6. Remove from the heat. Remove the cinnamon and cloves. Cover with a clean towel and allow to cool and settle before pouring into sterilized jars. Seal with paraffin.

Quince Preserves

About 2 pints

6 large quinces
3 cups granulated sugar
3 cups water
1 tablespoon lemon juice
1 stick cinnamon
2 whole cloves
½ cup blanched almonds

1. Pare and core the quinces. Carefully remove the seeds and tie the seeds in cheesecloth.
2. Dice or coarsely grate the quinces. Bring the sugar and water to a boil in a stainless steel or enamel pot and add the quinces, lemon juice, cinnamon, cloves, and seed bag.
3. Bring to the boiling point, then lower the flame and simmer about two hours, or until the syrup thickens and forms a soft ball when dropped from the spoon. Stir occasionally to prevent scorching.
4. Remove the seed bag, cloves, and cinnamon and add the almonds. Remove from the heat, cover with a clean towel, and let cool completely before pouring into sterilized jars. Seal with paraffin.

Tsoureki

(Easter Bread)

3 loaves

2 envelopes dry active yeast
2 cups milk, scalded and cooled to lukewarm
1 cup sweet butter
1½ cups granulated sugar
7 eggs
12 cups sifted all-purpose flour
½ teaspoon baking powder
½ teaspoon powdered masticha (see note)
1 tablespoon water
½ cup sliced almonds
6 hard-cooked eggs, colored

1. Soften the yeast in one-half cup of the milk. Beat the butter with the sugar until light and fluffy. Beat in six of the eggs, one at a time. Add the softened yeast and the remaining milk.

2. Sift together the flour and baking powder into a bowl and add the masticha.

3. Stir the butter and egg mixture into the flour to make a soft dough. Knead with a dough hook of an electric mixer or on a lightly floured board with the hands until smooth. Kneading may be done in two batches if you prefer.

4. Set the ball of dough in a clean greased bowl and cover with a damp cloth. Let rise in a warm place until doubled in bulk (two to three hours).

5. Punch down and shape into three loaves. They will fit into three round pans (9 x 3; spring forms work well) or loaf tins (9 x 5 x 3), or the dough can be braided into three free-standing loaves and placed on a greased baking sheet.

6. Cover with a cloth and let rise until doubled in bulk, about one and one-half hours.

7. Preheat the oven to 350 degrees.

8. Brush the tops of the loaves with the remaining egg beaten with the water. Sprinkle with the almonds and set the colored eggs on the loaves. Bake thirty minutes, or until done. If the loaves start to brown too quickly, cover with foil.

Note: Pieces of masticha are ground with a pestle and mortar before measuring.

Ravani

35 pieces

1 cup sweet butter
1¾ cups granulated sugar
7 eggs, separated
1 teaspoon vanilla extract
   Grated rind of one orange
2 cups self-rising flour
¼ cup farina
⅓ cup sliced almonds
2 cups water
6 cinnamon sticks
12 whole cloves
3 tablespoons Metaxa brandy
3 tablespoons Grand Marnier

1. Preheat the oven to 350 degrees.

2. Beat the butter together with one-half cup of the sugar until light and fluffy. Beat in the egg yolks, one at a time, and add the vanilla extract and orange rind. Stir in the flour, farina, and almonds.

3. Beat the egg whites until stiff. Gradually beat in another half-cup sugar until the meringue is glossy and very stiff. Fold into the batter.

4. Turn the mixture into a greased pan (10 x 14 x 2) and bake thirty-five to forty minutes, or until done. Cool to room temperature in the pan, then turn out onto a plate.

5. Make a syrup by placing the water, remaining sugar, cinnamon, and cloves in a small pan. Heat, stirring, until the sugar dissolves. Bring to a boil and boil five minutes. Strain and discard the spices, then add the brandy and Grand Marnier and spoon a little at a time over the cake.

Quince Torte

About 12 generous servings

2½ cups sifted all-purpose flour
1 cup sweet butter, softened
2 tablespoons granulated sugar
3 egg yolks
½ teaspoon ground cinnamon
Rind of 1 lemon, grated
3 cups Quince Preserves (page 336)

1. Place the flour in a large bowl. Make a well, then add the butter cut up into small pieces. Add the sugar, egg yolks, cinnamon, and lemon rind.

2. Knead well, until the dough is firm and holds together. Be sure the butter is thoroughly mixed with the flour.

3. Form the dough into a ball, cover with waxed paper, and refrigerate for one hour before using it.

4. Preheat the oven to 375 degrees.

5. Remove the dough from the refrigerator and roll out two-thirds of the dough between two pieces of waxed paper. Place this in a twelve-inch round cake pan with removable bottom and bake for about ten minutes.

6. Remove from the oven and spread the quince preserves evenly over the pastry. Roll out the rest of the dough, cut into strips, and make a lattice top. Return the cake to the oven and continue to bake for twenty to thirty minutes, or until golden brown. Cool and serve at room temperature. Whipped cream is great with it.

Koulourakia

(Sweet Butter Cookies)

5 to 12 dozen, depending on size

3 cups sweet butter
1½ cups superfine granulated sugar
4 eggs
1 teaspoon vanilla extract
8 cups sifted cake flour
2 teaspoons baking powder
¼ cup Cognac
2 tablespoons milk

1. Heat the butter to boiling. Cool and refrigerate until solid, overnight if needed.

2. Remove the solid butter and discard the liquid.

3. Beat the butter with the sugar until light and fluffy.

4. Beat three of the eggs until light and add to the creamed mixture. Stir in the vanilla extract. Sift together the flour and baking powder and stir into the batter alternately with the Cognac.

5. Mix with the hands or a wooden spoon. Divide the dough into four or six batches and wrap in waxed paper. Chill one hour, or until the dough is easy to handle.

6. Preheat the oven to 300 degrees.

7. Pinch off pieces of dough and roll into sausage shapes about one-half inch in diameter and two, three, or four inches long, according to the size you want the finished cookies. Bend each piece into a ring and pinch the ends together. Place on a lightly greased baking sheet and brush with the remaining egg beaten with milk.

8. Bake thirty minutes, or until the cookies are light brown. Cool on a rack.

Haiti

Haitian Bread and Pumpkin Soup

4 to 6 servings

2 onions, peeled and sliced
2 tablespoons butter
4 slices white bread
4 cups Chicken Stock (page 115)
2 sprigs parsley
1 clove garlic, peeled
1 tablespoon salt, preferably coarse
1 sliver of hot green pepper or a few drops of Tabasco
2 cups cubed, peeled pumpkin
¼ cup finely chopped parsley or chives

1. Cook the onions in the butter until translucent. Add the bread and then the stock. Bring to a boil.

2. Meanwhile, pound together or puree in an electric blender the parsley sprigs, garlic, salt, and hot green pepper. If a blender is used, it will be necessary to add a little of the hot stock. Add this mixture to the soup.

3. Add the pumpkin and cook until thoroughly tender. Pour the soup through a sieve or food mill. Add the chopped parsley, bring again to a boil, and serve hot.

Bananas au Rhum

4 servings

4 firm ripe bananas
¼ cup butter
¼ cup brown sugar
Lemon juice
½ cup rum

1. Preheat the oven to 450 degrees.

2. Peel the bananas and cut them into halves lengthwise. Melt the butter in an oven-proof baking dish and add the banana halves. Sprinkle with the sugar and bake for about ten minutes, or until the bananas are thoroughly hot and the sugar is melted. Sprinkle with lemon juice and baste briefly. Return to the oven for two minutes.

3. Warm the rum and pour it over the bananas. Ignite the rum and, when the flame dies, serve immediately.

Hungary

Hungarian Cheese

1¼ cups

1 8-ounce package cream cheese
¼ cup sweet butter
1¼ teaspoons salt
2 tablespoons sweet paprika
1 teaspoon dry mustard
4 teaspoons whole caraway seeds

1. Mix the cream cheese until it is soft. Add the remaining ingredients and cream until well blended. Chill.

2. Remove the mixture from the refrigerator about one hour before serving. Use as a first course or as a dip for vegetables.

Liptauer Cheese

About 2½ cups

½ pound cottage cheese
4 anchovy fillets
1 teaspoon dry mustard
2 tablespoons caraway seeds
2 tablespoons bright red, sweet Hungarian paprika
½ teaspoon white pepper
½ teaspoon salt
⅛ teaspoon monosodium glutamate
3 tablespoons capers
1 8-ounce package cream cheese, at room temperature
½ cup butter, at room temperature
2 tablespoons gin or schnapps (this helps ripen the mixture and the juniper berries in the gin give it flavor; optional)
4 tablespoons finely chopped chives

1. Blend the cottage cheese in a blender until smooth with the anchovy fillets, mustard, caraway seeds, paprika, pepper, salt, and monosodium glutamate.

2. Add the capers and blend a few seconds more. Turn into a mixing bowl and blend with the cream cheese, butter, and gin. Just before serving, add the chopped chives.

Note: Liptauer cheese is best if allowed to ripen, under refrigeration, for a week.

Köménymagos Leves Nokedival

(Caraway Seed Soup with Dumplings)

8 servings

SOUP:

2 tablespoons all-purpose flour
9 cups Beef Stock (page 115) or Chicken Stock (page 115)
2 tablespoons caraway seeds
2 tablespoons chicken fat or vegetable oil
½ cup cold water

DUMPLINGS:

1 egg
3 to 4 tablespoons all-purpose flour
¼ teaspoon salt

1. Place the flour in a small saucepan and cook it, stirring, over medium heat until the flour is lightly browned. Set aside.

2. Meanwhile, combine the stock and caraway seeds and bring to a boil. Simmer thirty minutes and strain. Discard the seeds.

3. Blend the browned flour with the chicken fat or oil. When smooth, stir in the water. Add this to the caraway broth, stirring rapidly, and bring to a boil.

4. To make the dumplings, beat the egg in a flat soup bowl with a fork and add the flour, beating. Add just enough flour to make a thin but manageable batter. The batter should have the consistency of pancake or waffle batter. Add the salt.

5. Use the edge of a soup spoon to scoop up a little of the batter at a time and spoon it off into the simmering soup. Continue until all the batter is used. Simmer five minutes. Serve the dumplings and soup piping hot.

Hungarian Apple Soup

4 to 6 servings

1 pound firm, ripe apples
2 whole cloves
¼ teaspoon ground cinnamon
Juice of ½ lemon
⅓ cup granulated sugar
½ cup dry white wine
2 cups milk
½ cup heavy cream
2 tablespoons all-purpose flour

1. Peel, core, and quarter the apples and place in a saucepan. Add water to cover, the cloves, cinnamon, lemon juice, and sugar. Simmer until tender. Put through a sieve or food mill. Return to a boil.

2. Add the wine and milk, stirring constantly. Remove from the heat. Blend the cream with the flour and stir into the soup. Return the soup to a boil and simmer five minutes. Chill.

Paprika Shrimp with Sour Cream

4 servings

There is little to be said about shrimp that has not already been said. It is America's favorite seafood. It is also one of the most versatile; in fact, it seems as if almost everything goes with shrimp (one great shrimp sauce contains catsup and Cognac, for instance). Herbs and cream are particularly excellent complements—and the variations on this theme are endless. Below is one with sour cream (to be served with rice).

2 tablespoons butter
24 medium raw shrimp, peeled and deveined
 Salt and freshly ground pepper to taste
¼ teaspoon cayenne pepper, or to taste
1 teaspoon paprika
3 tablespoons finely chopped shallots
⅓ cup heavy cream
2 teaspoons imported mustard, preferably Dijon or Düsseldorf
⅓ cup sour cream

1. Heat the butter, and when it is hot add the shrimp. Sprinkle with salt and pepper to taste, cayenne pepper, and paprika. Stir and cook just until the shrimp turn pink, turning each shrimp once. Do not overcook.

2. Sprinkle with the shallots and add the heavy cream. Stir the mustard into the sauce and remove the skillet from the heat. Stir in the sour cream and heat thoroughly without boiling. Serve immediately with rice.

Triple Goulash

6 servings

6 tablespoons butter
6 large onions, chopped
1 pound sirloin tip of beef, cubed
1 pound lean pork steak, cubed
1 pound veal stew meat, cubed
2 tablespoons paprika
1 teaspoon salt
1 teaspoon caraway seeds
2 large green peppers, seeded and cut into rings

1. Melt the butter in a deep kettle or heavy saucepan. Add the onions and simmer, covered, for thirty minutes, stirring occasionally.

2. Add the beef and cook, covered, for thirty minutes longer. Add the pork and cook, covered, for thirty minutes longer. Add the veal and continue to stew for one and one-half hours. When adding the meats to the onions, combine well by stirring with a large kitchen spoon. Add the meat quickly and re-cover the pan to prevent the liquids from evaporating.

3. Remove the pan from the heat and stir in the paprika, salt, and caraway seeds, blending well. Simmer for thirty minutes.

4. Add the peppers and bring to a boil, uncovered. Cover and cook until the peppers have lost their crispness. If the sauce is too liquid, uncover the pan and continue to cook for a few minutes until the sauce is reduced.

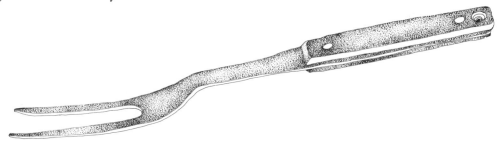

Sauté of Beef, Hungarian Style

4 servings

1½ pounds tenderloin of beef, cut into ½-
    inch slices
¼ cup butter
½ cup heavy cream
2 teaspoons paprika
1 teaspoon lemon juice
    Salt and freshly ground black pepper
    Cayenne pepper

1. In a large heavy skillet, brown the beef slices on all sides in the butter. Remove the meat and keep it warm.

2. Add the cream, paprika, and lemon juice to the skillet and bring to a boil. Season the sauce with salt, pepper, and cayenne to taste.

3. Return the meat to the skillet, spoon the sauce over, and heat through.

Hungarian Beef Goulash I

6 servings

3 tablespoons butter
3 cups thinly sliced onions
2 cloves garlic, finely chopped
1 teaspoon chopped fresh marjoram or ½
    teaspoon dried marjoram
3 pounds lean beef, cut into 1½-inch cubes
1 teaspoon salt
3 tablespoons paprika
3 tablespoons tomato paste
2 cups Beef Stock (page 115)
    Celery leaves from 2 ribs
4 sprigs parsley
1 bay leaf
¼ teaspoon ground thyme

1. Heat the butter in a saucepan. Add the onions and cook over low heat until lightly browned.

2. Add the garlic and marjoram and continue to cook for several minutes.

3. Add the beef cubes, salt, and paprika; mix well. Cover and simmer slowly for thirty minutes, stirring frequently. Stir in the tomato paste and stock.

4. Tie the celery leaves, parsley, bay leaf together and add, along with the thyme, to the meat. Bring the liquid to a boil. Reduce the heat, cover again, and cook slowly for about one and one-half hours, until the beef is tender when pierced with a fork.

5. Remove the celery bundle and discard. Skim off any excess fat. Serve the beef with noodles.

Hungarian Beef Goulash II

5 servings

3 medium onions, chopped
¼ cup melted chicken fat
2 pounds lean boneless beef chuck, diced
1 tablespoon sweet paprika
    Water
1 medium green pepper, sliced
1 medium tomato, peeled and sliced
1 tablespoon tomato paste
    Salt

1. Sauté the onions in the chicken fat until golden brown. Add the meat and paprika, cover the skillet, and simmer ten minutes. Stir twice, adding a little water if needed.

2. Add the green pepper, tomato, tomato paste, and one teaspoon salt. Add one and one-half cups water and cook, covered, over low heat until the meat is done, about two hours. During cooking time, stir occasionally and, if needed, add additional water. Add additional salt to taste, if desired. Serve with rice, noodles, or dumplings.

Meat Balls Paprikash

6 to 8 servings

½ cup finely chopped onion
1 clove garlic, finely minced
1 tablespoon butter
1½ pounds round steak, ground
¾ cup fresh bread crumbs
2 teaspoons salt
½ teaspoon freshly ground black pepper
1 egg, lightly beaten
¼ cup milk
2 tablespoons salad oil or shortening
2 tablespoons all-purpose flour
1 tablespoon paprika
¼ teaspoon cayenne pepper
1½ cups hot Beef Stock (page 115)
¾ cup sour cream

1. Preheat the oven to 300 degrees.

2. Cook the onion and garlic in the butter until wilted, then combine in a mixing bowl with the meat, bread crumbs, and salt, pepper, egg, and milk. Blend gently. Chill two hours.

3. Shape the meat into balls one and one-half inches in diameter. Brown a few meat balls at a time in the oil. As the meat balls brown, transfer them to a pie plate. Keep them warm in the oven.

4. Add the flour, paprika, and cayenne pepper to the skillet and stir in the hot beef stock. When the mixture is blended and smooth, remove the skillet from the heat. When the mixture cools slightly, add the sour cream, beating vigorously. When blended and smooth, reheat gently, but do not boil. Add the meat balls, heat thoroughly, and serve hot.

Meat Balls Smitane

About 6 servings

1½ pounds round steak, ground
    Salt and freshly ground black pepper
½ cup fresh rye bread crumbs
1 egg
¼ cup peanut or salad oil
1 cup finely minced onion
1½ cups thinly sliced mushrooms
2 tablespoons butter
1 cup Beef Stock (page 115)
1½ tablespoons all-purpose flour
    Ground mace or nutmeg
2 cups sour cream
¼ cup chopped fresh parsley

1. Combine the meat, salt and pepper to taste, bread crumbs, and egg in a mixing bowl. Blend with the fingers and shape into eighteen to twenty-four small balls. Brown them in the oil on all sides. Drain on paper towels.

2. Cook the onion and mushrooms in the butter until the mushrooms give up their liquid. Continue cooking until most of the liquid evaporates. Add the meat balls and stock and cook over low heat for thirty minutes.

3. To prepare the sauce, blend the flour, one teaspoon salt, mace to taste, and sour cream. Remove the meat balls from the heat and stir in the sour cream mixture. Return to the heat and heat thoroughly, but do not boil. Keep hot over simmering water, stirring occasionally, until ready to serve. Before serving, sprinkle with chopped parsley.

Pork Goulash

8 servings

1 pork loin (4 to 5 pounds), boned and cut into 1-inch cubes
3 tablespoons lard
4 large onions, sliced
2 tablespoons paprika
1 teaspoon salt
½ teaspoon dried marjoram
2 cloves garlic, minced
1 cup pork broth or Chicken Stock (page 115)
3½ cups (1 1-pound 13-ounce can) sauerkraut
1 cup sour cream
¼ cup kümmel or Tokay wine (optional)

1. Brown the pork cubes in the lard in a saucepan. Set aside.
2. Gently cook the onions in the saucepan until golden. Add the pork and sprinkle with the paprika and salt. Add the marjoram, garlic, and broth. Simmer, covered, for thirty minutes.
3. Add the sauerkraut and continue to cook for about thirty minutes, until the pork is tender. Stir in the sour cream and kümmel. Reheat, but do not boil.

Bakonyi Pork

(Paprika Pork)

4 to 6 servings

10 thin slices of pork cut from the leg (about 1½ pounds)
All-purpose flour
Salt and freshly ground black pepper
6 tablespoons lard, shortening, or salad oil
1 onion, peeled and sliced wafer thin
1 teaspoon Hungarian paprika
1½ cups water or Chicken Stock (page 115)
1½ pounds fresh mushrooms
½ cup sour cream

1. Have the butcher pound the pork slices as for veal scaloppine.
2. Dredge the meat in a mixture of flour, salt, and pepper until well coated. Heat four tablespoons of the lard in a skillet and cook the pork lightly on both sides. As it becomes golden, transfer the meat to a two-quart ovenproof casserole. Cover and cook over low heat.
3. Add the onion to the skillet in which the meat cooked and cook, stirring, until golden. Do not brown. Add the paprika and water. Simmer two to three minutes, then pour the mixture over the pork.
4. Meanwhile, slice the mushrooms. Heat the remaining lard in a skillet and cook the mushrooms, stirring, until wilted. Add the mushrooms to the meat and sprinkle with salt and pepper to taste.
5. Combine one tablespoon flour with the sour cream and dilute with a little of the liquid in the casserole. Blend well and stir the sour cream mixture into the casserole. Continue cooking five minutes. Do not boil. Serve with dumplings, if desired.

Braised Pork, Hungarian Style

8 servings

1 fresh shoulder of pork (6 pounds),
   boned and tied, with bones reserved
3 tablespoons peanut oil
   Salt and freshly ground black pepper
½ teaspoon dried thyme
½ teaspoon orégano
½ teaspoon fennel seeds, crushed
   All-purpose flour
2 cloves garlic, finely minced
1½ cups Chicken Stock (page 115)
½ cup dry white wine
2 tablespoons chopped parsley
1 bay leaf
2 tablespoons butter
1 cup sour cream

1. Rub the meat all over with one table-spoon of the oil. Rub the meat with a mixture of salt, pepper, thyme, orégano, and fennel seeds, then dust it lightly with flour.

2. Heat the remaining oil in a heavy casserole or Dutch oven. Brown the meat on all sides over moderate heat. When dark golden, add the garlic and cook briefly, without browning. Add the reserved pork bones, the stock, wine, parsley, and bay leaf and cover closely. Simmer two and one-half hours.

3. Transfer the meat to a hot platter and cover with aluminum foil to keep warm. Remove the bones from the casserole and skim off the fat.

4. Blend two tablespoons flour with the butter. Bring the liquid in the casserole to a boil and add the butter-flour mixture, bit by bit, stirring constantly. When the mixture is slightly thickened and smooth, strain the sauce into a saucepan. Stir in the sour cream and bring just to a boil, but do not boil. Slice the meat and serve the sauce separately.

Veal Goulash

About 6 servings

2 pounds veal, cubed
   Salt and freshly ground pepper to taste
2 tablespoons peanut oil
2 teaspoons butter
2 cups thinly sliced onions
1½ tablespoons paprika
1½ tablespoons all-purpose flour
1½ cups beer
½ cup Chicken Stock (page 115) or
   canned chicken broth
1 teaspoon Dijon or Düsseldorf mustard
1 teaspoon caraway seeds
1 cup sour cream

1. Preheat the oven to 350 degrees.

2. Sprinkle the meat with salt and pepper. Heat the oil and butter in a skillet and brown the meat on all sides. As it is browned, transfer it to a heavy casserole.

3. Add the onions to the skillet and cook, stirring, until wilted, adding a little more butter if necessary. Sprinkle with the paprika and flour and stir in the beer and chicken stock, using a wire whisk. Add the mustard and caraway seeds and bring to a boil. Add salt to taste and pour this over the meat. Cover and bake one to one and one-half hours. Just before serving, stir in the sour cream. Serve with noodles or dumplings.

Hungarian Veal

4 servings

1½ pounds veal steak
¼ cup all-purpose flour
3 tablespoons shortening
1 clove garlic, crushed
2 tablespoons minced onion
1 tablespoon chopped fresh parsley
½ teaspoon salt
¼ teaspoon paprika
¼ teaspoon celery salt
1 cup Chicken Stock (page 115)
½ cup sour cream

1. Cut the veal into one-inch pieces and roll in the flour.
2. Melt the shortening in a frying pan, add the garlic, and cook three minutes. Discard the garlic. Add the onion and veal to the pan and brown well.
3. Add the parsley, salt, paprika, celery salt, and stock. Simmer for one hour.
4. Add the sour cream and heat thoroughly, but do not boil. Serve immediately.

Chicken Paprikash

4 servings

2 large onions, chopped
¼ cup melted chicken fat
1 roasting chicken (4 pounds), cut into serving pieces
2 tablespoons sweet paprika
Salt
Water
1 medium green pepper, sliced
1 medium tomato, peeled and sliced
1 teaspoon tomato paste

1. Sauté the onions in the chicken fat until golden brown.
2. Add the chicken, paprika, and one teaspoon salt. Cover and simmer for ten minutes. During the simmering, stir twice and add a little water if needed.
3. Add the green pepper, tomato, and tomato paste and one cup water. Cover the skillet and cook over low heat for about fifty minutes, stirring and adding water as needed to prevent sticking. Add additional salt to taste. Serve with rice, noodles, or dumplings.

Smothered Chicken Smitane

4 to 6 servings

2 chickens (3 pounds each), cut into serving pieces
Salt and freshly ground black pepper
All-purpose flour
¼ cup butter
1 cup sour cream
1 teaspoon paprika or to taste

1. Dredge the chicken parts in a mixture of salt, pepper, and flour.
2. Heat the butter in a heavy skillet and brown the chicken in it on all sides. Cover and cook over low heat until the chicken is tender, thirty-five minutes to one hour.
3. Remove the chicken to a hot serving platter. Add the sour cream and paprika to the skillet and stir. Heat thoroughly but do not boil. Season with salt and pepper to taste and pour the sauce over the chicken or serve the sauce separately.

Chicken, Hungarian Style

4 servings

It is a pity that in this country the spice called paprika is thought of as something to dust on salads or fish. It is a seasoning that has long given a fillip to Hungarian cooking, and it is Hungary that produces the finest paprika of all. Below is a recipe for chicken that uses this seasoning in abundance.

1 chicken (3 pounds), cut into serving pieces
  Salt and freshly ground black pepper
6 tablespoons butter
2 tablespoons sweet paprika
2 medium onions, thinly sliced (about 2 cups)
8 mushrooms
1 cup heavy cream
  Broiled mushroom caps for garnish (optional)

1. Sprinkle the chicken with salt and pepper.
2. Heat four tablespoons of the butter in a large skillet and arrange the chicken pieces, skin side down, in it. Cook until the chicken is golden brown, fifteen to twenty minutes. Turn the chicken pieces and sprinkle with the paprika and onions. Cover.
3. Rinse the mushrooms in cold water and drain. Slice the mushrooms thinly and scatter them over the onions. Cover again and continue to cook twenty minutes. If there seems to be an excess of fat in the skillet, spoon the fat off and discard.
4. When the chicken is done, transfer it to a warm serving dish. Cover with aluminum foil and keep warm. Continue simmering the sauce in the skillet.
5. Add the cream and bring to a boil, stirring. Turn off the heat and swirl in the remaining butter by rotating the pan gently.

Pour the sauce over the chicken. Garnish, if desired, with mushroom caps broiled or cooked until tender in a little butter. Serve with buttered noodles.

Chicken Breasts Hungarian

4 servings

2 large chicken breasts, skinned, boned, and split in half
¼ cup butter
3 cups coarsely chopped Bermuda onion
1 clove garlic, finely minced
1 rib celery, chopped
1 carrot, scraped and chopped
1 bay leaf
2 sprigs parsley
¼ teaspoon dried thyme
2 tablespoons sweet paprika
1 tablespoon tomato paste
2 tablespoons all-purpose flour
1 cup Chicken Stock (page 115)
  Salt and freshly ground pepper to taste
½ cup sour cream

1. In a large skillet, brown the chicken breasts on both sides in half the butter. Transfer the chicken to a Dutch oven or other heavy utensil with a lid. Keep warm.
2. Heat the remaining butter in the same skillet and cook the onion, garlic, celery, carrot, bay leaf, parsley, thyme, and paprika until the onion is wilted. Stir in the tomato paste and sprinkle with the flour. Pour in the stock, stirring rapidly with a whisk. When smooth, simmer about five minutes. Discard the parsley and bay leaf.
3. Put the mixture through a food mill and pour over the chicken. Season with salt and pepper and bring the mixture to a boil. Simmer until the chicken is thoroughly tender, about twenty minutes. Stir in the sour cream and heat thoroughly without boiling.

Cabbage Strudel

8 to 12 servings

1 head cabbage (2 pounds)
  Salt
  Vegetable oil
  Freshly ground black pepper
8 strudel leaves
½ cup fine bread crumbs

1. Remove the core from the cabbage and discard it, then grate the cabbage fine. Sprinkle it with two teaspoons salt and let stand fifteen minutes. Squeeze to remove the moisture.

2. Heat two tablespoons oil in a heavy skillet and add the cabbage. Cook, stirring, until the cabbage is lightly browned. Add salt and pepper to taste. Let stand until thoroughly cool.

3. Preheat the oven to 375 degrees.

4. Cover a pastry board with a cloth. Arrange half the strudel leaves on the board and sprinkle lightly with oil. Sprinkle with half the bread crumbs and lightly with pepper.

5. Spoon a row of the cabbage filling—using half the amount—about four inches from the bottom edge of the dough. Fold this bottom edge over the cabbage. Then, using both hands, lift the cloth and let the cabbage roll fall over and over itself until the filling is completely enclosed in the pastry sheet. Repeat with the remaining cabbage filling, strudel leaves, pepper, and bread crumbs.

6. Lightly oil a jelly roll pan or other shallow baking dish and arrange the strudel on it, cutting the rolls in half if necessary to fit them inside the pan. Bake thirty minutes.

Transylvanian Layered Cabbage

6 or more servings

1½ cups water
   Salt
 ¾ cup uncooked rice
 ¼ cup lard, shortening, or salad oil
 2 onions, finely chopped
 1 clove garlic, finely minced
1¼ pounds pork, ground
   Freshly ground black pepper
 ½ teaspoon Hungarian paprika
 ¼ pound lean bacon, cut into small pieces
 ¼ pound smoked sausage, thinly sliced
 2 pounds sauerkraut
 1 cup sour cream

1. Bring the one and one-half cups water to a boil in a saucepan and add salt to taste and the rice. Cover and simmer ten minutes. Drain immediately.

2. Heat half the lard in a skillet and cook the onion until pale yellow. Add the garlic, pork, salt and pepper to taste, and the paprika. Cook, stirring, ten to twelve minutes.

3. In another skillet, cook the bacon and, when nearly done, add the sausage. Continue to cook about three minutes. Pour off most of the fat that accumulates in the skillet.

4. Preheat the oven to 250 degrees.

5. Place the sauerkraut in a large saucepan and add water to cover. Add salt to taste and simmer twenty minutes. Drain well.

6. Line the bottom of a large casserole with one-third of the sauerkraut. Add alternate layers of the bacon mixture, pork mixture, sour cream, rice, and sauerkraut, ending with a layer of sauerkraut. Dot with the remaining lard and cover. Cook one hour. Remove the cover and cook one-half hour longer.

Túrós Delkli

(Cheese Buns)

About 3 dozen

1 cup butter
1 cup plus 3 tablespoons granulated sugar
6 egg yolks
1 package dry active yeast
2 tablespoons lukewarm water
  Milk
½ teaspoon plus ⅛ teaspoon salt
3 cups sifted all-purpose flour, approximately
1 teaspoon ground cinnamon
1 pound farmer's cheese
1 8-ounce package cream cheese
1 teaspoon vanilla extract
1 egg white, lightly beaten

1. Beat the butter together with the three tablespoons sugar until light and fluffy. Beat in four of the egg yolks, one at a time, very well.

2. Dissolve the yeast in the water and stir into the creamed mixture with one-half cup milk, the one-half teaspoon salt, and enough flour to make a soft dough that will leave the sides of the bowl clean.

3. Divide the dough into two and wrap each piece in waxed paper. Chill in the refrigerator at least two hours, preferably four or five.

4. Combine one-half cup of the remaining sugar with the cinnamon and set aside.

5. Beat the two cheeses together with the remaining one-half cup sugar, the remaining egg yolks, the vanilla extract, and the one-eighth teaspoon salt.

6. Remove the dough from the refrigerator fifteen to thirty minutes before proceeding.

7. Preheat the oven to 350 degrees.

8. Roll one-half of the dough on a lightly floured board until it is about one-quarter inch thick. Cut into three-inch squares.

9. Brush the squares with milk and sprinkle with the sugar-cinnamon mixture, then put a spoonful of the cheese mixture on each square. Draw the four corners up together and pinch. Place on a greased baking sheet. Brush with egg white and bake twenty-five minutes, or until lightly browned. Cool on a rack.

10. Repeat with the remaining dough.

India

Most soups are thought of as the preface to a meal, but there are some that are so rich they comprise a meal in themselves. One such is the lightly curried East Indian mulligatawny —literally, "pepper water." The peppery nature of mulligatawny depends entirely on the cook: it can be hot or mild.

Mulligatawny Soup I

4 to 6 servings

1 chicken (3 pounds), cut into small serving pieces
6 cups Chicken Stock (page 115) or water, preferably chicken stock
1 onion, stuck with four cloves
2 small ribs celery with leaves
1 carrot, scraped and quartered
1 bay leaf
2 sprigs fresh parsley
Salt
14 peppercorns
½ small coconut
1 cup freshly cooked or canned chick-peas, drained
¼ cup butter
5 tablespoons all-purpose flour
3 tablespoons powdered turmeric
1 teaspoon grated fresh ginger or ½ teaspoon powdered ginger
1 teaspoon ground coriander
1 clove garlic, finely minced
Cayenne pepper
1 cup heavy cream
Freshly ground pepper
Lemon slices

1. Place the chicken in a saucepan and add the stock or water. Add the onion, celery, carrot, bay leaf, parsley, salt to taste, and peppercorns. Bring to a boil and simmer thirty minutes, or until the chicken is cooked and tender. Remove the chicken pieces and keep them warm. Strain the broth.

2. Remove the meat from the coconut shell. Pare away the dark coating and cut the meat into small cubes. Put the cubes in an electric blender and add two cups of the broth in which the chicken cooked. Blend on high speed. Line a sieve with cheesecloth and strain the coconut milk. Press to extract as much of the moisture as possible. Discard the residue.

3. Rinse out the blender. Return the coconut milk to the blender and add the chick-peas. Blend until the peas are thoroughly pureed. Add enough of the reserved chicken broth to make four cups.

4. Melt the butter in a saucepan and add the flour, turmeric, ginger, coriander, garlic, and cayenne pepper. Stir to blend and remove from the heat.

5. Gradually add the coconut milk mixture to the butter-flour mixture, stirring rapidly with a whisk. Add the cream and chicken parts, then season to taste with salt and pepper. Garnish with lemon slices and serve piping hot, with hot rice as an accompaniment.

Mulligatawny Soup II

3 or 4 servings

1 cup boiling water
¼ pound (1¼ cups) grated coconut
1 medium onion, sliced
¼ cup clarified butter (see note page 174)
1 tablespoon Curry Powder (page 33)
1 frying chicken (3 pounds), cut into serving pieces
1 teaspoon salt
4 cups Chicken Stock (page 115)
¼ cup dried lentils
4 bay leaves
  Hot, cooked rice
  Fresh limes

1. Pour the boiling water over the coconut and allow to stand.

2. Cook the onion in the butter until golden. Add the curry powder and cook for three to four minutes, then put in the chicken pieces and cook until the chicken is browned well on all sides.

3. Drain the coconut, pressing out the liquid and discarding the residue. Add this coconut milk and the salt to the chicken and cook for twenty minutes, or until tender. Select and reserve the best parts of the chicken.

4. To the remaining chicken, add the stock, lentils, and bay leaves. Simmer for two hours. Strain, forcing the lentils through the strainer. Add more salt if necessary.

5. Pour the soup into a heated tureen, add the reserved chicken, and pass with a bowl of flaky rice. The guests put a few spoonfuls of rice into their soup plates, then the soup, and then squeeze fresh lime juice over all.

Mulligatawny Soup III

4 to 6 servings

1 stewing chicken (5 pounds), cut into serving pieces
4 cups Chicken Stock (page 115)
1 carrot, scraped and sliced
1 whole onion
2 ribs celery with leaves
¼ pound mushrooms
3 sprigs parsley
3 tablespoons butter
½ cup finely chopped onion
1½ tablespoons all-purpose flour
1 tablespoon Curry Powder (page 33), or more to taste
½ cup heavy cream
¼ cup cooked rice

1. Combine the chicken, stock, carrot, whole onion, celery, mushrooms, and parsley in a saucepan. Bring to a boil and cook for ten minutes. Skim to remove the surface foam, partly cover, and continue to cook for one hour or longer, until the chicken is tender. Strain the broth. Reserve half a chicken breast, remove the bone, and cut it into very thin slices (julienne). The rest of the chicken may be refrigerated for another use.

2. Melt the butter and add the chopped onion. Cook, stirring, for about five minutes. Do not let the onion brown. Stir in the flour and curry powder. Gradually add the strained broth, while stirring, and bring to a boil, skimming as needed. Simmer for ten minutes. Adjust the seasoning if necessary.

3. Stir in the cream and rice and return to a boil. Serve in hot cups or soup bowls and garnish each serving with julienne strips of chicken.

Artichokes with hollandaise sauce (France

Lentil Soup

8 to 10 servings

2 cups dried lentils
¼ pound salt pork
9 cups water
Salt and freshly ground pepper to taste
1 cup finely chopped onion
1 cup finely chopped celery
½ teaspoon dried thyme
1 bay leaf
½ teaspoon granulated sugar
2 tablespoons butter
2 tablespoons all-purpose flour
Juice of 1 lemon
Thin slices of lemon for garnish

1. Place the lentils in a mixing bowl and add cold water to cover to a depth of one inch. Let stand overnight.

2. Drain and place the lentils in a large saucepan and add the salt pork and the nine cups water. Add salt and pepper to taste and bring to a boil. Simmer three hours, then add the onion, celery, thyme, bay leaf, and sugar. Simmer thirty minutes.

3. Remove the salt pork and bay leaf and put the soup through a food mill or puree it in an electric blender.

4. Heat the butter and stir in the flour, using a wire whisk. When blended, add about a cup of the pureed soup, stirring rapidly with the whisk. Stir this back into the soup and bring to a boil. Simmer about ten minutes, then add the lemon juice. Serve piping hot, with one thin lemon slice in each bowl.

resh ginger and spices enhance a curry (Ceylon)

Vindaloo Beef Curry

4 to 6 servings

1 cup chopped onions
1 clove garlic, finely minced
2 tablespoons butter
1 tablespoon ground coriander
½ teaspoon ground cumin
1 teaspoon ground turmeric
½ teaspoon dry mustard
½ teaspoon red pepper flakes, or more to taste
Freshly ground black pepper to taste
½ teaspoon ground ginger
2 tablespoons vinegar
2 pounds top round steak, cut into 1-inch cubes
2½ cups Beef Stock (page 115) or water
Salt
2 tablespoons fresh lemon juice
Hot, cooked rice

1. Cook the onions and garlic in the butter in a heavy kettle until the onions are wilted. Add the spices and vinegar and stir briefly.

2. Add the meat and cover. Cook, stirring occasionally, for about ten minutes, until the meat loses color.

3. Add the stock. Cover and cook for forty-five minutes, or until the meat is thoroughly tender. Add salt to taste and the lemon juice and serve piping hot over rice.

Koftas in Sour Cream

(Meat Balls)

6 servings

1 pound chuck, ground
¾ teaspoon garam masalah
1½ teaspoons ground cumin
2½ teaspoons ground coriander
¼ teaspoon or more ground red pepper
6 cloves garlic, finely minced
1 small onion, grated
2 teaspoons salt
Freshly ground black pepper
1 egg, beaten
½ cup mixed coarsely chopped pistachios, raisins, almonds, and pecans
Shortening
1 medium onion, finely chopped
1 teaspoon finely chopped or grated fresh ginger
1 tomato, peeled and chopped
1½ cups water
¼ teaspoon crushed red pepper
½ cup sour cream
1 teaspoon finely chopped parsley, preferably Chinese parsley (also called fresh coriander leaves)
⅛ teaspoon grated nutmeg

1. Place the chuck, one-half teaspoon of the garam masalah, one-half teaspoon of the cumin, one teaspoon of the coriander, the ground red pepper, half the garlic, the grated onion, half the salt, and pepper to taste. Blend thoroughly with the fingers.

2. Beat the egg in a mixing bowl. Break off small portions of the meat mixture and shape into balls the size of a walnut. Flatten slightly, then dip and coat in egg. Spoon one teaspoon of the chopped nut and raisin mixture into the center of each, then reshape each into a ball enclosing the chopped mixture.

3. Heat shortening to the depth of one inch in a skillet. Cook the meat balls in the hot shortening until golden all over.

4. Preheat the oven to 350 degrees.

5. Heat two tablespoons of shortening in a skillet and add the chopped onion, the remaining garlic, and the ginger. Cook until lightly browned. Add the remaining cumin and coriander. Stir constantly about five minutes, taking care that the ingredients do not burn. Add the chopped tomato and cook, stirring, ten minutes longer. Add the water, remaining salt, and crushed red pepper. Simmer half an hour, or until the liquid is reduced by one-third. Add the meat balls and simmer twenty minutes longer. Gently fold in the sour cream. Pour into a baking dish and cover. Bake fifteen to twenty minutes.

6. When cooked, turn off the oven and let the meat balls stand until ready to serve. Serve garnished with the chopped parsley, the remaining garam masalah, and the nutmeg.

Mahashes

(Stuffed, Spiced Vegetables)

5 to 10 servings

10 small green peppers or other vegetables for stuffing (see note)
1 pound beef or boneless chicken, ground
¼ cup uncooked rice, rinsed and drained
¼ teaspoon powdered turmeric
¼ teaspoon powdered cumin
¼ teaspoon ground coriander
1 tablespoon lemon juice
2 teaspoons brown sugar
½ teaspoon finely chopped garlic
½ teaspoon grated fresh ginger
1 small onion, finely chopped
2 teaspoons salt
1 tablespoon peanut oil
4 tablespoons water, approximately

1. Prepare the green peppers for stuffing. Trim off the tops of the peppers and pare away the white membranes. Shake out the seeds.

2. Combine the beef, rice, spices, lemon juice, brown sugar, garlic, ginger, onion, and salt in a mixing bowl and blend well. Stuff the peppers with the meat mixture.

3. Heat the oil in a large, heavy frying pan with cover. Lay the stuffed peppers on their side in the pan, cover, and cook over a low flame about ten minutes. Uncover and turn the vegetables to the other side. Cover again and cook until brown on the other side. Add three or four tablespoons of water to the skillet and cover. Cook over very low heat until all the liquid disappears, about forty-five minutes. Add a little water to the skillet if necessary to prevent burning.

Note: Other vegetables suitable for stuffing include green or yellow squash, cut into three-inch lengths and hollowed out; cabbage leaves, lightly parboiled; small eggplants, hollowed out; lettuce leaves, and so on.

Kebab and Kofte with Cherry Tomatoes

8 servings

2 pounds boneless leg of lamb, cut into 1-inch cubes
2 tablespoons olive oil
2 cloves garlic, finely minced
1 small onion, sliced
1 teaspoon crushed cumin seed
1 pound beef round, ground twice
1 onion, finely chopped
1 egg, lightly beaten
2 tablespoons tomato paste
1 tablespoon chopped parsley
1 teaspoon salt
¼ teaspoon freshly ground black pepper
1 teaspoon fresh snipped dill
24 cherry tomatoes

1. Marinate the lamb in the oil containing one garlic clove, the sliced onion, and cumin for two to three hours.

2. Mix the ground beef with the remaining garlic, chopped onion, egg, tomato paste, parsley, salt, pepper, and dill. Knead the mixture and shape into slightly flattened ovals approximately two inches in diameter.

3. Alternate the lamb cubes, tomatoes, and the beef patties on skewers, leaving a one-half-inch space in between the pieces. Broil over charcoal, or in an oven broiler, three to four inches from the source of heat, for six to eight minutes, turning several times during cooking.

Chicken and Beet Khuta

(Sweet and Sour Curried Chicken)

6 servings

2 chickens (3 pounds each), cut into serving pieces
3 cups finely chopped onion
1 clove garlic, finely minced
1 teaspoon chopped fresh ginger
½ teaspoon turmeric powder
½ teaspoon ground cumin
½ teaspoon ground coriander
½ teaspoon garam masalah or cayenne pepper
Salt and freshly ground pepper to taste
1 tablespoon tomato puree
1½ cups water
1 pound fresh beets or 1 1-pound can
3 tablespoons lemon juice
1 tablespoon brown sugar

1. Place all the pieces of chicken except the breasts in a heavy casserole or Dutch oven. Bone and skin the breasts and split each in half. Add the breasts to the casserole.

2. Add the onion, garlic, ginger, turmeric, cumin, coriander, garam masalah, salt, pepper, tomato puree, and water. Cover closely and bring to a boil. Cook over medium heat about one hour, or until almost all the liquid has evaporated.

3. Meanwhile, if fresh beets are used, trim them—but not too closely or they will "bleed" —and place them in a saucepan. Add water to cover and salt to taste. Partly cover and simmer until the beets are tender. Do not drain but set aside.

4. When the chicken is done, uncover and stir the pieces around while mashing the onion with the back of a spoon. Cook until the chicken starts to brown lightly. Add the beets (sliced), one cup of beet juice (either from the cooking liquid or from the can), the lemon juice, and sugar. Simmer slowly about fifteen minutes, or until all the flavors are well blended. If desired, correct the flavor by adding more lemon juice or brown sugar. Serve with a rice pilaf sprinkled with raisins and toasted almonds.

Chicken Bengal

6 to 8 servings

2 chickens (3½ pounds each), cut into serving pieces
1 cup Yogurt (page 554)
2 tablespoons finely minced garlic
Salt and freshly ground pepper to taste
2 tablespoons butter
2 tablespoons vegetable oil
2 cups finely minced onion
1 teaspoon freshly grated ginger or ½ teaspoon powdered ginger
3 cloves
1 hot red pepper (optional)
2 teaspoons ground coriander
1 teaspoon powdered turmeric
½ teaspoon ground cumin

1. Place the chicken in a mixing bowl and add the yogurt and half the garlic, salt, and pepper. Cover and let stand two hours, turning the pieces in the liquid.

2. Melt the butter in a heavy casserole and add the oil and onion. Cook, stirring, until the onion starts to brown. Add the remaining garlic and the spices and cook over low heat, stirring frequently, about two minutes.

3. Add the chicken and marinating liquid. If necessary, add salt and pepper. Cover and simmer until the chicken is fork tender, one and one-half to two hours. Serve with rice.

Chicken Tandoori

4 servings

2 chickens (3 pounds each), cut in half
2 cups coarsely chopped onion
1 clove garlic, finely chopped
2 green peppers, seeded and chopped
2 tomatoes, peeled and chopped
2 teaspoons salt
1 tablespoon each ground Curry Powder (page 33), coriander, and cumin
1 teaspoon turmeric
½ teaspoon cinnamon
1 teaspoon freshly ground black pepper
½ cup melted butter
2 cups Chicken Stock (page 115) or water

1. Preheat the oven to 375 degrees.
2. Place the chickens in a shallow baking pan, skin side up. Sprinkle with the onion, garlic, green pepper, tomatoes, salt, and spices. Pour the melted butter over all.
3. Add the stock and bake, basting frequently, fifty minutes. Serve hot, with rice.

Turmeric Chicken

4 to 6 servings

1 frying chicken (3 pounds), cut into serving pieces
1 cup uncooked rice
2 cups boiling Chicken Stock (page 115)
Salt to taste
1 tablespoon ground turmeric, or more to taste
½ teaspoon freshly ground black pepper
1 bay leaf
½ cup chopped onion, cooked in butter until wilted
1 tablespoon lemon juice

1. Preheat the oven to 325 degrees.
2. Combine all the ingredients in a two-quart casserole. Cover and bake for about one and one-quarter hours, until the rice and chicken are tender.

Indian Gobhi Musallam

12 or more servings

1 head cauliflower
  Salt
2 tablespoons vegetable shortening
¼ teaspoon mustard seeds
2 medium onions, cut in fine strips
1 large tomato, quartered
1 cup Yogurt (page 554)
¾ cup water
1 teaspoon grated fresh ginger
½ teaspoon ground coriander
½ teaspoon ground red pepper
½ teaspoon ground cumin
¼ teaspoon ground turmeric
  Pinch of asafetida

1. Cook the cauliflower in enough boiling salted water to barely cover. When nearly tender, eight to ten minutes, drain and set aside.

2. Heat the vegetable shortening in a flameproof casserole and add the mustard seeds. When they pop, add the onions and sauté until wilted. Add the tomato, yogurt, water, and spices. Cover and bring to a boil.

3. Put the cauliflower in, head down, and douse the whole cauliflower with the sauce. Cover and cook for thirty minutes. Serve head up in a shallow dish with the sauce, as part of a buffet.

Indian Chana

(Chick-Pea Casserole)

12 or more servings

4 cups dried chick-peas
  Salt
2 tablespoons vegetable shortening
2 medium onions, sliced
2 large tomatoes, chopped
1 cup tomato paste
1 cup water
1 teaspoon ground coriander
1 teaspoon cumin seed
¼ teaspoon powdered turmeric
1 teaspoon cayenne pepper
  Pinch of asafetida
  Rice
  Onion rings for garnish
  Chopped coriander leaves for garnish

1. Soak the chick-peas overnight in water to cover. Drain and add water to cover to a depth of one and one-half inches. Add salt to taste and simmer two hours or longer, until the chick-peas are tender.

2. Meanwhile, melt the vegetable shortening in a saucepan, add the onions, and cook until wilted. Add the tomatoes, tomato paste, water, and spices. Add the chick-peas and simmer thirty minutes longer. Serve hot over rice, garnished with onion rings and coriander leaves, as part of a buffet.

Indian Sambhar

12 or more servings

1 cup tamarind pods
  Water
1 cup arhar dhal (lentils)
  Salt
2 cups small white onions, peeled
2 teaspoons sambhar powder
¼ teaspoon powdered turmeric
⅛ teaspoon asafetida
2 teaspoons vegetable shortening
½ teaspoon mustard seeds
1 teaspoon urd dhal (lentils)

1. Soak the tamarind pods in hot water until softened. Squeeze the fruit in a cheesecloth and measure one cup of juice. Combine this cup of juice with one and one-half cups of water and set aside.

2. Meanwhile, place the arhar dhal in a saucepan and add water to cover to a depth of one and one-half inches. Add salt to taste and bring to a boil. Simmer until the lentils are tender, about forty minutes. Drain.

3. Combine the lentils, tamarind juice, onions, sambhar powder, turmeric, and asafetida. Cover and simmer until the onions are tender, about forty-five minutes.

4. Heat the shortening and add the mustard seeds and urd dhal. Cook until the mustard seeds pop. Add to the other mixture. Serve hot, over rice, as part of a buffet.

Indian Eggplant Rayatha

12 or more servings

1 tablespoon vegetable shortening
¼ cup mustard seeds
1 teaspoon urd dhal (lentils)
1 large onion, chopped
1 medium eggplant, peeled and finely chopped
1 teaspoon grated fresh ginger
  Pinch of asafetida
1 teaspoon coriander leaves, finely chopped
  Salt
1 large tomato, peeled and finely chopped
1 cup Yogurt (page 554)

1. Heat the vegetable shortening in a skillet and add the mustard seeds. Cook until the mustard seeds pop and then add the urd dhal.

2. Add the onion and saute until wilted. Add the eggplant, ginger, asafetida, coriander, and salt to taste. Cook for two minutes. Add the tomato, cover, and cook over medium heat thirty minutes. Let cool, then stir in the yogurt. Serve warm or cold, as part of a buffet.

Indian Aloo Dham

12 or more servings

2 tablespoons vegetable shortening
1 pound small, red-skinned potatoes, boiled until tender and peeled
  Crushed dried red peppers
3 cloves
½ teaspoon ground cinnamon
½ teaspoon ground cardamom
2 to 3 bay leaves
½ teaspoon grated fresh ginger (if available)
¾ cup Yogurt (page 554)
¼ cup water
  Salt

1. Heat the shortening in a skillet and add the potatoes. Fry until light brown on all sides, then remove and drain on paper towels.

2. Add crushed dried red peppers to taste, the cloves, cinnamon, cardamom, and bay leaves to the skillet and cook, stirring, for about two minutes. Add the ginger, yogurt, and water and simmer for three minutes. Add the potatoes and salt to taste and mix well. Cover and let simmer for five minutes. Serve hot or warm, as part of a buffet.

Smoked Eggplant Chutney

About 1½ cups

1 eggplant (about 1 pound)
2 teaspoons lemon juice
½ teaspoon salt
1 teaspoon olive or peanut oil

1. Place the unpeeled, untrimmed eggplant on the center of a gas burner. Using a very low flame, turn the eggplant every two or three minutes until the eggplant skin is slightly charred all over. Continue to cook on the flame about ten minutes longer, or until the eggplant is thoroughly soft throughout.

2. Cover the flame with aluminum foil and place the eggplant on top. Continue cooking about five minutes.

3. Let the eggplant cool. Pull off and discard the skin. Place the pulp in a mixing bowl and add the remaining ingredients. Stir to blend and chill several hours.

Yogurt with Cucumbers for Curry

6 servings

2 cups Yogurt (page 554)
1 clove garlic, finely minced
  Salt and freshly ground black pepper to taste
  Juice of ½ lemon, or to taste
1 cucumber, peeled, seeded, and finely chopped

Place the yogurt in a mixing bowl and stir in the remaining ingredients. Serve as an accompaniment to curries.

Raita

(Cucumbers with Yogurt)

6 servings

2 cups Yogurt (page 554)
1 cucumber, peeled and grated
¾ teaspoon freshly ground cumin
½ teaspoon salt or to taste
  Freshly ground black pepper
  Cayenne pepper
  Chopped parsley, preferably Chinese parsley (fresh coriander leaves)

1. Combine the yogurt, cucumber, one-half teaspoon of the cumin, salt, and black pepper to taste in a mixing bowl. Chill.
2. Serve sprinkled with black pepper, cayenne pepper, remaining cumin, and chopped parsley.

Indian Neruppu Vazhai

12 or more servings

6 firm bananas
¼ cup orange juice
½ cup light brown sugar
1 cup grated coconut
½ cup slivered blanched almonds
1 teaspoon ground cardamom
¼ cup melted butter
  Rum or Cognac (optional)

1. Preheat the oven to 400 degrees.
2. Peel the bananas and arrange them in a buttered baking dish. Pour the orange juice over them and sprinkle with the sugar, coconut, almonds, and cardamom. Pour the butter over them and bake twenty-five minutes. Serve, as a dessert, with a little rum or Cognac poured over, if desired.

Date Honey

(A Dessert Sauce)

About 2 cups

2 pounds pitted, pressed Iranian dates
4 cups water, approximately

1. Pull the dates apart and place them in a kettle. Add about four cups of water. The dates should be completely covered. Bring to a boil without stirring, then remove immediately from the heat. Let stand until thoroughly cool, four hours or longer.
2. Line a mixing bowl with a clean, damp linen towel. Cheesecloth will not do. Pour in the date mixture and bring the corners of the towel together. Press gently with the hands to extract as much liquid as possible but none of the pulp. Bring this liquid to a boil and simmer, skimming the surface often to remove the scum. Cook about two hours and let stand until cool. Serve over ice cream or sherbet.

Indonesia

Sambal Goreng Udang

6 servings

2 teaspoons vegetable oil
½ teaspoon laos
Salt to taste
½ teaspoon trasi (shrimp paste)
2 cloves garlic, finely minced
1 small onion, thinly sliced
1 salam leaf
1 teaspoon paprika
½ cup thinly sliced sweet pepper
¼ cup water
3 whole cloves
24 medium raw shrimp, peeled and deveined
¾ cup Coconut Milk Made in a Blender (page 34)
½ teaspoon brown sugar

1. Heat the oil in a saucepan and add the laos, salt, trasi, garlic, onion, salam leaf, paprika, and sweet pepper. Cook until the vegetables are wilted, about five minutes.

2. Add the water, cloves, and shrimp. Cook about five minutes, then add the coconut milk and brown sugar. Add salt to taste and simmer about five minutes.

Nasi Goreng

8 or more servings

3 cups uncooked rice
2 pounds chuck steak
¾ cup peanut oil
2 cloves garlic, finely minced
2 large onions, finely chopped
2 teaspoons ground coriander
3 or more tablespoons Curry Powder (page 33)
½ teaspoon cayenne pepper
Salt and freshly ground pepper to taste
2 whole chicken breasts
3 cups cooked shrimp (about one and one-half pounds in the shell)
6 tablespoons butter
¾ cup chopped green onions
Shredded Egg Pancakes (see below)
Chopped parsley or whole fresh coriander leaves
Broiled Banana Halves (see below)

1. Cook the rice according to package directions, or as you do ordinarily. To make this dish, the rice must be fluffy and have absorbed all the water. When cooked, set the rice aside.

2. Cut the beef into thin slices, then cut the slices into cubes or slivers and place in a

mixing bowl. Add one-quarter cup of the peanut oil, half the garlic, all the onion, half the coriander, one teaspoon of the curry powder, and half the cayenne. Add salt and pepper to taste. Mix well with the hands, cover, and set aside. Let stand at least one hour.

3. Skin and bone the chicken breasts. Cut the meat into thin slices, then into strips. Place in a mixing bowl and add one-quarter cup peanut oil, the remaining garlic, coriander, and cayenne and one teaspoon curry powder. Add salt and pepper to taste. Mix well with the hands, cover, and set aside. Let stand at least one hour.

4. When ready to prepare the nasi goreng, cook the beef in one skillet and the chicken in another. Cook, stirring, until the meat and chicken lose their color and are briefly cooked.

5. Cut each shrimp into three or four pieces.

6. Heat the butter and remaining oil in a large frying utensil, preferably a round-bottomed wok such as the Chinese use. Add the rice and sprinkle with the remaining curry powder. (Use the curry powder according to taste.) Cook, stirring, until the rice is well coated with oil and curry powder, then add the beef and chicken. Continue cooking, stirring frequently, letting the rice brown, about twenty minutes.

7. Add the shrimp and half the green onions and stir until well blended and thoroughly heated. Pour the nasi goreng onto a hot platter, sprinkle with the remaining green onions, shredded egg pancakes, and parsley or whole fresh coriander leaves. Garnish all around with the broiled banana halves. Serve with side dishes of chutney, cucumber strips, halved hard-cooked eggs, seedless raisins, chopped peanuts and macadamia nuts, and grated fresh coconut, with Krupuk (see below) on the side.

EGG PANCAKES:

About 15 pancakes

  5 eggs
1½ tablespoons all-purpose flour
  1 teaspoon granulated sugar
  1 tablespoon soy sauce
    Salt and freshly ground pepper to taste
    Butter for greasing pan

1. Combine the eggs, flour, sugar, soy sauce, salt, and pepper and beat well to make a thin batter. Strain.

2. Butter a crêpe pan. Pour in a very little batter, a tablespoon or less, and swirl it around in the pan. Cook until set on one side, then turn and cook briefly on the other. Continue greasing pan and cooking until all the batter is used. Slice the pancakes into thin shreds.

BROILED BANANA HALVES:

12 banana halves

6 small, ripe but firm bananas
2 tablespoons butter

Peel the bananas, slice them in half lengthwise, and arrange them, cut side up, on a baking dish. Dot with butter and place under a preheated broiler until nicely browned on top.

KRUPUK:

Krupuk are Indonesian wafers, and are available at some specialty shops. To cook them, heat an inch or so of vegetable oil in a skillet or other frying utensil. When it is quite hot, hold one krupuk at a time in the fat, using a pair of kitchen tongs. The krupuk will expand tremendously as they cook. Turn once in the fat.

Sate Kambing

6 servings

½ leg of lamb (about 3½ pounds)
2 tablespoons vegetable oil
  Freshly ground pepper to taste
1 clove garlic, finely minced
1 cup soy sauce, preferably dark
¼ cup dark brown sugar
1 small hot red pepper, finely chopped, or hot pepper flakes or pepper flakes in oil to taste
1 small onion, thinly sliced
1 thick slice of lime
2 tablespoons Deep-Fried Onion (page 365)

1. Cut the lamb into small bite-sized cubes and place it in a bowl. Add the oil, pepper, and garlic.

2. Combine the soy sauce with the brown sugar and stir to blend. Add half of this to the lamb and reserve the rest.

3. Let the lamb stand for fifteen minutes, then drain and arrange the meat on six skewers. Grill over charcoal, broil, or bake in an oven preheated to 500 degrees.

4. When ready to serve, place the chopped red pepper or pepper flakes, onion slices, and lime on an oval platter. Squeeze the lime and crush the onion. Add the remaining soy sauce and deep-fried onion rings and stir to blend. Arrange the skewered meat on the platter and serve immediately.

Sate Babi

(A Skewered Indonesian Pork Dish)

6 to 8 servings

3 pounds fresh pork butt, trimmed
¾ teaspoon salt
⅛ teaspoon freshly ground black pepper
1 tablespoon ground coriander
1 tablespoon cumin seed
½ teaspoon vegetable or peanut oil
½ cup sliced onions
1 tablespoon brown sugar
¼ cup soy sauce
1 teaspoon monosodium glutamate
¼ teaspoon powdered ginger
  Lime juice

1. Cut the meat into one-and-one-half-inch cubes.

2. Combine the salt, pepper, coriander, cumin seed, and oil. Add the meat and let stand for twenty minutes. Add the onions, sugar, soy sauce, monosodium glutamate, and ginger. Stir this into the pork mixture and let stand, refrigerated, at least one hour. The meat may stand overnight or all day before cooking.

3. Before cooking, prepare a charcoal fire or preheat the broiler. Thread the meat on skewers. If a broiler is used, broil about four inches from the heat for fifteen minutes, basting frequently and turning often. Reserve the cooking drippings. If charcoal is used, baste the meat and turn as it cooks. Serve sprinkled with lime juice to taste and, if available, the drippings. This dish may be served hot or cold.

Soto Ajam

6 servings

4 small, waxy new potatoes
2 eggs
2 large cloves garlic, peeled
¼ cup water
4 thin slices fresh ginger or one-half tea-spoon dried ginger
½ tablespoon ground turmeric
7 peppercorns
Salt to taste
1 tablespoon Deep-Fried Garlic (see below)
¼ cup Deep-Fried Onion (see below)
8 cups Chicken Stock (page 115) or water, or enough to cover the chicken when added
2 small, whole chicken breasts or 1 large, whole chicken breast, split in half
Vegetable oil for frying
1 djeruk purut leaf
½ teaspoon sereh
1 small package (2 cups loose) Japanese bean thread
½ cup finely chopped celery leaves
½ cup finely chopped green onions
1 lime, thinly sliced or cut into wedges

1. Boil the potatoes in their skins until tender, then drain and let cool. Peel and set aside.

2. Simmer the eggs in water to cover until hard cooked. Peel and set aside.

3. Place the garlic cloves, water, ginger, turmeric, peppercorns, salt, deep-fried garlic, and half the deep-fried onion in an electric blender. Blend into a paste, then set aside.

4. Bring the chicken stock or water to a boil. If water is used, add salt to taste. Add the chicken breasts and simmer, covered, skimming the surface as necessary, about five minutes for small breasts, ten minutes for large one. Drain; reserve the liquid.

5. Heat about one-half inch oil in a skillet and add the chicken breasts, skin side down. Cover and cook until golden on one side, then turn the pieces, cover, and cook until done. Drain on absorbent towels and set aside.

6. Meanwhile, simmer the liquid in which the chicken cooked. Spoon the pureed garlic mixture into the stock. Add the djeruk purut leaf and sereh. Cook, partly covered, about twenty minutes, skimming off all fat and foam from the surface.

7. Meanwhile, place the bean thread in a bowl and pour boiling water over it. Let stand until ready to serve, then drain.

8. When ready to serve, arrange the garnishes—the bean thread, chopped celery leaves, chopped green onions, the hard-cooked eggs cut into quarters, the potatoes, thinly sliced, and the fried chicken—on a large platter. To prepare the chicken as a garnish, cut the meat, including the skin, into bite-sized pieces. Place it in a mound on the platter.

9. To serve, keep the soup boiling at the table. Let each guest place one or some of each item on the garnish platter into a hot soup bowl. Add the boiling broth. Serve the remaining fried onions as a garnish. Serve the lime separately, to be squeezed into the soup.

DEEP-FRIED ONION OR GARLIC:

To prepare an onion for deep frying, peel it and slice it into the thinnest possible rings. To prepare garlic cloves, peel them and slice them thin. Drop the onion or garlic into hot fat and cook quickly, stirring, until golden brown.

Lumpia Goreng

(Fried Egg Rolls)

6 servings

1 cup sifted all-purpose flour
2 large eggs, beaten
1 cup water
1 teaspoon salt
3 cups vegetable oil
2 bean cakes, cut into thinnest possible strips (julienne)
1 medium onion, sliced
1 clove garlic, sliced
½ cup sliced pork or chicken
½ cup shrimp, cooked, shelled, and split lengthwise
2 tablespoons soy sauce
   Salt and freshly ground black pepper
1 cup bean sprouts
½ cup sliced cabbage
½ cup sliced bamboo shoots

1. Prepare a batter by mixing the flour with the eggs, water, and salt. Fry into about six to eight thin pancakes, about eight inches in diameter, as described in the recipe for Nasi Goreng (page 362). Reserve.

2. Heat about one-half cup of the oil in a large skillet. Fry the bean cakes in it until light brown. Drain off the oil, leaving one tablespoon in the pan. Fry the onion and garlic two minutes. Add the pork, shrimp, soy sauce, salt and pepper to taste, bean sprouts, cabbage, and bamboo shoots. Cook fifteen minutes, then cool.

3. Fill each pancake with about two tablespoons of the filling. Spread the filling out lengthwise and fold the pancake envelope fashion, first folding over the flap along the length of the filling and then folding over the two flaps along the ends of the filling. Moisten the edge of the last flap with salted water and seal.

4. Fry the egg rolls in a deep-fat bath with the remaining oil until golden brown. Drain on paper towels.

Gado-Gado

6 to 12 servings

SAUCE:

1 clove garlic, peeled and thinly sliced
1 small onion, thinly sliced
2¼ cups vegetable oil
½ cup freshly roasted, shelled, hulled peanuts
1½ tablespoons peanut butter
½ teaspoon powdered kentjur or 2 or 3 pieces whole
1 djeruk purut leaf
½ teaspoon trasi (shrimp paste)
3 tamarind pods
¾ cup water
1 small hot red pepper, finely chopped (optional), or Tabasco to taste
1 tablespoon brown sugar
1 tablespoon paprika
½ cup Coconut Milk Made in a Blender (page 34)

VEGETABLES:

2 small, waxy new potatoes
   Salt
1 pound green beans, trimmed and cut into 1½-inch lengths (about 4 cups when ready to cook)
1 pound spinach, picked over and tough stems removed
1 pound fresh bean sprouts or 1 1-pound can, drained
2 bean curds
   Fat for shallow frying

GARNISH:

2 hard-cooked eggs, thinly sliced
1 cucumber, peeled and thinly sliced

1. To prepare the sauce, cook the garlic and onion in half the oil until the onion is wilted. Spoon this into the container of an electric blender and add the peanuts, peanut butter, kentjur, djeruk purut leaf, and trasi.

2. Remove and discard the seeds from the tamarind and add the pulp to the blender. Add one-quarter cup of the water, the hot pepper, and brown sugar. Blend.

3. Heat the remaining oil in a skillet and add the paprika. Cook briefly, stirring, and add the blender mixture. Add the coconut milk and remaining one-half cup water to the blender to pick up any mixture remaining. Add this to the skillet and bring to a boil, stirring. Keep warm.

4. Meanwhile, cook the potatoes in boiling salted water to cover until tender. Drain and, when cool enough to handle, peel and slice.

5. Bring four cups of water to a boil, add salt and cook the green beans until crisp tender. Do not overcook. Remove them with a slotted spoon and set aside.

6. Cook the spinach in the liquid in which the beans cooked. Cook briefly, just until the spinach is wilted thoroughly. Remove the spinach with the spoon and drain well.

7. Pour the vegetable liquid quickly over the bean sprouts and drain quickly. Do not cook.

8. Fry the bean curds in hot oil until golden brown on one side, then turn and cook on the other side. Cut into bite-sized pieces.

9. To serve, arrange a layer of green beans on a platter. Cover with a layer of spinach and the bean sprouts. Garnish with the bean curd pieces, sliced potatoes, hard-cooked egg slices, and cucumber slices. Pour the hot sauce over all and serve immediately.

Atjar
(A Fresh Indonesian Pickle)

6 servings

1 cucumber
1 small onion
1 clove garlic, finely minced
  Salt to taste
¼ cup white vinegar
4 teaspoons granulated sugar
1 small hot red pepper, cut into fine circles (optional)

1. Peel the cucumber and split it in half. Scoop out the seeds with a spoon and cut the flesh into thin matchlike strips. Place in a bowl.

2. Peel the onion and slice it as thin as possible. Add it to the cucumber, then add the garlic and remaining ingredients. Chill until ready to serve.

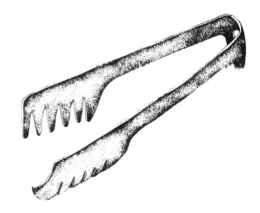

Israel

Mediterranean Fish

4 servings

¼ cup olive oil
1 cup finely chopped onion
1 green pepper, cored, seeded, and chopped
4 individual fish steaks such as salmon, small fish fillets such as flounder, or small whole fish
    Salt and freshly ground black pepper
    Cayenne pepper to taste
    Juice of 1 lemon
2 tomatoes, cored, seeded, peeled, and chopped (about 1½ cups)
½ cup Fish Stock (see below)
3 tablespoons taheeni (sesame paste)
¼ cup dry white wine
2 egg yolks, lightly beaten
2 tablespoons finely chopped parsley
8 stuffed olives
4 slices bread
    Vegetable oil for frying
1 clove garlic, cut

1. Heat half the oil in a large aluminum or enamelware skillet and cook the onion and green pepper until wilted.

2. In another skillet heat the remaining oil and cook the fish, first on one side and then on the other, until lightly browned. Transfer the fish in one layer to the skillet containing the onion mixture. Sprinkle with salt, pepper and the cayenne to taste and half the lemon juice. Spoon the tomatoes over the fish and add the fish stock. Cover with aluminum foil or parchment and cook over very low heat ten to fifteen minutes. Do not overcook.

3. Combine the taheeni and remaining lemon juice in a small mixing bowl. Start beating with a whisk and add salt and pepper to taste. Beat in the wine. Carefully pour the liquid from the cooked fish into the taheeni mixture and beat well. Beat in the egg yolks and parsley and spoon the mixture over the fish. Run the fish under the broiler until a brown glaze appears. Scatter the olives over the fish.

4. Meanwhile, fry the bread in oil and rub lightly with garlic. Serve the fish and toast while hot.

FISH STOCK:

About ½ cup

This is the simplest of stocks to make. Simply cover a few very fresh, broken fish bones with water. Add one small chopped onion, salt, pepper, half a bay leaf, and three parsley sprigs and simmer twenty minutes. Strain.

Israeli Sweet and Sour Meat Balls

24 meat balls

½ pound lean beef, ground
½ pound veal, ground
 1 large egg, lightly beaten
 1 clove garlic, finely minced
 1 onion, finely chopped
 6 tablespoons cooking fat
¼ cup finely minced parsley
   Salt and freshly ground black pepper
 1 hard roll
   Cold water
 3 tablespoons granulated sugar
 3 tablespoons vinegar or lemon juice
 2 cups boiling Beef Stock (page 115) or consommé

1. Combine the beef and veal in a mixing bowl. Add the egg and set aside.

2. Cook the garlic and onion in one tablespoon of the fat until the onion is wilted. Add this to the meat. Add the parsley and salt and pepper to taste.

3. Soak the roll thoroughly in cold water, then squeeze with the hands to extract most of the moisture. Break up the bread with the fingers and add to the meat. Using the hands, shape the meat into twenty-four balls.

4. Heat the remaining fat in a skillet and cook the meat balls until browned on all sides. Add the sugar, vinegar, and beef stock and pour everything into a saucepan. Simmer fifteen minutes and serve hot.

Nut Torte

8 servings

 6 eggs, separated
 1 cup granulated sugar
   Juice of ½ lemon
   Juice and grated rind of ½ orange
½ cup matzoh meal
 2 tablespoons cake flour
½ teaspoon salt
 1 cup walnuts, finely chopped

1. Preheat the oven to 350 degrees.

2. Beat the egg yolks, add the sugar gradually, and beat until the mixture is light in color. Add the lemon juice, orange juice, and orange rind. Mix in the meal, flour, salt, and walnuts.

3. Beat the egg whites until stiff but not dry. Fold into the walnut mixture. Bake in an ungreased eight-inch spring-form pan for forty-five minutes, or until the cake rebounds to the touch when pressed gently in the center.

Italy

Stuffed Clams

6 servings

Clams have a character all their own, a delicacy of flavor combined with a texture that makes them wholly unlike the oyster, their more sophisticated cousin. Whether littlenecks or cherrystones, they are marvelously versatile. They are delicious when accented with a simple squeeze of lemon, a blend of lemon and soy sauce, or a traditional tomato cocktail sauce. But, to some tastes, they are best of all when stuffed.

  1 dozen large cherrystone clams
1¼ cups bread crumbs
  ¼ cup freshly grated Parmesan or Romano cheese
  2 cloves garlic, finely minced
  2 tablespoons finely chopped fresh basil or 1 tablespoon dried basil
    Salt and freshly ground pepper to taste
  6 teaspoons olive oil
12 tablespoons Italian Tomato Sauce I (page 435)

1. Preheat the oven to 350 degrees.
2. Rinse the clams well. Place the clams in a small kettle and add about half a cup of water. Cover and cook about five minutes, or just until the clams open and give up their juices. Drain but reserve a little of the clam broth.
3. Break the clam shells apart and remove the clams. Set aside half the clam shells for stuffing.
4. Chop the clams and, in a mixing bowl, combine with one cup of the bread crumbs, the cheese, garlic, basil, salt, and pepper. Add enough of the reserved broth to moisten. Stuff the shells with this mixture. Arrange the clams in a baking dish containing a little water. Sprinkle the clams with the remaining crumbs, then sprinkle each clam with half a teaspoon of oil and cover each with a tablespoon of tomato sauce. Bake twenty minutes, or until piping hot and bubbling. Serve as an appetizer.

Kidneys on Skewers

20 servings

10 lamb kidneys
 3 sprigs fresh basil
 1 onion, cut into rings
 3 sprigs fresh thyme
   Juice and rind of 1 lemon
 1 bay leaf, crumbled
⅓ cup salad oil
   Salt and freshly ground black pepper to taste

1. Split the kidneys in half and remove and discard the white core. Cut each kidney into six pieces.

2. Combine the kidney pieces with the remaining ingredients and cover. Marinate, stirring occasionally, one hour or longer. Arrange the pieces of kidney on skewers and cook to the desired doneness over a very hot charcoal fire, or under a hot broiler, turning the skewers for even cooking. Serve as an appetizer.

Eggs in Green Sauce

8 servings

8 hard-cooked eggs
1 hard-cooked egg yolk
   Juice of 2 lemons
¾ cup olive oil
1 cup finely chopped parsley, preferably Italian
2 tablespoons chopped capers
3 anchovies, finely chopped
   Salt, if necessary
   Freshly ground black pepper to taste

1. Cut the eggs in half lengthwise and place them cut side down in a serving dish.

2. Sieve the egg yolk into a mixing bowl. Add the lemon juice and beat with a fork, gradually adding the oil. When well blended and of the right consistency, add the remaining ingredients. Pour over the eggs and serve as an appetizer.

Artichokes in Oil

6 servings

1½ cups olive oil
 2 cups finely chopped onion
 1 clove garlic, finely minced
 1 cup canned whole tomatoes, chopped
½ cup tomato paste
¼ cup finely chopped parsley, preferably Italian
   Salt
   Crushed pepper
 2 lemons
 6 medium artichokes

1. Heat the oil in a skillet or saucepan large enough to hold the artichokes. Add the onion and garlic and cook gently until the onion is wilted. Add the chopped tomatoes, tomato paste, parsley, salt and pepper to taste, and the juice of one lemon. Set aside.

2. Add the juice of the remaining lemon to a mixing bowl and add enough water to cover the artichokes as they are prepared.

3. Prepare one artichoke at a time. Pull off the tough outer leaves of each artichoke and cut off about one inch of the top. Cut the artichokes lengthwise and, using a melon ball cutter, remove the "choke" in the center. Add the artichokes to the tomato mixture and add enough water to cover. Cover and simmer thirty-five minutes, or until the artichokes are tender. Cool in the sauce, then chill. Serve as an appetizer.

Bagno Caldo with Celery

8 appetizer servings

2 large celery hearts, quartered lengthwise
1 cup boiling Chicken Stock (page 115)
6 tablespoons butter
½ cup olive oil
3 cloves garlic, finely chopped
2 cans (2 ounces each) anchovy fillets, chopped
2 tablespoons wine vinegar
    Lemon wedges

1. Place the celery hearts in a large skillet and add the chicken stock. Cover and simmer gently until the celery is barely tender, about ten minutes. Drain the celery and arrange on a warm platter.
2. Meanwhile, heat the butter and the oil in a small skillet and sauté the garlic and anchovies until the garlic is tender but not browned, about ten minutes.
3. Add the vinegar to the anchovy mixture, reheat, and pour over the celery. Garnish with lemon wedges and serve as an appetizer.

Bagno Caldo with Peppers

6 to 8 servings

6 tablespoons butter
½ cup olive oil
1 to 3 cloves garlic, finely chopped
2 cans (2 ounces each) anchovies
2 tablespoons wine vinegar
6 large green peppers, cored, seeded, and quartered

1. Heat the butter and oil in a saucepan and add the garlic and anchovies. Cook, stirring, about ten minutes. Stir in the vinegar.
2. Drop the peppers into boiling water to cover. Simmer, covered, about fifteen minutes. The peppers should remain firm. Drain.
3. Arrange the quartered peppers, skin side down, on a platter and spoon the hot sauce into the center of each. Serve hot, as an appetizer.

Mushrooms Parmigiana

4 to 6 servings

1 pound mushrooms
2 cloves garlic, finely minced
2 tablespoons finely chopped parsley, preferably Italian
3 tablespoons freshly grated Parmesan cheese
1 teaspoon orégano
½ cup bread crumbs
    Salt and freshly ground black pepper
    Water
½ cup olive oil

1. Preheat the oven to 350 degrees.
2. Wash the mushrooms and remove the stems. Chop the stems and mix with the garlic, parsley, cheese, orégano, bread crumbs, and salt and pepper to taste.
3. Place the mushroom caps cavity side up in an oiled shallow baking dish. Fill the cavities with the chopped mixture and fill the bottom of the baking dish with water to the depth of one-quarter inch. Pour the olive oil evenly over the caps and bake thirty minutes. Serve hot, as an appetizer.

Stuffed Mushrooms

6 servings

12 large mushrooms
¼ cup plus 1 tablespoon olive oil or butter
1 cup fresh bread crumbs
¾ to 1 cup freshly grated Romano or Parmesan cheese
1 tablespoon finely chopped parsley, preferably Italian
1 teaspoon finely chopped fresh basil or ½ teaspoon dried basil
1 or 2 cloves garlic, finely chopped
Salt and freshly ground pepper to taste

1. Preheat the oven to 350 degrees.
2. Carefully remove the stems from the mushroom caps. Chop the stems and cook them in the one tablespoon oil or butter until they give up their juices, then cook until the moisture evaporates. Let cool.
3. Combine the cooked stems with all the remaining ingredients, except the mushroom caps, and including the one-quarter cup oil, and set aside.
4. Rinse the mushroom caps in cold water, drain, and pat dry. Stuff the caps with the filling. Arrange the mushrooms in a baking dish and add a little water to prevent sticking. Bake twenty minutes, or until piping hot and golden. The stuffed mushrooms may be run under the broiler for a second at the last minute. Serve as an appetizer.

Mushrooms Stuffed with Anchovies

6 to 8 servings

24 medium to large mushroom caps, or 40 tiny caps
¼ cup olive oil
1 2½-ounce can anchovy fillets
1 clove garlic, finely chopped
1 teaspoon lemon juice
¾ cup bread crumbs
¼ cup chopped parsley, preferably Italian
Freshly ground black pepper

1. Preheat the oven to 350 degrees.
2. Sauté the mushroom caps in three tablespoons of the oil for two to three minutes.
3. Chop the anchovies with the garlic. Add the lemon juice, bread crumbs, and parsley and mix. Season with pepper to taste.
4. Fill the caps with the mixture, drizzle on the remaining oil and bake until hot, about fifteen minutes. Serve as an appetizer.

Roasted Italian Peppers

4 to 6 servings

Too often relegated to the role of accomplice for a main dish, vegetables can make (as all good Greeks and Italians know) an excellent first course. Peppers, roasted Italian style, have a special claim for consideration.

4 large green peppers, left whole
  Salt and freshly ground black pepper
1 clove garlic, finely minced
2 tablespoons finely chopped parsley, preferably Italian
1½ tablespoons wine vinegar
4½ tablespoons olive oil
  Lemon wedges

1. Place the peppers on a hot griddle or over hot charcoal, but not too close. Cook, turning occasionally, until the skin is roasted and almost black all over.

2. When cool enough to handle, peel away the charred skin, then remove the core and seeds. Cut the peppers into strips and arrange symmetrically on a dish. Sprinkle with salt and pepper to taste, the garlic, parsley, vinegar, and oil. Chill. Serve, garnished with lemon wedges, as an appetizer.

Mushrooms Stuffed with Pork and Veal

8 to 16 servings

32 large mushroom caps
6 tablespoons melted butter
4 shallots, finely chopped
½ pound lean pork, ground
½ pound veal, ground
½ cup soft fresh bread crumbs
1 2-ounce can flat anchovy fillets, chopped
½ teaspoon salt
¼ teaspoon freshly ground black pepper
1 egg, lightly beaten
¼ cup chopped parsley, preferably Italian

1. Preheat the oven to 375 degrees.

2. Rinse and dry the mushrooms and brush the outsides of the caps with four tablespoons of the butter. Place in a buttered shallow baking dish.

3. Pour the remaining butter into a skillet. Add the shallots, pork, and veal and sauté slowly, stirring occasionally, for about ten minutes, until the mixture is thoroughly cooked.

4. Add the bread crumbs, anchovies, salt, pepper, egg, and parsley to the cooked meat mixture.

5. Pile the mixture into the mushroom caps. Bake for fifteen to twenty minutes. Serve as an appetizer.

Potato and Cheese Mayonnaise alla Romana

6 servings

2 medium white potatoes
   Salt
¾ cup Mayonnaise (page 265)
   Juice of ½ lemon
   Freshly ground black pepper
   Cayenne pepper or Tabasco
¼ pound Swiss or French Gruyère cheese
¼ pound thinly sliced prosciutto
   Sliced white Italian truffles (optional)

1. Place a basin or mixing bowl under cold running water.

2. Peel the potatoes under cold running water. Slice them wafer thin, about one-sixteenth of an inch. It is best to use a hand slicer or an electric slicer for this. Drop the slices immediately into cold running water to prevent discoloration.

3. Remove the slices, a few at a time, from the water and drain. Place them in stacks and, using a sharp knife, make the thinnest possible matchlike strips (julienne). Drop these immediately into a saucepan and add cold water to cover. Add salt to taste and bring to a boil. Simmer about two minutes, more or less, until the potatoes are cooked but still firm and crisp tender. They must not overcook or they will be mushy. Drain well in a colander. Chill.

4. Combine the mayonnaise, lemon juice, and salt, pepper, and cayenne to taste. The lemon juice and cayenne should make this sauce a piquant one.

5. Place the cheese on a flat surface and cut it into the thinnest possible slices, about one-sixteenth inch. Cut the slices into the thinnest possible matchlike strips (julienne).

6. Cut the prosciutto into the thinnest possible strips.

7. Add the chilled potatoes, cheese, and ham to the mayonnaise. Toss gently but thoroughly. Chill. In Rome this salad is frequently served with sliced white truffles on top, an extravagant and delicious addition, but it is not essential. Serve cold as a first course or as a buffet dish.

Fritto Dolce

About 24 pastries

5   tablespoons sweet butter
1½ cups milk
1½ cups water
    Pinch of salt
3   tablespoons granulated sugar
½   cup farina
3   eggs
1   teaspoon grated lemon rind
¾   cup fine dry bread crumbs
    Confectioners' sugar
    Lemon slices

1. Combine one tablespoon of the butter, the milk, water, salt, and sugar in a saucepan and bring to a boil. Gradually add the farina, stirring constantly. Simmer, stirring occasionally, for about fifteen minutes. Remove from the heat and beat in one of the eggs and the lemon rind.

2. Spread the mixture onto a greased cookie sheet. The mixture should be about one-quarter inch thick. Cool overnight, then cut into rectangles (1 x 1½ inches).

3. Beat the remaining eggs. Dip each rectangle into the beaten eggs, then into the bread crumbs.

4. Heat the remaining butter and fry the pieces, several at a time, until they are golden brown on all sides.

5. Sprinkle with confectioners' sugar and garnish with lemon slices. Serve as an appetizer.

Cappon Magro

About 18 servings

1⅓ cups olive oil
6 tablespoons vinegar
Salt and freshly ground black pepper
1 small cauliflower, separated into flowerets and cooked
2 cups 1-inch pieces snap beans, cooked
2 cups sliced celery, cooked
2 cups each diced carrots, beets, and potatoes, cooked
3 tablespoons lemon juice
2 cups flaked boiled codfish
1 cup cooked lobster meat
2 dozen shrimp, cooked
1 9-ounce package frozen artichokes,
cooked
6 slices dry bread, crusts removed
1 clove garlic, halved
2 tablespoons water
Cappon Magro Sauce (see below)
2 dozen stuffed green olives
6 hard-cooked eggs, halved
12 anchovy fillets

1. Mix half of the oil, four tablespoons of the vinegar, and salt and pepper to taste. Marinate the cauliflower, snap beans, celery, carrots, beets, and potatoes separately in the oil and vinegar dressing.

2. Mix the remaining oil with the lemon juice and salt and pepper to taste. Marinate the codfish, lobster, shrimp, and artichokes separately in the lemon and oil dressing.

3. Rub the bread with the garlic and arrange the slices on a serving platter. Mix the water and the remaining vinegar, add salt to taste, and sprinkle over the bread. Spread the bread with some of the sauce.

4. Reserve the shrimp, olives, and four of the hard-cooked eggs for garnish. Pile the remaining foods in layers to form a pyramid based on the bread, ending with the fish and lobster.

5. Pour the remaining sauce over the pyramid. Pierce the olives and shrimp with picks and insert over the entire surface of the salad. Garnish the base with the reserved hard-cooked eggs and serve as an appetizer.

CAPPON MAGRO SAUCE:

About 2 cups

¼ slice white bread, crust removed
½ cup vinegar
⅓ cup parsley leaves, preferably Italian
1 small clove garlic, peeled
1 tablespoon pignoli (pine nuts)
1 teaspoon capers
2 flat anchovy fillets
2 hard-cooked egg yolks
6 green olives, pitted and sliced
1 cup olive oil
Salt and freshly ground black pepper

Drop the bread into the container of an electric blender and add two tablespoons of the vinegar, the parsley, garlic, pignoli, capers, anchovies, egg yolks, and olives. Add the remaining vinegar and the oil gradually while blending. Add salt and pepper to taste.

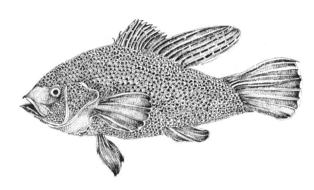

Cappelletti in Brodo

(Dumplings in Broth with Cheese)

6 to 8 servings

> 2 cups sifted all-purpose flour, approximately
> 3 eggs, lightly beaten
> ¼ pound lean pork
> ¼ pound lean veal
> ½ cup diced mortadella (Italian sausage)
> ½ cup diced, cooked breast of turkey
> 2 tablespoons butter
> 1¾ cups freshly grated Parmesan cheese
> 2 egg yolks, lightly beaten
>   Salt and freshly ground pepper to taste
>   Nutmeg to taste
> ½ teaspoon grated lemon rind
> 8 to 10 cups Chicken Stock (page 115) or Beef Stock (page 115)

1. Place one and three-quarters cups of the flour in a mixing bowl and make a well in the center. Add the eggs and blend quickly to make a dough, adding a little more flour as necessary to make a soft ball.

2. Turn the dough out onto a lightly floured board and knead until smooth, always keeping the board lightly floured.

3. Divide the dough in half and shape each half into a ball. Place in a small, lightly floured bowl and keep covered until ready to roll out.

4. To make the filling, grind together the pork, veal, mortadella, and turkey. Melt the butter in a skillet and add the ground meat mixture. Cook, stirring, until the meats lose their raw color.

5. Remove from the fire and cool briefly. Fold in three-quarters cup of the grated Parmesan cheese, egg yolks, salt, pepper, nutmeg, and grated rind. Set aside.

6. Roll out one ball of dough at a time into a square on a floured board. Cut the dough into two-inch squares. Place a little of the filling in the center of a square and fold the square over to make a triangle. Seal the edges with the fingers. Twist the points of the dough around and press them lightly to seal.

7. Bring the stock to a boil and add the cappelletti, or dumplings. Simmer about ten minutes. Serve the dumplings in the broth, with the remaining cheese on the side.

Clam Soup Italian Style

4 servings

40 littleneck clams, the smaller the better
⅓ cup olive oil
½ cup finely chopped onion
 4 cloves garlic, finely minced
 8 anchovies, finely chopped
 6 basil leaves, finely chopped, or 1 teaspoon dried basil
 3 tablespoons finely minced parsley, preferably Italian
 1 teaspoon orégano, or to taste
 1 teaspoon crushed fennel seeds
 1 teaspoon chopped leaf saffron (optional)
 1 6-ounce can tomato paste
 1 cup dry white wine
 2 cups water
   Salt and freshly ground black pepper to taste

1. Rinse the clams under cold running water to remove all sand from the shells.

2. Heat the oil in a large kettle and add the onion and garlic. Cook, stirring, until the onion is wilted. Add the anchovies, basil, parsley, orégano, fennel, and saffron. Cook, stirring, about five minutes. Add the tomato paste, wine, and water and stir. Simmer five minutes longer, then add the clams.

3. Cover and cook, stirring with a wooden spoon and shaking the kettle occasionally, until the clams open, five to ten minutes. Add salt and pepper. Serve in hot bowls with hot Italian or Garlic Bread (see below).

GARLIC BREAD:

Cut a loaf of French or Italian bread diagonally into one-inch slices without cutting through the bottom crust. Melt one-quarter cup of butter and to it add one-half clove of minced garlic. Brush the cut surfaces of the bread with the garlic butter. Wrap the bread in aluminum foil and bake in a preheated 350-degree oven until heated through, about fifteen minutes.

Escarole Soup I

8 servings

 5 pounds soup bones with marrow
 1 6-ounce can tomato paste
 2 quarts water
3¼ teaspoons salt
 ¾ pound chuck, ground
 ¼ teaspoon finely chopped garlic
 1 egg, lightly beaten
 ¼ teaspoon freshly ground black pepper
 3 tablespoons freshly grated Parmesan cheese
 1 pound escarole, chopped
 1 cup diced onion
 1 cup diced celery
 1 cup diced potatoes
 2 tablespoons chopped fresh parsley

1. Place the soup bones, tomato paste, water, and two and one-half teaspoons of the salt in a four-quart saucepan. Cover and simmer one hour.

2. Combine the chuck, garlic, egg, pepper, cheese, and remaining salt and shape into three-quarter-inch balls. Add to the hot soup and simmer ten minutes longer. Add the vegetables and simmer thirty minutes, or until the vegetables are tender. Remove the bones and serve the soup hot, with chopped parsley sprinkled over the top.

Escarole Soup II

6 or more servings

1 head escarole
¼ cup water
1½ quarts Chicken Stock (page 115)
2 eggs
¼ cup freshly grated Parmesan cheese
Salt and freshly ground black pepper

1. Cut out the center core of the escarole and discard. Rinse the escarole leaves in several changes of cold water and drain. Place the leaves in a large saucepan and add the water. Cover closely and cook until the escarole is tender, thirty minutes or longer. Drain and let cool, then press with the hands to remove excess moisture. Chop the escarole and set aside.

2. Bring the chicken stock to a boil and add the escarole. Beat the eggs well and beat in the cheese. Gradually add the egg mixture to the soup, stirring with each addition. When all has been added, add salt and pepper to taste and continue simmering about fifteen minutes. Serve in hot soup bowls.

Minestrone

4 servings

1 cup dried navy beans
5 cups Beef Stock (page 115) or water
Salt and freshly ground black pepper
¼ cup olive oil
1 cup finely chopped onion
½ cup chopped celery
1 clove garlic, approximately, finely minced
1 1-pound 3-ounce can tomatoes
½ cup finely chopped parsley, preferably Italian
1 cup finely chopped cabbage
2 zucchini, trimmed, left unpeeled, and cut into ¼-inch cubes
8 ounces ditalini (a form of macaroni)
Freshly grated Parmesan cheese

1. Place the beans in a mixing bowl and add water to cover to the depth of one inch. Soak overnight.

2. Drain and empty the beans into a kettle. Add the beef stock and salt and pepper to taste. Bring to a boil and simmer until tender, about one hour.

3. Heat the oil in a skillet and cook the onion and celery until wilted. Add the garlic and stir this mixture into the beans. Add the tomatoes and half the parsley and simmer twenty minutes. Add the cabbage, zucchini, and ditalini and cook about fifteen minutes longer, or until the ditalini is tender. Add the remaining parsley and, if desired, a little more freshly chopped garlic. Serve with Parmesan cheese.

Savoy Soup

4 to 6 servings

3 tablespoons olive oil
1 tablespoon butter
1 clove garlic, minced
1 large onion, chopped
½ teaspoon dried sage
1 cup chopped celery leaves
2 ribs celery, chopped
½ cup chopped parsley, preferably Italian
1 carrot, grated
2 tablespoons Italian Tomato Sauce I (page 435) or 1 large ripe tomato, chopped
3 black peppercorns, crushed
1 lemon slice, cut into quarters
1 thin slice smoked ham, cut into thin strips
1 2-inch piece cervelat sausage, peeled and cut into bits
4 cups Beef Stock (page 115)
1 head savoy cabbage, shredded
  Salt
  Freshly grated Parmesan or Romano cheese

1. Heat the oil and butter in a stock pot or kettle. Add the garlic and onion and sauté slowly for ten minutes. Add the sage, celery leaves, chopped celery, parsley, and carrot; cook for five minutes. Add the tomato sauce or tomato, the peppercorns, lemon slice, ham, and sausage and stir well. Add the stock and cover. Cook slowly for one hour after simmering starts, stirring well every twenty minutes.

2. Add the cabbage and one teaspoon of salt and cook for twenty minutes. Taste for seasoning and add more salt, if needed.

3. Pour the soup into a hot tureen, scatter grated cheese over, cover the tureen, and let the soup stand for ten minutes before serving. Serve with crusty French or Italian bread and more grated cheese, if desired.

Fish Fillets Piemontese

6 servings

4 cups water
  Salt
1 cup yellow cornmeal
6 tablespoons butter
¼ pound freshly grated Parmesan cheese
  Freshly ground black pepper
1½ pounds fish fillets such as whiting
  All-purpose flour
¼ cup peanut oil
½ cup clam broth or Fish Stock (page 116)
½ cup tomato puree
  Chopped parsley (optional)

1. Place three cups of the water in a kettle and add one teaspoon of salt. Bring to a boil. Combine the remaining cup water with the cornmeal and stir. Stir this into the boiling water. Cook until thickened, stirring frequently. Cover and cook over low heat ten minutes or longer. Stir in four tablespoons of the butter, the cheese, and pepper to taste. Set aside.

2. Meanwhile, dredge the fish pieces in flour seasoned with salt and pepper. Cook until golden on both sides in the oil, adding more oil if necessary. Drain on paper towels and keep warm.

3. Combine the clam broth and tomato puree in a saucepan and simmer briefly. Stir in the remaining butter.

4. Spoon the cornmeal mixture onto a hot oval dish and top with the fish fillets. Pour the tomato mixture over all. Garnish with chopped parsley, if desired.

Lobster Cardinal

6 servings

Whatever others may think, the lobster is a creature of extraordinary beauty to the world's gastronomes. Its flesh is dazzlingly versatile; it can be boiled, broiled, or served in sauces without number. One sublime creation, lobster cardinal, is outlined here.

    3 live lobsters (1½ pounds each)
    2 fresh thyme sprigs or ½ teaspoon dried
        thyme
    1 large or 2 small bay leaves
   12 peppercorns
        Salt
  5½ tablespoons butter
    4 tablespoons all-purpose flour
    1 cup milk
    ¼ cup tomato paste
  1½ tablespoons finely chopped shallots
        Freshly ground black pepper
    4 tablespoons Cognac
    ¼ cup heavy cream
    ¼ teaspoon cayenne pepper, or to taste
    1 egg yolk, beaten
    6 teaspoons freshly grated Parmesan
        cheese

1. Bring enough water to a boil in a large kettle to cover the lobsters. Add the thyme, bay leaves, peppercorns, and salt to taste; cover and simmer about five minutes.

2. Uncover the kettle and plunge the lobsters quickly into the boiling liquid. Cover and simmer exactly twenty minutes. Drain and let the lobsters cool. When they are cool enough to handle, split the lobsters lengthwise. Remove the tough sac near the eyes and discard. Remove and reserve the remaining body meat and green or yellow coral. Reserve the shells for stuffing.

3. Crack the lobster claws and remove the meat. Discard the claws. Chop the claw and body meat and set aside.

4. Preheat the oven to 400 degrees.

5. Melt four tablespoons of the butter and stir in the flour with a whisk. When blended and smooth, add the milk, stirring rapidly with the whisk. This will make a very thick sauce. Cook, stirring, about five minutes and remove from the heat. Stir in the tomato paste.

6. Melt remaining butter in a skillet and add the shallots. Cook briefly, then add the lobster meat and coral and salt and pepper to taste. Cook briefly, stirring, and sprinkle with two tablespoons of the Cognac. Stir in the sauce.

7. Stir in the cream and cayenne and bring to a boil. Remove from the heat.

8. Arrange the reserved lobster shells on a large baking dish and sprinkle the insides lightly with the remaining Cognac. Fill the shells with the lobster mixture but reserve approximately one-half cup. Combine the reserved half cup of lobster mixture with the beaten yolk and spoon this lightly over the tops of the filled lobsters. Sprinkle with the Parmesan cheese and bake ten minutes, or until hot and bubbling. Run the dish under the broiler briefly, just enough to give a brown glaze. Serve immediately.

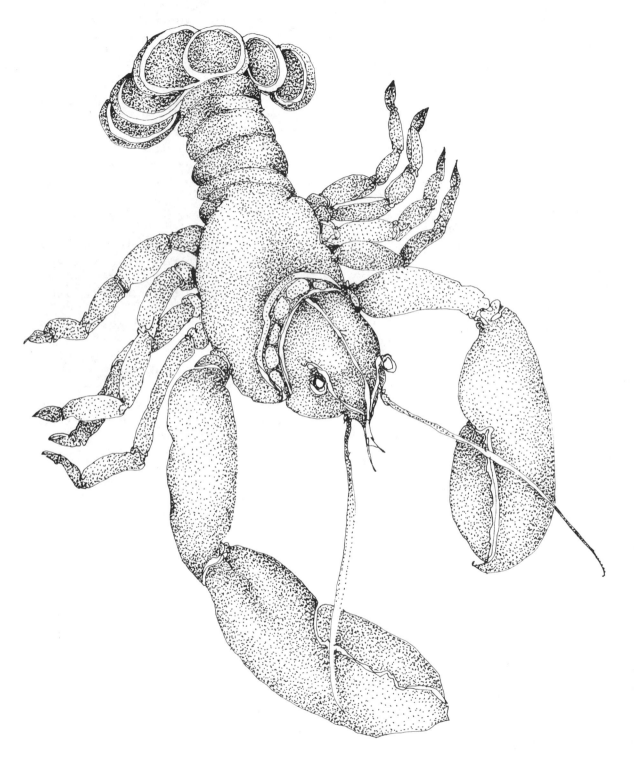

382   ITALY

Lobster Fra Diavolo

4 to 6 servings

2 live lobsters (1½ pounds each)
6 tablespoons olive oil
  Salt and freshly ground pepper to taste
2 tablespoons finely chopped garlic
¼ cup finely chopped shallots
½ cup dry white wine
½ cup finely chopped green pepper
¼ teaspoon hot red pepper flakes, or to taste
4 cups Italian canned tomatoes
2 tablespoons tomato paste
½ cup finely chopped Italian parsley
2 teaspoons chopped fresh basil or 1 teaspoon dried basil
1 teaspoon chopped thyme
1 bay leaf
1 teaspoon orégano
12 littleneck clams (optional)

1. Kill each lobster by plunging a knife into the place where tail and body meet. Break off the tail and cut it crosswise into thirds with the shell on, then cut the carcass (the main body) into quarters. Discard the tough sac near the eyes. Reserve the coral and liver for later use. Crack the claws.

2. In a large skillet, heat the oil and add the pieces of lobster, stirring frequently. Sprinkle with salt and pepper to taste. When the pieces are bright red all over, sprinkle with the garlic and shallots. Add the wine and cook until most of the wine evaporates.

3. Add the remaining ingredients except the clams and cover. Simmer, stirring occasionally, about twenty minutes. Add the clams, cover, and cook until the clams open. Put the reserved coral and liver through a sieve and add it to the sauce. Heat thoroughly. Serve with hot spaghetti.

Lobster with Linguine

4 servings

2 or 3 small live lobsters
1 2-pound 3-ounce can Italian plum tomatoes
½ cup olive oil
½ cup finely chopped Italian parsley
½ cup finely minced green pepper
2 cloves garlic, finely minced
3 tablespoons tomato paste
2 tablespoons chopped fresh basil or 1 tablespoon crushed dried basil
½ teaspoon Italian red pepper flakes
1 teaspoon chopped fresh mint leaves or ½ teaspoon dried mint
  Salt and freshly ground black pepper
1 pound linguine

1. Plunge a knife into the place on each lobster where the tail and body meet. This will kill them instantly. Set aside briefly.

2. Put the tomatoes through a sieve and set aside.

3. Pour the oil into a skillet large enough to hold the lobsters and add the parsley, green pepper, and garlic. Cook briefly, stirring, but do not brown. Add the tomato paste, stir, then add the sieved tomatoes. Add the basil, pepper flakes, mint, and salt and pepper to taste. Add the whole lobsters. Partly cover and simmer, stirring occasionally, about forty-five minutes. Turn the lobsters in the sauce occasionally.

4. Cook the linguine according to package directions while completing the recipe.

5. Remove the lobsters and continue simmering the sauce while they are being prepared. When the lobsters are cool enough to handle, break off the claws and crack them. Cut the bodies in half lengthwise and cut the tails crosswise into serving pieces.

6. Drain the linguine and pour onto a hot platter. Cover with the sauce and add the lobsters. Or, serve the linguine and sauce first and the hot lobster as a second course.

Cozze alla Marinara

(Mussels Marinara with Linguine)

4 to 6 servings

40 small to medium mussels
 1 onion, thinly sliced
 1 clove garlic, finely chopped
 3 tablespoons olive oil
 1 lemon, thinly sliced
 1 large can Italian plum tomatoes, mashed
 ½ 6-ounce can tomato paste
 5 or 6 leaves fresh basil, chopped, or 1 tablespoon dried basil
 1 tablespoon orégano
 ⅛ teaspoon red pepper
 ½ teaspoon freshly ground black pepper
 1 teaspoon salt
 1 cup red wine
 1 pound linguine

1. Rinse the mussels well in several changes of water. Set aside.

2. Sauté the onion and garlic in the oil in a large, heavy casserole or pot. When the onion is soft, add the lemon slices, tomatoes, tomato paste, basil, orégano, red and black pepper, and salt. Simmer over low heat, stirring occasionally, twenty-five minutes. Add the wine, stir, and simmer until the sauce is thickened, fifteen to twenty minutes longer.

3. Cook the linguine according to package directions, or to taste.

4. Meanwhile, add the mussels to the sauce, cover, and cook over high heat until the mussels are opened, about five minutes. Lower the heat and simmer the sauce, uncovered, until the linguine is cooked.

5. Empty the linguine into a very large bowl and pour the sauce and mussels over. Mix well and serve immediately. Any delay will cause the linguine to absorb the sauce and become dry.

Note: The sauce may be prepared in advance up to the addition of the mussels.

Roman Shrimp

4 to 6 servings

36 large raw shrimp
 ¼ cup butter
 4 to 6 large mushrooms, cut into matchlike strips approximately 1 inch long
 1 cup prosciutto or baked ham cut into finest possible strips (julienne) 1 inch long
     All-purpose flour seasoned with salt and pepper
 2 eggs, lightly beaten
     Vegetable oil for deep frying
     Juice of 1 lemon
 1 teaspoon Worcestershire sauce
     Lemon slices for garnish

1. Shell and devein the shrimp and rinse them under cold running water. Set aside.

2. Melt half the butter in a skillet. Sauté the mushrooms in the melted butter until soft, then add the prosciutto and cook for one to two minutes longer. Keep warm.

3. Roll the shrimp in the seasoned flour and shake each shrimp gently to remove most of the flour.

4. Dip the flour-coated shrimp in the beaten eggs and fry quickly in the hot oil until golden.

5. Arrange the prosciutto and mushroom mixture in the center of a serving plate and surround with the fried shrimp.

6. Mix together the remaining butter, melted, the lemon juice, and Worcestershire. Pour this mixture over the shrimp. Garnish with lemon slices and serve immediately.

Seafood crêpes with two sauces: deviled and curried (France

Shrimp Marinara

4 to 6 servings

- 2 pounds raw shrimp
- 2 tablespoons olive oil
- 2 cloves garlic, minced
- 1 6-ounce can tomato paste
- 2 teaspoons salt
  Freshly ground black pepper to taste
- 1 tablespoon minced fresh basil or 1 teaspoon dried basil
- ¼ teaspoon orégano
- ½ cup finely minced green onions
- 1 cup Chicken Stock (page 115) or clam broth

1. Shell the shrimp and remove the sand vein down the back. Heat the oil and cook the shrimp and garlic briefly, for about three minutes, just until the shrimp turn pink.

2. Stir in the remaining ingredients, bring to a boil, and simmer for about two minutes. Serve hot.

Scampi

4 servings

- ¼ cup butter
- 2 pounds large raw shrimp, shelled and deveined
- ½ teaspoon salt
- ¼ teaspoon freshly ground black pepper
- 2 cloves garlic, finely chopped
- ¼ cup chopped parsley, preferably Italian
  Lemon wedges

1. Heat the butter in a skillet and fry the shrimp on all sides for about five minutes, or until cooked, shaking the pan over high heat to turn the shrimp. Sprinkle the shrimp with the salt and pepper and place on a hot serving plate.

2. To the butter remaining in the skillet, add the garlic and parsley. Stir for thirty seconds and pour over the shrimp. Serve with lemon wedges.

Scampi Spaghetti

4 servings

There is "an idyllic country where no one works and all things are free, with a mountain of grated cheese in the middle of it," relates Boccaccio in the Decameron. *"On top of this mountain, there are people who do nothing but make pasta, which they cook in capon broth, and then dispense to all who want it." A glorious place to contemplate. Boccaccio should have added that pasta—which includes spaghetti, macaroni, rigatoni, and all the rest —also goes extraordinarily well with seafood.*

- ¼ cup butter
- 1½ pounds raw shrimp, shelled and deveined
  Salt and freshly ground black pepper
- 2 tablespoons chopped shallots
- 2 tablespoons warm Cognac
- ¼ cup tomato puree
- ½ cup plus 1 tablespoon heavy cream
- 1 tablespoon chopped fresh basil or ½ teaspoon dried basil
- 1 tablespoon finely chopped chives
- 1 egg yolk
- 1 pound spaghetti
- 2 tablespoons finely chopped parsley

1. Heat half the butter in a skillet and add the shrimp. Sprinkle with salt and pepper, and cook, turning once, until bright red on both sides.

2. Sprinkle with shallots and cook one minute, stirring. Add the Cognac and ignite it. Add the tomato puree and cook one minute over high heat.

3. Stir in one-half cup of the cream, the basil, and chives. Beat the yolk with the remaining tablespoon of cream and add to the sauce, stirring rapidly. Do not boil.

4. Cook the spaghetti according to package directions. Drain, toss with the remaining butter, and pour onto a hot platter. Pour the shrimp and sauce in the center and serve sprinkled with chopped parsley.

ettucine alla romana (Italy)

Snails, Sicilian Style

6 to 8 servings

2 pounds land snails
  Water
  Salt
2 cloves garlic, finely chopped
¼ cup olive oil
  Freshly ground black pepper to taste
½ cup lemon juice

1. There is a small membrane, known as an operculum, at the opening of each snail. Use a toothpick to remove this membrane and it will come off easily.

2. Place the snails in a basin and rinse thoroughly with cold water. Drain and rinse once more in cold water that contains a generous amount of salt. Rinse once more in cold water before cooking.

3. Add four quarts of cold water to a kettle and add the snails and about three tablespoons salt. Bring slowly to a boil and simmer six minutes, stirring occasionally.

4. Meanwhile, place the garlic and one teaspoon of salt in a small, heavy bowl. Crush the garlic with a pestle or the back of a heavy spoon to make a paste. Add the oil, pepper, lemon juice, and six tablespoons cold water. Stir with a whisk to blend.

5. Drain the snails and serve hot with the cold sauce.

Note: To eat the snails, pull out the meat with a pick and dip them one at a time in the sauce. The whole snail may be eaten, although the most fastidious prefer to skip the soft after end of the meat, which is the digestive tract.

Squid in Tomato Sauce

4 servings

1½ pounds squid
  2 tablespoons olive oil
  ¾ cup chopped onion
  2 tablespoons finely chopped parsley, preferably Italian
  1 clove garlic, finely minced
  ½ teaspoon crushed rosemary, or to taste
  2 tablespoons tomato paste
  ½ cup water

1. Clean the squid (see note) or have them cleaned at the fish market. Cut them into one-and-one-half-inch or other bite-sized pieces. The pieces will shrink as they cook.

2. Heat the oil in a saucepan with a lid. Add the onion and cook, stirring, until golden. Add the parsley, garlic, and rosemary and cook, stirring, about five minutes. Add the tomato paste, water, and squid and bring to a boil. Cover and simmer about forty minutes, or until the squid is tender. Serve with steamed rice.

Note: To clean squid, remove the spiny translucent portion and then pull the head and legs from the envelope-like covering. Removing the ink sac at the base of the head is optional.

Calamari Ripieni

(Stuffed Squid)

2 to 4 servings

6 large squid
¼ cup freshly grated bread crumbs
2 tablespoons finely chopped parsley, preferably Italian
2½ tablespoons freshly grated Parmesan cheese
2 teaspoons finely chopped garlic
1 egg, lightly beaten
¼ cup olive oil
  Salt and freshly ground pepper
4 whole cloves garlic, peeled
½ cup chopped, peeled tomatoes
¼ cup dry white wine

1. Put each whole squid under cold running water and get rid of the mottled outer skin by rubbing and pulling it away. Cut off the tentacles with a knife. Discard the ink sacs, the center bones, the eyes, and jaws. Wash thoroughly. What should be left of each squid is the white triangular body with an opening for stuffing, plus the tender parts of the tentacles.

2. Chop the tentacles and put them in a mixing bowl.

3. To the mixing bowl add the grated crumbs, parsley, cheese, one and one-half teaspoons of the chopped garlic, the egg, and about one tablespoon of the olive oil. Blend well with a fork. There should be enough oil to give the stuffing a slightly glossy look. Add salt and pepper to taste.

4. Spoon equal amounts of the stuffing into each of the squid bodies. Do not overstuff, for the squid will shrink.

5. Use thread to sew up the openings of each squid, or seal the openings with toothpicks.

6. In a skillet just large enough to accommodate the squid in a single layer, add the remaining oil. There should be enough to cover the bottom. Heat the oil and cook the garlic cloves, stirring, until golden brown. Discard the garlic cloves.

7. Add the squid and brown lightly and carefully on all sides. Add the tomatoes, the remaining chopped garlic, the wine, and salt and pepper to taste. Cover closely and cook twenty to thirty minutes.

8. Remove the thread or toothpicks from the squid. Cut the squid crosswise into half-inch slices, then line the slices up on a warm serving platter so that each squid is reassembled. Heat the sauce slightly and pour it over the squid. Serve with rice.

Italian Beef Roll

4 servings

1 slice round steak, ½ inch thick (1½ pounds)
½ pound pork, ground
¼ pound prosciutto, ground
¼ cup freshly grated Parmesan cheese
1 egg, lightly beaten
¼ cup chopped parsley, preferably Italian
   Salt and freshly ground black pepper
1 tablespoon olive oil
1 tablespoon butter
¾ cup chopped onion
1 clove garlic, finely minced
3 tablespoons Cognac
½ cup dry red wine
2 tablespoons tomato paste
1 teaspoon orégano
1 cup Beef Stock (page 115)

1. Pound the steak with a mallet until the steak is one-quarter inch thick.

2. In a mixing bowl, combine the ground pork, prosciutto, cheese, egg, parsley, and salt and pepper to taste. Spread the mixture on the flattened steak; roll up tightly like a jelly roll and turn in the ends to seal. Tie securely with a string.

3. Heat the oil and butter in a skillet and brown the roll on all sides. Add the onion and garlic and sauté until wilted. Remove from the heat. Warm the Cognac, add to the skillet, and ignite. When the flame has burned out, return to the heat. Add the wine and simmer until it is nearly evaporated. Stir in the tomato paste, orégano, and beef stock and simmer about forty-five minutes. To serve, remove the roll from the sauce and cut into one-inch slices. Pour the sauce over the slices and serve with noodles.

Sicilian Round Steak

4 or 5 servings

2 pounds round steak, ½ inch thick
¼ cup all-purpose flour
1½ teaspoons salt
⅛ teaspoon freshly ground black pepper
3 tablespoons lard or drippings
2 cups (1 1-pound can) tomatoes
½ teaspoon orégano
⅛ teaspoon dry mustard
1 clove garlic, minced
1 tablespoon chopped parsley

1. Cut the steak into four or five servings. Pound it to one-quarter-inch thickness.

2. Mix together the flour, salt, and pepper and dredge the meat with the mixture. Brown the meat in the lard in a heavy skillet. Pour off the drippings and add the tomatoes, orégano, mustard, and garlic to the skillet.

3. Cover tightly and simmer for about one hour, until done. Sprinkle with the chopped parsley and serve on a hot platter.

Brasciole all'Oreste Cianci

6 servings

6 thin slices round steak (about 2 pounds)
½ cup bread crumbs
Freshly grated Parmesan or Romano cheese
½ cup chopped parsley, preferably Italian
2 cloves garlic, finely chopped
Salt and freshly ground black pepper
½ cup olive oil
4 cups canned peeled Italian tomatoes
1 6-ounce can tomato paste
2 cups water, approximately

1. Using a mallet or other blunt instrument, pound the meat slices thin, or have the butcher do it.

2. Sprinkle the center of each slice with a mixture of bread crumbs, one-half cup cheese, parsley, and garlic. Sprinkle with salt and pepper and roll each slice like a jelly roll.

3. Tie the rolls securely with string and brown them in the olive oil, preferably in a Dutch oven. Add the tomatoes, tomato paste, and half of the water. Bring to a boil and simmer gently for one and one-half to two hours. Add additional water as the sauce boils down.

4. Season with salt and pepper to taste and serve with cooked pasta and additional grated Parmesan cheese.

Italian Beef Stew with Rosemary

4 servings

1½ pounds lean beef, such as top or bottom round or chuck
3 cups fresh or canned peeled tomatoes with basil
¾ cup chopped celery
½ cup chopped parsley, preferably Italian, loosely packed
¼ teaspoon orégano
¼ teaspoon dried thyme
2 tablespoons olive oil
Salt and freshly ground pepper to taste
Butter
1 teaspoon finely chopped garlic
½ cup dry white wine
1 sprig fresh rosemary or 1 teaspoon dried rosemary leaves
8 thin slices French or Italian bread
1 whole clove garlic, peeled

1. Trim the meat, if necessary, and cut it into one-inch cubes. Set aside.

2. In a saucepan or deep skillet, combine the tomatoes, celery, parsley, orégano, thyme, oil, and salt and pepper to taste. Cover and bring to a boil. Simmer about thirty minutes, or until the vegetables are tender. Put the sauce through a food mill and set aside.

3. Meanwhile, heat one-quarter cup butter in a wide flameproof casserole. Add the beef and cook, stirring, until the meat loses its red color. Add the chopped garlic and stir. Transfer the meat to another dish.

4. Add the wine to the casserole and cook over high heat until it is reduced by half. Add the meat, the rosemary, and the tomato sauce and, if necessary, salt and pepper to taste. Cover and simmer about one and one-half to two hours.

5. Meanwhile, spread the bread with butter and toast on both sides under the broiler. Rub on both sides with the garlic clove, place two slices in each of four hot soup bowls, and spoon the meat and sauce over all. Serve hot.

Sicilian Meat Balls

24 meat balls

2 pounds chuck, ground
1 clove garlic, coarsely chopped
¼ cup coarsely chopped Italian parsley
Salt and freshly ground pepper to taste
⅓ cup dry bread crumbs
⅔ cup grated cheese, preferably Locatelli, although Parmesan could be used
4 eggs
¾ cup water
Sicilian Tomato Sauce (page 394)

1. Place the meat in a mixing bowl and add the garlic, parsley, salt, pepper, bread crumbs, and cheese. Add the eggs and work the mixture with the hands until well blended.

2. Continue kneading while gradually adding the water. Shape the mixture into twenty-four balls. Drop the balls, without browning if desired, into the simmering Sicilian tomato sauce or any other tomato sauce and cook about one hour and fifteen minutes.

Stuffed Green Peppers Tuscany Style

6 servings

6 large green peppers
¼ cup melted butter
1 cup chopped onions
1 small clove garlic, finely minced
2 cups ground leftover roast meat or 2 cups ground raw round steak
Freshly grated Romano cheese
Soft fresh bread crumbs
¼ cup minced parsley, preferably Italian
2 eggs
Salt and freshly ground black pepper
Olive oil

1. Preheat the oven to 350 degrees.

2. Trim the stems from the peppers and remove the seeds and membranes.

3. Heat the butter and cook the onions and garlic in it until the onion is golden yellow. Add the ground roast or round steak. If the round steak is used, cook until the meat loses its red color. Stir in three tablespoons cheese, three tablespoons bread crumbs, parsley, eggs, and salt and pepper to taste.

4. Use the meat mixture to fill the peppers. Sprinkle the stuffed peppers with additional bread crumbs and cheese, if desired.

5. Arrange the stuffed peppers in an oiled casserole. Sprinkle the tops with olive oil and cover closely with aluminum foil. Bake for thirty minutes, then uncover and bake for twenty minutes longer.

Spit-Roasted Leg of Lamb

4 to 6 servings

1 leg of lamb (5 to 6 pounds)
¾ cup coarsely chopped parsley, preferably Italian
2 cloves garlic, peeled
3 shallots, peeled
½ cup wine vinegar
1 cup olive oil
1 cup dry white wine
Salt and freshly ground pepper to taste

1. Prick the lamb all over with the tines of a sharp fork or with an ice pick. Place the lamb in a close-fitting dish.

2. Combine the remaining ingredients in the container of an electric blender and blend well. Pour the mixture over the lamb and refrigerate twenty-four hours. Turn the lamb several times in the marinade as it stands.

3. Grill on a spit, or broil, basting often, about one hour. Serve the lamb sliced, with its natural juices.

Italian Stuffed Pork Chops

6 servings

1 cup fresh bread crumbs
1½ cups freshly grated mozzarella cheese
½ teaspoon chopped orégano
½ teaspoon dried thyme
  Salt and freshly ground pepper to taste
½ cup Chicken Stock (page 115), approximately
6 rib pork chops, each 1½ inches thick, with a pocket for stuffing
2 tablespoons vegetable oil
2 tablespoons butter
¾ cup Italian Tomato Sauce I (page 435)

1. Combine the bread crumbs, cheese, orégano, thyme, salt, and pepper. Moisten with about one tablespoon of the chicken stock.

2. Stuff the chops with equal portions of filling and skewer or sew the edges. Sprinkle with salt and pepper.

3. Heat the oil and butter and brown the chops on all sides. Pour off the excess fat and add the tomato sauce and about half the remaining chicken stock. Cover closely and simmer about one hour, or until the chops are tender. Add more chicken stock if necessary.

Bracciole in Tomato Sauce

8 servings

2 pounds sliced pork butt with bone
2 cloves garlic, cut into thin slivers
  Salt and freshly ground black pepper
¼ cup olive oil
2 cans (6 ounces each) tomato paste
2 cans (1 pound 12 ounces each) Italian peeled tomatoes
1 teaspoon granulated sugar
16 thin slices round steak, each about ¼ inch thick and measuring approximately 4 x 4 inches
16 teaspoons vegetable shortening, at room temperature
16 teaspoons freshly grated Parmesan cheese
16 teaspoons finely chopped parsley, preferably Italian
2 tablespoons or more finely minced garlic

1. Stud the pork with slivers of garlic and sprinkle with salt and pepper to taste. Heat half the oil in a Dutch oven and brown the pork on all sides. Add the tomato paste.

2. Put the tomatoes through a sieve or food mill and add the sieved liquid to the kettle. Add the sugar and bring to a boil. Add salt and pepper to taste. Let simmer, partially covered.

3. Meanwhile, place the slices of steak on a flat surface and pound lightly with the blade of a heavy knife. Do not pound hard enough to cut through. Turn the slices and pound lightly on the other side. Spread each slice evenly with one teaspoon of the shortening. Sprinkle each with one teaspoon of cheese and one teaspoon of parsley. Sprinkle with salt and pepper to taste, then sprinkle each slice lightly with minced garlic. Roll the slices jelly-roll fashion, seasoned sides inside, and tie to secure with string or food picks. Heat the remaining oil in another large skillet and brown the meat rolls on all sides. Add the rolls to the tomato sauce, partially cover, and continue cooking for about two hours. Serve hot, in the sauce.

Zampino or Ham with Beans Bretonne

40 servings

2 zampinos (7 to 8 pounds each; see note) or 1 ready-to-cook whole ham (15 pounds)
2 pounds white kidney beans
1 ham bone, cracked
3 sprigs fresh thyme or ½ teaspoon dried thyme
6 sprigs fresh parsley, preferably Italian
2 bay leaves
2 medium onions, whole
  Salt to taste
10 peppercorns
2 carrots, scraped and cut into cubes
¼ cup butter
2 cups chopped onion
2 tablespoons chopped garlic
4 cups chopped fresh, peeled tomatoes (or use canned Italian tomatoes)
  Freshly ground pepper to taste

1. If the zampino is used, place it in a kettle with cold water to cover and simmer until it is cooked thoroughly, about one and one-half to two hours. If the ham is used, cook it according to the recipe below.

2. Meanwhile, soak the beans overnight in cold water to cover. Drain and put in a kettle. Add cold water to cover the top of the beans by about one and one-half inches. Add the ham bone, thyme, parsley, bay leaves, whole onions, salt to taste, peppercorns, and carrots. Bring to a boil and simmer one hour, or until the beans are tender but not mushy.

3. While the beans cook, heat the butter and cook the chopped onion and garlic until the onion is translucent. Add the tomatoes and salt and pepper to taste. Simmer forty-five minutes.

4. When the beans are done, drain them and add to the tomato sauce. Simmer together about ten minutes. Serve the hot beans with sliced zampino or ham.

Note: Zampino is a European specialty that consists of a large pig's leg, boned and stuffed with sausage. It is available on order at Italian pork stores.

BOILED HAM:

15 to 20 servings

1 ready-to-cook whole ham (14 to 15 pounds)
3 bay leaves
1 onion, sliced
3 celery ribs with leaves
1 teaspoon thyme

1. Scrub the outside of the ham with a stiff brush, particularly if the ham has a pepper coating. Place in a deep, heavy kettle or casserole and cover with cold water.

2. Add the remaining ingredients. Bring to a boil, cover, and simmer gently for about three hours, or until the ham is fork tender.

3. Allow the ham to cool in the broth. Remove the skin and slice.

Tomato Sauce with Meat Balls and Sausages

About 2½ gallons

½ cup olive oil, approximately

3 cloves garlic, unpeeled

2 pounds Italian sausages (hot or sweet or a combination of both)

2½ pounds loin of pork, preferably the end cut, with bone in and cut into chops

6 cans (2 pounds each) Italian peeled tomatoes, preferably imported

12 cans (6 ounces each) Italian tomato paste

16 cups water, approximately
   Salt and freshly ground pepper to taste

1 cup finely chopped parsley, preferably Italian

2 tablespoons dried orégano

½ cup chopped fresh basil or 2 tablespoons dried basil

30 to 40 Meat Balls (see below), uncooked

1. Pour the oil into a large, heavy skillet. There should be enough oil to cover the bottom. Add the garlic, sausages, and pork. Cook, turning frequently, until browned on all sides.

2. Meanwhile, put the tomatoes through a food mill or sieve to remove the seeds (the seeds give a sauce a bitter taste). Pour the strained tomatoes into a large four- to five-quart kettle. Add the tomato paste and eight cups of the water, stirring until smooth. Add salt, pepper, parsley, orégano, and basil and bring to a boil. This sauce must be stirred frequently all over the bottom to keep it from sticking and burning. Stir, preferably with a wooden spoon.

3. As the sausage and pork are browned, transfer the pieces to the tomato sauce. After the meats are added to the sauce, the sauce must be simmered for at least five hours.

4. After all the meat and sausages are browned, add the meat balls to the skillet and brown them well on all sides. As the meat balls are browned, add them to the sauce and continue cooking. It should take about fifteen minutes to brown the meat balls.

5. Add about one-half cup of the fat in which the meats cooked to the sauce. Pour off all the remaining fat from the skillet. Add the remaining eight cups of water to the skillet and stir to dissolve the brown particles that cling to the bottom and sides of the skillet. Pour this liquid into a bowl and add, a little at a time, to the sauce as it cooks, to prevent the sauce from becoming too thick. Be sure to stir the sauce often.

Note: Leftover sauce may be frozen in small or large quantities and defrosted at will.

MEAT BALLS:

30 to 40 meat balls

4 pounds top round, ground

2 pounds lean pork, ground

1 cup fresh bread crumbs

2 cloves garlic, finely minced

1 cup finely chopped parsley, preferably Italian
   Salt and freshly ground pepper to taste

4 eggs, lightly beaten

½ cup freshly grated Locatelli or Parmesan cheese

Combine all the ingredients in a large mixing bowl and blend well with the hands. Shape the mixture into thirty to forty meat balls before browning as in the recipe for Tomato Sauce with Meat Balls and Sausages (see above).

Sicilian Tomato Sauce with Meat Balls

8 to 12 servings

2 cans (2 pounds 3 ounces each) Italian peeled tomatoes
  Water
¼ cup plus 3 tablespoons olive oil
1 pound boneless pork
½ cup finely chopped onion
1 7-ounce can tomato paste
1 clove garlic, cut into slivers
2 tablespoons granulated sugar
1 teaspoon black pepper
1 tablespoon dried basil
  Salt to taste
24 uncooked Sicilian Meat Balls (page 390)

1. Pour the tomatoes into a large skillet. Rinse out each can with a quarter cup of water and add it.

2. Using a large spoon, crush and press the tomatoes until broken up. Simmer fifteen minutes.

3. Meanwhile, heat the one-quarter cup oil in a deep casserole and add the pork. Cook on all sides over moderate heat until golden brown. Add the onion and cook briefly, stirring. Pour in the tomatoes and simmer twenty minutes.

4. Add the tomato paste. Fill the tomato paste can with water and add it while rinsing out the can. Add an additional cup of water. In a small skillet, heat the remaining three tablespoons oil and add the garlic. Brown briefly and add the garlic and oil to the sauce.

5. Add the sugar, black pepper, basil, and salt. It is not necessary to brown the meat balls before dropping, one at a time, into the simmering sauce. Stir briefly and gingerly with the spoon to see that the meat balls are covered with sauce, but take care not to break them. Simmer, partly covered, one hour and fifteen minutes, stirring gently around the bottom once in a while to see that the sauce does not stick or burn. Slice the pork and serve with the meat balls and sauce.

Veal Roast with Frankfurters

4 to 6 servings

1 boneless veal roast (3 pounds)
3 all-beef frankfurters or chorizos
  Salt and freshly ground pepper to taste
1 teaspoon powdered sage
2 tablespoons butter
2 tablespoons peanut or vegetable oil
¼ cup Chicken Stock (page 115), approximately
¼ cup dry sherry
½ cup light cream

1. Have the butcher make three holes in the meat so that the roast may be stuffed with the frankfurters or chorizos.

2. Stuff each of the holes with a frankfurter.

3. Season the meat with salt and pepper and sage.

4. Heat the butter and oil in a Dutch oven and sear the meat on all sides until golden. Add the stock. Cover closely and cook about one and three-quarters hours, turning the meat occasionally. Do not let it become dry.

5. Add the sherry and continue cooking fifteen minutes.

6. Remove the meat and add the cream to the pan juices. Bring to a boil.

7. Serve the meat, thinly sliced, with the cream sauce.

Veal Chops with Anchovies

6 servings

6 loin veal chops, each about 1 inch thick
Salt and freshly ground black pepper
2 tablespoons butter
2 tablespoons olive oil
1 2-ounce can flat anchovy fillets, chopped
1 tablespoon crumbled dried sage or 1 teaspoon ground sage
¾ cup dry white wine
1 tablespoon lemon juice
¼ cup canned beef gravy
Chopped parsley

1. Sprinkle the chops with salt and pepper. Heat the butter and oil in a heavy skillet and brown the chops on all sides. Remove the chops and reserve.

2. Add the anchovies and sage to the drippings left in the pan and cook for about five minutes. Add the wine and lemon juice, stir to loosen the brown particles, and simmer until the mixture is reduced by about a quarter. Stir in the beef gravy.

3. Return the chops to the pan and cover. Simmer gently for fifteen to twenty minutes, or until the chops are done.

4. Arrange the chops on a platter, around a mound of rice, if desired. Sprinkle the sauce left in the pan with parsley. Either pour the sauce over the chops or serve separately.

Veal Birds Salsicciana

6 servings

6 slices veal, cut from the leg (about 2 pounds)
All-purpose flour
1 cup sausage meat
12 stuffed olives
2 tablespoons butter
2 tablespoons olive oil
½ cup Chicken Stock (page 115), or dry white wine
¼ teaspoon ground thyme
1 bay leaf
Salt and freshly ground black pepper to taste
1 onion studded with 2 cloves
1 sprig parsley, preferably Italian

1. Bone the veal slices and pound them until very thin. Dredge the slices lightly with flour and place them flat on a chopping block.

2. Divide the sausage meat into six equal portions and place one portion in the center of each slice of veal. Push two olives into the sausage meat on each slice and roll the slices into cigarette shapes. Fasten with food picks or small metal skewers.

3. Brown the meat on all sides in the butter and oil. Add the remaining ingredients, cover, and simmer gently for about one hour, until the meat is thoroughly tender. Discard the bay leaf, onion, and parsley. Spoon the pan juices over the rolls and serve.

Veal Oreganata

4 servings

2 pounds veal, cut into thin slices
  Salt and freshly ground pepper to taste
3 tablespoons olive oil
2 cups thinly sliced onions
2 cups thinly sliced mushrooms
1 teaspoon dried orégano
½ teaspoon chopped fresh basil or ½ teaspoon dried basil
1 clove garlic, finely minced
1 tablespoon finely chopped parsley, preferably Italian
1 cup Chicken Stock (page 115)
½ cup dry white wine
2 cups canned Italian tomatoes

1. Sprinkle the meat with salt and pepper and brown the pieces, a few at a time, in the oil. Transfer the pieces to a heavy casserole with a tight lid.

2. Add the onions and mushrooms and cook, stirring, until wilted. Add the vegetables to the meat, along with the remaining ingredients and salt and pepper to taste. Bring to a boil and cover closely. Simmer until the meat is tender, thirty to forty minutes. Serve hot.

Veal Piccata

4 servings

16 small thin slices veal, cut from the leg
  Salt and freshly ground black pepper
  All-purpose flour
¼ cup butter
3 tablespoons water
3 tablespoons lemon juice
¼ cup finely chopped parsley, preferably Italian
  Lemon slices

1. Pound the veal slices lightly. Sprinkle them with salt and pepper and dredge lightly in flour.

2. Heat the butter in a large skillet and brown the veal in it quickly and lightly over moderately high heat, turning once. The meat should be cooked in one layer. If the skillet is not large enough to accommodate all the meat at once, cook it in several batches, adding more butter if necessary.

3. As the meat cooks, transfer it to a warm serving platter. Pour off most of the fat from the skillet, then add the water and swirl it around. Scrape around the bottom and sides of the skillet to loosen the brown particles. Add the lemon juice. Pour the sauce over the meat and sprinkle with parsley. Before serving, garnish the platter with lemon slices.

Veal Scaloppine with Lemon

6 servings

1½ pounds veal, cut into thin slices
2 eggs, lightly beaten
¾ cup all-purpose flour
  Salt and freshly ground black pepper
2 tablespoons oil
¼ cup butter
  Juice of 1 lemon
1 lemon, sliced wafer thin and seeded
2 tablespoons finely chopped parsley

1. Have the butcher pound the slices of veal until quite thin. Or place the veal between pieces of waxed paper and pound with a mallet or with the bottom of a skillet.

2. Dip the veal pieces in the egg and then dredge in the flour seasoned with salt and pepper to taste.

3. Brown the veal on all sides in the oil and half the butter. Remove the veal to a warm platter and add the remaining butter to the skillet. When bubbling, add the lemon juice and pour the sauce over the veal. Garnish with lemon slices and parsley and serve immediately.

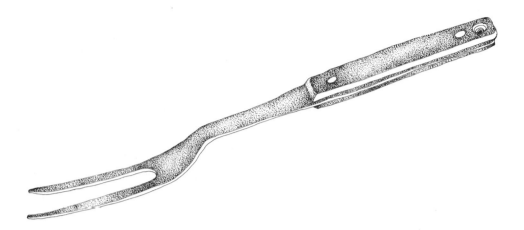

Veal Scaloppine with Marsala I

6 servings

6 veal scaloppine, pounded Italian style
  All-purpose flour
2 tablespoons butter
2 tablespoons olive oil
1 clove garlic, sliced
½ cup Marsala or sweet sherry
¼ teaspoon orégano
¼ cup Italian Tomato Sauce I (page 435)
1 teaspoon Worcestershire sauce
½ teaspoon granulated sugar

1. Dredge the scaloppine lightly with flour and pound slightly.

2. Heat the butter and oil in a large skillet and cook the garlic briefly. Remove the garlic and brown the meat lightly on both sides. Transfer the meat to a hot platter.

3. Add the wine to the skillet. Cook about five minutes, stirring. Add the remaining ingredients and cook briefly. Pour the sauce over the meat and serve immediately.

Veal Scaloppine with Marsala II

4 servings

1½ pounds boneless veal steak
  All-purpose flour
  Salt and freshly ground black pepper
2 tablespoons vegetable oil
1 tablespoon butter
½ pound mushrooms, sliced thin
1 clove garlic, finely minced
2 tablespoons finely chopped parsley, preferably Italian
1 teaspoon dried basil
1 cup peeled, seeded, and chopped tomatoes
½ cup Marsala

1. Preheat the oven to 350 degrees.

2. Pound the steak with a mallet or the flat side of a heavy knife until thin. Cut into two-inch squares and dredge the squares in flour. Sprinkle with salt and pepper.

3. Heat the oil and butter in a skillet and brown the meat on all sides, then transfer it to a casserole. Add the mushrooms and garlic to the skillet and cook briefly. Add the remaining ingredients to the skillet, then pour the mixture over the veal. Cover and bake for forty-five minutes.

Veal Scallops with Mushrooms

6 servings

6 slices veal, cut from the leg (about 2 pounds)
5 tablespoons melted butter
¼ cup olive oil
2 tablespoons chopped shallots or green onions
¼ cup dry white wine
⅓ cup Chicken Stock (page 115)
½ cup heavy cream
 Salt and freshly ground black pepper
½ pound mushrooms, sliced
2 tablespoons chopped parsley

1. Bone the veal scallops. Place them between pieces of waxed paper and pound with a mallet or the edge of a plate until they are one-quarter inch thick.
2. Sauté the scallops on both sides, a few at a time, in three tablespoons of the butter and three tablespoons of the oil for eight to ten minutes, until lightly browned. Transfer the cooked scallops to a warm dish.
3. Add the shallots to the skillet and sauté until tender but not browned. Add the wine and stock and stir to release all the brown particles in the skillet. Bring to a boil and simmer until the liquid is reduced by half. Add the cream, stirring. Season with salt and pepper to taste.
4. Sauté the mushrooms in the remaining butter and oil and add to the sauce, along with the veal scallops. Reheat but do not overcook. Sprinkle with parsley and serve immediately.

Veal Scaloppine with Parmesan

4 servings

1 egg
1 teaspoon water
½ cup fresh bread crumbs
3 tablespoons freshly grated Parmesan cheese
 Salt and freshly ground black pepper
¼ cup all-purpose flour
4 slices veal, cut from the leg (about 1 pound)
½ cup butter
4 lemon slices

1. Combine the egg and water in a shallow pie plate. Beat lightly.
2. Combine the bread crumbs, cheese, and salt and pepper to taste. Blend well.
3. Bone the veal slices and pound until thin. Dip the slices into the flour, then into the egg mixture, then into the crumbs.
4. When coated on both sides, cook the cutlets in the butter until golden brown all over. Serve garnished with lemon slices.

Bracciolini

8 servings

8 slices veal, cut from the leg (2½ pounds)
3 slices bacon, cut into small cubes
3 cloves garlic
3 tablespoons finely chopped parsley, preferably Italian
8 paper-thin slices prosciutto
¼ cup butter
1 cup Beef Stock (page 115), approximately

1. Bone the veal slices and pound them until thin. Lay the slices flat on a board.

2. Chop the bacon with the garlic and parsley and sprinkle an equal amount of the mixture over each veal slice. Place a slice of prosciutto in the center of each. Roll the veal and prosciutto in jelly-roll fashion and skewer or tie with string.

3. Heat the butter in a Dutch oven and brown the meat slowly on all sides, turning frequently. It should take fifteen to twenty minutes to brown.

4. Add the stock and cover. Simmer for thirty to forty-five minutes, depending on the size of the rolls. Add more stock if the pan becomes dry while cooking. Remove the skewers or string from the rolls and serve immediately.

Uccelleti Scappati

(Bracciolini)

4 to 6 servings

2½ pounds leg of veal, cut into approximately 8 thin slices (scaloppine)
⅓ pound fatback or salt pork
8 thin slices prosciutto
¼ cup finely chopped parsley, preferably Italian
1 teaspoon rubbed sage or ½ teaspoon ground fennel seeds
   Freshly grated Parmesan cheese
2 tablespoons butter
2 tablespoon olive oil
4 cups Italian Tomato Sauce I (page 435)

1. Place the scaloppine between pieces of waxed paper and pound lightly. Remove the slices and place them on a flat surface.

2. Chop the fatback as fine as possible and combine it with the prosciutto, parsley, and sage. Chop together to make a paste. Chop or mix in two tablespoons Parmesan cheese. Spread equal portions of this mixture over each piece of scaloppine. Roll the meat jelly-roll style and tie each with string.

3. Heat the butter and oil in a Dutch oven or heavy skillet with lid and brown the veal rolls on all sides. This should take about fifteen or twenty minutes. Remove the excess fat. Add the tomato sauce and cover. Simmer, stirring occasionally, about thirty minutes. Serve with hot, buttered green noodles and additional Parmesan cheese.

Vitello Tonnato

12 to 15 servings

3 to 4 pounds veal, cut from the leg
2 ribs celery with leaves, coarsely chopped
1 onion, skin on, sliced
1 7-ounce can tuna fish with oil
1 2-ounce can anchovy fillets with oil
2 cups dry white wine
2 to 3 cups Chicken Stock (page 115) or canned condensed chicken broth
Dash of white pepper
⅛ teaspoon dried thyme
Tiny pinch of sage
3 sprigs parsley, preferably Italian
1½ cups Mayonnaise (page 265)
Juice of 1 lemon
Capers, drained well
Minced parsley

1. Have the butcher roll and tie the meat.
2. Place the veal in a large, heavy kettle, along with the celery, onion, tuna, anchovies, wine, chicken stock, pepper, thyme, sage, and parsley sprigs. Bring to a boil slowly, skimming regularly. Place a piece of waxed paper over the top of the kettle and cover with a lid. Reduce the heat and simmer about one hour and ten minutes, or until the meat is tender when pierced with a fork. Immediately refrigerate the meat in the stock and leave overnight, or at least twelve hours.
3. The next day, lift the meat out of the broth. Wrap securely in foil or plastic wrap and refrigerate. Skim off the fat on the surface of the broth and discard. Place the broth back over high heat, bring to a boil, and reduce to about three cups. Put through a food mill, pushing through as much of the solids as possible. Discard the solids remaining in the mill. Cool.
4. Place the mayonnaise in large bowl. Beat in enough of the cooled, strained broth with a wire whisk to form a smooth sauce somewhat thicker than heavy cream. Add more mayonnaise or more broth, if necessary, to bring the sauce to the right consistency. Stir in the lemon juice, then chill.
5. Slice the cold veal into very thin slices and arrange, overlapping, on a platter. Spoon some of the sauce over the slices. Sprinkle with one tablespoon capers and minced parsley. Serve the remaining sauce on the side, garnished with more capers. Serve with cold, cooked rice mixed with finely chopped parsley.

Tomato Sauce with Tarragon Veal Balls

4 servings

SAUCE:
3 tablespoons olive oil
3 cloves garlic, finely minced
¼ cup finely minced green pepper
¾ cup finely minced parsley, preferably Italian
2 cans (1 pound each) Italian plum tomatoes
1 tablespoon chopped fresh or dried basil
1 teaspoon chopped fresh or dried mint
½ teaspoon salt
Cayenne pepper

MEAT BALLS:

1 pound veal or pork or veal and pork combined, ground
¾ cup fresh bread crumbs
  Salt and freshly ground black pepper
¼ teaspoon freshly grated nutmeg
1 egg, lightly beaten
2 tablespoons finely chopped parsley, preferably Italian
1 teaspoon finely chopped fresh or dried tarragon
1 clove garlic, finely minced
1 tablespoon freshly grated Parmesan cheese
  All-purpose flour
2 tablespoons vegetable oil
2 tablespoons butter

1. To prepare the sauce, heat the oil and cook the garlic and green pepper about one minute, stirring. Add the parsley, tomatoes, basil, mint, salt, and cayenne to taste and simmer for ten minutes.

2. To prepare the meat balls, place the meat, bread crumbs, and salt and pepper to taste in a mixing bowl. Combine the nutmeg, egg, parsley, tarragon, garlic, and cheese. Beat lightly and add to the meat and crumbs. Mix well with the fingers and shape into approximately fourteen one-and-one-half-inch balls. Dredge lightly in flour.

3. Heat the oil and butter in a skillet and brown the balls on all sides. When browned, add to the sauce and simmer for thirty minutes. Serve with cooked spaghetti and Parmesan cheese.

Veal Shanks with Prosciutto and Peas

6 to 8 servings

3 veal shanks, each sawed into 3 2-inch pieces
  All-purpose flour for dredging
  Salt and freshly ground pepper to taste
⅓ cup salad or vegetable oil
¼ pound prosciutto, cut into cubes
1 teaspoon dried mint
1 teaspoon rubbed leaf sage
1 bay leaf
2 sprigs fresh thyme or 1 teaspoon dried thyme
3 sprigs fresh parsley, preferably Italian
2 cups chopped onion
2 cloves garlic, finely minced
½ cup chopped celery
1 cup dry white wine
1¼ cups Chicken Stock (page 115)
2 tablespoons tomato paste
1 cup fresh or frozen peas

1. Dredge the shanks in the flour seasoned with salt and pepper.

2. Heat the oil and brown the shanks on all sides.

3. Arrange the shanks in an oval or round kettle or Dutch oven, standing the pieces on their sides so that the marrow does not fall out. Sprinkle the meat with the prosciutto, mint, sage, bay leaf, thyme, parsley, onion, garlic, and celery. Add the wine with the chicken stock and tomato paste. Cover and simmer two hours.

4. Add the peas and cook five minutes or longer, depending on the age and size of the peas. Frozen peas will, of course, require the least time. Serve with rice.

Pork Sausage with Fennel

3 pounds sausage

2 to 4 strands pork casings
3 pounds boneless pork butt
1½ teaspoons salt
2 tablespoons freshly ground black pepper
1½ teaspoons crushed fennel seeds
    Hot pepper flakes or cayenne pepper to taste (optional)

1. Rinse the pork casings well and let them soak in cold water at least one hour. Rinse well and drain thoroughly.
2. Remove most of the fat from the pork butt. Place the meat on a flat surface, slice it thin, then chop it coarsely. This method is preferable, although it may be coarsely ground in a meat grinder.
3. Blend the meat with the salt, pepper, fennel, and pepper flakes.
4. Stuff one casing at a time. To do this, slip one end of the casing over the mouth of a funnel with a big spout, or use a regular sausage stuffer. Use the fingers to push the casing down the spout or over the mouth of the sausage stuffer. Tie the end of the casing with string. Place the funnel in an upright position and start adding meat, pushing it through the funnel and into the casing, letting the casing slip away gradually as it is filled. Tie the sausage-filled casings every three inches to make links. If there are air holes, prick the sausage with needles to let the air escape. The sausage may be broiled or fried.

Sausage with Savoy Cabbage

4 to 6 servings

1 small head savoy cabbage
¼ cup olive oil
6 links uncooked Pork Sausage with Fennel (see above)
    Salt and freshly ground pepper to taste
2 cloves garlic, finely chopped

1. Rinse the cabbage head and drain. Cut into segments one and one-half to two inches thick. Set aside.
2. Heat half the oil in a skillet and add the sausage. Cook, turning as necessary, until golden brown and cooked through.
3. Heat the remaining oil in a casserole and add the cabbage, salt, pepper, and garlic. Cover tightly and simmer about fifteen minutes. It will not be necessary to add additional liquid unless the cabbage starts to stick or burn, in which case add just enough boiling water to keep it from sticking. Stir occasionally.
4. Add the sausage and cover. Cook until the cabbage is tender, fifteen minutes or longer.

Italian Sausages Marchigiana

6 servings

9 sweet or hot Italian sausage links or a
combination of both (about 1½ pounds)
1 large cauliflower, broken into flowerets
(quartered fresh fennel may be substituted)
2 tablespoons olive oil
2 onions, cut in half and thinly sliced
1 tablespoon crushed fennel seeds
1 tablespoon chopped fresh or dried basil
1 teaspoon finely chopped rosemary
½ teaspoon chopped Italian hot pepper
flakes
2 cloves garlic, finely minced
½ cup red wine vinegar
1 tablespoon tomato paste
½ cup warm water

1. Cook the sausages in a skillet, turning
frequently until brown and cooked through.
2. Cook the cauliflowerets in boiling salted
water for one minute. Drain.
3. Remove the sausage and cut into one-
inch lengths. Set aside. Pour off the fat from
the skillet and add the olive oil and cauliflower. Cook, shaking the skillet, until the
cauliflower is lightly browned. Add more oil
if necessary. Add the onions and cook, stirring, until they are wilted.
4. Add the fennel seeds, basil, rosemary,
and pepper flakes. Add the garlic and vinegar
and cook, stirring to blend, about five minutes over low heat. Dilute the tomato paste
in the warm water and add. Cover and simmer until the cauliflower is barely tender,
five to ten minutes. Return the sausage to the
skillet. Mix well and serve hot.

Sausage with White Beans

6 to 8 servings

1 1-pound cotechino (Italian sausage) or
fresh kielbasa (Polish sausage)
2 cans white kidney beans
6 green onions, green part and all
¼ cup olive oil
1 cup finely chopped parsley, preferably
Italian
Coarse salt to taste
Freshly ground pepper to taste
6 cloves garlic, finely chopped
½ cup dry white wine

1. Place the whole cotechino or kielbasa
in a saucepan and add water to cover. Bring
to a boil and simmer forty-five minutes.
2. Meanwhile, drain the beans in a colander and rinse them.
3. Trim the green onions and chop fine.
Cook briefly in the oil, then add half the
parsley. Add salt and pepper, the garlic,
beans, and wine. When the sausage is cooked,
add enough of the cooking liquid to barely
cover the beans. Cook over very low heat
about ten minutes, stirring carefully so as not
to break up the beans.
4. Remove the skin from the sausage, cut
the sausage into thin slices, and stir into the
beans. Sprinkle with the remaining parsley
and serve.

Rosemary-Stuffed Zucchini

4 servings

2 medium or 4 small zucchini
¼ cup butter
½ pound sausage, ground
1 clove garlic, finely minced
½ teaspoon finely chopped fresh or dried rosemary
2 tablespoons heavy cream
3 tablespoons finely minced parsley, preferably Italian
½ cup toasted bread crumbs
¼ cup freshly grated Parmesan cheese
1 egg, lightly beaten
   Salt and freshly ground black pepper
½ cup Chicken Stock (page 115) or dry white wine
½ cup tomato puree

1. Preheat the oven to 350 degrees.
2. Trim off and discard the ends of the zucchini. Split the zucchini in half. Using a melon ball cutter or a small spoon, scoop out and reserve the center pulp of each half, leaving a shell for stuffing.
3. Heat half the butter in a saucepan and cook the scooped-out pulp until wilted.
4. Meanwhile, cook the sausage, crumbling with a spoon, until done. Pour off all excess fat. Add the sausage to the pulp.
5. Add the garlic, rosemary, cream, parsley, crumbs, and half the cheese. Stir in the egg and salt and pepper to taste and, when blended, use the mixture to fill the zucchini halves. Sprinkle with the remaining cheese and dot with the remaining butter. Arrange the stuffed halves on a greased shallow baking dish. Pour the chicken stock and tomato puree around and stir. Bake twenty minutes, or until the zucchini are tender and the filling is golden brown.

Chicken Canzanese

4 servings

If chicken is not the most adaptable of foods, it is certainly a contender for the title. It marries well with most spices (and with many at once in curries); it blends with wine and cream, and crops up in the cooking of almost every culture on earth. The chicken Canzanese *here is an Italian dish from the Abruzzi region, a recipe of Ed Giobbi, the artist.*

1 chicken (3 pounds), cut into serving pieces
   Salt to taste
2 whole sage leaves
2 bay leaves
1 clove garlic, sliced lengthwise
6 cloves
2 sprigs fresh rosemary or ½ teaspoon dried rosemary
12 peppercorns, crushed
1 hot red pepper, broken and seeded (optional)
1 ½-inch-thick slice prosciutto (about ¼ pound)
½ cup dry white wine
¼ cup water

1. Place the chicken pieces in a mixing bowl and add cold water to cover and salt to taste. Let stand one hour, then drain and pat dry.
2. Arrange the chicken pieces in one layer in a skillet and add the sage and bay leaves, garlic, cloves, rosemary, peppercorns, and red pepper. Cut the prosciutto into small cubes and sprinkle it over the chicken. Add the wine and water. Do not add salt, since the prosciutto will season the dish. Cover and simmer forty minutes, then uncover and cook briefly over high heat until the sauce is reduced slightly. Serve hot.

Chicken Parmigiana

4 servings

1 frying chicken (3½ pounds), cut into serving pieces
   Salt and freshly ground black pepper
¼ cup butter or olive oil
1 cup sliced mushrooms
1 green pepper, cored, seeded, and finely chopped
½ cup finely chopped onion
1 clove garlic, finely minced
2 cups peeled, seeded, and chopped tomatoes
½ cup dry vermouth
½ cup sliced stuffed olives
¼ cup freshly grated Parmesan cheese

1. Preheat the oven to 350 degrees.
2. Sprinkle the chicken with salt and pepper and brown on all sides in the butter. Sprinkle with the mushrooms and cook for five minutes. Sprinkle with the green pepper, onion, and garlic, then add the tomatoes and vermouth. Cover closely and bake for thirty minutes.
3. Add the olives and cook for ten minutes longer. Serve with the grated cheese.

Chicken Romarin

6 servings

¼ cup all-purpose flour
   Salt and freshly ground black pepper
2 chickens (2½ pounds each), cut into serving pieces
2 tablespoons butter
2 tablespoons peanut oil
3 tablespoons finely chopped shallots or green onion
1 cup sliced mushrooms
¼ cup dry white wine
1½ cups drained canned Italian peeled tomatoes
1 teaspoon dried rosemary
1 tablespoon finely chopped parsley

1. Combine the flour with salt and pepper to taste. Dredge the chicken pieces in the mixture.
2. Heat the butter and oil in a large skillet and brown the chicken on all sides. Transfer the chicken to a warm platter. Add the shallots and mushrooms to the skillet and cook, stirring, until the mushrooms are wilted. Add the wine and cook, stirring to dissolve the brown particles that cling to the bottom and sides of the skillet.
3. Return the chicken to the skillet and add the tomatoes and rosemary. Sprinkle with salt and pepper to taste. Cover and simmer over low heat for thirty minutes, or until the chicken is tender. Before serving, sprinkle with chopped parsley.

Pollo alla Cacciatore

4 servings

1 chicken (2½ to 3 pounds), cut into serving pieces
  Salt and freshly ground black pepper
5 tablespoons butter
3 tablespoons peanut oil
¼ pound sliced prosciutto, cut into bite-sized pieces
1 tablespoon fresh or dried leaf sage (preferably sage with stems)
¾ cup dry white wine

1. Sprinkle the chicken pieces with salt and pepper.

2. Heat three tablespoons of the butter and the oil in a large skillet and cook the chicken pieces until golden brown all over. Pour off most of the fat from the skillet and add the prosciutto, sage, and wine. Cover and cook until tender, about twenty minutes. Remove the chicken to a hot platter.

3. Bring the pan juices to a boil, then remove the skillet from the heat. Swirl in the remaining butter by rotating the pan gently and serve the sauce separately.

Breasts of Chicken Gismonda

4 servings

2 large whole chicken breasts, halved, skinned, and boned
  All-purpose flour
  Salt and freshly ground black pepper
2 eggs, lightly beaten
1 tablespoon water
¼ cup freshly grated Parmesan cheese
½ cup fresh bread crumbs
¾ cup butter
1½ pounds fresh spinach
½ pound fresh mushrooms, thinly sliced
1 tablespoon lemon juice
¼ teaspoon nutmeg

1. Coat the chicken breasts lightly but thoroughly in flour seasoned with salt and pepper.

2. Beat the eggs with the water and dip the chicken in the mixture. Blend the cheese and bread crumbs and dip the pieces in this, coating thoroughly. Pat lightly to help the crumbs adhere.

3. Melt one-half cup of the butter in a large skillet and cook the chicken in it until golden brown on both sides, turning once.

4. Meanwhile, rinse the spinach well and place it in a saucepan with a tight-fitting lid. Do not add additional water or salt. Cover and cook briefly, stirring once or twice, until the spinach is crisp tender.

5. While the spinach cooks, heat half the remaining butter in a skillet and cook the mushrooms, stirring, until light brown.

6. Drain the spinach well and toss with the remaining butter and the lemon juice. Season with salt to taste and nutmeg.

7. Spoon the hot spinach onto four hot plates and top each with a chicken breast. Scatter the mushrooms over all and serve hot.

Chicken Breasts alla Parmigiana

4 servings

2 whole chicken breasts
½ cup all-purpose flour
¼ teaspoon freshly grated nutmeg
   Salt and freshly ground black pepper
2 eggs, lightly beaten
¾ cup bread crumbs
¼ cup grated Parmesan cheese
⅓ cup melted butter
4 lemon wedges

1. Have the chicken breasts split in half and boned. Remove and discard the skin.
2. Season the flour with nutmeg and salt and pepper to taste. Dredge the breasts lightly in the flour mixture. Dip the breasts into the eggs and then in a mixture of bread crumbs and Parmesan cheese, coating thoroughly. Brown on all sides in the melted butter and serve hot, with lemon wedges.

Chicken Breasts Siena Style

4 servings

2 whole chicken breasts, halved, skinned, and boned (this will yield 4 pieces)
¼ cup butter
½ tablespoon salad oil
   Salt and freshly ground pepper to taste
   Juice of 1 lemon
2 tablespoons finely chopped parsley, preferably Italian

1. Place the breast halves on a flat surface and, using a sharp knife, slice them in half. This will make two "fillets" of each breast half.
2. Heat the butter and oil in a large skillet and cook the fillets on both sides. Do not overcook. The entire cooking should involve only two or three minutes.

3. Transfer the chicken to a warm platter and sprinkle with salt and pepper.
4. Add the lemon juice to the skillet and stir with a wooden spoon to dissolve the brown particles in the skillet. Add the parsley and return the chicken to the skillet. Turn the chicken in the sauce and serve hot, with the sauce poured over.

Italian Olive Stuffing

(Poultry Stuffing)

*About 4 cups; enough for a
4- to 5-pound chicken*

¾ cup ripe olives, cut into wedges
4 cups day-old bread cubes, toasted
4 slices bacon, cooked until crisp and crumbled
1 clove garlic, finely minced
⅓ cup chopped onion
¼ cup butter
½ cup chopped green pepper
½ teaspoon dried orégano
½ teaspoon dried basil
⅓ cup tomato paste
¼ cup Chicken Stock (page 115)
½ teaspoon salt
¼ teaspoon freshly ground black pepper

1. Place the olives, bread, and bacon in a bowl.
2. Sauté the garlic and onion in the butter until tender.
3. Stir in the green pepper, orégano, basil, tomato paste, stock, salt, and pepper and bring the mixture to a boil.
4. Pour the onion mixture into the olive and bread mixture and toss all the ingredients together.

Mozzarella in Carrozza

3 to 6 servings

1 crusty loaf of Italian or French bread
1 6-ounce package mozzarella cheese
¼ cup warm milk
All-purpose flour for dredging
2 eggs, lightly beaten
Hot vegetable oil for deep frying
Anchovy Sauce (see below)

1. The trick in this recipe is making the hollowed-out bread boxes (or "railroad cars") for the cheese. When finished, they look like miniature shoe boxes without lids.

2. To make the boxes, cut the long loaf of bread into slices one and one-half inches wide. Trim off the crust of the bread and cut each slice into rectangles about one and one-half by two and one-half inches. Hollow out the rectangles, leaving the sides and bottom one-quarter inch thick.

3. Cut the mozzarella into rectangles that will fit inside the hollowed-out pieces of bread. The more snugly the cheese fits the better.

4. When the bread boxes are filled with cheese, smear or brush them all over lightly —cheese and all—with the warm milk. They must not become soggy.

5. Dredge the boxes all over lightly in flour, then dip into the beaten egg until well coated and dredge again in flour.

6. Heat the oil until it is almost smoking and drop the boxes, cheese side up, in the fat. When the bottom is brown, quickly turn them in the fat and cook just until the cheese melts. If the boxes have been properly coated with egg and flour, the cheese should not run out in the fat. When golden all over, drain on absorbent towels and serve hot with anchovy sauce.

ANCHOVY SAUCE:

About ⅓ cup

Melt six tablespoons of butter in a small saucepan and add six to eight flat anchovies. Stir with a wooden spoon until the anchovies dissolve in the butter. Serve hot.

Risotto

4 to 6 servings

¼ cup butter
½ cup finely chopped onion
1 cup uncooked rice
½ cup dry white wine
2 cups Chicken Stock (page 115) or canned chicken broth, approximately
½ teaspoon leaf saffron or ¼ teaspoon powdered saffron
¼ cup freshly grated Parmesan cheese

1. Preheat the oven to 350 degrees.

2. Heat the butter in an ovenproof casserole and cook the onion until wilted. Add the rice and cook, stirring, two to three minutes without browning.

3. Meanwhile, bring the wine and chicken stock to a boil and ladle approximately one cup of the liquid onto the rice. Cover tightly and place in the oven.

4. Keep the broth at the simmer. After five minutes, add a third of the remaining liquid to the rice and cover again. Five minutes later combine half the remaining liquid with the saffron and add to the rice. Cover and cook ten to fifteen minutes longer. If necessary, add the remaining broth. When the risotto is done, almost all liquid will be absorbed, but it is not a fluffy dish. Just before serving, stir in the Parmesan cheese.

Risotto Milanese

6 to 8 servings

½ teaspoon whole saffron
6 to 8 cups hot Chicken Stock (page 115),
   approximately
7 tablespoons sweet butter
   Salt to taste
3 tablespoons finely chopped onion
2 cups uncooked rice
¾ cup dry white wine
   Freshly ground pepper to taste
1 cup freshly grated Parmesan cheese

1. Chop the saffron and combine it with half a cup of the chicken broth. Set aside.

2. Melt three tablespoons of the butter in a heavy, fairly wide metal casserole (with a four- or five-quart capacity). Add salt and the onion and cook, stirring, until the onion is wilted but not brown. Add the rice and stir without browning. Add the wine and the saffron mixture.

3. Add three cups of chicken stock and stir with a wooden spoon. The heat for cooking the risotto should be moderate to high. As the liquid is absorbed, add more chicken stock, shaking the casserole frequently and stirring with the spoon. You must use your own judgment in deciding the quantity of stock to be added; it may or may not require eight cups. The important thing is to continue cooking the rice, adding liquid as necessary, until the rice is tender but not mushy and not soupy. All the liquid must be absorbed.

4. When the risotto is ready, sprinkle with pepper. Stir in the remaining butter and half the grated Parmesan cheese. Serve the remaining cheese on the side.

Risotto with Mussels

6 servings

3 pounds mussels, scrubbed and debearded
¾ cup finely chopped onion
3 tablespoons imported olive oil
3 tablespoons butter
2 cloves garlic, finely minced
¼ cup chopped parsley, preferably Italian
½ cup dry white wine
   Freshly ground pepper to taste
1¾ cups Chicken Stock (page 115) or
   canned chicken broth
1½ cups short-grain Italian rice
   Freshly grated Parmesan cheese

1. Using a sharp, thin-bladed knife, open the mussels. Remove the mussels from the shells, reserving both the mussels and juice.

2. Cook the onion in the oil and butter in a saucepan until golden brown. Add the garlic, parsley, wine, and pepper. Simmer five minutes.

3. Drain the mussel liquid into another small saucepan and add the chicken stock. Bring to a boil and keep hot while the risotto cooks.

4. Add about three-quarters cup of the broth to the onion and parsley mixture and bring to a boil. Add the rice and cook, stirring frequently, until all the liquid is absorbed. Add another small ladleful of liquid and cook, stirring frequently, until this liquid is absorbed. Continue adding liquid, stirring and cooking until the rice reaches the desired degree of doneness. In most Italian homes it is cooked *al dente*.

5. Shortly before the rice is cooked, stir in the mussels. Serve with freshly grated Parmesan cheese.

White Risotto with Mushrooms

6 servings

¼ cup olive oil
1 whole clove garlic, peeled
½ pound fresh mushrooms, thinly sliced
½ cup minced parsley, preferably Italian
    Salt and freshly ground black pepper
¼ cup butter
½ medium onion, thinly sliced
1½ cups uncooked long-grain Carolina rice
4 cups hot Chicken Stock (page 115)
½ cup dry white wine
½ cup freshly grated Parmesan cheese

1. Heat the olive oil and garlic clove. Add the mushrooms and parsley and season lightly with salt and pepper. Cook over medium heat, stirring constantly, for about five minutes, or until the mushrooms are almost tender. Remove from the heat and discard the garlic clove; reserve the mushrooms.

2. Heat the butter in a two-quart flame-proof casserole. Add the onion and cook over low heat until the onion is soft but still white. Add the rice and cook over medium heat, stirring constantly, about two minutes, or until the rice is opaque.

3. Add the hot chicken stock, one-quarter cup at a time, stirring constantly. When the rice has absorbed the stock, add more, stirring constantly to prevent scorching. Add the wine. When the rice is creamy and almost cooked, add the mushrooms. Because different kinds of rice absorb liquids differently, a little more hot stock may be needed. Add it a tablespoon at a time. Cook together until the mushrooms and rice are tender. Stir in the Parmesan cheese and serve hot.

Fettuccine Alfredo

2 servings

2 cups sifted all-purpose flour
½ teaspoon salt
4 egg yolks
4 to 6 tablespoons hot water
½ cup butter, cut into 8 parts
    Freshly ground black pepper
⅔ cup light cream
¼ pound Parmesan cheese, grated fresh
2 large white Italian truffles, sliced (optional)

1. To make the noodles, sift the flour and salt together onto a board. Make a well in the center and put in the egg yolks.

2. Gradually work the egg yolks into the flour until a stiff dough is formed, adding the hot water as necessary. Knead the dough until smooth.

3. Cut the dough into halves and roll out each piece on a floured board until paper thin. Allow the sheets to dry for fifteen to twenty minutes.

4. Fold the sheets of dough into rolls and cut them crosswise into strips one-half inch wide, using a very sharp knife. Toss the noodles gently with the fingers to unfold.

5. Spread the noodles on a floured board and let stand, covered with a towel, for not longer than one hour.

6. Cook the noodles in two quarts of boiling salted water for three to four minutes. Drain and place in a dry pan.

7. Gently heat the noodles. Toss them gently while adding the butter and grinding the pepper over them.

8. Add the cream and allow to heat thoroughly, tossing once or twice, until most of the cream has been absorbed.

9. Add the Parmesan cheese and the truffles. Heat, still tossing gently, for two to three minutes, until the noodles are evenly coated with the melted cheese. Serve immediately.

Fettuccine alla Romana

2 large or 4 small servings

To most Americans who dine in the Italian restaurants of Manhattan or San Francisco or Kalamazoo, the thought of pasta generally conjures up an image of spaghetti or lasagne bathed in tomato sauce. Italians, however, envision more glorious preparations. One of the great pleasures of dining in Rome or in Milan or Bologna—or whatever Italian town you will—is the infinite imagination the cooks employ in adorning pasta. Here is a Roman version of fettuccine.

½ pound fettuccine
    Salt
¼ cup butter, at room temperature, cut into 8 pieces
½ cup freshly grated Parmesan cheese
¼ cup hot heavy cream
½ cup freshly cooked peas, preferably freshly shelled
⅓ cup finely shredded imported or domestic prosciutto

1. The important thing about this recipe is to have all the ingredients ready. The fettuccine must be tossed and served with the other ingredients within seconds after they are cooked. Heat a serving dish for the fettuccine and have a colander in the sink.

2. Place the fettuccine into boiling salted water to cover and cook to the desired degree of doneness. This should not require more than eight or nine minutes for *al dente,* as preferred by Italians. It may require longer for those who prefer it softer.

3. Test the fettuccine for doneness a strand at a time. Remove the strand with a fork, let cool briefly, then bite into it. When nearly done, add the butter to the hot serving dish.

4. When done, pour into the colander. Drain quickly and not too thoroughly. Pour the moist pasta into the serving dish and toss quickly. Add the cheese, cream, peas, and prosciutto and continue tossing. Serve quickly on hot plates. Let each guest season his portion himself with a peppermill.

Lasagne for a Crowd

About 16 servings

1½ pounds lasagne noodles
    Salt
 ½ cup olive oil
 3 pounds whole-milk ricotta
 3 eggs
13 cups tomato sauce from Tomato Sauce with Meat Balls and Sausages (page 393)
 ¼ cup chopped parsley, preferably Italian
    Freshly ground pepper to taste
1¼ cups finely grated Locatelli or Parmesan cheese
 1 pound white American cheese, cut into small cubes
1½ pounds mozzarella cheese, cut into small cubes
1½ cups butter
    Meat balls, sausages, and loin of pork from Tomato Sauce with Meat Balls and Sausages (page 393)

1. Preheat the oven to 350 degrees. Have ready a baking utensil (17 x 11½ x 2¼). It must be the proper size.

2. Drop the noodles into several quarts of boiling water, adding salt to taste and the olive oil. The oil will keep the noodles from sticking. Cook the noodles until done, but do not overcook. They will bake further in the oven. When cooked, drain the noodles in a colander and run cold water over them.

3. Place the ricotta in a mixing bowl and add the eggs, one cup of the tomato sauce, parsley, salt, pepper, and one-quarter cup of the grated Locatelli cheese. Blend well.

4. Spoon a layer of tomato sauce all over the bottom of the baking dish. The layer should be about one-quarter inch thick. Carefully arrange a single layer of noodles, with the noodles slightly overlapping, over the baking dish. Add a layer of the ricotta mixture (use about one-third of the amount) and smooth it over the noodles. Sprinkle this with about one-third each of the American cheese, mozzarella, and the Locatelli. Dot everything with about one-third of the butter.

5. Remove several meat balls from the sauce and crush them with a fork. Crush enough to produce three cups of meat. Similarly crush enough sausages to produce three cups. Now shred enough of the pork loin to produce about two cups.

6. Sprinkle one-third of each of the meats (crushed meat balls, sausages, and shredded pork) over the baking dish.

7. Continue making layers, three layers in all, ending with a sprinkling of the meats and a layer of tomato sauce. Reserve a little of the Locatelli for sprinkling on the top. Pat this down gently with the back of a spoon and give a final sprinkling of grated Locatelli cheese. The baking dish should be almost if not completely full. Cover closely with aluminum foil.

8. Line the oven rack with aluminum foil to catch any drippings. Add the pan to the oven and bake one to one and one-half hours, uncovering the dish for the final fifteen minutes of baking. When ready, the lasagne should be thoroughly hot and bubbling. Serve cut into squares with additional grated cheese on the side, accompanied by crusty French bread and a tossed green salad.

Note: When the lasagne is ready for the oven and covered closely with aluminum foil, it may at that point be frozen. If frozen, the lasagne must not be defrosted before baking. It must be baked from the frozen state, two and one-half hours at 350 degrees.

Macaroni Leonardo

6 servings

2 pounds sweet Italian sausage
1 onion, finely chopped
1 clove garlic, finely minced
1 teaspoon salt
1 6-ounce can tomato paste
1 (1-pound 13-ounce) can tomatoes
1 teaspoon orégano
⅛ teaspoon freshly ground black pepper
1 pound elbow macaroni, cooked according to package directions

1. Cut the sausage into one-half-inch slices and brown them. Add the onion and garlic and cook until golden. Drain off the fat.

2. Add the salt, tomato paste, and tomatoes. Bring to a boil and simmer, uncovered, forty-five minutes. Add the orégano and pepper ten minutes before the end of the cooking time.

3. Arrange the macaroni on a serving dish and pour the sauce over the top.

Linguine with Red Clam Sauce

4 to 6 servings

48 littleneck or cherrystone clams in the shell or 1 cup canned minced clams
½ cup olive oil
2 large cloves garlic, finely minced
6 tablespoons chopped parsley, preferably Italian
2 teaspoons finely chopped fresh thyme or 1 teaspoon dried thyme
2 cups Italian Tomato Sauce I (page 435)
Salt and freshly ground pepper to taste
1 pound linguine

1. If fresh clams are used, open them (or have them opened) and save the clam juice. Drain the clams and save that juice, too. Finely chop the fresh clams and set them aside. If canned clams are used, simply open the can and set it aside.

2. Heat the oil and add the garlic. Cook briefly, without browning, and add the fresh clam juice. If canned clams are used, add the clams plus their juice.

3. Add the parsley, thyme, and tomato sauce and simmer briefly. Add salt and pepper.

4. Cook the linguine according to package directions.

5. If fresh clams are used, add them at the last minute to the sauce and bring just to a boil. Serve immediately with the hot linguine.

Pasta e Fagioli

(Macaroni and Beans)

8 servings

1 pound dried navy beans or other small white beans
2 quarts water
1 beef bone
¼ cup olive oil
2 cloves garlic, peeled
1 teaspoon dried basil
2 teaspoons salt
½ teaspoon freshly ground black pepper
1 cup Beef Stock (page 115)
3 tomatoes, peeled and chopped
1 pound medium macaroni
2 tablespoons minced parsley
  Freshly grated Parmesan cheese

1. Pick over the beans, wash thoroughly, and cover with the water. Allow to soak overnight, or bring to a boil, simmer for two minutes, and allow to stand for one to two hours before proceeding.

2. Add the beef bone to the beans, bring to a boil, and simmer for two hours, or until the beans are tender.

3. Heat the oil in a small pan and sauté the garlic in it. Add the basil, salt, pepper, stock, and tomatoes and bring the mixture to a boil. Pour into the cooked beans.

4. Cook the macaroni according to package directions. Drain and reserve the liquid. Add the macaroni to the beans and cook for five to ten minutes longer. Adjust the consistency of the dish by crushing some of the beans if it is too moist or by adding some of the reserved liquid if it is too dry. Discard any remaining liquid. Serve sprinkled with the parsley and the cheese.

Pasta with Ricotta

6 to 8 servings

2 pounds spinach
1 pound fresh ricotta cheese
3 eggs, lightly beaten
  Freshly grated Parmesan cheese
⅓ cup chopped parsley, preferably Italian
2 teaspoons salt
½ teaspoon freshly ground pepper
  Marinara Sauce I (page 436)
1 pound tubelike pasta such as macaroncelli, mustaccioli no. 84, elbow macaroni, or penne

1. Preheat the oven to 375 degrees.

2. Pick over the spinach, trimming away and discarding tough stems. Rinse the leaves well and drain. Cook the spinach briefly, tightly covered, in the water that clings to the leaves. Stir the spinach as it cooks just until the leaves are wilted. Drain well in a colander. When the spinach is cool enough to handle with the hands, press the spinach to remove most of the moisture and chop.

3. Combine the spinach, ricotta, eggs, two-thirds cup Parmesan cheese, parsley, salt, pepper, and marinara sauce. Blend.

4. Bring a large quantity of water to a boil and add the pasta, stirring rapidly. Cook, stirring, for two minutes, then drain the pasta in a colander and add to the ricotta mixture. Pour the mixture into a baking dish and bake twenty-five to thirty minutes, or until the pasta is tender but not mushy. Do not overcook. Serve with more Parmesan cheese on the side.

Homemade Noodles with a Machine

One of the easiest methods of making noodles in the home is with a small machine. To prepare homemade noodles by machine, spoon flour into a mixing bowl. For each cup of flour add one whole egg, lightly beaten, and a pinch of salt. Some cooks add a little salad oil.

Work the mixture quickly with the fingers and hands until all the flour is moistened with egg and forms a ball. The trick is in getting the right distribution of moisture in the dough. It may be necessary to add more flour or it may be necessary to add a little water. The first few tries with the dough may be frustrating, but with practice even a child can make noodles by machine. When the dough is ready it should be divided into thirds and put through the rollers according to the manufacturer's instructions.

Noodles and Chicken Campanini

4 to 6 servings

½ cup butter
⅓ cup all-purpose flour
2½ cups Chicken Stock (page 115)
¾ cup light cream
¼ cup dry white wine
2 teaspoons salt
¼ teaspoon freshly ground white pepper
1 cup sliced fresh mushrooms
6 mushroom caps
1 cup cooked ham cut in thinnest possible strips (julienne)
½ pound medium noodles, cooked according to package directions
2 cups cooked, diced chicken
⅓ cup freshly grated Parmesan cheese

1. Preheat the oven to 350 degrees.
2. Melt half the butter in a saucepan. Blend in the flour with a whisk. Gradually add the chicken broth, stirring constantly with the whisk. Add the cream and cook, stirring, until the sauce is thickened and smooth. Add the wine, salt, and pepper.
3. Sauté the sliced mushrooms, mushroom caps, and ham in the remaining butter. Add the sliced mushrooms, ham, cooked noodles, and chicken to the sauce. Turn the mixture into four or six greased individual casseroles. Top each with a mushroom cap and sprinkle with Parmesan cheese. Heat in the oven until the cheese is melted and golden brown, about ten minutes.

Noodles Florentine I

6 servings

2 pounds noodles, cooked according to
  package directions
½ cup olive oil
2 cloves garlic, finely chopped
½ cup freshly grated Swiss or Gruyère
  cheese
  Freshly ground black pepper
6 cups chopped, cooked spinach
2 teaspoons dried tarragon
2 tablespoons lemon juice
½ cup butter
  Salt
  Buttered, toasted bread crumbs
  Freshly grated Parmesan cheese

1. Preheat the broiler.
2. Drain the noodles and mix them with
the olive oil, garlic, Swiss cheese, and pepper
to taste.
3. Drain the spinach and to it add the tarragon, lemon juice, butter, and salt to taste.
Make a bed of hot spinach on the bottom of
a lightly greased baking dish. Place the
noodles on top and sprinkle liberally with
buttered, toasted bread crumbs and Parmesan cheese.
4. Put under the broiler for five minutes.
Serve at once.

Noodles Florentine II

4 servings

½ pound broad or medium noodles
2 tablespoons butter
2 tablespoons all-purpose flour
½ cup milk
½ cup heavy cream
  Salt and freshly ground pepper to taste
¼ teaspoon nutmeg
2 cups freshly cooked, chopped spinach
2 cups loosely packed grated Gruyère or
  Swiss cheese

1. Preheat the oven to 400 degrees.
2. Cook the noodles according to package
directions. Drain them and run them under
cold running water so that they will not stick
together. Drain well.
3. While the noodles are cooking, melt the
butter and stir in the flour with a whisk. Add
the milk, stirring constantly with the whisk.
Add the cream and stir until blended and
smooth. Add the salt, pepper, and nutmeg,
then stir in the spinach.
4. Line a buttered baking dish with half
the noodles and sprinkle them with half the
cheese. Spread this with the spinach mixture.
Sprinkle with the remaining cheese and top
with another layer of noodles. Bake ten minutes, or until brown.

Green Noodles with Garlic

4 servings

½ pound green noodles
¼ cup butter
1 clove garlic, finely minced
¼ cup freshly grated Parmesan cheese
¼ cup freshly grated Swiss or Gruyère
  cheese
  Freshly ground black pepper

1. Cook the noodles in boiling, salted
water according to package directions. Do
not overcook, however; the noodles should be
tender but not mushy.
2. Meanwhile, heat the butter in a skillet
without browning. Stir in the garlic.
3. Drain the noodles in a colander and return them to the hot kettle. Pour the garlic
butter over the noodles and quickly toss with
the cheeses. Sprinkle liberally with pepper
and serve immediately.

Ingredients for spaghetti with anchovy and clam sauce (Ital

Ravioli

About 18 dozen ravioli

4 cups sifted all-purpose flour
2 eggs
¾ cup water, approximately
    Pinch of salt
    Braised Veal Ravioli Filling (see below)
    or Veal Stuffing for Ravioli (see below)

1. Place the flour in a large mixing bowl and make a well in the center. Add the eggs and mix well with the fingers. Add the water gradually and work well to form a stiff dough.
2. Divide the dough into quarters. Roll each portion out into a sheet one-eighth inch thick. Place small mounds of filling at intervals on one sheet of dough. Cover with another sheet of dough and cut between the mounds with a ravioli cutter to form pillows. Press around the sides of each ravioli. Continue until all the dough is used.
3. Drop the ravioli, a few at a time, into boiling salted water and simmer until tender, five to eight minutes, depending on size.

Note: Leftover ravioli may be sprinkled with cornmeal, covered with waxed paper, and frozen in a box.

BRAISED VEAL RAVIOLI FILLING:

Filling for about 18 dozen ravioli

2 pounds lean veal, cut into small cubes
1 tablespoon butter or vegetable oil
    Salt and freshly ground black pepper
1 clove garlic, finely chopped
½ cup water
½ teaspoon chopped rosemary
½ teaspoon chopped sage

1. Brown the veal on all sides in butter or oil and sprinkle with salt and pepper to taste. Add the garlic and cook briefly.
2. Add the water and herbs. Cover and cook until the meat is tender, about one hour. Let the mixture cool before using.

VEAL STUFFING FOR RAVIOLI:

About 2½ cups

¼ cup butter
½ cup minced onion
½ pound veal, ground
¼ teaspoon freshly grated nutmeg
    Salt and freshly ground black pepper to taste
¼ cup chopped fresh basil or 1 teaspoon dried basil
¼ cup freshly grated Parmesan cheese
¼ cup fresh bread crumbs
1 egg, lightly beaten

1. Heat the butter in a skillet and cook the onion until wilted. Add the veal and cook, stirring, until the meat loses its color.
2. Remove the skillet from the heat and add the remaining ingredients. Let the mixture cool before using.

Pasta with Seafood

6 servings

¾ cup olive oil
¾ cup finely chopped parsley, preferably Italian
½ cup finely chopped green pepper
3 cloves garlic, finely minced
1 (2-pound 3-ounce) can Italian plum tomatoes
2 teaspoons finely chopped fresh basil or dried basil
1 teaspoon dried mint
Cayenne pepper
Salt
18 cherrystone or littleneck clams, well washed (if unavailable, use 1 small can of clams)
18 raw shrimp, shelled and deveined
½ pound boneless whitefish, cut into thin strips, or bay scallops
1 pound rigatoni (small tubular pasta)
3 tablespoons butter
2 tablespoons Cognac

1. Heat the oil in a kettle and add the parsley, green pepper, and garlic. Put the tomatoes through a sieve or food mill and add them. Add the basil, mint, and cayenne and salt to taste and simmer five minutes.

2. Preheat the oven to 350 degrees.

3. Add the clams in their shells, shrimp, and whitefish and simmer ten minutes.

4. Meanwhile, cook the rigatoni in boiling water for exactly ten minutes, stirring frequently. Drain and run under cold running water, then add to the seafood mixture. Add the butter and Cognac and cover with aluminum foil or turn into a casserole and cover. Bake twenty minutes.

Rigatoni con Quattro Formaggi

(Rigatoni with Four Cheeses)

6 servings

Pasta is one of the glories of cooking, but until the gastronomic revolution of the past decade the vast majority of home cooks in this country had the pitiful choice of spaghetti or macaroni. Only those who were in the know sometimes succeeded in finding spaghettini, lasagne, linguine, and vermicelli. But times have changed. Today, supermarket shelves are filled with such tantalizing forms as rigatoni, perciatelli, tripolini, tufoli, and rotelle. A recipe that uses rigatoni—and a marvelous blend of four cheeses—follows.

¼ pound pancetta (a rolled, cured pork product; see note)
¼ pound prosciutto
½ cup dried Italian mushrooms
½ cup boiling rich beef broth (may be made with bouillon cubes and boiling water)
½ cup butter
1½ cups chopped onion
8 tablespoons all-purpose flour
4 cups milk
½ pound rigatoni
¾ cup cubed Fontina cheese
¾ cup cubed Gruyère cheese
¾ cup cubed Swiss cheese (Emmenthal)
¾ cup cubed Bel Paese cheese
¼ cup freshly grated Parmesan cheese

1. Cut the pancetta and prosciutto into small dice and place in a saucepan. Cook, stirring occasionally, until the pancetta gives up its fat and the prosciutto starts to brown. Crush the mushrooms with the fingers and add them, along with the boiling broth. Simmer five minutes and set aside.

2. Melt the butter in a one-and-one-half-quart saucepan and add the onions. Cook, stirring, until translucent. Spoon the onions

into the container of an electric blender and blend until the onions are pureed.

3. Return the mixture to the saucepan, using a rubber spatula to scoop it out. Stir in the flour over low heat until well blended, using a whisk.

4. Bring the milk just to a boil and add to the container of the blender. Blend a second or two to capture what remains of the butter-onion mixture.

5. Gradually add the milk to the saucepan, stirring rapidly with the whisk. Continue cooking and stirring until the mixture thickens.

6. Preheat the oven to 350 degrees.

7. Meanwhile, cook the rigatoni in about six quarts of boiling salted water. Cook only until *al dente*, about nine minutes. Drain quickly and rinse lightly under cold water until cool enough to handle.

8. Place one layer of rigatoni in a two-quart casserole or soufflé dish. Add about half the pancetta-prosciutto mixture. Add a little of each of the four cubed cheeses and a layer of the sauce. Continue making layers in this fashion, ending with a layer of sauce. Sprinkle with Parmesan cheese.

9. Bake thirty minutes or longer, until the casserole is bubbling throughout and browned on top.

Note: If pancetta is not readily available, use proscuitto with the fat left on.

Rotelle with Mushrooms

4 servings

½ cup olive oil
1 clove garlic, chopped
1½ pounds fresh mushrooms, sliced
¼ teaspoon coarse salt
2 tablespoons chopped parsley, preferably Italian
1 pound rotelle (see note)
Freshly grated Parmesan cheese

1. Combine the oil with the garlic and mushrooms in a saucepan and cook fifteen minutes. Add the salt and parsley and cook five minutes more.

2. Cook the rotelle in boiling salted water to the desired tenderness. Drain and serve immediately with the mushroom mixture and Parmesan.

Note: Rotelle (springs) are available in many markets, but may be difficult to find in some communities. In that event, spirelle or rigoletti may be substituted.

Spaghetti with Anchovy and Clam Sauce

4 servings

3 salted whole anchovies or 8 canned flat anchovy fillets
2 dozen cherrystone clams in the shell
¼ cup olive oil
3 tablespoons butter
3 cloves garlic, finely minced
2 shallots, finely chopped
¼ cup finely chopped parsley, preferably Italian
½ teaspoon chopped rosemary
½ cup dry white wine
Freshly ground pepper
Salt (very little, since the clams and anchovies are salty)
1 pound spaghetti, cooked to the desired degree of doneness
Hot pepper flakes (optional)

1. If salted whole anchovies are used, wash them in cold running water to remove most of the external salt and any tiny scales that may be present. Use the fingers to pull the fillets from the bone. Discard the bones. Set the fillets aside.

2. Open the clams or have them opened and reserve both the clams and one cup of clam juice. Finely chop the clams (there will be about three-quarters cup) and set aside.

3. Heat the oil and butter in a skillet. Add the garlic and shallots and cook until lightly browned. Add the anchovies and stir until they dissolve. Add the parsley, rosemary, reserved clam juice, and white wine and bring to a boil. Add pepper to taste and a tiny bit of salt and simmer about fifteen minutes.

4. Add the chopped clams and cook five minutes. Serve piping hot over the freshly cooked spaghetti. Serve hot pepper flakes on the side, if desired, but no cheese.

Spaghetti Carbonara I

4 servings

1 pound bacon
½ cup finely chopped Bermuda onion
½ cup finely chopped green pepper
1 pound spaghettini or vermicelli
Olive oil
2 eggs
Freshly grated Parmesan cheese
Salt and freshly ground black pepper

1. Slice the bacon crosswise and sauté until crisp. Pour off all but three tablespoons of the drippings. Add the onion and green pepper and cook until the vegetables are tender. Set aside.

2. Cook the spaghettini in a large pot of salted water containing a dash of olive oil. Drain and rinse the spaghettini and put back into the pot. Keep warm. Break the eggs into the spaghettini and sprinkle moderately with cheese and salt and pepper to taste. Stir.

3. Reheat the bacon and vegetable mixture. Pour over the spaghettini, stirring thoroughly. Reheat and serve garnished with additional cheese.

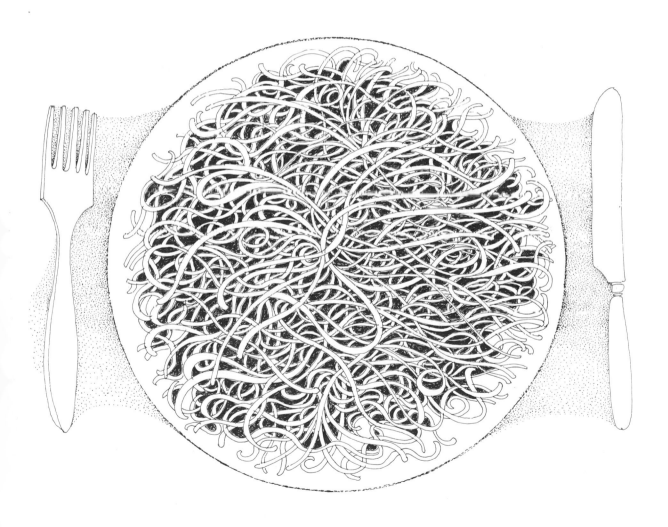

Spaghetti Carbonara II

4 servings

¼ pound bacon, cut into one-inch lengths
3 tablespoons olive oil
1½ cups chopped onion
½ cup finely chopped parsley, preferably Italian
1 cup finely diced Fontina cheese
⅔ cup finely shredded prosciutto or Virginia ham
2 egg yolks, lightly beaten
Hot red pepper flakes
1 pound spaghetti
Freshly ground pepper
1 cup freshly grated Parmesan cheese

1. Heat the bacon pieces in a heavy skillet and cook, stirring frequently, until crisp. Using a slotted spoon, transfer the bacon to paper toweling to drain.

2. Pour off almost all the fat from the skillet, but do not wash the skillet. Add the olive oil and onion. Cook the onion until tender.

3. Prepare the parsley, cheese, prosciutto, and egg yolks and keep these ingredients, plus the bacon bits and pepper flakes, close at hand. Have a hot dish ready for tossing the spaghetti and hot bowls ready to receive the portions.

4. Cook the spaghetti in boiling salted water to the desired degree of doneness. The moment it is done, empty it into a colander. Drain quickly, then pour the spaghetti into the hot dish.

5. Add the onion, bacon bits, parsley, Fontina cheese, prosciutto, beaten yolks and red pepper flakes to taste and toss quickly and thoroughly with a fork and spoon. Serve in hot bowls and pass the pepper and Parmesan cheese.

Spaghetti with Chicken Livers

4 to 6 servings

¾ pound chicken livers
Salt and freshly ground black pepper
3 tablespoons olive oil
½ cup finely chopped onion
½ clove garlic, finely minced
1 cup Chicken Stock (page 115)
1 cup tomato puree
½ cup tomato paste
½ teaspoon orégano
½ teaspoon dried basil
Cayenne pepper
½ pound thin spaghetti (spaghettini or vermicelli), cooked according to package directions
2 to 4 tablespoons softened butter
1 cup freshly grated Parmesan cheese

1. Sprinkle the livers with salt and pepper and brown lightly in oil. Remove the livers to a bowl and chop fine.

2. To the skillet in which the livers cooked add the onion and garlic and cook until the onion is wilted. Add the stock, tomato puree, tomato paste, orégano, basil, cayenne to taste, and the chopped liver. Cover and simmer one hour, stirring occasionally. Taste the sauce for seasonings and add them if necessary. Continue to cook fifteen minutes.

3. Toss the spaghetti in butter and serve with the sauce and cheese.

Spaghetti with Fish Balls

6 servings

2 whitings (1½ pounds each), filleted, heads and bones reserved
2 cloves garlic, finely chopped
2 tablespoons finely chopped Italian parsley
1 egg, lightly beaten
  Salt and freshly ground pepper to taste
½ cup freshly grated Parmesan cheese
1½ quarts peeled, seeded tomatoes, put through a sieve
½ cup olive oil
1 teaspoon dried basil
  Hot pepper flakes to taste (optional)
1 pound linguine

1. Chop the fish fillets as fine as possible. Add half the garlic and half the parsley and continue chopping until well blended. Scrape or spoon the mixture into a mixing bowl. Add the egg, salt, pepper, and cheese and mix well. Using the hands, shape the mixture into balls one to one and one-half inches in diameter.

2. In a skillet combine the remaining garlic and parsley, the tomatoes, oil, basil, and hot pepper flakes. Do not cover. Simmer ten minutes, then add the reserved fish heads and bones. Cook over high heat five minutes. Add salt and pepper to taste. Lower the heat and simmer ten minutes longer.

3. Add the fish balls and simmer one-half hour. Remove and discard the fish heads and bones. Then remove the fish balls, set aside, and keep warm.

4. Cook the linguine seven minutes and drain quickly. Add to the sauce and toss well. Cook only to the desired degree of doneness; do not overcook. Serve piping hot, with the fish balls.

Note: If fresh whiting is not available, use fresh pike, haddock, cod, or halibut.

Spaghetti with Mussels

4 servings

2 pounds mussels
½ cup water
2 shallots, coarsely chopped
3 sprigs parsley
½ bay leaf
½ teaspoon dried thyme
2 tablespoons olive or vegetable oil
1 clove garlic, finely minced
½ cup finely chopped parsley, preferably Italian
1 cup peeled Italian plum tomatoes
½ cup dry white wine
  Salt and freshly ground pepper to taste
1 pound spaghetti
¼ cup butter

1. Wash the mussels well and scrub them, then place in a kettle with the water, shallots, parsley sprigs, bay leaf, and thyme. Cover and bring to a boil quickly over high heat. Cook five to ten minutes, or until the mussels are opened, occasionally shaking the kettle back and forth, holding the lid tightly in place. Set aside to cool.

2. Heat the oil in a large saucepan and add the garlic. Cook briefly without browning, then add half the chopped parsley and the tomatoes and simmer thirty minutes over low heat.

3. Remove the mussels from the shells and reserve one cup of the broth. If desired, pull off and discard the tough, stringlike band from each mussel. Add the mussels to the tomato sauce, along with the wine, mussel broth, and the remainder of the chopped parsley. Add salt and pepper to taste. Simmer fifteen minutes.

4. Cook the spaghetti according to package directions or to the desired degree of doneness. Drain and toss with the butter. Serve hot, with the mussel sauce.

Spaghetti with Meat Balls and Bracciolini

12 servings

    2 cans (1 pound 12 ounces each) tomato
      puree
 4½ cups water
      Meat Balls (see below)
      Bracciolini (see below)
   12 hot or sweet Italian sausages, or com-
      bination of both
      Salt and freshly ground pepper to taste
    2 pounds spaghetti, cooked according to
      package directions and drained

1. Put the tomato puree in a large, deep skillet or kettle. Add three cups of the water. Rinse out the cans with another cup of water and add it.

2. Cook the meat balls as directed in the recipe for meat balls and set them aside. Cook the bracciolini in the same skillet when the meat balls are removed and set them aside. Add the sausages to the skillet and brown well on all sides. Add the sausages to the sauce.

3. Pour off the fat from the skillet in which the meats cooked. Add the half cup water to the skillet and cook, stirring, to dissolve the brown particles that cling to the bottom and sides of the pan. Add this to the sauce. Cook, partly covered, one hour, stirring frequently. Add the meat balls, bracciolini, salt, and pepper and partly cover. Continue cooking one hour longer. Serve with hot spaghetti.

MEAT BALLS:

6 to 12 servings

    1 pound lean beef, ground
   ¾ cup freshly grated Romano or Parmesan
      cheese
    2 slices bread, cut into small cubes
   ¼ cup water
    1 clove garlic, finely minced
   ¼ teaspoon nutmeg
      Salt and freshly ground pepper to taste
    1 tablespoon chopped fresh basil or 1½
      teaspoons dried basil
    2 tablespoons chopped parsley, preferably
      Italian
    2 eggs
   ¼ cup olive oil

1. Place the beef in a mixing bowl and add the cheese. Combine the bread cubes and water. Let stand five minutes, then add to the beef.

2. Add the garlic, nutmeg, salt, pepper, basil, parsley, and eggs and blend well with the fingers. Shape into twelve balls and cook in the oil until golden brown all over.

BRACCIOLINI:

6 to 12 servings

    2 pounds bottom round, cut into 4 slices
   ½ pound salt pork
    4 slices prosciutto
    1 clove garlic, finely minced
   ¼ cup finely chopped parsley, preferably
      Italian
    4 leaves fresh basil
    1 teaspoon orégano
      Salt and freshly ground pepper to taste
   ¼ cup olive oil

1. Trim the meat of all fat. Cut each slice into four pieces of approximately the same shape. Pound each piece as for scaloppine.

2. Cut the salt pork and prosciutto into small cubes and chop them together. Add the

garlic, parsley, basil, orégano, salt, and pepper and continue chopping to a fine, spreadable paste. Spread each slice of meat on one side with this and roll up jelly-roll fashion. Tie each piece with string.

3. Cook the roll-ups in the oil until golden brown all over.

Spaghetti all'Ortolana
(Spaghetti with Eggplant)

4 to 6 servings

1 medium eggplant
Salt
Olive or salad oil
1 teaspoon finely chopped garlic
1 tablespoon finely chopped parsley, preferably Italian
1½ to 2 cups peeled, cored, chopped tomatoes
Hot pepper flakes to taste
1 pound spaghetti or spaghettini, cooked according to package directions and drained

1. Cut off the ends of the eggplant and discard. Cut the eggplant into quarter-inch rounds. Place in a mixing bowl and sprinkle with salt. Let stand about half an hour, then squeeze the eggplant slices to remove most of the moisture.

2. Add about a quarter inch of oil to a skillet and cook the slices on all sides until golden brown, adding more oil as necessary. Drain the slices on paper towels.

3. Heat four tablespoons of oil in a skillet and add the garlic. Cook briefly and add the parsley, tomatoes, and hot pepper flakes. Simmer about ten minutes, or until the oil separates from the tomatoes.

4. Meanwhile, cut the eggplant slices into thin strips. Add the strips to the sauce and cook about three minutes. Serve with the hot spaghetti or spaghettini.

Spaghetti with Fresh Peas

6 to 8 servings

¼ pound prosciutto or bacon
1 medium onion
1 clove garlic, peeled
1 3-inch piece celery
1 cup parsley, preferably Italian
¼ cup olive oil
5 tablespoons butter
1½ pounds fresh peas
⅓ cup Chicken Stock (page 115) or Beef Stock (page 115)
1 large tomato, peeled, seeded, **and** chopped
2 tablespoons chopped fresh basil
Salt and freshly ground black pepper
1 pound spaghetti or linguine, cooked according to package directions
Freshly grated Parmesan cheese

1. On a chopping board, mince together the prosciutto, onion, garlic, celery, and parsley.

2. Heat together the olive oil and three tablespoons of the butter. Cook the minced ingredients in it over medium heat about five minutes.

3. Add the peas and stock. Cover and simmer, stirring occasionally, until the peas are tender. Toward the end of the cooking time, add the tomato and basil. Season with salt and pepper to taste. If there is too much liquid, cook uncovered to allow for evaporation. The peas should be dry, not soupy.

4. Toss the pasta with the pea mixture. Add the remaining butter and serve with grated Parmesan cheese.

Spaghetti with Peas

6 servings

½ cup finely diced salt pork
1 onion, finely chopped
2 cloves garlic, finely minced
2 cups diced, peeled ripe fresh tomatoes or canned tomatoes
3 tablespoons tomato paste
1 cup Beef Stock (page 115)
  Salt and freshly ground black pepper
1 cup fresh or frozen peas
1 green pepper, seeded and cubed
2 tablespoons chopped parsley, preferably Italian
1 pound spaghetti, cooked according to package directions and drained
  Freshly grated Parmesan cheese

1. Sauté the salt pork until lightly browned. Add the onion and garlic and cook slowly until just tender but not browned.

2. Add the tomatoes, tomato paste, stock, and salt and pepper to taste. Bring to a boil and simmer for thirty minutes, stirring constantly.

3. Add the peas. If fresh, cook until barely tender, add the green pepper and parsley, and cook for five minutes longer. If frozen, add the peas along with the green pepper and parsley and cook until barely tender.

4. Toss the spaghetti with the sauce and serve with grated Parmesan cheese.

Spaghetti with Stuffed Peppers

6 servings

1 egg, slightly beaten
½ cup milk
⅔ cup soft bread crumbs
  Salt
¼ teaspoon freshly ground pepper
  Celery salt
⅛ teaspoon rubbed sage
2 tablespoons raisins
1 pound chuck, ground
¼ cup chopped onion
1 clove garlic, minced
2 tablespoons olive oil
6 medium green peppers, washed, with tops and seeds removed
3 cups Italian Tomato Sauce I (page 435)
½ teaspoon orégano leaves
½ teaspoon basil leaves
¾ pound spaghetti

1. Mix together the egg, milk, bread crumbs, one teaspoon salt, the pepper, one-quarter teaspoon celery salt, the sage, and raisins and let stand five minutes. Add the meat.

2. In a Dutch oven or large kettle, sauté the onion and garlic in oil until the onion is crisp tender. Remove from the heat. Add half the onion-garlic mixture to the meat mixture; keep the remaining half in the pan. Stuff the peppers with the meat mixture.

3. To the onion-garlic mixture in the Dutch oven add the tomato sauce, orégano, basil, and stuffed peppers. Simmer, covered, forty-five minutes; uncover and simmer ten minutes longer, or until the peppers are tender, basting occasionally with the sauce.

4. Meanwhile, add one and one-half tablespoons salt to four quarts of rapidly boiling water. Gradually add the spaghetti so that the water continues to boil. Cook, uncovered, stirring occasionally, until tender, about nine minutes. Drain in a colander and serve on a platter with the peppers and sauce.

Spaghetti with Tarragon Meat Balls and Sausages

6 to 8 servings

¾ pound veal, beef, or pork or any combination of the meats, ground
¼ teaspoon nutmeg
½ teaspoon chopped fresh or dried tarragon
Salt and freshly ground black pepper
2 slices white bread, trimmed of crusts and cubed
3 tablespoons heavy cream
2 tablespoons butter
½ cup chopped onion
1 small clove garlic, finely chopped
1 egg, lightly beaten
1 tablespoon freshly grated Parmesan cheese
⅓ cup all-purpose flour
Vegetable oil
6 sweet or hot Italian sausages
6 cups Italian Tomato Sauce I (page 435)
1½ pounds spaghetti, cooked according to package directions

1. Place the veal in a mixing bowl and add the nutmeg, tarragon, and salt and pepper to taste.

2. Soak the bread cubes in cream, then squeeze to extract the liquid. Add the bread to the veal.

3. Heat the butter in a skillet and cook the onion and garlic until wilted. Add to the veal. Add the egg and Parmesan cheese and mix with the fingers until blended. Shape the mixture into sixteen to eighteen balls of equal size. Dredge the balls in flour.

4. Heat the oil to a depth of one-quarter inch in a skillet. Carefully cook the veal balls until golden brown on all sides.

5. Meanwhile, broil, bake, or fry the sausages until nearly done. Add the sausages and the veal balls to the tomato sauce and simmer thirty minutes. Serve hot, with the hot spaghetti.

Spaghetti with Pesto and Vegetables

4 servings

½ cup finely chopped fresh sweet basil
1 tablespoon finely chopped parsley, preferably Italian
⅓ cup Italian olive oil
½ cup freshly grated Pecorino or Parmesan cheese
1 pound spaghetti
Salt to taste
1 medium potato, cut into small cubes
¼ pound green beans, cut French style (slivered)
1 tablespoon butter
Freshly grated Parmesan cheese

1. Place the basil and parsley in a mixing bowl and stir in the oil. Add the cheese and blend well. Set this mixture, the "pesto," aside.

2. Bring a kettle of water to a boil and add the spaghetti and salt. Add the vegetables immediately and cook until the spaghetti is done to taste. Drain immediately into a colander and empty the spaghetti and vegetables onto a hot platter. Toss with the butter.

3. Add the pesto and mix quickly. Serve piping hot, with Parmesan cheese on the side.

One of the glories of the Italian table is that specialty of Genoa—pesto genovese, a spaghetti sauce made with fresh basil, butter, and, usually, garlic. The time of year to make it is when basil flourishes in local gardens and is available in many markets and nurseries. Lorane Schiff, who contributed one of the recipes below, informed us that the name of the sauce comes from al pesto *(literally, by pounding), since the ingredients used to be crushed with a mortar and pestle before the advent of the electric blender.*

Pesto Genovese I

4 servings

1 cup loosely packed basil
½ cup pignoli (pine nuts) or shelled walnuts
2 cloves garlic, peeled
¾ cup freshly grated Parmesan cheese
½ cup olive oil
1 pound spaghetti, cooked according to package directions
3 tablespoons butter

1. Place the basil in the container of an electric blender and add the pignoli and garlic. Blend, stirring down carefully with a rubber spatula if necessary. When well blended, add the cheese.

2. Gradually add the olive oil while blending on low speed.

3. When the spaghetti is cooked, drain it quickly and pour it into a hot serving dish. Toss with the butter. Serve the spaghetti immediately, passing the pesto sauce separately.

Pesto Genovese II

6 to 8 servings

3 cups (about 3 bunches) fresh basil
1 clove garlic, peeled
¼ cup pignoli (pine nuts)
¼ cup butter
¼ cup olive oil
　 Freshly grated Parmesan cheese
　 Salt to taste
2 pounds spaghetti

1. Wash the basil and pat it dry. Pull off the leaves, using part of the leaf stem if the herb is young and tender.

2. Put the basil leaves, garlic, pignoli, butter, oil, one-half cup Parmesan cheese, and salt in a blender and blend until pureed, stirring down with a rubber spatula. Blend two or three minutes until the pesto has the consistency of a thick puree.

3. Cook the spaghetti according to package directions or to the desired degree of doneness. Drain it quickly in a colander and empty it immediately into a hot serving dish. Add the pesto and toss quickly. Serve with additional Parmesan cheese.

Spaghettini Estivi

4 to 6 servings

2 pounds ripe tomatoes, peeled and chopped
1 tablespoon chopped Italian parsley
5 fresh basil leaves, chopped
  Juice of 1 lemon
3 tablespoons olive oil
1 clove garlic, finely chopped
  Salt and freshly ground pepper to taste
1 pound spaghettini
  Freshly grated Asiago or Parmesan cheese (optional)

1. Drain the tomatoes in a colander, then turn into a mixing bowl and add the parsley, basil, lemon juice, olive oil, garlic, salt, and pepper. Do not cook the sauce but set it aside. The sauce is served at room temperature.

2. Preheat four to six soup bowls and a bowl for tossing the spaghettini. Keep them hot.

3. Cook the spaghettini to the desired degree of doneness. If possible, use a pasta fork to remove the pasta directly from its pot, shaking the water back into the pot as the pasta is forked out. Failing this, quickly turn the pasta into a colander and immediately pour the pasta into the hot bowl. Spoon a little more than half the sauce over the spaghettini and toss quickly. Divide the mixture evenly into the hot soup bowls and divide the remaining sauce over the servings. Serve with grated cheese, if desired.

Spaghettini with Sausages

6 servings

6 links uncooked Pork Sausage with Fennel (page 402)
6 hot Italian sausages
1 cup imported olive oil
1 cup finely chopped parsley, preferably Italian
¾ cup finely chopped green pepper
3 tablespoons finely minced garlic
8 cups imported Italian plum tomatoes, put through a food mill or sieve
  Salt and freshly ground black pepper
2 teaspoons ground dried orégano leaves
1 tablespoon finely chopped basil
1 pound imported spaghettini, perciatelli, spaghetti, or other long pasta
¼ pound freshly grated imported Parmesan cheese

1. Preheat the oven to 350 degrees.

2. Place the sausages in a skillet and add enough cold water to barely cover the bottom. Place over high heat until the water starts to boil, then place the skillet in the oven. Bake until the sausages are browned and cooked through. Or, if desired, do not use the oven but broil the sausages.

3. Meanwhile, heat the oil in a casserole and add the parsley, green pepper, and garlic. Cook, stirring, over low heat for one to two minutes. Do not brown. Add the tomatoes and bring to a boil. Add salt and pepper to taste, the orégano, and basil. Simmer, stirring frequently, about one-half hour.

4. Drain the sausages and add them. Simmer about ten minutes longer.

5. Meanwhile, cook the spaghettini according to package directions. Drain. Serve hot with the sauce and sausages, with the Parmesan cheese on the side.

Note: Leftover sauce and sausages may be frozen.

Spaghettini with Little Veal Cubes

4 to 6 servings

2 tablespoons olive oil
2 tablespoons butter
2 white onions, chopped
1 pound veal steak, cubed
1½ tablespoons all-purpose flour
1 teaspoon salt
　Freshly ground black pepper
　Pinch of dried orégano
1 cup Chicken Stock (page 115)
　Juice of ½ lemon
¼ cup freshly grated Parmesan cheese
1 pound spaghettini

1. Preheat the oven to 400 degrees.
2. Heat the oil and butter and sauté the onions in it until soft.
3. Roll the veal cubes in the flour and season with salt, pepper, and orégano; brown in the oil and butter. Stir in the chicken stock and simmer, uncovered, for ten minutes.
4. Remove from the heat and stir in the lemon juice. Place the mixture in a baking dish, sprinkle with a little of the cheese, and cover. Bake for twenty minutes, or until the sauce is thickened and the veal fork tender.
5. Cook the spaghettini *al dente* (eight or nine minutes), drain, and place in a hot bowl. Toss with the remaining cheese, then with half of the veal mixture. Spoon the rest of the veal sauce atop individual portions in hot soup bowls.

Tortelloni di Biete

(Tortelloni with Swiss Chard Filling)

80 to 90 tortelloni

2 bunches Swiss chard
¾ cup finely chopped onion
5 tablespoons sweet butter
3 or 4 slices prosciutto, finely chopped
7½ ounces ricotta cheese
1 egg yolk
⅔ cup plus ½ cup grated Parmesan cheese
½ teaspoon nutmeg
　Salt to taste
　Pasta dough for ravioli made with 2 eggs and 1⅔ cups flour
　Olive oil
½ cup heavy cream

1. Pick over the chard to obtain the tender leaves. Discard any tough stems. Cook the leaves in a little boiling salted water until tender. Drain, cool, and squeeze to remove excess liquid. Chop very fine.
2. Cook the onion in two tablespoons of the butter until translucent. Add the prosciutto and chopped chard. Cook two minutes longer, stirring. Add this to a mixing bowl.
3. Add the ricotta, egg yolk, two-thirds cup Parmesan cheese, nutmeg, and salt to taste to the chard mixture.
4. Roll out the pasta dough made according to any recipe that calls for two eggs and one and two-thirds cups flour (see recipe for Ravioli, page 417, for instructions on mixing the dough). Use about one teaspoon of the chard mixture for stuffing and proceed to make small "pillows," as in making ravioli. Cook the tortelloni in boiling salted water to which a little olive oil has been added. Cook about two or three minutes, then drain.
5. Put the remaining butter and about half the cream in a heavy skillet. Stir over moderate heat about half a minute. Remove from the heat, add the drained tortelloni, and toss while adding the remaining cream and cheese. Add salt to taste. Serve immediately.

Ziti with Marinara Sauce, Sausage, and Cheese

30 servings

6 eggs
4 pounds cottage cheese
1 tablespoon dried thyme
1 tablespoon dried orégano
1 teaspoon dried basil
  Pinch of salt and freshly ground black pepper
5 pounds ziti, cooked according to package directions and drained
1 pound sweet Italian sausage, sliced into rounds
1 cup freshly grated Parmesan cheese
2 quarts Marinara Sauce II (page 436)
2 pounds mozzarella cheese, sliced

1. Preheat the oven to 400 degrees. Lightly oil or butter a roasting pan (17 x 12½).

2. Mix together the eggs, cottage cheese, thyme, orégano, basil, salt, and pepper.

3. Place the ziti in the roasting pan and top with the cottage cheese mixture and the sausage slices. Sprinkle with Parmesan cheese. Pour the marinara sauce over all and stir briefly to distribute the sauce. Bake for one hour.

4. Turn off the oven heat, top the noodles with the mozzarella cheese slices, and let stand in the oven's retained heat until the cheese is melted. Serve immediately.

Artichokes Roman Style

4 servings

4 large artichokes with stems
½ lemon
3 tablespoons finely chopped parsley, preferably Italian
1½ teaspoons finely chopped garlic
½ teaspoon dried mint
  Salt to taste
½ cup olive oil

1. Do not cut off the stems of the artichokes.

2. Cut away all the hard outer leaves of the artichokes. Using a paring knife, neatly trim all over the outside of the artichoke, including around the stem. Using a melon ball cutter or spoon, scoop out the center leaves and fuzzy central core. Rub the cut surfaces of the artichokes with the lemon to prevent discoloration.

3. Combine the parsley, garlic, mint, and salt and rub two-thirds of this mixture inside the artichoke bottoms.

4. Arrange the artichokes, stem up, in a heavy casserole with a tight-fitting lid. Sprinkle the remaining parsley mixture over all and add the oil. Add enough water to cover nearly one-third of the artichoke, not counting the stem.

5. Soak two sheets of paper toweling in water. They must be large enough to cover the casserole. Cover the casserole with the lid on top of the towels and cook over medium heat about thirty minutes, or until the artichokes are tender when pierced with a fork. If there is liquid remaining in the pot, turn up the flame and let the liquid evaporate. The oil, of course, will not evaporate. Serve the artichokes either lukewarm or at room temperature, never hot.

Sicilian Broccoli

4 to 6 servings

1 large bunch broccoli (approximately 2 pounds)
2 tablespoons butter
1 tablespoon finely chopped shallots or green onions, green part and all
1 clove garlic, finely minced
1½ tablespoons all-purpose flour
1 cup Chicken Stock (page 115)
4 anchovies, finely chopped
½ cup sliced black olives, preferably imported
  Freshly ground black pepper
2 cups shredded mozzarella or sharp Cheddar cheese

1. Cook the broccoli in salted water until tender.

2. As the vegetable cooks, melt the butter in a saucepan and add the shallots and garlic. Cook, stirring, about three minutes. Do not brown.

3. Sprinkle with the flour and add the stock, stirring vigorously with a wire whisk. When the mixture is thickened, simmer five minutes.

4. Add the anchovies, olives, pepper to taste, and cheese and stir until the cheese melts. Serve over the hot, drained broccoli.

Eggplant Parmigiana

6 servings

1 medium eggplant
  Salt
¾ cup olive oil
2 cups Italian Tomato Sauce II (page 435)
1 teaspoon orégano
  Salt and freshly ground pepper to taste
2 tablespoons finely chopped parsley, preferably Italian
1 teaspoon finely chopped fresh basil or ½ teaspoon dried basil
½ cup fresh bread crumbs
1 cup freshly grated Romano or Parmesan cheese
2 hard-cooked eggs, coarsely chopped
½ cup cubed mozzarella cheese

1. Preheat the oven to 350 degrees.

2. Do not peel the eggplant, but trim off the ends. With a sharp knife cut the eggplant into very thin slices, less than a quarter inch thick. Make layers of the eggplant slices in a dish, sprinkling between the layers with salt. Cover with waxed paper and weight the slices with cans. Let stand one hour. Liquid will accumulate from the slices.

3. Drain the slices and rinse them in cold running water. Cover with cold water and let stand about ten minutes. Drain the slices once more and squeeze between the hands to extract as much moisture as possible. Pat the slices between pieces of paper toweling.

4. Add about one-quarter cup of the oil to a large skillet and cook the slices, a few at a time, until lightly browned on both sides. Add more oil as necessary. Drain the slices on absorbent paper toweling.

5. Meanwhile, combine the tomato sauce with the orégano, salt, pepper, parsley, and basil. Simmer about ten minutes.

6. Spoon a thin layer of sauce in a baking dish and arrange one-third of the eggplant slices, overlapping, over the sauce.

7. In a mixing bowl, combine the bread

crumbs, one-quarter cup of the Romano cheese, the eggs, and mozzarella. Toss together to blend. Sprinkle half this mixture over the slices. Cover with half the remaining sauce.

8. Add another third of the slices, overlapping. Add the remaining crumb mixture and cover with the remaining slices, overlapping. Cover with the remaining sauce. Sprinkle with another quarter cup Romano cheese. Bake twenty minutes, or until piping hot and bubbling. Serve with the remaining half cup Romano cheese.

Stuffed Eggplant all'Italiana

8 servings

The eggplant, treasured in Far Eastern cookery for more than 3,000 years, is a relative newcomer to the cuisine of the Western world. Until a few hundred years ago it was linked with the deadly nightshade and known as the "mad apple." Today no such stigma is associated with it. The vegetable has a curious name, but not without reason. There are small, egg-shaped, egg-white eggplants that are available in autumn in New York's Chinatown. The recipes here, however, are for our domestic, deep purple, and altogether delicious variety.

4 small or 2 medium eggplants
6 tablespoons olive oil
3 cloves garlic, peeled
8 anchovies
6 sprigs parsley, preferably Italian
1 tablespoon capers
2 tablespoons coarsely chopped, pitted imported black olives
1 teaspoon orégano
1½ cups fresh bread crumbs

½ teaspoon chopped hot green or red pepper (optional)
8 to 12 thin slices tomato
    Salt and freshly ground pepper to taste

1. Preheat the oven to 350 degrees.

2. Cut the eggplants in half lengthwise and scoop out the pulp, leaving a half-inch shell. Chop the flesh fine.

3. In a skillet heat two tablespoons of the oil and add the eggplant flesh. Cook, stirring, about one minute.

4. Chop the garlic, anchovies, and parsley together and add the mixture to the skillet. Add the capers, olives, orégano, bread crumbs, hot pepper, and three tablespoons oil. Stir to blend and use to fill the eggplant shells.

5. Cover each filled shell with thin, slightly overlapping tomato slices and sprinkle with salt and pepper to taste. Dribble the remaining oil over the tomatoes and place the stuffed eggplant on a baking sheet. Bake thirty minutes, or until piping hot and bubbling.

ITALY   *433*

Funghi Trifolati

(A Mushroom Dish)

4 servings

½ cup olive oil
3 cloves garlic, peeled and left whole
4 cups thinly sliced mushrooms
¼ cup chopped parsley, preferably Italian
   Salt and freshly ground pepper to taste

1. Heat the oil in a saucepan and add the garlic. Cook until the garlic just starts to brown, then remove and discard the garlic.
2. Add the mushrooms and parsley to the pan. Do not add more liquid, as the mushrooms will give up their own. Cover and cook, stirring occasionally and shaking the pan, thirty-five minutes, or until most of the mushroom liquid is reabsorbed.
3. Season to taste with salt and pepper and serve as an accompaniment for meat or poultry.

Zucchini Flan

6 to 8 servings

2 tablespoons butter
3 tablespoons chopped onion
1 tablespoon finely chopped shallots or green onion
6 firm, unblemished zucchini
1 cup heavy cream
2 egg yolks, lightly beaten
1 egg, lightly beaten
¼ teaspoon nutmeg
   Salt and freshly ground black pepper
½ cup freshly grated Fontina, Swiss, or Gruyère cheese

1. Preheat the oven to 350 degrees.

2. Melt the butter in a large skillet and add the onion and shallots. Cook, stirring, until the onion is wilted.
3. Trim off and discard the ends of the zucchini. Slice the vegetable into thin rounds and add them to the skillet. Cook the zucchini in the skillet briefly, stirring.
4. Spoon the zucchini into a buttered ovenproof casserole. Blend the cream, egg yolks, egg, and nutmeg. Add salt and pepper to taste and strain the mixture over the zucchini. Sprinkle with the cheese and bake thirty minutes, or until the custard is lightly set. Serve hot.

Zucchini and Tomato Salad

12 servings

6 zucchini
   Water to cover
   Salt
24 slices red, ripe tomatoes
   Freshly ground black pepper
1 clove garlic, finely minced
¾ cup olive oil
¼ cup wine vinegar
⅓ cup chopped parsley, preferably Italian

1. Cut off the stem and bud end of each zucchini. Rinse well and dry. Cut the zucchini on the bias into slices about three-quarters inch thick. Place the slices in a saucepan and add water to cover and salt to taste. Bring to a boil and simmer gently just until the vegetable is crisp tender; do not overcook. Drain immediately. Let cool, then chill.
2. When ready to serve, arrange alternating slices of zucchini and tomatoes on a platter. Sprinkle with salt and pepper to taste. Combine the garlic, oil, and vinegar and beat with a fork. Pour the sauce over the vegetables and sprinkle with chopped parsley.

Italian Tomato Sauce I

About 6 cups

- 3 tablespoons olive oil
- 1½ cups finely chopped onion
- 1 clove garlic, finely minced
- 1 1-pound 3-ounce can Italian plum tomatoes
- 1 6-ounce can tomato paste
- 1½ cups water
   Salt and freshly ground black pepper to taste
- ½ teaspoon granulated sugar
- 2 sprigs fresh thyme or ½ teaspoon dried thyme
- 4 basil leaves, finely chopped, or 1 teaspoon dried basil
- 1 bay leaf
- 1 tablespoon finely chopped parsley, preferably Italian

Heat the oil in a kettle and cook the onion and garlic until the onion is wilted. Add the remaining ingredients and simmer, stirring occasionally, about thirty minutes.

Note: This sauce, like most tomato sauces, freezes well.

Italian Tomato Sauce II

2¼ cups

- 2 small white onions, peeled and sliced
- 1 clove garlic, peeled and halved
- 3 tablespoons olive oil, heated
- 2 cups thinly sliced celery
- 1 cup thinly sliced carrots
- 1 bay leaf
- 1 teaspoon salt
- 2 cups (1 1-pound 1-ounce can) tomatoes
- ¾ cup tomato puree
- 1 cup water
- ½ teaspoon granulated sugar
- ½ teaspoon chopped fresh basil
- ½ teaspoon orégano

1. Sauté the onions and garlic in the oil in a saucepan. Add the celery, carrots, bay leaf, salt, tomatoes, tomato puree, and water. Cover and cook slowly one hour.

2. Add the sugar, basil, and orégano to the saucepan. Cover and cook fifteen to twenty minutes. Put through a sieve or food mill or blend in an electric blender. Reheat before serving.

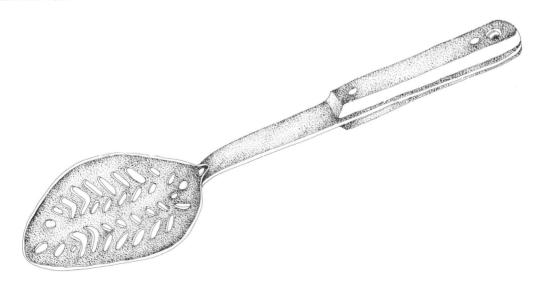

Marinara Sauce I

3 to 4 cups

¼ cup olive oil
2 cups coarsely chopped onion
1 small carrot, cut into rounds, about ½ cup
2 cloves garlic, finely minced
4 cups canned Italian plum tomatoes
  Salt and freshly ground pepper
¼ cup butter
1 teaspoon dried orégano
1 tablespoon chopped fresh basil or 1 teaspoon dried basil

1. Heat the oil in a large open skillet and add the onion, carrot, and garlic. Cook, stirring, until the vegetables are golden brown.

2. Pour the tomatoes through a sieve, pushing the pulp through with a wooden spoon. Discard the seeds. Add the pureed tomatoes to the vegetables and add salt and pepper to taste. Partially cover and simmer fifteen minutes. Put the sauce through a sieve, pushing the solids through with a wooden spoon. Return the sauce to the skillet and add the remaining ingredients. Partially cover and simmer thirty minutes longer. Serve with pasta.

Marinara Sauce II

About 2 quarts

3 cups chopped onions
4 cloves garlic, minced
5 tablespoons olive oil
6 cups canned Italian-style plum tomatoes, undrained
3 cans (6 ounces each) tomato paste
3 cups water or meat broth, approximately
1 bay leaf
1 teaspoon salt
½ teaspoon freshly ground black pepper
1 teaspoon dried orégano, or ½ teaspoon each dried orégano and basil

1. Sauté the onions and garlic in the olive oil until the onions are browned, stirring often. Add the tomatoes, tomato paste, water, bay leaf, salt, and pepper. Simmer, uncovered, stirring occasionally, for about two hours. Add more water as necessary.

2. Add the orégano and continue to cook for about fifteen minutes. Remove the bay leaf. The sauce should be thick. Serve with pasta.

Pesto

About 1½ cups

3 large cloves garlic, finely minced
20 fresh basil leaves, chopped
1¼ cups freshly grated Parmesan cheese
⅔ cup pignoli (pine nuts), finely chopped
1 teaspoon salt
1 cup olive oil

Mash together the garlic and basil to make a paste. Beat in the cheese and pignoli. Add the salt and gradually beat in the oil, most easily done in an electric blender. The resulting sauce should be smooth. Serve with noodles or other pasta.

Tomato and Caper Sauce

About 9 cups

3 cups chopped onion
3 large cloves garlic
⅓ cup olive oil
2 cups canned Italian tomatoes
2 cans (6 ounces each) tomato paste
6 cups water
2 bay leaves
1 teaspoon orégano
2 stalks fresh basil (10 leaves) or ½ teaspoon dried basil
1½ teaspoons salt
    Freshly ground black pepper
1 tablespoon capers, or to taste

1. Sauté the onions and garlic in the oil until well browned. Add the tomatoes, tomato paste, water, and bay leaves. Simmer, partially covered, for one hour, stirring frequently.

2. Add the orégano, basil, salt, and pepper to taste. Continue cooking, stirring often, until the sauce thickens, about one hour. Remove the bay leaves and add the capers.

Manicotti I

20 to 24 manicotti

4 eggs
1 cup sifted all-purpose flour
    Salt
1 cup water
½ pound ricotta cheese
¼ pound mozzarella cheese, cut into small cubes
¼ cup freshly grated Parmesan cheese
2 tablespoons finely chopped parsley, preferably Italian
    Freshly ground black pepper
    Italian Tomato Sauce I (page 435)

1. Break three of the eggs into a mixing bowl and beat well with a whisk or fork. Gradually add the flour, beating constantly. Add salt to taste and the water, beating and stirring to make a light, smooth batter.

2. Heat a small crêpe pan or cured black iron skillet about five inches in diameter. Brush with vegetable oil and add a couple of tablespoons of the batter at a time. Cook the "pancakes" on one side only until they are set; do not let them brown. Cook each crêpe for a minute, more or less. When they are done, transfer them to a piece of waxed paper.

3. In another mixing bowl combine the ricotta, mozzarella, remaining egg, Parmesan cheese, parsley, and salt and pepper to taste.

4. The manicotti may be assembled in advance and refrigerated. To assemble them, place one pancake, uncooked side up, on a flat surface. Add one or two tablespoons of filling and roll the pancake cigarette fashion. Arrange the manicotti in a baking dish or on a baking sheet with sides.

5. When ready to serve, preheat the oven to 350 degrees.

6. Spoon a generous amount of tomato sauce over the manicotti. Bake fifteen minutes, or until the manicotti are piping hot throughout.

Manicotti II

12 servings

2 pounds pot cheese
1 cup freshly grated Romano cheese, or more to taste
1 tablespoon finely chopped parsley, preferably Italian
1 tablespoon finely chopped fresh basil or 1½ teaspoons dried basil
  Salt and freshly ground pepper to taste
4 eggs
48 Pancakes for Manicotti (see below)
48 cubes mozzarella cheese
3 cups Italian Tomato Sauce I (page 435)
  Freshly grated Parmesan cheese

1. Preheat the oven to 350 degrees.

2. Combine the pot cheese with the Romano, parsley, basil, salt, pepper, and eggs. Beat well. Add more seasoning according to taste.

3. Place a spoonful or so of the cheese mixture in the center of a pancake, uncooked side up, and add a cube of mozzarella cheese. Fold the sides over. Fold again to enclose the filling, envelope fashion. Continue until all the pancakes, cheese mixture, and cubes are used.

4. Spoon a layer of tomato sauce on the bottom of one or two baking dishes. Arrange the manicotti over this. Cover with tomato sauce and bake until piping hot and bubbling. Serve grated Parmesan cheese separately.

PANCAKES FOR MANICOTTI:

About 48 pancakes

1 cup sifted all-purpose flour
¾ cup plus 2 tablespoons milk
6 eggs
  Salt to taste

1. Place the flour in a mixing bowl. Add the milk, a little at a time, stirring with a wire whisk.

2. Add the eggs, one at a time, beating well after each addition. Add salt to taste, then strain the batter.

3. Brush a crêpe pan, omelet pan, or griddle lightly with oil and wipe with paper toweling. Ladle or spoon two or three tablespoons of the batter into the pan and tilt the pan this way and that to distribute the batter, or smooth the batter with the bottom of a large spoon. If the batter seems too thick, stir in a little more milk. Cook just until set on one side only, about twenty or thirty seconds. Transfer the pancake to a piece of waxed paper. Continue making pancakes, always covering with waxed paper, until the batter is used.

stir until thickened and smooth. Add salt, pepper, and nutmeg to taste and simmer, stirring frequently, for one hour. If the mixture develops any lumps (which it should not), put it through a sieve.

2. Remove the sauce from the heat and stir in the egg yolks, Parmesan, Gruyère, and finely grated truffles. Stir until well blended and chill.

3. Place the crêpes, one at a time, on a flat surface and place one tablespoon of the chilled sauce in the center of each. Fold in flour, like a square envelope, and place folded side down in an ovenproof dish. Place the crêpes close together.

4. When almost ready to serve, preheat the oven to 375 degrees.

5. Melt the remaining two tablespoons butter and trickle it over the folded crêpes. Place in the oven and bake until the filled crêpes are piping hot. Serve on small, hot plates with wafer-thin slices of truffle on top.

Note: You may substitute chopped shrimp or anchovies for the grated truffles and eliminate the final sliced truffles.

Gruyère Crêpes with White Truffles

(Fagottini con Tartufi)

6 generous servings

½ cup butter
6 tablespoons all-purpose flour
4 cups milk, brought to a boil
Salt and freshly ground black pepper
Freshly grated nutmeg
5 egg yolks, lightly beaten (reserve the whites for the crêpes recipe)
¾ cup freshly grated Parmesan cheese
¾ cup freshly grated imported Gruyère cheese
2 ounces finely grated white truffles or canned truffle paste, if available (see note)
3 dozen Crêpes (see below)
2 ounces thinly sliced white truffles, if available (see note)

1. Melt six tablespoons of the butter in a large saucepan and stir in the flour with a whisk. When blended, add the hot milk, stirring vigorously with the whisk. Continue to

CRÊPES:

About 3 dozen

6 eggs
5 egg whites
3 tablespoons all-purpose flour
1 teaspoon salt
¾ cup milk

1. Combine the eggs and egg whites in a mixing bowl and beat lightly. Combine the flour, salt, and milk and add to the egg mixture.

2. Brush a crêpe pan or six-inch frying pan with clarified butter (see note page 174) and add a tablespoon or so of crêpe mixture. Swirl it around until all the pan is coated. Cook until set on one side; turn and cook briefly on the other side. Do not overcook or the crêpes will toughen.

Pizza

4 to 8 servings

1 package active dry yeast
1 cup lukewarm water
3 cups all-purpose flour
5 tablespoons olive oil
  Salt to taste
3 cups peeled, chopped tomatoes, fresh or canned (if canned, use the imported Italian kind)
2 teaspoons orégano
  Freshly ground pepper to taste
2 tablespoons anchovy paste
1 cup cubed mozzarella cheese
⅓ cup freshly grated Parmesan cheese

1. Soften the yeast in the water and stir.
2. Place the flour on a flat surface and make a hole in the center. Add one tablespoon of the oil and salt to taste. Start adding yeast, mixing in the flour with the fingers. Continue working the flour and yeast until all the liquid is used. The dough should be soft but not sticky. Add a little more water or flour if necessary to make a proper dough.
3. Turn the dough out onto a floured surface and knead until very smooth and elastic.
4. Place the dough in a greased bowl. Grease the surface, cover with a towel, and let rise in a warm place (80 to 85 degrees) until double in bulk, about one and one-half hours.
5. Meanwhile, heat three tablespoons of oil and add the tomatoes, half the orégano, salt, and pepper to taste. Simmer about five minutes and set aside.

6. Preheat the oven to 500 degrees.
7. Brush a jelly-roll pan (15 x 10) with the remaining tablespoon of oil. Sprinkle it lightly with salt.
8. Turn the dough out of the bowl onto a floured surface and shape it into a ball. Roll the dough into a rectangle about the size of the pan. Place the dough in the pan and press and stretch with the fingers until the dough touches the sides of the pan, including the rim. Trim off the excess dough.
9. Dot the surface of the dough at two-inch intervals with the anchovy paste. Spoon the tomato sauce evenly over the dough and sprinkle with the remaining orégano. Dot the top with mozzarella and sprinkle with the Parmesan.
10. Bake the pizza on the lower shelf of the oven until browned, fifteen to twenty minutes. Cut into squares and serve hot.

MUSHROOM PIZZA:

Omit the anchovy paste in the preceding recipe. After the tomato sauce and remaining orégano have been added, slice four large mushrooms and place the slices evenly over the surface of the pizza. Add the mozzarella, sprinkle with the Parmesan cheese, and bake as directed above.

PEPERONI PIZZA:

Omit the anchovy paste and dot the surface of the pizza with one sliced peperoni sausage before adding the mozzarella, sprinkling with Parmesan cheese, and baking.

Zuppa Inglese

12 servings

SPONGE CAKE:

6 eggs, separated
1 cup granulated sugar
1 tablespoon lemon juice
1 tablespoon grated orange rind
1 cup sifted cake flour
1½ teaspoons baking powder
¼ teaspoon salt

CUSTARD FILLING:

½ cup granulated sugar
¼ cup cornstarch
⅛ teaspoon salt
2 cups milk
3 egg yolks, lightly beaten
½ cup dark rum
½ teaspoon vanilla extract
2 tablespoons crème de cacao
¼ cup Marsala

TOPPING:

1 cup heavy cream, whipped
2 tablespoons chopped mixed candied fruits

1. To make the cake, preheat the oven to 350 degrees. Grease and flour a nine-inch spring-form pan.

2. Beat the egg yolks until they are very thick and pale, then gradually beat in the sugar until the mixture spins a rope when dropped from the beaters.

3. Beat in the lemon juice and the orange rind. Sift together twice the flour, baking powder, and salt and gently fold into the yolk mixture.

4. Beat the egg whites until stiff but not dry and fold into the cake batter. Pour into the prepared pan and bake about forty-five minutes, or until the cake rebounds to the touch when pressed gently in the center. Cool on a rack.

5. To prepare the filling, combine the sugar, cornstarch, and salt in a saucepan. Stir in the milk, bring to a boil, stirring, and cook one minute.

6. Pour a little of the hot mixture into the egg yolks, mix, and return all to the pan. Heat one to two minutes until the mixture thickens slightly.

7. Divide the custard into three bowls. Add two tablespoons of the rum to the first bowl and chill. Add the vanilla to the second bowl and the crème de cacao to the third bowl and chill.

8. Split the sponge cake into three layers and sprinkle all layers with the remaining rum mixed with the Marsala. Place the bottom layer in a shallow dish or deep plate. Spread with one of the cooled custards. Repeat with the other layers and the two other custards.

9. Frost with the whipped cream and serve immediately, or refrigerate until serving time. Just before serving, garnish with the candied fruit.

Amaretti Torte

6 to 8 servings

10 amaretti (Italian macaroons)
1 cup butter, at room temperature
1 cup granulated sugar
5 eggs, separated
½ cup all-purpose flour
4 squares (4 ounces) semisweet chocolate, finely grated
Confectioners' sugar

1. Preheat the oven to 350 degrees.
2. Pulverize the amaretti in an electric blender.
3. Cream together the butter and granulated sugar and beat in the egg yolks, one at a time. Continue beating for ten minutes.
4. Gradually add the flour and amaretti crumbs, beating after each addition.
5. Fold in the chocolate. Beat the whites until stiff and fold them in. Pour into a pan (8½ x 8½) that has been greased with butter and sprinkled with flour. Bake forty-five minutes. Before serving, sprinkle with confectioners' sugar.

Gali

(Deep-Fried Pastries)

About 8 dozen

3 cups sifted all-purpose flour
3 eggs
1 teaspoon vanilla extract
3 tablespoons or more granulated sugar
Lard for deep frying
Confectioners' sugar

1. Place the flour in a mixing bowl and make a well in the center. Break the eggs into the center and mix well with the hands. Add the vanilla and sugar and blend well.
2. Roll out the dough, a little at a time, on a lightly floured board and cut the dough into strips with a pastry cutter. Each strip should be about one inch wide and seven inches long. Tie each strip into a knot.
3. Heat the lard to 375 degrees on a deep-frying thermometer. Fry the pieces until golden brown. Drain on paper towels. Serve warm or cold, sprinkled with confectioners' sugar.

Zeppole di San Giuseppe

(Fried Cream Puffs for St. Joseph)

About 18 zeppole

Foods and feast days seem inalienably linked. March 17, of course, is Saint Patrick's Day and, in this country at least, the association is with corned beef and cabbage. But two days later is the lesser-known feast of Saint Joseph. In Italy—and in the Italian neighborhoods of New York—the traditional dessert for the festival is zeppole, *fried cream puff rings filled with sweetened ricotta.*

1 cup water
¼ cup butter
1 cup all-purpose flour
⅛ teaspoon salt
1 tablespoon granulated sugar
4 eggs
    Fat or vegetable oil for deep frying
    Ricotta Filling (see below)
    Confectioners' sugar
    Crystallized orange peel slices or candied cherries (optional)

1. Cut several circles of parchment paper or heavy brown paper the size of the bottom of the fry basket that fits the deep-fryer. Grease generously.

2. Place the water and butter in a small pan and heat gently until the butter melts and the mixture comes to a boil.

3. Mix the flour with the salt and sugar and add all at once to the boiling water mixture, beating well over moderate heat until the mixture forms a ball and leaves the sides of the pan.

4. Cool the mixture slightly and then beat in the eggs, one at a time, very well until the mixture is smooth and creamy.

5. Heat the fat in the deep-fryer to 350 degrees.

6. Spoon the mixture into a pastry bag fitted with a large fluted tube.

7. Pipe the cream-puff mixture into doughnut shapes about two inches in diameter, with three to four on each circle of parchment.

8. Take one piece of parchment, with the shapes on it, and turn upside down onto the surface of the hot fat. Taking care not to burn the fingers, remove the paper as the cakes loosen themselves from it.

9. Cook until the uppermost surface is set and then, with the bottom of the fryer basket, press the three or four zeppole into the hot oil and keep them there three to four minutes.

10. Remove the basket and continue cooking, first one side and then the other, turning with a slotted spoon until the zeppole are golden on all sides and cooked through, a total of six to ten minutes.

11. Remove with a slotted spoon and drain on paper towels.

12. When cool, split the zeppole and fill with the ricotta filling, dusting the tops with confectioners' sugar. Or spoon the ricotta mixture over the top and decorate with crystallized orange peel.

13. Once filled, the cakes must be refrigerated. They should be eaten the same day they are made.

RICOTTA FILLING:

About 2 cups

1 pound ricotta cheese
2 tablespoons chocolate bits, roughly chopped
⅓ cup granulated sugar
1 tablespoon grated orange peel
2 tablespoons crème de cacao (optional)

Combine all the ingredients in a bowl and mix well with a wooden spoon.

Note: If ricotta cheese is not available, very dry pot cheese may be substituted in this recipe.

In some Italian homes, candied fruit in various colors is added to the ricotta filling. Chopped candied fruit is available in jars.

St. Joseph's Cream Puffs

12 to 15 cream puffs

½ cup butter
1 cup water
1 cup all-purpose flour
  Few grains of salt
4 eggs
  Ricotta Filling for Cream Puffs (see below)
  Orange-Flavored Icing (optional, see below)

1. Preheat the oven to 400 degrees.
2. Put the butter and water in a saucepan and bring to a boil.
3. Combine the flour and salt and add to the water all at once. Mix well. Cook, stirring constantly, until the mixture forms a smooth, compact mass. Remove from the heat.
4. Add the eggs, one at a time, beating vigorously after each addition. Drop by tablespoonfuls two inches apart on a greased baking sheet. Bake for thirty-five minutes, or until thoroughly browned and set. Cool.
5. Make a slit with a sharp knife near the bottom of each puff. Fill with the ricotta filling. If desired, frost lightly with orange-flavored icing.

RICOTTA FILLING FOR CREAM PUFFS:

Combine one pound ricotta cheese with one-half cup sugar and mix thoroughly. Stir in two squares unsweetened chocolate, grated, and a few drops of almond extract.

ORANGE-FLAVORED ICING:

Combine one-half cup sifted confectioners' sugar with two and one-quarter teaspoons orange juice.

Sicilian Cannoli

6 to 12 servings

1 cup whole-milk ricotta cheese
  Granulated sugar
½ teaspoon finely grated lemon rind
1 tablespoon grated sweet or semisweet chocolate
1 teaspoon coarsely chopped sweet or semi-sweet chocolate
12 eggs
12 teaspoons butter
  Confectioners' sugar

1. Place the ricotta in a mixing bowl and add three tablespoons sugar, or more if you prefer. Beat thoroughly until smooth. Add the lemon rind, grated chocolate, and chopped chocolate. Blend well.
2. Beat one-quarter teaspoon of sugar and two eggs at a time with a fork until frothy and lemon-colored.
3. Heat two teaspoons butter at a time in a large crêpe or omelet pan or a skillet that will not stick. Pour in the two-egg mixture and swirl the pan around this way and that until the bottom is evenly coated. Do not stir, but cook until the mixture sets and is lightly browned on the bottom.
4. Meanwhile, sprinkle the bottom of a dinner plate generously with confectioners' sugar. Slide the pancake, browned side down, onto the plate. Continue making pancakes until all the eggs are used.
5. Spoon equal portions of the ricotta mixture down the center of each pancake and roll so that the filling is enclosed like a tube. Before serving, sprinkle with confectioners' sugar and cut each tube in half, if desired.

Chocolate Zabaglione Dessert

8 or more servings

10 eggs, separated
⅛ teaspoon salt
½ teaspoon cream of tartar
1 cup plus 10 teaspoons superfine granulated sugar
¾ cup finely chopped blanched almonds
6⅔ tablespoons Marsala
½ cup heavy cream
   Chocolate Frosting (see below)

1. Preheat the oven to its lowest setting, 170 to 225 degrees.

2. Moisten three large baking sheets with water and cover with unglazed brown paper, or lightly grease and flour the sheets, or line them with parchment paper. Using an eight-inch layer pan as a guide, mark five circles, at least one inch apart, on the paper.

3. Beat the egg whites with the salt and cream of tartar until just stiff but not dry.

4. Gradually beat in the one cup sugar, a tablespoon at a time, making sure that the mixture remains thick and smooth as marsh-mallow and that, at the end, no grains of sugar are felt when the mixture is rubbed between the fingers. Fold in the almonds.

5. Using a pastry tube fitted with a large plain tube, start in the center of one of the marked circles and press out a continuous strip, curling it around and around until the entire circle is filled in. Repeat with the other four circles.

6. Bake the circles about thirty minutes at 225 degrees, then turn off the heat and let the meringue remain in the warm oven until crisp and dry. Or bake at 170 degrees for forty-five to sixty minutes. Turn off the heat and leave in the warm oven about fifteen minutes, until crisp. Remove gently from the baking sheet or paper and cool on a rack.

7. To make the filling, place the egg yolks in the top of a double boiler. Add the remaining sugar and the Marsala. Beat with a wire whisk over hot, barely simmering water until thickened. Remove the sauce from the heat and continue beating until cold. Whip the cream and fold it into the sauce. Chill. Use the sauce as a filling for the meringue rings, starting with one meringue on the bottom and ending with a meringue on top. Cover the top and sides with the chocolate frosting and chill again before serving.

CHOCOLATE FROSTING:

About 2 cups

8 ounces bittersweet chocolate
2 egg whites
½ cup granulated sugar
2 teaspoons powdered cocoa
1 cup melted butter

Heat the chocolate over simmering water in the top of a double boiler, and when it starts to melt add the remaining ingredients. Stir slowly with a wooden spoon until blended and smooth. Cool before spreading on the dessert.

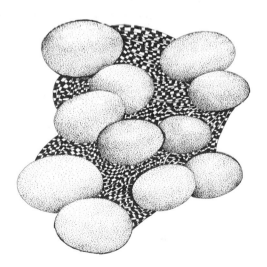

Biscuit Tortoni

About 12 servings

¾ cup granulated sugar
¾ cup water
 3 eggs, separated
12 almond macaroons
 2 teaspoons almond extract
 2 teaspoons vanilla extract
 2 cups heavy cream

1. Combine the sugar and water in a saucepan and cook until the mixture spins a thread (230 degrees on a candy thermometer).

2. Beat the egg whites until stiff but not dry. Slowly stir the sugar syrup into the egg whites and mix well. Beat the egg yolks until thick and lemon colored; add to the sugar mixture, stirring well.

3. Crush the macaroons into fine crumbs. This can be done in a blender. Reserving three tablespoons of the crumbs, add the balance to the sugar mixture along with the almond and vanilla extracts.

4. Whip the cream until stiff, then mix well into the sugar-macaroon mixture. Put into the freezing compartment of the refrigerator.

5. After twenty minutes, stir the mixture to keep the macaroons from settling. Then put the mixture into paper cupcake cups and sprinkle the reserved macaroon crumbs on top. Keep in the freezer until ready to serve, about four hours.

Bombe al Zabaglione

8 servings

¼ pound unsweetened chocolate
 7 egg yolks
¼ cup plus 5 tablespoons granulated sugar
¼ cup sweet butter
 2 egg whites
¼ teaspoon vanilla extract
 1 cup whipped cream
 5 egg yolks
10 tablespoons Marsala

1. Heat the chocolate over hot water until melted. Beat two of the egg yolks with the one-quarter cup sugar until thickened and lemon colored. Add the chocolate. Melt the butter and fold it into the chocolate mixture. Beat the egg whites until frothy and stir into the chocolate mixture. Add the vanilla extract and fold in one-half cup of the whipped cream. Lightly oil a melon mold and line it with the chocolate mixture, leaving the center hollow. The chocolate is only to be used as a shell for the following.

2. Place the remaining five egg yolks in a thin mixing bowl and place the bowl over boiling water. Beat rapidly with a rotary beater or whisk and add the remaining five tablespoons sugar and the Marsala. When the mixture is thick and foamy, remove from the water but continue beating until cool. Fold in the remaining one-half cup whipped cream and chill. Spoon this mixture into the hollow of the mold and place in the freezer until frozen, preferably overnight. When frozen, place a hot towel on the outside of the mold and work with the hands until the bombe can be unmolded onto a cold plate. Return to the freezer until ready to serve. Serve sliced.

Jamaica

Jamaican Codfish with Ackee

4 to 6 servings

1 pound salt cod, cut into large pieces
¼ pound salt pork, cut into cubes or thin slices
2 medium red, ripe tomatoes, cored and coarsely chopped
2 medium onions, peeled and thinly sliced
1 tablespoon coconut oil (see note)
1 1-pound 3-ounce can ackee
   Freshly ground black pepper
   Salt, if necessary

1. Place the cod pieces in a saucepan and add a generous amount of water. Cover, bring to a boil, and simmer three minutes. Drain. Add more water to cover, return to a boil and simmer two or three minutes longer. Drain well. Place the cod on a plate and flake, discarding any bones and skin. Set aside.

2. Heat the salt pork in a skillet and, when golden brown and rendered of fat, add the tomatoes, onions, and coconut oil. When the onions are wilted, add the flaked cod and ackee. Sprinkle generously with black pepper and simmer over medium heat fifteen minutes. Taste and, if desired, add salt. It may not be necessary because the cod is salty.

Note: Coconut oil is available in stores where West Indies food products are sold. It can be and frequently is made with freshly grated coconut in Jamaican homes. To make it, crack a coconut and grate the meat on a grater or in a blender. Line a mixing bowl with cheesecloth and add the grated meat and one quart of water. Squeeze to extract most of the liquid and pour the liquid into a saucepan. Bring to a boil and simmer until all the watery liquid evaporates and only the oil is left.

Jamaican Rice and Beans

10 to 12 servings

1   cup dried red kidney beans
1   rib celery, cut in half
1   small wedge green pepper
1   large coconut
6   cups water, approximately
    Salt
½   teaspoon dried thyme
2½ cups uncooked rice

1. Place the beans in a large kettle and add water to cover to a depth of one inch. Add the celery and green pepper, cover, and bring to a boil.

2. As the beans cook, prepare the coconut. There are three "eyes" on a coconut, and one of them is soft enough to pierce. Pierce that eye and drain the coconut water from the interior (see note). With a heavy hammer or mallet, crack the coconut shell in several places and, using a knife, remove the meat from the shell in large pieces.

3. Do not bother to cut away the dark outer coating of the coconut meat. Grate the coconut, using a fine grater, or cut the coconut into cubes and use an electric blender, blending a few cubes at a time.

4. Line a mixing bowl with cheesecloth and add the grated coconut. Add two cups of cold water and squeeze to extract the white liquid. This is coconut milk. Add two more cups of water and squeeze, then add the remaining water and squeeze. This should yield nearly six cups of liquid.

5. When the coconut milk is ready, add it to the simmering beans. Cover and continue to cook until the beans are tender, about one and one-half hours in all. Stir frequently to prevent the beans from burning.

6. Add salt to taste, thyme, and the rice. Stir once and cover. Continue to cook until the liquid is absorbed by the rice, about twenty minutes. If necessary, add a little water as the rice cooks. When done, the rice should be tender and all the liquid absorbed. Serve with any of the chicken fricassee recipes on pages 218–220 or with roasted or stewed beef.

Note: The coconut water drained from the whole coconut can be and generally is used as a beverage in Jamaica. The coconut water is often combined with white rum and ice and served as a spirituous beverage.

Jamaican Curried Goat

12 or more servings

12 pounds goat (leg, breast, neck, and all), cut into 1½- or 2-inch cubes
    Salt
2   teaspoons or more red pepper flakes
¾   cup Curry Powder (page 33) or more to taste
4   green onions, finely chopped
1   large onion, coarsely chopped

1. Rinse the meat under cold running water and pat dry with a clean towel.

2. Put the meat into a large, heavy casserole with a cover. Add salt to taste, a little at a time, and work the salt into each piece of meat with the hands. Add the red pepper flakes and curry powder, a little at a time, and continue rubbing the mixture into the meat. Add the green onions and onion and continue kneading briefly. Cover and let stand two hours or longer.

3. Do not add water. Place the casserole on the stove, cover and bring to a boil. The meat will give up a lot of liquid. When it becomes liquid on the bottom, stir to bring the bottom meat to the top and vice versa. Continue cooking, stirring occasionally, until the meat is tender, two to three hours. Serve with plain rice.

Japanese sou,

Fried Plantains, Jamaican Style

6 or more servings

4   large ripe plantains
¼   cup vegetable or peanut oil, approximately

1. Peel the plantains and cut them into one-quarter-inch slices lengthwise or crosswise. If lengthwise slices are used, cut each slice in half, if desired.
2. Heat the oil in a skillet and fry the slices, a few at a time, until golden brown on both sides. Add more oil as necessary. Drain and serve hot. Serve with Jamaican Codfish with Ackee (page 447) or with Jamaican Curried Goat (page 448).

Boiled Green Bananas

6 servings

6   green bananas
    Salt
3   thin slices salt pork
    Butter (optional)

1. Place the bananas in a container and add very hot but not boiling water. Let stand until the skin turns almost black. This will facilitate peeling.
2. Peel the bananas and put them in a kettle or large saucepan. Add water to cover, salt to taste, and the salt pork. Bring to a boil and simmer until the bananas are very tender, thirty minutes or longer. Serve hot. The bananas are generally served unbuttered unless they are mashed. If mashed, add butter to taste. Serve as a vegetable.

Rum Custard Pudding

5 servings

2   cups milk
5   eggs, beaten
2   tablespoons brown sugar
1   tablespoon cornstarch
¼   cup dark rum
    Whipped cream

1. Bring the milk to a boil, stirring constantly.
2. Combine the eggs, sugar, and cornstarch. Add to the hot milk and cook, without boiling, until the mixture is thickened, stirring constantly.
3. Remove from the heat and stir in the rum. Pour into sherbet glasses and chill until set. Serve garnished with whipped cream.

Koo chul pan, Korean nine-hole dish

Jamaican Rub-Up Cake

8 to 10 servings

2½ cups all-purpose flour
  4 teaspoons baking powder
  ½ teaspoon salt
  ½ cup butter
1½ cups granulated sugar
  3 eggs, lightly beaten
1½ teaspoons vanilla extract
  1 cup milk

1. Preheat the oven to 350 degrees.

2. Sift the flour, then resift it with the baking powder and salt. With the fingertips or a pastry blender, work the butter into the flour.

3. Add the sugar.

4. Add the eggs, vanilla, and milk all at once and stir to mix with a wooden spoon. There will be some lumps. Pour the batter into a greased, waxed-paper-lined two- to two-and-one-half-quart deep cake pan.

5. Bake forty-five minutes to one hour, or until a cake tester inserted into the center comes out clean. The cake will have a moist, open, muffinlike texture.

Japan

Suimono

1 serving

There is nothing more convincing than an Oriental soup to dispute the notion that food must be elaborate to be good. It may be only a clear broth with one leaf of watercress, a length of green onion, or a carrot slice to beguile the eye. The palate is seduced with the inherent goodness of the broth. Below is a recipe for suimono, *a soup from Japan, a simple, but excellent, introduction to almost any meal.*

  1 cup plus 2 tablespoons Dashi (see below)
1½ teaspoons granulated sugar
  4 teaspoons soy sauce
  ¼ cup sake
  3 small, bite-sized cubes raw chicken
    Salt to taste
  ¼ teaspoon ajinomoto (monosodium glutamate)
  1 green onion
  1 teaspoon grated fresh ginger

1. In a saucepan bring the one cup dashi, one teaspoon of the sugar, and three teaspoons of the soy sauce to a boil. Simmer about five minutes. When ready, set aside.

2. Meanwhile, combine the sake, chicken, remaining dashi, sugar, soy sauce, salt, and monosodium glutamate in a skillet and bring to a boil over high heat. Cook the chicken until done, about three minutes, shaking the skillet. Transfer the chicken pieces to a small soup bowl.

3. Trim the ends and green part from the green onion. Slice the white part lengthwise into the thinnest possible shreds (julienne). Rinse in very cold water, then drain and pat dry.

4. Spoon the piping hot dashi broth over the chicken pieces and add the green onion and ginger. Serve immediately.

Dashi

About 1 quart

  1 sheet black seaweed (yamadashi)
  4 cups water
  ½ cup bonito flakes

1. Place the seaweed in a large flameproof casserole and add the water. Bring to a boil and simmer about five minutes. Remove the seaweed.

2. Add the bonito flakes to the casserole and turn off the heat under the casserole. Let stand until the bonito flakes sink to the bottom, then strain. The broth from this recipe is the dashi. It is the foundation stock for thousands of Japanese dishes, principally soups.

Bean Soup

Combine two and one-half cups of Dashi (page 451) and three tablespoons soy bean paste. Stir until dissolved. Heat without boiling and add cubes of tofu (bean curd). Heat thoroughly and serve hot.

Elaborate Tempura

6 servings

24 raw shrimp
 6 Alaska king crab legs, thawed and patted to remove excess moisture
 6 green onions, cut into 3-inch lengths
 6 green beans, each about 3 inches long, trimmed at the ends
 6 snow peas
 6 to 12 large parsley sprigs
 6 pieces Fuji Foo Young (see below)
   Tempura Sauce (page 453)
1½ quarts peanut oil
   Tempura Batter (page 453)
   Grated Japanese white radish for garnish
   Sliced pickled radishes (available in bottles) for garnish

1. Peel the shrimp but leave the last tail segments intact. Split the last tail segments top to bottom. Run a knife down the back slightly and remove the intestinal vein. Rinse the shrimp and pat dry. Place each shrimp on its back and make a few widthwise slits down the underside of each. This will keep the shrimp from curling when they fry. Arrange the shrimp symmetrically on a platter.

2. Arrange the crab legs, vegetables, parsley sprigs, and fuji foo young on the same platter; refrigerate until ready to use. Finish preparing the tempura sauce (first preparations should be done a day ahead).

3. Heat the oil to 350 degrees. As it heats, prepare the batter. A skillet may be used for frying, but a Japanese or Chinese wok is preferable. Keep the oil at 350 degrees, more or less.

4. To prepare the tempura, use the fingers, tongs, or chopsticks and dip one piece of sea food or vegetable at a time into the batter. Drop each piece into the oil and cook, turning once or twice, until golden brown. Several pieces may be cooked at the same time, but do not crowd the pan. As the foods are cooked, drain on absorbent toweling. Serve hot, with the tempura sauce and garnishes.

FUJI FOO YOUNG:

6 servings

1 dried black mushroom
4 raw shrimp
2 water chestnuts, preferably fresh, but canned will do
2 green onions, trimmed
2 snow pea pods (optional)
¼ cup bean sprouts, preferably fresh, but canned will do
6 large, fresh mushrooms
1 small piece fresh ginger
  Salt to taste

1. Place the dried black mushroom in a mixing bowl and add boiling water barely to cover. Let stand until soft, about fifteen minutes.

2. Shell and devein the shrimp; dice them. If fresh water chestnuts are used, peel them. Cut them into thin slices and cut the slices into thin strips. Chop or slice the green onions and snow pea pods. If canned bean sprouts are used, rinse them and then chop lightly. Drain and chop the black mushroom

and remove and chop the stems from the fresh mushrooms, reserving the caps. Grate the ginger.

3. Combine all the ingredients except the mushroom caps in a mixing bowl and add salt to taste. Fill the mushroom caps with the mixture and stick one plain, wooden toothpick into each cap. The filled caps are now ready to be dipped into batter for deep frying along with the shrimp and vegetables on the tray.

TEMPURA SAUCE:

6 servings

  1 cup imported soy sauce
  6 tablespoons granulated sugar
  3 slices fresh ginger
    Juice of ½ lime
  ¼ cup dry sherry
  1 packet dashi-no-moto (dried bonito flakes) or use 1 tablespoon bulk dashi-no-moto
  1 cup boiling water

1. Combine the soy sauce, sugar, ginger, lime juice, and sherry in a pint jar. Cover and let stand overnight.

2. In a mixing bowl, combine the dashi-no-moto and the boiling water. Let stand one minute and remove the packet or, if bulk dashi-no-moto is used, strain and reserve the liquid. Stir this into the soy mixture. Pour the sauce into six individual dishes.

TEMPURA BATTER:

  2 egg yolks
1½ cups ice water
  2 cups sifted cake flour

1. Place the yolks in a flat-bottomed dish, such as a soufflé dish or earthenware casserole. Do not use a mixing bowl. Stir in the water, preferably using two large chopsticks. If you can't maneuver chopsticks use a fork, but stir lightly.

2. Sprinkle one-half cup of the flour over the liquid and chop in most of the flour rather than stirring it in. The object is a fairly lumpy, nonsmooth batter. Add another half cup of flour and repeat the chopping, pushing-down action. Add another one-half cup flour until the desired consistency is reached. The batter should be more or less the consistency of heavy whipping cream, and there should always be lumps. There should also be some flour on the surface. The quantity of flour to liquid cannot be precise. If the batter seems too heavy, add more ice water. If it seems too thin, poke in more flour.

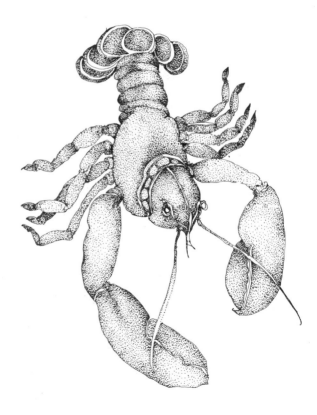

Beef Teriyaki I

4 servings

⅓ cup sake or dry sherry
⅓ cup soy sauce
¼ cup granulated sugar
1 teaspoon grated fresh ginger or ½ teaspoon ground ginger
1 clove garlic, finely minced
¼ lemon, thinly sliced
1 pound lean beef, preferably shell steak

1. Combine the sake, soy sauce, sugar,
ginger, garlic, and lemon and stir until the
sugar dissolves.

2. Cut the meat into thin strips and add to
the marinade. Marinate fifteen minutes or
longer, then drain and cook briefly in a hot
skillet. The beef is best if eaten slightly rare.

Beef Teriyaki II

30 sandwiches

1 cup soy sauce (preferably Kikkoman)
6 tablespoons granulated sugar
1 cup mirin (sweet Japanese cooking wine)
  or very dry sherry
1 tablespoon sesame oil
1 teaspoon grated fresh ginger
1 clove garlic, finely minced
30 boneless club steaks, cut from the rib
  (each ¼ inch thick)
30 sesame buns

1. Combine the soy sauce, sugar, mirin,
sesame oil, ginger, and garlic. Stir until the
sugar dissolves.

2. Make layers of meat in a large, flat dish
and cover with the sauce. Continue making
layers until all the meat and sauce are used.
Let stand an hour or more.

3. Split the sesame buns and lightly brown
the split halves under the broiler.

4. Grill the steaks quickly on both sides
and serve in the buns.

Mongolian Grill

6 servings

1½ cups thinly sliced onions
12 tomato slices, ½ inch thick
12 green pepper rings
2 bunches of watercress, trimmed
3 leeks, trimmed, cut into quarters, washed
  well, and dried
½ pound sirloin or fillet of beef, cut into
  thin slices
½ pound lean pork or chicken breasts, cut
  into thin slices
1 cup soy sauce
1 cup vegetable oil
  Beef fat

1. Arrange the vegetables and meat slices
symmetrically on one or more large platters.
Pour the soy sauce and oil into separate
serving dishes.

2. Heat charcoal in a hibachi or other
grill until the coals are white hot and ashes
start to form. Place the grill about five inches
above the source of heat. When it is hot, rub
it with beef fat.

3. Dip bite-sized portions of vegetables or
meat into oil or soy sauce and place on the
hot grill. Cook to the desired degree of doneness and serve while hot. Traditionally,
guests cook and serve themselves.

Shabu-Shabu

4 servings

The dish the Japanese call shabu-shabu *is sometimes called oriental fondue in this country. It consists of wafer-thin slices of beef (instead of chunks, as in an occidental meat fondue) cooked briefly in a boiling liquid and dipped into a savory sauce. As in the West, it is a communal dish and any number (depending on the size of the* shabu-shabu *pot) can play. Shabu-shabu is served at Saito, 131 West 52d Street, one of New York's best Japanese restaurants, and here we give the recipe of the Saito chef. Shabu-shabu is onomatopoeic; it imitates the sound of chopsticks as they swirl in the broth.*

4 cups water
1 2½-inch square kombu (sea kelp)
2 pounds well-marbled, uncooked rib of beef, sliced paper thin
½ Chinese cabbage, cut into two-inch lengths
1 large onion, sliced paper thin
2 pieces tofu (bean curd), each cut into 4 pieces (8 pieces in all)
8 thin slices carrot
8 slices bamboo shoots
4 raw mushrooms, sliced
1 bunch watercress
2 cups udon (Japanese noodles, preferably kishimen)

1. Bring the water to a boil in an electric skillet or flameproof casserole and add the sea kelp. Simmer three minutes and remove the sea kelp. Keep the water boiling throughout the meal to cook the ingredients.

2. Arrange the thin slices of meat on one platter, and the cabbage, onion, tofu, carrot, bamboo shoots, mushrooms, watercress, and noodles on another. Let each guest serve himself by taking a piece of beef with a fondue fork or chopsticks, dipping it into the boiling liquid, cooking it briefly, and then dipping it into one of two sauces, Ponzu (see below) or Gomatare (see below).

3. While eating the beef, add the various vegetables and cook briefly in the hot liquid, dip into the sauce of one's choice, and eat while hot. When all the vegetables and beef have been eaten, the noodles may be added to the broth, heated thoroughly, and eaten. Serve hot rice with the shabu-shabu.

PONZU:

(Soy and Lemon Sauce)

About 1 cup

½ cup lemon juice
½ cup soy sauce
½ tablespoon mirin (sweet Japanese cooking wine)
¼ teaspoon ajinomoto (monosodium glutamate; optional)
1 tablespoon finely chopped green onion Shichimi tongarashi (hot Japanese red pepper) to taste

Combine all the ingredients and serve.

GOMATARE:

(Sesame Sauce)

About 1½ cups

½ cup sesame seed or sesame seed paste
½ cup soy sauce
1 cup Dashi (page 451)
1 tablespoon mirin (sweet Japanese cooking wine)
1 tablespoon ajinomoto (monosodium glutamate; optional)

1. If sesame seeds are used, toast them lightly in a frying pan and then grind them fine.

2. Combine the ground sesame seeds or paste with the remaining ingredients and serve.

Pork Chops Teriyaki

5 servings

1 cup soy sauce
3 tablespoons sherry
¼ cup granulated sugar
½ teaspoon ground ginger
1 clove garlic, finely minced
10 loin pork chops
   Hot, fluffy rice

1. Preheat the oven to 425 degrees.
2. To make the teriyaki sauce, combine the soy sauce, sherry, sugar, ginger, and garlic. Bring to a boil, stirring to dissolve the sugar.
3. Dip each chop into the sauce. Place the meat in a baking dish and bake, uncovered, for fifteen to twenty minutes, until done. Serve the chops over the rice and serve the sauce separately.

Chawanmushi

(Steamed Egg Custard)

4 servings

10 eggs
1 teaspoon salt
2 tablespoons dry sherry
3 cups hot but not boiling water
½ pound ground pork or finely chopped shrimp (see note)

1. To make this dish, use a traditional Chinese wok fitted with a bamboo Chinese steamer with top. A roasting pan will serve if it is fitted with a rack placed above the water level to let the food steam.
2. Break the eggs into a mixing bowl and beat until foamy with a rotary beater. Add the salt and sherry and gradually beat in the water. Stir in the pork or shrimp. Pour the mixture into a round, ten-inch ovenproof glass or aluminum dish with a one-and-one-half-inch border. Place the dish in the wok over the boiling water, cover, and steam twenty to thirty minutes, or until a testing knife comes out clean.

Note: Substitutes for the pork or shrimp in this recipe include one-quarter pound lobster meat cut into one-half-inch cubes, and one-half cup chopped raw clams or oysters.

Oyako Domburi

1 serving

¾ cup uncooked short-grain Japanese rice
¾ cup water
½ boned chicken breast with skin left on
¼ cup sake
1¾ teaspoons granulated sugar
     Salt to taste
2½ teaspoons mirin (sweet Japanese cook-
     ing wine)
4 teaspoons soy sauce
     Ajinomoto (monosodium glutamate),
     optional
½ cup Dashi (page 451)
½ cup thinly sliced onion
3 or 4 sprigs trefoil or watercress
1 egg

1. Rinse the rice well in cold water. Drain and let stand thirty minutes.

2. Measure the rice and spoon it into a saucepan. Add an exactly equal amount of water. Do not add salt. Cover closely and bring to a boil. Boil furiously about fifteen minutes, then reduce the heat and cook about five minutes longer. Remove the rice from the heat. The grains should stick together, but all the water should be absorbed. The rice should be moist.

3. Meanwhile, cut the chicken breast into small, bite-sized cubes.

4. Add the sake, chicken breast, one-half teaspoon of the sugar, one-quarter teaspoon salt, one teaspoon of the mirin, one-half teaspoon of the soy sauce, and one-quarter teaspoon ajinomoto to a saucepan. Cook, stirring the chicken pieces with chopsticks, until done but not overcooked, about five minutes.

5. In another saucepan combine the dashi, remaining soy sauce, sugar, and mirin, dash of salt, and more ajinomoto, if desired. Cook five minutes. Pour into a small skillet and add the chicken pieces and onion. Simmer briefly and add the trefoil. Beat the egg thor-oughly, then hold a strainer over the skillet and strain the egg over the chicken. Turn the heat to high and stir gently. Cook about fifteen seconds, or just until the egg is set.

6. Spoon the hot rice into a Japanese bowl. Carefully transfer the chicken onto the rice. Serve hot.

Stashi

4 servings

1 pound spinach
     Japanese soy sauce
2 tablespoons sesame seeds, cooked in a slow oven until toasted
     Sesame oil

1. Wash the spinach well and place it in a kettle. Add water to cover, bring to a boil, and simmer one minute. Drain well, pressing with the hands to remove excess moisture.

2. Chop the spinach lightly and divide into four individual cups. Sprinkle with two to three tablespoons soy sauce, the sesame seeds, and a drop or two of sesame oil. Serve immediately, with more soy sauce, if desired.

Korea

Kori Kuk

(Oxtail Soup)

4 to 6 servings

1 oxtail
10 cups water
1 tablespoon sesame seeds
¼ cup imported soy sauce
1 tablespoon sesame oil
½ teaspoon freshly ground black pepper
2 tablespoons minced onion
1 tablespoon minced garlic

1. Have the butcher cut the oxtail into about eight pieces. Wash and place in a kettle with the water. Bring to a boil and simmer, removing the scum from the surface, three hours or until oxtail can be pierced easily with a fork or chopstick. Remove the oxtail from the broth and cut away the excess fat.

2. Place the sesame seeds in a pan and brown slowly over low heat, then grind in a mortar.

3. Combine the ground sesame seeds and remaining ingredients in a mixing bowl. Add the oxtail and stir until well coated. Return the oxtail and sesame mixture to the broth and bring to a boil before serving.

Korean Saewu Jun

(Shrimp Fried in Egg Batter)

4 to 6 servings

1 pound raw jumbo shrimp
1 teaspoon salt
  Freshly ground black pepper
¼ cup all-purpose flour
2 eggs, lightly beaten
⅓ cup sesame oil
  Imported soy sauce
  White vinegar

1. Shell and devein the shrimp, then slit them down the back, taking care not to cut all the way through the flesh. Flatten them out with the broad side of a knife and score lightly. Sprinkle with the salt and pepper to taste. Dredge in the flour, then dip in the egg.

2. Heat the oil in a skillet until very hot and sauté the shrimp about one minute on each side, or until brown. Turn off the heat and let shrimp cook about three minutes longer in the hot pan. Serve immediately, with a side dish of soy sauce and vinegar mixed in proportion of four parts soy sauce to one part vinegar.

Korean Bul-Kogi

(Barbecued Beef)

4 servings

One of the most typical of all Korean dishes is called bul-kogi, *the name of which is, of course, a translation from Korean characters. Americans frequently refer to* bul-kogi *as Korean barbecue, and it can be made with various meats, such as chicken or beef, thinly sliced, marinated and cooked quickly and directly over hot coals. For best results the meat should be cooked no more than thirty seconds.*

2 pounds beef, sirloin, rib steak, or flank steak
1 tablespoon sesame seeds
3 green onions, finely chopped
4 cloves garlic, finely minced
¼ cup plus 1 tablespoon soy sauce
2 tablespoons sesame oil
¼ cup granulated sugar
2 tablespoons sherry or Beef Stock (page 115)
¼ teaspoon monosodium glutamate
⅛ teaspoon freshly ground black pepper

1. Slice the steak very thin diagonally across the grain from top to bottom. Score each piece lightly with an X.
2. Place the sesame seeds in a pan and brown slowly over low heat, then grind in a mortar.
3. Combine the ground sesame seeds and remaining ingredients in a bowl and mix well. Add the meat to the marinade and stir until well coated. Let stand twenty minutes or longer. Grill, preferably over charcoal, or, failing that, on an open electric grill or under an oven broiler. Cook thirty seconds or so to each side.

Korean Meat Salad

8 to 10 servings

3 pounds top sirloin, eye round of beef, or other lean, good-quality beef
2 tablespoons peanut oil
5 dried mushrooms, preferably Chinese
1 4½-ounce jar sliced mushrooms
3 tablespoons soy sauce
1 tablespoon rice vinegar or white vinegar
1 tablespoon vinegar from bottled capers
3 cloves garlic, crushed
2 red onions, finely chopped
1 yellow onion, sliced into rings
6 green onions, green part and all, trimmed and sliced
1 tablespoon finely chopped shallots
2 tablespoons finely chopped parsley
3 tablespoons capers
2 teaspoons sesame oil

1. Trim the meat of all fat, then cut the meat into very thin strips, approximately ¼ x ¼ x 2 inches.
2. Heat the oil in a skillet and cook the beef, stirring, just until it loses color. Transfer the meat to a mixing bowl.
3. Place the dried mushrooms in another mixing bowl and add lukewarm water to cover. Let stand fifteen minutes or longer. Remove the mushrooms; discard their stems. Slice the caps and reserve.
4. To the skillet in which the meat cooked add the liquid from the jar of mushrooms. Add the soy sauce, vinegars, and juice that may have accumulated around the beef. Do not add the beef. Bring this liquid to a boil.
5. Combine the garlic, onions, green onions, shallots, parsley, capers, dried mushrooms, and mushrooms from the jar. Pour the skillet liquid over them and let stand until cool. Add the mixture to the beef, then stir in the sesame oil. Cover and refrigerate at least twenty-four hours, but serve at room temperature.

Kim Chee

(Korean Pickled Cabbage)

About 1 quart

2 pounds celery cabbage (Chinese cabbage)
½ cup coarse salt
4 cups water
1½ tablespoons crushed red pepper flakes
1 clove garlic, finely minced
1 teaspoon fresh ginger, minced
1 tablespoon granulated sugar
2 green onions, finely chopped

1. Rinse the cabbage in cold water and drain. Cut the cabbage into one and one-half-inch squares. Sprinkle with salt, add the water, and let stand overnight.

2. Rinse the cabbage in cold water and drain. Using a wooden spoon, blend the remaining ingredients and stir this well into the cabbage pieces. Pack into a quart jar and cover. Place the jar in a plastic bag to prevent the odors from spreading to other foods. Refrigerate and let stand four to five days to cure.

Koo Chul Pan

(Korean Nine-Hole Dish)

*6 to 8 servings, with approximately
3 filled pancakes per person*

18 to 24 thin Pancakes (page 461)
20 dried oriental mushrooms, or use fresh mushroom caps
2 tablespoons tree ears
Vegetable oil
Salt
1 cup finely shredded carrots, the shreds about 3 inches long
1 cup finely shredded green pepper, the shreds about 3 inches long
5 eggs, separated
1 teaspoon cold water
1 cup bean sprouts (optional)
½ pound Korean Beef Shreds (page 461)
1 cup thinly shredded green onions

1. Prepare the pancakes and set them aside. If a Korean nine-hole dish is available, use a very large biscuit cutter, a small saucer and a sharp knife or other device to cut each pancake into rounds that will fit the inside hole. If not, serve the whole pancake.

2. Place the dried mushrooms, if they are used, in a small mixing bowl and add boiling water to cover. Let stand fifteen minutes, then drain well. Cut away and discard the tough stems. Cut the mushrooms into shreds and set aside.

3. Place the tree ears in another bowl and add boiling water to cover. Let stand fifteen minutes, then drain well.

4. Heat a little oil in a skillet and add the shredded mushrooms. Sprinkle with a little salt and cook quickly, tossing quickly. Spoon the mushrooms out of the skillet and set aside. Or if fresh mushrooms are used, slice them thin and cook in a little oil with salt. Spoon them out of the skillet and set aside.

5. Wipe the skillet and cook the carrots quickly in a little oil with a sprinkle of salt.

Spoon the carrots out of the skillet and set aside. The carrots should remain crisp tender.

6. Repeat the procedure with the shredded green peppers. The peppers should remain crisp tender.

7. Beat the egg whites lightly with a teaspoon of oil. Heat a little oil in a stick-proof nine-inch skillet and add one-third of the whites. Cook until set but without stirring. Slip the egg out of the skillet and repeat until all the whites are used. Shred the hardened egg whites.

8. Beat the yolks with a teaspoon of cold water and a little salt. Heat a little oil in a stick-proof nine-inch skillet and make a layer of yolks. Cook until set without stirring or browning. Shred the hardened egg yolks.

9. If canned bean sprouts are used, rinse them off and drain. Heat a little oil in a skillet and add the bean sprouts. Cook quickly for one minute and set aside.

10. This dish is almost always served lukewarm or at room temperature. If a koo chul pan dish is not available, use eight individual ramekins and a plate for the pancakes. If the Korean serving dish is available, place the trimmed pancakes in the center and arrange the other ingredients, including the shredded beef and the raw green onions, in the surrounding holes. Let each guest serve himself. Pick up one pancake, add a little of each ingredient, and roll to enclose the filling. Eat with the fingers.

PANCAKES:

About 24 to 36 pancakes

1½ cups sifted all-purpose flour
  2 eggs, lightly beaten
    Salt
  2 to 2½ cups milk
  6 tablespoons melted butter

1. Place the flour in a mixing bowl.

2. Beat together the eggs, a dash or two of salt, and the milk. Add to the flour, stirring with a wire whisk. Whisk in the melted butter and strain.

3. Brush a seasoned six- or seven-inch crêpe pan with a cloth dipped in melted butter. Heat the pan and spoon in two tablespoons, more or less, of the batter, turning the pan this way and that in a circular pattern so that the batter neatly covers the bottom. Cook briefly until brown on the bottom and turn the pancake with a spatula. Cook briefly on the other side. Continue until all the batter is used.

KOREAN BEEF SHREDS:

About 1½ cups

½ pound chuck or round steak in one piece
  3 tablespoons soy sauce
    Freshly ground pepper
⅛ teaspoon monosodium glutamate (optional)
  1 tablespoon toasted sesame seeds
  1 tablespoon granulated sugar

1. Slice the beef, then cut it into very thin strips (julienne).

2. Heat the soy sauce in a small skillet and add the beef and remaining ingredients. Cook briefly, stirring, just until the meat loses its red color.

Lebanon

Lamb on Skewers

6 servings

2 pounds lean lamb, cut into small bite-sized cubes (smaller than for shish kebab)
¼ cup finely chopped onion
¾ cup dry white wine
2 tablespoons olive oil
2 teaspoons dried mint
  Salt and freshly ground black pepper to taste

1. Combine all ingredients in a mixing bowl. Cover and refrigerate overnight, stirring occasionally.
2. Drain the meat but reserve the marinade. Thread the meat on skewers. If wooden skewers are used, soak them in water first.
3. Grill the meat over hot charcoal or under the broiler to the desired degree of doneness. Baste with the marinade and turn the meat as it cooks.

Meat Balls, Middle Eastern Style

4 servings

1½ pounds ground lamb
  2 cloves garlic, finely chopped
  1 egg, lightly beaten
  1 teaspoon salt
  ¼ teaspoon freshly ground black pepper
  ¼ teaspoon allspice (optional)
  ½ cup pignoli (pine nuts)
  ½ cup chopped parsley
    Olive oil

1. Mix the meat lightly with the remaining ingredients except olive oil, then add a little olive oil to moisten the mixture. Form into small balls.
2. Cook the meat balls in hot olive oil until browned on the outside but still pink in the middle, about five minutes, depending on size. Serve with rice.

Lebanese Spinach Pies

About 12 spinach pies

2 cups sifted all-purpose flour
1½ tablespoons plus 1 teaspoon salt
   Salad oil
1 envelope active dry yeast
¾ cup lukewarm water
1½ pounds fresh spinach
1 cup coarsely chopped onion
6 tablespoons pignoli (pine nuts)
¼ cup lemon juice
2 tablespoons dried mint
1 teaspoon ground allspice
½ teaspoon freshly ground white pepper

1. Prepare the dough so that it will have a chance to rise. To do this, empty the flour into a mixing bowl and make a hole in the center. Add the one teaspoon salt and one tablespoon oil. Meanwhile, dissolve the yeast in the lukewarm water. Add to the flour mixture, stirring with the hands. Continue stirring and adding liquid until all is used. This should make a moist but manageable dough. Knead briefly. Shape the dough into a ball. Wipe out the mixing bowl and rub the bottom with oil. Rub the ball all over with oil and add it to the bowl. Cover with a towel and place in a warm place to rise, about one to one and one-half hours.

2. Meanwhile, pick over the spinach and discard all tough stems and bruised leaves. Rinse the spinach well in three changes of cold water and drain well, shaking to remove as much moisture as possible. Place on a flat surface and chop coarsely. Add the remaining salt and toss. Let stand an hour or so.

3. Preheat the oven to 500 degrees.

4. Squeeze the spinach with the hands to remove the liquid created by the salt. There should be about two and one-half cups of spinach. Place the spinach in a mixing bowl and add the onion, pignoli, lemon juice, mint, allspice, and pepper. Mix well with the hands.

5. When the dough is risen to twice its size, remove it from the mixing bowl and, without kneading, pull it into a thin roll, about eighteen inches long. Cut this roll into twelve equal pieces. Roll out each piece on a lightly floured board into a circle five or six inches in diameter.

6. Spoon about one-third cup of spinach mixture into the center of each circle and bring up three edges of the pastry, pressing with the fingers to seal. When the spinach mixture is sealed in the pastry, it should be the shape of a "tricorn" or three-sided pyramid. Continue filling and sealing the pastry until all the pieces are filled and most of the spinach mixture is used. (The mixture is also good served cold as a salad.)

7. Brush a jelly-roll tin lightly with oil and arrange the filled pastries on it. Brush the tops of the pastries with oil. Place the tin on the bottom of the oven (not on an oven rack). Bake eight minutes and place the pan on a middle rack. Immediately reduce the oven heat to 350 degrees and continue baking until golden brown, about eighteen minutes. Remove the pan from the oven and brush the tops of the pies with oil. Serve lukewarm.

Mexico

Guacamole I

6 servings

2 large, ripe avocados
1 small green chili serrano, chopped
1 medium onion, finely chopped
1 clove garlic, finely minced
1 small tomato, peeled, seeded, and finely chopped
   Salt and freshly ground black pepper
   Chopped fresh coriander leaves (cilantro or Chinese parsley)

1. Peel the avocados and reserve the seeds.
2. Mash the avocado pulp and combine it in a bowl with the chili, onion, garlic, tomato, and salt and pepper to taste. Blend well and place the avocado seeds on top of the mixture. This will prevent the guacamole from darkening as it stands; remove the seeds before serving. Serve, sprinkled with chopped fresh coriander, as an appetizer or salad.

Guacamole II

5 servings

4 avocados, pitted and peeled
3 ripe, red tomatoes, peeled and finely diced
3 onions, chopped
½ ajipepper (hot red pepper), chopped
1 tablespoon fresh coriander (cilantro or Chinese parsley), chopped
½ teaspoon salt
   Juice of 2 lemons
¼ teaspoon monosodium glutamate (optional)
10 tortillas (see note)
   Lard for deep frying

1. Mash the avocados coarsely with a fork. Avocados should not be pureed but mashed in small pieces.
2. Add the tomatoes, onions, ajipepper, coriander, salt, lemon juice, and monosodium glutamate. Mix with a spoon until all the ingredients are blended.
3. Cut the tortillas into quarters and deep-fry them in lard until a crisp golden brown. Cool.
4. Place the avocado mixture in a serving bowl and decorate with the tostadas (fried tortillas). Serve as an appetizer or salad.

Note: Canned or frozen tortillas are available in most specialty shops and in many supermarkets.

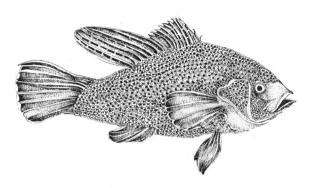

Seviche
(Pickled Raw Fish)

6 or more servings

3½ pounds fresh mackerel (1, 2 or 3 fish, depending on size)
    Juice of 3 fresh limes, approximately
    Salt to taste
6 tablespoons olive oil (preferably a full-bodied, not-too-refined oil)
½ teaspoon dried orégano
2 large tomatoes
2 canned chilies serranos
1 tablespoon coarsely chopped fresh coriander (cilantro or Chinese parsley)
1 small white onion, thinly sliced
    Freshly ground pepper to taste
1 ripe avocado

1. Have the fish merchant bone and skin the mackerel. Cut the fish into bite-sized pieces and place in a mixing bowl. Add lime juice to barely cover. Cover the bowl and refrigerate for at least five hours, turning the fish in the lime juice occasionally as it stands.

2. Add salt to taste, the olive oil, and orégano.

3. Drop the tomatoes into boiling water and let stand for about twelve seconds, no longer. Drain immediately. Pull the skin off the tomatoes and cut out the core, then cut the tomatoes in half and remove the seeds. Cut the tomatoes into cubes and add to the fish. Chop the chilies serranos fine and add. Add the coriander, onion, and pepper. Peel the avocado, cut into cubes, and add. Cover and refrigerate until serving, as an appetizer.

Guacamole III

6 servings

2 fresh or canned chilies serranos
½ cup finely chopped fresh coriander (cilantro or Chinese parsley)
2 red tomatoes, peeled, seeded, and cut into cubes
1 cup finely minced white onions
3 ripe avocados, peeled, seeded, and chopped to a puree (reserve the seeds)
    Salt to taste
3 tablespoons olive oil
1 teaspoon or more cider vinegar

1. Remove the stems and seeds from the chilies and chop the chilies.

2. Combine the chilies with the remaining ingredients and spoon the mixture into a serving dish. Place the avocado seeds in the center. This will prevent the guacamole from darkening as it stands; remove the seeds before serving. Serve as an appetizer, with warm tortillas, if desired.

Mexican Stuffed Olives

6 to 8 servings

1 1¾-ounce can flat anchovy fillets
1 7½-ounce can pitted olives, drained
1 4-ounce can pimentos, chopped
1 clove garlic, finely minced
⅓ cup wine vinegar
1 tablespoon olive oil
¼ cup minced parsley

1. Drain the anchovies and reserve the oil. Chop the anchovies and stuff the olives with them.

2. Combine the pimentos, garlic, vinegar, olive oil, and reserved anchovy oil. Pour the oil mixture over the olives and marinate overnight. At serving time sprinkle the parsley over all. Serve as an appetizer.

Tostadas with Cheese

6 servings

Heat lard or oil in a skillet and deep-fry six tortillas until crisp and golden brown on both sides. Drain and serve hot, topped with chili con carne, grated Cheddar cheese, chopped onions, and shredded iceberg lettuce. Serve as an appetizer.

Caldo Xochitl

6 to 8 servings

6 cups Chicken Stock (page 115) or canned chicken broth
1 whole chicken breast, split in half
¼ cup vegetable oil
¼ pound very thin spaghetti, such as vermicelli or capellini
1 ripe, unblemished avocado
2 hot green chilies (optional)
Salt and freshly ground pepper to taste

1. Pour the stock into a large saucepan and add the chicken breast. Cover tightly and simmer the chicken until it is cooked and tender, twenty to thirty minutes. Remove the chicken breast and, when cool enough to handle, remove the bones and skin. Cut or shred the chicken into bite-sized pieces and set aside.

2. Meanwhile, heat the oil in a skillet. Break the spaghetti into two-inch lengths and cook it in the oil, stirring, until golden. Do not burn. Drain the spaghetti on paper towels.

3. Return the chicken stock to a boil and add the spaghetti. Simmer until the spaghetti is tender, five to ten minutes, depending on the size. Add the chicken.

4. Peel and seed the avocado and cut the flesh quickly into half-inch cubes. Add the cubes to the soup. Chop the chilies, if used, and add them. Heat thoroughly and add salt and pepper to taste. Serve in hot cups.

Sopa de Mazorca con Pollo

(Chicken and Corn Soup)

6 servings

3 pounds chicken breasts
4 cups water
1 small onion
¼ teaspoon peppercorns
  Salt
½ teaspoon coriander seeds
1 rib celery, quartered
1 medium carrot, quartered
6 ears fresh corn
2 tablespoons catsup

1. Place the chicken, water, onion, peppercorns, one teaspoon salt, the coriander seeds, celery, and carrot in a saucepan. Cover and bring to a boil. Reduce the heat and simmer for forty to fifty minutes, until the meat is tender. Remove the chicken and reserve. Strain the stock into another kettle.

2. Cut the corn off the cobs. Add the kernels to the chicken stock, cover, and cook for ten minutes. Remove the chicken from the bones, cut into strips, and add to the stock. Stir in the catsup and add salt to taste. Serve hot.

HOW TO PREPARE FRESH CHILIES:

Chilies poblanos would be a rarity in local markets. This is how they are prepared, however: Hold the whole, firm green chilies over a flame and turn them until they blister on the outside. Place them in a container and cover closely with a wet cloth. Let stand until cool. Uncover and peel the chilies by hand. Slice them, discarding the stem and seeds.

Sopa de Chilies Poblanos

(Green Chili Soup)

4 to 6 servings

1½ cups mild green chilies, prepared fresh (see note) or canned
3 tablespoons butter
2 tablespoons finely minced onion
2 tablespoons all-purpose flour
¾ cup light cream
1 cup Chicken Stock (page 115)
  Salt and freshly ground pepper to taste

1. If fresh chilies poblanos—largely unavailable in local markets—are used, prepare them according to the instructions below and place them in the container of an electric blender. If canned chilies are used, drain them and place in the blender. Blend until smooth.

2. Melt the butter in a saucepan and add the onion. Cook briefly, stirring, without browning. Stir in the flour with a whisk. When blended, add the pureed chilies, stirring with the whisk. Cook over moderate heat, stirring, about three minutes.

3. Stir in the cream and chicken stock and simmer about ten minutes, stirring frequently. Season with salt and pepper and serve hot.

Mexican Corn Soup

6 servings

3½ cups fresh corn, cut and scraped from the cob (about 8 to 12 ears, depending on the size of the ears)
¾ cup water
¼ cup butter
2 cups milk
Salt to taste
2 tablespoons canned mild green chilies (Ortega or El Paso brand), cut into cubes
1 cup cubed white "melting" cheese, such as Monterey Jack, Muenster, or Fontina Granulated sugar (optional)
6 or more tablespoons deep-fried tortilla squares (see note)

1. Use a knife or corn scraper (available in hardware stores) to cut off the kernels. After cutting, scrape the cobs for the remaining "milk."

2. Place the kernels, "milk," and water in the container of an electric blender. Blend briefly to break up the kernels, but do not overblend.

3. Put the blended mixture through a fine sieve, pressing to extract as much liquid as possible. Pour the mixture into a saucepan and add the butter. Simmer slowly five minutes, stirring well because the corn tends to stick. Add the milk and salt to taste. Bring to a boil and add the green chilies.

4. When ready to serve, add the cheese and sugar, and when the cheese is melted and the soup is piping hot, serve immediately in soup cups. Garnish each serving with the deep-fried tortilla squares.

Note: Stack six or eight tortillas on a flat surface and use a sharp knife to cut them into cubes about half an inch square. Drop the cubes into hot fat and cook, stirring with a wooden spoon, until crisp and golden.

Puree of Pumpkin and Shrimp

6 servings

2 pounds pumpkin
1 rib celery, diced
3 cups scalded milk, approximately
2 cups Chicken Stock (page 115), approximately
Salt and freshly ground black pepper
⅓ pound raw shrimp, shelled and deveined
½ teaspoon lemon juice
⅛ teaspoon freshly grated nutmeg
Lemon slices
Chopped parsley

1. Peel the pumpkin and discard the seeds and cottony center. Cut the flesh into small pieces.

2. Place the pumpkin in a heavy saucepan with the celery, milk, stock, and salt and pepper to taste. Simmer for about thirty minutes, until the pumpkin is tender.

3. Puree the mixture in an electric blender or by forcing the mixture through a food mill or sieve. Return the puree to the pan.

4. Pound the shrimp in a mortar and add the lemon juice and one-quarter cup of the puree; or puree the shrimp in the blender with one-half cup of the pumpkin mixture and the lemon juice. Add the mixture to the remaining pumpkin, bring to a boil, and simmer for ten minutes. Add the nutmeg.

5. Reheat the soup and adjust the seasoning. Adjust the consistency, if necessary, with milk or stock. Garnish with lemon slices and chopped parsley.

Note: Pumpkin goes sour quickly, so the soup should be used within twenty-four hours.

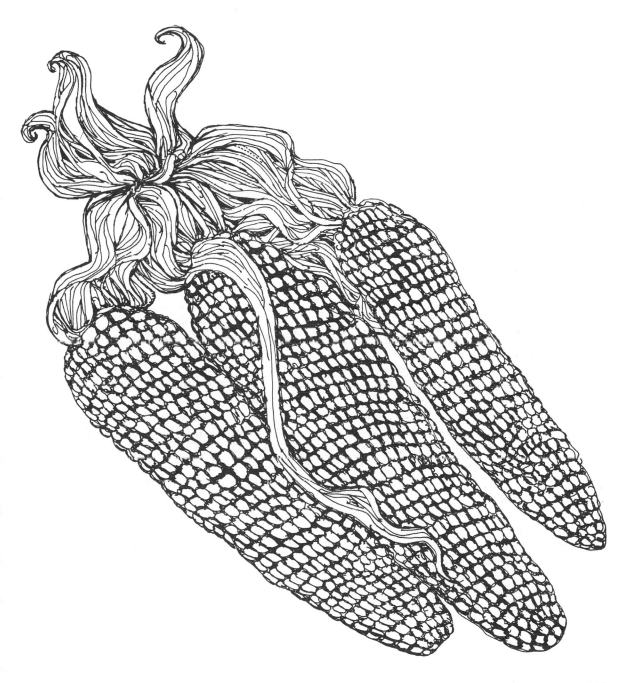

Puerco en Adobo

(Pork in Chili Sauce)

6 servings

2 pounds pork, cut into 1½-inch cubes
Salt
6 chilies anchos
6 chilies pasillas
2 sprigs fresh marjoram, if available, or 1 teaspoon dried marjoram
2 sprigs fresh thyme, if available, or 1 teaspoon dried thyme
5 whole cloves
1 1-inch piece cinnamon
6 peppercorns
6 cloves garlic, peeled
¼ small white onion
1 teaspoon cumin seeds
¼ cup vinegar
½ cup lard
3 tablespoons granulated sugar
2 bay leaves

1. Place the pork in a saucepan and add salted water to cover. Boil slowly until the meat is tender but not overcooked. Drain and save the cooking liquid.

2. Remove the seeds and veins from the chilies and add hot water to cover. Let stand fifteen minutes, then drain.

3. Grind the marjoram, thyme, cloves, cinnamon, peppercorns, garlic, onion, cumin seeds, and salt to taste. While grinding, add the vinegar to moisten. For this use a stone molcajete, mortar and pestle, or electric blender.

4. Grind the chilies separately and add them to the spices.

5. Heat the lard in a fireproof earthenware casserole or a skillet and brown the pork lightly. Drain the pork and set aside. In the same lard cook the spice and chili mixture, stirring constantly and taking care that the mixture does not burn. This should take about fifteen minutes.

6. Add the sugar and bay leaves. When the sauce is properly made, it is very thick and barely slides off the sides of a wooden spoon. At that point, add the meat and stir briefly. Add one and one-half cups of the liquid in which the pork cooked and simmer ten minutes longer. Serve with tortillas and Salsa de Tomate Verde (page 477).

Pork Chops Veracruz

6 servings

¼ cup bacon fat
1 to 2 cloves garlic, finely minced
6 thick pork chops
2 teaspoons dry mustard
Salt and freshly ground black pepper
¾ cup dry white wine
¾ cup freshly squeezed orange juice, preferably sour orange juice
1½ cups thinly sliced onions
2 green peppers, cored, seeded, and cut in strips

1. Heat the bacon fat and add the garlic. Cook, stirring, but do not brown.

2. Smear the pork chops with the mustard and sprinkle with salt and pepper. Brown on both sides in the bacon fat and add the wine and orange juice. Cook over low heat until the sauce is slightly reduced. Add the onion slices and green peppers. Cover the pan.

3. Continue cooking over low heat until the chops are tender, one to one and one-half hours. If desired, add more salt and pepper to taste. Serve hot, with rice.

Mexican Spareribs

4 to 6 servings

Salt and freshly ground black pepper
Pinch of monosodium glutamate
2 to 3 pounds spareribs, cut into individual ribs
2½ cups Salsa Fria (page 476)

1. Preheat the oven to 300 degrees.
2. Combine the salt and pepper to taste and the monosodium glutamate in a bowl. Blend well with the fingers and rub the mixture into the spareribs.
3. Place the ribs in a baking pan with a rim and bake one and one-half to two hours. Pour off the fat as it accumulates. Serve the hot ribs with salsa fria (see note).

Note: Although a salsa fria is recommended here, almost any hot barbecue sauce, perhaps one flavored with chili peppers, would be good served as a dip for the spareribs.

Cabrito Asada

(Oven-Roasted Kid)

12 servings

½ baby goat including legs, shoulder, and breast, cut into serving pieces
Salt and freshly ground pepper to taste
1 tablespoon orégano
5 cups Salsa (page 476)

1. Preheat the oven to 450 degrees.
2. Sprinkle the meat with salt and pepper and put the pieces in a large roasting pan. Do not add any fat or liquid. Cover and bake two hours, stirring the pieces occasionally.
3. Sprinkle the meat with the orégano and bake, uncovered, twenty minutes longer. Add the salsa and continue baking and basting, uncovered, twenty to thirty minutes longer.

Quail Mole

6 servings

1 cup solid vegetable shortening
12 quail, cleaned
4¼ cups Chicken Stock (page 115)
1 8½-ounce jar mole en pasta
1 cup chunky peanut butter

1. Heat the shortening in a casserole large enough to accommodate the quail. Add the quail and cook about thirty minutes (see note), stirring frequently, until the quail lose their raw color and start to brown. Cover and cook thirty minutes longer.
2. Pour one and three-quarters cups of the stock into another kettle and bring to a boil. Add the mole en pasta and peanut butter. When smooth, add all but one cup of the remaining stock. Add the quail.
3. To the casserole in which the quail cooked add the remaining cup of stock and stir to dissolve the brown particles. Add this to the quail and cover. Simmer thirty minutes longer.

Note: If the quail to be cooked are unusually tender, it may be necessary to reduce the cooking time in this recipe.

Chicken El Parador

4 servings

1 chicken (3 pounds), cut into serving pieces
¾ cup plus 6 tablespoons peanut oil or vegetable oil
2 cloves garlic, crushed
1 bay leaf, broken
1 teaspoon orégano
½ teaspoon paprika
   Salt and freshly ground black pepper
1 teaspoon monosodium glutamate
½ teaspoon finely minced garlic
2 tablespoons wine vinegar
⅛ teaspoon cayenne pepper or Tabasco
½ cup all-purpose flour
1 medium onion

1. Place the chicken parts in a large mixing bowl and add three tablespoons of the oil, the crushed garlic, bay leaf, orégano, paprika, salt and pepper to taste, and monosodium glutamate. Turn the chicken pieces in the mixture until they are well coated. Cover and refrigerate overnight. Turn the pieces occasionally.

2. Make a French dressing by combining three tablespoons of oil with the minced garlic, vinegar, cayenne pepper, and salt and pepper to taste. Beat with a fork and let stand until ready to serve.

3. Take the chicken from the refrigerator and dredge the chicken, piece by piece, in the flour seasoned with salt and pepper. All the chicken pieces should be well coated with the flour mixture.

4. Heat the remaining oil in a large skillet and add the chicken pieces, skin side down. Cook the chicken over moderately high heat until golden brown on one side, then turn and cook on the other side until golden.

5. Peel the onion and cut it into four thick slices. Add the whole slices to the skillet. Brown lightly on one side and then turn.

Cover the skillet and continue to cook for about five minutes, then pour off the fat.

6. Beat the French dressing lightly and strain it over the chicken. Cover and let stand about two minutes. Serve hot.

Chicken Mole Poblano

6 to 12 servings

½ cup toasted bread crumbs (made preferably from a toasted hard roll or end of a French loaf)
2 tablespoons sesame seeds
¼ pound almonds
3 tablespoons pepitas
¼ pound unsalted peanuts, out of the shell and without hulls
1 teaspoon anise seeds
1 small piece of chili ancho or other hot red dried chili
2 peppercorns
2 tablespoons white raisins
1 tortilla
3 tablespoons peanut oil
1 small onion, thinly sliced, about ½ cup
2 cloves garlic, peeled
2 small cans (1½ ounces each) powdered mole
1 1-pound can Italian plum tomatoes
1 1-inch length cinnamon stick
2 tablespoons powdered cocoa
4 cups chicken broth from Boiled Chicken (page 473)
   Boiled Chicken (page 473)
   Salt to taste

1. Make the bread crumbs in the container of an electric blender and set them aside in the blender.

2. Combine the sesame seeds, almonds, pepitas, peanuts, and anise seeds in a skillet. Do not add oil, but cook the seeds, shaking the skillet, until golden brown. Add to the blender.

3. Add the chili ancho, peppercorns, and raisins to the blender.

4. Cook the tortilla on both sides in the same skillet in which the nuts cooked. Do not add oil, but cook the tortilla until it is nutty and golden brown. Crumble it and add to the blender. Blend all the ingredients until well blended.

5. Heat a cured earthenware or other flameproof casserole over medium heat and add the oil. Add the onion and garlic and cook, stirring, until golden. Discard the garlic. Add the powdered mole and cook until smooth. Continue cooking, stirring, until the mixture darkens considerably, but without burning, about five minutes. Add the blender mixture and stir to blend well. Cook about five minutes, then add the tomatoes and stir to blend.

6. Add the cinnamon and cocoa and cook about ten minutes. Stir in the chicken broth and stir until smooth. Cook ten minutes, then add the chicken pieces and salt to taste. Simmer until the chicken is thoroughly hot, about twenty minutes. This dish is best if made one day in advance, refrigerated, and then reheated. Serve with black beans and rice.

BOILED CHICKEN:

8 to 12 pieces

1 stewing chicken (5 to 6 pounds), cut into serving pieces
1 onion, peeled
1 carrot, scraped and cut into quarters
½ bay leaf
1 large clove garlic, unpeeled
½ teaspoon orégano
Salt to taste
12 peppercorns

1. Combine all the ingredients in a deep saucepan and add water to cover.

2. Let simmer about one hour, or until the chicken is tender but still firm. Let the chicken sit in the cooking liquid until cool. The chicken may be chilled in its jelly overnight before using.

Escabeche of Chicken

4 servings

2 broiling chickens, split
2 tablespoons paprika
2½ teaspoons salt
½ teaspoon freshly ground black pepper
2 tablespoons vegetable oil
2 fresh hot green peppers, seeded and finely diced, or 1 4-ounce can chili peppers, diced
1 cup lime juice (about 8 limes)
1 large sweet onion, cut into rings
2 sweet red peppers, seeded and cut into rings
Fresh coriander (cilantro or Chinese parsley; optional)

1. Rub the pieces of chicken with the paprika, two teaspoons of the salt, and the pepper. Rub in the oil.

2. Place the chicken halves in a shallow ceramic or glass dish or casserole. Combine the hot peppers and one-half cup of the lime juice and pour over the chicken. Refrigerate overnight, turning once or twice.

3. Broil the chicken halves over a charcoal fire, basting and turning frequently until done.

4. Meanwhile, blanch the onion rings in boiling water for one minute. Remove and reheat the onion rings in the remaining lime juice heated with the remaining salt.

5. Preheat the oven to 350 degrees.

6. Top the cooked chicken with the onion rings and pepper rings and reheat in the oven for five minutes. Garnish with coriander, if desired.

Chilaquiles

6 servings

    1 chicken (3 pounds)
   18 two-day-old tortillas
       Fat for deep frying
    1 10-ounce can Mexican green tomatoes
    1 clove garlic, peeled
    1 onion, finely minced
    2 tablespoons fat
 1¼ cups Chicken Stock (page 115)
       Salt and freshly ground pepper
 1½ cups loosely packed, grated sharp Cheddar cheese
   ½ cup sour cream
    1 cup plus 3 tablespoons heavy cream

1. Cook the chicken in salted water to cover until tender (about one hour) and let it cool. Remove the meat from the bones. Set aside.

2. Preheat the oven to 350 degrees.

3. Cut the tortillas into small squares, one inch or less. Deep-fry them in hot fat until golden brown. Transfer the squares to absorbent toweling to drain well.

4. Pour the liquid from the tomatoes into the container of an electric blender. Remove the tough skins from the tomatoes and add the pulp to the blender. Add the garlic and blend until all is pureed.

5. Cook the onion in two tablespoons of fat until wilted. Add the pureed tomatoes, tortillas, and half a cup of the chicken stock. Season with salt and pepper. Cover and cook over low heat, without stirring, thirty minutes.

6. Pour half the sauce into an earthenware casserole. Sprinkle with one cup of cheese. Arrange the chicken over this and pour the remaining sauce over all. Blend the sour cream with the three tablespoons heavy cream. Pour this over the casserole and add the remaining cheese, cream, and chicken stock.

7. Bake thirty minutes, or until the cheese is melted and the casserole is bubbling.

Pollo con Calabacitas

(Chicken with Squash and Corn)

8 servings

    3 tablespoons lard, butter or vegetable shortening
    1 chicken (2½ pounds), cut into serving pieces
       Salt to taste
    1 teaspoon cumin seed, crushed
   ½ teaspoon coarsely ground pepper
    2 cloves garlic, finely minced
 1½ pounds zucchini, unpeeled and cut into quarter-inch slices (about 5 cups)
    1 cup finely chopped onion
 2½ cups fresh corn off the cob (scraped from about 4 ears) or 2 packages (10 ounces each) frozen corn
    2 small hot green peppers, chopped (optional)
    1 pound fresh tomatoes, peeled and cored

1. Heat the lard in a large casserole and add the chicken. Sprinkle with salt and cook until the chicken loses its raw look.

2. Add the cumin seed, coarsely ground pepper, and minced garlic, and cook, stirring occasionally, about ten minutes. Add the squash and onion. If the corn is fresh off the cob, add it. Do not add the frozen corn, if used, until later. Add the hot green peppers and tomatoes and cover. Do not add other liquid; as the mixture stews it will accumulate quite a bit of liquid. Cook one hour.

3. If frozen corn is used, add it now. In any event, uncover the casserole and cook thirty minutes longer. Serve with rice or boiled potatoes.

Pollo Estofado

8 servings

 7 cloves garlic, crushed
12 peppercorns
 5 teaspoons dried orégano
 3 tablespoons salt
 2 tablespoons vinegar
 4 broiling chickens (1½ to 2 pounds each), quartered
12 dried prunes, pitted
10 small whole onions, peeled
 4 bay leaves
12 green olives, pitted
 2 tablespoons capers
 1 tablespoon liquid from the jar of capers
½ cup white wine
¾ cup granulated sugar

1. Using a mortar and pestle, grind together the garlic, peppercorns, orégano, and salt. Add the vinegar and rub the mixture into the chicken pieces.

2. Place the chicken in a deep Dutch oven. Place the prunes, onions, bay leaves, olives, capers, and caper juice on top of the chicken. Cover and refrigerate overnight.

3. Cook over medium heat for ten minutes, then reduce the heat to low and cook for two hours. Add the wine and sugar and simmer for one hour longer.

Chilies Rellenos con Queso

(Fried Chilies Stuffed with Cheese)

6 servings

 6 large, dried chilies anchos
 6 slices Monterey Jack or mozzarella cheese, each ½ inch thick
   All-purpose flour for dredging
¼ cup vegetable oil
 3 cups Mexican Tomato Sauce (page 477)
 2 very large or 3 small eggs, separated

1. Place the anchos in a bowl and add scalding hot but not boiling water to cover. Let stand thirty minutes to one hour, or until they are soft.

2. Leave the stems on. Carefully make a slit down one side of each and remove and discard the seeds. Rinse the chilies carefully and drain. Place one slice of cheese inside each chili. Dust each chili lightly with flour.

3. Heat the oil and bring the tomato sauce to a simmer. Beat the egg yolks until thick and lemon colored. Rinse the beater well, then beat the whites until they stand in soft peaks. Fold the yolks into the whites and carefully dip each chili into the egg mixture until coated all over. Fry immediately, one at a time, in the hot oil, turning once and spooning the hot oil over the uncooked places. Cook until golden brown all over. As each stuffed chili is cooked, drop it into the simmering tomato sauce. Let cook about five minutes and serve piping hot.

Calabacitas en Crema

(Squash in Cream)

4 servings

1 pound zucchini (the smallest available)
½ pound tomatoes, peeled, seeded, and coarsely chopped
½ cup heavy cream
4 peppercorns
3 sprigs fresh coriander (cilantro or Chinese parsley)
1 sprig fresh mint, if available, or 1 teaspoon dried crushed mint
½ inch stick cinnamon
3 whole cloves
2 small fresh or canned hot green chilies, finely chopped (seed them for a milder dish)
Salt to taste

1. Preheat the oven to 350 degrees.
2. Clean and trim the squash, then slice into rounds.
3. Combine the tomatoes and squash and all the remaining ingredients except the salt in an earthenware casserole. Cover and bake 30 to 45 minutes or until the squash is tender. Sprinkle salt on top and bake five minutes longer.

Salsa

About 5 cups

⅓ cup vegetable shortening
2 cups coarsely chopped onion
1½ cups coarsely chopped green pepper
1 teaspoon cumin seed (not roasted)
1 teaspoon crushed peppercorns
3 cloves garlic, finely chopped
2 cans (1 pound each) Italian peeled tomatoes
Salt and freshly ground pepper to taste

1. Heat the shortening and add the onion, green pepper, cumin seed, peppercorns, and garlic. Cook, stirring, until the onions are slightly wilted.
2. Add the tomatoes and simmer five minutes. Season to taste with salt and pepper. Serve with Cabrito Asada (page 471).

Salsa Fria

About 2½ cups

1 no. 2 can solid-pack tomatoes
1 onion, finely chopped
1 can peeled green chilies or small hot peppers, chopped
1 teaspoon coriander, or to taste
1 clove garlic, chopped with 1 teaspoon salt
1 teaspoon crushed orégano
2 tablespoons wine vinegar
1 tablespoon olive oil
Salt and freshly ground black pepper to taste

1. Pour the tomatoes into a mixing bowl and chop fine.
2. Add the remaining ingredients and stir well. Serve cold as a dip for spareribs or as a relish for cold meats.
Note: Canned peeled tomatillo (whole green Mexican tomatoes) are recommended as an addition.

Red Chili Sauce

About 1 quart

3 tablespoons all-purpose flour
3 tablespoons chili powder, or more to taste
  Water
3 cups Mexican Tomato Sauce (below)
  Salt to taste
1 teaspoon orégano
1 clove garlic, finely minced

1. Combine the flour and chili powder in a saucepan and add enough water gradually, stirring, to make a paste. Stir in the tomato sauce and three cups of water and, when blended and smooth, add the remaining ingredients.

2. Simmer, uncovered, about two hours, stirring frequently to keep the sauce from sticking.

Mexican Tomato Sauce

About 3 cups

1 small onion, chopped, about ⅓ cup
3 cups canned Italian plum tomatoes
  Salt to taste
½ teaspoon orégano
2 tablespoons vegetable oil

1. Combine the onion, tomatoes, salt, and orégano in a blender and blend until smooth.

2. Heat the oil in a casserole and add the tomato mixture. Simmer ten minutes.

Salsa de Tomate Verde

(Green Tomato Sauce)

About 1 cup

1 8½-ounce can tomatitos verdes (green husk tomatoes)
1 small onion
1 small clove garlic, peeled
2 sprigs fresh coriander (cilantro or Chinese parsley)
1 small green chili, fresh if available and seeded if desired
  Salt, preferably rock salt, to taste

1. Open the can of tomatoes and drain, but save a little of the liquid. Set the tomatoes aside.

2. Coarsely chop the onion and combine with the garlic, coriander, chili, and salt. It is best to pulverize the mixture in a stone molcajete, if available; otherwise use a blender.

3. Add the tomatoes and continue pulverizing until well blended. Add two or three tablespoons of the reserved juice to thin the sauce to the desired consistency. This sauce may be made in advance, but it will have to be thinned before serving, since it becomes like a thin jelly on standing. Serve as a dip or spoon onto Mexican dishes for added piquancy.

Tomato and Green Chili Sauce

About 3 cups

6 medium red, ripe tomatoes
½ cup or more thinly sliced or diced canned California green chilies, seeds and pith removed
⅓ cup minced onion
1 teaspoon salt
  Minced canned jalapeno chilies (or other hot chilies) to taste

1. Peel and finely chop the tomatoes.
2. Combine the tomatoes with the California green chilies, onion, salt, and as many jalapeno chilies as suit your taste. One jalapeno to each cup of sauce will be amply hot for most palates.

Onion Relish

4 to 6 servings

3 medium onions, thinly sliced
1 green pepper, seeded, cored, and thinly sliced
1 tomato, peeled and thinly sliced
1 cucumber, peeled, seeded, and thinly sliced
  Tabasco to taste
3 teaspoons granulated sugar
  Juice of 1 lemon
½ cup wine vinegar
2 tablespoons salad oil

Combine all the ingredients and chill until ready to serve.

Chalupas

About 16 chalupas

2 cups masa harina
1⅓ cups warm meat or poultry broth
⅓ cup lard or other shortening
1 teaspoon salt
  Vegetable oil or lard for deep frying
2 cups shredded, cooked chicken
1 to 2 cups Tomato and Green Chili Sauce (see above)
12 tablespoons grated Romano cheese

1. Combine the masa harina with warm broth until the dough holds together.
2. Whip the lard until fluffy and beat in the masa mixture and salt. Cover with a damp cloth and keep cool until ready to use.
3. For each chalupa pat two tablespoons of the dough into an oval-shaped cake about four inches long. Bake this on a medium-hot, ungreased griddle or in a skillet over medium heat until the masa begins to lose its doughy look. Remove the cake from the griddle and let cool until you can touch it. Then pinch in the edges with fingers to make a rim. Deep fry in hot oil until lightly browned. Do not turn, but ladle hot fat onto the cakes as they cook. Drain on paper towels.
4. Cover each cake with about two tablespoons of the shredded chicken and top with one or two tablespoons of sauce. Sprinkle each with about two teaspoons of cheese.

Chongos

(A Mexican Custard)

12 or more servings

8 cups milk
4 rennet tablets
3 tablespoons water
¾ cup granulated sugar
3 tablespoons vanilla extract

1. Heat the milk until it registers exactly 110 degrees on a thermometer.
2. Crush the rennet tablets in the water and add to the milk. Let the mixture set for one hour, or until it has the consistency of custard. Cut it into squares.
3. Very carefully transfer the squares to a cooking pan and add the liquid that may have accumulated. Do not add other liquid. Add the sugar and vanilla. Let the squares simmer over very low heat, being careful not to burn, for six hours, until the milk turns a golden color.

According to some sources in the liquor industry, that strangely appealing Mexican import called tequila is the fastest growing white spirit from the standpoint of sales in America. No one predicts that it will ever equal or surpass vodka and gin in popularity, but imports have gone up nearly 400 percent in the last five years. Tequila, made from the mescal cactus, may have been the first liquor ever distilled in the Americas. Below are recipes for the most popular cocktail made with tequila, the margharita, as well as for a sangrita and a tequila sour. Instructions for drinking tequila Mexican-style are also given.

Sangrita

1 serving

3 ounces tomato juice
1 teaspoon grenadine syrup (or less, to taste)
Juice of ½ lime or lemon
1 ounce orange juice
Salt
Tabasco (see note)
1½ ounces tequila
Lime wedge

1. Combine the tomato juice, grenadine, lime and orange juices, and salt and Tabasco to taste. Add ice cubes and shake rapidly.
2. Strain the mixture into a glass and serve the tequila on the side. It is drunk in Mexico by sipping the tomato mixture alternately with the tequila. Many non-Mexicans prefer to add the tequila to the tomato mixture before shaking the cocktail. Serve with the lime wedge and additional salt.

Note: Tabasco sauce is a Yankee addition to this recipe. In Mexico, small, hot, chopped green serrano chilies are used as the fiery seasoning. A genuine sangrita is highly spiced.

Margharita

1 serving

1½ ounces tequila
  1 to 1½ ounces Cointreau or Triple Sec,
    depending on sweetness desired
  Juice of ½ lime or lemon
  Kosher salt

Combine the tequila, Cointreau, and lime
juice. Add ice cubes and shake rapidly. Rub
the rim of a small cocktail glass with the
squeezed lime half, then dip the rim into a
saucer of salt. Strain the mixture into the
prepared glass and serve.

Tequila, Mexican Style

1 serving

Pour one ounce or so of tequila into a
small glass to fill it. (In Mexico, tequila
glasses are generally cylindrical and have
more height than width.) Serve with a wedge
of lime and salt on the side. The procedure
is first to bite the lime, then place a dip of
salt on the tongue, then take a swallow of
tequila. Sometimes the tequila is consumed
with one gulp.

Tequila Sour

1 serving

1½ ounces tequila
  Juice of ½ lemon or lime
  1 teaspoon to 1 tablespoon granulated
    sugar, depending on sweetness desired

Combine the tequila, lemon juice, and
sugar in a cocktail shaker. Add several cubes
of ice and shake well. Strain into a cocktail
glass.

Mexican corn sou

Morocco

Pastels

40 pastels

20 sheets phyllo pastry, approximately
1 pound beef, ground
1 cup water
½ cup chopped parsley
   Salt and freshly ground pepper to taste
   Vegetable oil for frying

1. Cut the sheets of pastry in half. Stack them, cover with a cloth and set aside.

2. Place the beef in a skillet and add the water, parsley, salt, and pepper. Cook, stirring and breaking up any lumps with a large kitchen spoon. Cook until all the liquid is absorbed, then cool.

3. Fold each piece of pastry in half, then fold once more to make a rectangle. Make one pastel at a time. Shape the meat mixture into small balls and place one ball at the end of a rectangle. Fold the end of the rectangle over, triangular fashion, then fold the pastry over and over itself, tucking in the last fold of pastry. Continue until all the pastry rectangles and meat balls are used.

4. Heat about one-half inch of oil in a skillet and fry the pastels until crisp and golden brown all over. Serve as an appetizer.

Moroccan Carrot Appetizer

6 servings

2 carrots, trimmed and scraped
¼ cup olive oil, or to taste
1 tablespoon vinegar, or to taste
1 clove garlic, finely chopped
   Salt and freshly ground pepper to taste

1. Scrape the carrots on the coarse blade of a grater. Place in a mixing bowl and add the remaining ingredients.

2. Cover and refrigerate until thoroughly chilled.

Middle Eastern medley. Clockwise from left: raw kibbee, tabbouleh garnished with mato wedges, laban (all from Syria), and stuffed grape leaves from Greece

El Harirah

8 to 10 servings

½ cup barley
⅓ cup lentils
⅓ cup split peas
2 pounds shin of beef (meat and bones)
3 tablespoons vegetable oil
3 cups chopped onion
1 cup chopped celery
1 cup chopped carrot
1 tablespoon ground turmeric
10 cups Beef Stock (page 115) or water
Salt and freshly ground pepper
½ cup uncooked rice
1 cup canned, drained chick-peas
1½ tablespoons all-purpose flour
1 egg, lightly beaten
Lemon juice or vinegar to taste
¼ cup chopped fresh coriander (cilantro or Chinese parsley)

1. Place the barley in a mixing bowl and add water to cover. Soak overnight. If package directions indicate it, soak the lentils and split peas overnight.

2. Cut the meat from the bones of the shin of beef. Cut the meat into small cubes. Reserve the bones.

3. In a kettle, heat the oil and add the onion, celery, and carrot. Cook, stirring, until the vegetables give up most of their moisture. Add the meat and continue to cook, stirring frequently, until the mixture browns. Sprinkle with the turmeric and add the bones. Stir in the beef stock or water and add salt and pepper to taste. Bring to a boil, partly cover, and simmer, skimming the surface to remove foam and fat. Simmer, stirring occasionally, about one hour.

4. Drain and add the barley, lentils, and split peas and simmer fifteen minutes. Add the rice and chick-peas and cook thirty minutes longer.

5. Place the flour in a small mixing bowl and blend with a little of the soup. Return this to the kettle, stirring. Beat the egg with a little soup liquid and add it. Bring just to a boil, but do not boil. Add the lemon juice and coriander and serve in hot plates.

Note: If this soup stands, it will become thick. Therefore, if it is to be served later, it will be necessary to thin it with more beef stock.

Striped Bass, Moroccan Style

8 or more servings

1 striped bass (5 to 6 pounds)
Salt
½ cup vegetable oil
3 tablespoons crushed cumin seed
1 tablespoon paprika
1 clove garlic, finely minced
½ cup chopped parsley
Freshly ground pepper to taste
1 lemon, thinly sliced and seeded

1. Preheat the oven to 350 degrees.

2. Rub the fish generously inside and out with salt and let stand fifteen minutes.

3. Rinse the fish thoroughly.

4. Combine the oil, cumin seed, paprika, garlic, parsley, and pepper and salt to taste.

5. Lay the fish on a sheet of heavy-duty aluminum foil, large enough to enclose the fish. Rub the fish inside and out with the oil mixture and wrap tightly in the foil. Bake the fish for one and one-half hours, or until the fish is tender when tested with a fork. Open the foil during the last fifteen minutes of baking.

6. Garnish with lemon slices and serve.

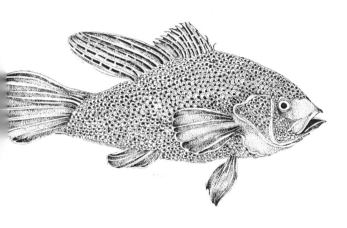

Lamb Marrakech

6 servings

1 cup white raisins
   Dry sherry
½ cup vegetable oil
3 pounds lean lamb shoulder, cut into 1½-inch cubes
2 large onions, finely chopped
3 cloves garlic, finely chopped
   Salt and freshly ground pepper to taste
   Red pepper flakes to taste
1 teaspoon ground turmeric
3 large, ripe tomatoes, peeled and chopped, or 3 cups Italian peeled tomatoes
1 cup Chicken Stock (page 115), approximately
1 cup toasted almonds (optional)
   French-fried onion rings (optional)

1. Soak the raisins in sherry to cover fifteen minutes or longer.

2. Heat the oil in a skillet. Brown the meat in the oil, then transfer it to a Dutch oven. Add the onions and garlic to the skillet and cook, stirring, until the onions are wilted. Add the onions to the meat. Add salt, pepper, red pepper flakes, and the turmeric and stir. Add the raisins, tomatoes, and enough chicken stock to cover. Bring to a boil, then cover and simmer one and one-half hours, adding more stock, if necessary. Serve garnished, if desired, with almonds and fried onion rings.

Fish au Citron

4 to 6 servings

1 porgy (3 to 4 pounds), cleaned
   Salt
¼ cup vegetable oil
1 cup water
1 tablespoon Saffron Water (page 490)
2 cloves garlic, finely minced
3 lemons, peeled, cut into thin rounds, and seeds removed

1. Cut the fish into one-inch steaks like salmon steaks or have this done at the fish market. Sprinkle the pieces of fish liberally with salt and set aside. Let stand one hour.

2. In a skillet combine the oil, water, saffron water, and garlic. Arrange the pieces of fish over all and cover with lemon slices. Cover and cook over gentle heat forty-five minutes to an hour.

Mussala

4 servings

3 tamarind pods or 1 teaspoon vinegar
1 onion, finely chopped
2 cloves garlic, finely minced
2 fresh or pickled small hot green peppers, seeded and finely chopped
6 slices green ginger
1 tablespoon ground coriander
1 teaspoon ground turmeric
½ teaspoon ground cumin
1 teaspoon ground poppy seed
½ teaspoon ground hot red chilies
¼ cup grated fresh coconut
¼ cup clarified butter (see note page 174)
1 pound lamb or beef, cut into 1-inch cubes, or 1 chicken (2½ pounds), cut into serving pieces
Salt to taste

1. Place the tamarind pods in a small saucepan and add water barely to cover. Bring to a boil and let cool. Remove and discard the seeds. Put the pulp through a sieve and set aside.

2. Combine the onion, garlic, hot green peppers, and ginger in a mortar and grind with a pestle or chop everything together. Place the mixture in a mixing bowl and set aside.

3. Combine the coriander, turmeric, cumin, and poppy seeds. Add the ground red chilies and the coconut. Stir in the tamarind pulp or vinegar and blend well to make a paste.

4. Heat the butter in a small frying pan and cook the paste briefly, about three minutes. Add the onion and garlic mixture and continue cooking and stirring about four minutes. Add the meat and cook, stirring, until the meat loses its red color or the chicken flesh turns white. Cook about five minutes and add salt to taste. Cover and cook over low heat until the meat is tender, adding a little liquid if necessary to prevent burning. Total cooking time should range from about thirty minutes to an hour, depending on the quality of the meat.

Les Truffes au Mouton
(Moroccan Truffles with Mutton)

6 or more servings

1 pound boned shin of mutton or lamb
  Salt to taste
¼ cup vegetable oil
1 cup water
1 clove garlic, chopped
2 tablespoons Saffron Water (page 490)
  Freshly ground pepper
1 14-ounce can white Moroccan truffles

1. Place the shin of mutton in a saucepan and add water to cover. Add salt and simmer for one hour, or until the mutton is fork tender. Set aside.
2. In a skillet heat the oil, water, garlic, saffron water, and salt and pepper to taste and bring to a boil. Simmer about three minutes.
3. Drain the meat and cut into bite-sized pieces, then add to the skillet. Drain the truffles and add them. Cover and simmer about fifteen minutes.

Veau aux Amandes
(Veal with Almonds)

8 to 12 servings

4 pounds boneless veal shoulder
2 cloves garlic, cut into thin slivers
1¼ cups vegetable oil
1 teaspoon paprika
1 teaspoon freshly ground black pepper
1 tablespoon orégano
  Salt to taste
  Juice of 2 lemons
1 pound dried prunes
2 cups water
½ cup brown sugar
1 cup blanched almonds (see below)

1. Using a small pick or a knife, make several insertions in the veal shoulder. Stick small slivers of garlic in the insertions.
2. Place the veal in a utensil with a cover and add one-quarter cup of the oil, the paprika, pepper, orégano, salt, and lemon juice. Cover and refrigerate overnight.
3. Preheat the oven to 400 degrees.
4. Transfer the veal to a baking dish and add the marinade. Cover with foil and place the veal in the oven. Bake one hour, then remove the foil and continue baking, basting occasionally, until the veal is tender, about one hour longer.
5. Meanwhile, place the prunes in a saucepan and add the water, brown sugar, and one-quarter cup oil. Bring to a boil and simmer, covered, half an hour, or until the prunes are tender. Keep warm.
6. Before the meat is done, heat the remaining three-quarters cup oil in a skillet and add the almonds. Cook, stirring, until they are golden brown. Drain on absorbent paper.
7. Slice the meat, put on a platter, and keep hot. Drain the prunes, arrange on a platter, and scatter the almonds over them. Serve the meat with the prunes and almonds as an accompaniment.

HOW TO BLANCH ALMONDS:
Drop the shelled almonds (with their brown skin) into boiling water to cover and boil exactly one minute. Drain. Press the almonds between the fingers until the almonds slip out of their skin. Pat dry.

Sweet Meat Balls for Couscous

6 to 8 servings

1½ pounds ground lean meat
1 small onion, peeled and grated
2 tablespoons chopped parsley
1 egg, lightly beaten
½ cup matzoh meal or bread crumbs
½ cup tomato juice
   Salt and freshly ground pepper to taste
¼ cup vegetable oil
6 onions, thinly sliced
1 quart water
½ cup raisins, soaked in warm water until plumped
8 dried prunes, soaked in warm water until softened
1 cup blanched almonds
1 pound peeled, prepared fresh pumpkin, if available, cut into 2-inch pieces
½ to 1 cup brown sugar, depending on sweetness desired
1 teaspoon ground cinnamon

1. Preheat the oven to 350 degrees.
2. Place the meat in a mixing bowl and add the grated onion, parsley, egg, and matzoh meal. Blend, then add the tomato juice, salt, and pepper. Knead until smooth. Add one tablespoon of the oil and knead again. Shape into small balls.
3. Cook the onions in the remaining oil until tender and brown. Add the water and bring to a boil. Add salt to taste. Drop the meat balls, one at a time, into the simmering liquid; simmer until firm.
4. Pour the meat balls and broth into a baking dish and add the drained raisins and prunes. Add the almonds and pumpkin. Sprinkle with the brown sugar and cinnamon and bake until golden brown and all the liquid disappears.

Chicken with Almonds

10 to 12 servings

5 chickens (3 to 3½ pounds each), cut into serving pieces
   Salt
10 cloves garlic, crushed
2 tablespoons ground ginger
1 to 2 teaspoons black pepper
1 tablespoon ground turmeric
¼ cup water
½ cup salad oil
5 onions, quartered
1 cup loosely packed parsley leaves
1 cup loosely packed fresh coriander leaves (optional)
2 onions, sliced
2 pounds shelled, unblanched almonds
3 cinnamon sticks
½ cup butter
½ teaspoon whole saffron, crushed

1. Rinse the chicken pieces thoroughly and pat dry. Remove and discard all evidence of chicken fat, but leave the skin on. Place the chicken in a bowl and add three tablespoons of salt, the garlic, ginger, black pepper, turmeric, water, and salad oil. Blend thoroughly, turning the pieces over and over with the hands until well coated. Cover and refrigerate overnight.
2. Place the quartered onions, a few at a time, in the container of an electric blender and add the parsley and coriander. Blend until all the onions are pureed.
3. Place the chicken in a large roasting pan or baking dish and add the onion mixture, salt to taste and sliced onions. Add water to barely cover and cover closely. Bring to a boil.
4. Meanwhile, cover the almonds with water and bring to a boil. Simmer two minutes, or until the skins slip easily off the almonds. Drain the almonds and slip off the skins with the fingers. Add the almonds, cinnamon sticks, and butter to the chicken.

Soak the saffron in a little warm water and add. Simmer everything until the chicken is thoroughly tender.

5. Remove the chicken pieces to a warm place and cook the sauce quickly over high heat, stirring often, until the sauce is reduced to a thick gravy. Return the chicken to the pot and reheat. Before serving, remove the cinnamon sticks.

Couscous may not be as refined as one of the great classics of the French cuisine, but it is one of the ultimate treats of the world—for those who dote on it, at least. Couscous, a semolina-like cereal, is the base for the dish, also called couscous, which consists of a bowl of the cereal accompanied by a stew of lamb or chicken. Here are three recipes picked up recently in Morocco, where couscous is, more or less, the national dish.

Couscous I

8 to 12 servings

1 pound couscous (cracked wheat)
1 breast of beef (3 to 4 pounds)
  Cracked soup bones
4 carrots, scraped and left whole
6 onions, peeled
6 ribs celery, trimmed and left whole
6 or more small turnips, peeled and left whole, or one small rutabaga (yellow turnip), peeled and cut into 2-inch cubes
½ pound washed Swiss chard (optional)
6 sprigs parsley
4 quarts water
  Salt and freshly ground pepper to taste
1 can chick-peas, drained

1. Place the couscous in a basin and add cold water to cover. Stir and drain.

2. Place the meat, bones, carrots, onions, celery, turnips, chard, parsley, water, salt, and pepper in the bottom of a couscous cooker or other steaming utensil (a colander over a kettle is good) and bring to a boil. Simmer, skimming the surface as necessary, about thirty minutes.

3. Work the couscous with the fingers to break up the lumps. Moisten it with stock from the boiling meat, then spoon the cereal into the top of the steamer or colander (lined with cheesecloth, if necessary). Place the couscous over the boiling meat and vegetables. Cover closely and steam one hour.

4. Pour the couscous back into the basin. Add more broth to moisten, then return the couscous to the steamer and cover closely. Add the chick-peas to the meat and vegetables in the bottom of the steamer. Steam once more for one hour. Serve the couscous moistened with a little of the soup stock and the vegetables. The meat may be served immediately or later. Or serve the couscous, if desired, with Sweet Meat Balls for Couscous (page 486).

Couscous II

6 servings

¾ cup butter, at room temperature
4 pounds very lean leg of lamb, cut into 1½- to 2-inch cubes
Salt to taste
1 teaspoon grated fresh ginger or ½ teaspoon ground ginger
Freshly grated black pepper to taste
1 teaspoon crumbled stem saffron or more to taste
¼ teaspoon ground cinnamon
3 cloves
¼ teaspoon nutmeg
7 cups water or lamb broth (see note)
1 pound couscous
1½ pounds onions, peeled and cut into inch-thick slices
5 white turnips (about 1 pound), peeled and halved or quartered, depending on size
3 carrots, scraped and quartered
3 medium zucchini, trimmed and cut into 1-inch lengths
½ cup raisins
1 cup cooked fresh or canned chick-peas
½ cup blanched almonds

1. It is best to use a specially made couscous cooker (couscoussière), although one may be improvised by placing a steamer with a perforated bottom or a colander over a kettle. The steamer must be close fitting, however.

2. Melt one-half cup of the butter in a kettle and add the meat, salt, ginger, pepper, saffron, cinnamon, cloves, and nutmeg. Turn the meat in the mixture without browning. Add the water or lamb broth and bring to a boil. Do not add the steamer, but cover the kettle and bring to a boil. Simmer about one hour (this time may have to be decreased if the meat is unusually tender).

3. Meanwhile, line a colander with cheesecloth and add the couscous. Run cold water over the couscous until it is thoroughly dampened and let stand about thirty minutes.

4. Line the steamer with cheesecloth. Crumble the couscous with the fingers to get rid of any lumps. Pour the couscous into the cheesecloth-lined steamer and place over the boiling stew. Do not cover. Let steam fifteen minutes.

5. Remove the steamer and set it aside. Combine one-quarter cup of water with salt to taste. Sprinkle this over the couscous and let stand.

6. Meanwhile, add the onions, turnips, carrots, zucchini, raisins, and chick-peas to the stew. Cover and cook fifteen minutes.

7. Stir the couscous once more to break up any lumps. Return the steamer to the kettle and continue to steam fifteen minutes longer.

8. The couscous is now ready to be served. Empty the cereal into a large, hot bowl and stir in the remaining one-quarter cup butter. Arrange the meat, vegetables, and raisins over the couscous, but do not add the liquid. Garnish with almonds. Serve the hot broth and Hot Pepper Sauce (see below) separately. Of course, you may, if you wish, serve the couscous in individual hot soup bowls and garnish with the meat and so on.

Note: Lamb broth may be made by placing a few meaty lamb bones in a kettle and adding eight cups of water and salt to taste. Simmer, covered, about one hour.

HOT PEPPER SAUCE:

About 6 tablespoons

12 dried hot red pepper pods
Salt to taste
3 tablespoons olive oil
1 tablespoon boiling water

1. Place the pepper pods in a saucepan and add water to cover. Bring to a boil and set aside. Let stand until the water is cold.

2. Drain the pepper pods and split them in half. Remove and discard the seeds. Place the pods, skin side down, on a flat surface and scrape off and accumulate the pulp in a small mixing bowl.

3. Add salt to taste and gradually beat in the oil with a wire whisk. Finally beat in the boiling water.

Couscous III

10 to 12 servings

4 cups small-grain couscous (cracked wheat)
1 pound lamb, such as neck, shoulder, breast, or shank, cut into large cubes
2 large onions, thinly sliced
1 tablespoon ground ginger
1 tablespoon ground turmeric
2 teaspoons black pepper
  Cayenne pepper to taste
¾ cup salad oil
¾ cup butter, at room temperature
  Salt to taste
¼ teaspoon whole saffron, crushed
3 large, tender carrots, scraped and quartered
4 white turnips, peeled and quartered
3 potatoes, peeled and quartered
3 zucchini, unpeeled, quartered
1 20-ounce can chick-peas with liquid
1 cup seedless raisins

1. Place the couscous in a large bowl and add about two cups of cold water. There should be just enough water to moisten the couscous thoroughly without making it soupy. Let the couscous stand one hour, mixing it with the hands occasionally to break up lumps that may form.

2. A specially made couscous cooker is ideal for this dish, but a colander snugly fitted into a kettle may be improvised. To the bottom section of the couscous cooker or to the kettle add the lamb, onions, ginger, turmeric, black pepper, cayenne, one-half cup of the oil, one-quarter cup of the butter, and salt. Soak the saffron briefly in a little warm water and add it. Add about two quarts of water. The level of the water should be about two inches above the level of the other ingredients. Place the steamer (or colander, if the kettle is used) on top of the couscous cooker and bring to a boil.

3. Using the hands, mix the couscous once more to break up any lumps. Line the steamer with cheesecloth and add the couscous. Cover and cook one hour, making sure that the couscous is steaming properly.

4. Remove the steamer and run cold water over the couscous for three minutes. Set aside to drain.

5. To the stew in the bottom of the couscous cooker, add the carrots, turnips, and potatoes and cook, covered, twenty minutes.

6. Pour the couscous into a large bowl and add the remaining oil and salt to taste. Mix thoroughly by hand until all the grains are coated. Return the couscous to the steamer or colander.

7. Add the zucchini, chick-peas, and raisins to the stew. Place the steamer or colander on top once more and continue cooking and steaming twenty minutes.

8. Pour the couscous into a warm bowl and add the remaining butter. While piping hot, stir with a kitchen spoon until well blended. To serve, heap the couscous onto a hot, shallow, round platter, make a well in the center, and fill with the drained vegetables. The lamb pieces may be removed and discarded or served separately.

Artichokes à l'Orange

6 to 8 servings

Juice of 2 lemons
15 small artichokes
1½ cups water
⅓ cup vegetable oil
2 tablespoons Saffron Water (below)
1 teaspoon salt
3 oranges, cut into ½-inch-thick slices, seeds removed

1. Place the lemon juice in a glass mixing bowl and add enough water to cover the artichoke bottoms when they are prepared. This is to keep the bottoms from discoloring.
2. Cut off the bottom stem of the artichoke. Cut off the upper quarter of the artichoke leaves, holding the knife parallel to the artichoke bottom. Carefully trim around the perimeter of the artichoke bottom. Using a silver spoon or a melon ball cutter, carefully scrape out the fuzz or "choke" in the center of each bottom. As the bottoms are prepared, drop them into the prepared lemon water. Let stand.
3. Heat the one and one-half cups water and the oil in a skillet and add the saffron water. Add the artichoke bottoms and the salt. Cover and simmer fifteen minutes.
4. Arrange the orange slices over all and cover again. Simmer forty-five minutes to one hour.

Hot Herb and Tomato Relish

About 4 cups

2 cups unpeeled, cored, cubed tomatoes
¼ cup finely chopped parsley
1 green pepper, cored, seeded, and coarsely chopped
1 cup chopped heart of celery
¼ cup drained capers
¼ Preserved Lemon (page 491), rinsed well and chopped (optional)
6 or more bottled hot Italian peppers (peperoncini) and/or chopped cherry peppers
Salt and freshly ground pepper to taste
Juice of ½ lemon
⅓ cup vegetable oil

Combine all the ingredients in a mixing bowl and blend gently. Refrigerate until ready to serve.

Saffron Water

½ cup

1 teaspoon ground saffron (if whole saffron is used, chop it to make 1 teaspoonful)
½ cup cold water

Combine the saffron and water in a small jar with a screw top. Keep covered in the refrigerator and use as needed.

Chicken with Lemon

4 to 6 servings

1 chicken (3 pounds), cut into serving
  pieces
1 pickled lemon (see below)
2 cloves garlic, finely chopped
3 tablespoons salad oil
1 teaspoon ground ginger
1 teaspoon turmeric
¼ teaspoon black pepper
  Salt
½ pound onions, sliced
¼ cup parsley leaves
¼ cup coriander leaves
 3 tablespoons butter
¼ teaspoon leaf saffron, crushed
 1 cup ripe Moroccan olives (see note)

1. Rinse the chicken pieces well in cold water and pat dry. Remove and discard all fat but leave the skin on. Place the chicken in a bowl.

2. Remove the pulp from the pickled lemon and rinse it briefly in cold water. Add it to the chicken. Rinse off the lemon peel. Add half the peel to the chicken and save the remaining half.

3. Add the garlic, one tablespoon cold water, the oil, ginger, turmeric, pepper and salt to taste. Blend well, turning pieces of chicken until coated. Cover and refrigerate overnight.

4. Place the onions, parsley and coriander in the container of an electric blender. Blend until pureed.

5. Arrange the chicken pieces in a flame-proof casserole. Add the onion mixture, salt to taste, water to barely cover and the butter. Soak the saffron in a little warm water and add it. Cover, bring to a boil and simmer about one hour, or until the chicken is very tender.

6. Remove the chicken to a warm dish and keep covered. Add the olives and reserved lemon peel to the casserole and cook the sauce quickly over high heat, stirring often, until reduced to a thick gravy. Return the chicken to the pan and reheat.

Note: If Moroccan olives are not available, you may substitute the large black Alfonso olives of Spain or the red-brown Kalamatas or green-brown Royal Victorias of Greece. California olives do not work well in this dish.

Pickled Lemons

*(Must be made
two weeks in advance)*

About 1 quart

6 to 10 lemons
  Salt

1. Set each lemon, one at a time, on the flat, stem end. Using a sharp stainless steel knife, cut straight down through the center of each lemon to about half an inch of the base.

2. Leave each sliced lemon on its base, but give it a quarter turn. Slice down once more to within half an inch of the base. Continue until all the lemons are prepared.

3. Make a quarter-inch layer of salt in a sterile quart Mason jar.

4. Pack the inside of each lemon with salt. As each lemon is prepared add it to the jar, pushing down. Make a layer of lemons, then a layer of salt, pressing down lightly on the lemons to make sure they are snug. They will, of course, give up much of their juices as they are pressed. Continue until the jar is packed full. Press down and fill the jar to the top with juice. Make certain that a little air space is left when the jar is sealed. Let stand in a not too warm place for at least two weeks until lemons are firm but tender.

Note: Always rinse before using. After the jar is opened, refrigerate. These lemons may also be used with baked fish dishes, in salads, and in marinades.

Norway

Red Caviar Dip

8 to 12 servings

1 3-ounce package cream cheese
1 tablespoon sour cream
1 tablespoon chopped chives or green onion
   tops
1 4-ounce jar red caviar

Blend the cream cheese, sour cream, and chopped chives together. Mix in the caviar, blending everything well together with a fork. Chill at least two hours before serving.

Note: This mixture can be used as a dip or spread on crackers. When it is first made it is fairly runny, but will stiffen up in the refrigerator. If used as a spread on crackers, do not prepare them ahead of time because the crackers will become soggy.

Leverpostej

(Homemade Pâté)

12 servings

2 tablespoons chopped shallots
¼ cup butter
½ pound chicken livers
3 tablespoons warm brandy
2 tablespoons heavy cream
   Pinch of dried tarragon
   Salt and freshly ground pepper to taste

1. Cook the shallots in one tablespoon of the butter until soft, then remove the shallots from the pan. Add the remaining butter and sauté the chicken livers over a hot fire for four or five minutes. Do not overcook.

2. Pour the brandy over the livers and ignite. Remove the pan from the heat and add the shallots to the livers. Add the cream, tarragon, salt, and pepper. Pour the mixture, in small quantities, into a blender and blend until smooth and creamy. Pour the mixture into a jar or bowl and chill at least four hours before serving as an appetizer.

Norwegian Meat Balls in Cream

6 servings

1 pound round steak, ground
½ pound pork, ground
1 egg, lightly beaten
½ cup mashed potatoes
½ cup dry bread crumbs
½ cup milk
2 teaspoons salt
¼ teaspoon each ground cloves, allspice, ginger, freshly ground black pepper, and nutmeg
½ teaspoon brown sugar
   All-purpose flour
2 tablespoons peanut oil
2 tablespoons butter
1 cup heavy cream

1. Preheat the oven to 325 degrees.
2. Combine the meats, egg, potatoes, bread crumbs, milk, salt, spices, and brown sugar. Blend well and shape into twenty-four meat balls. Roll the balls in flour.
3. Heat the oil and butter and brown the balls on all sides. Spoon the balls into an ovenproof casserole and pour the cream over. Set the casserole in a pan and pour boiling water around the casserole. Cover and bake forty minutes.

Norwegian Veal Chops

6 servings

6 veal chops, each about ½ inch thick
¼ cup butter
1 cup Chicken Stock (page 115)
6 tablespoons chopped onion
6 slices of nøkkelost (Norwegian spiced cheese)
6 tablespoons sour cream

1. Preheat the oven to 400 degrees.
2. Brown the chops on both sides in the butter, then remove to a warm plate. Add the stock to the skillet and stir to dissolve any brown particles around the bottom and sides of the pan. Return the chops to the skillet.
3. Spoon one tablespoon of chopped onion onto each chop. Cover each with a slice of cheese and top with one tablespoon of sour cream.
4. Bake the chops for about thirty minutes. Serve hot, with the pan gravy.

Kalvekarbonader

(Veal Patties)

About 12 patties

2 eggs
1¼ cups light cream or milk
8 zweiback
2 tablespoons finely chopped parsley
1 teaspoon salt
½ teaspoon freshly ground pepper
1 teaspoon freshly grated nutmeg
1 pound veal plus ¼ pound fresh pork, ground together twice
¼ cup butter
   Water or Beef Stock (page 115)

1. Beat the eggs and cream together slightly.
2. Crush or grind the zweiback into fine crumbs and add to the cream. Add the parsley, salt, pepper, and nutmeg. Blend well.
3. Gradually add the zweiback mixture to the meat. Form the meat mixture into round cakes two inches in diameter. Cook in the butter over fairly low heat until the cakes are cooked through, about ten minutes, turning once. Add a little water or stock to the skillet and simmer to make a light sauce.

Cauliflower with Shrimp and Dill Sauce

6 servings

1 large head cauliflower, trimmed
1½ tablespoons butter
1½ tablespoons all-purpose flour
1 teaspoon paprika
¼ cup liquid in which the shrimp cooked
¼ cup milk
½ cup heavy cream
   Salt and freshly ground pepper to taste
   Tabasco to taste
1 teaspoon lemon juice
1 cup shrimp, cooked, shelled, and deveined
1 tablespoon finely chopped fresh dill or parsley

1. Cook the cauliflower until tender either by steaming or by simmering in salted water. Do not overcook.

2. While the cauliflower cooks, make the sauce. Heat the butter in a saucepan and stir in the flour and paprika. When blended, add the shrimp liquid and milk, stirring vigorously with a whisk. Stir in the cream, salt and pepper, Tabasco, and lemon juice. Add the cooked shrimp and bring to a boil.

3. Drain the cauliflower. Pour the sauce over it and sprinkle with the dill or parsley.

Peru

Bistec a la Caserola

4 servings

4 hip steaks or shell steaks, each ½ to 1 inch thick
3 tablespoons white vinegar
Salt and freshly ground pepper to taste
½ to 1 teaspoon ground cumin
2 cloves garlic, finely minced
2 tablespoons butter
2 tablespoons vegetable oil
2 large onions, coarsely chopped
1 large, red, ripe tomato, peeled and chopped
½ cup coarsely chopped fresh coriander leaves (cilantro or Chinese parsley)
1 large green pepper (hot, if available), cored, seeded and cut into strips
Beef Stock (page 115) or other stock (optional)

1. Place the steaks in a dish and add the vinegar, salt, pepper, cumin, and garlic. Let stand, turning occasionally, at least three hours.

2. Heat the butter and oil in a large, oven-proof skillet and sear the steaks on each side. Sprinkle with the onions, tomato, coriander, and green pepper. Add salt and pepper to taste.

3. Cover and cook over low heat on top of the stove or in a 400-degree oven about forty minutes, basting occasionally, reducing the heat as necessary. If the meat becomes too dry, add a little beef stock or other stock. Serve with hot, fluffy rice.

Potatoes a la Huancaina

6 servings

½ cup cottage cheese
4 hard-cooked egg yolks
1 teaspoon finely grated onion
1 tablespoon finely chopped mild green chilies, fresh or canned, approximately (the amount will depend on the strength of the peppers)
½ cup heavy cream
½ cup vegetable oil
Salt and freshly ground pepper to taste
6 large or 12 small hot, freshly cooked boiled potatoes
Olive slices, radish slices, and sliced hard-cooked eggs for garnish

1. Put the cottage cheese through a sieve and into a mixing bowl. Put the egg yolks through a sieve and add to the cheese. Beat with a wire whisk until smooth.

2. Beat in the onion and chopped chilies and gradually beat in the cream alternately with the oil. Season to taste with salt and pepper. Serve over very hot potatoes, garnished with olive, radish, and hard-cooked egg slices.

Picante de Gallina

(Spiced Chicken)

10 or more servings

1 chicken (5 to 6 pounds)
  Salt to taste
2½ cups olive oil
3 medium onions, finely chopped
1 or more cloves garlic, finely minced
8 ounces (½ loaf) white bread
1 14-ounce can evaporated milk, or 1½ cups heavy cream
1 cup finely chopped walnuts
1½ cups freshly grated Parmesan cheese
1 dried hot chili pepper, seeded and soaked in water
  Freshly ground pepper to taste
  Sliced potatoes, sliced eggs, and olives for garnish

1. Place the chicken in a kettle and add water to cover to the depth of one inch. Add salt, bring to a boil, and simmer two hours, or until the chicken is tender but not falling from the bone. Let cool in the broth.

2. Remove the chicken from the broth, reserving the broth. (Any not used may be frozen.) Remove and discard the skin and bones. Cut the meat into pieces, then chop it.

3. Heat the oil in a large skillet. Add the onions and garlic and cook until light brown. Let cool slightly. Add one cup of the broth and simmer briefly. Add the chicken and stir. Simmer about five minutes.

4. Trim away and discard the crust from the bread. Soak the bread in enough broth to moisten. Squeeze lightly, then put the bread through a sieve or strainer. Add the crumbs to the chicken, along with the milk, stirring. Stir in the walnuts and cheese, then chop the chili pepper and add. Stir to blend. Season with salt and pepper, simmer briefly, then serve, garnished with sliced potatoes, sliced eggs, and olives.

Poland

Mushroom Piroshki

40 to 50 piroshki

1 recipe for Duxelles (see below)
1 cup sifted all-purpose flour
½ cup butter
3 tablespoons sour cream, approximately
   Salt to taste
   Cornstarch

1. Prepare the duxelles and chill.
2. Place the flour in a mixing bowl and add the butter. Cut it in with a pastry blender until the mixture has the texture of coarse cornmeal. Add the sour cream and salt and blend with the hands until the dough holds together. Wrap in waxed paper and chill four hours.
3. Preheat the oven to 400 degrees.
4. To make the piroshki, pull off one piece of dough at a time about the size of a small walnut and shape it into a ball. Roll it lightly in cornstarch and place between two sheets of waxed paper. Roll lightly with a rolling pin. Remove the dough from the waxed paper and add about half a teaspoon of filling. Moisten the edge of the dough with water and fold over. Press with the tines of a fork and place on an ungreased cookie sheet.
5. Continue making piroshki until all the dough is used. Bake fifteen to twenty minutes. Serve hot, as an appetizer.

DUXELLES:

(A Mushroom Paste)

1 to 1½ cups

½ pound fresh, edible wild mushrooms, although fresh cultivated mushrooms may be used
½ cup butter
1 cup finely chopped onion
   Salt and freshly ground pepper to taste
¼ teaspoon nutmeg, or to taste

1. Rinse and pick over the mushrooms to remove all traces of soil, sand, and so on. Drain well. Chop the mushrooms fine.
2. Heat the butter and add the onions. Cook over low heat, stirring frequently, until the onions are golden brown. Do not burn.
3. Add the mushrooms and cook, stirring frequently, until the mushrooms give up their liquid. Continue cooking and stirring until most of the liquid evaporates, about fifteen minutes. Season to taste with salt, pepper, and nutmeg and set aside to cool.

Wild Mushroom Soup

6 to 8 servings

¼ pound dried wild mushrooms, preferably boletus edulis (see below)
9 cups strong, not too salty Beef Stock (page 115)
¼ cup butter
1 cup finely chopped onion
1 tablespoon cornstarch
Salt to taste
Sour cream

1. Soak the mushrooms overnight in cold water to cover. Drain the mushrooms and reserve the soaking liquid. Put the liquid through a fine cloth.

2. Rinse the mushrooms well in cold water to remove any remaining trace of sand. Slice the mushrooms and put them in a three-quart saucepan. Add eight cups of the beef stock and the mushroom-soaking liquid. Simmer four hours.

3. Meanwhile, heat the butter in a heavy skillet and cook the onion in it, stirring frequently, until golden brown. Add the onion to the soup.

4. Blend the cornstarch with the remaining one cup of stock and stir it into the soup. Continue to simmer until thickened slightly. Season with salt and serve in individual cups. Top each serving with one tablespoon of sour cream.

HOW TO DRY WILD MUSHROOMS:

Have ready a square or rectangle of one-quarter-inch hardware cloth. It resembles chicken wire with very small holes. It should be just the size of the inside of the oven.

Prepare the mushrooms. One of the best mushrooms for drying is the boletus edulis. Brush the mushrooms thoroughly all over to clear away all debris, sand, soil, etc. Remove the stems and slice both the stems and the caps.

Preheat the oven to its lowest possible heat.

Place the mushrooms on the hardware cloth and place them in the oven. Leave the oven door slightly ajar. The purpose is to dry the mushrooms without cooking them.

Let the mushrooms stand in the oven until they are crisp and will crackle between the fingers, about twenty-four hours. Store the dried mushrooms in airtight containers.

To use the mushrooms, soak them several hours or overnight and add them directly to a sauce, stew, or soup.

Bigos

4 to 6 servings

2 pounds sauerkraut
4 dried mushrooms
2½ cups canned tomatoes
10 peppercorns
1 bay leaf
2 cups diced Polish sausages or frankfurters or leftover meat such as beef, veal, pork, or lamb
1 cup cubed salt pork or bacon
2 medium-sweet apples, peeled, cored, and sliced

1. Wash the sauerkraut in cold water and squeeze dry.

2. Soak the mushrooms in water to cover for several hours. Bring to a boil and simmer until the mushrooms are soft. Slice the mushrooms and add them, along with the liquid in which they were cooked, to the sauerkraut. Add the tomatoes, peppercorns, and bay leaf. Cover and simmer for one hour.

3. Add the diced meats and salt pork to the sauerkraut and cook for one hour longer. Add the apple slices and cook for fifteen minutes longer. Serve the bigos with steamed potatoes.

POLAND   *499*

Pickled Mushrooms

About 2 cups

1 pound mushrooms, preferably fresh, edible wild mushrooms, although small cultivated mushrooms may be used
Salt to taste
½ cup chopped fresh leek or onion
¼ cup white vinegar
¾ cup water
1 tablespoon mixed pickling spices
2 tablespoons granulated sugar

1. Rinse and pick over the mushrooms to remove all traces of soil, sand, and so forth. Drain well. If the stems are tough, remove them.

2. Place the mushrooms in a saucepan and add cold water to cover and salt to taste. Simmer twenty minutes, then drain well. Place the mushrooms in a bowl and add the chopped leek.

3. Meanwhile, combine the remaining ingredients and bring to a boil. Simmer about three minutes and pour the mixture over the mushrooms and leek. Let stand until cool. Store in a jar with a tight-fitting lid and keep refrigerated.

Portugal

Fish, Portuguese Style

4 servings

4 sole or flounder fillets
    Salt and freshly ground black pepper
1 tablespoon butter
¼ cup Fish Stock (page 116) or clam juice
½ cup dry white wine or water
½ cup canned tomatoes, drained
2 tablespoons minced parsley
2 tablespoons chopped onion or shallot

1. Roll the fillets and secure them with food picks. If the fillets are large, it may be necessary to cut them into halves lengthwise. Sprinkle lightly with salt and pepper to taste.

2. Rub a skillet with the butter and arrange the fillets in the pan. Pour the stock and wine over them. Add the tomatoes, parsley, and onion and bring to a boil. Cover with aluminum foil and cook for ten to twelve minutes, or until the fillets are done, turning them once as they cook.

3. Remove the fillets to a hot serving dish and cook the sauce remaining in the pan over high heat for one minute. Season the sauce with salt and pepper to taste and pour over the fish.

Chicken Breasts in Port

4 servings

2 whole chicken breasts, skinned, boned, and split in half
½ cup all-purpose flour
1 teaspoon salt
¼ teaspoon nutmeg, preferably freshly grated
¼ teaspoon freshly ground black pepper
6 tablespoons butter
1½ cups heavy cream
¼ cup port wine
½ pound fresh mushrooms, sliced

1. Place the chicken breasts between pieces of waxed paper and pound lightly with a wooden mallet or the bottom of a skillet.

2. Combine the flour, salt, nutmeg, and pepper and dredge the chicken pieces in the mixture.

3. Melt four tablespoons of the butter in a heavy skillet and brown the chicken on both sides. Remove the chicken from the skillet and add one cup of cream, stirring. Bring to a boil and simmer two minutes. Add the wine and return the chicken pieces to the skillet. Cover and simmer about twenty minutes.

4. Meanwhile, in another skillet melt the remaining butter and cook the mushrooms, stirring, until they are wilted. Add the remaining cream and bring to a boil. Pour this over the chicken and add salt and pepper to taste. Cover again and simmer ten minutes longer. Serve hot.

Puerto Rico

Pastellios

About 30 turnovers

1 cup water
2 tablespoons butter
1½ teaspoons salt
2 cups sifted all-purpose flour
¼ pound Cheddar cheese, cut into thin slices
1 pound lard

1. Heat the water, butter and salt. Add flour, all at once, stirring rapidly with a wooden spoon. Still stirring rapidly, cook briefly to avoid lumps. Remove the mixture from the heat and continue stirring until smooth.

2. Turn the hot dough out onto a lightly floured board and knead while hot for about two minutes. Shape into a ball, place in a mixing bowl, and cover with cloth. Let stand one hour.

4. Shape the dough into a roll about two inches thick. Cut the roll into slices about one-half inch thick and roll each slice with a floured rolling pin into a round about a quarter-inch thick. Use a biscuit cutter to cut each slice into a circle about the size of a doughnut. Place a thin slice of cheese in the center of one circle of dough and cover with another circle. Press the edges together, first with the fingers and then with a lightly floured fork. When all the circles are used, refrigerate one-half hour.

5. Heat the lard to 400 degrees. Fry the turnovers, three at a time, until golden brown. Drain on absorbent paper. Serve hot, as an appetizer.

Cornmeal Sticks

About 50 sticks

2 cups water
1¼ teaspoons salt
1½ cups cornmeal
1 cup grated Edam cheese
Lard for deep frying

1. Combine the water and salt in a saucepan. Heat to the boiling point and gradually stir in the cornmeal. When thoroughly blended, cook for five minutes, stirring almost constantly. When ready the mixture should separate from the bottom and sides of the pan.

2. Remove the mixture from the heat and stir in the cheese.

3. When cool enough to handle, shape the mixture, one heaping teaspoonful at a time, into balls. Using the palms of the hands, roll each ball into small cigar shapes, about one-half inch thick.

4. Drop the sticks, a few at a time, into lard heated to 375 degrees. Cook until golden brown and drain on absorbent paper. Serve as an appetizer.

Cazuela

(A Casserole Pudding)

10 servings

4 cups fresh or canned pureed sweet potatoes
4 cups fresh or canned puréed pumpkin
1 cup Coconut Milk Made in a Blender
(page 34)
¼ cup butter
3 eggs, lightly beaten
2 cups granulated sugar
1 teaspoon salt
¼ cup all-purpose flour
½ cup water
1 small piece fresh ginger, mashed, or ½
teaspoon dried ginger
1 4-inch length cinnamon stick
¼ teaspoon aniseeds
5 whole cloves

1. If fresh potatoes and pumpkin are used,
they should be pared and cubed and cooked
in boiling salted water until tender, about
forty-five minutes. They should then be
drained and put through a food ricer.

2. Preheat the oven to 350 degrees.

3. Combine the puréed potatoes and
pumpkin with the coconut milk, butter, eggs,
sugar, salt, and flour. Blend well.

4. Combine the remaining ingredients in
a saucepan and bring to a boil. Simmer five
minutes and strain into the other mixture.
Blend well.

5. Butter a nine-and-one-half-inch earthenware casserole. Line it either with plantain
leaves that have been rinsed and dried or
with parchment paper. Butter this generously.
Pour the pumpkin mixture into the casserole
and fold leaves or paper over the top.

6. Bake about one and one-half hours. Let
cool completely before unmolding. Remove
the leaves or paper and serve.

Arroz con Gandules

(Rice with Pigeon Peas)

4 servings

3 tablespoons diced salt pork
2 green peppers, chopped
2 tomatoes, peeled and chopped
1 onion, finely chopped
2 cloves garlic, finely chopped
1 tablespoon capers
2 cups uncooked long-grain rice
1 teaspoon salt
1 tablespoon achiote (a spice that gives a
yellow color)
1 pound cooked fresh pigeon peas or 1
1-pound can peas
3 cups water, approximately

1. Sauté the salt pork until most of the fat
has been rendered. Add the peppers, tomatoes, onion, and garlic and cook five minutes.

2. Add the remaining ingredients, bring
to a boil, and simmer, covered, until all the
liquid has been absorbed, about fifteen minutes. Continue to cook, stirring occasionally
to prevent sticking, until the rice is cooked
and very dry and fluffy.

Pineapple Flan

6 to 8 servings

3 cups pineapple juice
3 cups granulated sugar
¼ cup water
7 eggs

1. Combine the pineapple juice with two cups of the sugar and bring to a boil. Cook until a thin syrup is formed (it will measure 222 degrees on a candy thermometer). Remove the syrup from the fire and let it cool completely.

2. Preheat the oven to 350 degrees.

3. Combine the remaining cup of sugar with the water and let simmer for eight minutes. Pour the mixture immediately into a nine-inch cake tin and place over low heat. Cook just to caramelize, taking care not to let the syrup burn. Immediately swirl the pan around to coat the inside bottom and sides.

4. Use a fork to stir the eggs, but do not beat them. When the yolks and whites are blended but not frothy, strain them into the pineapple syrup. Strain this mixture into the caramel-lined pan.

5. Set the pan in a vessel containing hot water and bake one hour, or until set. Let cool thoroughly before unmolding onto a platter.

Pineapple Rum Punch

20 servings

6 cups pineapple juice
2 cups granulated sugar
½ cup fresh lime juice
5 cups white Puerto Rican rum

1. Combine two cups of the pineapple juice and the sugar in a saucepan; bring to a boil, stirring. When the sugar has dissolved, remove from the heat and add the remaining juice.

2. Add the lime juice and rum and blend well. Place in a bowl and freeze. Spoon the mixture into daiquiri glasses and serve frozen or partly frozen with spoons or straws.

Templeque
(A Chilled Coconut Milk Pudding)

8 to 12 servings

4 cups Coconut Milk Made in a Blender (page 34, and see note below)
½ cup cornstarch
3½ cups boiling water
⅔ cup granulated sugar
½ teaspoon salt
1 tablespoon orange blossom water

1. Pour the coconut milk into a large saucepan.

2. Combine the remaining ingredients and stir into the coconut milk. Cook, stirring constantly with a wooden spoon, over medium-low heat for fifteen minutes.

3. Rinse a two-quart mold with cold water. Pour the coconut mixture into the mold and refrigerate until thoroughly set. Unmold and serve.

Note: If fresh coconuts are not available, canned coconut cream, which can be purchased in Spanish markets, may be used. If so, use three cups of the coconut cream, eliminate the sugar and increase the boiling water to four cups.

Russia

Caviar with Blini

6 to 8 servings

1 pound cold fresh caviar
28 Blini for Caviar (see below)
1 cup melted butter
2 cups sour cream

Spoon a little cold caviar onto each hot blini and pour a generous amount of butter over each. Serve as an appetizer, with the sour cream on the side.

BLINI FOR CAVIAR:

About 28 small blini

¾ cup buckwheat flour
¼ cup all-purpose flour
½ package active dry yeast
2 tablespoons lukewarm water
1⅜ cups lukewarm milk
2 whole eggs
½ tablespoon granulated sugar
½ teaspoon salt
1½ tablespoons melted butter
2 egg whites

1. The preparation of the blini requires about two and one-half hours. Sift the buckwheat flour with the all-purpose flour. Measure three-eighths cup of the combined flours into a mixing bowl.

2. Dissolve the yeast in the water and add three-eighths cup of the lukewarm milk. Add the yeast mixture gradually to the flour to make a smooth batter. Cover and let rise in a warm place for two hours.

3. Beat the whole eggs. Add the sugar, salt, and melted butter and stir the egg mixture into the yeast mixture. Add the remaining milk and flour and mix well. Beat the egg whites until stiff and fold into the batter.

4. Bake on a lightly buttered griddle, using about one tablespoon of batter for each small pancake. Serve immediately.

Pickled Herring in Milt Sauce

12 to 16 servings

6 firm schmaltz herring or salt herring
¾ cup white vinegar
2¼ cups water
1 tablespoon pickling spices
⅔ cup granulated sugar
1 teaspoon salt, if desired, if schmaltz herring are used
3 very large Spanish onions
Milt of 6 to 8 herring (see note)

1. If schmaltz herring are used, soak them overnight in a large bowl of ice water in the refrigerator. If salt herring are used, soak them forty-eight hours in ice water in the refrigerator, changing the water twice.

2. Combine the vinegar, water, and pickling spices in an enameled saucepan. Bring to a rolling boil, then stir in the sugar. If schmaltz herring are used, add the salt (the salt is supposed to give herring firmness while they pickle, but the validity of this has not been checked). Let the mixture stand overnight at room temperature.

3. The next morning, make a thick layer of newspaper on which to work. With scissors, cut off the fins of the herring. Slit open the abdomens with the scissors and remove and reserve any milt. With a sharp knife, make an incision down the backs, cutting to the bone. Fillet the herring, starting from the tail. This is a comparatively easy job because it is more a matter of pulling the meat from the backbone than using a knife. Do not be concerned about the small bones that will remain in the herring. These seem to dissolve or disappear after a few days in the pickling mixture. After the herring have been filleted, remove the skin by pulling it off. Rinse and dry the herring on paper towels.

4. Peel the onions and cut into fairly thick slices. Separate into rings.

5. Whirl the milt in an electric blender or force through a food mill or sieve. Pour off the vinegar mixture from the spices, discarding the spices. Stir the vinegar into the pureed milt.

6. Make alternate layers of herring slices and plenty of onions in a two- to three-quart crock. When the crock is almost full, pour the vinegar-milt mixture over all to cover. Cover the crock and chill in the refrigerator at least five days, up to four months. The pickled flavor will get stronger as the herring stands. Serve as an appetizer.

Note: Ask the fish man if the herring have milt in them. If there is no milt, or very little, as is often the case with schmaltz herring, he will sell you some separately.

Creamed Pickled Herring

12 to 16 servings

Pour the pickled herring mixture from Pickled Herring in Milt Sauce (see above) into a colander or strainer to drain off all the pickling mixture. For each six schmaltz herring to be creamed, use about one quart thick sour cream about three or four days old so it will be very thick. Combine the herring and sour cream in a bowl and stir together gently. Serve, garnished with chopped fresh dill, as an appetizer.

Rollmops

12 servings

6 firm schmaltz or salt herring, soaked, filleted, and skinned (see page 506)
3 tablespoons prepared hot mustard
12 small slices onion
½ carrot, scraped and cut into 12 matchsticks
½ sour pickle, cut into 12 matchsticks
2 large Spanish onions
Pickling mixture with milch from Pickled Herring in Milt Sauce (page 506)

1. Spread the herring fillets with the hot mustard. Place an onion slice, carrot stick, and pickle stick on the narrow end of each fillet. Roll up the fillets jelly-roll style and skewer with food picks.
2. Peel the Spanish onions and cut up coarsely. Make alternate layers of rollmops and onions in a crock until all are used. Pour over the pickling mixture to cover. Cover the crock and place in the refrigerator at least one week before serving as an appetizer.
Note: If smaller appetizers are desired, the herring may be quartered lengthwise and prepared as above.

Cream Cheese Pastry

About 36 small pastries

½ cup butter
¼ pound cream cheese
1 cup sifted all-purpose flour

1. Cream the butter and cream cheese until well blended. Add the flour and mix until smooth. Chill.
2. Roll out on a lightly floured pastry cloth to the desired thickness and shape as suggested below.
3. Bake in a preheated 425-degree oven until golden brown. Serve warm or cool.

SEEDED SHAPES:
Roll the pastry to a thickness of one-sixth inch and cut into one-inch squares, rounds, or triangles. Brush the top of each with lightly beaten egg and dip the moist surface into sesame, poppy, or caraway seeds.

PASTRY HEARTS:
Roll the pastry to a thickness of one-eighth inch and cut into strips about five inches wide and as long as the pastry sheet. Fold the long edges to the center and press down. Fold the folded edges to the center and cut the roll into one-quarter-inch slices. For filled hearts, spread the pastry with one of the fillings given below before folding.

PINWHEELS:
Roll the pastry to a thickness of one-eighth inch and cut into a strip five to six inches wide. Spread with one of the fillings given below and roll like a jelly roll. Cut into one-quarter-inch slices.

FILLED SLICES:
Roll the pastry to a thickness of one-eighth inch. Spread half of it with any filling given below and fold the plain pastry over the filled half. Press the top gently and then cut into small fingers, squares, or triangles.

ANCHOVY FILLING:
Cream together one part anchovy paste and two parts heavy cream.

ROQUEFORT CHEESE FILLING:
Cream the cheese with enough heavy cream to give a spreading consistency.

DEVILED HAM FILLING:
Mix one two-and-one-quarter-ounce can deviled ham with one teaspoon prepared mustard, two tablespoons grated Parmesan cheese, and enough heavy cream to give a spreading consistency.

Borscht I

About 2 quarts

 5 large beets, peeled and grated
1½ quarts water or Chicken Stock (page 115)
 1 onion, chopped
 1 cup tomato puree
 1 tablespoon lemon juice
   Salt and freshly ground black pepper
 1 teaspoon granulated sugar
 2 eggs, lightly beaten
 1 cup sour cream

1. Combine the beets, water or stock, and onion in a heavy kettle. Bring to a boil, then cover and simmer for forty-five minutes.

2. Add the tomato puree, lemon juice, salt and pepper to taste, and sugar. Cook for forty-five minutes longer. If desired, the soup may be strained and the vegetables discarded.

3. Combine the eggs with some of the hot soup. Stir the egg mixture into the remaining soup and reheat, but do not allow to boil. Serve the soup hot or chilled, topped with spoonfuls of sour cream.

Borscht II

About 6 servings

 2 cups finely shredded cabbage
 2 cups boiling salted water
 ½ cup chopped onion
 ¼ cup butter
 1 1-pound 4-ounce can whole beets
 1 quart Chicken Stock (page 115)
 2 teaspoons caraway seeds
 1 teaspoon granulated sugar
   Salt and freshly ground black pepper
 3 tablespoons lemon juice
 ¼ cup dry white wine
   Sour cream

1. Cook the cabbage for ten minutes in the boiling salted water. Cook the onion in the butter for a few minutes without browning. Drain the beets, saving the juice, and chop them fine until you have two cups of beet shreds.

2. Add the stock to the onions. When it comes to a boil, add the cabbage and the water in which it cooked. Add the beets, one cup of the beet juice, the caraway seeds, sugar, and salt and pepper to taste. Simmer for ten minutes, skimming carefully.

3. Remove the soup from the heat. Add the lemon juice and wine and heat to the boiling point. Serve with sour cream.

Borscht III

8 or more servings

1 shin of beef (3 to 4 pounds), cut into 3 or 4 pieces
Salt to taste
1 1-pound 13-ounce can tomato puree
1 carrot, grated on a coarse blade
1 onion, diced
1 1½-pound cabbage, cut in half and finely shredded
3 sprigs fresh dill, or to taste
1 whole green pepper, cut in half and seeded
1 1-pound can whole beets with their liquid
Chopped fresh dill to taste (optional)
Sour cream

1. Place the beef in a kettle and add a generous amount of water to cover. Add salt to taste and simmer, skimming the surface as necessary, about one and one-half hours. Do not cover.

2. Add the tomato puree, carrot, and onion. Simmer about one hour longer, skimming the surface as necessary. Do not cover. If too much liquid evaporates, it may be necessary to add boiling water. Add the cabbage, dill sprigs, and green pepper and cook, uncovered, about thirty minutes longer.

3. Discard the dill sprigs and green pepper. Add the beet juice. Grate the beets, add them, and bring to a boil. The soup is now ready. Serve in deep dishes with a little of the shredded meat in each bowl and garnished with chopped dill. Serve the sour cream on the side.

Note: The more you reheat this soup, the better it becomes.

Shchi

(Russian Sauerkraut Soup)

About 8 servings

1 pound sauerkraut, fresh or canned
1 large firm cabbage
3 tablespoons butter or bacon fat
1 large onion, peeled and sliced thin
1 rib celery, finely chopped
2 cloves garlic, finely minced
2 cups canned Italian-style plum tomatoes
2 pounds shin of beef or short ribs of beef
2 quarts Beef Stock (page 115)
Salt and freshly ground black pepper
Juice of 1 lemon
2 tablespoons granulated sugar (optional)
2 tablespoons all-purpose flour
1 tablespoon finely minced parsley
1 tablespoon finely minced dill
1 cup sour cream

1. Drain the sauerkraut and empty it into a basin of cold water. Rinse well and squeeze dry. Pull apart to remove any lumps.

2. Remove and discard the core from the cabbage, then shred the cabbage with a sharp knife. Place the sauerkraut and cabbage in a large kettle.

3. Heat two tablespoons of the fat and cook the onion, celery, and garlic in it until the onion is translucent. Add to the kettle.

4. Add the tomatoes, beef, stock, and salt and pepper to taste and bring to a boil. Simmer for about two hours, or until the beef is tender, skimming the surface as necessary to remove foam and scum. Add the lemon juice and sugar and cook for ten minutes longer.

5. Cook the flour in the remaining tablespoon of fat until golden in color. Stir into the soup and cook for about twenty minutes.

6. To serve, slice the meat and discard the bones. Place the meat in the bottom of a soup tureen and sprinkle with parsley and dill. Pour in the soup. Serve the sour cream separately.

Coulibiac

12 servings

BRIOCHE DOUGH:

½ cup milk
½ cup butter
⅓ cup granulated sugar
1 teaspoon salt
1 package active dry yeast
¼ cup lukewarm water
1 egg yolk
3 whole eggs, beaten
3¼ cups sifted all-purpose flour

FILLING:

1 onion, chopped
¼ cup butter
½ pound mushrooms, sliced
1½ pounds boneless, skinless salmon
¾ cup dry white wine, or Fish Stock (page 116) seasoned with salt and freshly ground black pepper to taste
¼ cup fresh snipped dill weed
4 cups cold cooked rice (1 cup uncooked) Salt and freshly ground black pepper
1 egg white, lightly beaten

1. The day before, prepare the brioche dough. Scald the milk and cool it to lukewarm.

2. Cream the butter, adding the sugar gradually. Add the salt.

3. Soften the yeast in the water. Blend the milk, creamed mixture, and yeast. Add the egg yolk, whole eggs, and flour and beat with a wooden spoon two minutes.

4. Cover and let rise in a warm place (80 to 85 degrees) until more than double in bulk, about two hours or less.

5. Stir down and beat thoroughly. Cover tightly with aluminum foil and refrigerate overnight.

6. Preheat the oven to 425 degrees.

7. To prepare the filling, sauté the onion in the butter until tender, add the mushrooms, and cook three minutes. Allow to cool. Poach the salmon in the wine or stock.

8. Cool the salmon and, when cool, break up into bite-sized pieces. Mix together the vegetables, dill, rice, salmon, and one-half cup of the liquid in which the fish was cooked. Season with salt and pepper to taste.

9. Remove the dough from the refrigerator, stir down, and turn out onto a lightly floured pastry cloth on a board. Roll the dough into a rectangle at least eighteen by sixteen inches.

10. Pile the salmon-rice mixture into a meat-loaf shape in the center of the dough, leaving at least four inches on all sides clear.

11. Draw the long edges of the dough together over the filling and pinch to seal. Cut off a triangle from each corner, then fold the ends like envelope flaps over the covered filling.

12. Place a lightly greased and floured baking sheet face down on the seam side. Holding the cloth firmly, turn the cloth, filled roll, and pan over all together so that the smooth dough is uppermost.

13. Brush the coulibiac with the egg white. Make two or three steam holes along the length of the dough and bake ten minutes, or until well browned. Reduce the oven heat to 350 degrees and cook ten to fifteen minutes longer, or until cooked. Serve with warm clarified butter (see note page 174).

Beef Stroganoff

About 6 servings

¼ cup all-purpose flour
½ teaspoon salt
1 pound filet mignon, cut in ¼-inch-wide strips
¼ cup butter
1 cup thinly sliced mushrooms
½ cup chopped onion
1 clove garlic, minced
1 tablespoon tomato paste
1¼ cups Beef Stock (page 115) or 1 can condensed beef broth
1 cup sour cream
2 tablespoons dry sherry

1. Combine one tablespoon of the flour with the salt and dredge the meat in the mixture.

2. Heat the skillet, then add half the butter. When melted, add the meat strips and brown quickly, flipping the meat to brown on all sides. Add the mushroom slices, onion, and garlic. Cook three to four minutes, or until the onion is barely tender.

3. Remove the meat and mushrooms from the skillet and keep warm. Add the remaining butter to the pan drippings. When melted, blend in the remaining flour with a whisk. Add the tomato paste. Slowly pour in the meat stock. Cook, stirring constantly with the whisk, until the mixture thickens.

4. Return the meat and mushrooms to the skillet. Stir in the sour cream and sherry and heat briefly.

Cutleti

6 servings

1 pound chuck, ground
4 to 6 slices white bread
2 eggs, lightly beaten
1 onion, grated
1 teaspoon freshly grated cheese, such as Sap Sago or Parmesan
Salt and freshly ground pepper to taste
1 cup or more fresh bread crumbs
Vegetable oil for frying

1. Place the meat in a mixing bowl.

2. Moisten the bread with water, then squeeze it to remove as much of the water as possible. Using the fingers, work the bread into crumbs or tiny pieces. Add the bread to the meat. Add the eggs, onion, cheese, salt, and pepper and blend. Shape the meat into six oval patties.

3. Dredge the patties lightly on all sides in bread crumbs, pressing lightly to make the crumbs adhere. Make light crisscross (waffle) patterns on both sides of the patties.

4. Heat a little oil in a skillet and cook the patties until brown, about five minutes to a side. If desired, serve with Mushrooms in Sour Cream (page 514).

Transylvanian Pork and Sauerkraut

6 generous servings

2½ pounds lean pork, cut into 1-inch cubes
¼ cup all-purpose flour
   Salt and freshly ground black pepper
1 tablespoon sweet paprika
½ pound lard
2 large white onions, peeled and chopped
¾ cup water, approximately
1 pound sauerkraut
1 cup sour cream
½ cup uncooked rice
1 pound smoked Polish sausage, cut into thin rings

1. Dredge the pork cubes with a mixture of the flour, salt, pepper, and half of the paprika. Heat all but two tablespoons of the lard in a skillet and lightly brown the meat in it. Transfer the meat to another container and add the onions to the skillet. Cook until the onions are light brown.

2. Return the meat to the skillet. Add one-half cup of the water, cover, and cook over low heat for about one hour, until the meat is tender. Add more water if necessary.

3. Wash the sauerkraut under cold running water. Drain and squeeze gently to remove excess water. Place the sauerkraut in a saucepan and add two tablespoons of the liquid in which the meat is cooking. Add half the remaining paprika, cover, and simmer slowly for thirty minutes.

4. Remove the meat from the skillet and set aside. Turn off the heat under the skillet and stir the sour cream into the sauce remaining in the skillet. Stir vigorously until the sour cream is mixed in well. Add salt to taste.

5. Cook the rice, stirring, in the remaining lard for about five minutes. Add the remaining water, cover, and steam until the rice is tender, about twenty minutes. Add the remaining paprika.

6. Preheat the oven to 350 degrees.

7. Arrange the foods in alternate layers in an ovenproof casserole as follows: sauerkraut, pork cubes, rice, sausage rings, and sauce. Continue building up layers until all the ingredients are used, ending with the sauce and a garnish of sausage rings.

8. Bake the casserole for thirty minutes, or until the top is golden brown and crisp.

Paschka, the traditional Russian Easter desse

Chicken Cutlets Pojarski

4 servings

Once upon a time, according to legend, there was a small and prosperous town between Moscow and St. Petersburg called Torjok. Travelers changed horses there. And in the town was a tavern. The tavernkeeper was named Pojarski and the specialty of the house was an excellent dish made of finely chopped meat, shaped like a cutlet and sautéed. Called Pojarskiya kotleti *or Pojarski cutlet, the dish was made of game or of game and beef together. Today it is usually made of chicken, as in the recipe below, accompanied by a recipe for a paprika sauce.*

2 large whole chicken breasts, skinned and boned
Salt and freshly ground pepper, preferably white
¼ teaspoon freshly grated nutmeg, or to taste
11 tablespoons butter
½ cup all-purpose flour
1 egg
1 teaspoon vegetable oil
1 tablespoon water
1½ to 2 cups fresh bread crumbs
Paprika Sauce for Chicken Cutlets Pojarski (see below)

1. Chill a mixing bowl in the freezer.
2. Care must be taken that all bones are removed from the chicken breasts. Place the boned chicken meat on a board and chop thoroughly with a sharp knife, or grind the meat, using a fine blade. There should be about one and one-half cups chopped or ground meat. Add the meat to the chilled bowl. Add salt and pepper to taste, nutmeg, and five tablespoons of the butter, melted. Beat well. Chill in the freezer; do not freeze.
3. Season the flour with salt and pepper and place on a length of waxed paper.

4. Break the egg into a pie plate and beat with the oil and water.
5. Place the bread crumbs on another length of waxed paper.
6. Divide the chicken mixture into six to eight portions and shape each portion into a ball. Flatten each ball one-half inch thick and shape each into the shape of a small cutlet or pork chop. Dip one cutlet at a time into flour, then in egg, then in bread crumbs. Press the crumbs in gently, then chill briefly.
7. Heat the remaining butter in a large skillet and carefully add the cutlets. Cook until golden brown on one side, then turn and cook on the other. Arrange on a hot platter and spoon the paprika sauce over or serve separately. Serve immediately.

PAPRIKA SAUCE FOR CHICKEN
CUTLETS POJARSKI:

About 1½ cups

2 tablespoons butter
3 tablespoons finely chopped onion
2 teaspoons paprika
1 tablespoon all-purpose flour
½ teaspoon dried thyme
½ cup Chicken Stock (page 115)
½ cup heavy cream
2 teaspoons lemon juice
Salt and freshly ground black pepper
1 teaspoon Cognac
¼ cup sour cream

1. Melt one tablespoon of the butter in a small saucepan and cook the onion until wilted. Sprinkle with the paprika, flour, and thyme, stirring. Stir in the stock, using a whisk, and simmer about three minutes. The sauce may be made in advance to this point.
2. Add the cream and bring to a boil. Add the lemon juice, salt and pepper to taste, and the Cognac. Strain the sauce through a sieve. Return to the heat and stir in the remaining butter and the sour cream. Bring just to a boil, but do not boil.

Chicken cutlets Pojarski (Russia)

Mushrooms Smitane

4 servings

¼ cup butter
1 cup finely chopped green onion
1 pound mushrooms, sliced
   Salt and freshly ground black pepper
½ teaspoon paprika
½ teaspoon dried marjoram
3 tablespoons finely chopped parsley
1 cup sour cream

1. Heat the butter and add the green onion. Cook over low heat until the onion is wilted. Add the mushrooms. Cover and cook until the mushrooms give up their liquid. Continue to cook for ten minutes.

2. Add salt and pepper to taste, the paprika, marjoram, and parsley. Stir well. Add the sour cream and heat thoroughly, but do not boil.

Mushrooms in Sour Cream

About 3 cups

1 pound mushrooms, thinly sliced
1 medium onion, split in half, then sliced wafer thin
2 tablespoons butter
1 cup sour cream
1 teaspoon all-purpose flour
1 teaspoon powdered mushrooms (available on spice racks)
   Salt to taste
1 teaspoon freshly grated cheese, such as Sap Sago or any firm white grating cheese

1. Place the mushrooms in a deep mixing bowl and pour over them enough boiling water to cover. Let stand about ten minutes.

2. In a saucepan cook the onion in butter, without browning. Stir the onion until wilted and translucent.

3. Drain the mushrooms and add them to the onion. Cook, stirring occasionally, five or ten minutes over low heat.

4. Blend the sour cream and flour and stir this into the mushroom mixture. Add the remaining ingredients and continue to cook, stirring, over low heat until the sauce is piping hot. Do not boil the sauce.

Potatoes Alexandre

8 servings

One of the most unlikely combinations might seem to be baked potato with caviar. But it is, in fact, one of the most interesting (and hedonistic) liaisons of this or any age. When the potatoes are baked, scooped out, and mashed—as for more down-to-earth preparations—they are then blended with sour cream and chives. The caviar is added last, black and pearly and in quantity according to conscience—the more the better. The best, of course, is Russian or Iranian, but even black Danish or red caviar will do, although the latter—lesser breeds—should be added in smaller quantities.

8 large Idaho potatoes
2 tablespoons butter
1 cup sour cream
2 tablespoons chopped fresh chives
¼ teaspoon nutmeg or more to taste
   Salt and freshly ground pepper
1 pound caviar, preferably fresh Beluga or Sevruga (see note)
8 lemon wedges
   Dill or parsley sprigs

1. Preheat the oven to 400 degrees.

2. Bake the potatoes forty-five minutes to one hour, depending on size.

3. When the potatoes are done and still hot, cut off a slice from the top. The slice should be about a quarter-inch thick, but large enough to remove the potato pulp for stuffing. Scoop out the pulp but leave a shell for stuffing. Spoon the pulp into a saucepan. Turn off the oven heat and place the potato shells briefly in the oven to keep them hot.

4. Place the saucepan over low heat and immediately add the butter, sour cream, chives, nutmeg, salt, and pepper. Stir rapidly with a wooden spoon to blend thoroughly, breaking up the potato pulp. If desired, add more butter or sour cream. The important thing is to have the mixture piping hot. Stuff the potato shells with the potato mixture. Top each serving with equal amounts of caviar and garnish each with a lemon wedge and dill sprigs. Serve as a luncheon dish.

Note: Substitutes for fresh caviar would include pressed caviar, pasteurized caviar, black Danish caviar, and red caviar.

Russian Mustard

About 1 cup

1 4-ounce tin dry mustard
1½ cups water
¾ cup granulated sugar
2 tablespoons white vinegar

1. Place the mustard in a small round mixing bowl and add enough water to make a stiff paste. Smooth over the top.

2. Meanwhile, bring about one and one-half cups of water to a boil. Pour half a cup of boiling water over the mustard, but do not stir or blend. Let stand until cool, then pour off the water. Add another half cup of boiling water and let cool. Pour it off. Add the third half cup of water and let cool. Pour this off.

3. Stir in the sugar and vinegar and work with a fork or spoon to blend well and remove all lumps.

Salat Olivet

6 servings

1 whole chicken breast, cooked and cooled
2 tablespoons chopped pitted green olives
1 tablespoon capers
2 tablespoons chopped pickles, preferably sour pickles
1 tablespoon grated onion, or more to taste
¼ cup finely diced heart of celery
½ cup green peas, cooked
1 large or 2 small hard-cooked eggs, sliced or cut into eighths
½ teaspoon granulated sugar
1½ to 2 cups Mayonnaise (page 265)
   Lemon juice to taste
   Salt and freshly ground pepper to taste
1 cup peeled, diced, hot boiled potatoes

1. Remove and discard the skin and bones of the chicken breast. Cut the meat into small cubes.

2. Combine the chicken cubes with all the remaining ingredients except the potatoes. Stir lightly to blend.

3. At the last, add the hot boiled potato cubes. If necessary, add more mayonnaise. Serve cold.

Paschka

16 servings

The dessert called paschka, *traditionally served at the Russian Easter, is as rich as Solomon's mines and as elegant as a crown jewel. There are traditional molds for making the dish, but a well-washed clay flowerpot will do.*

2¼ pounds farmer's pot cheese (dry-curd cottage cheese)
15 tablespoons butter
7 egg yolks
1½ cups granulated sugar
1½ cups heavy cream
⅓ cup chopped candied fruits
3 tablespoons slivered blanched almonds
¼ cup currants (optional)
2 teaspoons pure vanilla extract
Fresh and glazed fruits for garnish

1. Scrub a six-inch clay pot (measured across the top) thoroughly with a brush and soap and water. Rinse inside and out with hot running water; wipe dry and bake in a 300-degree oven for an hour or until thoroughly dry. (It can be kept from year to year if it is wrapped in clear plastic.)

2. Meanwhile, let the pot cheese, the butter and the egg yolks stand (covered) at room temperature for two hours. Place the sugar and egg yolks in a mixing bowl and beat until light and lemon-colored. Set aside briefly. Scald the cream and set aside.

3. Break up the cheese and put half of it in the container of an electric blender. Add half the yolk mixture. Blend together at low speed until smooth. Add half the scalded cream, blending until smooth. Empty into a pan. Repeat with remaining ingredients.

4. Heat the mixture, stirring until it thickens slightly. Do not allow it to boil. Remove from the heat and add the chopped candied fruits, almonds and (if desired) the currants. Put the mixture in a cool spot or in the refrigerator until it is cool.

5. Place the butter in a mixing bowl and beat it with a rotary or electric mixer until soft, fluffy and pale. This will take several minutes. Using a rubber spatula, stir and fold this into the cooled mixture. Add the vanilla and fold until very well blended.

6. The flowerpot must be thoroughly cooled before using. Cut off a large length of cheesecloth, rinse in cold water and squeeze until almost dry. Line the flowerpot with a double layer of the damp cheesecloth, allowing a generous portion of the cheesecloth to extend over the edges of the flowerpot.

7. Place the pot on a rack over a shallow pan. Pour in the paschka mixture. Fold edges of the cheesecloth over the top. Cover with foil. Fit a small saucepan into the top of the flowerpot and weight it to press down on the mixture. Place the whole assembly in the refrigerator for twenty-four hours. The whey will drain into the shallow pan.

8. Run a knife around between cheesecloth and flowerpot to loosen paschka. Turn a serving plate upside down over the pot and reverse to ease paschka out. Remove the cheesecloth gently. Garnish the paschka with fresh and glazed fruits. Cut in small wedges to serve.

Spain

Galician Soup

6 servings

1 cup dried white beans
6 cups water
1 pound lean beef
½ pound lean smoked ham, trimmed
¼ pound salt pork
1 onion, studded with two cloves
2 or 3 cloves garlic, peeled
2 large tomatoes, peeled, cored, and quartered
  Salt and freshly ground black pepper
1 frying chicken (3 pounds), cut into serving pieces
1 pound firm potatoes, peeled and cut into cubes
1 small bunch of white turnips, peeled and cut into cubes
1 pound cabbage, cored and cut into 1-inch squares

1. Soak the beans overnight in water to cover. Or, to use a quicker method, add the water to the beans, bring to a boil, simmer for two minutes, and let stand for one hour.

2. Drain the beans and put them in a large kettle with the six cups fresh water.

3. Cut the beef and ham into small strips and add to the beans. Cut the salt pork into cubes and add it. Add the onion, garlic, tomatoes, and salt and pepper to taste and bring to a boil. Partly cover and simmer gently for one hour.

4. Add the chicken and cook for about thirty minutes, until the beans, meat, and chicken are tender. Add the remaining vegetables and simmer until the vegetables are tender. Add more salt, if necessary.

Málaga Gazpacho

6 servings

In the middle of June with simmering days and sweltering nights, there is nothing so rare as a well-chilled soup. It could be one of those silky and gratifying French creations enriched with cream, or it might be a simple gazpacho, that scintillating Spanish mixture of red-ripe tomatoes, cucumbers, oil, and vinegar.

3 cups cored, coarsely chopped fresh tomatoes
1½ cups peeled, coarsely chopped cucumber
1 green pepper, cored, seeded, and coarsely chopped
1 clove garlic, sliced
½ cup water
5 tablespoons olive or corn oil
¼ cup or more wine vinegar
Salt to taste
2 slices untrimmed fresh bread, cubed

1. In the container of an electric blender, combine all the ingredients. Blend on high speed, stirring down with a rubber spatula as necessary.

2. Place a large, ordinary kitchen sieve inside a mixing bowl. When all the ingredients are blended, pour the mixture into the sieve. Press and stir with a wooden spoon to extract as much of the juices as possible. Discard the solids in the sieve. Taste the soup for seasoning and add more salt and vinegar, if desired. Chill the soup thoroughly before serving.

Swordfish Steak, Spanish Style

3 or 4 servings

1 swordfish steak (1 pound)
Salt and freshly ground black pepper
6 tablespoons olive oil
1 medium onion, finely chopped
1 clove garlic, finely minced
¼ cup chopped parsley
½ teaspoon chopped thyme
1 large tomato, peeled and chopped
1 bay leaf
2 tablespoons tomato paste
½ cup dry sherry or clam broth
½ cup water
3 lemon slices

1. Preheat the oven to 350 degrees.

2. Sprinkle the fish with salt and pepper. Pour two tablespoons olive oil into a shallow baking dish, then add the fish.

3. Cook the onion, garlic, parsley, and thyme in the remaining oil until wilted. Add the tomato, bay leaf, and salt to taste. Cook until well blended. Add the tomato paste, sherry, and water and simmer five minutes longer. Pour the mixture over the fish. Add the lemon slices and bake thirty minutes, basting occasionally.

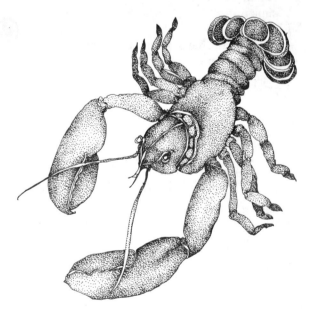

Shrimp Granados

4 or more servings

2½ dozen raw medium shrimp or 18 raw extra jumbo shrimp
2 cups water
2 ribs celery, chopped
⅛ teaspoon dried thyme
   Salt
¼ cup butter
2 tablespoons all-purpose flour
1 small bay leaf, crumbled
2 cloves garlic, finely minced
   Tabasco to taste (the dish should be hot)
2 whole pimentos, chopped
2 tablespoons chopped chives

1. Shell and devein the shrimp. Reserve the shells.

2. Place the shrimp shells in a saucepan and add the water, celery, thyme, and salt to taste. Bring to a boil and simmer fifteen minutes. Drain and reserve the cooking liquid. If necessary, reduce by boiling to one and one-half cups.

3. Heat the butter in a skillet and add the shrimp and salt to taste. Cook over low heat, shaking the skillet or turning, until the shrimp are bright red and the flesh is firm, about five minutes. Transfer the shrimp to a warm bowl and cover to keep warm while making the sauce.

4. Add the flour to the butter in the skillet and cook, stirring with a whisk, until blended. Add the shrimp liquid, stirring vigorously with a whisk. Transfer the sauce to a saucepan and add the bay leaf, garlic, and Tabasco. Continue cooking, stirring frequently, for fifteen minutes. Strain. Add the shrimp, pimentos, and chives and heat through.

Shrimp with Saffron

4 servings

24 large raw shrimp
½ cup peanut or vegetable oil
   Juice of 2 lemons
1 teaspoon whole saffron
3 sprigs parsley
1 teaspoon finely chopped fresh thyme or ½ teaspoon dried thyme
1 clove garlic, peeled
½ bay leaf
   Salt and freshly ground black pepper
¼ cup butter

1. Preheat the broiler.

2. Shell the shrimp and remove the intestinal vein down the back. Rinse under cold running water and dry on paper towels. Place the shrimp in a bowl and add the oil, lemon juice, and saffron.

3. Place the parsley on a chopping surface and chop. Add the thyme and garlic and continue chopping. When the herbs are chopped together, add the bay leaf and continue chopping until the bay leaf is finely chopped. Add this to the shrimp and sprinkle with salt and pepper. Stir until the shrimp are well coated with the mixture.

4. Place the butter in a saucepan and heat thoroughly.

5. Transfer the shrimp to another pan and pour the remaining marinade into the hot butter. Do not boil.

6. Broil the shrimp about four inches from the source of heat. As liquid accumulates in the shrimp pan, pour it into the butter mixture. Cook the shrimp, turning once, until they are red and cooked, four to five minutes. Do not overcook or they will toughen. Arrange the shrimp in a warm serving dish.

7. Stir the butter sauce with a wire whisk while heating, but do not boil. Pour the butter sauce over the shrimp and serve immediately.

Paella

8 to 10 servings

¼ pound salt pork, diced
2 cloves garlic, finely chopped
½ teaspoon dried thyme
  Salt
1 tablespoon wine vinegar
¼ cup olive oil
½ teaspoon ground coriander
1 chicken (2½ pounds), cut into serving pieces
1 pound raw medium shrimp, shelled and deveined
1 lobster (2 pounds), cut into serving pieces
2 chorizos (Spanish sausages) or hot Italian sausages
¾ cup chopped onion
1 teaspoon whole saffron or ¼ teaspoon powdered saffron
2 tablespoons capers
⅓ cup chopped fresh or canned tomatoes
½ cup dry white wine
2½ cups uncooked rice
3½ cups Chicken Stock (page 115), approximately
  Freshly ground pepper to taste
20 mussels, well scrubbed (optional)
20 small clams, well rinsed
1 package frozen artichoke hearts, partly thawed
½ cup freshly cooked or frozen peas
1 4-ounce can pimentos
1 teaspoon anise liqueur, such as Pernod or Ricard
  Lemon wedges

1. In a heavy four-quart ovenproof skillet, casserole, or paella pan, sauté the pork until the fat is rendered and the pork bits are brown. Remove the pork and reserve.

2. Chop the garlic with the thyme and one teaspoon salt. Scrape into a bowl, then add the vinegar, oil, and coriander. Coat the chicken pieces with the mixture and allow to stand at least thirty minutes before cooking.

3. Meanwhile, in the pork fat remaining in the pan sauté the shrimp quickly until bright pink; remove and reserve. Do the same with the lobster.

4. Fry the chorizos in same pan until cooked, about twenty minutes. Slice and reserve.

5. Brown the coated chicken pieces in the fat remaining in the pan. Sprinkle with the onion, saffron, capers, and tomatoes.

6. Return the pork pieces to the pan. Add the wine, rice, and chicken broth. Season with salt and pepper to taste. Cover and simmer gently about fifteen minutes.

7. Meanwhile, steam the mussels and the clams in one-quarter cup of water until they open, about five minutes. Discard any that do not open.

8. Preheat the oven to 350 degrees.

9. Add the shrimp, lobster, artichoke hearts, and peas to the chicken and rice. Cook, uncovered, five to ten minutes. If all the liquid has been absorbed, add the liquid from the mussels and clams or more chicken broth. The rice should be moist, but there should be no excess moisture.

10. Add the pimentos, liqueur, and reserved chorizos. Garnish with the mussels and clams, cover, and place in the oven to reheat. (If the dish is to be kept warm for as long as half an hour, reduce the oven heat to 200 degrees.) Serve with lemon wedges.

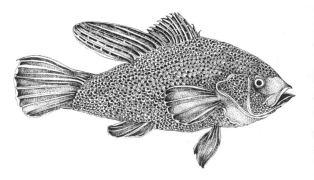

Cazuela

6 servings

1 teaspoon whole saffron
½ cup boiling water
¼ cup corn oil
¾ cup coarsely chopped green pepper
1 medium onion, thinly sliced
2 whole cloves garlic, peeled
2 unpeeled tomatoes, cored and sliced
1 1-pound baby octopus, cleaned and cut into bite-sized pieces
⅓ cup dry white wine
1 bay leaf
¼ cup finely chopped parsley
1 teaspoon paprika
½ teaspoon dried thyme
  Salt and freshly ground black pepper
1 pound shrimp, shelled and deveined
1 dozen littleneck clams, the smallest available, thoroughly rinsed
12 mussels, well scrubbed

1. Place the saffron in a measuring cup and add the boiling water. Let stand for an hour or so.

2. Heat the oil in a large saucepan or casserole and add the green pepper and onion. Cook, stirring frequently, until the onion just starts to turn color.

3. Add the garlic, tomatoes, octopus, and the water with the saffron. Add the wine, bay leaf, parsley, paprika, thyme, and salt and pepper to taste. Cook, uncovered, ten minutes.

4. Cover the casserole and cook ten minutes longer.

5. Add the shrimp, clams, and mussels and cover. Cook five minutes, or just until the clams and mussels open. Serve immediately, with rice.

Cocida Español
(Spanish Boiled Dinner)

8 servings

1 pound dried chick-peas
  Salt
½ pound salt pork, in one piece
½ pound ham hock or other smoked ham, in one piece
1 pound soup meat, in one piece
1 shin bone, cracked
1 medium head cabbage, quartered
1 large carrot, cut into thirds
4 potatoes, peeled and halved
1 bouquet garni (3 ribs celery, 2 sprigs parsley, and 1 leek, trimmed, washed, and tied in a bunch)
2 pounds chorizos (Spanish sausages)
1 pound vermicelli or thin spaghetti

1. Place the dried chick-peas in a cloth bag and tie with a string. Cover with cold water and add two teaspoons salt. Let stand for twenty-four hours, then drain.

2. Cover the salt pork and the ham hock with cold water and soak for one hour.

3. Pour about six quarts of water into a large soup kettle and bring to a boil. Add the soup meat, shin bone, and drained salt pork and ham hock. Return to a boil and simmer for one hour. Add the chick-peas, still tied in the bag, and simmer for forty-five minutes. Add the vegetables, bouquet garni, and chorizos. Add salt to taste and cook for one hour longer.

4. Discard the bouquet garni and pour most of the soup stock into another large saucepan. Keep meat and vegetables warm.

5. Bring the soup stock to a boil and cook the vermicelli in it until tender, according to package directions. Serve this soup with pasta as a first course.

6. Cut the meat into serving portions. Arrange the chick-peas in the center of a hot serving platter and arrange the meat and vegetables around it symmetrically.

Saffron Beef

8 servings

Saffron may be the most expensive spice in the world. And understandably. It is the dried stigmas of the flowering crocus and it takes more than 200,000 stigmas—hand-picked—to make a pound. The spice comes in whole stem form and in powder. It is generally quite pungent—a little goes a long way—and gives foods (rice, for instance) a magnificent golden color. A tablespoonful is called for in the recipe below, on this page, but the amount may be varied according to conscience and pocketbook. It could be omitted altogether, but then, of course, it would scarcely be saffron beef. Saffron is usually available wherever fine spices are sold.

¼ cup butter, chicken fat, or vegetable oil
3 pounds onions, cut in half and thinly sliced
1 large clove garlic, peeled and thinly sliced
  Salt and freshly ground pepper to taste
1 green pepper, cubed
5 pounds bottom round of beef, cut into cubes each about one and one-half inches
1 pound tomatoes, cored, peeled, and cubed
1 teaspoon chopped fresh thyme or ½ teaspoon dried thyme
1 tablespoon loosely packed whole saffron
1 15-ounce can tomato puree

1. Preheat the oven to 325 degrees.
2. Heat the butter in a large casserole with a close-fitting lid.
3. Add the onions and garlic and sprinkle with salt and pepper to taste. Cook until the onion is wilted, stirring gently. Add the green pepper and beef. Spoon the tomatoes over all and add the thyme, more salt and pepper to taste, and the saffron. Add the tomato puree and stir. Bring to a boil on top of the stove. Cover and place the casserole in the oven and bake three hours.

4. Remove the casserole from the oven and uncover. Skim off all the fat. If a thicker sauce is desired, strain the liquid and keep the meat hot. Reduce the sauce by half, stirring frequently, to make certain it does not stick or burn. Add the meat and heat through. Serve with rice.

Lamb Stew, Spanish Style

6 servings

2 pounds breast of lamb
⅓ cup all-purpose flour
1 medium onion, chopped
3 tablespoons shortening
3 cups hot water
1 bay leaf
3½ teaspoons salt
½ teaspoon whole black peppercorns
¼ cup sweet pepper flakes
½ cup uncooked rice
2 cups (1 1-pound 3-ounce can) tomatoes
1 cup frozen peas, thawed
1 egg, beaten
1 teaspoon olive oil
½ teaspoon cider vinegar

1. Wipe the lamb and cut it into one-and-one-half-inch pieces. Dredge in the flour.
2. Cook the onion in the shortening until golden. Add the lamb and cook until brown.
3. Add the hot water, bay leaf, salt, and peppercorns. Cover and cook slowly one and one-half hours, or until the lamb is almost tender.
4. Add the sweet pepper flakes and rice and simmer thirty minutes longer. Add the tomatoes and peas ten minutes before cooking time is up.
5. Mix the egg, olive oil, and vinegar and add to the stew, stirring, without letting it boil, until thickened. Serve hot.

Chicken Español

4 to 6 servings

1 roasting chicken (4 pounds), cut into serving pieces
All-purpose flour
Salt and freshly ground black pepper
¼ cup olive oil
¾ cup chopped onion
1 clove garlic, finely minced
2 ribs celery, finely chopped
1 small green pepper, seeded, cored, and chopped
1½ cups Chicken Stock (page 115)
½ pound mushrooms, sliced
2 tablespoons butter
12 stuffed olives, sliced

1. Preheat the oven to 325 degrees.

2. Dredge the chicken pieces with flour seasoned with salt and pepper, then brown on all sides in the oil. Transfer the chicken to a small casserole.

3. Add the onion, garlic, celery, and green pepper to the skillet and cook, stirring, for about five minutes. Pour the vegetables over the chicken.

4. Bring the stock to a boil and pour it over the chicken. Cover the casserole and bake for thirty to forty-five minutes, or until the chicken is tender.

5. Meanwhile, cook the mushrooms in the butter for about five minutes. Five minutes before the chicken is done, add the mushrooms and olives to the casserole. This dish will keep for an hour or so before serving, but it must be served hot.

Chicken and Pork Español

6 servings

6 chicken legs
¾ pound lean pork, cut into strips ½ inch wide
2 tablespoons cider vinegar
1 bay leaf
1 teaspoon crushed peppercorns or ½ teaspoon freshly ground black pepper
2 tablespoons finely chopped onion
1 clove garlic, finely minced
1 tablespoon salt
6 stuffed olives, sliced
1 cup canned tomatoes
1 cup uncooked rice

1. Combine the chicken legs, pork, vinegar, bay leaf, peppercorns, onion, garlic, and salt. Let stand for one hour, or longer if there is time.

2. Preheat the oven to 350 degrees.

3. Combine the meat and seasonings with the olives, tomatoes, and rice. Pour into a casserole, cover, and bake for one to one and one-half hours, or until the chicken and pork are tender when tested with a fork and the rice has absorbed most of the liquid. Serve hot.

Chicken with Saffron Cream Sauce

6 to 8 servings

2 chickens (2 to 2½ pounds), cut into serving pieces
2 sprigs parsley
1 rib celery with leaves
1 onion, quartered
2 quarts water
  Salt and freshly ground pepper
5 tablespoons butter
¾ cup finely chopped onion
2 shallots, finely chopped
1 tablespoon whole saffron, more or less to taste
¼ cup dry vermouth
3 egg yolks
1 cup heavy cream

1. Make a chicken stock with the wing tips, necks, and backs of the chickens. Combine these parts with the parsley, celery, quartered onion, water, and salt and pepper to taste. Cook one hour and strain.

2. Heat the butter in a large skillet and add the chicken parts, skin side down. Sprinkle with salt and pepper and cook gently about fifteen minutes, barely browning. Cover and cook about fifteen minutes longer, or until tender and cooked.

3. Remove the chicken and add the chopped onion, shallots, and saffron. Stir briefly, then add the vermouth. Stir with a wooden spoon to dissolve the brown particles on the bottom and sides of the pan. Add two and one-half cups of the chicken stock and bring to a boil.

4. Beat the egg yolks lightly and stir in the cream. Add a little of the hot broth, then stir the egg mixture into the hot sauce, stirring rapidly with a wire whisk. Return the chicken to the sauce; heat briefly. Serve with rice.

Spanish Duck, Mountain Style

4 servings

¼ cup olive oil
  Paprika
1 duck (4 to 5 pounds), quartered
1 medium onion, chopped
¼ cup all-purpose flour
2 cups Chicken Stock (page 115)
½ cup sherry
1 medium tomato, sliced
¼ cup chopped pimento-stuffed green olives

1. Combine the olive oil and one tablespoon paprika in a Dutch oven. Mix well. Add the duck and cook until browned on all sides. Remove the duck and set aside.

2. Add the onion to the drippings in the pan and cook for five minutes. Add the flour and mix well. Gradually add the stock and sherry and cook over low heat, stirring constantly, until thickened.

3. Add the tomato and olives and return the duck pieces to the pan. Cover and cook over low heat for about one hour, until the duck is tender. Sprinkle with additional paprika and serve.

Rice Andalouse

4 to 6 servings

2 tablespoons butter
¼ cup chopped onion
1 cup uncooked rice
2 cups Chicken Stock (page 115)
  Salt and freshly ground pepper to taste
1 bay leaf
2 sprigs parsley
¾ cup hot, freshly cooked green peas
¼ cup chopped pimento

1. Heat the butter in a saucepan and add the onion. Cook until the onion is translucent. Add the rice and stir. Add the chicken stock, salt, pepper, bay leaf, and parsley. Cover and bring to a boil. Simmer until the rice is cooked and all the liquid is absorbed, about twenty minutes. Discard the bay leaf and parsley.

2. Carefully stir the peas and pimento into the rice. Cover and let stand until ready to serve.

Rice with Chicken and Sausage

6 to 8 servings

3 slices bacon, cut into small squares
2 cups finely chopped onion
3 cloves garlic, finely minced
2 green peppers, cored, seeded, and chopped
1 pound Spanish or Italian sweet sausage
½ pound Spanish or Italian hot sausage
4 cups Chicken Stock (page 115), approximately
   Salt and freshly ground black pepper
12 stuffed green olives
1 tablespoon capers
1 teaspoon whole saffron, crushed, or ½ teaspoon powdered saffron
1 chicken (3 pounds), cut into serving pieces
1 tablespoon paprika
¼ cup olive oil
2 cups uncooked rice
1 cup cooked green peas
   Pimento for garnish

1. Preheat the oven to 400 degrees.

2. Combine the bacon, onion, garlic, and green peppers in a skillet. Slice all the sausages into one-half-inch lengths and add. Cook all together until the onions are wilted.

3. Spoon the mixture into an earthenware casserole and add one-quarter cup of the stock. Add salt and pepper to taste, the olives, capers, and saffron.

4. Sprinkle the chicken pieces with salt, pepper, and the paprika. Cook in the olive oil until brown on all sides, then add to the casserole.

5. Rinse the rice in a colander and add to the casserole. Add the remaining stock and cover. Bake thirty-five to forty minutes, stirring once during the baking. If the rice becomes too dry, add more stock. When the rice is tender, uncover and reduce the oven heat to 300 degrees. Add the peas and cook ten minutes longer.

6. Garnish with pimento and serve with a chilled dry white wine or cold beer.

Valencian Rice

8 servings

2 tablespoons butter
2 tablespoons finely chopped onion
2 young, tender zucchini, cut into small
  cubes (there should be about 1½ cups)
¾ cup peeled, cubed fresh tomatoes
2 cups uncooked rice
2 cups water
  Salt and freshly ground pepper to taste
½ cup Chicken Stock (page 115)
2 sprigs fresh thyme or 1 teaspoon dried
  thyme
2 sprigs fresh parsley
½ bay leaf
2 tablespoons chopped pimentos
½ package frozen green peas, cooked according to package directions
3 tablespoons butter

1. Preheat the oven to 400 degrees.
2. Melt the butter in a flameproof casserole and add the onion. Cook, stirring, until
the onion is wilted. Add the zucchini and
tomatoes and stir. Cook until most of the
liquid evaporates. Add the rice and stir.
3. Add the water, salt, pepper, and chicken
broth and bring to a boil on top of the stove.
Tie together the thyme, parsley, and bay leaf
and add it. Cover and bring to a boil once
more.
4. Place the casserole in the oven and
bake eighteen minutes, or until the moisture
is absorbed and the rice is tender. Off the
heat add the pimento, green peas, and butter
and toss until all is incorporated.

Spanish Caramel Custard

4 servings

½ cup granulated sugar
1 teaspoon water
4 egg yolks or 3 whole eggs
2 cups milk, scalded
½ teaspoon vanilla extract

1. Place six tablespoons of the sugar and
the water in a heavy skillet. Heat over low
heat, shaking or stirring with a wooden spoon
occasionally to prevent burning, until the
sugar turns into a golden syrup.
2. Immediately pour the caramel syrup
into a shallow baking dish (8 x 8) or pie
plate. Cool until firm.
3. Preheat the oven to 325 degrees.
4. Beat together either the egg yolks or
the whole eggs. Combine with the milk,
vanilla extract, and remaining sugar and
beat until well blended. Pour over the cooled
caramel.
5. Set the baking dish in a pan of hot
water. Bake for one to one and one-half
hours, or until set. Cool and chill. To serve,
carefully invert onto a serving platter.

Sweden

Inlagd Sill

(Swedish Pickled Herring)

12 pickled herring fillets

6 salt herring
4 cups white vinegar
1 cup granulated sugar
4 medium red onions
5 whole sprigs fresh dill
1 carrot, sliced
6 peppercorns
4 bay leaves
2 tablespoons or more chopped fresh dill
2 teaspoons whole allspice, crushed

1. Place the herring, one at a time, on a flat surface. Using a sharp knife, neatly cut away and discard about one-half inch of the "belly." Clean the inside of the fish cavity.

2. Fillet the fish. To do this, hold the knife horizontal to the table and run the knife along the main bone structure of the fish from the head section toward the tail. Then repeat, turning the fish over to remove the other fillet. Using the fingers and the knife, pull away the skin from both fillets.

3. As the herring are filleted, drop the fillets into a basin of cold water and let stand overnight.

4. Combine three cups of the white vinegar and three-quarters cup of the sugar in a saucepan.

5. Cut three of the onions into eighths and add to the vinegar-sugar mixture. Add the dill sprigs, carrot, peppercorns, bay leaves, and half the allspice. Bring to a boil and stir until the sugar is dissolved. Let cool.

6. Arrange the herring fillets in one or two glass jars or crocks and pour the liquid and vegetables over the fillets. The fillets should be covered with the marinade. Cover and refrigerate one week or longer.

7. When ready to serve, drain the herring and discard the original marinade and vegetables. Or, if desired, remove only a few fillets at a time from the marinade and keep the remainder refrigerated. Slice the herring crosswise into bite-sized pieces and arrange neatly in serving dishes.

8. Combine the remaining cup of vinegar and the one-quarter cup of sugar. Stir until sugar dissolves. Divide this mixture equally over the herring. Cut the remaining onion into wafer-thin slices and scatter it over the fish. Sprinkle with the chopped dill and the remaining teaspoon of crushed allspice. Serve as an appetizer.

Pickled Salmon

12 or more servings

1 4-pound section of salmon, preferably
   middle cut
3 tablespoons salt
1 teaspoon white peppercorns, crushed
3 tablespoons granulated sugar
   Twigs of pine or spruce, if available
3 bunches fresh dill
2 tablespoons Cognac
   Fresh dill for garnish
1 lemon, cut in wedges, for garnish

1. Bone the fish and separate it carefully into two sections or fillets. Do not scrape or rinse, but dry with paper towels.

2. Mix together the salt, pepper, and sugar and sprinkle the mixture on the boned (flesh) side of both pieces of fish. Spread some of the twigs and one bunch of dill on the bottom of a deep, flat dish and place one of the pieces of fish on this bed, skin side down. Spread another bunch of dill over the fish, sprinkle on the Cognac, and place the second piece of fish on it, skin side up. Turn the fish to make the most compact "sandwich," putting the thin end of one piece over the thick end of the other. Cover with the remaining dill and twigs and put a board or plate with a weight on top. Keep in a cool pantry or the bottom of the refrigerator for thirty-six hours.

3. Scrape off the spices and slice thin like smoked salmon or in regular serving pieces. Garnish with fresh dill and wedges of lemon, and serve, as an appetizer, with any mustard sauce or a sweetened mustard vinaigrette.

Note: Pickled salmon will keep a week in the refrigerator.

Beef à la Lindstrom

4 servings

1¼ pounds round steak, ground
  2 boiled potatoes, peeled and chopped
  2 egg yolks
  ½ cup heavy cream
    Salt and freshly ground pepper to taste
  ¾ cup finely diced pickled beets
1½ tablespoons capers
  2 tablespoons finely chopped onion
  3 tablespoons butter

1. Place the meat in a mixing bowl and add the potatoes and egg yolks. Beat with a wooden spoon. Add the cream gradually while beating vigorously. Beat in the salt and pepper.

2. Stir in the beets, capers, and onion and refrigerate one hour.

3. Shape into four cakes about one inch thick. Heat the butter in a skillet and brown the patties on both sides, turning once. Remove the patties to a warm platter and add a little water to the skillet. Stir to dissolve the brown particles. Pour over the meat and serve hot. Serve with sautéed potatoes and pickled gherkins.

Swedish Meat Balls I

6 to 8 servings

¼ pound lean veal
¼ pound lean pork
1 pound round steak
1 egg, lightly beaten
½ cup milk
1¼ cups heavy cream
½ cup fresh bread crumbs
2 tablespoons grated onion
 Salt and freshly ground pepper to taste
¼ teaspoon ground allspice
3 tablespoons butter
2 tablespoons all-purpose flour
1 cup boiling Beef Stock (page 115) or canned beef broth

1. Have the veal, pork, and beef put through a grinder four times. Put the ground meat into a mixing bowl and add the egg, milk, one-half cup of the cream, bread crumbs, onion, salt, pepper, and allspice. Mix well with the hands, then shape into thirty to forty balls of equal size.

2. Heat the butter in a large skillet and brown the balls on all sides. Pour off most of the fat and sprinkle the flour over the meat balls. Shake the balls around in the skillet so that they are coated with flour.

3. Add the boiling stock and cover. Simmer forty-five minutes, then pour in the remaining cream. Bring to a boil and serve hot, with boiled potatoes.

Swedish Meat Balls II

4 to 6 servings

½ pound round steak, ground
½ pound veal, ground
¼ pound pork, ground
1 cup bread cubes
3 tablespoons milk
3 tablespoons cream
3 tablespoons finely grated onion
1 clove garlic, finely minced
 Salt and freshly ground pepper to taste
¼ teaspoon freshly grated nutmeg
¼ teaspoon freshly grated allspice
1 egg, lightly beaten
2 tablespoons salad oil, approximately
¼ cup butter, approximately
2½ cups Beef Stock (page 115) or canned beef broth
2 tablespoons all-purpose flour

1. Preheat the oven to 350 degrees.

2. Combine the ground steak, veal, and pork and put the mixture through a food grinder twice. Or have the meats ground together three times by the butcher.

3. Place the meats in a mixing bowl. Soak the bread cubes in the milk and cream until the liquid is absorbed. Add this to the meat. Add the onion, garlic, salt, pepper, nutmeg, allspice, and egg and blend all together with the hands. Shape the mixture into thirty to forty small meat balls.

4. Heat the oil and half the butter in a skillet and brown the meat balls on all sides. As they brown, transfer them to a baking dish. Add the beef stock and bake half an hour, or until thoroughly cooked.

5. Pour off the liquid from the baking dish into a saucepan. Keep the meat balls hot. Blend the remaining butter with the flour and stir this, bit by bit, into the boiling broth. Pour the sauce over the meat balls and serve piping hot.

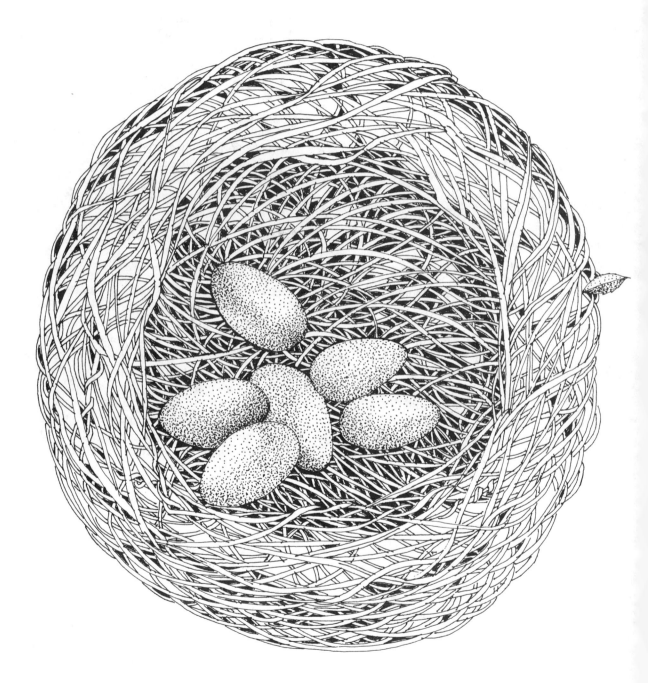

Swedish Meat Balls III

About 50 meat balls

2¼ pounds beef, pork, or veal or a combination of the 3, finely ground
1 cup heavy cream
4 slices white bread
3 eggs
4 teaspoons salt
1 teaspoon freshly ground white pepper
1¼ cups finely minced onion
¼ cup melted butter
½ teaspoon ground allspice (optional)
Vegetable oil for frying

1. The meat should be put through a grinder four times, the last time using a fine blade of the grinder. Place the meat in a mixing bowl.

2. Pour the cream into the container of an electric blender.

3. Trim away and discard the crusts from the bread. Cut the white part into cubes and add to the blender. Let stand until the cream is absorbed. Add the eggs and blend just until the bread and eggs are thoroughly blended. Add this to the meat, then add the salt and pepper.

4. Cook the onion in butter until wilted. Do not brown. Add this to the meat mixture and, if desired, add the allspice.

5. Blend the mixture with the fingers, then shape the mixture into meat balls the size of walnuts.

6. Pour the oil into a skillet to a depth of about one-quarter inch and cook the meat balls, turning gently, until browned and cooked through. Serve hot.

Lamb with Dill

8 or more servings

5½ pounds lamb shoulder or breast of lamb, cut into serving pieces
   Salt
½ cup chopped fresh dill
2 carrots, finely chopped
2 ribs celery, finely chopped
2 medium onions, finely diced
12 peppercorns
3 tablespoons butter
3 tablespoons all-purpose flour
1 tablespoon granulated sugar
¼ cup vinegar
2 egg yolks
½ cup heavy cream

1. Place the lamb in a kettle and add water to cover and salt to taste. Do not oversalt because the cooking liquid will be boiled down later. Bring to a boil and skim off the fat. Add one tablespoon of the dill, the carrots, celery, onions, and peppercorns. Return to a boil and skim again. Simmer until the meat is thoroughly tender, about one hour.

2. Drain the broth from the kettle into a saucepan and cook over high heat until reduced to about two cups. Keep the meat hot.

3. Melt two tablespoons of the butter in a saucepan and stir in the flour with a wire whisk. Add the broth, stirring rapidly with the whisk. When the mixture is thickened and smooth, continue to cook for about ten minutes.

4. Stir in the remaining dill, sugar, and vinegar. Blend the egg yolks with the cream.

5. Remove the sauce from the heat and stir in the cream mixture. Add the meat to the sauce and reheat just to the boiling point. Just before serving, and off the heat, swirl in the remaining tablespoon of cold butter by rotating the pan gently.

Swedish Christmas Ham

15 to 20 servings

1 fresh leg of pork (10 to 12 pounds)
1 tablespoon saltpeter
  Salt (see note)
3½ tablespoons sugar
1 egg
½ tablespoon prepared mustard
¼ teaspoon ground ginger
3 tablespoons fresh bread crumbs

1. First, cure the ham (three to six weeks). Select a crock large enough for the ham.

2. Place the leg on a tray. Combine the saltpeter, two tablespoons of salt, and three tablespoons of the sugar. Blend well, then rub this mixture into the ham on all sides. The ham must be massaged well with the mixture. Let the ham stand in a cool place overnight.

3. Meanwhile, prepare a brine. In a kettle add enough water to cover the ham and start adding salt, stirring until the salt dissolves. Test the salt content with the egg. Enough salt should be added and dissolved to make the raw egg float in the brine. Bring the brine to a boil, then let it cool overnight.

4. The next day, place the ham in the crock and pour the brine over it. Let the ham stand three to six weeks in a cool place.

5. When the ham is cured, remove it. Soak it in fresh water to cover overnight. Drain and add fresh water to cover. Bring to a boil and cook three to four hours, or until thoroughly tender. Cool in the cooking liquid.

6. Preheat the oven to 500 degrees.

7. Remove the ham from the liquid and pat dry. Carefully pare away the rind.

8. Blend the mustard, the remaining sugar, and the ginger. Mix well, then smear the mixture over the ham. Sprinkle with bread crumbs and bake for five to ten minutes, or until the crumbs are golden brown.

Note: Do not use iodized salt in this recipe. Use pure salt or kosher salt.

Swedish Liver Pâté

4 to 6 servings

2 pounds pork liver or calves' liver
1 medium onion
1 pound pork fat
¼ cup butter
¼ cup all-purpose flour
2 cups light cream
2 eggs, well beaten
2 teaspoons anchovy paste, or to taste
2 teaspoons salt
1 teaspoon freshly ground black pepper
½ teaspoon ground ginger

1. Preheat the oven to 325 degrees.

2. Grind the liver and onion twice with the finest blade of the meat grinder. Grind the pork fat twice.

3. Melt the butter and stir in the flour with a whisk. Gradually stir in the cream. Cook over low heat, stirring constantly with the whisk, until thickened and smooth. Add the ground pork fat and stir until the fat has melted.

4. Remove the mixture from heat. Add the liver and the remaining ingredients and blend thoroughly. Spoon into a two-quart baking dish. Place the dish in a baking pan containing hot water and bake one and one-half to two hours, or until a cake tester inserted in the center comes out clean. Cover with a lid or aluminum foil if the top of the pâté browns too quickly. Replenish the water in the baking pan if necessary. Cool before serving.

Jansson's Temptation

6 servings

1 tin (3¼ ounces) anchovy sprats
1 cup finely diced onion
¼ cup butter
3 to 4 large Idaho potatoes
1½ cups light cream
    Freshly ground black pepper

1. Preheat the oven to 350 degrees. Butter a one-and-one-half-quart baking dish.

2. Open the tin of anchovy sprats, taking out the sprats and saving the juice. Chop the sprats and set aside.

3. Cook the onion in butter until translucent and set aside.

4. Wash and peel the potatoes, then drop into a basin of water until ready to use. Drain one potato at a time and cut it into thin slices. Cut the slices into very thin strips (julienne). There should be about three and one-half cups. Working quickly, place the potatoes in a saucepan. Add the cream and immediately bring to a boil. Pour the potatoes and cream into the baking dish and stir in the chopped sprats, the liquid from the tin, and the chopped onion. Add pepper to taste and bake, uncovered, for fifty minutes to one hour.

Swedish Cucumber Salad

12 servings

6 cucumbers
¾ cup wine vinegar
2 tablespoons cold water
⅓ cup granulated sugar
    Salt and freshly ground black pepper
1 tablespoon freshly chopped dill (optional)

1. Peel the cucumbers and slice thin. Place the slices in a basin of ice water. When ready to use, drain and dry between towels.

2. Combine the vinegar, water, sugar, and salt and pepper to taste. Pour the mixture over the cucumbers.

3. Chill for an hour or longer before serving. Garnish with dill, if desired.

Glögg

20 or more servings

2 bottles red Bordeaux wine
2 bottles port wine
2 tablespoons grated orange peel
4 broken cinnamon sticks
20 whole cloves
20 cardamom seeds
2 cups blanched almonds
1 pound seedless raisins
1 pound lump sugar
2 cups Cognac

1. Combine the Bordeaux and port in a large stainless steel, ceramic, or porcelainized serving vessel. Heat very gently and stir in the grated orange peel.

2. Tie together the cinnamon, cloves, and cardamom in a cheesecloth bag. Add this to the glögg and steep over very low heat. The liquid should be barely boiling. Simmer fifteen minutes, then add the almonds and raisins and continue simmering fifteen minutes.

3. Place a wire grill over the vessel and arrange the sugar on the grill. Spoon the Cognac over the sugar and ignite the cubes. When the sugar is melted, remove the grill. Cover the serving vessel until the flame dies. Serve in after-dinner coffee cups or in glögg cups.

Laggtarta

8 servings

One of the delights of a Swedish kitchen is an easily made confection known as Laggtarta *(literally, pan cake). The layers, light as eiderdown, are lavishly spread with apple-sauce and served with fruit and whipped cream. The trick in making the dessert is the use of a seasoned griddle or its equivalent. Select an eight- or ten-inch cast-iron griddle, an omelet pan or a heavy cast-aluminum skillet with heatproof handle. To season, grease lightly with shortening and heat slowly until fat smokes; wipe with paper towels, allow to cool, and repeat the process once more.*

> 3 eggs
> 1 cup granulated sugar
> 1 cup sifted cake flour
> 1 teaspoon baking powder
> ½ cup butter
> 1 cup thick applesauce
> ⅓ cup pureed strawberries or raspberries (optional)
> Confectioners' sugar
> Sweetened fresh fruit (strawberries or blueberries)
> Sweetened whipped cream

1. Preheat the oven to 425 degrees. Have ready a seasoned griddle, pan, or skillet as outlined in the introduction to this recipe. Beat the eggs and sugar together, using an electric beater on high speed, until the mixture is lemon yellow and quite thick.

2. Sift the flour and baking powder together. Use a rubber spatula, and with a gentle motion, fold the flour mixture into the egg mixture. Cut through the center of mixture, then around the bottom of the saucepan, then draw the spatula up and out.

3. Meanwhile, clarify the butter. To do this, let the butter melt in a small pan over very low heat. Let it cool slightly, then gradually add the clear, yellow liquid to the batter, folding it in with the spatula. Discard the white sediment.

4. Grease and heat the griddle or pan. Pour and spread one-sixth of the batter (about two-thirds cup) onto an eight-inch griddle or pan (or one-quarter of the batter onto a ten-inch griddle or pan). Bake five to seven minutes, or until the "cake" is lightly browned.

5. Loosen all around and underneath the cake layer with a spatula and gradually ease out onto a cake rack. Clean the griddle or pan thoroughly, regrease, and heat before repeating with successive sixths (or quarters) of the batter. Continue until all the batter is used.

6. In a mixing bowl, combine the applesauce with the pureed berries, if a pink filling is desired, and use between the layers, stacking the cake layers carefully. Sprinkle the top with confectioners' sugar and serve fruit and whipped cream separately.

Switzerland

Veal Cutlets from Ouchy

4 to 6 servings

> Butter
> 1 tablespoon anchovy paste
> 1½ pounds veal scallops
> Thin slices of boiled ham
> Thin slices of Gruyère cheese
> 1 egg, beaten with 1 tablespoon water
> All-purpose flour

1. Soften one-quarter cup of butter and mix with the anchovy paste.

2. Trim the meat so that the slices are all of the same size. Spread the anchovy butter on half of the meat slices. Top each with a slice of boiled ham and a slice of cheese. Cover with the remaining veal as if making sandwiches. Secure each meat sandwich with a food pick or tie with string. Take care that the cheese is well covered by the meat, or the cheese will ooze out during the cooking.

3. Dip the meat sandwiches in the beaten egg and then in the flour. Sauté in hot butter for three to five minutes on each side, or until golden brown. Serve very hot, with any green vegetable.

Veal Scallops with Cheese

4 servings

> 8 thin slices Italian-style veal (scaloppine)
> 2 eggs, lightly beaten
> Juice of ½ lemon
> Salt and freshly ground black pepper
> Nutmeg
> ¼ cup butter
> 8 thin slices Gruyère or Swiss cheese
> ½ cup Chicken Stock (page 115)

1. Have the veal slices pounded or pound them between pieces of waxed paper with a flat mallet.

2. Blend the eggs, lemon juice, and salt and pepper to taste in a large pie plate or baking dish. Dip the meat, one slice at a time, in the mixture to coat well. Sprinkle lightly with nutmeg to taste.

3. Cook the meat quickly, first on one side, then the other, until lightly browned on each side. Cover each slice with a slice of cheese and cover the pan. Cook over low heat just until the cheese melts. Transfer the meat to hot serving dishes and keep warm.

4. Add the chicken stock to the skillet, let the stock boil briskly for about one minute, and pour the hot drippings around the veal. Serve immediately, with rice.

Veal Cordon Bleu

6 servings

One of the simplest, most delicate, and most gratifying dishes of any cuisine is sautéed-in-butter, breaded veal scallops. Rich in flavor to begin with, the dish is enhanced by such additions as lemon and anchovies and capers. Stuffed with ham and cheese, when it is known as cordon bleu *it is an absolute delight, particularly if the cheese used is a Gruyère and the ham is prosciutto.*

12 veal scallops (3 to 4 ounces each), preferably cut from the leg
Salt and freshly ground pepper to taste
6 round, thin slices prosciutto or ham
6 thin slices Gruyère or Swiss cheese
2 eggs, lightly beaten
1 teaspoon water
All-purpose flour
1½ cups fresh bread crumbs
½ cup butter
Parsley sprigs

1. Place each veal scallop between pieces of waxed paper and pound with a flat mallet or the bottom of a small, heavy skillet until thin. Sprinkle lightly on both sides with salt and pepper.

2. Place one slice of ham in the center of each of six scallops and top each with a slice of cheese.

3. Beat together the eggs and water. Brush the outside perimeter of the veal with the beaten egg and top with another slice of veal.

4. Carefully dredge the filled pieces of meat in flour on both sides. Dip the pieces in the beaten egg and then in the crumbs until well coated. Pat the pieces lightly with the side of a heavy kitchen knife to help the crumbs adhere.

5. Transfer the meat to a wire rack and refrigerate one or two hours. This, too, will help the breading adhere to the cutlets as they cook.

6. Heat the butter in a large skillet and, when it is hot but not brown or smoking, sauté the cutlets in it until golden on all sides.

7. Arrange the cutlets on a heated platter and garnish each serving with a sprig of parsley.

Wienerschnitzel

4 servings

4 veal scallops (6 ounces each), preferably cut from the leg
Salt and freshly ground pepper to taste
All-purpose flour
1 egg
1 teaspoon water
1 cup fresh bread crumbs
½ cup butter
Lemon wedges

1. Place each scallop between pieces of waxed paper and pound with a flat mallet or the bottom of a small, heavy skillet until thin. Sprinkle lightly on both sides with salt and pepper. Dredge lightly but thoroughly with flour.

2. Beat the egg lightly with the water and dip the floured cutlets in the mixture. Turn the veal in the crumbs until well coated. Pat them lightly with the side of a heavy kitchen knife. This will help the crumbs adhere. Transfer the meat to a wire rack and refrigerate one or two hours. This, too, will help the breading adhere to the cutlets as they cook.

3. Heat the butter in a large skillet and, when it is hot but not brown or smoking, sauté the cutlets in it until golden brown on both sides.

4. Arrange the cutlets on a heated serving platter and garnish with lemon wedges. Serve immediately.

Veal, Swiss Style

4 servings

The veal-in-cream dish on this page is as thoroughly Swiss as edelweiss and alpenhorns. It is absolutely delectable and—adding virtue to virtue—phenomenally easy to prepare. Once the ingredients are ready for the skillet, it cooks in less than ten minutes.

1 pound boneless veal, preferably from the leg
  Salt and freshly ground pepper to taste
3 tablespoons corn oil
¼ cup butter
2 tablespoons finely chopped shallots
¼ cup dry white wine
½ cup Chicken Stock (page 115) or Beef Stock (page 115)
1 cup heavy cream
1 tablespoon minced parsley

1. Cut the veal into half-inch cubes or smaller pieces. Sprinkle with salt and pepper to taste.

2. Heat the oil to almost smoking in a skillet and add the veal. Stir rapidly with a two-pronged fork. The meat will cook quite rapidly, and it should not brown.

3. Use a slotted spoon and transfer the meat to a warm dish.

4. Immediately wipe out the skillet and add the butter. When it is frothy, add the shallots and stir. Do not brown. Add the wine and let it reduce almost completely. Add the stock and cook down by half. Add the liquid that has accumulated from the meat, but do not add the meat. Simmer about one minute, then add the cream. Simmer one minute, stirring, then add the meat and salt and pepper to taste. Bring to a boil and serve hot, sprinkled with chopped parsley.

Potato Croquettes

4 servings

5 medium Idaho potatoes
2 tablespoons butter
½ teaspoon nutmeg
  Salt and freshly ground black pepper
⅓ cup grated Swiss or Cheddar cheese
1 egg yolk
½ cup all-purpose flour
1 egg, lightly beaten
1 teaspoon vegetable oil
2 tablespoons water
1 cup bread crumbs
¼ cup freshly grated Parmesan cheese
  Vegetable oil for deep frying

1. Preheat the oven to 400 degrees.

2. Bake the potatoes until tender, forty-five minutes to one hour. Scoop out the flesh and put it through a sieve or ricer into a heavy flameproof casserole. Place over very low heat.

3. Using a wooden spoon, beat in the butter, nutmeg, and salt and pepper to taste. Beat in the Swiss or Cheddar cheese and the egg yolk over low heat. Beat and stir until the mixture comes away from the sides of the pan. Cool, then chill.

4. Shape the mixture into approximately eighteen balls. Dredge in the flour.

5. Combine the egg with the teaspoon oil, water, and salt and pepper to taste. Dip the balls into the mixture. Combine the crumbs with the Parmesan cheese and roll the balls in this mixture. Deep-fry at 360 degrees until golden brown, then drain on paper towels. Keep warm, if necessary, in a 300-degree oven.

Gruyère Potatoes

4 servings

1½ cups milk
2 tablespoons butter
   Salt and freshly ground pepper
3 medium baking potatoes
1 teaspoon finely minced garlic
½ cup freshly grated Gruyère or Swiss cheese

1. Preheat the oven to 325 degrees.
2. Combine the milk, butter, and salt and pepper to taste in a saucepan. Bring to a boil.
3. Rinse the potatoes under cold running water and peel them. Cut the potatoes into slices one-eighth inch thick but do not drop the slices into cold water as usual. Drop them instead into the hot milk. Add the garlic. Partially cover and return to a boil. Simmer about fifteen minutes. Pour the potatoes into a buttered one-and-one-half-quart baking dish and sprinkle the cheese on top. Bake until the sauce thickens and the top is golden brown.

Swiss Rosti Potatoes

4 servings

1 pound potatoes
6 tablespoons butter
   Salt and freshly ground pepper

1. Boil the potatoes. Cook large potatoes about twenty minutes, medium ones about fifteen minutes. Let cool, then chill. Peel and grate finely.
2. Heat four tablespoons of the butter in a black iron skillet and, when it is hot, add the potatoes. Smooth them down gently with the back of a kitchen spoon. Add salt and pepper to taste and dot with the remaining butter. Let cook over moderate heat until quite brown underneath, taking care that the potatoes do not burn.

3. Slide the potatoes onto a plate and invert the skillet over the uncooked side. Quickly invert both plate and skillet so that the uncooked side is at the bottom of the skillet. Continue cooking that side until it is browned. Serve hot.

Swiss Squash

6 servings

6 medium yellow squash
6 tablespoons butter
1 cup finely chopped onion
½ cup finely minced ham
3 cloves garlic, finely minced
3 sprigs fresh thyme, finely chopped, or ½ teaspoon dried thyme
½ bay leaf
   Salt and freshly ground black pepper
1 cup bread crumbs
1½ cups freshly grated Gruyère or Swiss cheese
2 egg yolks

1. Preheat the oven to 350 degrees.
2. Pare off the ends of the squash and split each in half. Scoop out the center of each squash, leaving a quarter-inch-thick shell. Drop the shells into boiling salted water and simmer three minutes. Drain.
3. Chop the scooped-out squash pulp fine.
4. Heat four tablespoons of the butter in a skillet and add the onion. Stir until the onion is wilted and add the ham. Cook two minutes, then add the chopped squash.
5. Meanwhile, chop together the garlic, thyme, and bay leaf until it is a fine mixture. Add to the stuffing, along with salt and pepper to taste. Cook, stirring occasionally, about five minutes, or until slightly dry. Add the bread crumbs, half the cheese, and the yolks. Fill the shells with the mixture and sprinkle with the remaining cheese. Dot with the remaining butter and bake thirty minutes. Brown quickly under the broiler. Serve hot.

Syria

Raw Kibbee

8 servings

¾ cup fine (no. 1) burghul or cracked wheat
1 pound lean lamb, ground
1 large onion, finely chopped
¼ cup ice water
  Salt and freshly ground black pepper
  Radish slices
  Hot melted butter

1. Cover the burghul with cold water and let stand twenty minutes. Drain and squeeze out the extra water.
2. Combine the burghul, meat, and onion and grind twice through a fine blade. Knead in ice water and season with salt and pepper to taste. Form into a flat cake and score into a diamond pattern. Garnish with radish slices and serve, with hot melted butter, as an appetizer.

Tabbouleh I

6 servings

1 cup fine (no. 1) burghul or cracked wheat
¾ cup finely chopped onion
½ cup finely chopped green onion, green part and all
1 teaspoon salt
¼ teaspoon freshly ground black pepper
1½ cups finely chopped Italian parsley
½ cup finely chopped fresh mint leaves
½ cup lemon juice
¾ cup olive oil
2 tomatoes, skinned and cut into wedges or chopped

1. Cover the burghul with cold water and allow to stand one hour. Drain and squeeze out the extra water.
2. Add the remaining ingredients except the tomatoes and mix well with the hands. Pile into a dish and garnish with the tomatoes. Serve as an appetizer.

Tabbouleh II

8 to 12 servings

1½ cups no. 2 burghul or cracked wheat
 5 green onions
 1 bunch parsley
 1 tablespoon vinegar
 2 tomatoes, peeled, cored, seeded, and chopped
    Salt
    Juice of 2 lemons
10 fresh mint leaves
½ cup olive oil, or to taste
12 tender heart of romaine leaves

1. Place the burghul in a large mixing bowl and add two quarts of water. Let stand two hours, or until softened. The burghul will expand to three or four times its original size. Drain the burghul in a colander lined with cheesecloth and then squeeze thoroughly with the hands to extract as much water as possible. Place the burghul in a mixing bowl.

2. Trim the green onions at the root end, then rinse, dry, and chop them fine. Add to the burghul.

3. Wash the parsley well in cold water, then wash in a mixture of cold water and the vinegar. Drain and dry on paper towels, then chop. There should be about one cup chopped parsley. Add to the burghul.

4. Add the tomatoes, salt to taste, and lemon juice and toss well. Refrigerate until ready to serve. Before serving, empty the tabbouleh into a wooden salad bowl. Tear the mint leaves into bits, using the fingers, and add. Add the oil and toss. To serve, arrange the romaine leaves on plates and spoon the tabbouleh down each. Serve as an appetizer.

Laban

About 1½ cups, or 6 servings

 4 cups Yogurt (page 554)
½ teaspoon salt
⅓ cup olive oil
 2 tablespoons chopped fresh mint leaves
    Mint leaves for garnish

1. Mix the yogurt and the salt and put in a bag made of several layers of cheesecloth. Tie the bag and suspend it over a bowl to catch the drips. Leave overnight.

2. Remove the solid cheeselike mixture from the bag and either form into balls or make a mound with a depression in the middle. Place in a serving dish. Pour the olive oil over the balls or into the depression and sprinkle with chopped mint. Garnish with the mint leaves and serve as an appetizer.

Hummus

About 3 cups, or 8 to 10 servings

 2 cups cooked or canned chick-peas, drained
⅔ cup taheeni (sesame paste)
¾ cup lemon juice
 2 cloves garlic
 1 teaspoon salt
    Italian parsley leaves

Place the chick-peas, taheeni, lemon juice, garlic, and salt in a blender and blend until smooth. Alternatively, the chick-peas may be sieved and mashed along with the remaining ingredients. Pile into a small bowl and garnish with the parsley leaves. Serve as an appetizer.

Baba Ghanouj

8 servings

2 large eggplants
Juice of 2 lemons
2 tablespoons taheeni or sesame paste
Salt
1 large clove garlic
¼ cup chopped parsley or pomegranate seeds
2 tablespoons olive oil

1. Cook the eggplants until soft over charcoal or on top of a gas flame. If a gas unit is used, line the metal around the burner with aluminum foil. Place the whole, unpeeled eggplants over charcoal or over a slow-to-medium gas flame. Cook the eggplants on all sides, turning as necessary, until soft throughout and the skin is charred. Eventually the eggplants will "collapse." Set them aside for about one hour to cool.

2. Peel the eggplants and discard the skin. Put the flesh into a mixing bowl and immediately add the lemon juice. Mash well. Add the taheeni and blend well. Add salt to taste.

3. Place the garlic clove between sheets of waxed paper and mash and pound gently with a mallet or the bottom of a skillet. The garlic should be mashed as fine as possible. Add to the eggplant mixture, stir well, and chill. Place in a flat serving dish and garnish with parsley or pomegranate seeds. Pour olive oil over the dish and serve as an appetizer.

Cold Eggplant with Pine Nuts

6 servings

1 medium eggplant
¾ cup olive oil, approximately
10 cherry tomatoes
1 clove garlic, finely minced
2 tablespoons finely chopped onion (optional)
½ cup pignoli (pine nuts)
Salt and freshly ground black pepper
¼ cup finely chopped parsley
Lemon wedges

1. Trim off and discard the ends of the eggplant. Cut the eggplant into slices one-quarter inch thick or less.

2. Heat a little oil in a skillet and cook the eggplant slices until golden brown on both sides, adding more oil as necessary. As the eggplant is cooked, drain the slices on paper toweling. Chop the eggplant and place in a mixing bowl.

3. Meanwhile, drop the cherry tomatoes into boiling water and let stand about nine seconds. Drain immediately. The tomatoes will now be easy to peel; use a paring knife to pull away the skin. Chop the tomatoes and add to the mixing bowl. Add the garlic, onion, and pignoli. Season liberally with salt and pepper to taste and spoon the mixture into a serving bowl. Chill and sprinkle with chopped parsley before serving. Serve, with lemon wedges and sesame bread, as an appetizer.

Cracked Wheat with Lamb and Chick-Peas

4 servings

1½ pounds lamb, cut into 2-inch cubes
    Salt and freshly ground black pepper
1 tablespoon lamb fat or peanut oil
1 cup chopped onion
3 tablespoons butter
1 cup burghul or cracked wheat
1 can chick-peas, drained

1. Sprinkle the lamb cubes with salt and pepper and brown on all sides in the lamb fat or peanut oil. Add the onion and cook briefly, until the onion is light brown.

2. Add the butter and enough water to cover the lamb. Simmer until the lamb is almost tender, forty minutes to one hour.

3. Rinse the burghul under cold water and squeeze to remove excess moisture. Add the burghul to the kettle and cook twenty minutes longer, or until all the liquid has been absorbed. Add the chick-peas and cook until the peas are heated through. Serve with Yogurt (page 554).

Baked Kibbee

8 to 12 servings

2 cups no. 3 burghul or cracked wheat
4 pounds round steak, ground
1 onion, finely minced
    Salt and freshly ground black pepper
3 tablespoons butter
6 small white onions, peeled and finely chopped
½ cup pignoli (pine nuts)
¼ teaspoon ground allspice, or to taste

1. Place the burghul in a mixing bowl and add two quarts of boiling water. Let stand three hours, then drain in a colander lined with cheesecloth and squeeze dry with the hands.

2. Preheat the oven to 350 degrees.

3. Place three pounds of the meat in a large mixing bowl and add the finely minced onion and salt and pepper to taste. Add the burghul and blend with the hands. Place the mixture in the center of an oval ten-inch ironstone platter or use a two-quart rectangular glass baking dish. Spoon the mixture evenly over the bottom of the baking utensil, then make a wide cavity so that there is a rim of the meat and burghul mixture about one or one and one-half inches high.

4. Heat the butter in a skillet and cook the finely chopped onions until wilted. Add the pignoli and cook, stirring, until the nuts are golden. Sprinkle with allspice and add the remaining ground meat, then add salt and pepper to taste. Break up the meat with a fork. Do not allow the meat to brown. When it has lost its red color, pour into the center of the cavity. Bake twenty-five minutes. Serve, sliced, with cold Yogurt (page 554).

Lentils with Tomatoes

3 to 4 servings

1 cup lentils
2 quarts water
    Salt
1 onion, finely chopped
1 green pepper, finely chopped
¼ cup olive oil
3 pimentos, chopped
2 cups peeled, chopped tomatoes
    Freshly ground black pepper

1. Rinse the lentils in cold water and drain. Bring the two quarts water to a boil and add the lentils and salt to taste. Simmer twenty minutes, or until tender. Drain.

2. Cook the onion and green pepper in the oil until wilted. Add the pimentos and stir. Add the tomatoes and salt and pepper to taste. Stir in the lentils and cook, uncovered, one-half hour. Serve hot.

Tahiti

Tahitian Poisson Cru

(A Version of Seviche)

8 or more servings

2 pounds freshly caught ocean fish fillets such as mackerel, salmon, red snapper, or tuna
Salt to taste
6 to 8 limes
1 teaspoon mustard, preferably Dijon
1 cup vegetable oil or peanut oil
¼ cup red wine vinegar
2 cloves garlic, finely minced
1 teaspoon granulated sugar
Freshly ground pepper to taste
¾ cup Coconut Cream (page 544; optional)
4 hard-cooked eggs, finely chopped
½ cup finely chopped green onions
½ cup finely chopped celery
¼ cup finely chopped parsley
4 medium tomatoes, peeled, seeded, and cubed
Tomato wedges for garnish
1 hard-cooked egg, put through a sieve, for garnish

1. Cut the fish fillets into long, thin strips or small cubes.

2. Place the fish in a mixing bowl, add salt, and mix thoroughly. Add the juice of the limes. Cover and let stand several hours. Drain.

3. Combine the mustard, oil, vinegar, garlic, sugar, salt, and pepper. Beat well with a whisk to blend. Stir in the coconut cream, if available. Add the chopped eggs, green onions, celery, parsley, and cubed tomatoes. Pour this over the fish and stir to blend. Chill until ready to serve. Pour the mixture into a bowl and garnish with the tomato wedges and sieved hard-cooked egg. Serve as an appetizer.

543

Chicken Rea

(Chicken Turmeric)

4 to 6 servings

2 chickens (2½ pounds each), cut into serving pieces
  Salt and freshly ground pepper to taste
3 tablespoons butter
3 tablespoons vegetable oil
1 large onion, thinly sliced
2 cloves garlic, finely minced
2 cups Coconut Cream (see below)
2 to 3 tablespoons turmeric

1. Sprinkle the chicken pieces with salt and pepper, then brown on all sides in a mixture of butter and oil. Transfer the browned chicken pieces to a Dutch oven with a close-fitting lid.

2. Add the onion and garlic to the skillet and cook briefly, until the onion wilts. Spoon this over the chicken and cover closely. Cook over low heat until the chicken is fork tender, forty-five minutes to an hour.

3. Blend the coconut cream with the turmeric and pour the mixture over the chicken. Add salt and pepper to taste and bring just to a boil. Do not boil, but serve piping hot.

COCONUT CREAM:

About 2 cups

Crack the shell of a coconut and remove the meat. Pare away the dark skin from the meat, then grate the white meat and place in a piece of cheesecloth. Bring up the ends of the cheesecloth to make a bag. Squeeze to extract the juice. If more coconut cream is desired, empty the squeezed coconut into a mixing bowl and add one cup of water. Let stand, then squeeze once more in the cheesecloth.

Baked Papaya

6 servings

3 ripe but firm papayas
6 small pieces vanilla bean
6 teaspoons butter
12 teaspoons brown sugar

1. Preheat the oven to 350 degrees.

2. Peel the papayas with a potato peeler and split each in half. Remove the seeds.

3. Arrange the papaya halves, cut side up, in a baking dish with about one-half inch of water over the bottom. Dot the center of each papaya half with a small piece of vanilla bean, a teaspoon of butter, and two teaspoons of brown sugar. Bake until thoroughly tender, forty-five minutes to an hour.

Trinidad

Glorified Bulljoul

8 or more servings

2 pounds *baccalao* (salt cod)
1½ pounds fresh shrimp, cooked, shelled, and deveined
2½ lemons
1 teaspoon coarsely ground black pepper
½ teaspoon dried thyme
1 large red onion, finely chopped
2 large bell peppers, preferably red, although green will do, chopped
1 10-ounce bottle whole green olives
1 bunch watercress leaves
2 ribs celery, finely chopped
2 tomatoes, peeled and cut into small pieces
1 large or 2 small, ripe, unblemished avocados, peeled and cubed
1 cup olive oil
Lettuce leaves, sliced tomatoes, and avocado wedges for garnish

1. Soak the salt cod overnight in cold water to cover.

2. Drain and place in a saucepan. Add more cold water to cover and bring to a boil. Simmer five minutes, then remove from the heat and drain. Remove any bones from the cod and squeeze the flesh with the hands. Shred the cod and place it in a mixing bowl.

3. Add the shrimp and stir until well blended. Add the juice of the lemons, the pepper, thyme, onion, bell peppers, olives, watercress, celery, and tomato pieces.

4. Place the avocado cubes in the container of an electric blender and blend, gradually adding the oil. Add this to the cod mixture and stir gently to blend everything. Pour the mixture into a serving dish and garnish with lettuce, tomatoes, and avocado wedges.

Trinidad Roast Pork

About 12 servings

1 pork butt (4 to 5 pounds)
½ lemon
1 tablespoon onion juice (made by grating an onion and squeezing through cheesecloth)
1 tablespoon finely minced garlic
1¼ cups soy sauce
2 teaspoons sage
¼ cup finely chopped parsley
2 teaspoons dried chervil (optional)
3 tablespoons finely chopped fresh chives or 4 teaspoons dried chives
2 tablespoons finely chopped fresh tarragon or 4 teaspoons dried tarragon leaves
2 tablespoons finely chopped fresh basil or 4 teaspoons dried basil
2 teaspoons finely ground black pepper
1½ pounds bulk sausage
1½ cups finely chopped onion
1 large bell pepper, preferably red, but green will do, chopped
2 ribs celery, finely diced
1 teaspoon dried rosemary
6 slices bacon

1. Have the butcher bone the pork butt, but leave the rind on and do not let him "open up" or butterfly the butt. Simply have the bone removed.

2. Preheat the oven to 450 degrees.

3. Rub the pork all over, inside and out, with lemon. Squeeze the lemon juice over and inside the butt. Combine the onion juice, half the garlic, and one-half cup of the soy sauce, and massage the mixture inside and outside the meat.

4. Combine half the sage, parsley, chervil, chives, tarragon, basil, and black pepper and rub this mixture inside and outside the meat.

5. In a mixing bowl combine the sausage, chopped onion, bell pepper, celery, rosemary, and all the remaining ingredients except the bacon and one-quarter cup of the soy sauce.

6. Stuff the meat with this mixture and arrange the bacon slices over the large opening. Tie the roast like a rolled roast, using string to secure the bacon. Wrap the roast in two lengths of heavy-duty aluminum foil. It must be tightly sealed. Place the roast in a baking dish containing a little water and bake thirty minutes.

7. Reduce the oven heat to 400 degrees and continue baking one and one-half hours.

8. Open the foil and continue baking one and one-half hours, basting the meat frequently with the juices in the foil and the remaining soy sauce. When cooked, the roast will be quite dark. If necessary, reduce the oven heat to prevent the roast from burning, but this should not be necessary if it is basted often enough.

9. Remove the roast from the oven and let stand thirty minutes before slicing. Remove the string and serve the roast cut into half-inch-thick slices.

Note: If desired, the pan juices may be skimmed of fat and a sauce made by adding one chopped onion, two chopped tomatoes, and one clove of garlic finely minced.

Coucou

12 or more servings

8 cups cold water
3½ cups white cornmeal
1 pound fresh okra
Salt to taste
1 teaspoon dried orégano
¼ cup butter

1. Lightly butter a three-quart dish for molding the coucou.

2. Place two cups of the cold water in a saucepan and gradually add the cornmeal, stirring constantly. The texture should be like damp sand.

3. Trim the stem ends of the okra and slice thin. Place in a saucepan with the remaining six cups water and bring to a boil. Add the salt and orégano. Cook five minutes, then gradually add the cornmeal mixture, stirring constantly with a wooden spoon until the mixture becomes volcanic. Lower the flame and cook, stirring constantly, about five minutes. Stir in the butter and cook, stirring, ten to fifteen minutes longer. Pour the mixture into the buttered mold and press firmly. Smooth the top. To serve, unmold onto a hot serving dish and slice like cake.

Note: Leftover coucou may be refrigerated and reheated in hot butter in a skillet.

Trinidad Torte

8 to 10 servings

Fine dry bread crumbs
2 cups sifted all-purpose flour
1 teaspoon baking powder
1 teaspoon baking soda
4 ounces grated walnuts
1 cup butter
1¾ cups granulated sugar
3 eggs, separated
¾ cup sour cream
2 tablespoons grated orange rind
2 tablespoons grated lemon rind
⅛ teaspoon salt
2 tablespoons orange juice
2 tablespoons lemon juice

1. Preheat the oven to 350 degrees.

2. Butter a nine-inch spring-form pan. Coat the pan with the bread crumbs.

3. Sift together the flour, baking powder, and baking soda. Stir a few spoonfuls of the dry ingredients into the walnuts and set both mixtures aside.

4. Cream the butter and one cup of the sugar together, and beat in the egg yolks one at a time.

5. Add the dry ingredients alternately with the sour cream. Add the nuts and stir in the grated rinds.

6. Beat the egg whites with the salt until they hold a peak, then fold into the batter. Pour the batter into the pan and smooth the top by shaking briskly back and forth.

7. Bake one hour, or until a cake tester inserted into the center of the cake comes out clean. A few minutes before removing the cake from the oven, prepare a glaze by mixing the remaining sugar and the orange and lemon juices in a small saucepan. Bring to a boil, stirring to dissolve the sugar.

8. When the cake is removed from the oven, prick the top quickly with a small sharp knife and brush the hot glaze over the hot cake until all absorbed. Cool in the pan.

Trinidad Punch

About 20 servings

1½ cups granulated sugar
  2 cups lemon juice
  8 cups dry white wine
  2 quarts light or dark rum
 ½ teaspoon Angostura bitters
  1 cup maraschino cherries
1½ cups diced fresh fruit
  2 cups fresh or canned pineapple in chunks
    Orange slices for garnish

1. Combine all the ingredients except the orange slices and place in a bowl. Put the bowl in the freezer overnight, removing one hour before the guests are to arrive.
2. Garnish with orange slices and serve.

Turkey

Tripe Soup

10 to 12 servings

Patricians, to quote again that venerable and out-of-print tome, The Wise Encyclopedia of Cookery, *relished tripe in Babylon's gardens; plebeians have always welcomed it as good—and cheap. The world's most famous dish of tripe is* à la mode de Caen, *flavored with Calvados and named for the Norman town, but there are also tripe dishes from other parts of the world that enjoy considerable esteem. Below is a tripe soup from Turkey.*

4 pounds honeycomb tripe
  Water
  Salt and freshly ground pepper to taste
¼ cup butter
2 tablespoons all-purpose flour
2 eggs
  Juice of 2 lemons
1 teaspoon paprika
  Cayenne pepper to taste
6 tablespoons vinegar
6 cloves garlic, finely chopped
  Croutons (see below)

1. Wash the tripe thoroughly, then cut into large pieces and put in a saucepan. Add five cups of water, cover, and simmer over medium heat for about three hours. Add more liquid as it boils away.

2. Remove the tripe and reserve the stock. Put the tripe through a meat grinder or cut it into small cubes. Return the tripe to the stock and season with salt and pepper. Cover and simmer two hours longer. Add more liquid if necessary.

3. Melt half the butter in a saucepan and stir in the flour, using a wire whisk. Cook briefly without browning. Stir in about one cup of the soup, then return the mixture to the saucepan. Stir to blend. Simmer two minutes longer, stirring with a spoon.

4. Beat the eggs with a rotary beater and add the lemon juice. Remove the soup from the heat and stir in the egg and lemon mixture. Bring the soup almost but not quite to a boil. If the soup boils, it might curdle.

5. Melt the remaining butter in a small saucepan and add the paprika and cayenne.

6. Pour the soup into a hot tureen and pour the butter and paprika mixture on top.

7. Blend the vinegar and garlic in a small bowl. To serve, add a few croutons and a little of the vinegar sauce to hot soup plates. Spoon the soup on top.

CROUTONS:

Preheat the oven to 400 degrees. Trim the crusts off three or four slices of white bread. Cut the bread into half-inch cubes and arrange the cubes on a baking sheet. Bake, stirring the cubes, until they are golden brown. Let cool.

Serbian Fish

6 servings

1 whole whitefish (3 pounds)
  Salt and freshly ground black pepper
2 slices of smoked bacon, each cut into 8 pieces
1 tablespoon all-purpose flour
1 teaspoon paprika
3 large potatoes, peeled
2 green peppers, seeded and cut into ½-inch rings
3 tablespoons dry bread crumbs
3 firm, ripe medium tomatoes, sliced
⅔ cup sour cream
⅓ cup milk

1. Have the fish cleaned, boned, and split lengthwise, but leave the skin intact. Sprinkle the fillets on both sides with salt and pepper. Place the fillets, skin side up, on a board. Using a sharp, pointed knife, make eight incisions through the skin of each fillet. Plug each incision neatly with a piece of bacon. Dredge the fillets with a mixture of the flour and paprika.

2. Place the potatoes with salted water to cover in a saucepan. Bring to a boil and parboil for five to ten minutes. Drain, then cut into half-inch slices.

3. Drop the pepper rings into boiling water and cook for two minutes. Drain.

4. Preheat the oven to 350 degrees.

5. Butter or grease an oblong ovenproof baking dish large enough to accommodate the fish. Sprinkle the dish with bread crumbs, then arrange the sliced potatoes over the bottom of the dish. Arrange the pepper rings over the potatoes, and top each ring with a tomato slice. Sprinkle the vegetables with salt and pepper.

6. Place one fillet, skin side down, on the bed of vegetables. Cover with the other fillet, skin side up. Bake.

7. Blend the sour cream and milk. When the fish has baked for about fifteen minutes,

baste it with the cream and milk mixture. Baste several times during baking with the mixture and the juices in the baking dish. Bake for thirty to thirty-five minutes, or until the potatoes are tender and the fish flakes easily when tested with a fork.

Swordfish Shish Kebab

4 servings

If all the frankfurters barbecued on a typical summer weekend were placed end to end, they would doubtlessly stretch from here to Honolulu and back. While it is true that franks and their kindred—hamburgers, steaks, and chicken—are delicious, skewered foods are more dramatic. We recommend an old-fashioned shish kebab of beef or lamb or, and this is a Turkish idea, a shish of fish. Swordfish is an excellent choice. A recipe for a swordfish shish is given below.

1 clove garlic, smashed with the flat side of a knife
¼ cup finely chopped parsley
¼ cup lemon juice
⅔ cup peanut oil or salad oil
1 teaspoon chopped fresh thyme or ½ teaspoon dried thyme
3 drops Tabasco
  Salt and freshly ground black pepper
1½ pounds swordfish, cut into neat cubes
12 cubes sweet onion
12 cubes green pepper
12 unpeeled cherry tomatoes
1 stick butter
  Juice of ½ lemon

1. Combine the garlic, parsley, lemon juice, oil, thyme, Tabasco, and salt and pepper to taste. Stir to blend and add the swordfish. Refrigerate one hour or so. Turn the swordfish occasionally in the marinade.

2. Arrange cubes of swordfish, onion, and green pepper and the cherry tomatoes on skewers. Grill, turning once, until the fish flakes easily. When pushing the mixture off onto a plate, push off one unit at a time or the tomatoes will shatter.

3. Melt the butter, combine it with the lemon juice, pour over all, and serve.

Note: The dish may also be made with salmon or any other large, fresh, firm-fleshed fish.

Media Dolma

6 servings

50 to 60 mussels, the largest available, scrubbed and debearded
2 cups natural mussel liquid
  Salt
3 cups finely chopped onion
1 cup olive oil
½ cup uncooked, long-grain rice
¼ cup currants
¼ cup pignoli (pine nuts)
½ teaspoon freshly ground black pepper
½ teaspoon ground allspice
½ teaspoon ground cinnamon
  Lemon wedges

1. Each mussel has a straight-sided "hinged" back, a large rounded end, and a short rounded end. To open the mussels for stuffing, plunge a sharp, thin paring knife midway into the back of each, with the blade facing the large rounded end. Carefully work the knife blade clockwise, taking care to catch all the mussel liquid in a mixing bowl. When the muscle of the mussel is cut through, the shell can easily be pried open with the fingers like a purse or pocketbook. Open the mussel to receive the stuffing, but take care not to break the hinged back.

2. Measure the mussel liquid. If there is not two cups, add enough water to make two cups and a little salt to taste.

3. Cook the onions in oil over low heat until they are soft and translucent, about ten minutes. Add the rice, currants, nuts, one teaspoon salt, the pepper, allspice, and cinnamon.

4. Use a small spoon to fill each mussel lightly with the rice mixture. Remember that the rice will expand as the mussels cook, so do not overfill them. Close the mussel shells with the fingers and place them in layers in a deep, wide kettle. When all the mussels are layered, add the mussel liquid and cover closely with an inverted plate. Add the pot lid and cook over high heat until the steam escapes from the pot, about five minutes. Reduce the heat immediately and cook over very low heat two hours.

5. Let the mussels cool thoroughly. Several hours before serving, take the mussels from the pot and reverse the layers. That is, put the top layers on the bottom and vice versa so that the mussels remain equally moist and marinate equally in the pot broth. To serve, remove the mussels from the pot and arrange them symmetrically on a large platter. Garnish liberally with lemon wedges.

Stuffed Mussels

4 servings

2 dozen raw mussels
½ cup chopped parsley
2 tablespoons chopped fresh basil or 1 tablespoon dried basil
1 tablespoon crushed orégano
½ cup freshly grated Parmesan cheese
2 cloves garlic, finely minced
 Salt and freshly ground black pepper
1 cup fresh or dried bread crumbs
 Milk (optional)
¼ cup olive oil

1. Preheat the oven to 500 degrees.

2. Using a sharp, thin knife, open the mussel shells, running the knife horizontally so that the mussel shells are separated. Discard one shell, but leave the mussel in the other. Cut around the mussel to loosen.

3. Combine the parsley, basil, orégano, cheese, garlic, and salt and pepper to taste in a mixing bowl.

4. If soft fresh bread crumbs are used, add them directly to the herb mixture. If dried bread crumbs are used, moisten them with a little milk. Squeeze to remove most of the moisture. Add the crumbs to the herb mixture and toss all the ingredients until well blended. Stir in the olive oil.

5. Spoon or sprinkle equal parts of the mixture onto the mussels. Arrange on a baking sheet and bake five minutes or longer, or until the crumb mixture is golden brown. Serve hot.

Turkish Meat Balls on Skewers

4 servings

1 large onion
2 tablespoons salt
2 pounds lean lamb or beef, ground twice
2 eggs, lightly beaten
 Freshly ground pepper to taste
1 tablespoon salad oil
4 slices toasted white bread
2 cups cold Yogurt Sauce (page 554)
2 tablespoons butter
1 tablespoon paprika

1. Grate the onion into a mixing bowl and add the salt. Let stand fifteen minutes.

2. Place the meat in another bowl. Pour the grated onion into a square of cheesecloth and squeeze the onion juice over the meat. Add the eggs and pepper to the meat and mix well.

3. Divide the mixture into eight portions and shape each portion into sausage shape, about one inch in diameter and four inches long. Brush the surface of each sausage with oil. Oil eight skewers and shove them through the meat. Cook over charcoal or under the broiler to the desired degree of doneness.

4. Place two sausages on each piece of toast and spoon the yogurt sauce on top.

5. Heat the butter and stir in the paprika. Spoon this over the yogurt and serve immediately.

Chicken with Walnut Sauce

4 to 6 servings

1 chicken (4 to 5 pounds)
1 onion, peeled
1 carrot, scraped
1 rib celery with leaves
3 sprigs parsley
½ bay leaf
  Salt
12 peppercorns
3 quarts water
3 cups Walnut Sauce (see below), approximately
  Paprika

1. Place the chicken in a large kettle and add the onion, carrot, celery, parsley, bay leaf, salt to taste, peppercorns, and water. Bring to a boil and simmer one to one and one-half hours, or until the chicken is tender. Cool the chicken in its stock.

2. Remove the chicken from the kettle, reserving one cup stock for use in making the walnut sauce. Slice the chicken and arrange the slices on a platter. Set aside until the sauce is made.

3. Spread the chicken with walnut sauce and sprinkle with paprika. Serve cold.

WALNUT SAUCE:

Combine three slices white bread, trimmed of crusts and cubed, with one cup of the stock in which the chicken was cooked in the container of an electric blender. Cover and blend on high speed. Gradually add two cups shelled walnut meats (available in cans) and blend to make a paste. Add salt to taste.

Serbian Chicken Casserole

4 servings

1 frying chicken (3 pounds), cut into serving pieces
½ cup butter
2 cups finely chopped onion
1 green pepper, seeded and chopped
½ cup chopped celery
1 teaspoon paprika
1 tablespoon salt
  Freshly ground black pepper
2½ cups (1 1-pound 3-ounce can) whole tomatoes
1 cup Chicken Stock (page 115)
1 cup uncooked rice

1. Preheat the oven to 350 degrees.

2. Wash the chicken parts in cold water and dry well.

3. Heat the butter in a large skillet and cook the onion, green pepper, and celery in it until the onion is translucent.

4. Add the paprika, salt, pepper to taste, tomatoes, stock, and rice. Stir briefly and pour the mixture into a one-and-one-half-quart casserole. Arrange the chicken pieces on top and sprinkle with salt. Bake for one hour, or until the chicken is tender and the rice has absorbed the liquid. Add more stock as the dish cooks if the rice becomes too dry.

Dried Fava Bean Salad

6 to 8 servings

1½ cups shelled dry fava beans
1 large onion, quartered
2 quarts cold water, approximately
1 teaspoon granulated sugar
  Salt to taste
6 tablespoons lemon juice
6 tablespoons salad oil
1 tablespoon sour cream
1 bunch green onions, trimmed and chopped
2 tablespoons chopped dill
2 tablespoons chopped parsley
6 imported black olives
6 radish roses

1. Soak the beans overnight in a generous amount of water.

2. Drain the beans and rinse well, then place in a saucepan with the onion and the two quarts cold water. Bring to a boil and simmer, stirring frequently, until tender. Add more water as necessary. When the beans are done, most of the water should be absorbed.

3. When the beans are thoroughly tender, remove them from the heat. Mash the beans with a potato masher or put them through a food mill. Add the sugar, salt, two tablespoons of the lemon juice, two tablespoons of the oil, and the sour cream. Spoon the mixture (it should have a consistency like thick mashed potatoes) onto a plate and shape it with a spatula into a flat, round cake about one inch thick. Let cool. Garnish with the green onions, dill, parsley, olives, and radishes. Chill. To serve, slice the "cake" into wedges.

4. Blend the remaining lemon juice with the remaining oil and salt to taste and serve separately.

Yogurt

About 2 quarts

2 quarts milk
½ cup commercially made yogurt

1. Bring the milk to a boil and remove from the heat. Let the milk stand until it is at room temperature.

2. Combine the yogurt with one-half cup of the milk and stir until blended. Stir this into the remaining milk and pour the mixture into a clean glass bowl. Cover with clear plastic wrap, then cover with a towel and let stand at 70 degrees. (A good place, if convenient, would be on the floor at the exhaust of your refrigerator.) If you wish the yogurt on the "sweet" side, let it stand twelve hours. If you want it on the "sour" side, leave it eighteen hours.

Yogurt Sauce

About 2 cups

2 cups Yogurt (see above)
1 teaspoon salt
2 cloves garlic, finely minced

Combine all the ingredients and blend well. Serve on fried vegetables, meat kebabs, stuffed vegetables, etc.

Yogurt Dessert

About 12 servings

1 cup Yogurt (page 554)
1½ cups confectioners' sugar
3 eggs
¼ cup melted butter
2 cups sifted all-purpose flour
1 tablespoon grated orange or lemon rind
1 teaspoon baking powder
2½ cups granulated sugar
3½ cups water
1 tablespoon lemon juice
2 tablespoons ground pistachio nuts (see note)
Sweetened whipped cream
2 cups strawberries

1. Preheat the oven to 350 degrees.
2. Grease a baking pan (9 x 9 x 2).
3. Place the yogurt in a mixing bowl. Using an electric beater, gradually beat in the confectioners' sugar, eggs, butter, flour, and orange or lemon rind. The batter should be smooth. Add the baking powder, beating lightly. Do not overbeat.
4. Pour the batter into the prepared pan and bake forty to forty-five minutes.
5. Fifteen minutes before the cake is done, prepare a syrup by combining the granulated sugar, water, and lemon juice in a saucepan. Bring to a boil, stirring constantly until the sugar is dissolved. Simmer ten minutes without stirring. Remove from the heat and keep hot.
6. Cut the cake into the desired shapes, squares or diamonds. Pour the hot syrup over all, a little at a time, until all the syrup is absorbed. Cover with a tray and let cool several hours. This cake may be prepared one day in advance and kept in the refrigerator.
7. To serve, sprinkle the cake with the pistachio nuts. Arrange the pieces on a serving dish and serve with whipped cream and strawberries.

Note: To prepare the pistachio nuts, place the whole shelled nuts in a saucepan, cover with water, and simmer five minutes. Drain, pour two cups of cold water over them and slip off the dark skins of the nuts. Dry on toweling and grind as desired.

United States

New England Clam Chowder

6 to 8 servings

¼ pound salt pork, cut into small cubes
2 cups finely chopped onion
3 cups diced raw potatoes (½-inch cubes)
½ teaspoon dried thyme
2 cups water
4 cups finely chopped raw chowder clams, with their liquid
4 cups milk
2 tablespoons butter
Salt and freshly ground pepper to taste

1. Put the salt pork cubes in a kettle and cook until rendered of their fat. Add the onions and cook, stirring, until the onions are wilted. Add the diced potatoes, thyme, and water and cook until the potatoes are nearly tender, about ten minutes.

2. Add the remaining ingredients and cook about ten minutes longer. Serve with pilot crackers.

Clam Chowder from Long Island

8 to 10 cups

1 peck large quahog (chowder) clams
4 large ribs celery with a few leaves left on, trimmed and cut into 2-inch lengths
½ pound small onions, quartered
1 pound potatoes, peeled and quartered
2 large carrots, trimmed and scraped and cut into 1-inch lengths
1 pound fresh tomatoes, peeled and chopped, or one 1-pound can
1 teaspoon dried thyme (optional)
6 tablespoons butter
½ cup chopped parsley
4 cups heavy cream
Salt and freshly ground pepper
Milk (optional)

1. When the raw clams are opened, all the clam meat and the juices must be retained. This may be done at the fish store or at home. To do this, rinse each clam well and open with a clam knife. Line a colander with cheesecloth and set the colander over a large mixing bowl. Open the clams over the colander, then drop the clams into the colander and let the juice drain. One peck of clams produces about one quart of clam meat and six to eight cups of juice.

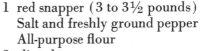

Red Snapper Creole

4 to 6 servings

1 red snapper (3 to 3½ pounds)
   Salt and freshly ground pepper
   All-purpose flour
3 slices lemon
¼ cup butter
1½ cups coarsely chopped onion
2 whole cloves
1 cup coarsely chopped celery
1 cup coarsely chopped green pepper
1 strip lemon rind
2 cups canned Italian tomatoes
¼ cup chopped parsley
½ teaspoon crushed rosemary
½ teaspoon crushed peppercorns
1 bay leaf
2 cloves garlic, finely chopped
½ teaspoon dried thyme
1 tablespoon Worcestershire sauce
   Tabasco

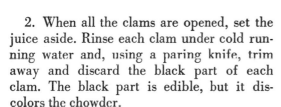

2. When all the clams are opened, set the juice aside. Rinse each clam under cold running water and, using a paring knife, trim away and discard the black part of each clam. The black part is edible, but it discolors the chowder.

3. Put the celery, onions, potatoes and carrots through the fine blade of a meat grinder and place the mixture in a heavy kettle. Add the tomatoes and thyme.

4. Put the clams through the meat grinder and add them to the vegetables. Add the clam juice and bring to a boil. Cook, uncovered, skimming the surface as necessary, about two hours.

5. Stir in the butter and chopped parsley.

6. When ready to serve, remove the chowder from the heat and add the heavy cream and salt and pepper to taste. Bring just to a boil, but do not boil or the chowder will curdle. If the chowder is too thick, add enough milk to thin it to the desired consistency. Heat thoroughly but do not boil.

1. Have the fish cleaned. The head may be left on or removed.

2. Preheat the oven to 350 degrees.

3. Sprinkle the fish inside and out with salt and pepper to taste, then dredge the outside lightly with flour. Place the fish in a greased baking dish and arrange the lemon slices on top.

4. Meanwhile, heat the butter in a skillet and add the onion, cloves, celery, and green pepper. Cook briefly until the onions are slightly wilted.

5. Add the lemon rind, tomatoes, parsley, rosemary, peppercorns, salt to taste, bay leaf, garlic, thyme, Worcestershire sauce, and Tabasco to taste. Bring to a boil and simmer five minutes.

6. Pour the sauce around the fish and bake, basting frequently, about forty-five minutes, or until the fish flakes easily when tested with a fork.

Note: Other firm-fleshed fish such as cod may be substituted for the red snapper.

Clam Pie à la Springs

6 to 8 servings

2¼ cups sifted all-purpose flour
 1 teaspoon salt
 ¾ cup vegetable shortening
 6 tablespoons water
 3 cups ground clams, preferably quahogs
    (chowder clams)
 ½ cup finely chopped onion
 ¾ cup fresh cracker crumbs, preferably
    made from pilot crackers
    Freshly ground black pepper
    Dried thyme (optional)
 ¾ cup light cream

1. Preheat the oven to 375 degrees.
2. In a mixing bowl, combine the flour and salt. With a pastry blender or two knives, cut in the shortening until the mixture looks like coarse cornmeal.
3. Sprinkle the water over the mixture, one tablespoon at a time, and mix lightly with a fork until all the flour is moist.
4. With the hands, gather the dough into a ball and divide it in half. On a lightly floured board, roll out each half into a circle one-eighth-inch thick and about one and one-half inches larger in diameter than the pie plate to be used. Line a nine-inch pie plate with one circle of dough, leaving one-half inch overhanging.
5. Combine the clams, onion, crumbs, and pepper and thyme to taste and all but one tablespoon of the cream in a mixing bowl. Pour the filling into the lined pie plate. Cover with the remaining circle of dough and neatly trim the edges. Fold the edge of the top pastry under the edge of the lower pastry and seal by pressing together. Flute the edges, if desired. Brush the top of the pie with the remaining cream, then prick the top, and bake the pie for forty minutes, or until golden brown and baked through.

Barbecued Spareribs

12 servings

3 racks spareribs
    Salt and freshly ground black pepper
1½ teaspoons monosodium glutamate
 1 cup tomato catsup
    Juice of ½ lemon
 1 teaspoon Worcestershire sauce
 ½ teaspoon Tabasco

1. Preheat the oven to 350 degrees.
2. Lay out three large lengths of heavy-duty aluminum foil, each large enough to envelop one rack of ribs. Sprinkle the ribs with salt, pepper, and the monosodium glutamate. Place one rack of ribs on each length of foil and bring up the sides. Enclose the ribs securely, sealing the foil so that the juices will not escape. Place the ribs in the oven and let them bake, without opening the foil, for one to one and one-half hours. (Baking time will depend on the size of the ribs.) Remove the ribs from the oven, open the foil, and let stand until ready to grill. The juices in the foil may be added to the barbecue sauce or discarded.
3. Meanwhile, prepare a charcoal fire. When the coals are hot and have a white ash on top, the fire is ready.
4. Arrange the cooked ribs over the coals. Combine the catsup, lemon juice, Worcestershire sauce, and Tabasco. If desired, add the sparerib drippings from the foil. Stir and bring to a boil. Brush the mixture over the ribs and grill until the ribs are brown on one side. Turn them carefully and brush again. Grill until browned on both sides. Note that the ribs need very little cooking on the grill, because they are already done.

Deep South Veal Grillades

4 to 6 servings

2 veal steaks, each about ½ inch thick (about 1½ pounds)
Salt and freshly ground pepper
½ cup vegetable oil
6 tablespoons all-purpose flour
1½ cups chopped onion
½ cup tomato paste
1 cup Chicken Stock (page 115) or canned chicken broth, approximately
1 cup dry white wine
4 cloves garlic, finely minced
½ cup finely chopped parsley
½ cup finely chopped celery
1 cup chopped green pepper
1 cup finely chopped green onion
1 teaspoon chopped fresh thyme or ½ teaspoon dried thyme
1 bay leaf

1. Cut the veal into serving portions and sprinkle the pieces with salt and pepper. Heat half the oil in a large skillet and brown the meat well on all sides. When the meat is browned, transfer it to a casserole.

2. Add the remaining oil to the skillet, then add the flour. Cook, stirring with a wooden spoon, until the flour is browned. Add the onions and cook until soft. Blend the tomato paste and the one cup chicken stock and add it to the skillet.

3. Stir in the wine, and, when all is blended and smooth, pour the mixture over the meat. There should be enough liquid to cover the meat. If not, add more chicken stock. Add the remaining ingredients, plus salt and pepper to taste, and cover. Simmer for forty-five minutes, or until the meat is fork tender.

Chicken Jambalaya

6 to 8 servings

1 chicken (3 pounds), cut into serving pieces
Salt and freshly ground black pepper
¼ cup butter
1 cup finely diced raw ham
½ cup finely chopped onion
1 cup uncooked rice
1 cup drained tomatoes, preferably Italian plum style
2 cups boiling Chicken Stock (page 115) or water, approximately
½ teaspoon dried basil
½ bay leaf
¼ teaspoon dried thyme
¼ cup finely chopped parsley

1. Sprinkle the chicken with salt and pepper. Heat the butter in a skillet and cook the chicken until golden brown on all sides. Add the ham and cook briefly, stirring. Spoon the chicken and ham into another dish and reserve.

2. Add the onion and rice to the skillet. Cook, stirring, until the onion is translucent. Add the tomatoes, the chicken, ham, and boiling chicken stock to barely cover. Add the seasonings and more salt and pepper, if necessary. Cover and cook over low heat until the chicken is tender and most of the liquid is absorbed, thirty to forty minutes.

3. About fifteen minutes before the chicken is done, preheat the oven to 350 degrees. When the chicken is done, remove the cover and place the chicken in the oven just long enough to dry slightly.

Barbecued Chicken

4 to 8 servings

To judge from the sale of barbecue equipment these days, that form of primitive cookery borders on a national mania. Sauces for barbecued meats range from an elegant tarragon butter with a dash of Chablis to basic red—the Maine-to-Hawaii favorite that uses catsup as a blast-off point. Southern catsup sauce is listed here, and you can't get more basic than that. The thing to remember about barbecued chicken is that—if you can't manage to barbecue it to a turn—it is better overcooked than undercooked.

2 chickens (2½ pounds each), split for broiling with backbones removed
Salt and freshly ground pepper
⅓ cup white shortening or salad oil
10 tablespoons catsup
½ cup vinegar
8 teaspoons Worcestershire sauce
½ cup brown sugar
1 tablespoon dry mustard
2 tablespoons chili powder, or to taste
1 teaspoon grated fresh ginger or ½ teaspoon ground ginger
1 clove garlic, finely minced
2 tablespoons butter
2 slices lemon

1. Each chicken should be split into two halves. Place each half skin side up on a flat surface and pound with a flat mallet or the bottom of a skillet. This will make them lie flatter and cook more uniformly on the grill. Sprinkle the chicken with salt and pepper and rub all over with shortening or salad oil.

2. Combine all the remaining ingredients and salt and pepper to taste in a saucepan. Stir over moderate heat until blended.

3. Place the chicken halves, skin side up, on a prepared grill over hot coals. Brush the sauce over the skin side and let cook, without turning, about ten minutes. Turn and baste the other side. Continue turning and basting every ten minutes or so until the chickens are thoroughly done, brushing after they are cooked with any remaining sauce. Cooking time will depend on how hot the coals are and how close the chicken is to the coals.

Southern Fried Chicken

4 to 6 servings

1 chicken (2½ to 3 pounds), cut into serving pieces
Milk
Tabasco
1 tablespoon or more freshly ground black pepper
1 pound lard
¼ pound butter
All-purpose flour
Salt to taste

1. Place the chicken parts in a mixing bowl and add milk to cover. Add a few drops of Tabasco and about half a teaspoon black pepper. Let stand an hour or longer or refrigerate overnight.

2. When ready to cook, begin melting the lard and butter in a large, heavy skillet.

3. Drain the milk off but do not dry the chicken. Place in a large bowl enough flour to coat the chicken; add salt to taste and the remaining black pepper. (Remember that the secret of good southern fried chicken is black pepper used liberally and ample salt.) Dredge the chicken parts in the flour.

4. While the lard and butter are still melting, start to add the chicken pieces, skin side down. Turn the heat to high and cook the chicken until it is appetizingly brown on that side, then turn the pieces, using tongs. Turn the heat down to moderately low and continue cooking the chicken pieces until golden brown on the other side. Cook until the meat is cooked through, twenty minutes or longer. Drain well on paper toweling.

Corn Bread Stuffing

*Stuffing for a 12- to 15-pound turkey
with leftover stuffing to bake*

There was a chef in France some years ago who stanchly refused to stuff a turkey with oyster dressing for a rich American client on the grounds that it was cannibalism. He may not have been aware that holiday birds in this country have been stuffed with all sorts of exotica, including water chestnuts and hot chilies. Be that as it may, some of the best dressings are still the old-fashioned kind. This one, using corn bread and sweet herbs, is not only delicious but carries no connotation of cannibalism.

3 cups crumbled day-old corn bread
3 cups cubed white bread
   Liver, gizzard, and heart of a 12- to 15-pound turkey
1 cup butter
2 cups chopped onion
2 cups chopped celery
1 cup chopped green pepper
3 cloves garlic, finely minced
1 teaspoon chopped fresh thyme or ½ teaspoon dried thyme
⅓ cup finely chopped parsley
1 tablespoon chopped fresh basil or 1½ teaspoons dried basil
   Salt to taste
¾ teaspoon or more freshly ground black pepper, or to taste (black pepper is a vital flavor in this dressing)
1 bay leaf, finely chopped
   Tabasco to taste

1. Crumble the corn bread into a large mixing bowl.

2. Toast the white bread under the broiler, tossing to distribute the cubes, and let them brown evenly. Add the toasted white bread to the corn bread.

3. Put the turkey liver, gizzard, and heart through the fine blade of a meat grinder.

4. Heat half the butter in a skillet and add the liver mixture, onion, celery, green pepper, garlic, thyme, parsley, basil, salt, pepper, bay leaf, and Tabasco. Cook, stirring, over moderate to low heat about twenty minutes. Add the remaining butter, and, when it melts, add the contents of the skillet to the mixing bowl. Stir to blend well.

5. Use the filling to stuff a twelve- to fifteen-pound turkey. Leftover stuffing may be placed in a baking dish, dotted with butter, and baked to serve with the turkey.

New Orleans Remoulade Sauce

About 1¾ cup

2 cups fresh Mayonnaise (page 265)
1 teaspoon grated onion
1 clove garlic, finely minced
½ cup Creole mustard (bottled in Louisiana)
1 cup finely chopped parsley

Combine all the ingredients and use as a sauce for chilled cooked shrimp. This is enough for about three pounds of shrimp.

Cheesecake

12 or more servings

Butter
½ cup graham cracker crumbs, approximately
2 pounds cream cheese, at room temperature
4 eggs
1¾ cups sugar
Juice of 1 lemon
Grated rind of 1 lemon
1 teaspoon vanilla extract
Strawberries, blueberries or other fruit for garnish (optional)

1. Preheat oven to 325 degrees.
2. Butter the inside of a metal cake pan eight inches wide and three inches deep. Do not use a spring-form pan. Sprinkle with the graham cracker crumbs and shake the crumbs around the bottom and sides until coated. Shake out the excess crumbs and set the pan aside.

3. Place the cream cheese, eggs, sugar, lemon juice, lemon rind, and vanilla extract into the bowl of an electric beater. Start beating at low speed and, as the ingredients blend, increase the speed to high. Continue beating until thoroughly blended and smooth.
4. Pour and scrape the batter into the prepared pan and shake gently to level the mixture.
5. Set the pan inside a slightly wider pan and pour boiling water into the larger pan to a depth of about half an inch. Do not let the edge of the cheesecake pan touch the rim of the other, larger pan. Set the pans inside the oven and bake two hours. At the end of that time turn off the oven heat and let the cake sit in the oven one hour longer.
6. Lift the cake out of its water bath and place it on a rack. Let the cake stand at least two hours.
7. Invert a plate over the cake and carefully turn both upside down to unmold the cake. Invert a cake plate over the bottom of the cake and carefully turn this upside down so that the cake comes out right side up. Garnish with berries or fruit.

Brandy Alexander Pie

1 envelope unflavored gelatin
½ cup cold water
⅔ cup granulated sugar
⅛ teaspoon salt
3 eggs, separated
¼ cup Cognac
¼ cup crème de cacao
2 cups heavy cream, whipped
1 Graham Cracker Crust (see below)
Chocolate curls

1. Sprinkle the gelatin over the cold water in a saucepan. Add one-third cup of the sugar, the salt, and the egg yolks. Stir to blend.

2. Heat over low heat, stirring, until the gelatin dissolves and the mixture thickens. Do not boil.

3. Remove from the heat and stir in the Cognac and crème de cacao. Chill until the mixture starts to mound slightly.

4. Beat the egg whites until stiff. Gradually beat the remaining sugar into the egg whites and fold into the thickened mixture. Fold in one cup of the whipped cream. Turn into the chilled crust and chill several hours or overnight.

5. Garnish with the remaining cream and chocolate curls.

GRAHAM CRACKER CRUST:

1 9-inch piecrust

1¼ cups graham cracker crumbs
¼ cup granulated sugar
⅓ cup melted butter

Combine all the ingredients and press evenly against the bottom and sides of a nine-inch pie plate. Chill until ready to use.

Pecan Pie

6 servings

1 cup granulated sugar
1¼ cups dark corn syrup
4 large eggs
¼ cup butter, at room temperature
1½ cups broken pecans
1 teaspoon vanilla extract
¼ teaspoon salt
1 unbaked 8-inch Pastry Shell (page 289)

1. Preheat the oven to 350 degrees.

2. Put the sugar and corn syrup into a saucepan and cook until the sugar dissolves.

3. Beat the eggs lightly and gradually pour in the corn syrup mixture, beating constantly. Add the butter while beating, then stir in the pecans. Add the vanilla extract and salt and pour the mixture into a pie shell.

4. Bake about forty-five minutes, or until set.

Juiced Apple Pie

6 to 8 servings

6 Stayman winesap apples
1¼ cups granulated sugar
1 teaspoon cinnamon
⅛ teaspoon nutmeg
¼ teaspoon salt
  Pastry for a Two-Crust Pie (see below)
2 tablespoons all-purpose flour or 1½ tablespoons tapioca
3 tablespoons butter

1. Peel, core, and slice the apples.

2. Combine the sugar, cinnamon, nutmeg, and salt and coat the apples with the mixture. Let stand at least two hours. Drain and reserve both apple slices and the syrup that forms.

3. Preheat the oven to 450 degrees.

4. Roll out half the dough and line a nine-inch pie plate with it. Arrange the apple slices over the bottom of the pastry, packing the slices closely and letting them pile up.

5. Roll out the remaining dough and cut two holes near the center, each hole about the size of a dime. Wet the rim of the bottom crust and put the top crust on. Trim and crimp the crust. Bake the pie forty-five minutes.

6. Meanwhile, put the drained syrup in a saucepan and stir in the remaining ingredients. Bring to a boil.

7. When the pie is done, hold a funnel over one of the holes and then the other, adding the syrup gradually. It must be added gradually or it will overflow. The pie will become firm when it cools. Serve warm or cool.

Note: The pie may be frozen if desired. If frozen, let it thaw five hours before warming it up.

PASTRY FOR A TWO-CRUST PIE:

Pastry for a 2-crust, 9-inch pie

2 cups sifted unbleached flour
1 teaspoon salt
1 cup solid white vegetable shortening
¼ cup ice water

1. Sift the flour and salt into a mixing bowl and cut in the shortening, using a pastry blender or two knives, until the mixture resembles coarse cornmeal.

2. Add the ice water gradually, tossing the mixture with a two-pronged fork. Handle the dough as little as possible but shape it into a ball. Divide the dough in half and roll out one-half at a time on a well-floured board.

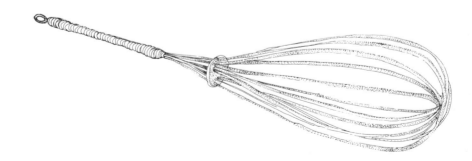

Lime Pie

8 servings

    3 tablespoons cornstarch
 1¼ cups plus 6 tablespoons granulated sugar
    ¼ cup fresh lime juice
    1 tablespoon grated lime rind
    3 eggs, separated
 1½ cups boiling water
    1 baked 9-inch Pastry Shell (page 289)

1. Preheat the oven to 425 degrees.

2. Combine the cornstarch, the one and one-quarter cups sugar, lime juice, grated lime and rind. Beat the egg yolks and add to the lime juice mixture, then gradually add the boiling water. Heat to boiling over direct heat and boil gently four minutes, stirring constantly. Pour into the pastry shell.

3. Beat the egg whites until stiff but not dry and gradually beat in the remaining six tablespoons sugar. Spread the meringue over the top of the pie, carefully sealing in all the filling and being sure to touch the edge of the pastry shell all around. Bake for four to five minutes, or until browned. Cool on a cake rack.

Lemon Chess Pie

6 servings

    2 cups granulated sugar
    ⅛ teaspoon salt
    2 tablespoons grated lemon rind
    1 tablespoon all-purpose flour
    1 tablespoon cornmeal
    4 eggs
    ¼ cup melted butter
    ¼ cup lemon juice
    ¼ cup milk
    1 unbaked 9-inch Pastry Shell (page 289)

1. Preheat the oven to 350 degrees.

2. Mix the sugar, salt, lemon rind, flour, and cornmeal together.

3. Beat in the eggs thoroughly, then add the butter, lemon juice, and milk. Pour into the prepared pastry shell and bake fifty to sixty minutes, or until set.

Index

ABOUT THE AUTHOR

Food News Editor for *The New York Times* for many years, Craig Claiborne is well known for his books and articles on cuisines around the world and for his knowledge of the art and enjoyment of cooking. He has traveled widely and has prepared and tasted countless dishes of every variety from many lands and cultures. In 1953–1954 he was a student in cuisine and table service at the Ecole Hôtelière, the professional school of the Swiss Hotelkeepers' Association, Lausanne, Switzerland. Upon his return to the United States he was on the staff of *Gourmet* magazine, where he wrote a column and features.

Born in Mississippi in 1920, Claiborne attended high school there. He went to Mississippi State College for two years, and received his Bachelor of Journalism degree from the University of Missouri in 1942.

He served with the U.S. Navy from 1942 to 1945 in both the European and Far Eastern theaters. From 1945 to 1949 Claiborne was assistant director of publicity for the American Broadcasting Company, midwest division, in Chicago. The next year he attended the Alliance Française in Paris. With the outbreak of the Korean War, he again served in the U.S. Navy. From 1950 to 1953 he was a lieutenant aboard a destroyer escort.

Among his cook books are *Cooking with Herbs and Spices, Craig Claiborne's Kitchen Primer* and *The New York Times Cook Book*.